The Nightmare Decade

For CAREY McWILLIAMS

FRED J. COOK

The
Nightmare
Decade

The Life and Times of Senator Joe McCarthy

Random House   *New York*

ISBN: 0-394-46270-X

Library of Congress Catalog Card Number: 74-102320

Manufactured in the United States of America
by The Book Press, Brattleboro, Vermont

9 8 7 6 5 4 3 2
First Printing

Contents

Foreword

THERE IS A NEW GENERATION of young Americans, many of whom have only the vaguest ideas about Joseph R. McCarthy and what the McCarthyism of the 1950s represented. When you mention the name McCarthy, they think you are talking about Senator Eugene McCarthy and the campaign of 1968; and when you explain that there was another and earlier Mc-Carthy, an entirely different McCarthy, the reaction is often a vague look and the murmured reply, "Oh, I don't know much about him."

I began writing this book more than two years ago with the idea that it was time to fill this particular generation gap and put in perspective McCarthyism and the decade of the 1950s that it so greatly influenced. The idea originated with my publishers. When we first discussed the project, we both thought that the book would deal with history, not with current events.

Then, on the night of November 13, 1969, Vice President Spiro Agnew delivered the first of a series of slashing attacks on the media. The major television chains had presumed to offer some criticism—the very mildest criticism, it seemed to me—of President Richard M. Nixon's major nationally televised November 3 speech on Vietnam. Agnew argued that the President should be allowed to speak without having his words subjected to instant analysis, and he pictured the President as the victim of Eastern intellectuals with a stranglehold on the media.

The next evening I walked into a suburban store to pick up my newspapers, and the proprietor, an archconservative, shouted at me: "Did you see that, buddy boy? Did you see that speech of Agnew's? Wasn't he *something?* There's your next President, buddy boy!"

I found myself in instant confrontation. "What do you people want?" I asked him. "The President spoke to the nation on TV; he had his say. Isn't anyone supposed to have any opinions about what he said? What are you trying to do? Revive the age of Joe McCarthy, when the truth was what *he* said it was, and any newspaper or TV chain that disagreed was an affiliate of the *Daily Worker?*"

From behind me came the roaring voice of a new customer: "Joe McCarthy! He was *the one*—the only good one we've ever had!"

Vice President Agnew, intentionally or not, had the old McCarthy legions baying. They had never gone away. They had subsided for a time because they had lost their leader, but now they were rallying to a new voice.

I came away angry and shaken, convinced that a large number of older Americans, frustrated by the Vietnam stalemate, alarmed by the issues of race and the ghettos and the revolt of the young, were ready to follow the new Pied Piper, blaming all the nation's ills on such scapegoats as the "effete," the "intellectuals" and some unnamed "conspirators" against the American way. This was the old McCarthyism resurgent, hate-filled, appealing to a blind superpatriotism; impervious to reason.

Were we going to travel that road again? The mounting

evidence in the weeks that followed seemed to say that we had already started out along it. Bumper stickers proliferated everywhere—"America, Love It or Leave It." Would we go the full paranoid route of the old McCarthyism? Only time could answer that question. Meanwhile, the mere thought that McCarthyism had again reared its head was sickening. This book had acquired —for its author at least—a new and ominous relevance.

Interlaken, N.J.
July, 1970

PART ONE

Build-up
to Hysteria

1

The Way It Was

IT WAS A TIME OF NATIONAL PARANOIA in which
the greatest power on earth expended its energies hunting for
communists under every bed; in which millions of average Americans looked fearfully over their shoulders, wondering whether
they would be tapped next to explain themselves before the grand
inquisitors.

It was a decade of upheaval in the world. Age-old colonial
dynasties were crumbling before a new wave of nationalism;
ancient regimes were toppling in revolution. And so it was a
period when experts in government were needed as never before
—and it was precisely at this time in America that many of these
experts were exiled from government.

It was a decade that saw the basis of all human existence altered. The hydrogen bomb hung menacingly over the heads of men, capable of turning the earth into a wasteland as barren as the moon. And so it was a time when man's fullest intellectual powers should have been exercised to devise antidotes to self-destruction—and it was precisely at this time in America that intellectualism was most derided, that the intellectual became known as an "egghead"—and somehow associated with communism.

It was an era in which the second industrial revolution, wedding computers to technology, was transforming the circumstances of human life, offering man a vision of plenty, yet presenting him with complex new problems—and frustrating millions of the still-deprived by the gap between glorious possibility and the harsh reality of their own lives. And so, it was an age in which perception and foresight were needed as never before, when only the freest debate could have brought understanding of a new world. But in America it was precisely at this time that the mind was most shackled, that the kind of dissent and freewheeling philosophy in which the nation had been born became virtually a badge of treason. The result was a smothering blanket of inertia, the timorous conformity of an entire generation.

It was a period dominated by the most effective demagogue ever to practice the arts of mass passion on this continent—Senator Joseph R. McCarthy of Wisconsin. These were the 1950s—the Nightmare Decade.

Looking back after the sixties, marked by Vietnam protests and college riots, it may seem incredible that this is the same nation that rolled over and played dead at the first raucous shout of a junior Senator. To the young generation of today, clamoring for change, provoked to violence, it may seem fantastic that for a whole decade there was hardly a whisper of dissent in the land. But it is true—and it must be understood. For the failures of the fifties are our legacy.

A S A M A N, Joseph McCarthy was a paradox. He wanted everyone to love him, and yet he did and said the most outrageous things. He had what many called a "shaggy-dog" friendliness; "He comes at you with his tail wagging," as one put it—and yet he was uninhibited in invective, using terms ranging from "nit-wit" to "traitor" to brand those who crossed him. In private conversation, he spoke in terms of moderation and reason like the most sensible of men; on the Senate floor, he adopted all the tactics and manner of rational discourse. A demagogue by the very nature of his business is inevitably a hypocrite. He appeals to passion, he hurls the most sensational and unwarranted accusations—always in the name of principle, high honor and patriotism. No man ever mastered the technique more perfectly than Joe McCarthy. He would take the Senate floor and fire broadsides accusing scores of officials of treason, and then he would protest that he must not be asked to name them because it would not be *fair* to them to do so before they had a chance to answer. By this device he not only avoided the necessity of substantiating anything that he had said; he managed to accuse an entire Administration and create the impression that the nation was being betrayed on a wholesale scale. Only on those relatively rare occasions when he was seriously challenged, when the pose of principle and patriotism he had adopted for himself was threatened by scorn or ridicule—only then would the gentlemanly veneer shred away, and in its place would come the scowl and the snarl and the harsh hectoring voice that derided a foe's intelligence and courage, even his paternity and patriotism.

In appearance, he was a bulky man, with broad shoulders and powerful, hairy arms. His head was large, the face heavy, the features big; and yet there was about him, especially in profile, a certain aquiline sharpness. It was an impression created by his long, pointed nose and by the receding hairline, with the thin front strands combed straight back—strands that he kept forever fingering and rubbing backward in times of stress. The combination gave him at times the look of an unhooded hawk, a predator —from the snap of the heavy-browed eyes to the clamp of the wide-curved lips.

Such was the man who made himself in two years his party's most dreaded political weapon. In the Presidential election of 1952, he was loosed by the Republican hierarchy to pin the label of "twenty years of treason" on every Democrat in sight. He was the man chosen to link Adlai Stevenson to the dark designs of Moscow.

One image of the 1952 campaign remains unforgettable—that

of Joe McCarthy campaigning on television in his native Wisconsin. Shirt sleeves rolled up as if for a fight, brawny arms pumping, the large-featured face grimacing in the intensity of what seemed like genuine passion, he thundered: "If somebody would only smuggle me aboard the Democratic campaign special with a baseball bat in my hand, I'd teach patriotism to little Ad-lie."

That was just the opening salvo. He stormed on, clutching a sheaf of papers in one upraised fist. This organization led to that —and that to another and another and yet another. It all went so fast, the organizations cited so obscure, that one could never know just what connected with what or whom; but somehow it all circled back to the impression that "little Ad-lie" was a dangerous "fellow traveler," if not an outright subversive.

The effect was that of a Nazi bullyboy glaring at you from your television screen, but few persons seemed to see this or to care. The Associated Press carried a paragraph on the performance; a few columnists gave it passing notice; and one Wisconsin paper asked editorially, "Are McCarthy Storm Troopers Coming?" But there was no gale of unfavorable publicity, no cry of public outrage. Republicans, in their desperation to capture the White House after twenty years of banishment in the political desert, hailed McCarthy as a mighty champion. The party's Presidential candidate, five-star hero-general Dwight David Eisenhower, deleted from his prepared Wisconsin speech an unflattering reference to McCarthy, suffered a public McCarthy bear hug, and proclaimed that he was for "good" Republicans everywhere.

WALTER LIPPMANN, for generations one of the most sagacious American commentators, afterward explained that he had favored a Republican victory in 1952 because he had felt that this was the only way to restore the nation to sanity. The Republicans had been getting so wild and irresponsible in their charges, frustrated as they had been by the long hegemony of Roosevelt and Truman, that he had believed only a dose of the responsibilities of power could cure them and, in addition, that only they could take care of the excesses of McCarthyism. And that, he noted with satisfaction, was just about the way it had turned out.

It is hardly a healthy thought that the reward for outrageous demagoguery should be the investiture of national power. Even as pragmatism, Lippmann's reasoning had its flaws. For the Republicans, once victorious, were as terrorized by their own special weapon as the Democrats had been; and for almost two years, McCarthy roared on like an unguided missile, demoralizing friend as well as foe.

The State Department cowered before him. It had been assumed that Secretary of State John Foster Dulles, a stalwart Republican, prestigious and highly press-agented, would stand as an impregnable buffer between McCarthy and the much-abused departmental personnel. But Dulles cringed. His first speech to members of the department was an almost McCarthy-like diatribe on loyalty, and soon he was changing policies back and forth at the mere whisper that McCarthy might be displeased.

In the White House, one of the most beloved Presidents of modern times sat aloof. To pleas that he squelch McCarthy as Lippmann had anticipated, President Eisenhower retorted, "I just will not—I *refuse*—to get into the gutter with that guy." The result was a creeping demoralization at the highest levels of government.

Emmet John Hughes, who was a Presidential speech writer and White House adviser in those years, later took up the Lippmann theme of the sobering responsibilities of power in his book *The Ordeal of Power*, writing: "There is a nightmarish quality to even the memory of McCarthy's storming through Washington at this time—promptly after the election of a Republican leadership supposed to neutralize him politically. Day after day, he seemed to rant through the front pages of the press—denouncing the Voice of America, demanding censorship of American embassy libraries overseas, inflaming public libraries across the country to purge their shelves of 'subversive' literature, isolating government officials for inquisition, exploiting the malicious allegations of disappointed government employees."

Martin Merson, who went to Washington in the early Eisenhower days as an aide of Dr. Robert L. Johnson in the International Information Administration, later acknowledged that he "felt ashamed" at having been part of "the web of expediency and appeasement" of McCarthy in the capital. In his *mea culpa* in *The Reporter*, he wrote: "The obsession with security, which set the prevailing tone in Washington then as it does now [in 1954], ranged all the way from the frivolous to the salacious. The irresponsible charges and countercharges, the 'secret' name lists, dog-eared from constant circulation, and the little black books, the hurried tipoffs by phone, and the double talk in crowded rooms and corridors, most of it so contradictory, so wildly improbable—all this gave me at times the feeling that mutual espionage had become a new kind of intramural sport or political parlor game . . ."

My own memories of that time are vivid, but they relate mainly to the latter years of the decade after McCarthy had faded as a force but remained as a pervasive presence. For me, it all began with my involvement in the case of Alger Hiss—the watershed case of the entire era; the case that, perhaps more than any other single domestic event, made McCarthy possible.

Hiss was the young, bright, extremely capable State Department official who was accused by Whittaker Chambers of being a communist and a spy. Chambers produced documents he said Hiss had forwarded to him in 1938 that seemed to support his story and that sealed Hiss' fate, resulting in his conviction in late January, 1950, on charges of perjury stemming from his denial of Chambers' accusations.

At the time, like most Americans, I had had no doubt about Hiss' guilt. Documents are so convincing, so impressive—especially to Americans, who are relatively unsophisticated about the forgeries and high-level intrigues that have marked political life in other lands—that it had never really occurred to me to question them. I had looked upon Hiss with revulsion and had no desire to examine his case; but Carey McWilliams, editor of *The Nation,* kept insisting to me that he believed that an examination of the actual trial records might prove to be shocking. I shook him off, but he broached the subject again and I finally yielded. The agreement was that if I analyzed the evidence and still felt the same repugnance I was perfectly free to turn down the assignment.

An examination of the records quickly raised some doubts. Chambers had repeatedly asserted under oath before both the House Un-American Activities Committee and a federal grand jury that *the one thing* that had *never* been involved in his relationship with Hiss was espionage. He had done a complete about-face, committing perjury himself, and had produced his documents in the most melodramatic fashion only after the re-election of President Harry S Truman in 1948 had made him fear that he might face punitive action by the Democrats for his sensational tales of communist infiltration in high places. In his book *Witness,* Chambers later revealed that he had felt threatened by the surprise reelection of Truman. And well he might. He had certainly made himself a target for the politically vengeful by providing so much headline ammunition for the Republicans during the campaign. In such circumstances, the sudden escalation of his charges against Hiss became infinitely suspect. The imputation of treason—the accusation that Hiss had taken and copied secret State Department documents and passed them on to Chambers, knowing that Chambers was a Russian spy —was the one step that could remove the threat to Chambers and transfer it to Hiss. For no government can condone treason; no government can place itself in the untenable position of protecting a traitor and at the same time persecuting the patriot who is trying to unmask him.

There were other elements of doubt. Chambers had insisted that *all* of the documents he had produced had been given to him by Hiss and that *all* had been copied on Hiss' old Woodstock typewriter. But trial testimony showed that some of the documents had never gone to Hiss' division in the State Department, that he could not have had them; and even a Federal Bureau of Investigation expert admitted that one of the documents had been typed not on the Woodstock but on either an Underwood or a Royal. Chambers could not explain it. In addition there was the mystery of the ancient Woodstock itself. It seemed to me that the late Chester Lane, Hiss' counsel on appeal, had made quite a convincing demonstration that the documents had been forged and that the typewriter introduced in evidence at the trials, the machine that supposedly had produced them, had been deliberately doctored to reproduce the typing. Most peculiar of all was the fact that the experts of the FBI had never been called in to examine the machine whose validity Lane challenged. The government had been content to rest the heart of its case on a legal quibble: the argument that the defense, had it used "due diligence," should have raised this issue during the trials.

At this point I began to be scared of my own thoughts, which were forcing me to the conclusion that Hiss had been framed for political advantage. Some wrong convictions are the result of mistakes. A witness may be lying; events may seem to fall neatly into a pattern of circumstantial evidence, only to take on a quite different complexion when a missing piece of evidence is added. Such was not the case here. If the documents that had condemned Hiss were not legitimate, there must have been a deliberate conspiracy to manufacture them. And it seemed unlikely that the FBI and the Justice Department, with their scientific resources, could have been completely hoodwinked.

I was mulling over this problem in the late summer of 1957 when I walked into Chester Lane's office to pick up some volumes of testimony. Mrs. Helen Buttenwieser, his associate on the Hiss case, was there, and we talked briefly. She told me that I could have as much or as little contact with them as I wanted (at this point I wanted little), but that they would be glad to make all the hearing and trial records available to me—and any other records or correspondence that I needed. Before I left, she said one other thing: "If you decide to write this story, make no mistake about it, you will be asking for trouble. Almost certainly, you will be investigated, and you had better think about it very carefully first. You have a job and a family to support, and if you decide you can't do it, or don't want to do it, we will understand."

I felt certain that she was not exaggerating. At that time I was working for the New York *World-Telegram and Sun,* and the owner and editor of that paper, the late Roy W. Howard, had long been one of the most passionate anticommunist crusaders in journalism. The Hiss case was his especial pride and joy; it was the case that proved everything. I knew that if I challenged this concept I could well be fired.

At this juncture, I tried to take a close look at myself. Fortunately, I am not a joiner. Perhaps I have covered too many futile meetings as a reporter ever to be enamored of sitting through interminable discussions. I had never had any fondness for communism, had never signed petitions or belonged to "front" organizations. So there was no avenue by which I could be legitimately attacked. It all boiled down to a simple question: Did I dare? I began to get angry at myself and the world around me: at myself because I knew I wanted to chicken out; at the atmosphere of the times because it was downright degrading to have to worry and ponder and hesitate about pursuing the truth.

The result of this inner rebellion was that I wrote a scathing article for *The Nation,* later expanded into a book, *The Unfinished Story of Alger Hiss.* The backfire was exactly what had been anticipated. Friends began to get checkup telephone calls about me from a variety of sources, including former FBI agents. My editor was noncommittal, hardly daring to speak to me for weeks, and I was told he suffered a secret anguish, anticipating that at almost any moment he might get the order to lop off my head. When my book appeared in the spring of 1958, John Wingate asked me to appear on his night television show, and on the day of the broadcast (to me a harrowing prospect) one of the Hearst papers headlined its radio and television column: "See Red Tonight Over Channel 13."

I, at least, saw red. So did John Wingate. He made it clear on his show that he wasn't endorsing my thesis, but was outraged that it was impossible to have a frank discussion of facts and opinion without being smeared.

O N E   D I S T I N C T I V E   H A L L M A R K of that whole preposterous time was that it seemed that almost everywhere one could see the legions of the paranoid running around, carrying under their arms those green-covered volumes of committee testimony issued by the Government Printing Office.

We had hardly finished broadcasting the Wingate show before a beefy character emerged from the dark shadows of the studio, one of those green-jacketed tomes tucked under his arm. He hopped a cab with us to downtown New York and during the whole ride he kept babbling.

He was a good friend of "Freddie's," he said, referring to Frederick Woltman, my fellow journalist on the *World-Telegram and Sun* and he had never been able to understand why "Joe" and "Edgar" had put such faith in the turncoat informer Harvey Matusow. (McCarthy had planted Matusow in New York to inform on suspected communists in the press; and Matusow, who had served McCarthy well for a time, ultimately had embarrassed everybody by announcing that the testimony he had given for the government had been a tissue of lies—a declaration of conscience that had led to his prompt jailing for perjury, on the contention that he had lied the second time by saying that he had lied the first time.) "You know, I roomed with Harvey for a while," my new acquaintance said. "I knew he wasn't reliable, and I tried to warn Joe and Edgar about him, but they went right on using him. Why do you suppose they did that?"

I wasn't supposing. I had the uncomfortable feeling that *he* might have been sent to spy on *me*. All I wanted was to get rid of him.

The incident and my reaction to it symbolized for me the insanity of the time. Another of these testimony-toting characters rode our commuter train from the Jersey shore to New York. He had his own brokerage firm on Wall Street. Day after day, he rode the train, cuddling his favorite reading matter. He made no secret of the fact that he felt all newspapermen were dangerous liberals and potential subversives, and one day he challenged me about the play of our front-page stories. Senator McCarthy had made some pronouncement (I forget now what it was, but I remember it struck me at the time as something he had said many times before), and the *World-Telegram and Sun* had given the item a mere three or four paragraphs and an inconspicuous head. Why hadn't that story led the paper with the eight-column line? the broker wanted to know. Didn't we know what people wanted to read? It was obvious he thought I or some subversive friend of mine in the newsroom had sabotaged his hero.

The climax of my encounters with the paranoid broker came one day when he flipped open his favorite volume of testimony to the table of contents. "Here, look here." His object of concern was Professor Owen Lattimore, of Johns Hopkins University, whom McCarthy had accused of being the Number 1 Soviet spy in America. "Look at the number of times his name is listed," the broker said. "Just look at *that*, will you?"

It was obvious that to him the mere listing of a name represented proof of guilt. It was useless to argue. I simply changed my car on the train, riding in what we called "the working man's club car" with the refinery workers from Bayonne, a gang that filled the air with tobacco smoke and beer fumes, and that I found infinitely more compatible.

.   .   .

THE ENTIRE NATION RAN COWED. A whisper out of the night could ruin a life, a career. Just to have a name similar to someone else's could be fatal. If one had ever in all innocence signed petitions or joined groups working for what had seemed at the time estimable causes, one became extremely vulnerable in the changed political climate a decade later when the Attorney General's office belatedly labeled many such groups communist fronts. To have been connected with any of them, however tentatively or remotely, automatically stigmatized one as "a communist fronter."

Such "communist fronters" had no recourse. It was not necessary to prove they had been communists. It was not necessary to show they had known that the groups with which they had been connected had communists in them. Such persons were not accused of any crime. They were not brought to trial in any court of law. They were simply branded—and, often, professionally ruined. Equally ruined by mistake or mischance were others who had not even been "communist fronters," but whose names were similar to those so accused.

In the early 1950s an actress named Madeline Lee, who specialized in making baby noises on the radio, was suddenly blacklisted and became virtually unemployable. It was charged that on one occasion five years earlier she had given a party in her home to raise funds for an organization later listed as a "Communist front," and that in 1949 she had performed at a benefit in Carnegie Hall for another "front" organization. Even if Madeline Lee had been the most dedicated communist—and even the most rabid didn't contend this; they merely labeled her a "fronter"—it is difficult to see how the soul of America could have been contaminated by the baby gurgles she made on the radio.

Even more ridiculous than what happened to Madeline Lee, however, was the fate that befell three other actresses whose identities became confused with hers. Out on the West Coast there was an actress named Madaline Lee who appeared regularly as Miss Blue on the *Amos 'n' Andy* TV show. Although she had no political blackmarks against her name, she suddenly was hit with a deluge of protests against her television appearances. The campaign against her became so vicious that even one of the right-wing blacklisting sheets of the time was impelled to print a notice calling off its baying hounds by advising them they had treed the wrong quarry.

Another actress, Camilla Ashland, resembled the blacklisted Madeline Lee. She had a role in the TV show *Danger,* and after an appearance the barrage of anonymous protesting telephone calls began. Like Madeline Lee, Miss Ashland had never been a political activist, and she was completely mystified by the attacks. It was not until months later that a friend showed her a newspaper clipping indicating that her trouble had all stemmed from her physical resemblance to Madeline Lee.

The third actress to be affected was Madeline Pierce, who had been on the radio for twenty years. She, too, was uninvolved politically; but unfortunately she was a baby-gurgler—and her first name was Madeline. Suddenly her telephone line virtually went dead. Agencies that had given her regular employment for years called no more. The blacklist had descended upon her as silently as a smothering fog. Eventually she deduced the reason: all Madeline baby gurgles were suddenly suspect.

Americans have always admired the "stand-up guy," but in these years few stood up. Most ran for the storm shelters. The cravenness was most serious in the very circles that should have provided leadership. The movie industry abjectly capitulated to the witch hunt. So did radio and television. So did the publishing industry. So did the press, large and influential segments of which whooped the madness on; and so did the colleges, the advertising agencies, business and industry.

On the highest levels, both in government and industry, one tactic became standard. If an employee was called before a Congressional committee because it was charged that he had been a communist or had associated with communists, his only recourse was to abase himself. It did not matter that he might have acted in perfect innocence and from high motives; all he could do was confess. He must denounce the waywardness of his past thoughts and actions; he must inform fully on any others who had been associated with him in his now-dubious adventure. Only if a man was willing to shed his manhood, to disown his past and crawl, could he be sure that he would be "cleared" and allowed to retain his job.

Incident after incident demonstrated the intensity of the pressure—and the almost universal absence of the "stand-up guy."

In 1952 one of the oldest and most prestigious American publishing firms forced the resignation of its editor-in-chief. The books that he had edited had accounted for more than half of the firm's lucrative sales to book clubs, but many of the authors on his list were progressives and some were downright radicals. In the summer of 1951 another publisher dared to issue a book by an author noted for his dissents; almost instantly, the landlord of the New York office building in which the firm was located threatened to evict. He subsided only when the publisher told him he would fight any attempted eviction all the way to the Supreme Court.

Such defiance was rare. Joseph L. Rauh, Jr., Washington lawyer and long-time liberal, a leader in Americans for Democratic Action, comments: "The lesson of the times was that decent people don't stand up to this kind of attack; and every time someone tells me the German people were bad because they didn't stand up to Hitler, I tell them few people stood up to McCarthy—and this in a country where McCarthy couldn't begin to do to them what Hitler did to the Germans. I want to tell you it was mighty lonesome. I probably handled more loyalty cases than anyone in the district, and it was a mighty, mighty lonesome business."

If it had been possible to erect a dam anywhere to hold back the tides of hysteria, one might have expected that it would have been at the center of intellectual life—the colleges and universities, where the tradition of the open mind was most sacred. But the fact is that most college administrations crumpled before the onslaught like a row of jerry-built houses in a hurricane.

The atmosphere that prevailed in the institutions of higher learning has been most vividly recreated in a survey initiated in 1964 by the late Professor Paul Tillett, of the Eagleston Institute of Politics, Rutgers University. Professor Tillett died before he could finish his work, but the detailed replies he received to hundreds of questionnaires recreate the panic of the times.

Admittedly, some of the professors who were dismissed for their refusals to cooperate with inquisitorial committees were or had been communists and this was the basis for one of Joe McCarthy's most insidious ploys: labeling all such naysayers "Fifth Amendment Communists." This simply was not true. Some were liberals of varying persuasions—men who felt that a vital democratic principle was involved, that no agency of government had a right to pry into their individual beliefs, and that no one could "walk with dignity and without fear," to use Justice William O. Douglas' phrase, if such invasions of individual rights were permitted. They felt that they had to take a stand. But when they did, they were deserted.

One young professor who was being groomed to head the political science department in a Washington, D.C., university was summoned to testify before the House Un-American Activities Committee in 1959. He had been "an active Leftist in graduate school a decade before," but he had no sinister ties at the moment, he wrote, and "could have answered all the questions asked me by those Congressmen in the negative." But he decided that an important principle was involved, and he resolved not to testify. When his decision was made known to the faculty and administration, he became virtually a leper. He described the experience: "Not one individual that I had known previously in the University . . . offered me one syllable of solace . . . the wife of a department member used the word 'treason' in front of me and was not challenged; on hearing that I would not accept the one and only proposition offered—that I tell all and hope for mercy—the head of the department lost his meal in front of me. . . . When a son was born to me in this trying time, not one called to congratulate me; when I was fired, almost without salary, three days before Christmas, not one called to offer aid."

In the Los Angeles area, an assistant professor of English defied the HUAC. As he later wrote, he belonged to no organizations at the time except the American Association of University Professors, the association of Rhodes scholars, and Phi Beta Kappa. He could have testified, but he was outraged and wouldn't. "I did not *want* to have legal aid," he wrote, "because I feel a citizen should be able . . . to defend himself against such bastards. Did not want to stand on any amendment or any part of the Constitution. Was argued out of this position and accepted legal aid, took dozens of amendments and have regretted it since."

The college president who fired him "also said that I was an exemplary teacher and offered to write me a letter of recommendation!" As for support from his colleagues on the faculty, "there was some 'moral' support by letter, telephone or when they thought none of their colleagues were looking. As to reaction—

many thought that I was getting a bad deal, that HUAC was a monstrous thing; but these were opinions privately held. Others simply could not understand how anyone could oppose *any* kind of authority, especially anything related to government. (I think this was the first time I knew why fascism had such an easy time of it with professors in Germany. . . .)"

The cowardice of college administrations and faculty is a constant theme running through the Tillet survey. Sometimes students and faculty members protested, but the predominant mood was one of spiritless acquiescence to authority, no matter how humiliating its demands on the individual. One dismissed instructor of humanities and history, who had taken the Fifth Amendment, put it this way: "Having been treated almost like a pariah . . . I shall never again view friendship with anything but a cautious, even cynical eye. It isn't simply that people are self-interested (I've always known that), but that almost everyone lacks the simplest requirement of courage. Among intellectuals, this lack of courage paralyzes their minds so that often they are incapable of doing the very thing they are trained to do—to think according to the rules of evidence and logic."

A one-time Rhodes scholar wrote: "I would say the episode *destroyed* a life . . . it was largely responsible for destroying a marriage and a family because of the lack of money to live on, lack of security, the resultant anxieties." One Negro instructor in a large Midwestern university, a socialist who described himself as an outspoken critic of the existing order, a gadfly in the pattern of Socrates, was fired for his beliefs just before he would have been given tenure. "My wife . . . 'went along' with me," he wrote, "then she got scared (for she, too, was one of the Negro firsts in the social agency where she was employed), and told me she could not afford to jeopardize her job." Again, the result was divorce. One professor, dismissed by a large Michigan university, unable to get another teaching job in the United States, moved to Canada and settled there permanently. His dismissal, he wrote, "had a relatively permanent effect on our eldest son, who was 7 at the time of my dismissal. He was subjected to a considerable amount of both verbal and physical abuse and has never forgotten it . . ."

Frequently the harrowing experiences of these intellectuals resulted in their virtual divorce from politics. Some hesitated to participate because they feared that any organization with which they became affiliated could be damaged by another witch-hunting resurrection of their past. One, a liberal, limited his political activities to casting his vote in the polling place. Explaining, he wrote: ". . . these experiences have compelled me to be *cautious* in everything so that I am not as effective as I should be in promoting a better world."

O N T H E H I G H E S T L E V E L S of intellect and leadership, the abdication of responsibility was all but complete. The Democratic-liberal establishment, which should have provided a rallying point, virtually disintegrated before the first onslaught and sought to camouflage itself by riding to hounds with the foe.

Why should this have been so? There were many reasons, but a British journalist, R. H. S. Crossman, writing in October, 1954, probably analyzed the disarray of liberal forces as perceptively as any:

"It is only the joiners and opinion-framers who supported the New Deal, Republican Spain and the Russian alliance that get it in the neck when the Americanism of yesterday becomes the treason of today. Those who suffer are the civil servants, journalists, radio and television commentators and trade union officials in exposed positions. And for them it was the Hiss case, not the activities of Joe McCarthy, which was the real disaster . . . Hundreds of thousands of American liberals felt themselves on trial along with Hiss; and all of them—apart from the few who still believe Hiss innocent—share a sense of guilt now that he has been proved guilty, which inhibits not only free discussion but free thought as well. This sense of guilt may partly explain the eagerness with which so many have jumped on the anti-Communist band-wagon. Since they are no longer certain that their previous views were right, why not seek safety in conformism?"

Crossman pointed out that leading liberal Democrats had adopted the tactic of trying to outdo McCarthy; that Senator Hubert H. Humphrey had upstaged McCarthy by introducing a bill to outlaw the Communist Party and that Senator Paul H. Douglas, the Illinois Democrat who fought so many valiant battles on behalf of the common man, had given the measure his fullest support. Crossman had an interview with Senator Douglas, and of this he wrote:

"When I asked Douglas about this measure, he replied very fiercely that the Republican Party does not really want to destroy the Communist Party. 'They keep it in existence,' he said, 'and use it to smear Democrats like myself. We liberals must destroy the Communists if this dirty game is to stop.' Is it unfair to suggest that his attitude is not unlike that of the Germans in the late 1920s who tolerated Jew-baiting in order to preserve the Weimar Republic?"

Compromise on principle led to "punch-pulling" in journalism and in the classroom "to the avoidance of dangerous subjects." "Worst of all," Crossman wrote, "they [the liberals] have willingly or unwillingly come to terms with the New Loyalty. By accepting it and seeking only to modify its excesses, the liberal movement is conniving at its own destruction."

He might have added that this conniving was also weakening the fiber of the nation. The effect showed most clearly in the attitude of the college generation of the 1950s, which became known as "the silent generation" or "the conforming generation." Jules Feiffer, the dramatist and cartoonist noted for his savage caricatures, has recalled the academic atmosphere of the era as he felt it during lecture tours of college campuses. He would often make what he thought was a most provocative speech on the issues of the day, and when he finished, there would be that abysmal silence that signifies a total lack of reaction. "Then," he said, "someone might ask me a question like 'Where do you get your ideas?' or 'What size drawing paper do you use?' "

Near the end of the decade, the attitudes of the college class of 1958 were capsuled in articles written for *The Nation* by graduating students from major colleges. A typical student attitude, according to a paper written by two students at Stanford University, was this: "As for politics, what can I do? The odds against me are too great. For one thing, the problems are too complicated; for another, national politics is a dirty business . . . As for employment in a large corporation, well, I have to eat. I want a wife and children . . . I'll conform eight hours a day and be a free man in my own home. The world will probably be better off without my messing in it."

Another university student wrote: "In a local history class, a majority of the students voted in favor of Socrates's execution. It made quite a stir among the professors, but the students showed little surprise . . . or concern."

Such was the mood of a generation that cringed before the witch hunters. In this atmosphere, as in the time of Robespierre, any accusation was tantamount to conviction and brought a thumbs-down vote from the Madame LaFarges eager to guillotine reputations. Elmer Davis, one of the most powerful radio voices of the day, recalled that early in the McCarthy hysteria he had broadcast an appeal for calmness and sanity, pointing out that McCarthy was hurling unproven allegations and arguing that "we had better wait and see if the evidence justified conviction."

"Whereupon," he wrote, "an infuriated citizen, apparently a man of standing in his community, wrote me, 'We cannot wait for convictions; what we want is confessions.'"

This was hardly the America envisioned by the Founding Fathers.

The panicked flight of the American public from the noblest traditions of our past was demonstrated time and again by inquiring reporters. On July 4, 1951, the Madison *Capital-Times* in Wisconsin drafted a petition made up entirely of quotes from the Declaration of Independence and the Bill of Rights of the Constitution. A reporter was sent out on the streets to test public reaction. He stopped 112 persons; 111 refused to sign the petition, reacting with horror. They considered the sentiments taken verbatim from our two basic national documents positively subversive.

In another Midwestern town, only two persons out of a hundred were willing to sign a similar document. Ninety-eight either did not want to get "involved" in any statements so "controversial," or they felt that the phrases must have been written by dangerous persons, radicals or communists. In the South, the New Orleans *Item* tried the same experiment. A reporter accosted thirty-four persons; twenty-eight refused to have anything to do with the ideology expressed in our Declaration and Constitution. Many even urged that the FBI should be called in to inquire into this suspicious business.

How did it come about that "100-percent Americans" were afraid to be associated with the basic American documents of freedom?

2

The Roots Go Deep

EX-PRESIDENT WILLIAM HOWARD TAFT, reflecting on the victory of Calvin Coolidge in 1924, came up with an observation that is as valid today as it was then. "This country is no country for radicalism," he said. "I think it is really the most conservative country in the world."

The performance of the American electorate in the tug-of-war just concluded had given Taft adequate basis for his belief. The Presidential election had been a three-way contest among laconic Calvin Coolidge, stodgy Democrat John W. Davis, and the elder Robert M. La Follette, champion of Wisconsin and Midwestern progressivism. La Follette's third-party movement, like that of Theodore Roosevelt in 1912, had been predestined to failure in the power complex of the American two-party system —this despite the fact that La Follette as a political leader was a giant running against two dwarfs. What the dwarfs had going for them, however, was something that La Follette did not—an image of sober, stable leadership. La Follette's image was that of the windmill battler, the challenger of the established order.

The issue, Republican spokesmen declared, was whether the American people would choose common sense with solid and silent Cal or "the sinking sands of socialism with Robert M. La Follette." Presented in those terms, there was really no choice. As a boy aware for the first time of a Presidential election, I can remember how deadly the tactic was. Many of my elders, men who admired La Follette's courage and liked much that he had done, became possessed by that inbred American fear that he was perhaps a bit too wild-eyed—somehow not quite "safe." It was no surprise when Calvin Coolidge won in a landslide.

Time and again in American history a similar set of circumstances calling for a similar choice has produced a similar result. William Jennings Bryan, most famous orator of his day, reached three times for the Presidential prize—and three times the American people shied fearfully from what they regarded as his dubious and dangerous "free silver" doctrine. More recently, at the other end of the spectrum, Barry Goldwater triggered the same reaction in 1964 when he became identified in the public mind as a dangerous extremist. The voters fled, seeking what they had always sought—a centrist whom they saw as more restrained and responsible.

In 1968 the protest demonstrations at the Democratic convention in Chicago—protests marked by police brutality so outrageous it was later labeled in the Walker Report as tantamount to a "police riot"—elicited a public reaction the reverse of what might have been expected. Though police beatings of helpless demonstrators and even of innocent bystanders had been shown on nationwide television, public sympathy quickly coalesced around the police. This again was typically American. Many of the demonstrators had been the bearded and unwashed; they had tried to disrupt orderly processes; they had created "scenes." To the cautious middle-class American mind they were the personification of anarchy, a threat to peace and stability; they represented a menace to the fixed order of things; and in this situation even police brutality could be rationalized as a necessary antidote.

Such an episode is revealing of the American character. Americans empathize with plain, common, "good" men possessing qualities much like their own (the image of a Truman or an Eisenhower), or they become enraptured with a charismatic leader possessed of buoyancy and wit, like John F. Kennedy, whom they see as calling forth the best in themselves. But there it stops. Americans have no sympathy for a man who proposes to upset hallowed traditions, who advocates extreme measures. There is built into the American character an instinctive prejudice against the usual source of such proposals for drastic change—the innovative and agitating left.

The right is relatively immune to such reaction. The right does not stand for disruptive and unpleasant change; its traditional role is defender of the status quo. Only when it blatantly steps over the boundary into extremism does it provoke adverse reaction. Only when the John Birch Society labels an Eisenhower a Communist, or when a Barry Goldwater proclaims that "extremism in defense of liberty is no vice" and advises leaving life-and-death decisions to the generals, does the political right suffer the rejection of the American people. And even then the stigma is usually for the moment only. When the right reverts to its customary role as guardian of the gates against change, its excesses are quickly forgotten.

Such are the characteristics that make this the most inhospitable nation for the propagation of communistic doctrines. Only idealists divorced from contact with political realities, or psychotic individuals seeking to trample their way to power, could ever have deceived themselves into believing that communism would be "the wave of the future" in America. Elmer Davis, writing of the communist/ex-communist syndrome in his essay on doublethink, propounded the thesis that Communists were wrong when they were Communists and equally wrong when they became ex-communist witch hunters. They were wrong in the first instance because they so completely failed to comprehend the American character; and they were wrong the second time around because, unable for their own egos' sake to acknowledge the magnitude of their original error, they had to convince themselves and everyone else that it had not been all a mirage, that their nightmare had been horribly and dangerously real, and that what they had renounced was still a threatening demon.

Every statistic that we have ridicules the premises of these switch-artists. In 1932, in the pit of the worst economic disaster the nation had ever suffered, when the entire economic system toppled toward collapse—even in such a time of utter desperation, only a scant 100,000 out of 40 million Americans who cast their ballots in the Presidential election voted for the Communist ticket. Even in 1944, in a national mood softened toward Russia as a result of our wartime alliance, the Communist Party could muster a membership of only 80,000, by J. Edgar Hoover's own figures—and this was the highest peak it ever reached. For two decades one of the most vociferous Congressional redbaiters was Rep. Hamilton Fish, the ultraconservative New York Republican. Fish admired dictators of many stripes, ranging from the Dominican Republic's Trujillo to Hitler, and in 1933 he even wrote a glowing American introduction to a Nazi propaganda book trumpeting the wonders of National Socialism. Yet even Fish in 1947 acknowledged that communists and communist sympathizers constituted *less than one percent* of America's adult population.

Yet it was this less than one percent that this mighty nation was soon to view as a threat so pervasive that it justified every American in suspecting his neighbor.

A T T H E C O R E of the American character lies the concept of the private possession of land and the private ownership of business. It could hardly be otherwise, for it was this concept that played a fundamental role in the initial colonization and in three centuries of expansion westward through the wild spaces of a magnificent continent.

There were, of course, many and mixed motives that impelled the original settlers to brave the rigors of the Atlantic in cockleshell boats, and to face the additional hardships of taming a wilderness. Many came to escape religious persecutions or political reprisals, but others were impelled by one strong motive—the quest of the poor, the homeless, for land, for farms and homes that they could call their own. A man who had been a virtual serf in Europe could stand tall and strong, his feet planted firmly in the fertile soil of *his own* land.

Inevitably, the idea of the sanctity of property, of a man's inalienable right to the possession of his own hard-won acres became basic to the American character. For a people with such a tradition there could be no more heretical creed than communism, with its threat of collectivization of farms, seizure and nationalization of industry. This was an ideology that threatened everything the average American and his ancestors had held dear; and so, here were the seeds of a national paranoia—waiting for the proper combination of circumstances.

The Russian revolution in 1917 led to the first shock-wave of hysteria—a relatively brief flash of insanity that left, most would have said, no permanent scars on the nation. But it had been a warning, much like that given a man who has a first mild heart attack.

This first aberration contained all the seeds of the second. Rarely in history have two periods—their antecedents, their atmosphere, their contending forces—been so similar as the postwar periods of World Wars I and II in America.

Prior to World War I, the national mood had been one of growing liberalism, and its product had been an unprecedented spate of liberal legislation during the first New Freedom Administration of Woodrow Wilson. Prior to World War II, the New Deal of Franklin D. Roosevelt had changed historic concepts of the role of the federal government in national life and had produced a flood of basic liberal reforms. World War I brought an end to the liberalism of Wilson, restoring to the seats of power, as he himself had prophesied, the very big-business and ultraconservative interests his New Freedom had battled; World War II similarly ended Rooseveltian domestic innovation and developed for the first time a military-industrial complex dominated by reactionary forces. In World War I, the Russian Revolution established communism as a reality, not just a crackpot theory. American conservatives in their panic promoted an irrational propaganda campaign that envisioned blood-dripping Bolsheviki hiding under every other American bed; in the aftermath of World War II, the demon Russian ideology emerged stronger than ever, and conservatives phantasied virtually nonexistent American communism into a kind of national Loch Ness monster. The results in both periods were the same. Liberalism, equated with radicalism, died. After World War I, the nation drifted into the do-nothing "normalcy" of Harding and Coolidge, a path that led directly to the Great Depression. After World War II, there was a similar slowing of the pace of change in the euphoric Eisenhower years—followed by the chaos of the sixties, when the nation began to pay the penalty for long neglect of its domestic affairs.

The Nightmare Decade can best be understood if one realizes that it had all happened the same way before, in briefer and milder form. It has worked with clock-like precision twice, and logic says that unless it is understood and combatted it could work just as infallibly again.

The Russian Revolution shook the established order. At one extreme, radicals envisioned replicas of the communist coup sweeping the world; at the other, conservative business and financial powers were haunted by the specter of the Bolsheviki. In between, disregarded in the calculations of both sides, was the overwhelming mass of stable, practical American people.

Postwar disturbances played into the hands of business and its vigilantes. Workers had been caught in a wartime bind. Food prices had increased 84 percent, the cost of living had risen 99 percent—but wages had gone up, at most, only 5 to 10 percent, and in many cases not at all. These pressures created a wave of strikes involving more than four million workers in 1919, and disturbances of such magnitude gave the management class an ideal propaganda weapon. A small band of radical extremists furnished additional fuel for the propaganda fires. These crackpots, most of them anarchists, went around the country planting bombs at the doors of prominent officials or sending bombs through the mail. These explosions frightened the great mass of the American people, lending a semblance of credibility to the outcry in the headlines that the Bolsheviki were about to take over the country. Though the most rigorous investigations, backed by all the authority of government, never could establish the existence of more than a handful of bomb-plotters, the frenzy was incredible.

On one occasion, the sheriff of Delaware County in Pennsylvania proclaimed that he had uncovered a Bolshevist plot that "threatens to engulf" the city of Chester. He had, he said, arrested "sixty-four Bolsheviki," and he had enrolled deputies, police, the state police and the citizens' home guard in a small army to place a special cordon around the jail. The menace that this army had been marshaled to fight never developed, and the whole wild, one-day alarum dropped quickly out of sight.

This failure of the menace to accommodate the headlines in case after case had relatively little effect on journalists. The one-sidedness of the American press showed in its handling of any dispatches dealing with the new regime in Russia. The Soviet rule was pictured as one of diabolical cruelty. One dispatch claimed that in Petrograd the Bolsheviki operated an electrical guillotine that lopped off five hundred heads an hour. The Bolshevik rule was said to be a "compound of slaughter, confiscation, anarchy and universal disorder." Russian women had been nationalized, ran another myth, and cartoonists pictured wealthy and cultured women cleaning the streets. One artist portrayed the Soviet government as a smoking gun, a bomb, and a dangling hangman's noose.

Only in a few liberal weeklies of limited circulation was any serious attempt made to enlighten the American people about the actual aims of the revolution or the conditions that had produced it. Even *The New York Times* was infected. A study of the *Times* from 1917–46 has shown that the Russians were almost invariably described as "enigmatic," "incomprehensible" people whose behavior was "a riddle." Their leaders were "immoral," "unethical," "perfidious," "treacherous," "unjust," "unreasonable" and "arbitrary" men. Between November, 1917, and November, 1919, the *Times* reported solemnly on no less than ninety-one occasions that the Soviet regime was about to fall.

The hysteria eventually subsided. The reason was that the myth of a national Red menace was slain by the myth-makers themselves. In early January, 1920, Attorney General A. Mitchell Palmer, who had visions of becoming President, ordered a sweeping series of dragnet raids in major American cities. Literally thousands of alleged Bolsheviki were rounded up and incarcerated—and eventually released. The overwhelming majority turned out to be innocent and baffled workers, some of whom had been attending social functions or English classes. The excesses perpetrated by the witch hunters in this dragnet roundup had the effect of killing the witch hunt. By the end of January, 1920, the Red menace had practically vanished from the headlines.

But the frenzy, though of brief duration, had had its effect. Robert K. Murray, assistant professor of history at Pennsylvania State University, later wrote that business had wanted to roll back the present and the immediate past and to return to "normalcy." "It was the normalcy of the pre-Spanish-American War era," he wrote. "Normalcy (to the businessman) meant freedom from government regulations, from labor unions, from public responsibility—the freedom of laissez-faire." The scare campaign designed to achieve this, Murray added, had led the nation to desert "its most honored principles of freedom—principles which had made it great and had given it birth."

The atmosphere was perhaps best described by a British journalist, A. C. Gardiner, in phrases that could just as well have been penned thirty years later: "No one who was in the United States as I chanced to be, in the autumn of 1919, will forget the feverish condition of the public mind at that time. It was hag-ridden by the spectre of Bolshevism. It was like a sleeper in a nightmare, and the horrid name 'Radical' covered the most innocent departure from conventional thought with a desperate purpose. 'America,' as one wit of the time said, 'is the land of liberty—liberty to keep in step.'"

THEODORE ROOSEVELT, the only Republican President in this century with a claim to greatness, had been unable to imbue the party with his own political philosophy. His mild liberalism and willingness to reform were traits conspicuously absent in the Republican Administrations of the roaring twenties, when business leadership under the banner of "normalcy" led the nation into an orgy of speculation and the inevitable crash of 1929. This business dominance of national affairs for an entire decade would have been abhorrent to Roosevelt, who had had little respect for the acumen of "the moneyed men," as he called them, in running the affairs of state. He had written during the panic of 1907: "I neither respect nor admire the huge moneyed men to whom money is the be-all and end-all of existence; to whom the acquisition of untold millions is the supreme goal in life, and who are too often utterly indifferent as to how these millions are obtained."

And later he commented: "I do not dislike, but I certainly have no especial respect or admiration for and no trust in, the typical big moneyed men of my country. I do not regard them as furnishing sound opinion as regards either foreign or domestic policies." There was absolutely nothing to be said, he argued, for "government by a plutocracy, for government by men very powerful in certain lines and gifted with 'the money touch,' but with ideals which in their essence are merely those of so many glorified pawnbrokers."

With the election of Warren G. Harding, the "glorified pawnbrokers" were in the saddle. This was again the golden age of business in politics, a return to the "normalcy" of William McKinley. And a return, too, to the ethics of the "black-horse cavalry," those agents of business who had casually bought and sold legislatures from the Presidency of Ulysses S. Grant down to the turn of the century. The scandals created new symbols: Teapot Dome would forever stand as the epitome of political corruption, and the name of Samuel Insull for the pyramiding of watered stock and the fleecing of investors.

The speculative orgy in Wall Street had to be experienced to be believed. One underpaid editor I know tells how he went out to dinner with friends. One of them had a hot tip on a stock that was "going places," and he urged my editor friend to get in on the ground floor. "But I haven't any money," the editor protested. "That doesn't make any difference; you can't lose," his friend insisted. "Here, go call my broker."

Quaking because he didn't know what he would do if he did have to put up money, the editor did as he was told. Describing his experience later, he said: "I went back and we had dinner, and when we finished, my friend said, 'Let's give a call and see how that stock is making out.' So we did. And the stock had gone up like a rocket—and I sold out. I had made $1,400 while I was having dinner—and I hadn't put up a cent."

Sanity said that such a gambling fever could lead only to destruction, but men with faith that business could do no wrong sat in the White House. Harding had died, and Coolidge kept faith at the shrine. "The chief business of the American people is business," he said once. And again: "The man who builds a factory builds a temple . . . The man who works there worships there."

Such was the official religion. And when "silent Cal" decided he "did not choose to run," eagerly waiting in the wings was the even more perfect symbol of the business dynasty—Herbert Hoover, the great engineer, the perfectionist. After Hoover was elected it happened—the great stock market collapse of 1929 and the succeeding, harrowing years of an ever-deepening depression.

It was useless for Republicans to shout that this was just the inevitable aftermath of the dislocations of World War I; *that* depression had been overcome in 1921, and the nation had had eight years of frenzied prosperity. It was ridiculous to contend, as Hoover did for so long, that such trials were just temporary maladjustments of the business cycle and that a return to prosperity was "just around the corner" if people would only be patient. The truth was that the Great Depression had been caused primarily by the mentality and ethics of the "glorified pawnbrokers."

But to have acknowledged this would have been an admission of fundamental error. The business community's faith in itself, its enduring memories of the trials of Wilson's New Freedom, and its psychotic fear of the specter of Bolshevism, all contributed to its obdurate blindness. For if business was not a god, and the factory not a temple, then the only alternative was that government must have a responsibility for the welfare of the worker, and the duty to avoid economic collapse.

This fundamental clash of ideology underlay the tumult of the Roosevelt and Truman years and was fundamental to McCarthyism. The extent of the split is illustrated by an anecdote recounted by Frances Perkins, one of the closest aides of Franklin Roosevelt. Describing the early years of the depression when Roosevelt was Governor of New York, Miss Perkins wrote: ". . . He was fully appreciative of the enormous advances in the standard of living which has come about through the utilization of machinery, efficiency, and system under private ownership and management. But he could not accept the cruel philosophy then being peddled in some quarters that, since the system was so good on the whole, the only thing to do when it struck one of its periodic crises was to let it plunge to the bottom where it would right itself and gradually begin to move up again.

"I once saw Roosevelt listening to this argument from a man he had known for years and who called himself an economist. I shall never forget the gray look of horror on his face as he turned on this man and said, 'People aren't cattle, you know.' "

Herbert Hoover faithfully waited for "the plunge" to hit bottom, and for the system to "right itself and gradually begin to move up again." But this oft-predicted, "natural" correction of the laws of economics refused to take place. The plunge went on into a seemingly bottomless abyss.

In many towns and cities, every bank collapsed; money became, for many, practically nonexistent. Policemen, firemen, teachers could be paid only in script—promises of the town fathers to put up hard cash later, if and when it became available. Some merchants refused to accept the script at all; others would take it only at a discount. In one family I knew, the father, like 25 percent of the labor force, was out of a job and could not find one; the mother, a schoolteacher, was being paid in script—and too many merchants just wouldn't take the script. At one point it was necessary to break up the furniture to get heat in a bitterly cold winter.

When Franklin Roosevelt took office in March, 1933, the whole nation was in a state of paralysis. In many states the epidemic of bank failures had closed the doors of every bank. The entire structure on which generations of businessmen had built their faith was crashing down around them. "We are at the end of our rope," Herbert Hoover cried on the verge of retirement. "There is nothing else we can do."

The business community was in the wildest panic. "Over champagne and cigars at the Everglades in Palm Beach," Arthur Schlesinger has written, "a banker declared the country on the verge of revolution; another guest, breaking the startled silence, advised the company 'to step without the territorial bounds of the United States of America with as much cash as you can carry just as soon as it is feasible for you to get away.' 'There'll be revolution, sure,' a Los Angeles banker said on a transcontinental train. 'The farmers will rise up. So will labor. The Reds will run the country—or maybe the Fascists. Unless, of course, Roosevelt does something.' "

Roosevelt, of course, did something. He plunged into the furious activity of the hundred days, fighting the depression with all the powers of government just as he would have fought a war. The banks were saved, bank deposits insured; the farmers and home owners were helped with loans; a farm price and production control system was devised. Labor legislation freed the hands of unions. The Security and Exchange Commission was created to supervise Wall Street. Ultimately, the Social Security Act, a great cornerstone of the modern economy, became law. Unemployment insurance guaranteed that, in depressions, workers would not be left destitute—and so purchasing power would not completely dry up. Old-age pensions shored up the economy in times of trouble with a floor of guaranteed buying support. And finally the Wages and Hours Act in 1938 mandated the forty-hour week, provided for a scale of minimum wages, and made necessary the payment of overtime for any labor in excess of the legislated maximum.

This was interference of government in the hallowed affairs of business—with a vengeance. The nation had been saved; it had not been necessary for the wealthy to skip out of the country with all the cash they could carry. They retained, in fact, most of their wealth and special privileges—but they hated it. The medicine that had cured them was foul-tasting stuff that stuck in their gullets. The Roosevelt break with all the sacred traditions of laissez-faire capitalism had been, due to the necessity of the times, sharp and complete; the sudden wrench from old ways was traumatic for these men. They still dreamed of an era when all would work out perfectly for "the moneyed men" who just had to be right about everything because they were right about ways of making money. This was the faith that would not die, and in it were the seeds for the schisms of our times. Roosevelt, the hero of the great mass of Americans, was the detested "that man" of business and finance. Because he had such a tricky, damnably effective personality, because the people were so gullible and so mesmerized by his radio voice, there was only one way he could be attacked—through a propaganda campaign that would equate all liberalism with socialism and communism in a formula designed to frighten the wits out of the least volatile electorate in the world. It was a campaign that did not really take while Roosevelt was alive, but it was conducted with unremitting determination for the better part of fifteen years—and in the end, helped by the conspiracy of circumstance, it produced the Nightmare Decade.

3

The Equation of the "Ism"

IT WAS THE EVENING of January 25, 1936, and some 2,000 guests, representing the most powerful economic forces in the nation, were gathered in the ballroom of the Mayflower Hotel in Washington to see the propaganda techniques of Joseph Goebbels tried out on the New Deal. The method is simplicity itself. All change—all economic or social legislation that impinges on the holdings, privileges and power of the extremely rich—is equated with communism.

This Mayflower Hotel rally of the millionaires' club and representatives of industries controlled by them marked the climactic effort of the American Liberty League to scare the American people out of their strange devotion to the heresies of Franklin

Roosevelt. The audience represented, according to *The New York Times,* "either through principals or attorneys, a large portion of the capitalistic wealth of the country." The attitude of this emperor class had already been spelled out in a series of lavishly printed pamphlets, redolent of the skills of Madison Avenue.

The message of the Liberty League was unadorned and unequivocal: the United States under Franklin Roosevelt was headed straight for socialism, bankruptcy and tyranny. The league mixed fascism and communism almost indiscriminately in its catalogue of horrors, but it bore down most heavily and consistently on the communist menace. It saw the Agricultural Adjustment Administration, Roosevelt's effort to bring some stability to farm prices, as a "trend toward the Fascist control of agriculture." The Utility Holding Company Act, designed to protect investors against the kind of stock-watering and fleecing that had marked the career of Samuel Insull, was pictured in a series of full-page newspaper advertisements as a device intended to rob widows and orphans of their mite and as "a blow at invested capital." Relief programs to help the poor and the Social Security Act marked "the end of democracy." The menace of every foreign "ism" under the sun to the "American way" had all been wrapped up in one emotional bundle by John W. Davis, the 1924 Democratic Presidential candidate, the Wall Street lawyer and spokesman for Morgan interests, and a prime mover in the Liberty League. Davis predicted that the American Congress would soon amount to little more "than the present Congress of the Soviets, the Reichstag of Germany or the Italian Parliament."

This creed had been having little effect, strangely enough, upon the American people. They had somehow gotten it into their perverse heads that federal relief programs were to be preferred to the bread lines, near-starvation and economic collapse of the Hoover days. They somehow felt that the Social Security program was for their benefit. It was in their desperation to effect a change in this mass delusion that the Liberty Leaguers now made their last great play for publicity.

Their standard-bearer was a convert—Alfred E. Smith, the one-time "Happy Warrior" and 1928 Democratic Presidential candidate, now an embittered old man because his protégé, Franklin Roosevelt, had captured the prize he so long had coveted. Eaten up by envy, Smith had proclaimed he was going "to take a walk" from the party of his lifelong allegiance in the campaign of 1936. He had even gone to San Simeon and conferred at the summit with one of the emperors of American journalism, his old enemy William Randolph Hearst. They had issued a joint communiqué denouncing the "imported, autocratic, Asiatic Socialist party of Karl Marx and Franklin Delano Roosevelt." The Liberty League program had been underwritten and financed by corporations possessing assets of more than $37 billion. The league's directors had been identified as men having affiliations with such power complexes as U.S. Steel, General Motors, Standard Oil, the Chase National Bank, Goodyear Tire and Rubber Company, the Baltimore and Ohio Railroad. The Du Ponts, inveterate backers of right-wing causes, had financed the Delaware branch with contributions amounting to $10,357.

Such had been the build-up for the final blare of ideological trumpets in the Mayflower Hotel. In the Mayflower audience as Smith spoke, newsmen noted the presence of the economically powerful and politically disaffected; almost at random they jotted down such names as businessman Winthrop Aldrich; Ernest T. Weir of National Steel; no less than a dozen Du Ponts; John W. Davis; even the young Dean Acheson (no shouting liberal he, though he was to become one of those most foully smeared in the McCarthy era).

To these and others like them Al Smith, in white tie and tails, delivered the message about New Dealers they had come to hear. "It is all right with me," he cried, "if they want to disguise themselves with Karl Marx or Lenin or any of the rest of that bunch, but I won't stand for allowing them to march under the banner of Jackson or Cleveland."

In his peroration, he hammered home the theme: "Let me give this solemn warning: There can be only one capital, Washington or Moscow. There can be only one atmosphere of government, the clean, pure, fresh air of free America, or the foul breath of communistic Russia."

In the White House, Roosevelt sat baffled, unable to understand what possessed the wits of his old friend and mentor. "It was perfect," said Pierre S. Du Pont, giving the reaction of the millionaires' club to the performance. In the nation as a whole, the public yawned. But the failure of the Mayflower Hotel rally to bring the American people screaming to their feet did not daunt these powerful men.

DID THEY REALLY BELIEVE that the New Deal could be equated with communism? Or did they use these slogans in a callous and cynical play to regain political power? Only they themselves could ever know, and the answer of course varied with the individual. In the end, however, it made little difference whether they were self-deluders or unconscionable schemers; the result was the same. They were united on the tactics that must be used to unseat "that man" in the White House.

Right-wing extremist organizations proliferated, heavily financed in many instances by the same angels who had backed the Liberty League. An all-out attempt was made to appeal to self-interest groups of every variety, and to all types of religious and racial prejudice. One such organization, the Farmers' Independence Council, operated out of the Liberty League office in Washington. Its largest contributor was Lammot Du Pont, who put up $5,000. Others who became exercised about the farmers' independence—and so poured their contributions into the council —included those well-known agriculturists Alfred P. Sloan of General Motors, banker Ogden Mills, Winthrop Aldrich, and J. Howard Pew of Sun Oil.

A more sinister organization went by the inspiring name of Sentinels of the Republic. In the spring of 1936, Senator Hugo Black's Special Committee to Investigate Lobbying Activities turned a spotlight on the Sentinels and showed that these defenders of the gates were backed by such wealthy industrialists as Pew, A. Atwater Kent, and Nicholas Roosevelt, of the New York *Herald-Tribune*. The Sentinels were opposed to the twentieth century in almost every way. They frowned on the Child Labor Amendment, fought the Social Security Act, advocated repeal of the welfare clause of the Constitution. Such themes were stressed in editorials that the Sentinels supplied free to some 1,300 newspapers, "urging a return to American principles." Some of their principles could hardly be described as American: the Black committee investigators uncovered correspondence that showed the Sentinels were dyed with a deep stain of anti-Semitism. According to them, FDR had brought "the Jewish brigades" to Washington; "the enemy is world-wide" and "is Jewish in origin."

Exposure of such crackpot ideas in the prevailing liberalism of the times made the wealthy classes the laughingstock of most of the nation. By midsummer the Republican Party was pleading with the Liberty Leaguers not to identify themselves with the national ticket. Yet the tactics of the league remained the tactics of the party. As the candidacy of Alfred M. Landon faltered, Republican desperation mounted, and the charges became ever more wild and irresponsible. Colonel Frank Knox, a Bull Mooser in his youth and now the Republican Vice Presidential candidate, became the redbaiting echo of Hearst and Al Smith.

"The New Deal candidate," he cried, "has been leading us toward Moscow," and the Democratic Party "has been seized by alien and un-American elements." He was preaching, he thundered, "the doctrine, not of the soft and spineless kept citizens of a regimented state, but of the self-respecting and self-reliant men who made America . . . Next November you will choose the American way."

As the campaign went into its final weeks, no scare tactic was too despicable. Knox shouted: "Today no life insurance policy is secure; no savings account is safe." The Hearst newspaper chain splashed a front-page editorial charging that the communists, on the orders of Moscow, were working for the reelection of Roosevelt. The Republican National Committee called Roosevelt "the Kerensky of the American revolutionary movement." And William Lemke (the Presidential candidate of the Union Party, organized by the anti-Semitic, profascist radio priest Father Charles Coughlin) chimed in:

"I do not charge that the President of the United States is a Communist, but I do charge that [Earl] Browder, [David] Dubinsky and other Communist leaders have laid their cuckoo eggs in his Democratic nest and that he is hatching them."

Roosevelt met the attack head-on, with scorn and his own priceless brand of satirical humor. The attempt to put the communist label on the Democrats, he said, was a red herring dragged out to hide the fact that the opposition had no program and no ideas. There was no difference between the major parties on the issue of communism; it was abhorrent to both of them; and he personally repudiated "the support of any advocate of communism or of any other alien 'ism which would by fair means or foul change our American democracy." And then he told this story:

"In the summer of 1933, a nice old gentleman wearing a silk hat fell off the end of a pier. He was unable to swim. A friend ran down the pier, dived overboard and pulled him out; but the silk hat floated off with the tide. After the old gentleman had been revived he was effusive in his thanks. He praised his friend for saving his life. Today, three years later, the old gentleman is berating his friend because the silk hat was lost."

The chuckles of most of the nation drove the Republicans to new extremes. One of the last pieces of legislation during Roosevelt's first term had been the Social Security Act, which was to go into effect January 1, 1937. This had been one of the measures closest to Roosevelt's heart; he felt deeply, as Frances Perkins later wrote, that this protection was desperately needed, as had been demonstrated by the Depression of 1929–33. But the Republicans now turned to an all-out attack on the Social Security Act. In the closing days of the campaign, they charged that it would literally enslave the American people.

Powerful industrialists took up the theme. Placards went up in factories across the nation: YOU'RE SENTENCED TO A WEEKLY PAY REDUCTION FOR ALL YOUR WORKING LIFE. YOU'LL HAVE TO SERVE THE SENTENCE UNLESS YOU REVERSE IT NOVEMBER 3. This referred to the 1 percent payroll tax that would go into effect the first of the year; it made no mention, of course, of the fact that employers would also have to contribute to the Social Security fund for each of their employees. When workers opened their pay envelopes, they found in them further messages of concern from the kindly management. These notes warned that the tax in future might go much higher than the 1 percent (this much, at least, was right), then resorted to a scare technique, casting doubt on the integrity of the system. "You might get this money back . . . but only if Congress decides to make the appropriation for this purpose," the messages read. "There is NO guarantee."

Landon charged that Social Security raised the specter of a police state. "Are these 26 million [workers] going to be fingerprinted? Are their photographs going to be kept on file in a Washington office? Or are they going to have identification tags put about their necks?" he asked. Republican National Chairman

John D. M. Hamilton went further (using the tactic that was to make Joe McCarthy famous fourteen years later in Wheeling). In a speech in Boston, he declared that each of the 26 million enslaved workers would be compelled to wear a metal dog tag— "such as the one I hold in my hand."

This attack provoked Roosevelt to fury. In his final campaign speech in Madison Square Garden, he declared, in terms that brought the massive crowd roaring to its feet, that "only desperate men with their backs to the wall would descend so far below the level of decent citizenship." They were, he said, "already aliens to the spirit of American democracy."

When the votes were counted the result astounded everyone, even Roosevelt himself. The Republicans went down to the most catastrophic defeat in their history; they carried only Maine and Vermont.

One might have thought that such a decisive verdict would carry a message to even the most insensitive of men, but it did not. The faith that business knows best remained unshaken by the evidence of the past or the verdict of the present.

THE CRUSHING DEFEAT OF 1936 drove the wealthy classes of America deeper into paranoia. They convinced themselves and tried to convince everyone else that Roosevelt was a virtual dictator, that the American system had been subverted by foreign "isms," and that only the most desperate measures could save the nation. In an effort to reverse completely the public verdict rendered so emphatically at the polls, one of the most effective propaganda organizations ever put together in this nation was swiftly formed by leading newspaper publishers and industrialists. It became marked in time with obviously fascist and anti-Semitic overtones. For two decades it conjured up the horrors of the Red menace, and some of its propaganda offshoots remain active on the American scene today. The counsel to a House of Representatives subcommittee on lobbying in 1950 called it "the most comprehensive lobby I have found in my study."

The organization was known originally as The National Committee to Uphold Constitutional Government. In 1941 that somewhat unwieldy title was changed to The Committee for Constitutional Government.

The committee was organized in February, 1937. Frank E. Gannett, of Rochester, N.Y., owner of a chain of eighteen small-city daily newspapers, was its president and moving spirit. Gannett, who had been a vice chairman of the Republican National Committee and who was to become a candidate for the Republican Presidential nomination in 1940, drew into his organization a number of newspaper publishers and powerful industrialists, combining propaganda outlets with an unlimited flow of cash. From the moment of its birth, finances were no problem for The National Committee to Uphold Constitutional Government; in the first twelve to thirteen months of its existence, it spent more than $300,000, and conducted one of the largest mail-order campaigns this country has ever seen.

The field director of the new committee, the man who was in direct charge of its operations and of the affiliates it soon spawned, was Edward A. Rumely, a Germanophile who had been convicted and had served a brief term for having operated a German propaganda machine through his ownership of the New York *Daily Mail* in World War I days (he was later given a full pardon by Coolidge). Rumely and Gannett were far more sophisticated propagandists than the bumblers of the Liberty League. The huge headline-making splash was not for them. Their method was to till the grass roots, to play on every kind of self-interest and prejudice, to try by subtle means to meld together any and every group that could serve a reactionary purpose.

They compiled elaborate mailing lists. Rumely told the House of Representatives committee investigating lobbying in 1950 that they had spent $15,000 drawing up a list of 40,000 farm leaders, and he added with satisfaction: "That list is productive. We get action on it." Other lists were compiled containing the names of doctors and professional men, newspaper editors and publishers, leaders of industry and millionaires who could be tapped for instant revenue for the nationwide distribution of books and pamphlets describing the "pure" American creed. In 1948 Rumely wrote, "we asked Ed Hutton [Edward F. Hutton, who headed one of the largest Wall Street brokerage firms] to write to 20,000 individuals worth $500,000 to $1 million and over."

The response to such appeals kept the committee's treasury constantly replenished. The committee and one of its affiliates, America's Future, a book distribution and radio propaganda arm, received hearty contributions from some of the most powerful corporations and individuals in America. There were J. Howard Pew and various Du Ponts. The 1950 House investigation showed that corporations contributing to both the committee and America's Future included Armco Steel, Champion Spark Plug, Cities Service, Connecticut Light & Power, Kennecott Copper, S.S. Kresge, Eli Lilly & Co. and Republic Steel. Correspondence uncovered in the House investigation indicated that Eli Lilly & Co. alone had contributed $25,000 to the committee in 1950 and that H. R. Cullen, the Texas oil tycoon, had put up $1 million to keep America's Future programs on the air over a hundred stations of the Liberty network.

Fortunately for the committee, unfortunately for the nation, Roosevelt's greatest political blunder coincided with the committee's birth. In 1937, perhaps carried away by his overwhelming victory at the polls, Roosevelt sprang upon a startled nation a devious plan that would have enabled him to pack the U.S. Supreme Court with Justices of his own choosing. The plan would have permitted the President to appoint one new Justice for every Justice on the court who had failed to retire after his seventieth birthday. Since there were six septuaginarians on the court that had been blocking New Deal legislation, Roosevelt could have named six more Justices and assured favorable decisions for his programs.

It was an action that cut across all political lines, violating a most sacred American tradition—the separation of powers in a system of checks and balances designed to prevent any branch of government from becoming dictatorial. Roosevelt's action demonstrated to the conservatives that he was exactly the symbol of authoritarianism that they had been denouncing, and even many of his liberal supporters were shocked. A mood of distrust and uncertainty swept the nation. As President Lyndon B. Johnson, then a Congressman from Texas, was to comment years later, Roosevelt by this one action had torn apart his great consensus and was never again to have the kind of power he had wielded in his first Administration.

The occasion was perfect for the first offensive of the newly formed Committee to Uphold Constitutional Government. Rumely and Gannett swung into action, distributing 200,000 copies of the Senate Committee report condemning the court-packing bill. They sent 32,000 telegrams urging defeat of the bill to voters in eleven states where wavering Senators lived; and they used the Congressional frank of friends in Congress to distribute 15 million pieces of literature free of charge through the mail. In the end, when the bill was ignominiously buried, the committee claimed—and with good reason—that it had played a major role in its defeat. It was just the first of many victories.

The motivations of the Committee for Constitutional Government became apparent in the pamphlets it distributed under its own name and in the books it endorsed, for which it got its millionaires to underwrite nationwide distribution. In a "Voters Questionnaire" widely distributed in the early 1940s, the committee launched an all-out campaign to send "strong men" to Congress, and it spelled out just what these "strong men" would do. They would save "free enterprise" by lowering the taxes on the very rich; they would "avert inflation" by raising the taxes on the poor; and they would press for "legislation with teeth in it" to curb "predatory" labor unions.

The soak-the-poor, be-kind-to-the-rich motif showed up time and again in the committee's propaganda. As early as July, 1941, it launched a campaign to make families with incomes of less than $2,500 pay their "share" of taxes so that an "unfair and crushing burden" should not be placed on the "thrifty." It argued that the Sixteenth Amendment had been "misused" and that it should be supplanted by a Twenty-second Amendment that would impose a limit of 25 percent on taxes that could be levied on the highest-income brackets. In effect, this meant that persons with incomes of $1 million a year would pay only $250,000 in taxes—and that, to make up for it, families subsisting on $2,000 a year, who had been paying $175, would have to pay $500.

Rep. Wright Patman (D., Tex.), long a battler for the common man, denounced the committee on the floor of Congress as the "most sordid and sinister lobby ever organized"; he called the proposed Twenty-second Amendment "the millionaires' amendment to make the rich richer and the poor poorer"; and added: "If this amendment were to become law, in a few years a few families would own the entire wealth of this nation. Is that not fascism?"

The Committee for Constitutional Government's fondness for millionaires was matched in intensity only by its detestation of labor. It was outraged by the last great piece of social legislation of the Roosevelt Administration—the 1938 Wages and Hours Act, which imposed a limit of forty hours on the work week and provided for payment at overtime rates beyond that. The newspaper affiliates of the Gannett propaganda enterprise were especially incensed because this meant that for the first time in history they could not work reporters and other journalists sixty hours a week at salaries of thirty to forty dollars a week with no overtime. And so the propaganda campaign against the bill began. The shorter workweek would ruin American manhood; men would become puny, flabby creatures; a man was not a man if he did not work at least forty-eight hours a week. Such arguments were advanced in all seriousness.

When World War II broke out, the press-industrial combine behind the Committee for Constitutional Government saw an opportunity to scuttle the whole nefarious wage-hour act. It promptly demanded the abolition of the forty-hour week, and some of those in the CCG hierarchy began to write of establishing a standard fifty-six-hour week. Front-page stories pictured inevitable defeat by the Axis if we tried to win the war by working just forty hours a week. Patriotism demanded that we back up our boys at the front by shunning such socialistic restraints.

I remember that campaign well. My publisher at the time was one of those dedicated to the promotions of the CCG. When the furor about the forty-hour week started, Roosevelt was away from Washington, and in his absence, the campaign caught on and spread like fire on a tinder-dry prairie. The wire services, properly alerted by the front offices of their newspaper clients, turned out new leads every day on the rising ground swell of support for junking the forty-hour week; and for a time it seemed to us in the newsroom that the act was doomed. "You boys are going to lose your overtime," the boss said one day, rubbing his hands in anticipatory glee. Then Roosevelt came back to the capital and held a press conference. When my publisher came bouncing in, burning to learn what "that man" could possibly have said, I told him with what I'm certain was undisguised relish: "He said we would work forty hours a week, fifty hours a week or sixty hours, whatever is necessary to win the war—but we'll work it at over-time rates with cost-plus contracts for industry."

The smile vanished. The boss whipped around on his heel and fled back to the haven of the front office—and the whole news-room grinned. Everybody knew that those words "cost-plus con-tracts" had scuttled the whole CCG drive. However many hours might be worked, the costs would be borne by the government, and industry would be assured of a percentage of profit above cost. Indeed, it might even work out that the greater were the costs, the greater would be the profits. In this happy world of guaranteed profit, the forty-hour-week issue became irrelevant.

The collapse of this effort did nothing to alter the CCG's fundamental conviction that the free-enterprise system could only be saved by tearing down the house of labor. When the Taft-Hartley Act was being debated in 1947, labor was roused to fury about its new restrictions on unions, but for the CCG the bill was a namby-pamby proposition, not half strong enough. In the midst of the debate, the committee sent to every member of Congress a copy of a new book, and started a drive to place a million copies in the hands of those in the professions. The book was entitled *Labor Monopolies—or Freedom.*

Senator George Aiken, a conservative Vermont Republican, generally regarded as one of the most upright men in the Senate, was so enraged by what he found in this volume that he took the floor and read quotations from it. "There should be no laws that recognize strikes as legitimate and lawful . . . A strike should be considered an offense against society." Another sentence read: "Some day it may dawn on the majority of our citizens that the abuse to be eliminated is collective bargaining itself."

"This is an alien doctrine," Aiken told the Senate. And he added that he thought it was time for government agencies "which are concerned with inquiring about organizations in the United States which preach Nazi or Fascist doctrines to look into this matter . . . if such activities are carried far enough, the final result will be the destruction of democracy . . ."

The committee was indeed allying itself ever more closely with admittedly profascist elements in American society. It worked hand-in-glove on various issues with Father Coughlin— and Coughlin, in turn, backed Gannett for the Republican Presidential nomination in 1940, calling him a man who would not "obey the orders . . . of Jew masters." At one point seven of the fifteen members of the Committee for Constitutional Government's advisory board were also prominent in the activities of organizations run by Merwin K. Hart, apologist for Franco, avowed anti-Semite, advocate of white supremacy, and eventually an organizer for the John Birch Society.

In the years immediately prior to America's entry into World War II, the committee had equally close ties with the America First movement. America First, which claimed the allegiance of many prominent businessmen, gave covert aid to the Fascist powers by campaigning against every move Roosevelt made to help the embattled democracies with war materiel. After Pearl Harbor the wrong-headedness of its policy became obvious to virtually everyone, but up to that final moment it continued its propaganda for complete isolationism.

In this, America First and the Committee for Constitutional Government were close allies. The committee's vice chairman, a trustee, and former Congressman Samuel Pettengill, who succeeded Gannett as CCG chairman in 1940, all were involved with America First. The committee's attitude was uncompromising. It denounced the Lend-Lease Act as "a monstrous measure," one that "strikes at the roots of the American system of free, constitutional government and sets up a dictatorship on American soil." Just a few weeks before Pearl Harbor, Pettengill, in a speech in Philadelphia, proposed "taking care of" the "traitors" who put the interests of the British Empire ahead of those of America.

Even after Pearl Harbor, when Hitler was claiming that an "international Jew-Communist conspiracy" had pitted America against fascism, the Committee for Constitutional Government was echoing almost the same thought. It claimed that "an international group surrounding the President" was responsible for policies that had dragged us into war; that the "intellectual switchboard" for this group was the British Jew Harold Laski; that, with the exception of the American Jew Felix Frankfurter, Laski had more influence with Roosevelt "than any one individual"; and that Laski, Frankfurter, and other members of the "international group" were sympathetic to communism.

During the war years, the committee concentrated much of its propaganda on the farm belt, raising the specter of collectivization. On July 30, 1943, Gannett himself dispatched a flier to all editors, disclosing that he had learned of the Administration's "plans for controlling our six million farmers" and expressing anxiety about "the possibility of our farmers becoming sovietized."

On other fronts, the committee fought federal aid to depressed areas, federal aid to education, Social Security, the income tax, the Wagner Health Bill, the Federal Communications Commission, and federal administration of farm and price-support policies. Like the John Birchers of the 1960s, it would have been satisfied only with the dismantling of the federal establishment and a return to the laissez-faire creed of Mark Hanna and William McKinley, the only faith it recognized as true Americanism.

In pursuit of its broad spectrum of anti-causes, the House probe of 1950 showed, the committee spent approximately $2 million in the seven-year period from 1937 to 1944. This huge bankroll enabled it to distribute 82 million booklets and pamphlets. It sent out more than 10,000 transcriptions of fifteen-minute radio talks on national issues; it dispatched 350,000 telegrams urging citizens to take action on specific measures; it flooded the press with uncounted thousands of releases; and it took out full-page advertisements in "536 different newspapers with a combined circulation of nearly 20 million."

The effectiveness of such propagandizing was demonstrated time and again in the roadblocks thrown up in Congress against progressive legislation. Harvey Fruehauf, of the Fruehauf Trailer Company of Detroit, wrote a letter in October, 1948, soliciting funds from 17,000 corporation presidents. In it he cited a report by the *Congressional Quarterly* ranking the Committee for Constitutional Government the second most effective lobby on the Hill. Only the National Association of Manufacturers surpassed it. NAM had battled six Truman Administration proposals, had scored five clear-cut victories, and on the sixth, federal aid to education, the House didn't act—so the NAM won there, too. The Committee for Constitutional Government, Fruehauf explained, "went to bat eight times and struck out only once, when it sought to prevent passage of the European Recovery Program."

4

The Tide Changes

WHILE ULTRARIGHT ORGANIZATIONS like the Committee for Constitutional Government have usually found it fairly easy to whip up a headline campaign for free enterprise or "100-percent Americanism," liberal or left-wing groups have a much harder time in promoting their causes in the national press. Somehow, a campaign like the one to abolish the forty-hour week seems always to be urgent, page-one news; but agitation for a national health plan, for instance, rates only the twenty-fifth page, if it rates at all. In the contrast one finds expressed the prejudices of a predominantly one-party press, ruled by press lords who cherish the anti-causes of CCG or the National Association of Manufacturers.

During the 1968 Presidential campaign, *Editor & Publisher,* the trade bible of the newspaper industry, took a poll of the nation's press and reported that 483 newspapers with a circulation of 21 million copies had endorsed Richard M. Nixon; only 93, with a circulation of 4 million, had thought Democrat Hubert H. Humphrey worthy of their support. Granted that this was one of our least inspiring elections, with vast portions of the electorate disenchanted with both candidates, is it not nevertheless remarkable that editors by 5 to 1 preferred the Republicans in a contest that, in the popular vote, was a cliff-hanger almost to the end?

No one who is familiar with the record of the American press since 1932 could have been surprised, however, by such a result. In 1936 Franklin Roosevelt wrote about the coming campaign in these words: "If the Republicans should win or make enormous gains, it would prove that 85 percent of the press and a very definite campaign of misinformation can be effective here just as it was in the early days of the Hitler rise to power."

He exaggerated to some extent, Arthur Schlesinger has written, but not so very much. A study of big-city dailies showed that about 75 percent were for Landon, only some 20 percent for Roosevelt. Whole days went by when Roosevelt did not make the front page of the Chicago *Tribune,* the most powerful paper in the upper Midwest; and there was one day when his name did not get into the paper at all. During the same period the *Tribune* bannered the great "crusade" of Alf Landon.

After 1936 and Roosevelt's court-packing fiasco, the lopsidedness of the American press became even more pronounced. In campaign after campaign, any foible or faux pas of a Democratic Administration became headline news; but somehow if a Republican committed a similar blunder it didn't seem to be so important. In the Truman years, especially after the stunning upset of 1948 in which only the Chicago *Tribune* headlined the election of Thomas E. Dewey as President, the frenzy reached almost insensate proportions. There were the mink coat scandals, the deep freeze scandals, the "5 percenter" scandals; there was the alleged "sellout" at Yalta, the "theft" of our nuclear secrets, "betrayal" in the State Department. The press had a field day; yet, looking back, the only charges that were ever really established involved the petty chiseling of underlings.

The contrast between the way the press treated the Truman

and Eisenhower Administrations was stressed by Richard Rovere, writing in June, 1953. Commenting on the dangers of a one-party press, Rovere said: "Because big money is almost solidly Republican, Republicans control the mass-communications industries. Newspapers are overwhelmingly favorable to the Republican side; so are the big-circulation magazines. Recalling what the press did whenever any mischief came to light in the Truman administration, and comparing that with the almost total blackout on the early examples of Republican waywardness, one has the eerie feeling that the one-party press may shortly put an end to the two-party system . . ."*

The way the scales were weighted in the journalistic joust was perhaps most significantly illustrated by the situation in New York City in the late 1940s and early 1950s. Here was the largest city in the nation, Democratic, liberal. Its newspapers had not yet killed themselves off one by one. Eight major dailies were then in existence, but only the smallest and weakest financially, the New York *Post,* could be counted on to support a Democratic Presidential candidate. On the other side were ranged the *Sun,* the *World-Telegram, The Daily News* (with the largest circulation in the nation), the *Daily Mirror,* the *Journal-American,* the New York *Herald-Tribune*—and, generally, *The New York Times.* It was hardly what one would call an even battle for the public mind.

When a nation has a one-sided press, it gets one-sided news. A vivid example of the discriminatory coverage of news came in the days just before American involvement in World War II, when Attorney General Robert H. Jackson addressed the Law Society of Massachusetts. Jackson, who was later to become a

* The frustration of a dedicated reporter shows in a letter written by the late Ronald W. May to Carey McWilliams, editor of *The Nation,* on October 22, 1959. May, who was the Washington correspondent for a string of medium-sized daily newspapers, reported he had "some 25 first-rate stories" partially developed in his files—and no one was interested in doing anything about them. The stories ranged, he wrote, from the misuse of money donated by alarmed citizens to an agent of the House Un-American Activities Committee to "fight communism," to the strange financial support given a wiretapper who had been caught wiretapping in the Senate Office Building; to the way "Eisenhower's millionaire cronies" were raising money for Richard M. Nixon; to the way the late Senator Robert M. Kerr had "bought an Oklahoma county and then [as chairman of the rivers and harbors committee] got a small river deepened for hundreds of miles to his property."

Supreme Court Justice and the prosecutor of war criminals at Nuremberg, was disturbed about attacks being made by powerful interests on the very processes of democracy, and he challenged the House Un-American Activities Committee to investigate American fascists.

"Lately there has arisen in this country what appears to be a school of thought which denies that our government is or ought to be democratic . . . ," he said.

He quoted General Van Horn Moseley, who had been labeled by the House Un-American Activities Committee as a profascist, as saying he was "doing all I can to get the word 'democracy' out of literature . . . A democracy pulls everything and everyone down to the level of an average and makes it communism."

Moseley perhaps could be dismissed as an irrational fringe figure. But Jackson made the point that there were a lot of others occupying respectable, power-brokerage positions who were peddling the same line. He cited H. W. Prentis, Jr., president of the National Association of Manufacturers, for having delivered an address "in which he assailed what he called 'the pitfalls of democracy.' Among the democratic institutions which Mr. Prentis attacked were the direct election of U.S. Senators, the primary, referendum and recall . . . 'Hope for the future of our republic,' said Mr. Prentis, 'does not lie in more and more democracy.'"

And then, a year later, continued the Attorney General, "we find the same thing being taken up by *The Saturday Evening Post*," then the most widely circulated weekly magazine in the nation. The *Post*, Jackson said, had "editorially asserted that 'this was not a democracy. The founders dreaded democracy almost as much as they feared despotism.'" The magazine had spelled out specifics. First, there was universal suffrage, whereas originally only those who owned property could vote; second, the election of a President had become more and more dependent on the popular vote; third, Senators were now elected by popular vote; and fourth, there was the graduated income tax. "Thus *The Saturday Evening Post* deplores these developments because they are steps in the direction of democracy," Jackson said.

He continued his attack by naming other individuals and organizations in the antidemocracy cabal. He bore down heavily on the Committee for Constitutional Government; Merwin K.

Hart, who headed the so-called New York State Economic Council, later the National Economic Council; and Charles A. Lindbergh, the national hero who had become bemused by the power of Hitler's air force and had opposed the draft in a speech in which, Jackson said, he made "a sneering reference" to democracy.

"We are witnessing," the Attorney General concluded, "the most ominous gathering of forces against freedom and democracy that has been seen in my time . . ."

By any standard of judgment, the speech had to be labeled important. Here was the Attorney General of the United States isuing a flat challenge to the House Un-American Activities Committee to investigate fascists and profascists in the same manner that it had pursued communists and procommunists. The committee, of course, turned a deaf ear to the challenge. Only Moseley, who commanded no great power complex and so was fair game, got a rap on the knuckles; the far more important forces Jackson had named were ignored. This see-no-evil, speak-no-evil position of the House committee was abetted to a great extent by the see-no-evil, speak-no-evil attitude of the American press.

George Seldes, who made a career of pointing out the sins and omissions of the press, conducted an exhaustive search of newspaper files to determine just what happened to this speech by Attorney General Jackson. He found that only the New York *Herald-Tribune* carried Jackson's speech in full and printed all the names. The *Times* printed a few small paragraphs buried far back in the paper and used no names but Lindbergh's. This was a tactic adopted by most papers. The New York *Sun* suppressed the whole Jackson speech, but then used a story headlined BARTON ASSAILS ACTS OF JACKSON, thus compounding the felony by using an attack on an official whose own words it hadn't reported. The Bruce Barton so favored by the *Sun* was incidentally head of one of the four largest advertising agencies in the nation.

"A search of one hundred important newspapers in the New York Public Library, including the Washington *Evening Star* and the Philadelphia *Ledger*, showed all of them suppressed the Jackson indictment," Seldes later wrote.

.   .   .

THE PREDOMINATELY ONE-PARTY PRESS and information media were playing to what should have been a receptive audience, an essentially conservative people. Public opinion polls and other studies showed time and again that Americans were more sympathetic to fascism than to communism.

Studies of public school textbooks in use in the two decades between the wars showed that scant attention was given to Russia and the Russian Revolution. And when they were mentioned, it was almost invariably in derogatory terms that explained little, but contributed mightily to aversion.

Texts emphasized, for example, the Russian "betrayal" of the Allies by signing a separate peace treaty with Germany in World War I, but they gave no indication that this was a deed of which the Russians themselves were not proud, an act to which they had been compelled by the military ineptness and wholesale slaughter of the Czar's bumbling armies. The Soviet regime was almost always described as one of "confiscation, terror and dictatorship of the lower class," or as one of "violence, bloodshed and the disorganization of industry and decline in production." In several texts there occurred the phrase "scratch a Russian and find a Tartar." Photographs emphasized the "Mongolian" features of many Russians, raising the image of the wild hordes of Genghis Khan. With this kind of educational background, it was little wonder that a study of the attitudes of high school students in 1927 showed that 54 percent regarded the Russians as an inferior people.

There was no comparable repugnance to the rise of the Fascists in Italy or the Nazis in Germany. A series of public opinion polls taken prior to the outbreak of World War II in September, 1939, were unvarying in their findings: most Americans, when confronted with a hypothetical choice between communism and fascism, chose fascism. In 1940, despite the European war precipitated by Hitler, more than half of the Americans polled considered the communists "mostly bad or misguided." Even Hitler's sweeping victories in Europe and the threat posed to a desperate Britain had little effect on this deeply ingrained American prejudice. Throughout most of 1941, though American involvement in Hitler's war crept daily closer, "numerous polls showed that the overwhelming majority of Americans considered Communists to be the single greatest menace to our way of life."

This public climate was nourished by official actions. During the decade of the 1930s when the Axis powers were becoming steadily more aggressive and clearly posed the greatest threat to our own peace and that of the world, the original House Un-American Activities Committee headed by Rep. Martin Dies (D., Tex.), expended its energies primarily in the pursuit of communists. As measured by its reports, some 63 percent of its time and effort was spent in ferreting out communists; only 23 percent was directed at Nazi agents and German-American Bundists, despite the fact that the latter were holding martial drills and mass rallies in many sections of the nation.

Doubtless, the presence of large German and Italian ethnic groups in big cities had an impact on American public opinion and official life. Certainly the existence of these powerful voting blocs was a consideration to politicians. But ethnic influence alone could not explain the lopsidedness of American public opinion. Even many American liberals in the 1930s favored Mussolini. He made the Italian trains run on time; the efficiency of his Fascist regime was widely praised. While communism was viewed as a threat to the established order, Mussolini's regime appeared to many as the defender of the status quo and the upholder of traditions and institutions Americans held most dear—religion, patriotism, private property and capitalism. John F. Diggins, in a study he called "Flirtation with Fascism: American Pragmatic Liberals and Mussolini's Italy," wrote in the *American Historical Review:*

"A middle-class, property-conscious nation, confronted by the towering figures of Lenin and Mussolini, would naturally turn to the charismatic Italian who paraded as the savior of capitalism. A nation of churchgoers, faced with a crisis in moral values, would understandably respond to the image of Mussolini as the redeemer who turned back the tide of materialism and anti-clericalism in Italy. And a nationalistic people reacting to Wilsonian internationalism could readily applaud Mussolini's scorn for the League of Nations and praise the fascist virtue of patriotism."

In a national climate so weighted in one direction, the wonder is not that the Nightmare Decade descended upon us in the 1950s but that it took so long in coming.* Yet, despite these conditions favoring conservatism, the American people for twenty years kept in power in Washington the liberal regimes of Roosevelt and Truman. Why? This paradox can be explained by two factors: Roosevelt himself and the sheer thrust of events that helped to make the Bourbons of the old order look like frustrated, ridiculous men.

Roosevelt in himself was worth an army. He went over the heads of the press lords and talked directly to the American people in his homely, down-to-earth radio "fireside chats," one of the most effective methods of communication between a leader and his people ever devised. As the public listened and put its trust in him, the frustration of his opponents grew. This, too, played into his hand. The most reputable sources spread the most scurrilous stories about him. Spokesmen for the Liberty League and other business organizations went to idiotic extremes to smear the President. An entire faked genealogy was worked out, purporting to show that Roosevelt was of Jewish ancestry. Other tales insisted "his smile had been grafted on his face by a plastic surgeon; he was insane, as evidenced by his maniac laughter; he and his family were drunk all the time; he was having an affair with Frances Perkins; Mrs. Roosevelt was a Communist, and it was arranged she would succeed him in the Presidency and turn the country over to Russia . . ." Reciting this litany, John Brooks wrote in his account of the Wall Street boom and bust: "Meanness of spirit had become an epidemic sickness among the rich, and the contagion had spread beyond them."

Such smallness and spitefulness was its own undoing. With his matchless gift of ridicule, Roosevelt turned such canards back upon their authors. The "silk hat" anecdote during the 1936 campaign was just one example of this technique. In his 1944 race against Thomas E. Dewey, Roosevelt found himself at one point of the campaign in a difficult spot. Dewey had just made a very effective speech on the labor issue, and Roosevelt did not want to put himself in the position of appearing to respond to Dewey. Fortunately for him, the opposition had been trying to

---

* This basic American conservatism still endures. A Gallup poll, reported on April 15, 1970, showed that Americans prefer to be labeled conservative instead of liberal by a margin of 3 to 2. Another Gallup poll three days later found that the public preferred the appointment of conservatives to the U.S. Supreme Court by a margin of 5 to 3.

make an issue out of his attachment to his favorite dog, a Scottie named Fala, that appeared with the President constantly. And so Roosevelt, in one of his most brilliant sallies, made a speech in which he mocked the Republicans for their attacks on "my little dog Fala," and implied that they were reduced to such straits because they had no real political issues. A good part of the nation was convulsed by laughter, and again the old American business dynasty tasted the bitter ashes of a defeat it had helped to bring upon itself.

Aside from the political magnetism of Roosevelt, the second factor in building a new political constituency was to be found in the conditions of the times. The Chicago *Tribune* and other papers might try to picture Alf Landon as conducting a "great crusade," but it was always obvious that the real purpose of such crusades was to return to the past. And the past reminded the American voter only of what had happened to him under Herbert Hoover. Roosevelt, it was true, had not solved all the nation's ills with a magician's wand; there was the slump that was called the "recession" of 1937; millions were still unemployed. But such misfortunes were only a pale shadow of the terrible days of the depression. Times, for most people, were much better. The banks had been saved, jobs had been saved, wages had improved, complete chaos had been averted. The voter had only to recall how things had been just a few years before and suddenly the panicked outcries of the former ruling interests seemed to him words of selfishness and folly. The public, which had once paid the editorial pages great respect, began to laugh at the press; newspapers were jeered instead of cheered, losing steadily in respect and influence—and Roosevelt and the Democrats, aided by the backfiring tactics of the opposition, happily gathered in the votes and kept returning to Washington.*

* Arthur M. Schlesinger, Jr., has described the public rebellion against press leadership in *The Politics of Upheaval.* In the 1936 campaign, he writes, Chicago crowds shouted epithets at press cars of the Chicago *Tribune* and Hearst's *Herald-Examiner.* "Down with the *Tribune!* To hell with the *Tribune!*" they shouted. Thomas Stokes, Pulitzer Prize-winning Washington columnist, commented: "These people no longer have any respect for the press, or confidence in it. The press had finally overreached itself." The frustration of the press lords grew as the wisdom of their editorial pages was ignored by the public in election after election. In the late 1940s, Roy W. Howard, editor and publisher of the New York *World-Telegram,* became so incensed at the loss of his editorial page's influence that he adopted the radical expedient of making the editorial page the first page of the second section. Not even this prominent display of the publisher's opinions could recoup lost prestige, however, and the experiment lasted only a short time.

It was a political show unlike any other in our history and a thing to marvel at while it lasted. But even the most cursory analysis shows that it all depended on two forces that were not immortal and immutable—the life of Franklin D. Roosevelt and the direction of national events. In 1945 both of these forces came abruptly to an end. Roosevelt, stricken by a cerebral hemorrhage, died in Warm Springs, Ga., and instantly the President was Harry S Truman, a far different man, lacking the political skills that had made Roosevelt a one-man host. A few months later the greatest war in America's history ended in America's greatest victory—and led directly to America's greatest frustration. Victory, which should have brought the relaxation of tensions, brought instead the intensification of tensions. We had fought, as we had fought in World War I, if not precisely to make "the world safe for democracy," at least to make the world safe for peaceful living—and all our sacrifices had produced a world in upheaval, the Cold War and the nuclear bomb. Something had gone wrong. A sense of frustration and betrayal seeped out across the land. Roosevelt was gone, and the tide had turned.

The reaction was remarkably swift. The midterm elections of 1946 marked the turning point. The "communism in government" label, which the far right had been trying so desperately for so long to pin on the Democrats, finally registered for the first time with the voters. One of the reasons that it did, aside from the gathering postwar disillusion, was that the most intensive effort was made to unite the right-wing forces and bring to a new pitch of effectiveness the propaganda line that had been promoted for a decade.

The prime movers in this endeavor were the powers in the Committee for Constitutional Government and the old America First Committee, with which CCG had been so closely if unofficially allied. It was an effort that has become typical of the radical right—one that wedded the so-called "respectables" of business and finance with rabble-rousers. The "respectables" contributed to the alliance their money, influence and publicity techniques; the not-so-respectables furnished grass-roots muscle.

Throughout the war years, the Committee for Constitutional Government had kept up its steady propaganda barrage against the Roosevelt Administration, distributing leaflets with titles like

"As We Go Marxing On." It also began to use its influence in an effort to unite all dissident factions into one overall Red-menace combine. One of its first moves in this direction was the adoption of a frankly white-supremacy line, designed to bring in the conservative Democrats of the South. One CCG leaflet appealed to Republican leaders to unite with Dixiecrats. "Will Republican leaders be patriotic and effect an American coalition [with right-wing Southerners] against the New Deal Nazis in 1944?" it asked.

Prior to the 1944 Democratic National Convention, a white-supremacy propaganda organization known as the American Democratic National Committee was spawned. Officially, there was no link between this committee and the Committee for Constitutional Government; unofficially the ties were extremely close, for many leaders of CCG and the old America First group occupied positions of power in the new white-supremacy front. Gleason Archer, who was a member of the advisory board of CCG, became chairman of the new American Democratic National Committee. General Robert E. Wood, the one-time head of Sears Roebuck who had been a leader of America First and was soon to become a trustee of CCG's satellite, America's Future, contributed $1,500 to the white-supremacy effort.* H. R. Cullen, the Texas oil baron who had bankrolled America's Future so lavishly, donated $5,000 to the new ADNC, Irénée Du Pont, E. F. Hutton and T. R. Ewart, a Texas fund-raiser and publicity man, also helped. Samuel B. Pettengill, the former chairman of the Committee for Constitutional Government, wrote an article praising the new ADNC as representing "American" Democrats. CCG itself helped the drive along by issuing a twenty-four-page brief, "Debunking the Poll Tax Assault." The poll tax device had been one of the principal means by which Southern states had kept millions of Negroes from voting, and now CCG found this disenfranchisement both legal and constitutional.

The attempt to force a white-supremacy plank into the Democratic platform in 1944 failed, but the racist and big-money

* America's Future and the Committee for Constitutional Government eventually became separate organizations. America's Future, perhaps to protect its tax-exempt status, always claimed that it was independent of CCG, but the House committee investigation in 1950 showed that some of its files were stored in the office of CCG. Earl Harding served as treasurer of both America's Future and CCG. And America's Future checks were all countersigned by Edward A. Rumely, the director of CCG.

forces that had been brought together in the effort did not abandon the field. A fundamental lesson of our times, dramatized by the takeover of the Republican Party in 1964, is that the forces of reaction never give up. Since ADNC had failed to accomplish its objective, it was allowed to wither on the vine, and still another organization, American Action, Inc., was formed in January, 1946, with the "respectables" and the not-so-respectables once again merged in a political action coalition.

Merwin K. Hart, avowed racist and profascist, became the executive director of American Action. Pettengill, a pillar of CCG, attended the organizing meeting and became one of the original members of American Action's national executive committee. E. F. Hutton, long closely linked with CCG enterprises, ran two organizing and fund-raising drives for American Action. Malcolm McDermott, a member of the CCG advisory board, was on the national executive committee of American Action. So was Robert E. Wood, the old American Firster. So was John T. Flynn, the journalist who had headed the New York chapter of America First and who was to produce one of the most widely disseminated political tracts of this or any other decade.

Contributions to American Action came from a host of highly placed "respectables." Col. Robert McCormick, publisher of the Chicago *Tribune*, attended one AA conference and gave $1,000. Lammot Du Pont, Ernest T. Weir and John J. Raskob all helped to bankroll the new organization. Edward A. Hayes, a former commander of the American Legion, was brought in to serve as field director. It all added up to a well-financed, well-coordinated drive to seize control of Congress from the Democrats in the 1946 election. The American Action war chest for this purpose was reported to be approximately $1 million.

American Action literature diligently equated all liberalism with the Red menace. "Leftist minorities terrorize and dictate to Congress and to legislatures," one of its releases read. "Leftists fill many key government offices, local and national. Leftists largely control American movies and the American theatre; and to a larger extent, radio."

Such scare tactics were backed up with grass-roots work. A "confidential" AA letter later uncovered by Congressional committees reported that the group was "developing door-bell ringing organizations in districts in Missouri, Oklahoma, Illinois, Wisconsin, New York and Washington to assist congressional candidates" who were opposed to "leftist" influences. "As rapidly as additional funds will justify," the letter added, "we intend to expand into similarly selected marginal districts in other states."

Across the nation the theme that liberals were "leftists" or "subversives," indistinguishable from communists, was used with devastating effect in contest after contest. Richard M. Nixon, then a political unknown, won his first election in California with the aid of this technique, and so began his long climb to the Presidency. Nixon's opponent in this first campaign was a liberal Democratic Congressman, Jerry Voorhees. A compilation of votes on selected issues indicated that Voorhees and New York's procommunist Congressman Vito Marcantonio had on occasion cast similar ballots, and this comparative tally sheet was printed on pink paper—the "pink sheets," as they came to be called; the color was calculated to make a voter think "pinko." The tactic was vicious and ignored all political realities. In the real world of politics, it is not uncommon to find politicians who hold divergent basic beliefs voting together on certain issues (Senator Robert A. Taft, as conservative a Republican as one could find, was an advocate of public housing). Such votes do not make the politicians casting them ideological bedfellows, as Nixon in his "pink sheet" campaign implied. This must have been obvious to any responsible politician, but Nixon built his early career on such distortions. He used the "pink sheet" technique again a few years later in unseating U.S. Senator Helen Gahagan Douglas, and in the early 1950s when he was Vice President, his ruthless use of the smear (to the extent of implying in one speech in Texarkana, Tex., that Harry Truman had been a traitor) made him the favorite high-titled hatchetman of his party.

Nixon was not the only beneficiary of such tactics in the pivotal campaign of 1946. Midterm Congressional elections have a tendency to go against the party in power; and, in this instance, the long Democratic rule in Washington, along with world turmoil, increased popular disenchantment. Grass-roots reaction was further inflamed in state after state by American Action and similar ultraconservative forces. Karl Mundt was elected to Congress in South Dakota. And in Wisconsin, American Action sent an organizer into the state and poured out money for full-page newspaper advertisements backing the candidacy of another political unknown—Joseph R. McCarthy. The result was that the "class of '46," as it became known, was the most conservative to come to Washington in twenty years. The Democrats were overthrown, and the Republicans organized the Eightieth Congress.

THE DEMOCRATS were at a crossroads after the election of 1946. They could draw the ideological and political battle line clearly and forcefully, as Attorney General Jackson had tried to do a few years earlier—or they could try to outdo the opposition in the witch hunt.

It is indisputable that no democracy can remain virile in a smothering atmosphere of conformity. Walter Lippmann wrote in 1953: "In the democracies that are foundering, and there are many of them, the underlying bonds have been ruptured which hold men together in all their differences in one community. The parties deny the good faith and loyalty of the opposition. Partisanship is a license to outlaw and ruin political opponents. When such a rupture of faith and confidence has occurred, democratic government and free institutions are no longer workable."

Thomas Jefferson in his first inaugural address had expressed the same thought. Speaking at a time when the French Revolution and its Napoleonic aftermath had thrown the whole world into turmoil and had made the conservative classes of that day as paranoid as the Russian Revolution was to make those of a century later, he said:

". . . Having banished from our land that religious intolerance under which mankind so long has bled and suffered, we have yet gained little if we countenance a political intolerance as despotic, as wicked, and capable of as bitter and bloody persecutions. During the throes and convulsions of the ancient world, during the agonizing spasms of infuriated man, seeking through blood and slaughter his long-lost liberty, it was not wonderful that the agitation of the billows should reach even this distant and peaceful shore; that this should be more felt and feared more by some and less by others, and should divide opinions as to measures of safety. But every difference of opinion is not a difference of principle. We have called by different names brethren of the same principle. We are all Republicans, we are all Federalists. If there be any among us who would wish to dissolve this union or to change its republican form, let them stand undisturbed as monuments of the safety with which error of opinion may be tolerated where reason is left free to combat it . . ." In the free give-and-take of ideas, the collective wisdom of a nation thrashes out issues and finds the right road. But this can happen only when every citizen can think and express any thought. When dissent is equated with treason, all thought is muted, and the climate of a democracy has been prepared for the man on horseback.

A Jefferson, faced with the issue that confronted the Democrats after the election of 1946, would have based his political stance upon the sanctity of those "inalienable" rights about which he had written in the Declaration. (Anyone who doubts it has only to recall how, in a similar climate, he had pounced upon the Alien and Sedition Acts, those repressive measures of conservatives in John Adams' day, and used the issue to set the nation back on the road to democracy and to rebuild the political fortunes of his own shattered party.) Unfortunately, Truman was no Jefferson. In a panicked reaction to the reverses of 1946, he joined and tried to outdo his critics.

The decisive day was March 12, 1947, when President Truman issued Executive Order 9835 setting up a loyalty security program. In explaining his purpose, he said he was motivated by a desire "to protect the security of the Government and to safeguard the rights of its employees." By its very nature, however, such a program placed all emphasis on "protection" and came to disregard "rights."

The word loyalty, admirable in itself, became the cloak for repression. Every employee of government, no matter how humble his post, was subjected to the scrutiny of the secret police, and a past thought, deed or association that might be considered in the least wayward could become on the instant sufficient grounds for suspension, humiliating loyalty hearings and possibly ultimate dismissal. It became the fashion later to associate the pernicious doctrine of "guilt by association" with Joseph McCarthy, but its real author was Harry S Truman. His loyalty order of 1947 provided as one standard for dismissal "membership in, association with, or sympathetic affiliation with any . . . organization, movement, group or combination of persons, designated by the Attorney General as . . . subversive." Even a "sympathetic affiliation," whatever that might be, with a "combination of persons," whatever that might be, was enough to make a man suspect.

The Attorney General by the new loyalty decree became, in his individual wisdom and individual prejudices, the arbiter of a man's fate. He drew up lists of "subversive" and "front" organizations. The lists searched back into political activities that had taken place a decade earlier—at the time of the Spanish Civil War when many Americans rebelled against the action of Hitler and Mussolini in turning Spain into the proving ground of World War II. Many of the organizations formed at that time were now labeled "Communist fronts," and many who, for idealistic motives, had participated in their activities or signed their petitions could now be smeared as a "dupe" or a "fellow-traveler" —and, if they were public servants, their jobs and livelihood were put in jeopardy.

This was a road we had never traveled before, not even in our most irrational moments, not even in the Palmer witch hunt of 1919–20. Writing at the time, Carey McWilliams noted: ". . . under the criminal syndicalism statutes and similar measures it was always necessary to prove that a particular organization had in fact advocated the overthrow of the government by force and violence or that the individuals charged with sedition or criminal syndicalism had in fact conspired to overthrow the government by such means. But under the new inquisition organizations are in effect banned by the simple technique of listing them as subversive without proof or evidence or an opportunity to be heard, and individuals are branded as disloyal and subversive solely by reason of their membership in such organizations. At the height of the delirium of the Palmer raids, organizations were not banned without hearing nor were citizens deprived of civil rights merely by listing their names in a political rogues' gallery."

Contrary to all principles of American justice, the burden of proof now rested, not upon the machinery of government to prove a man's guilt, but upon the accused individual to prove his innocence. The principle that the accused shall have the right to confront his accuser and cross-examine him, enunciated in the Sixth Amendment to the Constitution, was now scuttled. The accused was not to be informed of even the name of his accuser; he had to guess at the identity of the malevolent neighbor or cheap informer who had furnished what often proved to be merely a potpourri of gossip and suspicion. Repeated exposures of the unreliability of such information could not shake the conviction that it still represented the true word. In this atmosphere of delusion, men's livelihoods were placed in jeopardy by the flimsiest of concoctions. The cargo of innuendo and unsifted rumor in the colossal secret files of the Federal Bureau of Investigation now became the determinant of a man's career; for it was now no longer necessary for the government to prove an employee guilty of any specific misdeed—all it had to show was that some past association or deed gave grounds for the *belief* that he *might be* a security risk.

The psychological effect on the nation was almost instantly apparent. By August, 1947, the American Civil Liberties Union was writing in its annual report that "the national climate of opinion in which freedom of public debate and minority dissent functioned with few restraints during the war years and after has undergone a sharply unfavorable change."

There were some perceptive liberals in the Truman Administration who had questioned the wisdom of the loyalty program. One of those so concerned was Clifford J. Durr, a Montgomery, Ala., lawyer who was then a member of the Federal Communications Commission. Durr discussed the matter with Truman himself. He later wrote:

"In a talk with President Truman at the White House in June 1948, he frankly told me that he had signed the Order to take the ball away from Parnell Thomas. [This was Rep. J. Parnell Thomas, the archconservative New Jersey Republican who headed the House Un-American Activities Committee in the Eightieth Congress.] When I pointed out to him that the Order would be construed as giving Presidential sanction to the fears Thomas was trying to create, he assured me that if any injustices resulted he would modify the Order and even repeal it, if necesrary. So I left him feeling quite cheerful, but as you well know, the 1948 campaign was based on the issue of who was tougher on communism, and there seemed to be no turning back after that."

. . .

The 1948 Presidential campaign, with the Republicans in control of both houses of the Eightieth Congress, did indeed mark the point of no return. With J. Parnell Thomas heading the House Un-American Activities Committee, with Republicans dominating its Senate counterpart, the entire campaign summer and fall was marked by an almost daily succession of headlines dealing with the testimony of typical "doublethink" informers. Their distorted versions of the menace threatening America were presented to the public with the imprimatur of Congressional committees virtually as holy writ.

It did not matter that Whittaker Chambers in accusing Hiss could not keep from committing perjury himself. It did not matter that Elizabeth Bentley in accusing William Remington could not tell the same story twice, could not decide whether she had met Remington alone or in the presence of his estranged wife, could not even fix permanently on the details of the secret formulas she said he had passed to her. It did not matter that wildest rumor was the only basis for headlines proclaiming that traitors in the Roosevelt Administration had given Russia atom bomb secrets and had even air-freighted to the Soviets the raw material for the bomb itself. It did not matter that the House Un-American Activities Committee, as the campaign neared its climax, proclaimed the imminence of public hearings that would reveal even more horrendous tales of espionage—and then failed to hold the hearings. All that really mattered was that the incessant barrage of headlines was brainwashing the American people. You could almost feel their acceptance of the proposition, "Where there's smoke, there's fire."

When Hiss and Remington were convicted—both in courtroom trials in which the original charges given under oath were altered almost beyond recognition—the Democrats and the Roosevelt and Truman Administrations stood condemned, in effect, of having been "soft on communism," and thus the harborers of treason.

Such was the suicidal effect of Truman's short-sighted decision in 1947, to try to steal the opposition's thunder. As Durr had feared, the sweeping nature of the loyalty procedures made all the more credible every irresponsible charge that the government was riddled with spies. Truman's Attorney General became the defender of perjured informers in the attempt to avoid the accusation of having been "soft" on the Remingtons and the Hisses.*

Truman, in an attempt to avert the damage resulting from fanatical charges, placed the loyalty machinery largely in the hands of conservative Republicans of impeccable reputation. The State Department's Loyalty Board and the Loyalty Review Board were both headed by such stalwarts in an effort to see that not even a gnat could get through the meshes of security screening.

The result was that some 2.5 million federal employees were run through the loyalty mill. Of these, 6,412 came under suspicion under the hazy standards of the program. After hearings were held, this impressive number was reduced to a mere 270 who were dismissed. Of those dismissed, however, 69 were later reinstated on appeal so that, at the end of December, 1949, only 201 federal employees out of a total of 2.5 million had failed to qualify—and this under a program in which mere *belief* that a man *might be* a risk was grounds for dismissal. Only one-tenth of one percent of all those investigated had remained under suspicion, and *The New York Times* reported on April 6, 1950, that after three years of the most diligent investigation *not one single case of espionage had been discovered.*

Other nations did not handle this same problem of security in so paranoid and disruptive a fashion. England, for example,

---

* The Justice Department's protection of informers who perjured themselves cannot be questioned. Whittaker Chambers had clearly perjured himself in the Hiss case, and the federal grand jury that had indicted Hiss had wanted to indict him, too—but was talked out of it on the grounds that it would be difficult to prosecute Hiss if the government's own star witness was under indictment for perjury. The pattern was typical. In 1954 Joseph and Stewart Alsop, after examining court records, denounced the department's practice of paying and protecting informers. They pointed out that Paul Crouch, one of the department's favorite witnesses, had testified in great detail at one trial about his personal knowledge and acquaintanceship with a Communist leader—but that, in 1949, in an earlier trial, he had testified "no less than four times, and in the most specific manner," that he did not even know the man. The Alsops also wrote that "Manning Johnson [a witness in a loyalty case brought against Dr. Ralph Bunche, the Negro leader and United Nations official] has testified under oath that he would lie under oath, if directed to do so by his present employers." The testimony against Bunche was so suspect that the Loyalty Board cleared him by a unanimous vote and recommended that the Justice Department examine the testimony of his accusers. But in this, as in other cases, no action was taken. Informers continued to be paid and protected despite the fact, as the Alsops wrote, that the practice "has been regularly denounced as pernicious and dangerous since the time of the Roman historian Tacitus."

while realizing the dangers of communist infiltration, limited its loyalty procedures to areas "vital to the security of the State." The British used their loyalty program to test the qualifications of an employee for a particular, sensitive job—not to keep him from all public employment.

Truman's decision to appease the Republicans had effects on the national psyche as disastrous as the appeasement of Hitler at Munich had had on the international scene. The undermining of American ideals is well illustrated by the inaugural address given on May 1, 1949, by the new president of Georgetown University, in Washington, D.C., which trains a large number of our diplomatic personnel:

"It is not surprising to note that states have found it necessary to control opinion exactly as they found it necessary to control economics. *The state's thinking in this matter is much sounder than that of the resentful individual whose opinion is controlled.* Despite the dramatic but puerile dictum of Helvetius there is nothing essentially sacred about an opinion. In fact, in the field of religion, where God has been merciful enough to reveal the truth to mankind, opinion can be blasphemous. At best, opinions are blind gropings for the truth; at worst, they are the stubborn vaporings of ignorance. Actually, an opinion is grounded on nothing but the limited experience and personal interests of the individual. It is not supported by a universal, eternal, immutable law as is truth. *The state's opinion, then, is just as good, just as sacred, and just as accurate as the individual citizen's opinion or the majority opinion of all citizens . . .* With man's normal aspirations reduced by university training from a thirst for truth to the spawning of opinion, *there is every reason to expect that the state for its own preservation will be forced to establish an opinion-control bureau.* There are definite forewarnings of such a necessity." (Italics added.)

This philosophy was looked upon with such approval by one Democratic Senator that he inserted the full text in the *Congressional Record*. And President Truman had such high regard for that Senator, J. Howard McGrath, that he named him in 1949 to be Attorney General of the United States.

.   .   .

T H E   A B D I C A T I O N of the domestic ramparts by the Truman Administration coincided with what Professor Eric F. Goldman has called "the year of shocks." The year was 1949—a calamitous year in which disaster was piled upon disaster.

In January, Chiang Kai-shek's inept and corrupt Nationalist government abandoned the field in China to the Communists, fled to the island of Formosa, slaughtered Formosans right and left, and then hunkered down in its captured island sanctuary.

We had given Chiang more than $2 billion in grants and credits, plus another $1 billion in military equipment left behind at the end of World War II. Any government that received such substantial assistance—if it had any grass-roots support among its own people—should have been able to survive. The measure of the alienation of Chiang and his warriors from China's millions is that with all this assistance he couldn't put up even a respectable fight. But all the American people could see was that we had "lost" China—of course, the presumptuousness of thinking that China was ours to "lose" did not register with us.

This was bad enough, but worse was to come. President Truman announced on September 23, 1949, that Russia had exploded an atomic device; our most precious secret was a secret no longer. Now not only could we destroy Russia, Russia could destroy us.

It did not matter that the most eminent of our scientists had tried to tell the Truman Administration that this development was inevitable. Scientists realized that the knowledge on which development of the bomb had been predicated was world-wide; the only real secret we had possessed was that the bomb would work—and we had surrendered that secret at Hiroshima. The generals, of course, had refused to believe it; they had thought we had a secret we could keep for fifteen or twenty years—and here it was, barely four years after Hiroshima, and Russia had the bomb. It did not matter that Russia had some of the best scientific brains in all the world or that Russian science had been aided by German experts captured in the invasion. What registered with new impact now were those outcries about espionage and atomic bomb thefts that had been pumped into the headlines by Republican Congressional committees during the 1948 campaign. It began to look as if they had been right after all; we *must* have been sold out. Only a sellout could explain how those ignorant Cossacks of our high-school texts had drawn abreast of us so swiftly.

Boiling along throughout the long months of that year were other incitements to domestic frenzy. The trial of Alger Hiss, dragged out in the press day by day, reminded readers constantly of the subversive potential of communism. Hiss himself came to personify a new group in American government—the always slightly suspect "brain trusters" whom Franklin Roosevelt's New Deal had lured to Washington. Slender, handsome, urbane, the polished product of the finest Eastern universities, Hiss came to represent to the public those superior and perhaps slightly snobbish intellectuals who had set the tone of the New Deal and the Fair Deal. And so, in the imagination of the people Hiss became a symbol. The fate of two decades of Democratic Administrations became inseparably entwined with his.

Dean Acheson, Truman's Secretary of State, heightened the symbolism. Tall, suave, impeccably groomed, with a trim little mustache, he was Social Register, Groton, Yale and Harvard Law School. It did not matter that he had been so little of a shouting liberal that he had flirted with the Liberty League in his youth and disliked many New Deal domestic policies. It did not matter that as early as 1946 he had adopted a strongly anticommunist creed and had become a Cold War warrior. What registered was his clothes, his appearance, his cultured manner—plus the fact that he had been closely associated with Hiss in the State Department and that Hiss' brother, Donald, had been a member of his law firm. And so when Hiss was convicted and Dean Acheson said that, despite this, "I do not intend to turn my back on Alger Hiss," fanatics of the right leaped upon the statement in rage and glee, insinuating that here was proof positive of the perfidy of the Truman Administration.

Dean Acheson's statement may have done him credit as a man, but politically it was dynamite. Americans have always been slightly suspicious of the too-polished, too-intellectual college-educated man, who is not possessed of "the common touch." This tendency is perhaps most pronounced in the Midwest, where a regional antagonism intensifies resentment of such "pretension" when it occurs in Easterners.

"I look at that fellow," said Senator Hugh Butler of Nebraska, speaking of Acheson, "I watch his smart-aleck manner and his

British clothes and that New Dealism, everlasting New Dealism in everything he says and does, and I want to shout, Get out, Get out. You stand for everything that has been wrong with the United States for years."

It did not matter that Harry Truman had bawled out Soviet Foreign Minister Vyacheslav Molotov in what Drew Pearson called "Missouri mule-driver's language"; it did not matter that Truman's Marshall Plan had salvaged the economies of Western Europe and built a barrier against Russia and the spread of communism; it did not matter that Harry Truman had "stood up to" the Russians with the Berlin air lift. What registered was the shocks and the personalities. The fall of China. The atom bomb in Russian hands. Hiss. Acheson. The world seemed literally to be going to the devil, and this couldn't have happened to great, all-powerful America unless we had been betrayed.

THE TIMES WERE RIPE for a propaganda breakthrough, and the Committee for Constitutional Government was ready. John T. Flynn, the journalist who had been a leader in America First and American Action, had kept on cultivating the radical right front, and now in 1949, with the year of shocks making its impact on the psyche of the nation, he produced a book, *The Road Ahead*.

Benedict Fitzgerald, counsel for the 1950 lobbying committee headed by Rep. Frank Buchanan (D., Pa.), read into the record an extended analysis of everything *The Road Ahead* was against. He said the book: advocated repeal of the emergency powers of the President; opposed compulsory national health insurance; opposed public housing; called for a reduction in federal spending; opposed public power projects; opposed government regulation of credit; opposed government lending agencies like the Farm Credit Administration, home-loan banks, federal savings and loan associations, the Home Owners Loan Corporation, the Federal Housing Administration, the Federal Deposit Insurance Corporation, the Reconstruction Finance Corporation, the Export-Import Bank. It urged repeal "of all federal labor laws on wages, hours of labor, collective bargaining, minimum wages, etc." and the abolishment of "all boards, bureaus and commissions that result from these laws." The book also parroted a favorite line of

CCG: "A strike should be considered an offense against society."

A reading of *The Road Ahead* shows that Fitzgerald did not exaggerate. Flynn attacked Truman's effort to show that he was tough on Communists as a phony ploy designed to blind Americans to the real menace—which was not communism. "I insist," he wrote, "that if every Communist in America were rounded up and liquidated, the great menace to our form of social organization would still be among us . . ." He spelled out the threat: "The real enemy we must identify and fight at every crossroads and at all points is the American edition of the British Fabian Socialists, who is engaged in a sneak attack here as his comrades were in England, who denies that he is a Socialist and who operates behind a mask which he calls National Planning."

The theories of John Maynard Keynes, which have been so important in the management of national economies, and which have had much to do with the long unparalleled prosperity of the 1960s, were anathema to Flynn. National planners, he wrote, "wrap themselves in a mantle they call anti-communism. But they are pro-Socialist. They are not willing, of course, publicly to concede that. They are planners. That is, they are Socialist Planners—and unless they are identified, recognized for what they are and are stopped *they will destroy this country*." (His italics.)

Liberals and planners were the stalking horses for communism. There was no room for a middle way: the choice lay between the era of McKinley and a rampant Bolshevism. Here in *The Road Ahead* were expressed the rigidities of the American business class.

Fitzgerald said that the eminent Catholic magazine *America* in its issue of March 7, 1950, had characterized *The Road Ahead* as "the road to nowhere," but the Committee for Constitutional Government did not see it this way. Edward A. Rumely, the CCG director, testified that *The Road Ahead* had had only a modest bookstore sale until the committee took it up. Then distribution boomed.

In a confidential memo sent to persons on its varied mailing lists, CCG put it this way: "John T. Flynn's book, 'The Road Ahead,' is the most important book of this decade. It exposes how, in secret, planners at top level in Washington have been working for a stealthy revolution in collaboration with labor monopolists

. . . It shows that, in reality, the mislabeled 'Welfare State' is a *hand-out, pickpocket state*, by which bureaucrats buy, with other people's money, control of the entire nation and subject citizens to the serfdom of the state."

The capitalists to whom CCG appealed opened their bulging wallets. Ernest T. Weir, chairman of National Steel, distributed 5,000 copies. Harvey C. Fruehauf, a member of the CCG advisory board, wrote his fellow industrialists, urging everyone to read and distribute the book, making sure it got into the hands of workers in their plants. "This book, widely enough distributed, can become the 'Uncle Tom's Cabin' of the twentieth century from the standpoint of public impact," he wrote enthusiastically. The *Reader's Digest* treated its millions of readers to a twenty-page condensation in its issue of February, 1950 (an issue that, coincidentally, was on the newsstands at the moment McCarthy delivered his opening salvo at Wheeling), and copies of this condensation were printed and distributed throughout the country. By midsummer, 1950, when the lobbying hearings were held, CCG was well on the way to its objective: the distribution of one million copies of the full text.

Fitzgerald read into the record of the lobbying investigation a letter from Sumner Gerard, a trustee of CCG, in which Gerard had said: "Unlike most of those groups that flourish for a while like the green bay tree and then fade out of sight, our committee has been functioning for over ten years, and we have many scalps in our belt."

Fitzgerald then asked Rumely if his committee took credit for the primary defeats of liberal Democratic Senator Claude A. Pepper in Florida and another Democratic Senator in North Carolina. Rumely replied: "We do not; but the people we have inspired over the years distributed a whole lot of 'The Road Ahead.' " Continuing the disclaimer that sounded more like a claim, he added that some of CCG's faithful in North Carolina had purchased 60,000 copies of the Digest condensation "and put them into rural mail boxes."

It was the mightiest propaganda effort in the history of CCG, and it was taking hold as public events conspired to give it impact. All that was needed was the catalyst—the *man*—and he was there, too, ready to step to front and center stage.

PART TWO

The Man

5

The Kind of Man He Was

J O S E P H R . M C C A R T H Y at the height of his fame liked
to tell this story about himself. One day in the Senate he had
delivered one of his fiercest attacks on the State Department, and
as he came off the floor and entered the Senate cloakroom, he
was greeted by Senator John Bricker (R., Ohio). "Joe," Bricker
told him, "you're a real S.O.B. But sometimes it's useful to have
S.O.B.'s around to do the dirty work."

Most men would hardly have accepted this as an accolade,
but McCarthy relished it, and repeated the anecdote to almost
everyone he met.

The man who could be so unabashed about his own rascality
was a riddle. He was two men. He could turn on Irish charm

like water from a spigot—and in the next instant he could be a ruthless predator. Or he could reverse the process, attacking with primordial savagery one moment, then turning upon his astonished and humiliated victim the sunshine of his smile.

On one occasion, he became incensed at a Republican Senator who had been critical of him, the late Robert C. Hendrickson of New Jersey. Now, one of the most inviolate rules of the Senate calls for the preservation of the amenities at all times. If a member wishes to imply that another is a scoundrel, he prefaces his denunciation by calling his target "honorable," and then proceeds to skin him most politely. Such a subtle code was not for Senator McCarthy. On the floor, he informed his colleagues that Senator Hendrickson was "a living miracle, born without brains and without guts."

A short time afterwards in the Senate cloakroom, he threw a brawny, hearty arm about the shoulders of Hendrickson. "You know I didn't mean that, Bob," he said. "I'll change it in the Record."*

"Oh, don't bother, Joe," Hendrickson said. "As it is now, you've made me a living miracle. What other man can say that? You wouldn't want to take that distinction away from me, would you?"

Telling me about the incident months afterward, Hendrickson chuckled. Perhaps his satisfaction at his own repartee had taken away the sting, but he seemed to harbor no particular animosity. His attitude seemed to be that it had all been "just Joe"—and that allowances should be made for him, as for some wildly rampaging force of nature.

The ruthlessness, the brute headlong charge, the uninhibited tongue-lashings, these were the trademarks of the McCarthy on constant public display. But there was another McCarthy, a private McCarthy—who wanted desperately to be loved by everyone and who really, it seems, could never understand why the deeds of the first caused such animosity toward the second. This second McCarthy mixed easily in all kinds of company, called everyone by his first name, backslapped, laughed uproariously at a good joke, and was a hail-fellow well met.

---

* The *Congressional Record* that prints verbatim the debates in Congress. It is common practice for members to edit their remarks before the transcript goes to the printer.

How much of this was surface show, how much the real man? This was one of the conundrums to which few pretended to have an answer. Sometimes, standing at a party, a drink in his hand, listening to a funny story, he would seem to be with it all the way; and yet an observer, watching him closely, would sense a kind of tense alertness beneath the façade of jollity. Under the heavy brows his eyes would be dark and wary; he would look a person up and down, searching, intent, even while listening to an anecdote—as if he were measuring the fellow as a possible future opponent. One got the feeling that he was ready to shift gears in the middle of a laugh and launch into a full-scale onslaught.

According to Richard Rovere, a couple of our more eminent psychiatrists were induced to make studies of him, analyzing him not on the couch but simply by observing him in daily action. Under these limitations their diagnoses could not be fully professional, but still, these were acute observers, experts in their field.

The first report, which was summarized for Rovere, "stressed the elements of classical paranoia in McCarthy's actions: life was a series of conspiracies, the most fiendish of which were directed at him; no one acted except from base motives; delusions of persecution were manifest and were accompanied by delusions of grandeur."

The second analysis, from which Rovere quoted at length verbatim, reported: "The significant thing about McCarthy is the extraordinary intensity of his neurotic drives . . . The key to understanding is the recognition of his basic insecurity, self-doubt, and self-contempt . . . [Some] highly neurotic individuals are able to turn on a gush of good will, which conceals their inner doubts, hatreds, and feelings of unworthiness.

". . . Truth and justice are recognized by him only when they serve his ends. When they do not serve his ends, they are unrecognized or cleverly distorted 'to make the worse appear the better reason.' This seems to be overtly a shrewd opportunistic maneuver but basically is a sinister neurotic trait."

This was a description of the man who cast his long shadow over all America.

.   .   .

J O S E P H   R A Y M O N D   M C   C A R T H Y was born on November 14, 1908, the fifth of seven children of Timothy and Bridget McCarthy. The McCarthy home was an eight-room, white clapboard house located on a 142-acre, worn-out farm in Grand Chute Township near the north shore of Lake Winnebago, some hundred miles north of Milwaukee. The area of cut-over timberland had been settled by hard-muscled lumberjacks of German, Irish and Scandinavian extraction, and the McCarthy farm was in the heart of what was known as "the Irish Settlement."

Timothy McCarthy was a hard-driving taskmaster, and his sons, almost as soon as they could toddle, became inured to long and hard labor on the farm. Joe was probably the least prepossessing of the brood. Barrel-chested, with short, heavy arms, he resembled nothing so much as a bear cub, and his older brothers, with the cruelty of the very young, took delight in ridiculing him. Hurt, he became shy and withdrawn. When neighbors came to visit, he fled and sometimes hid out in the barn. Perhaps it was this sensitiveness and shyness that made him Bridget McCarthy's special darling. She kept prodding him, encouraging him: "Some day you get ahead, you *be* somebody."

Joe McCarthy was endowed with a keen mind and an almost inexhaustible physical energy. Boy and man, he seemed always to be trying to outwork and outdo everybody else. He had a thirst for ceaseless activity, for strenuous physical exertion. Even after he had become a U.S. Senator, he took off for North Dakota one summer and worked incognito as a farm hand, drawing down ten dollars a day for operating a combine. He was eternally driven, it seemed, by a compulsion to spend, to exhaust himself.

He left school when he was fourteen to work on his father's farm. Soon he branched out on his own, raising chickens. When a misfortune wiped out most of his flock, he packed all his belongings in an old truck and drove thirty miles to the little town of Manawa to start life anew. He was then nineteen.

"Joe was steamed up when he came to Manawa," a friend of those years later recalled. "I never saw anybody so steamed up. He just couldn't ever relax; he worked at everything he did. He was pushing all the time."

He became the manager of the local store of a grocery chain, turned on the charm for his customers, engaged the young men of the town in debate on local issues. Soon, recognizing his educational handicap, he crammed four years of high school into a year of intensive studying, then entered Marquette University, intending to become an engineer.

As a schoolboy, he had never been able to make the basketball team. "He was too rough and couldn't work with the team," a classmate later recalled. "And he couldn't seem to learn the rules." At Marquette, he went out for boxing and became known as a wild slugger. Finesse was a word he never understood. At the sound of the bell, he would rush from his corner, a human windmill pumping blows from all directions. Many opponents were overwhelmed by his headlong attack, but when Joe came up against an antagonist who knew how to box, he absorbed some fearful beatings. Even then, he seemed to relish the brutality. Backed up against the ropes, both eyes blackened, blood dripping from his slashed face, he would wave his gloves and taunt, "Come on! Come on!"

Even this early in his career, he recognized "truth and justice" only when they served his ends. He ran for president of his senior class against Charles Curran, a student who had previously defeated him for presidency of the debating club. In a display of good sportsmanship, McCarthy and Curran both pledged publicly that each would vote for the other. When the votes were counted, the result was a tie. Curran wanted to cut a deck of cards to settle the issue, but Joe wouldn't hear of it. The class must vote again, he said. This time McCarthy won by two votes, meaning that just one voter had switched. Curran had a suspicion who that voter was.

"Joe," he asked, "did you vote for yourself?"

McCarthy gave his roguish grin.

"Sure," he said. "You wanted me to vote for the best man, didn't you?"

Curran, who became a successful Wisconsin lawyer, recalled the incident years later for Ronald W. May, a Wisconsin journalist. He made it clear that he remembered his classmate not with bitterness but with affection. And with good reason. For once McCarthy's ends had been served in the class election, he became the other McCarthy—that generous, jolly fellow.

"My father died in 1933 while I was in school," Curran said. "Just before the funeral Joe drove all the way out to our house in an old Model A he'd borrowed. He cut classes, left his job, and borrowed money to get there. He did that for me, and he'll always be my friend."

After two years of engineering studies at Marquette, McCarthy switched to law, receiving his LL.B. in 1935. He began the practice of law in the county-seat town of Waupaca, about thirty miles from Appleton. He had only four skimpy cases in the whole time he was in Waupaca and made most of his living playing poker. In the back room of a tavern on the outskirts of town, a game went on night after night. McCarthy became one of the regulars. He played poker, as he did all else, with a kind of concentrated fury. As one friend later phrased it, "He was brutal. He'd take all the fun out of the game because he took it too seriously." He bluffed so outrageously that his opponents never knew whether he held deuces or aces. "You could usually beat him with a pair of jacks," one said later. "But whenever you'd come up with a full house or a flush and bet your wad on it, he'd come up with something better." When this happened, he would rake in pots from a hundred to two hundred dollars, a rewarding windfall in that north country region in those depression days.

Besides playing poker and handling the rare law cases that came his way, Joseph McCarthy adopted the favorite tactic of all up-and-coming politicians—he became the joiningest man in town. He embraced every civic group that would have him, made speeches whenever he could wangle an invitation, and cultivated the habit of picking up tabs, especially for newsmen. McCarthy, at this time, was a shouting Democrat. He got himself elected president of the Young Democrats in the eleven-county Seventh District of Wisconsin, and in the fall of 1936 he ran for District Attorney on the Democratic ticket. He was beaten by a margin of 2 to 1, and it may be that this experience disillusioned him about riding to fame on the back of the donkey.

In any event, it was not long before McCarthy formed a new and surprising connection. Mike G. Eberlein, a veteran north country lawyer, invited him to join the Eberlein law firm in Shawano. What made the move seem odd at the time was that McCarthy was supposed to be such a solid Democrat, while Eberlein was a prominent Republican. He had keynoted Republican state conventions and had run unsuccessfully for State Attorney General and U.S. Senator.

Eberlein now had one supreme ambition: to become a circuit court judge. He talked about it incessantly as the 1939 campaign neared, and the personality-boy McCarthy backslapped him and agreed he'd make a fine judge. How was Mike Eberlein to know there was another McCarthy? He found out one morning when he awoke to a shocking discovery—his own right-hand man had announced his candidacy for the very judgeship on which Mike Eberlein had set his heart.

Eberlein parted company with his ambitious colleague. "I simply told him it would be better if he left," Eberlein said afterward frostily. McCarthy always contended that he had departed of his own volition because he knew he would be spending so much time campaigning it wouldn't be "fair" to stay in Eberlein's office—and accept pay from the hand he'd just bitten.

McCarthy's candidacy was regarded at first as little more than a joke. After all, he was barely thirty years old, and in experience, knowledge and deportment, he was probably the least qualified lawyer in the district to aspire to a judgeship. But those who sold him short at the outset of this campaign, like those who were to sell him short later, were to be taught a grim lesson.

The inexhaustible energy went to work. McCarthy thrived on a twenty-hour campaign day. He whirled into virtually every town and hamlet. He visited back-country farms all over the district. He sweet-talked housewives, played with their children, discussed the ills of cattle and crops with farmers. And he did something else that was characteristic: he distorted truth to serve his purpose.

The unlucky man in the path of the McCarthy juggernaut was Judge Edgar V. Werner, a distinguished jurist with an unblemished record. Since he was actually above reproach, it would require some effort "to make the worse appear the better reason." First, McCarthy raised the age issue. Judge Werner was sixty-six years old—a fact promptly exaggerated by constant reference to "my seventy-three-year-old opponent." When Werner tried to answer that he really wasn't *that* old, he only advertised the age issue. Next, McCarthy tried to make it seem that the judge had been all but looting the public till, pointing out that Judge

Werner in his thirty-five years in public office had drawn down "$170,000 to $200,000." If voters had paused to do a little simple division, they might have figured out that this averaged out to only $4,800 to $5,700 a year; but, as McCarthy knew, not many would stop to make such a computation—only those horror figures would count. And so, indeed, it was. When the votes were tallied, McCarthy had whipped the veteran judge, 15,160 votes to 11,154.

There was a significant epilogue. Some years later, McCarthy's former boss Mike Eberlein fulfilled his lifelong ambition and became a circuit judge, with McCarthy's blessing and help. After that he always said that McCarthy "has one of the finest legal minds I've ever known." And McCarthy always said the same about him. After all, once the end had been served, there shouldn't be any hard feelings about the means, should there? Wasn't that the way the game was played?

N O T   M A N Y   J U D G E S turn the bench into a platform for higher office (it usually works the other way around), but Joseph McCarthy, flush from his first great political success, was already looking to a limitless future. When a former classmate told him that if he played his cards right he could be Governor some day, McCarthy loftily informed him: "No, thanks. I'm not interested in the small jobs." The indication was that he was already thirsting for a U.S. Senatorial seat.

McCarthy attacked his judicial duties with furious drive. When he took his seat on the bench, there was a backlog of 250 cases on his calendar. This gave him the opportunity to show Wisconsin what a real hard-driver of a judge could do. In one forty-four-day period, he kept his court in session until after midnight no less than twelve times. "Joe wanted to try every case in the United States," one Appleton lawyer later remarked. In any event, he rapidly cleared his own calendar and then looked around the state for other districts in need of his judicial energies.

It was customary for Wisconsin circuit court judges to exchange positions on occasion, and McCarthy seized upon the opportunity to travel from one end of the state to the other. Wherever he went, he made it a practice to look up lawyers, local judges, politicians—and newsmen. He kept a black book in which he jotted down the name of every important politico in the areas he visited, and he never was so busy with judicial business that he couldn't find time to chat with them. He was so solicitous of the welfare of newsmen in particular that some reporters began to keep a watch on the court calendar to see when Judge McCarthy was coming to town, confident that he would pick up all the bar tabs.

By all this activity in the courtroom and fence-building outside it, young Judge McCarthy began to acquire a statewide reputation as a speedy dispenser of justice. He sometimes disposed of divorce cases in five minutes. Wisconsin, it seemed, had a veritable Lochinvar of the bench—and yet, as usual, there was a second and seamier Joe McCarthy story.

This was illustrated by the Quaker Dairy case. Quaker Dairy had been squeezing Appleton area farmers on the prices it paid for their milk, and the Wisconsin Department of Agriculture finally stepped in, seeking an injunction to prevent this price-cutting, which was barred by Wisconsin law. With Judge McCarthy's complaisant nod, action on the case was stalled for some six weeks; when a hearing was finally held, Quaker Dairy had had the perspicacity to hire as one of its lawyers a good friend of Judge McCarthy to help out its regular counsel.

First, Judge McCarthy granted a temporary injunction—then, in a complete about-face, dismissed it. In his final ruling he held that Quaker Dairy had indeed been violating the state's price-cutting statute. *But,* he said, the law was scheduled to expire in six months anyway, so it would work "undue hardship" on Quaker Dairy to make it obey the law now. Case dismissed.

Gilbert Lappley, the young Agriculture Department lawyer who had been trying the case, was shocked. What about Quaker Dairy's actions in the past? He demanded an immediate trial on these violations, but Judge McCarthy airily waved him off, declaring that such a trial would be "a waste of the court's time."

Lappley stormed out and took an appeal to the State Supreme Court in Madison. The high bench responded: "We are cited no authority and we find none which justifies a court suspending the operation of a statute on the ground that it will work a hardship if it is enforced. It must be concluded that the grounds on which the trial court acted did not constitute a sufficient or proper legal reason therefor and that this action constituted an abuse of judicial power."

When the court asked for a transcript of what had transpired in McCarthy's courtroom, Joe replied that he had ordered his court reporter to destroy his notes "because they weren't material." This cavalier destruction of his own ruling caused the Supreme Court to deliver a scathing rebuke to Judge McCarthy: "Ordering destruction of these notes was highly improper . . . We can only say that if it were necessary to a decision, the destruction of evidence under these circumstances would be open to the inference that the evidence destroyed contained statements of fact contrary to the position taken by the person destroying the evidence."

The high court ordered McCarthy to restore the original injunction against Quaker Dairy. He had no choice but to obey. But when the retrial was held, it was not the genial judge Wisconsin knew who took the bench; it was the scowling and savage McCarthy. At the close of the proceedings, he viciously turned on Gilbert Lappley for "causing all this trouble." The dressing down was so intemperate and humiliating that the chief judge of the Supreme Court later asked Lappley why he hadn't walked out of the courtroom. "That was what McCarthy wanted me to do," Lappley replied, "so he could hold me for contempt of court"— (the one judicial power from which there is no appeal).

Though Lappley had restrained himself in the courtroom, he was not the kind of man to accept humiliation meekly. He tried to get a transcript of Judge McCarthy's tirade, but once again the transcript of the judge's remarks was unavailable.

What happened next now seems like the portent of things to come. Lappley began to get telephone calls and letters upbraiding him for having attacked so fine a judge. Wisconsin newspapers had been remarkably silent about the whole affair, and Lappley was compelled to take his own savings out of the bank to buy radio time with which to get his side of the story before the public. Political powers pressured him to shut up; when he refused, he was summarily fired by his superiors in the Department of Agriculture. Even the dismissal of Lappley was kept out of the newspapers as a blanket of silence was cast over the entire proceedings. Gilbert Lappley had been the first to discover what happened to a "stand-up guy" who opposed Joe McCarthy when there were no "stand-up guys" at the top.

Years later there was an indication of the extent to which the conspiracy of silence protected McCarthy. When Jack Anderson and Ronald W. May tried to investigate the Quaker Dairy case for their book on McCarthy, they went to the State Supreme Court Library in Madison in an effort to get the briefs that had been filed with the court. But the briefs were missing. It was the first time in history, an attendant said, that such important legal papers had vanished into the pure Wisconsin air, and nobody could explain how it had happened.

JUDGE MC CARTHY, having gotten as much prestige as he could from judicial robes, now turned to another garb as a means of advancing his fortunes. It was 1942. The Japanese had attacked Pearl Harbor. And, as everyone knows, war heroes—or just plain war veterans—have a tremendous advantage in the political contests of any postwar era.

Anderson and May in their detailed study of McCarthy's early life indicate that his plunge from the bench into uniform was stimulated by a budding political rivalry. Carl Zeidler—tall, blond and handsome—was the Republican glamour boy of the moment. He had scored an upset to become mayor of Milwaukee, and was generally regarded as the state's top Republican, the man of the future. Zeidler had added to his glamour by joining the Navy. A picture of him, handsome in ensign's uniform, adorned the front pages of Wisconsin papers. It was apparent that such a war hero, if he survived (unfortunately Zeidler was later lost with his ship), would have a decided advantage in the political battles of the future. It became essential for McCarthy to trump Zeidler's move.

In tracing what happened next, it is perhaps instructive to bear in mind an analysis of Joe McCarthy made years later by Oliver Pilat and William V. Shannon, of the New York *Post*. Both knew McCarthy well and had watched him closely as he careened through Washington, and they spotted in him one trait that was as natural to him as breathing. They wrote:

"In all dialogue, he instinctively edges over the line by tidying up the truth a little. (If the story concerns a Buick, call it a Cadillac, if it concerns two drinks make it four, etc., etc.) For years he has gone on and on this way until, as was inevitable, all restraint vanishes, the line between fact and falsehood blurs, and the foreground of truth fades into the murky background of lie."

This trait was never more clearly demonstrated than in McCarthy's account of McCarthy in uniform. On June 2, 1942, Judge McCarthy wrote a letter to Major Saxon Holt, the marine recruiting officer in Milwaukee. He used circuit court stationery and set forth all the reasons why he should be honored with an officer's commission.

The application for a commission was significant, for this wasn't the way McCarthy, who habitually turned a Buick into a Cadillac and two drinks into four, was to tell it. He had no sooner applied to the Marines than he rushed off to inform the Milwaukee *Journal* about the sacrifice he was prepared to make. The *Journal,* temporarily hoodwinked, reported: "Judge McCarthy, who has been earning $8,000 a year, applied to Marine headquarters here Wednesday, offering to enlist 'as a private, an officer or anything else you want me to be. I want to join for the duration.' "

This was the beginning of a sedulously cultivated myth. In 1944, in a campaign release, McCarthy authorized this statement: "Though automatically deferred from the draft, he left the bench and enlisted as a buck private in the Marine Corps." And still later, in 1947, while a Senator, he inserted in his biography in the *Congressional Directory* this detail: "In June of 1942 he applied for enlistment in the Marine Corps as a buck private and was later commissioned."

He told this story so often that it may be he came to believe it himself. Even when Pilat and Shannon asked him about it directly, McCarthy insisted he had indeed been a buck private. "I never did apply for a commission . . . After screening, they decided to send me to aviation school and make me an officer. I was a private weeks or at the most a month or two."

The records make clear that he never served for a minute as a buck private. He was sworn in as a first lieutenant in the Marines, and he even made his final appearance in court in his lieutenant's uniform before going off to Quantico for basic training.

The implication in the Milwaukee *Journal* account that he had sacrificed his judicial post was also untrue. He hadn't resigned; he had merely taken a leave of absence. He had persuaded his fellow judges to double up and handle his cases while he was away at war—a procedure against which Judge Arnold F. Murphy, chairman of the board of circuit judges, protested in vain as unfair to both jurists and litigants.

The legerdemain continued when McCarthy went out to the Pacific battlefront. In later political campaigns, Wisconsin was to be flooded with publicity about "Tail Gunner Joe." (Actually, Joe was never a tail gunner, he was simply an intelligence officer stationed well to the rear on island bases that had been pacified months earlier.) Then there was the sensational "war wound."

Service records show that the injury occurred on June 22, 1943. On that date, indisputably, McCarthy was an officer-passenger on the seaplane tender *Chandeleur* crossing the Pacific toward the battlefronts. One of his shipmates, who kept a diary, was later interviewed by the Milwaukee *Journal*, and described the "shellback" ceremony that took place as the ship crossed the equator.

"McCarthy was nearly through his initiation when he was hurt," he said. "He was going down the ladder with a bucket fastened to his foot when he slipped. His other foot caught on a lower rung—an iron pipe a few inches from the steel bulkhead—and he fell backward injuring his foot."

McCarthy's unit did not actually see action until "ten weeks after he was hurt," his shipmate said. Confirmation of this version later came from then Secretary of the Navy Dan Kimball, who examined McCarthy's official records in the Pentagon. They showed only this one injury.

It was characteristic of McCarthy that a fractured leg received during a shipboard prank became magnified into a war wound suffered at death's door. During one of his subsequent Wisconsin campaigns, a heckler in the audience asked him why he wore elevator shoes. "I'll tell you why I wear this shoe," McCarthy replied. "It's because I carry ten pounds of shrapnel in this leg."

Such a leg would have been a medical marvel, composed of almost solid metal. Evidently aware of this, he later denied having made this claim—but still he couldn't refrain from adorning the facts. When Pilat and Shannon asked him directly about what had really happened, he came up with a new, but no less heroic version.

"It was a plane crash on a runway at Guadalcanal," he said. "The plane I was in turned over."

"Was that when you got the citation from Admiral Nimitz for refusing medical attention?" he was asked.

"Nothing heroic," the modest hero said. "We were a long way from a hospital."

The greatest of all the McCarthy wartime myths, outshining even the image of the wounded hero, was the saga of "Tail Gunner Joe."

There is no question that he flew a lot, but there is also no evidence that he ever flew where there was any chance Japanese Zeroes could get at him. His was a dive-bomber squadron, and the planes had room for only two men, the pilot and the tail gunner. When things were quiet, intelligence officers sometimes flew in the tail gunner's seat to get the feel of things, but when it was a question of firing and being fired at, the man with the pilot was always a professional tail gunner.

The glamour of McCarthy's role as an aerial marksman was to be magnified the oftener he told the tale. He had a cavalier disregard for the sanctity of numbers. Thus, in a 1944 campaign leaflet in Wisconsin, it was reported that he had "participated in 14 dive-bombing missions over Japanese positions." A few years later, in 1948, furnishing biographical material for the *Congressional Directory,* he wrote that he had had "17 official missions in the South Pacific." And in 1951, testifying in a legal proceeding, he claimed, "I was on 30 dive-bombing missions, plus liaison missions." Significantly, his Marine Corps "jacket" failed to list a single one of those 14 or 17 or 30 missions.

The reason was that they weren't real missions; they were for fun and frolic, not for war. Lt. P. T. Kimball, a public relations officer in his squadron, subsequently put the actual situation into focus for the Milwaukee *Journal:*

"I remember a day when we were both at Munda when Joe's squadron was flying a 'milk run' to Bougainville. The job was bombing runways on old airfields to make sure the Japs didn't try to come back. It was dull duty, and the bored fliers decided to see how many flights they could make in a day. McCarthy, like other ground officers, joined in the fun to ride as a tail gunner.

"As public relations officer, I wrote a form story about 'the record-breaking day of bombing,' filled in the names of the men involved and sent them along slugged 'from an advance Marine base.' I forgot the whole thing till McCarthy came around with a handful of clippings from Wisconsin papers.

" 'This is worth 50,000 votes to me,' McCarthy said. 'Come, have a drink on it.' "

On those joy rides in the tail gunner's seat, he liked to blast away with the machine guns. In 1943 another item concerning his exploits found its way to the Associated Press wires. This recounted how "Tail Gunner Joe" had set what was claimed to be a new military record: he had touched off 4,700 rounds of ammunition in a single day. Any innocent reader of that item would have to be forgiven for assuming that he must have been in desperate combat: the story, of course, gave no indication that the only targets had been jungle growth and coconut trees! McCarthy loved to blast those trees—so much so that on one occasion a huge sign was erected across the base camp's recreation area. It read: PROTECT OUR COCONUT TREES. SEND MC CARTHY BACK TO WISCONSIN.

Some years later and thousands of miles removed from those coconut trees, McCarthy described on nationwide American Broadcasting Company radio "the rough days when we lost a number of our pilots and gunners" in attacks on the Japanese airfields at Rabaul. With a throb in his voice, he told how "my task at night was to write home to the young wives, to the young mothers, with the hope that we might be able to make the blow fall less heavily." On the night after the first Rabaul raid, he said, "a great number of letters had to be written." He depicted himself as struggling through the night "in my dugout" to ease the pain of the loved ones back home. This description bore no relation to the actual facts. For one thing, McCarthy was never in a "dugout," but always at a safe and secure base camp; for another, according to the official Marine Corps history of his unit, VMSB-235, his squadron lost just *five officers and two men during its entire tour of duty in the South Pacific.*

There was no limit to Joe's ingenuity. Ingratiating himself with his commanding officer, he persuaded that gentleman to recommend him for a citation; and, sure enough, apparently acting on the assumption the recommendation was valid, Admiral Chester W. Nimitz's office at Pearl Harbor came through with a formal citation lauding Joseph McCarthy for his "meritorious and efficient performance of duty" and his "refusal" to be hospitalized "although suffering from a severe leg injury." As the citation makes clear by use of the date, June 22, 1943, this indeed referred to the broken leg received that day during the crossing-the-line horseplay on the *Chandeleur.*

Citations are, of course, always impressive, but in World War II, they flew out of the services' mimeographing machines like leaves in the autumn wind. Something better was needed. And so in 1952, backed by his prestige as the most feared Senator in Washington, McCarthy applied to the Navy for medals in recognition of his fanciful wartime feats. His application, according to columnist Doris Fleeson, was accompanied "by what are said to be 'certified copies from his flight log book.'" The Navy responded by awarding him the Distinguished Flying Cross and the Air Medal with four stars. The Air Medal was awarded in World War II for five bona fide missions; the Distinguished Flying Cross, not for fourteen or seventeen missions, the figures McCarthy himself had sometimes used, but for a minimum of twenty-five.

This official anointment of McCarthy's wavering claims and statistics soured some stomachs. Leonard Burns, of Milwaukee, a "staunch Republican" by his own account, announced he was mailing his Distinguished Flying Cross and four Air Medals to McCarthy. Burns had received his awards for flying thirty torpedo bombing missions from the aircraft carrier *Hornet,* and said he was "disgusted" at McCathy's tinsel heroics. In his letter to McCarthy, Burns asked whether Senator McCarthy had threatened to expose someone in the Marine Corps "as being a Communist" in order to get his medals. "Joe," he wrote, "was it necessary for you to apply for the medals? I never heard of anyone having to remind one of the various branches of the service that he was a hero and deserving of medals."

FOR MOST OF THE MILLIONS of young Americans who fought in it, World War II was a dirty, hateful business; a nightmare of insect-infested jungles, of hardships and horror, of fighting and dying. But for Joe McCarthy it was a world of high profit, synthetic glory and political propaganda.

Here was a man with a genius for making all ends come together in one neat package. While he was performing his duties as an intelligence officer at South Pacific base camps, he was reaping a small fortune back home by successful gambles in a stock market that, thanks to wartime pressures, rose and rose. While the money piled up in his brokerage account, he joy-rode in a marine plane, touching off those record-breaking bursts of machine-gun fire that devastated the coconut trees. And as the clippings from Wisconsin papers telling the legend of "Tail Gunner Joe" came back to him in the South Pacific, his ambitions soared, and he decorated the scenery with huge banners proclaiming MC CARTHY FOR SENATOR.

It was an incredible performance—so incredible that some of Joe's marine buddies considered him little more than a likable buffoon, hardly to be taken seriously. And how could one blame them for not taking seriously a MC CARTHY FOR SENATOR sign erected against a South Pacific jungle backdrop?

Only later did some of McCarthy's wartime comrades vent their feelings in firsthand accounts. One of those who spoke out was Marine Captain Jack Canaan, of Los Angeles. After pointing out that McCarthy was not a tail gunner but an intelligence officer, Canaan said:

"His only air experience was two missions in one day. He told me he did it for publicity value. In a hospital in the New Hebrides, he personally showed me the AP clipping about firing more rounds than any other gunner in one day. At the time I didn't understand the significance of his knowing wink that this clipping and picture of himself in a helmet 'would help out back in the states . . .'

"When I next saw McCarthy it was in Bougainville. He was still intelligence officer of his squadron. His presence was known there by two trucks and a jeep with large signs on them saying 'McCarthy for Senator.' Most of us thought it was a gag."

It was, of course, no gag at all as the voters of Wisconsin were soon to discover.

6

How to Make the Most Out of War

JOSEPH MC CARTHY was a wild man with money, and his financial wheeling and dealing represented one of the most tangled aspects of his stormy career. In his early years in law practice he was always broke, or nearly so. When he joined Mike Eberlein's law firm in the 1930s, Eberlein paid him a starting salary of $200 a month, ample in those times in that area for a single man. But McCarthy was always spending next month's salary this month. "He had a poor business head," Eberlein said later. "He could never save. It went as fast or faster than he got it. If he ever saved a cent, it would be a surprise to me."

Eberlein tried rationing him, paying half his salary in cash and withholding the rest so that he would have $1,200 coming to him at year's end. But this didn't work either; McCarthy always found some way to borrow against his prospects.

After he became a judge, his financial affairs suddenly blossomed. Though he had been on the bench only a relatively short time, though he had never been known to save, he nevertheless came up with a lump sum of $2,200 (then, quite a large nest egg), and in 1942, before he left for the South Pacific, he invested this sum in a trading account with the brokerage firm of Wayne Hummer & Company in Chicago. In the market as in all else he was a reckless plunger. He put his money into an extremely risky 40-percent margin account—and, wartime pressures being what they were, he hit it rich.

McCarthy apologists still try to belittle his financial manipulations as matters of no moment. Roy Cohn, who later became counsel for McCarthy's Senate investigating committee, attempted to brush the whole matter under the rug in his 1968 book, *McCarthy.* Cohn wrote:

"Anyone who tries to fault McCarthy on profit-seeking grounds comes up against a blank wall, yet it is surprising how many have tried it. Various biographers have accused him of trying to make big money through investments. The truth is that he made small investments all the time, but he played around the way the average man would play gin rummy. He would come up with a 'sensational' idea upon which he would proceed to place a small bet in the form of an investment. Then he'd forget about it. He dabbled in the stock and commodities markets. He was in and out all the time I knew him; it was a form of relaxation, without much common sense or judgment or even real interest."

At the very least, this account glosses over the facts. In 1952 a Senate investigating committee examined the Wayne Hummer account and reported that, "supported by sensational advances in security prices, he [McCarthy] was enabled to build up his initial investment into such substantial proportions that in 1943 he realized a net profit of $40,561.67." There was an additional $1,293 in dividends, giving McCarthy a total taxable income of $41,854.67 from his stock market operations in this one year. This was hardly playing gin rummy.

There was another significant angle: McCarthy decided he just wasn't going to report it for tax purposes. From the marine air station at El Toro, Calif., he wrote state tax officials:

"During the entire year of 1943 I was serving in the armed forces of the United States, during which time I spent no time in Wisconsin. I had no property in the state and received no income from within the state (having waived my salary as Circuit Judge). Therefore, I assume it is unnecessary under the present laws to file a return. If you do not so understand the law I shall be glad to file a return."

This neatly put the onus on the Wisconsin income tax officials who, of course, could not know what McCarthy and his brokers knew. Since servicemen's pay was exempt from taxation, since few had additional taxable income, the responsible state officials let this alibi for not filing pass. It was not until 1947, after Mc-Carthy had been elected a United States Senator, that tax officials began to catch on to his 1943 stock-market bonanza. On February 13, 1947, the federal government announced it was assessing him an additional $3,500 on his 1943 income, and this prompted Wisconsin tax collectors to reexamine McCarthy's 1943 no-tax statement.

J. L. Tibbetts, Assessor of Incomes at Appleton, wrote Mc-Carthy on Feb. 20, 1947, that "the Department now has knowledge that you had income for the year 1943 other than pay for military service." McCarthy repeated his original contention that he had not been "a Wisconsin resident" in that year, but Tibbetts wrote him on April 24: "I am advised by the legal division that it is of the opinion that you were a resident of Wisconsin in the year 1943 and therefore required to file a return of your income for that year with the Wisconsin Department of Taxation."

Tibbetts gave McCarthy thirty days in which to pay up. Mc-Carthy, fuming, denounced this deadline as "arbitrary in the extreme." Finally, however, he yielded and paid a tax of $2,359 and $218.32 interest.

The facts were clear: McCarthy had tried to duck paying taxes, and had paid both the state and federal governments only after the hidden facts about his windfall had caught up with him. This was to be just the first of several murky financial transactions.

THOSE MC CARTHY FOR SENATOR SIGNS that had blossomed against the jungle background of Bougainville ceased to be a topic for jest in mid-1944. "I want to join for the duration," Judge McCarthy had said when he enlisted in the marines, and the duration obviously was not yet. Some of the toughest fighting in the Pacific island-hopping campaign lay ahead, but back in Wisconsin there was a U.S. Senate seat up for grabs. The incumbent was Alexander Wiley, a formidable Republican vote-getter, seemingly an impossible man to beat in the party primary. But McCarthy never had had a respect for odds.

Two circumstances at this time would seem to have barred a McCarthy candidacy. First, he was a marine captain on duty in the South Pacific, and service regulations were specific: no one in the armed forces was permitted to campaign for public office, using the uniform to lure votes. In McCarthy's case there was a second and equally unequivocal prohibition. He was still a Wisconsin judge, and the Wisconsin Constitution provided that, if any supreme or circuit court judges should run for office, "all votes for either of them for any office . . . shall be void." But military regulations and provisions of a state constitution existed for Joe McCarthy only as rules to be ignored.

It is obvious that his ambition was no secret to political cohorts back in Wisconsin. They began to beat the drums for the dashing marine who had been so widely publicized as the redoubtable "tail gunner" of the South Pacific. They wrote to McCarthy, asking whether by any possibility he would be willing to serve if they drafted him. His answer was a model of modesty, dedication and willingness:

"Some time ago I received your letter in which you, in behalf of the committee, ask whether I would be willing to serve if elected to the U.S. Senate. This is the first opportunity I have had to answer, but I have given the matter serious consideration.

"My answer is yes.

"You understand, of course, that I shall take no part in the campaign. In fact, I do not even expect to be in the United States before the election, and I cannot, because of military regulations, discuss political issues. But I do have a program, and this I will submit to the people of Wisconsin as soon as the time permits.

"I must, of necessity, leave this campaign to my friends and the voters of Wisconsin, because I shall continue on out here, doing to the best of my ability those tasks assigned to me."

Thus, after making the proper obeisance to "military regulations" that forbade the discussion of "political issues," he announced that he had "a program" which he would submit to the Wisconsin electorate. After saying that he must "leave this campaign to my friends" and stay "on out here" fighting the war, he managed to arrange a thirty-day leave from the marines and get back to Wisconsin in time to appear in person during the final crucial two weeks of the campaign.

Handsome in his marine captain's uniform, he energetically plunged into his noncampaign. He dashed about the state, coralling voters on every street corner. The pretense that he wasn't campaigning became ludicrous. Time and again, he said what he had to say after disclaiming he was saying it. "I wish I could discuss the importance of oil and the importance of maintaining a strong army and navy to be used in the event any international organization breaks down, but I may not do so," he told the Milwaukee League of Women Voters. Another favorite formula became the one he used before the Appleton League of Women Voters. Appearing before them resplendent in uniform, he pointed out that service regulations unfortunately muzzled him. "If I were able to speak, here's what I'd say," he said—and then proceeded to say it.

This dodging of all regulations finally became too much for the Wisconsin Secretary of State. He pointed to the constitutional provision against judges running for other political office and inquired of the Attorney General whether he shouldn't strike McCarthy's name from the ballot. The Attorney General, a staunch Republican, got around the constitutional roadblock with a ruling admirable for its sophistry. "Judge McCarthy, as we understand it," he wrote, "has filed the required number of signers and his papers are otherwise in order. You should certify his name on the official ballot, and any question with regard to his eligibility to hold the office of United States senator must await future determination."

So McCarthy was permitted to run even though the constitution clearly said he couldn't. All he had to do was defeat Alexander Wiley. And that was a task that proved too much for even the brash young marine. Wiley was renominated handily and went on to reelection, but "Tail Gunner Joe" polled almost 100,000 votes and finished well ahead of two other challengers. He had made his first deep impression on the voters of Wisconsin; he had made contacts and gained followers throughout the state; he had laid the foundation for his next big try.

T H E D E F E A T B Y A L E X A N D E R W I L E Y left Joseph McCarthy in a curious kind of wartime limbo. He was a Wisconsin judge—and he was still a marine, subject to the inconvenience of military orders. He tried to reconcile the incompatible by applying for another sixty-day leave, pleading the pressure of his judicial duties; but the Marine Corps decided that Captain McCarthy, having just had one leave, wasn't entitled to another. Fight or resign, the corps said; he resigned.

Back on the bench, disregarding once more the Wisconsin prohibition against a judge's engaging in politics, McCarthy began to build his political fences. He limped all around Wisconsin, the picture of a wounded wartime hero, and he spoke to gatherings all over the state about his experiences, his voice throbbing with emotion as he talked about "my boys" and the hazards they had shared together in the South Pacific.

He was searching for a political base, and he quickly found it in the Wisconsin Young Republicans. To them he had the glamour of a war hero; he was young like them; and they could easily envision him as the champion who would lead them in the assault against the old-guard of the GOP and catapult them to positions of political prestige and power.

In currying favor with the Young Republicans, Judge McCarthy performed a curious feat; he transplanted Reno to Wisconsin. In his court, the "quickie divorce" became the rule, if one had a lawyer with the proper political connections. This practice broke radically with Wisconsin traditions. The state had pioneered a domestic court system designed to save marriages rather than dissolve them. A county divorce counsel would sit down with estranged couples, talk over their problems, advise them and try to bring about a reconciliation. Many marriages were saved by this system. But now, in Judge McCarthy's court, the whole procedure was junked, and divorces were issued at the rap of the gavel, sometimes almost before the disputing parties had had a chance to settle into their seats in the courtroom.

One of these "quickie divorces" that raised eyebrows involved

Mr. and Mrs. Chester Roberts. Roberts was chairman of the Young Republicans of Milwaukee and one of McCarthy's most ardent political backers. He had made dozens of speeches glorifying McCarthy, who had reciprocated by telling one and all that "nothing's too good for my friend Chet Roberts." Roberts was a $186-a-month public utility employee who was having domestic difficulties, and when his wife sued him for divorce, he was only too happy to let her go. But under the slow Wisconsin system, the case dragged on for months—and no end was in sight. Finally, Mrs. Roberts and her attorney decided to seek a swifter solution.

"My wife and her lawyer headed for Marinette to get the divorce before Judge Harold Murphy," Roberts later recalled. "It was perfectly all right with me; the sooner they got it over with the better. On the way, they went through Appleton and happened to bump into Joe. Next thing I know, Joe had settled the whole mess."

Mrs. Roberts and her attorney had this fortuitous meeting with the judge in Appleton on September 5, 1946. The three had lunch together, and in less than two hours, Mrs. Roberts had her divorce. This swift action scandalized the independent Milwaukee *Journal,* the state's largest daily newspaper. "It was quick, it was quiet, it was without publicity. And no doubt it was legal," the *Journal* commented. But it saw larger issues involved in the case: "Is Wisconsin justice to be used to accommodate political supporters of a presiding judge? Are Wisconsin courts the place in which to settle political debts?" After answering its own questions with a resounding "No," the *Journal* concluded: "Judge McCarthy, whose burning ambition for political advancement is accompanied by an astonishing disregard for things ethical and traditional, is doing serious injury to the judiciary of this state."

The reprimand bothered McCarthy not a whit. He kept right on running his divorce mill for parties who had the perspicacity to retain lawyers with the appropriate political connections. On one occasion, participants later recalled, he began holding the hearing while the parties were walking up the courthouse steps.

"Are you the lawyer for the plaintiff?" McCarthy asked one of the attorneys climbing the steps with him. The lawyer said he was.

"And are you the lawyer for the respondent?" the judge asked another. The lawyer said he was.

"Are these stipulations correct?"

Both attorneys agreed they were correct.

"Is there anything anyone wants to say before we proceed?"

He was assured there was nothing anybody wished to say, and so, hustling into the courtroom, donning his robe and taking his seat on the bench, he rapped his gavel once and declared the warring couple divorced. The wife was stunned by the swiftness of it all. "Am I divorced?" she asked.

"Yes, you are now a free woman," McCarthy told her.

"But is that all there is to it? I thought there would be a court trial."

"We're efficient around here. You wanted a divorce and now you have it."

One reason for this judicial favoritism, and for the round of speech-making and posturing as a wounded war hero, was that another crucial political contest was brewing. In the election of 1946, Wisconsin's second Senatorial seat was at stake, and Judge McCarthy intended to capture the prize. At first glance, his task appeared even more difficult than had been his challenge to Alexander Wiley; for the Senator he would have to defeat was none other than Robert M. (Young Bob) La Follette, Jr.

La Follette, the son and namesake of Robert M. (Fighting Bob) La Follette, had held his seat in the U.S. Senate for twenty-one years. During that time, he had acquired a reputation as a fighting liberal, and he was often called the best Senator in Washington. It seemed the height of folly to challenge so distinguished a figure.

The La Follettes had originally been Republicans, but Fighting Bob, finding his party ruled by a dynasty of selfish and corrupt business interests, had been compelled to go outside the organization to achieve much-needed reforms. He had organized the Wisconsin Progressive Party, and he and his sons, Robert and Philip, had run as Progressives, assured of their party's nomination and drawing votes from all factions in the fall general election contests against Republicans and Democrats. It was a third-party system that had worked long and well in Wisconsin, and the successes of decades had clothed the La Follette name with political magic.

However, with the pressures of the wartime era, the well-springs of Progressive support had begun to dry up, and the La

Follettes had felt compelled to disband the Progressive Party. The result was that, in 1946, Senator La Follette was faced with the necessity of seeking the nomination of one of the two major parties. His liberal stance on national issues made him ideologically akin to the Democrats; but the Republican Party was by far the stronger party in Wisconsin; it was also the party of his father's early allegiance, and so the Senator decided to declare for the Republican nomination. It was a decision that entailed great risks—how great La Follette did not at first appreciate.

The Republican Party in Wisconsin had a strong conservative base. It was a conservatism fueled by injections of big money and aided by the tide of postwar disillusionment that had begun to sweep across the nation. The combination put La Follette in the position of seeking the nomination of a party many of whose old-guard leaders disagreed with his political philosophy and many of whose followers were becoming disenchanted with Washington. There was yet another, and perhaps even more crucial, drawback. La Follette, as he had advanced in power and seniority in the Senate, had become ever more deeply engrossed in national crises. He concentrated on the great issues of the day, got back to Wisconsin less and less frequently, and so committed the cardinal indiscretion for a politician: he lost touch with his constituents, his base of power. It was a situation ideally suited to the opportunism of his rival.

McCarthy's announcement of his candidacy was greeted with guffaws in many quarters of Wisconsin. Who was this upstart north-country judge who thought he could defeat the distinguished Senator La Follette? As was always to be the case, the laughter that belittled the political prospects of McCarthy was decidedly premature. He was determined to muscle aside every other aspirant and win the endorsement of the old-guard party organization for the test against La Follette. When local committees listened to him with a cool politeness, he adopted the technique of the face-to-face confrontation. He drove to the homes of potential rivals and tackled them head-on. "After all," he said to one, "you can't expect to beat a veteran, can you?" The prospective opponent, who had spent World War II safely at home in Wisconsin, acknowledged that he couldn't. When McCarthy, with the enthusiastic backing of the Young Republicans, bulldozed his way to a preliminary endorsement at the Republican State Convention, the political bosses were horrified at what they considered his poor chances. They began to cast around for a candidate who was better known. McCarthy, aware of their maneuvers, drove directly to the office of his new rival. This political leader had recently been divorced. As McCarthy later told the story, he reminded his prospective opponent—in a voice syrupy with regret—that divorced men make poor candidates, and explained how sorry he would be if, in the heat of the campaign, the details of the divorce were spread all over the press and radio. The threatened politician decided not to tackle McCarthy.

In the end, the old-line organization was left, willy-nilly, with Joe McCarthy and no one else—unless, of course, it was willing to accept La Follette. It was not. Thomas Coleman, known throughout the state as the "boss" of the Republican organization, made the final choice: he threw his full weight behind McCarthy's candidacy, sending out a flood of pamphlets endorsing him, extolling his wartime sacrifices and attacking La Follette. The battle was on.

With organization backing assured, McCarthy pulled out all the stops. Every possible campaign gimmick was trotted out and tried. An airplane flitted all around the state; speakers invaded bridge parties and poker games to laud McCarthy; and there was a blizzard of direct-mail advertising. The central theme of the campaign was the legend of "Tail Gunner Joe." Some 750,000 pieces of a twelve-page brochure glorifying his supposed wartime feats were circulated throughout the state. One large advertisement in the Milwaukee *Journal* read:

"JOE MC CARTHY WAS A TAIL GUNNER in World War II. When the war began Joe had a soft job as a Judge at EIGHT GRAND a year. He was EXEMPT from military duty. He resigned his job to enlist as a PRIVATE in the MARINES. He fought on LAND and in the AIR all through the Pacific. He and millions of other guys kept you from talking Japanese. TODAY JOE MC CARTHY IS HOME. He wants to SERVE America in the SENATE. Yes, folks, CONGRESS NEEDS A TAIL GUNNER. Now, when Washington is in confusion, when BUREAUCRATS are seeking to perpetuate themselves FOREVER upon the American way of life, AMERICA NEEDS FIGHTING MEN. These men who fought upon foreign soil to SAVE AMERICA have earned the right to SERVE AMERICA in times of peace."

Another device, which McCarthy had used with great effect

in previous campaigns, was the handwritten note. In the last few days of the campaign, some half-million postcards flooded the mails, reaching virtually every voter in Wisconsin. The salutation was personal; "Dear ——," followed by this message: "Your vote Tuesday will be greatly appreciated by Joe McCarthy." The McCarthy name was dropped down to the bottom of the note and handwritten to simulate his signature. Hundreds of different hands signed the name, but many bedazzled voters, unaccustomed to such personal attention, doubtless remained under the delusion that the candidate had taken a direct interest in them.

The Republican machine, before it covered the state with this paper blizzard, had carefully tested out the effectiveness of the technique in selected guinea-pig areas. A poll taken in Two Rivers originally showed McCarthy trailing La Follette by a 1-to-3 margin; after the postcard blitz, another poll showed that McCarthy had pulled even. In De Pere, La Follette had led McCarthy by 2 to 1; but after this tactic had been used, McCarthy pulled slightly ahead. So it went, in district after district.

To this direct-mail barrage was added the indefatigable campaigning of the office-seeker himself. He hurtled around the state, thriving on twenty-hour campaign days and hurling a barrage of charges at La Follette. His philosophy in politics was the same as it had been in the college prize ring: he was convinced that if you threw enough punches and never stopped throwing the law of averages dictated that you were bound sometime to land a haymaker. He denounced La Follette for making a handsome yearly profit out of a family-owned radio station, insinuating that the radio license was a kind of Senatorial payoff. His supporters tagged La Follette with a fascist label; and then McCarthy, in the next breath, called him a communist sympathizer, evidently seeing no incongruity. "Senator La Follette is playing into the hands of the Communists by opposing world cooperation," he cried in one radio speech.

It all seemed so wild and reckless that La Follette was apparently deluded into believing that such tactics could not possibly register with the independent and usually intelligent electorate of Wisconsin. He felt himself especially invulnerable to McCarthy's fellow-traveling charges—and with good reason. On May 31, 1945, he had taken the Senate floor and made one of the first and most blistering attacks on the Soviet designs in the postwar era. This was at a time, it must be remembered, when Russia was still our wartime ally and when even many staunch conservatives were predicting a peaceful postwar coexistence with the Soviets. La Follette was a bit of a Midwest isolationist; he looked with skepticism upon the United Nations as an effective peace-keeping force; and he was fearful of the extent of our growing world-wide commitments. At the same time, he condemned the ruthless Russian surge into Poland and Eastern Europe; and, in the May 31 speech and others that followed, he called for eternal American vigilance against communist designs.

The speech had aroused American Communists to fury; and, since some major labor unions were dominated at that time by Communist leadership, this meant that powerful segments of labor were being conditioned to bury the knife in La Follette's back—despite the well-established fact that he had been one of the best friends labor had ever had in the Senate. There were other hazards in the La Follette situation. Two months before primary day, the Milwaukee *Journal* noted that, under Wisconsin laws, it would be perfectly possible for thousands of Democrats to cross over and vote in the Republican primary. The normal assumption might be that these voters would be La Follette adherents, but this was not necessarily so. The *Journal* pointed out that many Democrats were angry with La Follette for spurning their party and designating himself a Republican; many believed, too, that if La Follette were defeated in the primary, McCarthy would be a much easier foe to handle in the general election.

All of these currents were running at flood level before La Follette recognized that he was in trouble. It was not until two weeks before the primary election that he returned to Wisconsin to campaign, and even then he did not tear into McCarthy as McCarthy had been tearing into him. He ran a lofty campaign, basing his appeal on his name and record. It was the wrong tactic at the wrong time. McCarthy had raised such a storm that voters could believe almost anything they pleased about La Follette unless they were presented with a solid case to the contrary. And this La Follette did not do.

Still it was close. As the votes were counted on election night, McCarthy, who had been at his cockiest, started to worry. The rural counties, on which he had counted for his heaviest support, began to go for La Follette. With almost all the back-country vote

tallied, La Follette led by some 3,000 votes, and still to be reported
were tallies from his labor strongholds in Milwaukee, Racine and
Kenosha, wards that had always favored him by overwhelming
margins in the past. But now there came a strange shift in the
returns. The Milwaukee precincts, where McCarthy had expected
to be weak, began to go for him; district by district, the La
Follette lead was whittled away until it evaporated, and McCarthy
surged to the front. When the tally was complete, incredibly, the
upstart had defeated the Senator with the famous name by
207,935 votes to 202,539—a margin of 5,396.

What could possibly have happened? The answer involves
what is doubtless one of the supreme ironies of American politics: though many factors contributed to the defeat of La Follette,
the final turning edge was supplied by the Communists; they had
elected their own Nemesis.

The vital narrow margin that the Communists had supplied
was demonstrated by an analysis of the vote in those labor districts that La Follette had been expected to carry overwhelmingly.
The Communists controlled the huge Allis-Chalmers CIO local
in Milwaukee; the Milwaukee garbage men were under Communist influence; the head of the Milwaukee CIO was a Communist and so was the state secretary. Unions in Racine and
Kenosha were similarly infected; and, in the weeks before the
election, the Wisconsin edition of *The CIO News* had brainwashed union members with a barrage of anti-La Follette propaganda. A series of headlines blasted away: UNION CALLS LA FOL-
LETTE ATTACK A BETRAYAL, BLAST LA FOLLETTE PLEA FOR
TOLERANCE TOWARD NAZI GERMAN, FASCIST LEADERS. The effect
was seen when the votes were counted, when the labor wards
that had been La Follette's bulwark in the past deserted him.

Before the year was out, a rank-and-file revolt purged communists from leadership in the CIO unions, and the new anti-
Communist leaders conceded that La Follette's defeat had been
largely the work of Communist conniving. But McCarthy didn't
care. When asked about his Communist support, he offered a
rationalization that, had it been made a few years later by
anyone appearing before his committee, would certainly have
condemned its author to a traitor's purgatory. Said he: "Communists have the same right to vote as anyone else, don't they?"

.   .   .

THERE HAS BEEN a long-enduring misconception about
the political wellsprings that gave birth to McCarthy's career.
Even as late as 1969, talking in Washington to some fairly high
former officials in the Truman Administration, I found that some
still harbored the idea that McCarthy originally was a maverick
offshoot of agrarian radicalism. "When he first came to Washington," said one, "he seemed to come out of left-field; there was
a tinge of Populism about him." Many analysts have endeavored
to demonstrate that McCarthy's original political appeal was to
the heirs of nineteenth-century Populist radicalism.

No assumption could be more wrong. Michael Rogin, in a
study of voting trends in the upper Midwest, published in 1967,
has showed that McCarthy's support derived from an archconservative base. Noting that the plains states consistently sent to
the Senate right-wing Republicans who supported McCarthy to
the end, Rogin wrote that "McCarthy was not the agent who disrupted the traditional agrarian radical base. Before these states
supported McCarthy, they had already undergone an evolution
from agrarian radicalism to extreme conservatism."

"In so far as McCarthy's appeal transcended anticommunism," Rogin added, "its roots were in groups disturbed about
cosmopolitanism and about the prestige given to the educated
and established families and businesses of the East . . . The midwest political elite, however long established, was still upset about
striped-pants diplomacy, intellectuals in the State Department,
Harvard intellectuals, and British 'pinkos.' "

Rogin commented on the attitude of small-town newspapers
throughout the plains states, which had "led the opposition to
every agrarian radical movement from Populism to La Follette
to the contemporary Farmers Union. . . . The Populists and the
Non-Partisan League, for example, had to start their own newspapers because the existing local press would not give them a
fair hearing in their news columns, much less support them on
the editorial page. The small-town press may be suspicious of
certain authorities and institutions, but it is supported by others
—particularly local business interests. The role of this press
provides evidence for McCarthy's conservative inheritance, not
his 'populist' roots."

In September, 1946—after McCarthy had defeated La Follette, but before he had been elected to the Senate—Felix Belair, Jr., a *New York Times* journalist, was making a swing through the Midwest, sampling the political winds. He called upon Colonel Robert McCormick, the publisher of the Chicago *Tribune* and the generally acknowledged Republican boss of Illinois at that time. McCormick had been one of the leaders of America First, with which the Committee for Constitutional Government had been so closely allied, and now he and former cohorts from CCG were putting together their new American Action movement, designed to alter the political complexion of America in the 1946 election.

Felix Belair found Colonel McCormick in a most ebullient mood. He first congratulated himself upon having hurried the political demise of Wendell Willkie, the Republican Presidential hopeful in 1940. When Willkie sought the nomination again in 1944, he entered the Wisconsin primary and lost decisively to Thomas E. Dewey. "Poor fellow," McCormick said, "he thought Dewey beat him in the Wisconsin primary, but it wasn't Dewey —I beat him. And the issue was Americanism. That's *Tribune* territory over there."

He continued with this political insight: "Everybody knows that the Democratic Party is the party of the Russian-loving Communists in this country . . . Everybody knows that Jimmy Byrnes [Truman's Secretary of State] is just a junior clerk for the British Foreign Office."

Belair commented: "The apparent inconsistency of a pro-British Secretary of State in a 'pro-Russian' administration was a phenomenon that Colonel McCormick seemed to think not worth explaining."

The interview was suddenly interrupted when McCormick's secretary announced that Judge Joseph R. McCarthy was waiting to see the publisher. McCormick promptly hustled Belair out of his office and warmly greeted the miracle worker who had just demolished the myth of La Follette invincibility.

Belair's account of this meeting of minds in the Chicago *Tribune*'s Tower caused some ripples of reaction in Wisconsin political circles. It was the first time some of those misguided laborites who had voted for McCarthy in the primary got an inkling of his allegiance with the far right. They began to stir a bit uneasily, and to quiet them, McCarthy rushed into print with a statement in which he belittled the significance of the rendezvous. Colonel McCormick, he said, had expressed a desire to see him; and so, as a matter of simple courtesy, he had dropped in to shake hands. "We had a little chat, that's all," McCarthy explained.

But the Chicago *Sun-Times* and the Milwaukee *Journal* began to look into the McCormick-McCarthy tie, and they came across the spoor of American Action. They discovered that the organization's reputed million-dollar war chest for the 1946 campaign had been raised by old America Firsters and CCG collaborators like McCormick, some of the Du Ponts, Robert E. Wood, Merwin K. Hart, Samuel B. Pettengill and E. F. Hutton. They discovered, too, that American Action was making its influence felt at the grass roots in Wisconsin. Not long after the McCarthy-McCormick tête-à-tête, Lansing Holt, who had been Wisconsin chairman of American First, became American Action's advance man in the state, and he announced publicly that American Action was supporting McCarthy because "he has a good war record and he's in favor of the American Constitution."

As Holt discussed the campaign issues, the themes and purposes that had been promoted for so long by the ultrareactionary millionaires behind America First and CCG clearly emerged. "If we gain control of the House of Representatives and the Senate, we will have accomplished our objectives," Holt said. "We will then control the purse strings. The New Deal will be busted and without money to spend. It won't take long then to put the radicals and Communists in their places."

Just as was the case with Van Horn Moseley, spokesman for CCG and the National Association of Manufacturers, and the editorial writers of *The Saturday Evening Post* whom Attorney General Jackson had attacked, Holt explained in all seriousness that American Action wanted nothing to do with that devil-word "democracy." It preferred "republic" to describe America because "democracy" was a Russian word that was used as a cover-up for communism.

This was pretty extreme even for the increasingly conservative upper Midwest, and on October 17, 1946, reporters asked McCarthy about American Action's role in his campaign. And here is what he said:

"If it is, as some newspapers have said, the old America First crowd, I want nothing to do with it. I want nothing to do with any group that goes in for racial and religious hatred. But if it was organized to fight communism and to oppose those who are communistically-inclined, then I welcome its support."

It was a statement that admirably covered both sides of the fence. American Action was not offended by such a split verdict, and it began to put advertisements in Wisconsin newspapers endorsing the candidacy of Joe McCarthy. This was the first really coordinated, big-money backing that McCarthy had received in his political campaigns; and, a significant point, it was used directly for his benefit—it was not funneled through the normal channels of the state Republican machine headed by Thomas Coleman. One might have thought that McCarthy would have remembered such potent assistance, especially since he had commented about American Action himself in the October, 1946, interview; but five years later, when Oliver Pilat and William Shannon asked him about the organization, he responded crisply: "Never heard of it."

M C C A R T H Y ' S D E M O C R A T I C O P P O N E N T in the fall election was Professor Howard J. McMurray, a political science instructor of New Dealish persuasion at the University of Wisconsin. Never was there a greater mismatch. The wave of anti-intellectualism, the aversion to striped-pants diplomacy, the rural distrust of the polished Eastern elite had begun to surge through Wisconsin—and Joe McCarthy took full advantage of the popular mood. "I'm just a farm boy, not a professor," he proclaimed.

He had no program, and when he tried to develop one, he sometimes forgot what the details were supposed to be. One ludicrous self-exposure of his uncertain grasp of issues came while he was making a speech discussing his five-point program to bring peace to labor and industry. He got to point three—and there he became stuck. He began to stammer and fumble around, unable to recall what point four was supposed to be until someone in the audience shouted helpfully, "Compulsory arbitration!" McCarthy grabbed the cue so quickly, announcing that this was indeed his fourth point, that the audience broke into gales of laughter, and he had to quit.

This was not advancing his candidacy, and soon McCarthy switched to out-and-out redbaiting. In a speech before an audience of 450 attending a League of Women Voters rally in Milwaukee, he casually mentioned that Professor McMurray was "Communistically inclined."

No matter how offhandedly it was made, this was a deadly charge, and the audience hushed. McMurray, who was present to debate with McCarthy, leaped to his feet and said slowly and impressively:

"I have never heard a responsible citizen—I say a *responsible* citizen—challenge my loyalty as an American before. I am sure my friends and my many students in my political science courses of the past years will not challenge my loyalty." He paused, and then, white and shaking with rage, continued: "This statement is a little below the belt. I'll leave the answer to the voters."

Any other man might have been abashed, but it was characteristic of McCarthy that he never faltered on the attack. And it was equally characteristic of him that, no matter how foul the blow he struck, he always placed himself upon a pedestal of unassailable principle and virtue in striking it. He did that now.

"I said that for the benefit of Howard McMurray," he replied smoothly, just as if he had done his foe a kindness. "But I also want to ask him: Does he then not welcome the endorsement of the *Daily Worker*, a Communist newspaper, which referred to him in a recent issue as 'a fellow traveler,' according to quotations in the Appleton *Post-Crescent* and the Green Bay *Press Gazette?*"

McMurray was on his feet in an instant. "I welcome that question," he said. "I have not seen the reported statement in the *Daily Worker*, nor the comments of those two most reactionary papers, the Appleton and Green Bay papers. But if I have the support of the *Daily Worker*, I certainly repudiate that paper and their whole tribe."

The statement was in stark contrast to McCarthy's failure to repudiate the communist support that had helped him win over La Follette—but no one at that time was making the comparison.

A week later in a speech in Appleton, McCarthy again dragged out the Red smear, a bit regretfully as if he was such a decent fellow himself that he hated to mention it. "The *Daily Worker* called you a fellow traveler, meaning Communist," he told McMurray. "I regret bringing this up, but you've forced me to do it."

McMurray's anticommunist credentials would appear to have been impervious to challenge. On one occasion, a Democratic candidate for Congress from Milwaukee had been discovered to be a Communist. The Democratic National Committeeman had publicly repudiated him and withdrawn party support. McMurray contended that he himself had written the repudiation statement and that he had been the first to give it to the press. But McCarthy charged that McMurray had done nothing, that he had sat back and remained silent until "he saw how the political winds were blowing."

McCarthy's patriotic camouflage was so convincing that finally even the church became involved. A priest in St. Joseph's Catholic Church in Appleton urged his flock to "vote against the Communist candidate" in the coming election—and no one had any doubt whom he meant.

McMurray was outraged. "I am ashamed of the fact that men in their pulpits have used the epithet 'Communist candidate,' " he said. "I am ashamed—because I am a Christian."

There was no corresponding shame in Joseph McCarthy. He was out to win, and he would use any method that furthered the end. An advertisement he placed in the Wausau *Record-Herald,* read:

"Some of the Democratic candidates for high offices in the government have been repudiated by the party because they have been proven to have Communist backgrounds and Communist ways of thinking. Others have been touched with suspicion, but the proof is lacking. Joseph R. McCarthy is 100 per cent American in thought and deed. No one can say that he believes in any foreign isms that have plagued the Democratic party throughout their reign. This is America. Let's have Americans in the government."

Howard McMurray wore himself hoarse denying and protesting. The more he defended himself, the more he raised the issue; the more a lot of voters began to suspect that "Joe must have something there." The result of a battle fought on these terms was inevitable. McCarthy polled 620,430 votes; McMurray, 378,772. Wisconsin had a new "100 percent American" junior Senator in Washington.

7

The Worst Senator

JOSEPH MC CARTHY'S WASHINGTON DEBUT took
place under auspices that, in retrospect, seem most appropriate:
he was the guest of honor at a victory bash arranged by John
Maragon, the "5 percenter" whose influence-peddling around the
White House was soon to leave a deep scar on the Truman
Administration. The victory celebration was held on the evening
of February 2, 1947.

Maragon was an immigrant from Greece whose scholastic
career had ended with the sixth grade. He had knocked about
Washington for years in a variety of nondescript jobs—bootblack,
newsboy, loan company collector, railroad detective. When

Truman became President in 1945, he was an obscure agent for the Baltimore & Ohio Railroad, earning $2,700 a year.

Then, abruptly, by some mysterious process that has never been satisfactorily explained, Maragon blossomed into a fast-talking, ubiquitous man-about-town. He had only a slight acquaintance with Truman before the latter became President, but now he seemed to have the run of the White House and he bragged to one and all about his gilt-edged contacts. Administration apologists were later to try to brush him off as an "utter nonentity," not in the same league with the big-name lawyers and public relations agencies that are the real power brokers in Washington. But Johnny Maragon was not to be dismissed quite so lightly. He developed a mysterious affluence. He began to live the good life in the swank Carlton Hotel, and he dined regularly in the Old New Orleans Restaurant. He entertained lavishly, and he seemed to have entrée to circles of officialdom important to interests that wanted "to get things done."

One of the firms for which Maragon peddled influence was Allied Molasses, of Perth Amboy, N.J., a company that was soon to play a decidedly sticky role in McCarthy's burgeoning career. Allied Molasses was headed by Harold Ross, and another part-time lobbyist for the firm was Ross' uncle, Milton R. Polland. Polland was a prominent Milwaukeean, a staunch Republican, and an ardent backer of McCarthy.

As the story was later put together, Polland thought it would be a fine gesture to launch the career of Wisconsin's junior Senator with a victory celebration in Washington. He suggested the idea to Otis (Bully Boy) Gomillion, who had been disappointed in a sheriff's election contest back in Wisconsin and was now about to settle into a permanent role as McCarthy's bodyguard. Gomillion in turn carried the victory party idea to Maragon. Maragon, who knew how to handle such affairs, was to arrange all the details, and McCarthy's Wisconsin backers would foot the bill.

Not at all loath to curry favor with a new and possibly puissant Senator, Maragon reserved thirty hard-to-get rooms in the Carlton Hotel. He also set up a subsidiary banquet for the more lowly Wisconsin field workers in the Old New Orleans Restaurant.

The main party in the thirty rooms of the Carlton seems to have been a swinging affair. McCarthy appeared, escorting an attractive young Wisconsin girl named Patricia who had worked in his campaign and had come to Washington, entertaining the idea that she might possibly become his secretary. With his irrepressible habit of transforming a Buick into a Cadillac, he introduced her all around the thirty rooms of the Carlton as "my fiancée."

Sometime after midnight, McCarthy rushed up to Maragon, wild-eyed, his wispy hair disarranged. "I'm glad to find you," he said. "Patricia lost her pocketbook."

Instantly assessing the seriousness of the crisis, Maragon searched frantically through the thirty rooms for the missing purse. It was not to be found.

This contretemps affecting the "fiancée" of the guest of honor put a damper on the hilarity of the evening and disturbed Johnny Maragon. He approached some of his friends the next day, and suggested that it would be "a nice gesture" if they all chipped in and bought Patricia a new purse. And so they did, shelling out sixty-five dollars for a handbag worthy of a Senator's bride-to-be.

Maragon, elated at having redeemed this delicate situation, arranged for another little party at which the handbag would be presented with appropriate ceremony. The party was a bit of a letdown for one reason: Patricia wasn't there. The "fiancée" had already returned to Wisconsin. McCarthy himself accepted the new handbag for her in absentia; Maragon personally donated a bottle of expensive perfume to go with it; and the package was mailed.

"The Senator was very appreciative of my help on that occasion," Maragon later said, describing the event. He added: "I never asked McCarthy for a damned thing. I never got even a cigarette out of it."

The evidence indicates that McCarthy fared much better. It was symbolic that he made his debut upon the Washington scene under the aegis of Maragon, for the Senator from Wisconsin was soon to become known as the lobbyists' fair-haired boy in the capital.

M C C A R T H Y began his senatorial career under a cloud arising from the very conditions under which he had gotten himself elected Senator. Just as he had flouted the constitutional provisions forbidding judges to run for office in his campaign against Alexander Wiley, so he had thumbed his nose at the same prohibition in his primary battle against Senator La Follette and his general election duel with Howard McMurray. Campaign literature soliciting funds for him had been sent out on circuit court stationery. Circuit court letterheads and envelopes had been used to send out copies of a ten-page speech he had made to the Wisconsin Young Republicans. The Madison *Capital-Times,* one of the nation's best small-city dailies, had denounced him by writing that Judge McCarthy "has not only refused to recognize the moral issue involved but is openly and brazenly using his office as circuit judge to advance his candidacy."

When McMurray had charged that he was not only violating the state constitution but the canon of ethics of the American Bar Association, McCarthy had replied that he wasn't a member of the bar association, and took a backhanded slap at the association's "code of ethics written by a few lawyers . . . without the force of law."

Efforts had been made to get McCarthy's name stricken from the ballot, but the Wisconsin Supreme Court, in one of those ambivalent performances that often characterize courts juggling sensitive public issues, had agreed that he might be wrong, but had contended it was powerless to act because he was running for a *federal,* not a *state* office—and besides the voters might not have him.

After the voters took him, Miles McMillin, a lawyer and editorial writer for the *Capital-Times,* petitioned the State Board of Bar Commissioners to study McCarthy's violation of the state constitution, of his oath of office and of the lawyer's code of ethics. Four of the state's most distinguished lawyers sat on the bar commission, and they had before them, as one of the key exhibits, McCarthy's signature to the oath of office he had taken on December 1, 1945, after he had been elected to the bench. In this, he had solemnly pledged himself to "support the Constitution of the United States and the Constitution of the State of Wisconsin," which forbade judges to run for other office while wearing judicial robes. The bar commissioners, after studying the evidence, took an unprecedented step. They petitioned the Wisconsin

Supreme Court to disbar McCarthy for "violating the public policy of the State of Wisconsin, the Code of Judicial Ethics, his Oath of Office as a Judge, and his Oath of Office as a Member of the Bar."

Harlan B. Rogers, counsel for the commission, minced no words in the supporting brief he filed in what became known as the *State of Wisconsin vs. Joseph R. McCarthy.* He said:

"It is difficult to conceive of any conduct upon the part of a presiding judge which would bring judges into greater disrepute and contempt than the conduct of the defendant in this proceeding. The defendant, by his conduct, chose to defy the rules of ethical conduct prescribed by the Constitution, the laws of the State of Wisconsin, and the members of the profession in order to attain a selfish personal advantage. The gratification of his ambition was in defiance of the declared policy and laws of Wisconsin . . ."

Striking directly at the court's earlier quibble that running for state office was one thing, for federal office another, the petition charged:

"The breach of official trust and obligation is as great when applied to a candidate for the office of United States Senator as it would be if applied to one for governor of the state. In either situation, to have a judge passing on the rights of litigants appearing before him and using his judicial position and power to influence votes for his candidacy and others in his political party, constituted a violation of the State Constitution and state laws and was in direct conflict with the duties and obligations of trust which he assumed by his Oath of Office."

The action of the bar commission put the Wisconsin Supreme Court in a quandary. How could it uphold ethics and the constitution on one hand—and McCarthy on the other? The court proved itself equal to the task. It wrote:

"Under the facts of this case we can reach no other conclusion than that the defendant [McCarthy], by accepting and holding the office of United States Senator during the term for which he was elected Circuit Judge, did so in violation of the terms of the Constitution and laws of the State of Wisconsin, and in doing so violated his oath as a Circuit Judge and as an attorney of law."

But, said the court with smoothest sophistry, the offense "is one in a class by itself which is not likely to be repeated"—that is, McCarthy almost certainly wouldn't return to sit on the circuit court bench and run for Senator again!

This judicial hair-splitting was greeted with derision in some Wisconsin circles. One political observer said it reminded him "of the case of the man who stabbed his wife, threatened to shoot a neighbor, and drove a car while drunk, but who was turned loose by the judge on the ground that he was a veteran carpenter and was not likely to repeat his offense (after all he only had one wife)."

Almost any other politician who had just squeaked by on such a technical clearance after being found guilty of violating his oath as a judge and a lawyer would have been content to let the whole matter be forgotten. But Joe McCarthy was not the man to bury an affront to his dignity. Apprised of the court's decision, he came out swinging:

"In view of the unanimous decision of the court in dismissing the case as having no merit," he said, "it must be assumed that the bar commissioners knew their case had no merit and were playing politics or that they were completely incompetent as lawyers. In either event their actions are a disgrace to every honest, decent lawyer in the State of Wisconsin and they should resign."

IN HIS FIRST THREE YEARS in the Senate, McCarthy laid the foundation for the judgment rendered by capital newsmen in 1951 in a poll conducted by *Pageant* magazine that he was "the worst Senator" in the entire body of ninety-six. He spent relatively little time on the floor of the Senate. He attended fewer roll calls than any able-bodied Senator. His votes and major activities reflected either the archconservative ideology of the old America Firsters and right-wingers who had backed his candidacy or the desires of special-interest groups. Ironically, he opposed the major Truman Administration proposals to combat and contain communism. He cast "No" votes against the Marshall Plan, which was so instrumental in rehabilitating Western Europe; against the Point Four program designed to prop up the faltering economies of underdeveloped nations; against military aid to free nations. It may be argued that such votes reflected the Midwestern isolationism that infected large segments of his Wisconsin electorate. But if it was true, as McCarthy was to contend, that communism represented a world-wide menace, such negativism regarding programs designed to combat it was utterly inconsistent.

Some of his other stands reflected the pressures of his farm-state constituency. He backed most Administration farm-aid programs, and opposed a bill that would have permitted oleo-margarine to be packaged like butter, a bitter consumer issue at that time—but then he had a lot of dairy farmers among his constituents, and such a vote is the kind that can be excused by a Senator's need not to alienate the home folks. Less defensible were a number of other public positions that followed faithfully the desires of his secret backers.

He voted for tax measures that favored the rich; opposed public housing that was so desperately needed in the postwar era that even the conservative Robert A. Taft favored it; supported the Taft-Hartley Act and other restrictive labor laws. Perhaps one of the most significant of his votes was cast on March 29, 1950, when he voted for the Kerr natural gas bill which would have exempted natural gas interests from regulation by the Federal Power Commission. This measure had been opposed by both the Republican and Democratic parties in Wisconsin; by the Governor of the state, the Attorney General and the legislature. All had based their opposition on the sound belief that passage of the bill would mean higher gas rates for Wisconsin consumers. Out of the entire Wisconsin delegation in both houses of Congress, only McCarthy and one Republican Congressman sided with the powerful oil and gas interests against the people of Wisconsin as the Kerr measure was approved by Congress, only to run into a veto by President Truman.

Equally illustrative of the manner in which Senator McCarthy cast his influence on the side of powerful special-interest groups seeking to dip their fingers into the federal till was his sponsor-ship of a bill that would have given some of his wealthy backers a windfall in real estate. Oliver Pilat and William V. Shannon described this effort in their series in the New York *Post:*

"He sponsored a bill to allow a group of his Milwaukee friends to purchase for a few hundred thousand dollars the federally constructed town of Greendale, Md., which cost the government millions to develop. Denounced by housing experts as a steal, the bill was eventually amended so drastically that McCarthy's real estate cronies never went ahead with their plans to take it over."

One of his more extreme involvements earned him the sobriquet "the Pepsi-Cola Kid" among Washington newsmen. Appropriately enough, this was a situation that found him hobnobbing with John Maragon and the Allied Molasses crowd.

During the immediate postwar years, many commodities were scarce and had to be rationed. One in especially short supply was sugar. Housewives wanted more sugar for canning. Industry wanted more for soft drinks. Both wanted quotas raised in their favor. Out of such shortages, such pressures, was fashioned a lobbyist's paradise.

Pepsi-Cola was engaged in a fierce sales contest with its great rival, Coca-Cola, and it desperately needed sugar. Allied Molasses, the firm for which Maragon labored so zealously, had managed to get possession of 1.5 million gallons of sugar cane syrup. This it refined, selling the sugar to Pepsi-Cola at a high price. It was a deal that circumvented rationing regulations; and the Department of Agriculture, learning of it, banned further deliveries of sugar to Allied Molasses until it had compensated for the Pepsi-Cola deal. Maragon and his associates used all their influence to get the department to soften this hard-hearted attitude; and eventually, by methods undisclosed, they succeeded.

McCarthy was in the thick of these involved negotiations. Through Maragon, he became acquainted with the Pepsi-Cola hierarchy. Soon he was sharing breakfasts, lunches and dinners with Pepsi-Cola President Walter Mack, and he was turning up at Pepsi-Cola lobbying parties. He was also becoming acquainted with a flamboyant character, Russell M. Arundel, a sportsman and *bon vivant,* a free-wheeling spender, and a lobbyist who represented both Puerto Rican sugar interests and Pepsi-Cola. Arundel had bestowed upon himself the noble title of Prince of Outer Baldonia, the name deriving from an island off the coast of Nova Scotia where he took partying weekend guests.

With these contacts, it was not long before "the Pepsi-Cola Kid" began to carry the ball on the floor of the Senate for an immediate end to sugar rationing. There were, at first, some preliminary maneuvers designed to get sugar quotas increased, and McCarthy in one speech tried to demonstrate that so much sugar was available strict rationing was no longer necessary. In a manner that was to become familiar later in his communist exposés, he piled figure upon figure until he reached the triumphant conclusion that the nation had "791,000 tons of sugar upon which we had not counted."

One of the Senators who watched this virtuoso performance with a skeptical eye was the white-maned, Bible-quoting Charles W. Tobey, a New Hampshire Republican who was to become a colorful figure during the Kefauver committee's investigation of organized crime. Tobey was concerned about the canning housewives of New Hampshire, his constituents, and he noticed that McCarthy was arguing for more sugar for industrial producers, but was silent on the subject of canning housewives. He rose and challenged McCarthy.

Joe promptly claimed that he was for good canning housewives everywhere, and he went on to make this assertion: "Within the past ten minutes I have received word from the Department of Agriculture that they . . . wish to discuss with us the possibility of agreeing to make available to the housewife during the third quarter—that is, during the canning season— a total allotment of 20 pounds of sugar . . ."

Senator Tobey doubted it. Quietly he left the floor and telephoned Secretary of Agriculture Clinton P. Anderson. What Anderson told him fired the righteous wrath for which Tobey was to become famous during the Kefauver probe. Claiming the Senate floor, he said:

"The Department of Agriculture's announced position was misrepresented by the Senator from Wisconsin today. Here is the answer which came from Secretary Anderson just three minutes ago, over the telephone, to me: 'I authorize you to state that I have not at any time made a statement that we can give more sugar for home consumption now . . . there is no more sugar available for home consumption . . .' That is Secretary Anderson's statement, and it refutes the statement which has been made by the Senator from Wisconsin."

As usual, lacking the decency to be embarrassed, the Senator from Wisconsin leaped to his feet and shouted: "Then . . . let me say in view of the unquestioned figures, I don't give a tinker's damn what Secretary Anderson says about the matter. The sugar is here."

Senator Tobey replied that the Secretary of Agriculture was the man in a position to know all the facts and figures. "On the question of veracity," Tobey concluded acidly, "I would not choose between the two gentlemen, but on a question of fact, I take the Secretary of Agriculture any time."

McCarthy was enraged, and the knee-and-gouge instinct in him erupted. He charged that he had been talking to Senator Tobey only a few days before, and Tobey had told him he was "going to introduce some type of fictitious amendment [to the sugar bill] which in effect will do nothing more nor less than deceive the housewife."

Tobey leaped instantly to his feet, demanded the floor, and in a voice shaking with rage roared out, "I take exception to his [McCarthy's] derogatory remarks. The Senator's statement, I submit, far contravenes the truth, to put it plainly . . ."

McCarthy tried to interrupt, but Tobey cut him off.

"I am not quite through yet, sir," he said sternly. "I point out that the Senator is confusing the Senate of the United States by a heterogeneous mass of figures which will not stand the test of accuracy . . ."

It was a prophetic remark.

In the end, with McCarthy playing a leading role, the date for the lifting of sugar controls was advanced from March 31, 1948, to October 31, 1947. It was an action that Senator Tobey denounced as opening "the flood-gates" to speculators. "The speculators are singing a Te Deum in their hearts tonight throughout the country," he said. "They are singing, 'Hail, hail, the gang's all here. We are ready for the kill.' "

Joe McCarthy was certainly ready. He had continued plunging in the stock and commodity markets, buying on margin, mortgaging himself to the hilt. If his wartime speculations had borne little relation to the innocent game of gin rummy Roy Cohn described, his postwar sallies bore even less. He gambled so recklessly with borrowed money that it seemed at times as if his whole Ponzi-like structure was about to collapse and engulf him in ruin. To save himself he needed well-heeled angels.

His first angel was the Appleton State Bank in Wisconsin. Matt Schuh, its president, was a longtime friend, and the bank granted McCarthy loan after loan. In late December, 1945, having reduced an earlier $73,000 loan to a mere $20,000, Mc-

Carthy asked his old friend and his old friend's bank for a real whopper—a new loan of $149,176. In making this loan, the bank broke all the rules and regulations that put a limit of $100,000 on an individual grant of this kind; and so, to make the thing look better in the eyes of the bank examiners, $69,540 of the loan was registered in the name of H. F. McCarthy, one of Joe's brothers.

This combined loan of $169,540 was to be the cause of infinite future difficulty. The year 1947 was a bad one in the stock market. McCarthy sustained losses of $28,000; and, since he had been buying stocks on margin with borrowed money, he needed more collateral to put up with the Appleton State Bank. Matt Schuh, pressured by the bank's board of directors and under the fire of state bank examiners, barraged McCarthy with frantic letters seeking either cash or more collateral to guarantee the loan. In this exigency, a Senate investigating committee later found, McCarthy turned to his Pepsi-Cola sidekick, Russell M. Arundel, the Prince of Outer Baldonia.

"The Prince" endorsed a McCarthy note for $20,000. But was this applied against the old loan? It was not. In an incredible sequence, on the basis of this note, on January 3, 1948, the Appleton bank loaned McCarthy another $20,000, which was used to purchase six hundred shares of Chicago, Milwaukee, St. Paul and Pacific Railroad preferred stock which, of course, was held by the bank as collateral. "This increase in an already hazardous loan was directly contrary to the expressed wishes of the Board of Directors of the bank," the Senate investigating committee later wrote. The Senate probe showed this sequence: McCarthy explained his financial dilemma to Arundel on either December 5 or 6, 1947, according to Arundel's own testimony; Arundel, who was never pressed to make the note good, endorsed the $20,000 certificate on December 8; and on December 9, McCarthy, in his official capacity as a Senator, made a "special appearance" before the Appropriations Committee to question the Army Secretary about the Army's purchase of Cuban sugar—a transaction that had been previously criticized by Pepsi-Cola.

Summing it all up, the Senate committee wrote:

"His [McCarthy's] acceptance of a $20,000 favor from the Washington representative of the Pepsi-Cola Company at the very time he was attacking the Government for its manner of handling sugar control makes it difficult to determine whether Senator McCarthy was working for the best interests of the Government, as he saw it, or for Pepsi-Cola."

TO THE COAT OF ARMS of "the Pepsi-Cola Kid," there was soon added another heraldic description—"water boy of the real estate lobby." That was the title conferred by the mayor of Racine, Wis., after McCarthy had done his industrious best to discredit public housing.

Housing had been a prime casualty of more than fifteen years of crisis—first of the great depression, then of World War II with its concomitant material shortages; the population was increasing at a rapid rate and returning veterans were establishing families and clamoring for living space. The acute housing shortage was widely recognized as one of the nation's most pressing problems. Even Senator Taft had joined in the sponsorship of a public housing bill, the Taft-Ellender-Wagner Bill. Freshman Senator McCarthy might have been expected to follow his party leader in supporting such an obviously necessary program—but not so; he had even more powerful interests to cultivate.

He had been backed in his Senatorial campaign by potent Wisconsin business figures, and their self-interest told them that there was a windfall to be made in producing prefabricated and inexpensive housing. A vast public-housing program, however, could well take the edge off this boundless free-enterprise opportunity. And so they needed a champion in Congress who would head a drive to kill off public housing.

It is an unwritten rule of the Senate that freshmen Senators, like children, are better seen than heard, but McCarthy gave this tradition the brush-off. Congress had created a Joint Housing Committee composed of fourteen members of the House and Senate. The public-housing advocates on the committee were in the majority, and it was widely assumed that Senator Tobey would be its chairman.

One hot summer day in 1947 Senator Tobey walked into the committee room for that first session. Only nine members of the committee were present, but this did not disturb him because, of the five absentees, he held in his pocket proxies from four enabling him to cast their votes as he wished. But, as he entered the hearing room, he noticed that McCarthy was whispering to his colleagues; and as Senator Tobey called the meeting to order, the junior Senator made his move. He proposed that no proxies be accepted—that only the votes of those present should be counted.

A quick nose count showed the motive. The conservative minority of the committee was present in force; if proxies were disallowed, they would name the committee chairman and organize the investigation. Senator Tobey was almost apoplectic. The voting of proxies in committee had never been questioned before in his long experience, he said. Rep. Wright Patman, a Texas Democrat, supported Tobey. In his twenty years in Congress, he said, the wishes of absentee members had always been respected, their proxies accepted. "We are all gentlemen here, aren't we?" he asked mildly.

It quickly became obvious that they weren't.

The indignant Senator Tobey thundered: "McCarthy whispered around and found out what proxies we had before he made his motion. Frankly, I can't take it. Let's lay our cards on the table here."

Blandly McCarthy insisted that the committee vote on his motion. It did. And by a 5-to-4 vote the conservative minority organized the committee. McCarthy was now in control. He proposed that Rep. Ralph Gamble, a New York Congressman, a nonentity and a perfect pawn, be named chairman; himself, vice chairman. When the new chairman wondered about assembling an investigative staff, Joe assured him he had "a couple of good people in mind."

It quickly developed that the "good people" were employees of Bill, Jones & Taylor, a New York public relations firm that represented the real estate lobby. The National Public Housing Conference denounced the hiring of such partisan "experts," declaring: "Seldom has there been in the history of Congress such a blatant attempt to slip professional representatives of a lobby into positions of control." And later, in reviewing the staff's work, the conference charged that McCarthy's "good people" had worked "almost as a part of the staff of the National Association of Real Estate Boards, the United Savings & Loan League, and the National Association of Home Builders."

The record certainly justified the accusation. With the committee organized and its staff assembled, McCarthy quickly brushed aside the figurehead chairman and took off on a cross-continent tour, holding housing hearings. His technique was brazenly simple. His first witnesses, who testified uninterrupted and at inordinate length, were almost invariably spokesmen for the private building and real estate interests. Advocates of public housing had to cool their heels for hours, waiting to be heard— and then, when they did get a chance to testify, they were some-times cut off because it was by now so late in the day that the Senator just had to leave to catch a plane for another city and another hearing.

This tactic, so helpful in compiling a one-sided record, was well demonstrated when McCarthy held his one hearing in Wis-consin. It was on November 10, 1947, in Milwaukee, and Mayor Bohn of Milwaukee was present to testify on the serious housing problem in his city. By all the rules of courtesy and customary procedure, he should have been the leadoff witness. McCarthy proved equal to the challenge. He greeted the mayor with elab-orate courtesy, brought him up to the committee table, and seated him in the position of honor, at McCarthy's own right hand. And there Mayor Bohn sat hour after hour, unheard, while McCarthy listened to the testimony of lumbermen, electrical contractors and real estate interests. Finally, unable to wait any longer, Mayor Bohn had to file his prepared statement with the com-mittee and depart.

Occasionally, when such delaying tactics failed, McCarthy would resort to other weapons. When a witness who favored public housing had the floor, the personality kid who had listened so understandingly to the testimony of real estate in-terests, would be suddenly replaced by a scowling, hectoring bully. What did the witness think, McCarthy would demand, of paragraph 5, subsection 10, page 19? What did he think of this phrase and that sentence of that paragraph? In no time, he would have the poor witness lost in a mass of pettifogging detail; and then McCarthy would remark sadly that it was perfectly obvious the witness didn't know what he was talking about.

On one occasion he visited the 1,124-unit Rego Park Veterans Housing Project in New York. "This is the first time I've seen a deliberately created slum area, at federal expense," McCarthy told the press, and he added, on the basis of no evidence whatsoever, that the place was "a breeding ground for communism." The tenants admitted that their housing was far from ideal, but they contended that McCarthy had woefully maligned it—and them. He was interested, they said, "not so much in seeing to it that veterans are provided with a place to live, but with arousing sentiment against continuing the very vital program of public housing."

When the hearings ended, the official record of testimony taken at the hearings was printed, and public housing advocates were outraged. They charged that the record had been falsified; that their views had been either deleted or so altered as to make them look ridiculous. Mayor Francis H. Wendt, of Racine, Wis., wrote the committee, denouncing its vice chairman as "the water boy of the real estate lobby." And he added: "The homeless people of Wisconsin can thank McCarthy for keeping them homeless."

When the public relations men whom McCarthy had loaded on the staff prepared the final committee report, their product was so one-sided and outrageous that the full committee rejected it. A second modified version was also turned down. Finally, the Senatorial staffs of Senators Tobey, Robert F. Wagner (D., N.Y.), and Ralph Flanders (R., Vt.) collaborated on a more balanced report that was approved by the committee. McCarthy's figure-head chairman wept at this development because, he said, the committee had "repudiated" his leadership.

It had indeed, but all was not yet lost. McCarthy asked the committee for permission to print a limited number of copies of the original repudiated report. The committee agreed, providing the copies bore the notation on the first page that this version did "not reflect the views of this committee." When the copies rolled off the Government Printing Office presses, however, it was discovered that the disclaimer nowhere appeared. Furthermore, the number of copies printed seemed virtually unlimited, and when interested persons wrote in for the committee's report, they received the McCarthy version as the "official" findings.

When the bill came to the floor, McCarthy continued his attack. With a proponent of the bill like the mild-mannered Senator Flanders, he would interrupt, asking for interpretations of obscure paragraphs and offering modifications of his own until Flanders became lost in the maze. McCarthy would then sympathize with him, a purr in his voice, for not being able to understand so complicated a measure. With a true housing expert like Alabama's Senator John J. Sparkman, McCarthy did not attempt such obfuscation, but would interrupt to fire oratorical broadsides about the dangers of such "socialistic" legislation. Such harassments finally led Senator Taft to take the floor and denounce McCarthy's "confusionist" tactics.

Taft had to throw all his great prestige behind the housing bill to salvage it in the Senate. Even so, he gained only a temporary victory. When the bill went to the House, it ran into further opposition; it was emasculated by amendments; and when it came back to the Senate, McCarthy mangled it with more amendments. In the end, Taft was forced to abandon sponsorship of his own brainchild. Public housing for veterans was killed, and young families continued to live in garages and attics, thanks to Senator Joe McCarthy and a real estate lobby that, it was estimated, had spent more than $300,000 in its campaign to influence Congress.

THE CHAIRMAN of a Congressional committee is, in his way, a small potentate. If his performance attracts attention or appeals to organizations with vested interests, he gets speaking invitations to conventions and banquets, receiving a fee that is politely called an "honorarium." Senator McCarthy now began to rake in such honorariums. There were a couple of $500 lecture fees, plus wine and entertainment, from a Columbus, Ohio, prefab builder named Robert Byers, and then there was a far more luscious reward—a $10,000 check from the Lustron Corporation, another Columbus manufacturer of prefabricated housing.

Lustron was a scandal from its inception to its costly demise. It had a multi-million-dollar vision—and little else. The vision was based on the prefabrication of pastel-tinted porcelain-and-aluminum houses, but to translate the vision into reality, capital was needed—and Lustron had none. The answer seemed to be the Reconstruction Finance Corporation, a federal agency created to make government loans to worthy businesses in critical situations. After looking into Lustron's plea for help, the RFC protested that there was hardly any private risk money invested in Lustron and that if the federal taxpayers financed the enterprise through RFC the risk-taking would be almost 100 percent theirs.

All such protests were futile. E. Merl Young, a one-time messenger boy who, like Maragon, had become a lobbyist with White House contacts, evidently had a persuasive way about him; RFC began to pour millons into Lustron—and Young was rewarded for his services by being made Lustron's $18,000-a-year vice president.

Another who helped himself generously out of the taxpayer-supplied kitty was Lustron's president, Carl Strandlund, whose talent was valued at $50,000 a year. With money flowing in from the reluctant RFC, Lustron led a short and colorful life. Between June 30, 1947, and August 29, 1949, the RFC made a series of seven loans to Lustron, totaling $37,500,000. When Lustron finally went bankrupt in February, 1950, Uncle Sam and the American taxpayers were left holding an empty $30 million bag. It was a sequence in which Joe McCarthy played at times a pivotal role.

In the series of amendments by which he had helped to emasculate Senator Taft's housing bill, he had repeatedly trumpeted the virtues of prefabricated housing as the solution to the nation's housing crisis. And he had taken steps to assist all who would join him in this free-enterprise crusade. One of his measures had raised the salary of Housing and Home Finance Administrator Raymond Foley. Another and more significant amendment had authorized the RFC to make loans not to exceed $50 million to manufacturers of prefabricated homes. This provision was vital to Lustron. The corporation had already dissipated RFC's previously loaned millions, and federal limitations prevented the agency from giving it more. But once McCarthy got the loan ceiling raised to $50 million, the RFC could come once more to the assistance of Lustron—and this it did on February 14, 1949, bestowing upon the prefab manufacturer another $7 million.

"A few days subsequent to the passing of the new Housing Act," the Senate committee that investigated McCarthy's affairs later reported, "Senator McCarthy contacted Administrator Foley to request his assistance for Miss Jean Kerr, of his office, who was working on a housing manuscript."

Foley assigned Walter Royall, of his staff, to help Miss Kerr with the research and preparation of a manuscript that would explain the virtues of prefabricated housing.

Even as this literary effort was being born, a small cloud appeared on the horizon. The Senate Investigating Committee had become disturbed about the huge loans to Lustron, and its counsel, William P. Rogers, had written RFC Director Walter L. Dunham requesting information about the firm's production and signs of progress. Dunham tried to get the information from Strandlund, but encountered arrogance in place of facts. He wrote Rogers:

"Mr. Strandlund . . . intimated that he had powerful friends within the administration and in Congress. He said he thought the RFC, Congress and the administration had a moral commitment to him to carry on this obligation regardless of expense until its complete success had been established."

McCarthy was not only the dominant force on the Joint Housing Committee, he was also a member of the Senate Investigating Committee which had just exhibited a curiosity about the tangled affairs of Lustron. And so it just happened that, on November 12, 1948, one week to the day after the investigating committee decided to peek, a few days after the passage of the new housing act that made greater loans possible, the Lustron Corporation made out a check for $10,000 payable to one Joseph R. McCarthy.

The check ostensibly was to pay McCarthy for his literary labors on what he described as a "book." Actually all he had contributed was a seven-thousand-word section in the middle of a ninety-four-page booklet put out by Lustron under the title *How to Own Your Own Home Now*. In order to pad out the effort into something that might conceivably be called a book, Lustron went to the further expense of hiring Maron Simon, a New York literary technician. Simon spent four days with Miss Kerr touring federal housing agencies and another six weeks building the "book" around McCarthy's seven-thousand-word contribution. Cynics later computed that novice author McCarthy had been paid for his literary skill at the rate of $1.43 a word—a fee that made Winston Churchill, with his dollar-a-word rate, seem like a piker.

There was little secret at the time about this foul-smelling deal. Strandlund, when first asked about it, just shrugged and said he had "purchased the name of a Senator." McCarthy himself swelled up with the pride of synthetic authorship. Even though the work had been done by his staff, housing agency experts and

Maron Simon, it was *his* name that was on the cover; and on February 28, 1949, he called a press conference to announce the birth of his brainchild. In talking to Washington reporters, he was coy about just one detail—the rewards of authorship. He shrugged off his fee as nothing much.

"It's embarrassingly small," he told the Milwaukee *Journal*. "Besides, I have to split it with ten people who helped me."

It is to be hoped that those "ten people" didn't hold their breaths waiting for the split, for canceled checks later uncovered by the Senate committee showed that McCarthy shared with no one. "The Lustron check for $10,000 was endorsed in blank over to Wayne Hummer & Co., the Senator's broker, to purchase additional stock of the Seaboard Airlines Railroad," the committee reported. This stock was pledged with the Appleton Bank as additional security for the loans that had been driving Matt Schuh to desperation.

In the subsequent 1951–52 investigation of McCarthy, Carl Strandlund described how his acquaintance with the Senator had begun. He had been at the Laurel, Md., racetrack in September or October, 1948, when "a complete stranger" appeared at his box and asked him to cash a check "in the hundreds." The stranger turned out, of course, to be McCarthy. Though it would seem that the request was decidedly unusual, Strandlund never hesitated for a moment; he was only too happy to indulge a United States Senator.

This racetrack practice grew to be a habit, if one can believe the testimony that E. Merl Young, vice president of Lustron, later gave another Senate committee. Young insisted that McCarthy used to get Strandlund to cash checks to make up for his losses on the ponies—and that Strandlund most obligingly used to tear up the checks.

It was in October, 1948, Strandlund testified, that McCarthy approached him about the purchase of his housing manuscript. Though McCarthy admitted the literary effort wasn't "in publishable form," he set a price tag of $10,000 on it. And Strandlund didn't haggle. He didn't even consult his own public relations men or other officials in the firm; he simply ordered the check made out. Strandlund admitted the transaction "scared me some," and well it might have. Clyde M. Foraker, who later became receiver for the defunct Lustron firm, called the whole deal "unethical," and added: "I'll bet he [McCarthy] wouldn't have gotten $10,000 if he hadn't been a Senator."

The Senate investigators of McCarthy's affairs asked this biting rhetorical question: "How can Senator McCarthy justify acceptance of a $10,000 fee from Lustron, which, in effect, was a fee being paid out of public funds, at a time when Lustron's continued operations and financing depended entirely upon the RFC, and which Agency, in turn, was dependent upon the Congress and, more particularly, the Banking and Currency Committee, of which he was a member, for its continued authority and operation?"

IN HIS FIRST THREE YEARS in Washington, McCarthy had already been designated "the Pepsi-Cola Kid" and "the water boy of the real estate lobby." And he was soon to be identified in another, far more devastating, way—as defender of the Nazi SS troops at Malmédy.

MALMÉDY HAS GONE DOWN IN HISTORY as one of the horror words of World War II. It was in this small Belgian crossroads town at Christmastime in 1944 that the First SS Panzer Regiment under Colonel Joachim Peiper wrote a new chapter in depravity. Colonel Peiper's elite outfit had become known as the Blowtorch Battalion after it had burned a couple of Belgian villages and slaughtered everyone in them. With these deeds on its record, it came to Malmédy at Christmastime and rounded up some hundred-fifty captured American soldiers and a hundred Belgian civilians. Colonel Peiper told his men Germany had her back to the wall; she could not afford the luxury of prisoners. So the captives were taken out into the fields and machine-gunned to death by the Nazi troopers—who laughed hilariously at the sport.

In the subsequent war-crimes trials, seventy-four members of the Blowtorch Battalion were tried for their roles in the Malmédy massacre; forty-three were convicted and sentenced to die. But legal maneuvers stalled the immediate execution of the sentences. Months dragged by, and the American public began to forget.

With interest flagging, the condemned men now took the

offensive. From their death block cells, a stream of affidavits poured forth. These accused their American captors of the most hideous tortures. In almost identical language, the affidavits alleged that false confessions had been wrung from the captured SS troopers by lighting matches thrust under their fingernails and by brutal beating of their abdomens and genitals. In Germany, these charges generated headlines, and the headlines began to create a wave of anti-American feeling.

The mood of the times was also changing. The wartime thirst for vengeance against the Nazis was being tempered by the strains of the Cold War. Russia, so recently our ally, loomed as the new threat to the peace of Europe and the world, and American foreign policy was being recast on the premise that we would need West Germany's help in the trials of the future. Such pressures made American officials exceptionally sensitive to the torture charges of the Nazi SS troopers.

In this atmosphere, the U.S. Supreme Court granted a review of the Malmédy death sentences. It upheld the verdicts. In Germany, the communist press seized upon the decision and twisted it for its own propaganda purposes. The Supreme Court decision demonstrated, it contended, that it was impossible for Germans to obtain justice in America.

The propaganda in Germany became so intense that the U.S. Senate began to worry. In April, 1949, the Senate Armed Services Committee appointed a three-man subcommittee to investigate the Malmédy massacre. The committee was headed by Senator Raymond Baldwin, a mild-mannered and thoroughly decent Republican from Connecticut. McCarthy was not one of the members of the committee, but he demanded the right to "sit in" at the hearings. Baldwin granted him permission. McCarthy pressed more demands. He submitted a list of witnesses he wanted the committee to call; again the committee acquiesced. He demanded the right to cross-examine witnesses—and again Baldwin yielded. From that point on, there was almost no chance of holding orderly hearings, for McCarthy virtually took over the investigation, castigating witnesses, storming through the hearing room, impugning the motives of the committee and its counsel, Marine Colonel Joseph Chambers, a Congressional Medal of Honor winner.

Why had McCarthy gone to such lengths to insinuate himself

into the dispute? Why did he rage in defense of the Nazi murderers of American soldiers?

The answer lies in the influence exerted by some of McCarthy's ultraconservative, even pro-Nazi, backers in Wisconsin. McCarthy had been bankrolled in his political campaigns by such leaders of Wisconsin's powerful German-American community as Frank Seusenbrenner and Walter Harnischfeger. Seusenbrenner was the president of the Kimberly Clark Paper Company and president of the board of the University of Wisconsin; Harnischfeger was president of the Harnischfeger Company, of Milwaukee, makers of traveling cranes, overhead machinery—and prefabricated houses. Both men were known as being fiercely pro-German.

McCarthy showed not the slightest repugnance for Harnischfeger's passionate ultrarightism and admiration for Hitler. Before the war, one of the manufacturer's nephews attending the University of Wisconsin had shocked fellow students by displaying an autographed copy of *Mein Kampf*, and flaunting a watch-chain swastika. During the war, Harnischfeger had advocated a negotiated peace with Germany, and as soon as the war ended, he played a leading role in organizing a German relief society. The Harnischfeger Corporation was one of eight Midwestern concerns holding war contracts that were ordered by the President's Fair Employment Practices Commission to stop discriminating against workers because of race or religion. The commission charged, on April 12, 1942, that these firms had refused to employ Jews or Negroes and had advertised for only Gentile, white Protestant help.

After 1945 Harnischfeger made several trips to Germany. He criticized the dismantling of German factories, denounced the war-crimes trials, and urged the restoration of Germany's colonies. After Joe McCarthy became a Senator, he inserted Harnischfeger's pronouncements in the *Congressional Record;* and Upton Close, the profascist radio commentator, parroted the views to his radio audience.

McCarthy's 1947 financial troubles, stemming from his stock market reverses and his heavy overload of loans from the Appleton State Bank, appear to have been cured by this Wisconsin angel. "I have made complete arrangements with Walter Harnischfeger to put up sufficient collateral to cure both our ulcers,"

McCarthy finally wrote to his harried banker friend, Matt Schuh. At the time of the 1948 Presidential election, McCarthy listened to the returns in Harnischfeger's home. The industrialist's interest in prefabricated housing was believed in Washington to have been one of the reasons that McCarthy had so interested himself in the issue.

In terms of the Malmedy investigation, Anderson and May described the McCarthy-Harnischfeger axis in these terms: "Ten days after the Malmedy investigation was begun, a young man named Tom Korb arrived to act as McCarthy's brains on the case. Korb worked for six weeks, carried on the books as McCarthy's 'administrative assistant.' He stayed long enough to help Joe write a speech on the Malmedy Massacre, delivered on July 26, 1949, and then he went back to his job as a lawyer and corporation official in Milwaukee. His employer: the Harnischfeger Corporation."

The first witness called by Senator Baldwin at the hearings was Lt. Col. Burton F. Ellis, who had been the chief prosecutor of the Malmédy Nazis. Ellis had been testifying for approximately one minute when McCarthy interrupted and denounced him for making "phenomenal statements."

One of the Senators who was on the committee—as McCarthy was not—tried to set the record straight with a mild observation. "This hearing is not a prosecution. What we are attempting to do is just get the witnesses' statements, and we will be the judge of whether they did things in the right manner."

"I entirely disagree," snapped McCarthy. "If that is the purpose, I am wasting my time."

On April 22, 1949, the committee called Kenneth Ahrens, one of the twelve American survivors of the massacre. Ahrens testified that he had escaped execution only by tumbling into a ditch and pretending to be dead, and he described how the Nazi machine-gunners roared with laughter as they went about their work.

This testimony sent McCarthy into one of his typical rages. He accused the veteran of trying to turn the hearing into a "Roman holiday," denouncing Ahrens for attempting to "inflame the public." He charged that some of the American interrogation team that had questioned the Malmédy Nazis were Jewish; that a few of them were "39ers," meaning refugees from Hitler in that year; and that they constituted "a vengeance team." He lashed out at the military court judges as "morons"; and then he thundered:

"I think you are lying. You may be able to fool us. I have been told you are very, very clever. I am convinced you cannot fool the lie detector!"

He wound up this tirade with an ultimatum: either the Americans who testified against the Nazis would be compelled to take lie-detector tests—or he would withdraw from the hearings. The effrontery of it was stunning. Here one who had no legitimate status in the hearing room, except as a matter of courtesy, was laying down conditions about the conduct of the hearings.

As a former judge, McCarthy certainly knew that lie-detector tests have no validity in American courts, but he pressed his demand so strenuously that Senator Baldwin finally put the issue to the full Senate Armed Services Committee. The committee, of course, voted it down, and McCarthy did indeed storm out of the hearings, calling them "a shameful farce" and "a deliberate and clever attempt to whitewash the American military." Senator Baldwin, he charged, was "criminally responsible."

This final McCarthy eruption occurred on May 20, 1949, and a witness to it was Richard H. Rovere, *The New Yorker*'s man in Washington. Rovere, who was unfamiliar at the time with the background details of the Malmédy investigation, happened to walk into the hearing room as McCarthy was hurling his final denunciations and stuffing voluminous documents into a bulging brief case. Impressed by the performance, Rovere followed McCarthy as the latter stalked out of the hearing, and in the corridor, he told the Senator that he would like to know more about the case. Instantly, McCarthy went to work.

"These documents will speak for themselves," he said, impressing Rovere by the sheer bulk of the brief case. "When you've looked at a few of my documents you will agree with me that this is one of the most outrageous things the country has ever known."

He adopted a pose that was to become a favorite of his—that of Joe McCarthy, the all-American boy, battling for the people against some shadowy and overwhelming conspiracy of evil. He was, he told Rovere, "through with this lousy investigation." He was going to take his case to the public. He struck Rovere as "being a bit overwrought," but on the whole "an earnest and plausible young Senator." And he kept talking about "the magnitude of his revelations" until Rovere could hardly wait to see what the brief case held.

"We reached his office at last and sat down at his desk," Rovere later wrote. "He emptied the brief case and piled up the papers in front of him. 'Let's see now,' he said as he thumbed his way down toward the middle of the pile, 'I've got one document here that's a real eye-opener. Oh, yes, here we are now.' He pulled out several pages of photostat paper and handed them to me. 'I think the facts will mean more to you than anything I could say.'

"I read rapidly through what he gave me. Then I read it a second time, more carefully. When I'd finished the second reading, I was certain that the Senator had selected the wrong document. I no longer recall just what was in it, but it was a letter from one Army officer or government official to another, and it didn't seem to me to prove anything about anything. I told McCarthy that as far as I could see it was a pretty routine piece of correspondence.

" 'You're certainly right about that,' he said. 'Don't get me wrong, now. I didn't mean you'd find the *whole* story there. Standing alone, it doesn't mean much. I know that just as well as you do. But it's a link in a chain. It's one piece in a jigsaw puzzle. When you've seen some of these other documents, you'll know what I mean.' "

"This was reassuring. In fact, I felt a bit ashamed of myself for expecting to master a complex situation in a few minutes. I read the next document McCarthy handed me. 'Now when you put these two together,' he said, 'you get a picture.' The second document was mainly a listing of names. None of them meant anything to me. I tried to think what connection they might have with the letter I'd just read or with Senator Baldwin. I tried to 'put them together,' as McCarthy had advised, and 'get a picture.' No picture came . . ."

The farcical performance continued. Each time Rovere confessed he wasn't getting "a picture," McCarthy agreed with him and advised him just to wait until he saw the next document. Rovere was overwhelmed with lists of names, pictures of Germans who had accused American officers of brutality, pictures of American officers who had been accused of brutality by the Germans, pictures of Malmédy farmhouses, pictures of American barracks in occupied Germany. The climactic evidence was a swatch of affidavits from the condemned Nazis, all alleging that American officers had subjected them to "the most hideous mistreatment." Rovere read these, and remarked that it seemed to him possible a man under sentence of death might be telling the truth, but that it was at least equally conceivable he could be lying in an attempt to save his skin. "You've put your finger on it," McCarthy said, oblivious to the fact that Rovere was in effect saying his case had been demolished. "Those are precisely the facts that Baldwin and the administration don't want me to bring out. That's why I walked out of that hearing. They're concealing all the evidence . . ."

Rovere came away shaking his head. "I was not aware then of having been switched, conned, and double-shuffled by one of the masters," he later wrote.

The fact that a Senator of the United States adopted as truth the contentions in the affidavits lent credence to the Nazi charges. The communist press in Germany had a field day. Mass meetings were held, and anti-American feeling was fomented on a wide scale. Public sentiment became so aroused that, to prevent the hate-America feeling from becoming a dominant force, the sentences had to be commuted.

There could be no doubt about the truth of the matter; Baldwin's Senate committee established that. Through the testimony of men like Ahrens who had escaped the slaughter, through the words of respected American officers and officials who had investigated the case, the committee established beyond question that the Nazi SS troops had indeed committed the Malmédy massacre. But facts and evidence meant nothing against the wave of propaganda to which McCarthy had given the validating prestige of an American Senator. The committee left no doubt as to how it viewed his actions. It wrote:

"Through competent testimony submitted to the subcommittee, it appeared that there are strong reasons to believe that groups within Germany are endeavoring . . . to discredit the American occupation forces in general. The subcommittee is convinced that there is an organized effort being made to revive the nationalistic spirit in Germany through every possible means. There is evidence that at least part of this effort is attempting to establish a close liaison with Communist Russia. Due to the manner in which the allegations in this case were handled [by McCarthy], it was also clear that no matter what the facts were in the case, in the minds of practically all Germans, the allegations were accepted as fact. This was certain to damage the American position in Germany."

This finished the labors of the Baldwin committee. It also finished the Senatorial career of Baldwin himself. This Republican, "a man with a considerable reputation for probity," as Rovere wrote, frankly acknowledged that he felt the Senate of the United States was no place for him with Joe McCarthy rampaging around. So Raymond Baldwin resigned in the middle of his term and went back to Connecticut to become a judge of the Supreme Court of Errors.

Senator Baldwin was not alone in his disgust. When McCarthy delivered his long tirade on the Senate floor, calling the conclusions "a whitewash" and charging again that Baldwin was "criminally responsible," Senator Estes Kefauver (D., Tenn.) denounced him, and Senator Tobey demanded that he be ruled out of order. But McCarthy brushed their objections contemptuously aside and went right on reading thousands of words of manuscript, arraigning American military officers, the courts and the Senate and implicitly upholding the moral purity of the Nazis at Malmédy.

The Senate of the United States has a strong stomach for this kind of stuff on most occasions, but McCarthy had overstepped the bounds of its tolerance. On August 19, 1949, the full Senate Armed Services Committee met and issued a formal statement, signed by twelve of its members, in which it praised Senator Baldwin for his "integrity, character and personality." The statement continued, "We . . . take this unusual step in issuing this statement because of the most unusual, unfair, and utterly undeserved comments that have been made concerning Senator Baldwin and his work as chairman of this subcommittee of the committee on armed services." In such terms the powerful hierarchy of the Senate publicly rebuked Joseph R. McCarthy.

A question remained: Where had McCarthy obtained all those documents that had bulged his brief case? In a moment of carelessness, he himself had supplied the answer. One day in his haste he had mislaid a brown manilla envelope in the Congressional hearing room. The envelope bore the return address of Rudolph Aschenauer in Frankfurt, Germany. Aschenauer was a communist agent. Questioned in Germany, he admitted that he had sent affidavits made out by the condemned Nazis to Senator McCarthy so that McCarthy might be "informed of the various statements that had been made." And, subsequently, when McCarthy parroted the charges as facts, Aschenauer had had no trouble in getting them splattered all over the front pages of the German press.

Incredibly, Joe McCarthy had himself become the willing dupe and tool of a communist agent. But then it is a generally unappreciated irony of history that, when it will advance their different purposes, extremists of the right and left often wind up as bedfellows.

8

"I Have Here in My Hand—"

J O S E P H   M C   C A R T H Y faced an uncertain future. He would
have to stand for reelection in Wisconsin in 1952. He now recognized that in his first years in the Senate he had hardly compiled
a record that would recommend him to the voters. The Pepsi-Cola
Kid. Water boy of the real estate lobby. Defender of the Nazi
murderers of Malmédy. These were hardly the images a politician
would care to flaunt before his constituents. He began to worry
about what kind of an issue he could champion that would appeal
to the voters of Wisconsin.

The result of this concern was a dinner with three personal
friends in Washington's swank Colony Restaurant on January 7,
1950. His consultants were three fellow Catholics of varying

political faiths. One was a well-known Washington attorney, a big, tough-talking liberal named William A. Roberts, a legal adviser of columnist Drew Pearson. The other two were from Georgetown University. One was Professor Charles Kraus, a political science instructor at Georgetown; the other, Father Edmund Walsh, was vice president of Georgetown and regent of its ultraconservative School of Foreign Service, probably the largest single supplier of State Department talent.

Father Walsh, who as head of the Papal Relief Mission had waged a futile battle with the Soviet state in the 1920s in an effort to capture the religious allegiance of the Russian people for the Catholic Church, had developed, perhaps as a result of this experience, what Robert Bendiner has described as "a morbid fear" of communism. The foreign service school at Georgetown inevitably reflected his views. During the Spanish Civil War, Father Walsh had denounced the Loyalist government of Spain in harshest terms.

More recently Father Walsh had written an all-out attack on communism entitled *Total Power*. Professor Kraus, who greatly admired Father Walsh and wanted McCarthy to meet him, had sent the Senator a copy of the volume because he had spoken of a desire "to read some meaty books." Kraus and Roberts, like McCarthy, were Marine veterans of World War II.

Now the three men were gathered for dinner at the Colony to help their friend find an issue.*

The Senator outlined his plight. Here he was nearing the end of his first term, and he had attracted little favorable national publicity. Worse still, he had no specific issue that would excite the voters back in Wisconsin. His dinner companions began to make suggestions.

"How about pushing for the St. Lawrence Seaway?" Roberts asked.

---

* Roy Cohn in *McCarthy* disputes this account of the significance of the Colony dinner and tells a much more cloak-and-daggerish version, which he had from McCarthy: An intelligence officer in the Pentagon became concerned because a one-hundred-page FBI report on Communist infiltration had been neglected for two years. The G-2 officer was shocked, got a group together, and began to try to find a Senator who would speak out. The search ultimately led to McCarthy. Joe took the copy of the FBI report, read it, spent a sleepless night—and then decided he was "going to take it on." Cohn acknowledges that the Colony dinner was held, but sloughs it off as of no importance.

McCarthy considered, shook his head. "That hasn't enough appeal," he said. "No one gets excited about it."

Joe next tested out an idea of his own on his companions. How about a Townsend-type pension plan? How about paying a hundred dollars a month to everyone over sixty-five? His companions quickly argued him out of this plan on the grounds that it was economically unsound.

After the four finished dinner, they went to Roberts' office in the nearby DeSales Building and continued their discussion. McCarthy and Roberts did most of the talking, but at one point Father Walsh broke in and took up his favorite theme—the menace of communism. He was convinced that this was a vital issue, one that would be as important in 1952 as it was in 1950.

The suggestion struck a responsive chord in McCarthy. After all, he had experimented in the La Follette and McMurray campaigns with the vote-getting possibilities of anticommunism, and he had more recently, as in his visit to the Rego Park housing development, thrown out a redbaiting phrase to catch a headline. These had been merely offhanded barbs uttered for immediate political profit. But the trial runs had been good, and they raised an obvious question: What could a man do if he took up anticommunism as a holy crusade—if he went all out with it? McCarthy began to get excited.

"The Government is full of Communists," he declared on the spot, cutting in on Father Walsh. "The thing to do is to hammer at them."

Roberts, with a liberal's instinct, spoke a blunt warning. Such a campaign, he said, would have to be solidly based; there had been enough "Wolf! Wolf!" cries about Reds. McCarthy brushed aside these words of caution. Getting facts, he said, would be no problem.

Professor Kraus, Father Walsh and Roberts had no idea at the time of what they had started. All three were soon to repudiate McCarthy and his methods, but no repudiation could stop the juggernaut they had set in motion.

THE TIMING WAS PERFECT. McCarthy's new tactic was devised in an atmosphere that may best be described as the product of a conspiracy of men dovetailing with a conspiracy of events.

The 1949 "year of shocks"—that had seen the fall of Chiang Kai-shek in China, the Russian explosion of the A-bomb—was barely over. The shocks had not ended. The very air seemed to breathe of intrigue.

First, shortly after the turn of the year, came the ultimate conviction of Alger Hiss. The one-time glamour boy of the State Department had been tried twice for perjury resulting from his denials that he had ever passed government documents to Whittaker Chambers. The first trial had ended in a hung jury, and the fury of Republicans and right-wingers had known no bounds. There was an outcry for the impeachment of the first trial judge because some of his rulings had favored Hiss. Jurors who had refused to vote for conviction were hounded in the press, subjected to insinuations that they must be ideologically tainted. Reacting to such outcries, Truman's Justice Department made certain that no charges of favoritism could be leveled at it the second time. The second trial jurist was a Republican of impeccably conservative faith, and the atmosphere of the courtroom, with a daily delegation of highly placed Republican women sitting in the front rows and staring at the jurors like so many Madame LaFarges waiting at the foot of the guillotine, seemed to say that anything less than a conviction would be a betrayal of the American way. The result in the circumstances was inevitable. On January 21, 1950, the second trial jury announced that Alger Hiss had been convicted.

There were other sensations. On March 6, 1949, Miss Judith Coplon, a Barnard graduate and an employee of the Justice Department in Washington, had been arrested in New York during a night-time rendezvous with an attaché of the Soviet delegation to the United Nations. In her purse was a handwritten note, evidently intended for her Russian contact, in which she explained her difficulty in getting access to a secret FBI report. Her trial, conviction, appeal and retrial kept the espionage-in-government charge constantly in the headlines and ever fresh in the public mind.

And then, on February 3, 1950, came the disclosure that provided the final jolt. The British government announced the arrest of Dr. Klaus Fuchs, a high-level atomic scientist who had worked in the United States during the war on the development of the first atomic bomb. Dr. Fuchs had confessed, the British announced, that he had been a spy for Russia; he told a vague story about contacts with an American go-between—a thread that was to lead ultimately to the confessed spy courier Harry Gold and the trial and execution of Ethel and Julius Rosenberg. Fuchs' British superiors described his betrayal as "of the highest value to a potential enemy" and estimated that he had speeded up Russian bomb development by "at least a year."

This succession of headlines meshed with another awesome development. On January 21, 1950, President Truman disclosed that, since the Russians now had the A-bomb, it had become necessary for us to press one step further: we were going to develop "the so-called hydrogen or super-bomb," a weapon of virtually limitless destructive capacity, a thousand times more devastating than the puny atomic bombs that had obliterated Hiroshima and Nagasaki. The decision to develop such an ultimate horror weapon divided the scientific community. Albert Einstein, the godfather of the nuclear age, proclaimed the inevitability of the "annihilation of any life on earth" if such bombs were ever used.

During such a parade of frightening events the need was for sober and responsible leadership; precisely the brand of leadership that was not forthcoming from either political party.

The Republicans, frustrated by the successive defeats of two decades, were incapable of responding to the call for national sanity. Neurotic after the final humiliation of the Presidential election of 1948, they were possessed by the dread that their whole party might expire if they lost once more; and so they were ready to go to any lengths in the struggle for restoration to power. They began to bellow, as did Senator Homer Capehart, the conservative Indianian, "How much more are we going to have to take? Fuchs and Acheson and Hiss and hydrogen bombs threatening outside and New Dealism eating away at the vitals of the nation. In the name of Heaven, is this the best America can do?" The appeal brought a storm of applause from the Senate floor and galleries. For the first time in twenty years, events were working in favor of the Republicans. Many strands in the public psyche were weaving together in a single pattern. Who were they, the parched political outcasts of two decades, to turn their backs on this windfall?

The heavy Catholic voting blocs in the great cities had been a major source of strength in the political coalition that Franklin Roosevelt had put together. If these voters should desert their long-time Democratic allegiance, the effect upon the party would be disastrous; and it was precisely at this time that vast numbers of Catholics began to bolt to Republicanism. The Democratic Administration in Washington made every effort to conciliate this religious following by appointing to high position devout Catholics like Attorney General McGrath or running for office men like Senator Thomas Dodd, of Connecticut—who were in many instances indistinguishable in their attitudes from the ultraright opposition.

Though it would be unfair to give the impression that the Catholic Church spoke with one voice, the preponderant weight of the church hierarchy was cast on the side of a delusional anti-communism. The 1937 encyclical of Pope Pius XI, *Atheistic Communism*, had ruled out any cooperation or compromise with the heathen ideology. "Communism is intrinsically wrong, and no one who would save Christian civilization may collaborate with it in any undertaking whatsoever," Pius XI had decreed.

Under wartime exigencies, driven by the need of national survival, the United States had violated this flat prohibition, allying itself with Soviet Russia. This pragmatic tie had disturbed a large portion of the American Catholic hierarchy. Francis Cardinal Spellman, its most widely publicized and authoritative voice, began as early as 1946 to issue warnings. He feared that communists were "digging deep inroads into our own nation"; in 1947–48, he spoke of the hour "of dreadful, desperate need." By 1949 he was declaring that America would not be safe "until every Communist cell is removed from within our government, our own institutions, not until every democratic country is returned to democratic leadership . . ." In February, 1949, speaking from the pulpit of St. Patrick's Cathedral in New York, he warned that America was in imminent danger of "Communist conquest and annihilation."

Such exaggerations reached a peak in a comic-strip pamphlet distributed by the Catechetical Guild of St. Paul. Entitled *Is This Tomorrow?* the pamphlet pictured communist mobs attacking St. Patrick's Cathedral with blazing torches, and nailing the Cardinal to the door. A widely read Catholic magazine gave this terror tract its imprimatur by including it as a supplement in its regular issue, and one New York priest sold more than 7,000 copies of the booklet from the pamphlet rack in the back of his church.

Ironically, it was just at this time that internal danger, to whatever degree it had actually existed, had been virtually expunged.

The Communist Party in America had reached the peak of its membership, prestige and influence during the war years of the alliance with Russia; after that it swiftly declined. The five years between 1945 and 1950 (a span during which McCarthy expressed no great awareness of the menace) was the period during which others more perceptive were battling communist influence. Undeniably, during the early 1940s, the communists, despite their lack of numbers, had wormed their way into isolated positions of considerable power. They had gained control of several large and influential labor unions; they had gotten into strategic spots in some local governments—and certainly some had been hidden in the mammoth bureaucracy in Washington. But battles had been fought on a rank-and-file level in the unions, and communist leadership in instance after instance had been effectively purged.

Walter Reuther, though he was widely denounced as a dangerous radical, the *bête noire* of industrial leadership, had in fact risked his future in battling the hidden communist control of the mighty United Automobile Workers union. In a bitter internecine fight that raged through 1946 and 1947, he ultimately succeeded in ousting communists from positions of power and influence. Though McCarthy would later try to show that the New York newspaper world was dangerously tainted, the fact remained that a rank-and-file revolt had overthrown communist leadership of the New York Newspaper Guild in the late 1940s, and installed a more conservative and representative administration. Even John F. Cronin, S.S., assistant director of social action of the National Catholic Welfare Council and one of the foremost authorities on communist infiltration of the labor movement, was later to write that a great change in American attitudes took place between 1948–50 and that the crucial problems had been "mostly solved by 1950."

The insidious charge of treason on the highest levels in Washington had also been exposed by that time for the myth it was. The Republican-controlled Eightieth Congress in 1948 was a highly partisan legislature slavering for Democratic blood in the upcoming Dewey-Truman campaign. The Hiss and Remington cases had stemmed from the hearings conducted at that time by the House Un-American Activities Committee and its Senate internal security counterpart. Even if one were to accept the validity of these two dubious cases, the fact remains that they stood in isolation. Though it was never properly appreciated by an excited public nor adequately explained by a partisan press, these were the only cases that the Congressional majority could make stick in court—and this despite the fact that Republican committees for a considerable period of time had full access to the government's personnel files. Four Republican-dominated committees of the Eightieth Congress examined, for example, the personnel files of the State Department and kept their mimeograph machines working overtime making copies of all the raw, unevaluated gossip found in them. The committees were the House Committee on Appropriations, the House Committee on Foreign Affairs, the House Committee on Expenditures in the Executive Department and the Senate Committee on Appropriations. The manner in which the most irresponsible innuendoes seemed to flit out of the supposedly secret files and into the press finally had led President Truman in March, 1948, to close the executives files to Congressional inspection; but by that time most of the potentially damaging information had been inspected. And so it has to be held of some significance that the verdict of even these Republican-controlled committees seeking explosive political material seems to have been summed up in the words of Rep. Bartel Jonkman, of Michigan, who had served as a one-man subcommittee of the House Foreign Affairs Committee in its investigation of the State Department. On August 2, 1948—with the Presidential campaign entering a heated stage—he told the House:

"But before the 80th Congress adjourns, I want the members to know that there is one department in which the known or reasonably suspected subversives, Communists, fellow-travelers, sympathizers and persons whose services are not in the best interests of the United States, have been swept out. That is the Department of State."

Such an explicit exoneration, one might have thought, would

have foreclosed the possibility of Republicans returning to rake over the old terrain. But then came 1950, the conviction of Hiss, the arrest of Fuchs, and the increasingly distrustful national mood. Sniffing the winds of change, the Republican leadership acted with cynical alacrity. On February 6, 1950, the Republican National Committee and the party leadership in Congress drew up a so-called statement of principles. In this, they excoriated the Truman Administration for "the dangerous degree to which Communists and their fellow travelers have been employed in important Government posts" and for permitting vital secrets to fall into the hands of "alien agents and persons of questionable loyalty . . ." The Republicans demanded a thorough "overhaul" of the loyalty security program and the banishment of communists and subversives from government.

Thus was laid down the campaign line designed to save the GOP from annihilation—and just three days later Joe McCarthy fired the opening salvo in his speech in Wheeling, West Virginia.

AFTER THE DINNER at the Colony, McCarthy set out to get the "facts" that he had assured his three companions he would have no trouble finding. His friendly relationship with the Chicago *Tribune* may have been the reason for his confidence. In any event, his principal source of information for what was to follow appears to have been Willard Edwards, of the Chicago *Tribune,* who had long been hatcheting the Roosevelt and Truman Administrations for their supposedly Red bias. Edwards sent McCarthy a file of his stories. The Senator whipped up a rough draft, then he informed the Senate Republican Campaign Committee that he would be available for a series of Lincoln Day speeches.

Early February is the traditional rallying time for Republicans. In honor of the party's first and greatest President, GOP national leaders and lesser orators crisscross the country, sounding the themes that they hope will arouse the passions of the electorate in the next great test of national will.

In the campaign now to be mounted along the lines prescribed in the Republican policy statement of February 6, the little-known Senator from Wisconsin did not rate the big speaking engagements. He was assigned to lesser ports of call. The first stop on his itinerary was Wheeling, West Virginia, the grubby little mining and industrial city tucked away in the northward-thrusting arm of the state, with Ohio just beyond the river.

Late on the afternoon of February 9, McCarthy's plane arrived in Wheeling. He was met at the airport by a local delegation of just three persons: Tom Sweeney, who was to be his host; Republican Congressman Francis J. Love; and Frank Desmond, a reporter for the Wheeling *Intelligencer*.

On the ride to town from the airport, Desmond asked McCarthy if he had a copy of his speech, and the Senator said he had a rough draft. Sweeney remarked that the local radio station, WWVA, was going to carry the speech and wanted an advance copy to guard against libel. McCarthy gave both Sweeney and Desmond a copy of the ideas he had jotted down, and they went on to the McClure Hotel, where a suite of rooms had been reserved.

Senator McCarthy had time only for a brief reception with local Republican leaders, a drink or two, a chat with Desmond, and then he was onstage—in what was to be the first act of the Nightmare Decade.

Waiting in the Colonnade Room of the McClure were some 275 party faithful, guests at the dinner sponsored by the Ohio County Women's Republican Club. William Callahan, a Wheeling attorney and executive director of the Ohio Valley Republican organization, introduced McCarthy.

There was to be an interminable debate later about precisely what he said, but Frank Desmond was there, with McCarthy's rough draft in his pocket, and Desmond reported it as he heard it. Most accounts later agreed—and anyone who ever saw him in action must recognize the description—that McCarthy moved all around the platform, waved his brawny arms, and worked himself up into a fine lather as he thundered his lines. Far from being a polished orator, he gave the impression of an earnest country boy, a little crude perhaps but struggling to get across the truth as he saw it. This made him all the more effective. Audiences came away shaking their heads, some of them instant disciples. "Gee, you couldn't fail to be impressed by that man," hearers would say. "He was *so* sincere."

Of great significance was the ever-present religious motif.

Frank Desmond wrote in his lead paragraph in the next morning's *Intelligencer* that McCarthy got "a rousing ovation" when "he declared bluntly that the fate of the world rests with the clash between the atheism of Moscow and the Christian spirit throughout other parts of the world." Here was the theme which McCarthy was to use time and again to rally disturbed Catholics and equally disturbed Protestant fundamentalists.

Following the motif of the Republican National Committee directive of February 6, McCarthy next stressed the guilt of Alger Hiss. "As you heard this [Hiss] story of high treason," McCarthy told his Wheeling audience, "I know that you are saying to yourself—well, why doesn't Congress do something about it?"

His answer was that there was "a lack of moral uprising on the part of 140 million American people," the result of "an emotional hangover and the temporary moral lapse" that follows war.

He now came to the statement that was to resound across the nation: "While I cannot take the time to name all the men in the State Department who have been named as members of the Communist Party and members of a spy ring, I have here in my hand a list of 205 that were known to the Secretary of State as being members of the Communist Party and who, nevertheless, are still working and shaping policy in the State Department."

As subsequent investigations disclosed, McCarthy held no such list in his hand. So undeniable is this that some of his apologists have gone to great lengths, as he himself was soon to do, to cast doubt on whether he had ever uttered those specific words. But the phrase "I have here in my hand" was to become a trademark, the gimmick that convinced credulous millions. McCarthy himself, after much hedging, finally admitted to *U.S. News & World Report* in September, 1951, that he had indeed used such a figure as 205. Its source and its irrelevancy to the specific charge that he made became apparent later, but one mystery has always remained: Just what was on that piece of paper Joe waved aloft in Wheeling?

A personal friend of mine, a journalist who was once a close friend of McCarthy's, asked him on one occasion: "Joe, just what did you have in your hand down there in Wheeling?"

McCarthy gave his characteristic roguish grin, and replied, "An old laundry list."

. . .

ONE OF THE MOST AMAZING ASPECTS of the Wheeling performance is that hardly anybody paid much attention to it at the time. Even those in McCarthy's audience in the Colonnade Room of the McClure seem not to have been especially startled by his declaration. Frank Desmond noted that, in the question-and-answer period after the speech, McCarthy was asked not so much about his communists-in-government charges as about the Agriculture Department's plan "to destroy millions of tons of potatoes, eggs, butter and fruit." Other questions dealt with "old-age and social security problems."

Ironically enough, one of those most stunned by the ensuing furor over McCarthy's speech was the Ohio Valley Republican leader who had introduced him, William Callahan. Callahan recalls that he was busy with "the radio man" from WWVA while McCarthy was speaking. While he was so preoccupied, "McCarthy said something about communism. Afterward I wondered what in the world had happened. The newspapers seemed to think he had said something very momentous."

When reporters and Senate investigators later came around questioning him, Callahan says, he didn't know quite what to tell them. His best recollection was that McCarthy had used two figures, apparently the sensational 205 and the more modest 57 that was soon to emerge in his other speeches, but in just what connection these figures had been used Callahan couldn't say.

The rest of the nation almost slept through the great speech, too. Days passed before the first obscure mentions of McCarthy began to creep into even the redbaiting newspapers.

The major news of the day for the afternoon papers of February 10 and the morning papers of February 11 was the Klaus Fuchs story from London. Fuchs had been arraigned in court; journalists had gotten their first look at him; and the details of his public confession and demeanor filled columns in the press. *The New York Times* on February 11 described his statement as one of "controlled schizophrenia" and added: "It was a confession such as might have come from behind the Iron Curtain."

Redbaiting journalists had a glorious time with the Fuchs confession, pairing this overseas sensation with dramatized domestic versions of their own. In New York, Hearst's *Journal-*

American was running a long spy-subversion series written by
the late Howard Rushmore, based largely on the half-baked disclosures of the Republican investigating committees in 1948. In
Chicago, the journalist who had supplied McCarthy with much
of his material, Willard Edwards, was giving the Administration-
baiting Chicago *Tribune* the raw meat on which this tiger fed.
TELL HOW RED SPIES ESCAPED PROSECUTION, ran the headline
on his contribution of February 9, the day of the Wheeling
speech. The next day, the *Tribune* made no mention of McCarthy
and the Wheeling detonation, but it had another Edwards horror
tale headed: TELLS HOW FDR SHRUGGED OFF RED SPY NEWS. It
was not until the third day after McCarthy's Wheeling speech
that it all began, and even then it was in a spotty, tentative way.
The Associated Press had picked up Frank Desmond's Wheeling
story with its "I have here in my hand" paragraph about 205
Communists in the State Department, and it had moved a brief
item on its national wires. Most news editors apparently put the
item on the spike of discarded wire-copy chaff. But out West, in
conservative country where McCarthy was going on his Lincoln
Day tour, this paragraph pricked the curiosity of some newsmen.
Everywhere McCarthy went, he began to be bombarded with
questions about communists and spies and subversives. Mc-
Carthy, shilly-shallying nervously at first about whether to admit
he had said what he had said, could sense before long that he had
touched a sensitive nerve; and, as the days passed, he became
incredibly bold. He challenged the State Department; he challenged President Truman; he challenged the Democrats—already
he was assuming what was to become one of his favorite roles,
that of the all-American boy, ready to take on all comers.

And the Democrats, to their eternal regret, took up his challenge just as though it had been legitimate.

THE MC CARTHY STORY now began to shift like the
sands of the desert in a windstorm. Each retreat was cloaked, however, by an outcry so fierce and a new stance so challenging that
the fact of change was camouflaged. This is what Richard Rovere
called the multiple big-lie technique.

It seems obvious from the Wheeling speech that there had to
be 205 Communists at work at that moment in the State Depart-

ment—or McCarthy was a liar. Though the press hadn't reacted, the State Department had sent off a wire to McCarthy demanding the 205 names and promising a swift investigation. This prompt response apparently gave McCarthy a temporary case of jitters. In Denver, en route to Salt Lake City, he told reporters that he had been misquoted in Wheeling. He had not charged that there were 205 Communists in the State Department, he said, but had spoken only of "bad security risks," quite a different matter, since a number of other species—alcoholics and homosexuals, for instance—would fall into this category.

Why this sudden retreat?

The foray into communism had been launched in such slap-dash fashion that McCarthy actually had no real information and, furthermore, he was uncertain about what he himself had said. If he had retained a copy of the notes from which he spoke at Wheeling, he apparently had already mislaid or lost it, for in the next few months, in the furor over the 205 figure, he went through a hilarious interlude trying to track down and identify his own words. Frederick Woltman later recalled how "on a number of occasions . . . I heard McCarthy and his advisers wrack their brains for some lead as to what he had said in that Wheeling speech. He had no copy . . . he could not find the notes . . . The Senator's staff could find no one who could recall what he had said precisely. He finally hit on the idea of appealing to ham radio operators in the area who might have made a recording of the speech. He could find none."

By the time he had reached Salt Lake City, however, McCarthy had bounced off the ropes and was once again the slugger that boxing fans at Marquette had come to recognize. The 205 figure was now forgotten as if it had never been; the new magic number was 57. About three-quarters of the Communists in the State Department had vanished in a single day, but still 57 was a good, shocking number.

A Salt Lake City radio personality named Dan Valentine interviewed McCarthy on February 10, and a tape of this interview was preserved. From the tape, then, here is what McCarthy said:

McCarthy: Last night I discussed Communists in the State Department. I stated that I had the names of 57 card-carrying members of the Communist Party . . . Now, I want to tell the Secretary this: If he wants to call me tonight at the Utah Hotel,

I will be glad to give him the names of those 57 card-carrying Communists. . . .

Valentine: In other words, Senator, if Secretary of State Dean Acheson would call you at the Hotel Utah tonight in Salt Lake City you could give him 57 names of actual card-carrying Communists in the State Department of the United States—actual card-carrying Communists.

McCarthy: Not only can, Dan, but will . . .

Valentine: Well, I am just a common man out here in Salt Lake City, a man who's got a family and a son and a job. You mean to say there's 57 Communists in our State Department that direct or control our State Department policy or help direct it?

McCarthy: Well, Dan, I don't want to indicate there are only 57, I say I have the names of 57.

More than six weeks later, at a time when he had raised the number to 81, McCarthy testified under oath before a Senate committee, admitting: "At this particular moment I could not give you the names of half of these persons." Since he had had six weeks to do research and was still in this state of ignorance, one can imagine how prepared he was to give Secretary Acheson the 57 names over the telephone from the Hotel Utah.

From Salt Lake City it was on to Reno and another speech on February 11. Here again he stuck to his charge of 57—but just barely. He was still beguiled by that more grandiose figure of 205, and his uncertainty about how far to go was revealed in a paragraph in a news story written by Edward Conners of the *Nevada State Journal.* Conners apparently had been given an advance copy of McCarthy's speech, and had spotted a change in the numbers game. He wrote:

"Sen. McCarthy, who had first typed a total of 205 employees of the State Department who could be considered disloyal to the United States and pro-Communists, scratched out that number and mentioned only '57 card-carrying members,' whom Acheson should know as well as members of Congress."

This genius of effrontery now did something so daring that he at last captured the headlines he had been seeking. McCarthy fired off a telegram to the President of the United States, challenging him to a duel of truth.

In the telegram, he repeated: "I have in my possession the names of 57 Communists who are in the State Department at present." Then, cannily, he shifted his ground. It was up to Truman to check, to get the names. He could do this easily, McCarthy said, because the State Department's Loyalty Board "did a painstaking job and named hundreds which had been listed as dangerous to the security of the nation because of communistic connections." This was far different from the flat accusation of "card-carrying Communists." It was marvelously indefinite. Might not one man's "communistic connection" be another man's mild liberalism?

McCarthy had given himself all kinds of room to maneuver. He was to need all the room he could get, as quickly became obvious. For, in Reno, he ventured a bit further than he had in the past. For the first time, he named some names—and fell flat on his face doing it.

After denouncing the supposed communist infiltration of the State Department, he said he would cite some specific cases. He named four persons who, he implied, were in the State Department: John W. Service, Mrs. Mary Jane Keeney, Gustavo Duran and Dr. Harlow Shapley. But in what connection did he name them? This was something of a mystery. The Chicago *Tribune* in a specially written story from Reno reported: "He said he did not accuse them of being either traitors or Communists, but added: 'I don't care if these people sue me. It might give me a platform on which to expose them.'" Expose them as what?

One might logically assume that the names first mentioned would be the best he had to support his charges of subversion in the State Department. But of the four persons named, only one was still in government service, two hadn't been for years, and one *never* had been. In the still-active category was John S. Service (not John W.), a Far Eastern specialist who had been investigated in 1945 in connection with the *Amerasia* case, had been cleared of all charges by a federal grand jury and then had been reinstated. This was the closest McCarthy came to pay dirt. His other charges were ludicrously wide of the mark.

Gustavo Duran hadn't been employed in the State Department for more than three years. He had seen three years service in its auxiliary foreign service division, had resigned on October 4, 1946. Mrs. Mary Jane Keeney had been employed by State for less than four months, had resigned June 21, 1946. Dr. Harlow

Shapley was an astronomer who in his private capacity had supported a number of left-wing causes and had served on American delegations to various scientific and astronomical conferences, and he was at this time one member of a large American delegation to a conference of the United Nations Educational, Scientific and Cultural Organization (UNESCO), representing the prestigious American Association for the Advancement of Science. Dr. Shapley had *never* been employed by the Department of State.

W H E R E D I D those entrancing, shifting figures—205 and 57 and 81—come from? The answer is that they came from records hoary with time; from records that, even when they were fresh, had been considered virtually worthless by four separate committees of the Republican-dominated Eightieth Congress.

It all began with a letter written July 26, 1946, by then Secretary of State James F. Byrnes, a conservative South Carolina Democrat. Wild rumors had been flying around that hundreds, perhaps thousands, of Communists had found shelter in the State Department. Rep. A. J. Sabath (D., Ill.) had asked Byrnes for the facts.

In his reply Byrnes wrote that, when the war ended, some 3,000 employees were transferred to the State Department from such wartime agencies as the Office of Strategic Services and the Office of War Information. Preliminary security investigations had been made on all of these, and as a result the departmental screening committee had "recommended against permanent employment" of 284. Of this number, 79 had been discharged when Byrnes wrote, and investigations of the others were continuing. Any grade-school student by subtracting 79 from 284 would come up with a remainder of 205—and this was precisely what McCarthy had done, as he later admitted to *U.S. News & World Report* when he said he had taken the Byrnes letter as the basis for his Wheeling speech.

It was after Byrnes wrote his letter that Truman's loyalty program got into full swing, and the merest suspicion led to suspension. Thus these figures were hopelessly out of date. It mattered not to McCarthy. Actually, at the time of the Wheeling speech, only about 65 of the 284 employees originally questioned were still on the State Department payroll—and this after passing the most severe of loyalty tests.

Between Wheeling and Salt Lake City, McCarthy shifted from 205 to 57. Where did this figure come from? It came from another of those years-old Republican committee investigations. In mid-1947, the Republican-controlled House Appropriations Committee of the Eightieth Congress spent six weeks rummaging through hundreds of State Department personnel files. The committee culled out 108 cases that it considered possibly suspect. Hearings were held, beginning in January, 1948. Names were not revealed, a significant detail in view of McCarthy's later difficulty with names, but the cases were discussed by number. State Department security officers testified, giving the results of investigations undertaken after the original charges were filed, and they pointed out—another significant point in view of Mc-Carthy's subsequent charges—that the 108 cases involved, not just employees of the department, but also *applicants* for department jobs. In March, 1948, the department compiled a statistical summary showing that 57 of the 108 were on the department's payroll. Also as of March, 1948, more than half of the 57 who had been retained had been cleared after a full FBI investigation, and 22 remaining cases were still under the FBI microscope. McCarthy, of course, ignored the fact that the FBI, whose director was one of the most dedicated anticommunists in the nation, had passed on all of these 35 cases, and that the cases involved all kinds of other derogatory charges in addition to that of communism. Only by cavalierly ignoring all such relevant details, only by concealing the fact that he was dealing with data two years old, and with cases that were then under intensive investigation—only by such distortion had McCarthy been able to create the impression that there were 57 Communists still actively at work making policy in the State Department.

THE HIGHEST LEADERSHIP of the Republican Party —the eminent "respectables"—were just as irresponsible, just as much to blame, as Joe McCarthy. He increasingly became their national mouthpiece; they never repudiated his tactics until he attacked *them*. The party leadership was deeply involved in his excesses; its spokesmen were doing exactly what he was doing, lacking only his demagogic skill. Having every reason to know better after their own committee probes in 1948, the Republican hierarchy now embarked on a campaign of vilification without precedent on the part of a major party in American politics.

This is not to suggest that politics is ever a lily-white profession. The Democrats for twenty years had certainly taken excessive advantage of the Hoover Administration's disaster in the Great Depression, reminding the electorate every four years (and on appropriate occasions in between) that the Republican Party had been the architect of that disaster. Nevertheless, most politicians in the past at least retained the decency to consider their opponents patriotic Americans. The final smear to which no responsible party should ever stoop is to impute disloyalty and treason to the opposition. Such a charge is an appeal to the height of unreason; a charge against which there is no possible defense. For the inevitable retort to denial by the accused is that, of course, a traitor would never admit his treason.

Yet it was just such an appeal to passion and unreason that the hierarchy of the Republican Party had unleashed by its directive of February 6, 1950. And McCarthy was by no means alone in his irresponsible attack on the State Department.

The prestige of the party's foremost leaders, naturally, was not put on the line at this point. This is a standard political tactic. The big men must maintain their lofty images while, just an echelon or two down, the lesser workers fling the mud pies. And so one finds that in this February of 1950 Senator Taft, Mr. Republican, speaking at Miami University in Ohio, was expanding on the comfortable Republican theme of liberty versus socialism. At the same time, Senator Everett McKinley Dirksen was putting his mellifluous magic to work extolling the virtues of Abraham Lincoln. But down in West Virginia there was meatier fare.

On February 10, the day after McCarthy's Wheeling speech, Republican National Chairman Guy Gabrielson, in a Lincoln Day address in Charleston, demanded an overhaul of all loyalty and security procedures by the federal government. He pledged the party's support to the FBI in weeding Communists and "sympathizers" from federal payrolls. And he lambasted President Truman for failing "to recognize fully the implications of this threat and the dangerous degree to which Communists and fellow-travelers have been employed in government posts, especially the State Department."

On February 13, in Morgantown, West Virginia, Republican National Committeeman Walter S. Hallanan held up the Hiss case as typical of communist infiltration of the State Department, and said the secrets of the atom and hydrogen bombs had been given to the Russians by "traitors who had been planted in the inner sanctums of our government." These "traitors," he said, had "enjoyed the protection of the administration in Washington," and Americans were "terrified at the realization that the State Department and other agencies of our government are still permeated with Communists and fellow-travelers."

In all three of these speeches—McCarthy's, Gabrielson's and Hallanan's—the basic theme was the same. Traitors had done us in. The Truman Administration had coddled them. The specific target was the State Department—the one department that had been examined by four Republican committees in the Eightieth Congress and found clean. And McCarthy had had the cheek to stand up and proclaim "I have here in my hand" . . .

McCarthy's indulgence in the big-lie technique made him overnight an invaluable party property. Back in Washington after his Lincoln Day tour, he found, perhaps to his own amazement but certainly to his gratification, that his wild-swinging charges had given him a national forum. All that remained was for him to carry his attack to the floor of the Senate, and this he did on February 20, just eleven days after Wheeling.

This was the Pepsi-Cola Kid, the water boy of the real estate lobby, the defender of the Nazis at Malmédy. Yet, almost the instant he began to speak, many of his colleagues in the Senate made it clear that in their view he was a statesman whose charges should be regarded with the utmost seriousness.

The debate began with McCarthy's sparring with his Democratic critics. He squirmed and wriggled to avoid being hooked on the 205 fantasy. He told the Senators he didn't believe he had used any such figure; that the speech he had delivered in Wheeling was "the same speech" he had made in Reno. At this point, before McCarthy had produced a single item of proof, Senator Henry Cabot Lodge injected himself into the discussion.

Lodge said he was "interested and concerned" as a member of the Senate Foreign Relations Committee, and he promised "at the earliest appropriate opportunity to make a motion to have a subcommittee of the Senate Foreign Relations Committee take up every single one of the accusations which the Senator from Wisconsin makes."

"I was hoping the Senator would," McCarthy replied, perhaps indicating that there had been a private understanding. The impression was strengthened by McCarthy's next few words that showed he had some prior knowledge of Lodge's plans. "In case the Senator from Massachusetts is not able to remain and listen to all my remarks—" he began.

Lodge cut in: "I cannot remain and listen to the whole of the Senator's speech because I have another engagement, but I shall read it all in the morning with the utmost care."

One of the most prestigious Republican names in the Senate was backing McCarthy, demanding an investigation, without waiting to see whether an investigation was justified—whether the Senator held in his hand anything more significant than an old laundry list.

9

The Mad Hatter's Nightmare

THE SENATE OF THE UNITED STATES, for all its
"gentlemen's club" tradition, has witnessed many a mad scene.
In 1856, in the passion of pre-Civil War debate, courtesy was
junked for violence on at least one occasion, when a South Caro-
linian trapped abolitionist Senator Charles Sumner in his chair
behind his desk and beat him senseless with a heavy cane. In
more recent times, the Senate had been filled with the sound and
fury of Huey Long and the Bilbos of the South trying to read the
menace of communism into the Negro demand for equality. But
it is to be questioned whether this chamber, sometimes called
the world's greatest deliberative body, had ever abandoned more
completely all claims to legislative sanity than it did on the late

afternoon of February 20, 1950, when Senator Joseph McCarthy took the floor. What followed was a mad hatter's nightmare.

From about six o'clock until nearly midnight, McCarthy held the center of the stage. He came equipped with his trademark, the bulging brief case, and as he spoke he scattered mounds of files on his desk. Richard Rovere has commented that it seemed obvious from McCarthy's befuddlement with his own material that he was reading these case histories for the first time; the record supports that judgment.

He put on a performance bewildering in its paradoxes, chameleonlike in its changes of manner. He spewed forth in the most indiscriminate manner the most sensational charges—then posed as the most responsible and considerate of men, one who wouldn't think of naming names lest he injure the innocent. To his fellow Senators, he was by turns a model of courtesy and gentlemanliness—and their arrogant instructor in the intricacies of black arts they did not have the wit to fathom. In the first role, he was always elaborate in his willingness to yield the floor to colleagues asking a question; in the second, when the questions became too sharp and pressing, he became patronizing, almost contemptuous of the intellect of skeptics who would question his facts, and haughty with the haughtiness of the utterly righteous where his own conduct and prestige were concerned.

All of this is there in the *Congressional Record*. Some description of his telltale shifts of mood and manner, some hint of his patent confusion and uncertainty with his own facts, might have been expected to seep into the press accounts the next day— but did not. The headlines and stories featured the sensational charges, unadorned with any indication that they were perhaps unreliable. Because McCarthy was a Senator, because he made his charges on the Senate floor, it followed that he must be treated like a statesman. His lurid tales must be reported "straight" as he gave them, without analysis of the gaps in his facts and figures, without background. This "tape-recorder reporting" that is part of the tradition of Olympian impartiality that governs the American press furthered the propagation of the big lie and helped insure the future of McCarthy.

Looking back on that evening in the Senate, three salient features emerge. The first is that the documents McCarthy read were raw, unevaluated gossip and rumor, not containing one countervailing word—all out-and-out indictment. Second, this act was put onstage with the full power and prestige of the Republican establishment behind it. And third, the Democrats, prisoners of the Truman Administration's devotion to its own milder brand of witch hunt, played—with only rare exceptions—the role of gullible fools.

What was the performance like on February 20? Watch as the curtain lifts.

M C C A R T H Y B E G A N by reading the telegraphic challenge he had wired to Truman from Reno. He had had no reply from the President, he said; Truman's only reaction had been to tell a press conference that there wasn't a word of truth in anything McCarthy had said. This cavalier treatment of a serious challenge by a responsible Republican statesman seemed to shock the GOP faithful. Time and again as he spoke, they interrupted to cluck-cluck about the fact that nine full days had passed since Reno, and Truman hadn't even deigned to answer. McCarthy saw the Presidential contempt for his veracity as a demonstration of the Administration's determination to cover up its own scandals. He thundered on: "I do not feel that the Democratic Party has control of the executive branch of the government any more . . . I think a group of twisted-thinking intellectuals has taken over the Democratic Party."

Senator Scott Lucas (D., Ill.), the majority leader, inter-rupted. Had McCarthy in Wheeling charged that there were 205 Communists active in the State Department? McCarthy said he didn't believe he had used that figure. Lucas challenged him again, reminding him of the press reports of his speech, arguing that if he had the 205 names he should produce them, and point-ing out that he could do so with perfect immunity on the Senate floor.

At this suggestion, Joe McCarthy became as righteous as a Puritan divine. It would not be "fair" to make the names public, he said. And, carried away by his sense of "fairness," he made a pledge that was to haunt him:

". . . I will not say anything on the Senate floor which I will not say off the floor. On the day I take advantage of the security we have on the Senate floor, I will resign from the Senate."

Lucas harassed him further. Had he used the figure 205? Certainly he must know whether he had; clearly he could answer yes or no. McCarthy replied by starting to read into the record the full text of his Reno speech. "It was the same speech," he said. Patently, since he had named names at Reno and had named no names in Wheeling, it was not.

When McCarthy had finished reading, Lucas returned to the attack, repeating his question about the 205 Communists mentioned in Wheeling. Joe slapped down this persistent gadfly: "I may say, if the Senator is going to make a farce of this, I will not yield to him. I shall not answer any more silly questions of the Senator. This is too important, too serious a matter for that."

Senator Herbert H. Lehman spoke up. He wondered whether it was not McCarthy's duty to reveal those names to the State Department so that subversives, if they existed, could be smoked out immediately. McCarthy took refuge in hauteur. "If the Senator will sit down and let me make my report to the Senate, he will have all the information he wants," he said. "The Senator from Wisconsin does not need any advice on his duty as a Senator in this respect."

Throughout it all, the Republican leadership threw the Senate into parliamentary turmoil in its support of the Senator from Wisconsin. Lodge had departed, but Kenneth Wherry, the Nebraska Republican who was the minority leader, protested from the beginning about the sparse attendance in the Senate chamber. He observed that there were only nine or ten Senators on the floor (not an unusual circumstance for any speech at this late hour of the day), and he declared that McCarthy's subject "seems to me of such importance" that he felt there should be a recess or quorum call to round up absentees. "I believe more Senators should be on the floor to hear this statement," he said.

Wherry finally agreed, reluctantly, to let McCarthy begin his speech, but at 7:30 P.M. he again provoked the quorum issue.

"I think the Senator from Wisconsin is presenting a serious challenge," he said. "I think it desirable to have all the Senators present, if possible, to hear his remarks . . ."

This precipitated an involved debate. McCarthy ended it by demanding a quorum call. The Democrats yielded, as under parliamentary rules they had to, and the sergeant at arms was instructed to use his power to "compel" members to come to the floor. It was the first time in five years that such a drastic step had been taken.

JUST WHAT EVIDENCE did McCarthy present that day on the Senate floor? He had announced that he had 81 documented cases involving Communists in the State Department— but he couldn't add. Some case numbers were missing altogether, and some were duplications. When he had finished, Cases 15, 27, 35, 37 and 59 hadn't showed up at all in his recital. He prefaced the speech by calling attention to Cases 1, 2, and 81. "Those, I think, represent the big three . . . if we can get rid of those big three, we will have done something to break the back of the espionage ring in the State Department." It was typical of McCarthy that this was almost the last anyone heard of "the big three," though he took a couple of subsequent stabs at harvesting some headline capital out of Case 2.

He was presumably discussing the menace of Communists in the State Department—but some of his cases dealt with other types of security risks like homosexuals and at least a few concerned persons who were specifically *not* Communists, according to his own description.

In addition he admitted: "I may say that I know that some of these individuals whose cases I am giving the Senate are no longer in the State Department. A sizeable number of them are not."

Time and again, he assured various Senators: "The names are available. They may have them if they care for them . . . The Senator [Lucas] can come to my office as soon as I finish and receive the names." But, always, and clearly, he took it all back in the same speech, usually on the grounds that the Democrats said they would reveal the names once they got them, and this, of course, would not be "fair" to the individuals he was accusing.

He gave a cloak-and-dagger account of the manner in which he had penetrated "Truman's iron curtain of secrecy." His disclosures had been made possible, he assured the Senate, only because he had had the help "of some good, loyal Americans in the State Department," and he would refuse to disclose the sources of his information because "I know the State Department is very eager to know how I have secured all this information. I know that the jobs of the men who helped me secure this material would be worth nothing if the names were given."

The "iron curtain of secrecy" charge was based on Truman's action in closing the executive files to prying Republican committees of the Eightieth Congress in 1948. A full set of the files dealing with the delinquencies of the 108 suspects had apparently found its way into the hands of Joseph Kamp, the anti-Semitic, profascist pamphleteer, who had produced a sixty-four-page broadside entitled *America Betrayed, The Tragic Consequences of REDS on the Government Payroll.*

Director Leon Birkhead of Friends of Democracy later made a comparison of the McCarthy and Kamp charges, showing that the source of both was quite obviously this list of cases investigated by the Republicans and dismissed even by them as unworthy of credence. The remarkable similarity of the Kamp and McCarthy cases is evident. For example:

McCarthy Case Number 3: " . . . was employed with OSS in 1942. In 1945 he transferred to the State Department. He is a member of a number of Communist-front organizations, and . . . his friends are known Communists . . . He was very friendly and sympathetic toward Harry Bridges, and strongly opposed any move to deport Bridges . . . sympathetic to Russia and the Communist experiment . . . blamed the capitalists . . . praised Russia . . ."

The Kamp version: ". . . came from OSS to the Intelligence Division in Sept. 1945 . . . he was a member of several Communist-front organizations . . . he associated openly with Communists . . . he was very friendly and sympathetic toward Harry Bridges and strongly opposed moves to deport him . . . sympathetic to Russia and the Communist experiment . . . blamed the capitalists . . . praised Russia . . ."

Another case, McCarthy's Number 5: "The report dated May 4, 1946 . . . shows that this individual has strong Communist leanings . . . This individual was discharged from a Navy school during the war for bad grades and for Communist activities . . ."

The Kamp version: "An investigation report dated May 4, 1946 says . . . 'strong Communist sympathies' . . . 'has been discharged from a Navy school during the war' for poor grades and for pro-Communist activities . . ."

The Democratic leadership had had eleven days after Wheeling in which to do their homework. They certainly should have known the antecedents and history of the two-year-old 108 list compiled by Republicans in the Eightieth Congress. Yet they sat there for the most part like so many zombies. They sniped at McCarthy about whether he had used the figure 205, about whether he would reveal the names; but there was no all-out challenge, no real confrontation.

It would have been so easy to spell out the fraud. Time and again, McCarthy gave the game away. Even in his own telling, aside from the numbered cases that simply were not there, his charges transparently were not what they purported to be.

Case 14 was "primarily a morals case." Case 41 concerned a staunch *anti*communist. As for Case 62, "This file is not important insofar as Communistic activities are concerned." He would "hesitate in naming" the employee in Case 65 as a Communist. Again, in Case 72, "I do not confuse this man, as I said, as being a Communist." And Case 76 "does not involve Communist activities."

At one point, Senator Homer Ferguson, the Michigan Republican who had headed one of the Red-hunting committees in the Eightieth Congress, interrupted McCarthy to note with some concern that he had skipped Case 37. Did he have such a case? ". . . I assume I had a case No. 37," McCarthy replied, explaining it must be mixed up in his papers somewhere. ". . . I get the impression that the Senator may have a file of his own, and apparently I do not have the same cases he has . . ."

How could Ferguson have a file of cases if McCarthy had just discovered fresh and sensational material by penetrating "Truman's iron curtain of secrecy"? How many files were there? And where did they come from? No one asked.

Even more ludicrous was McCarthy's entrapment in the convolutions of his own material. He was roaring along in his finest, most denunciatory style on Case 77, when suddenly he came up short with a confession. "Mr. President," he said to the Senate's presiding officer, "I believe I have covered this case before, and what I have just said seems to be a repetition . . ."

It was a perfect moment to hoist him with his own petard—

but the Democrats just sat there. At the very outset, as soon as Lodge had finished speaking, they had agreed to give McCarthy the Senate committee inquiry he demanded—and so assured him the national forum he sought. Their reaction, like Truman's in the loyalty program following the 1946 election, was to proclaim their patriotism and agree to join in the hunt. It was a tactic that sanctified McCarthy's charges, sight unseen and nothing proven, and for the Democrats it was suicidal. By joining their accuser, they helped to implant in the public mind the suspicion that there must be substance to his accusations.

T H R O U G H O U T the long and acrimonious evening, the Democrats made only two passes at sanity, and one of them was half-hearted. At one point, Majority Leader Scott Lucas inquired whether McCarthy was familiar with the make-up of the loyalty boards that had been passing on State Department employees. McCarthy confessed that this was a matter he hadn't investigated. Didn't the Senator know, Lucas wondered, that the Loyalty Review structure was headed by Seth Richardson, an eminent attorney and a Republican of impeccably conservative persuasion?

Taken aback for a moment, McCarthy confessed that he had not been aware of this. He appeared to be almost sagging on the ropes, but his Republican cohorts came to his aid. They pointed out that Seth Richardson headed the top Loyalty Review Board with broad jurisdiction over government departments, not the departmental Loyalty Board that had initial jurisdiction over questionable cases. So reprieved, McCarthy instantly recovered his aplomb and proclaimed that it seemed to him one of the first agencies communists would try to infiltrate would be the loyalty boards. He was obviously offering a debater's argument, but the Democrats let him get away with it. No one had the energy or wit to point out that the State Department's Loyalty Review Board was headed by a Republican just as irreproachable as Richardson—General Conrad E. Snow. No Democrat made the point that Truman deliberately had put the loyalty machinery in the hands of the opposition; and that if the State Department was riddled with subversives as McCarthy was suggesting, eminent Republicans on the loyalty boards must themselves have been largely responsible.

The second joust with reason was much more energetically fought. Its champion was the late Senator Brien McMahon, of Connecticut, the only Democrat who came out of the affair with high credit. McMahon had been summoned by the sergeant at arms from a dinner party in Georgetown, and he came on the floor late in the evening in white tie and tails. After listening for a time to McCarthy's case-history citations, he interrupted in an attempt to introduce some logic into the whole eerie performance.

He asked whether McCarthy had the "full files" of the cases he was discussing. "Has the Senator both the derogatory information and any good information that is in the file?"

McCarthy: The Senator asks whether I have the complete State Department files. The answer is "No."

Having obtained this admission, McMahon, who had begun his career as a Justice Department attorney in the Roosevelt Administration, bored in to the attack.

"The Senator does not have in his possession any information which will indicate that the derogatory statement is true," he said. "Does not the Senator realize that, if I were to send investigators into his State, perhaps I could obtain 105 or perhaps 1,005 witnesses who would make statements about the Senator that would be totally untrue and incorrect, and the same investigators might go to 2,000 other persons who would say, 'Those 105 people are not telling the truth at all. They are angry with the Senator because he voted for this bill or that bill that they did not like.' Did the Senator ever think of that?"

McCarthy responded that he was giving, he believed, a "fair" digest of what the files showed, though obviously, since hardly a good word was said about any of his suspects, he was presenting the kind of version one might expect from a prosecutor hell-bent on obtaining a conviction.

McMahon, harking back to the earlier days of his career when he had seen the contents of secret dossiers, drove home his point: "I tell the Senator that in the course of my career I have examined many Government files and many investigation records, and I have seen in the files statements that 'This man McCarthy,' or 'This man—' "

McCarthy: Make it Jones.

McMahon: Or this man Smith is a terrible person. He is not to be trusted. He defrauds his creditors. He even beats his wife. He has been seen going around the corner with suspicious persons.

And then if we go to other persons in the community, they say, "I am not at all surprised that you have been told that, because Smith had a fight with a man named Jones, who lives down the street. I will bet that you got an interview with him, and that in it he said that this fellow Smith is a terrible person."

I call attention to the possibility that, if we had the whole file before us, as undoubtedly the State Department has, the information the Senator from Wisconsin is giving the Senate might be contradicted to the point where creditable witnesses or creditable evaluators of the files would say, "In that event, we cannot believe that information."

It was an appeal to common sense—and not a line of it lived in the press the next day. All that survived was a passing reference, buried far down in a United Press wire story, to an angry exchange between McMahon and Senator Karl Mundt, the South Dakota Republican.

McMahon's onslaught had set the Republicans off like so many Roman candles, and Mundt and Capehart clamored for the floor at the same time. Mundt got it and promptly twisted McMahon's words.

"I hope the Senator [McCarthy] will not follow the suggestion of the Senator from Connecticut and discontinue his efforts to purge Communists from the government," he said.

"Mr. President, the Senator from Connecticut made no such statement," McMahon roared.

According to the United Press account, McMahon then rushed over to Mundt's desk, fist upraised and shouted angrily: "I say to the Senator that what we have to be careful of is that we do not imitate the very thing we are against. Star chambers are not for the United States of America, nor are trials ex parte, on the basis of part of the files of the persons concerned, on the floor of the United States Senate, the way to handle this matter."

Mundt replied almost as angrily that, if Congress had depended on due process, Alger Hiss would never have been convicted. Capehart chimed in, hissing Hiss, always Hiss. If the

President was permitted to "freeze" the files, Mundt said, "that would be the complete way to cover up every Communist in government."

McMahon snapped back: "What I do not see is how anyone can form an intelligent judgment simply by reading what a half a dozen people say, because perhaps they are rogues, scoundrels, and thieves. Perhaps they have some ulterior motive for making the statements that they do."*

Unsupported by Senators from his own party, he was drowned out in the partisan clamor. McCarthy droned on in his first major role as a Republican statesman, shuffling his mixed-up dossiers, piling case upon case in bewildering confusion until finally, at 11:43 P.M., the entire performance whimpered to a close.

THE WISE ADVICE of Senator McMahon is vindicated every time one probes for some bedrock of fact to support the horror tales about the State Department. In no instance, however, was the exposure so swift and complete as in the ludicrous tangle involving McCarthy's Cases 14 and 41—whereby the villain of the former case was the martyr of the latter.

In his February 20 oration, McCarthy had described the man in Case 14 as having "a bad background from the standpoint of security." A translator in the State Department, "he was fla-

---

* The FBI files at this time contained unevaluated data on more than 70 million Americans. The names of every federal employee and of every applicant for a federal job were checked out in this massive file. If derogatory information of any kind was turned up, the FBI conducted a full field investigation of the individual, questioning everyone it could find who had ever known him. Describing this process, Cabell Phillips wrote in *The New York Times* on March 26, 1950: "Someone 'seems to recall' that he was a sort of a radical in his younger days and was mixed up in a number of left-wing organizations. Another is 'almost certain' he used to pal around with a fellow named Bill Smith, and everybody knew, of course, that Smith was a Communist . . . With dead-pan objectivity, the FBI faithfully records everything everybody tells its agents about the person in question. It doesn't weigh or evaluate the data, separate the chaff of gossip from the kernels of fact. It turns its complete and unexpurgated report over to the loyalty board of the agency in which the person in question is employed and considers itself through with the case." It was from such compilations of the worst possible scuttlebutt about individuals that McCarthy read on February 20, ignoring the fact that in the years since the data had been gathered his "cases" had been weighed by the conservative-oriented State Department Loyalty Board and the Loyalty Review Board to see whether there was enough to justify even "the belief" that a person might be disloyal.

grantly homosexual," McCarthy declared, and some of his friends were "active members of Communist-front organizations, including the Young Communist League." The translator was fired on February 19, 1946, but reinstated April 1. McCarthy charged that this reinstatement resulted from the efforts of "a high State Department official" who made the rounds, pressuring signers of adverse affidavits to repudiate them.

More than two weeks later, on March 8, McCarthy admitted to reporters that he still did not know the name of "the high State Department official" whom he had accused of using such undue influence. It was a pity because, though he did not realize it, the man whom he had pictured as the arm-twisting scoundrel in this case was the same man whom he had praised in Case 41, explicitly and by name, as an official who had made herculean efforts to clean Communists out of the State Department.

Case 41, McCarthy said, illustrated a different point than his other cases. In this instance, a dedicated State Department official had striven for the dismissal of "an assistant chief in the division of occupied areas." Investigation had disclosed, said McCarthy, that most of the assistant chief's "close friends and associates have records as fellow travelers and Communists. He admitted to having contributed money to Communist-front organizations.

"There is a memorandum in the file to the effect that Joe Panuch had made considerable efforts to get this man out of the State Department. He was not successful, however . . ."

McCarthy continued that it was his understanding "this man Panuch tried to do a job of housecleaning" under Secretary of State Byrnes, but that he was fired for his efforts, a martyr to the cause of anticommunism, almost the instant George C. Marshall became Secretary of State. And this, McCarthy hinted darkly, resulted from Dean Acheson's inordinate influence with Marshall.

In both cases, the man in question was Joseph A. Panuch, a New York lawyer of considerable reputation—and, like Seth Richardson and General Snow, a Republican whose loyalty could not be doubted. He had been brought into the State Department by Secretary Byrnes for this very reason—to make certain that no suspicion could ever be attached to the disposition of loyalty cases.

Though McCarthy by his own admission didn't know even as late as March 8 the identity of the dastardly official of Case 14, Joseph Panuch recalled the details very clearly. The accused State Department translator in Case 14, he said, had been neither a homosexual nor a communist. He had investigated the case thoroughly, and he had found a man who was the victim of malicious gossip. Panuch said:

"That man was being railroaded. There was a routine hearing and he was ordered fired. He appealed to Secretary Byrnes, and Byrnes referred the case back to me.

"We then had an intensive proceeding and weighed a hell of a lot of evidence. We got new evidence, additional evidence and some changed evidence. There is a formal paper signed by me in the files completely clearing him. There's a huge file on the case. It must weigh five pounds.

"There is nothing on either count against this man. He is neither a homosexual nor a Communist. He is a German and never associated with Communists. He went through hell in that case, and I will stand on my opinion which is in the files. McCarthy must be crazy if he is raising that case."

Summing up, Panuch rendered this verdict: "If that's the best McCarthy's got, he's going to be blown out of the water."

Panuch did not realize that McCarthy could transmute such an exposure into victory; nor could he imagine that this feat of legerdemain would be made possible, not by just McCarthy's own efforts, but by powerful forces in American society.

SKIPPING AHEAD, it is perhaps instructive to see how much substance there was in the tale of "the 81" with which McCarthy regaled the Senate on February 20. Alfred Friendly, of the Washington *Post*, after a meticulous examination of the "cases," concluded that, when omitted numbers and duplications were eliminated, "the 81" boiled down to just 66 identifiable individuals. What happened to them?

The furor and the almost incessant review and rereview of these cases continued well into the Eisenhower era—into a time when McCarthy headed his own investigating committee, when the Justice Department was in the hands of a Republican Attorney General most anxious to validate his party's charges of subversion under the Democrats. Even under these circumstances, with the exception of Owen Lattimore, only *one* of "the 81"—or the 66, if you will—was ever indicted. And that indictment, in the end, disgraced not the defendant, but the government that procured it.

This lone unfortunate was Val R. Lorwin, who had been Case 64 in McCarthy's February 20 catalogue of betrayal. McCarthy described Case 64 this way:

"This individual is presently employed in Research and Intelligence in the State Department . . . The investigative files show that informants stated that he and his wife maintained a communistic and un-American attitude. The file further shows that he is a close friend of a number of Russian agents connected with a major espionage case . . . This individual apparently still enjoys clearance to top-secret documents."

McCarthy's charges precipitated an investigation. Harold W. Metz, subsequently employed by the Hoover Commission on Organization of the Executive Branch of the Government, told the FBI that communist meetings had been held in Lorwin's apartment and that Lorwin had showed him a Communist Party membership card.

On October 16, 1950, disloyalty charges were filed against Lorwin; Loyalty Board hearings were held; and in February, 1951, Lorwin was suspended. He fought the verdict; and, more than a year later, after further review of the case, he was reinstated with back pay from the time of his suspension. Lorwin then resigned and became an assistant professor at the University of Chicago.

There the matter rested for a time; but on December 3, 1953, after the Eisenhower Administration had been in office for nearly eleven months, Lorwin was indicted for perjury, based on his denial under oath that he had been a Communist. The battle lines were drawn for a court fight, but it was a contest that never came off because the government's case collapsed at the first challenge.

Lorwin's attorneys asked the court for a transcript of the Loyalty Board hearings, and the court ordered the Justice Department to produce the record. Attorney General Herbert Brownell refused, contending the files were secret, and Lorwin's lawyers asked that he be cited for contempt.

Matters had reached this impasse when, on May 25, 1954, Assistant Attorney General Warren Olney III walked into Federal District Court in Washington and asked Judge Edward M. Curran to dismiss the indictment. It had been obtained, he acknowledged, only through the misrepresentations made to the grand jury by the government prosecutor.

This overzealous gentleman had told the grand jurors it would be pointless to try to question Lorwin or his wife because obviously, since they were Communists, they would claim the privilege of the Fifth Amendment against self-incrimination. He also assured the jury that the testimony of the principal accusing witness would be supported by that of two FBI agents. On both counts, Olney said, the information given to the grand jury by the government was incorrect. Actually, both Lorwin and his wife had refused to avail themselves of the Fifth Amendment privilege and had denied under oath that they had ever been Communists, and there had been no additional witnesses against them. As a result of the deception practiced on the grand jury, Olney said, the prosecuting attorney who had obtained the indictment had himself been suspended by the Justice Department.

Lorwin's lawyers subsequently outlined the background of the case that never came to trial. Lorwin and his wife were socialists, they said. Far from being identical with communists, socialists are actually at war with them; Norman Thomas himself, the grand old man of American Socialism, respected for his personal integrity even by the conservative American press, had led a parade of ninety-one witnesses who had testified on Lorwin's behalf at the loyalty board hearings.

The whole case, it appeared, had stemmed from a bit of injudicious horseplay on Lorwin's part. There is sometimes an almost irresistible temptation for a liberal to twit and try to shock a conservative, whose mind he feels is buried in a frozen past. Lorwin on one occasion, in a party atmosphere, had yielded to this impulse by flashing under Metz's conservative nose a card that Metz took for a Communist Party membership card. Actually, said Lorwin's attorneys, it had been something quite different.

The extensive Loyalty Board hearings had apparently established that Lorwin, if judged by his official actions, not by his horseplay, was a proven anticommunist, and this had been the reason for his reinstatement. After the perjury indictment had been dismissed and he had been finally exonerated, Lorwin expressed his feelings in a statement issued through his attorneys.

"In asking today for the dismissal of the indictment against me," he said, "the Government has admitted the obvious fact that there could be no other case against me than that based on misrepresentation, falsehood or obstinate misunderstanding.

"The allegations of communism were particularly outrageous in view of the long record of vigorous anti-communism in my work and outside activities. No responsible official of the Department of Justice who took the trouble to read the record could have had the slightest doubt that the department was prosecuting an innocent man."

That was the closest Joe McCarthy ever came, with the exception of the Owen Lattimore case, to proving anything about the mythical "81."

M C C A R T H Y ' S P E R F O R M A N C E on the Senate floor that memorable night of February 20, 1950, had been so outrageous that, in the immediate aftermath, the leaders of his party and leading anticommunist agitators virtually disowned him. "It was a perfectly reckless performance," said Senator Taft.

Richard Rovere later summed up the reaction this way: ". . . In the ranks of the militant anti-Communists which McCarthy sought to join, dismay prevailed. Richard Nixon and other members of the House Un-American Activities Committee considered him a disaster. In New York, Eugene Lyons, a journalist eminence grise of the movement, took the view in the *New Leader* that 'the luck of the Communists . . . held good' when McCarthy cast himself as the latest Hercules. The earlier stable cleaners—Martin Dies, of Texas, John Rankin, of Mississippi, J. Parnell Thomas, of New Jersey—had been fools or worse, but now the ultimate fool, a paragon of ignorance and innocence and irresponsibility, had come to succeed them and to make a mockery of true, disinterested anti-Communism."

But those who, for the sake of their own reputations—and of the anticommunist cause as they saw it—would have dissociated themselves from McCarthy did a somersault and became his most ardent supporters. He became the embattled champion of his party. Why? Because a great portion of the American public had swallowed in one credulous gulp the insubstantial, inconsistent concoction McCarthy had presented on the floor of the Senate.

The cynical Republican leadership was content to ride along with the mood of the moment. An eloquent example was the way the revered Senator Taft quickly recovered from his first qualms about McCarthy's recklessness. He told *The New York Times* in an interview that he had given Senator McCarthy a bit of advice —the kind of advice that McCarthy hardly needed since it fitted perfectly into the tactics that came so instinctively to him. Senator Taft's advice was simple: "If one case doesn't work, try another."

10

The Tydings Saga Begins

THERE WAS NO investigative incentive in the American press; no fight and no dedication to vital issues in the Democratic high command; no consideration of the higher ethics of public service among the Republicans—and so there was created the perfect vacuum in which a master manipulator like Joe McCarthy could operate. Of all the short-sighted Democratic blunders, beginning with Truman's indiscriminate loyalty program and his guilt by association criteria of 1947, none transcended the colossal miscalculation that led the Democrats, at the very beginning of McCarthy's February 20 speech, to yield him the vital point and accord him a national platform before a subcommittee of the prestigious Senate Foreign Relations Committee.

Instead of giving themselves an opportunity for reflection, instead of taking the floor in full-scale debate in the tradition of Daniel Webster to expose the tawdriness of McCarthy's charges, the Democrats put their reliance on two tactics, one ineffective, the other highly dangerous: they relied on the press conference for immediate replies to McCarthy and on the full-scale committee hearing to demolish him.

The futility of the first technique was demonstrated in the press conference held on February 24 by Secretary of State Acheson. He denied to reporters that there were any Communists still active in the State Department. He pointed out that the department had been unable to get any names or specifics from McCarthy—this despite the fact, though Acheson didn't stress the point, that McCarthy had been so anxious to give him 57 names over the telephone from the Hotel Utah—and he finally got to the nub of the matter, explaining that McCarthy's "descriptions" of cases sounded suspiciously like the descriptions given two years earlier during the department's appropriations hearings. *The New York Times* dealt with this fundamental disclosure in this brief sentence: "The comparison revealed such a striking similarity between the two lists that it led to the conclusion that they were the same cases aired at that time, Mr. Acheson said."

Such treatment of the issue made no public impact. The accused Secretary of State had denied the charges, but then what would the accused be expected to do? The complaint that McCarthy hadn't furnished names or specifics was only half-heartedly made, with no hard-hitting comparison with his Western braggadocio, and in the circumstances it sounded more plaintive than challenging. And there was no development specifically, case by case, of the fact that McCarthy had presented a mishmash of old and exploded cases and had perpetrated a fraud upon the Senate by dressing them up as new. It was a technique that earned the Democratic defense only an obscure paragraph in an obscure story in *The New York Times*—and that, in many papers, did not rate even that. Perhaps a courageous and investigative press would have said to itself at this point: "Well, let us compare. Acheson says these are the same old charges, aired two years ago and dismissed. Is that true? Let us examine case by case and find out." Unfortunately, with rare exceptions, America does not have a press so dedicated to ferreting out the difficult truth.

WHAT DID DEMOCRATS THINK of these develop-ments? One former Senatorial administrative assistant, an aide to one of the more courageous Democratic Senators of that time, makes two major points. In the first place, he feels there was a lamentable weakness on the part of the Democratic floor leader-ship in the Senate.

"When Lyndon Johnson was majority leader," he says, "he knew all the ways there were to sidetrack issues that he didn't want to come up. That is part of the job of a good majority leader. Probably Johnson, if he had been the majority leader at that time, would have found some way to put the whole issue on the calendar and get it lost."

Failing that, this Senatorial assistant explains, it apparently was considered wiser to handle McCarthy in a committee hearing instead of in open debate on the floor. McCarthy's rough-house tactics were well known to his colleagues, and few wanted to risk tangling with him on so politically explosive an issue as communism in a jittery nation. It took no great imagination for a Senator contemplating such a head-on confrontation to envision the McCarthy counterattack and the headlines it would produce. To conduct the investigation in committee seemed far more discreet.

"You must understand," the former Senatorial assistant ex-plains, "that Senators do not normally fear each other. Each one of them has a high opinion of his own competence, and each feels that, if he heads a committee, he is in the driver's seat, fully capable of dealing with everything and anything that may come before *his* committee."

The Senator who was chosen to head the subcommittee in-vestigating McCarthy's charges fitted perfectly this description of Senatorial overconfidence. He was Millard E. Tydings, of Maryland, tall, aristocratic, endowed with conceit concerning his own abilities. A point to bear in mind is that Tydings was one of the "old guard" ultraconservatives of the Democratic Party. A veteran of twenty-four years' service in the Senate, he had earned for himself the label of one of the most intransigent intraparty opponents of Franklin Roosevelt and the New Deal. The band of Senatorial rebels who had led the successful fight against Roosevelt's court-packing proposal of 1937 had met for the first time and organized for the battle in Tydings' home. Tydings had been, indeed, such a prickly thorn in Roosevelt's hide that he had been one of four Democratic Senators whom the President had tried unsuccessfully to purge in the primaries of 1938. Subsequently, Tydings had opposed Roosevelt's break with the no-third-term tradition, and he had joined the coalition of favorite sons who had been put in nomination for the Presidency at the 1940 Democratic Convention in a futile effort to block the Roosevelt bid.

There were some indications that he might be the very type of committee chairman to commit the blunder of playing to one of McCarthy's greatest fortes—his role of the lone 100-percent American boy battling against some overwhelming conspiracy on behalf of justice and the people. This had been one of his ploys in disrupting the activities of the Baldwin committee in the Malmédy investigation, and it was easy to imagine what he might do were *he* ever cast in the role of badgered defendant. Yet Tydings—by no means alone among Senate committee chairmen—had shown a tendency in the past to conduct one-sided investigations along preconceived lines in the endeavor to tailor truth to fit his personal predilections.

Secretary of the Interior Harold L. Ickes, the crusty old curmudgeon of Bull Moose days who was one of the more doughty battlers of the Roosevelt era, has left a scathing description of one such Tydings probe. This occurred in 1935 when Tydings, in an effort to embarrass the Administration, decided to pillory Paul M. Pearson, the father of columnist Drew Pearson and the then Governor of the Virgin Islands. Since Pearson's administration was under Ickes' jurisdiction and any reflection on Pearson would be a reflection on Ickes, the Secretary tried to get Tydings to agree in advance of the public hearings to let him make an opening statement and to permit his department to cross-examine witnesses. Though Tydings originally agreed to the second request on cross-examination, he later reversed himself and turned Ickes down on both counts. Then, for a week, in a purring examination, he put on the stand a parade of witnesses hostile to Pearson, Ickes and the Administration.

One of Tydings' stellar performers was Judge Thomas W. Wilson, who had been the Federal Judge in the Virgin Islands, whose own conduct had come in for some criticism and who obviously bore no love for Governor Pearson. As Judge Wilson testified, Senator Tydings interrupted and praised him as one of the finest of men, rendering the judgment that nothing that had happened reflected upon him. This verdict in advance of the evidence sparked Ickes' notoriously short fuse, and he dashed off a statement to Tydings and the press. "Senator Tydings became berserk when I gave out to the newspapers a copy of my letter to him in which I accused him of gross partiality, white-washing Judge Wilson and failure to keep his promise that we could cross-examine witnesses," Ickes wrote in his diary of Thursday, July 11, 1935. "Late in the afternoon he wrote a letter to me that was a perfect tirade. He scolded like a fish wife and made wild charges that cannot be sustained by the facts."

In an entry for the next day, July 12, Ickes continued:

"At Cabinet meeting today the President told about his interview with Senator Tydings yesterday. With great gusto he said that at the very beginning he said to Tydings: 'Millard, if I had been the Secretary of the Interior, I wouldn't have written you that letter.' According to the President, Tydings quite expanded on that suggestion. The President went on, 'Neither would I have given out a statement to the press,' whereupon Tydings could be seen to unfold like a flower. Just as he was thinking as well as possible of himself, the President added: 'No, I would have gone to your office and punched you in the nose.'"

Such was the Senator whom the Democrats had selected to take on Joe McCarthy.

THE WAY MCCARTHY was later to tell it was the way much of America was to see it; his perceptions became a nation's truth. In this version he was the courageous underdog battling a conspiracy so colossal that it embraced virtually every member of the Democratic Party and virtually all of the information media. The communist menace was so pervasive, it had infiltrated every sector of the American Establishment to such a degree that only the poor farm boy from Wisconsin had the temerity to stand against it. To get the full flavor of the myth, it helps to quote at some length from Joe McCarthy himself as he told the story in his subsequent book, *McCarthyism, the Fight for America.* He wrote:

"When the inter-office buzzer across the room on my desk sounded, it seemed as though only ten minutes had passed since I had stretched out on the leather couch in my office after a night's work.

"Actually, an hour had passed since I had asked my office manager to wake me at 10:15 A.M.

"It was now 10:15 A.M.

"This was March 8, 1950.

"In fifteen minutes I was due in the Senate Caucus room to begin testifying before the Tydings Committee . . .

"I quickly shaved and checked through my briefcase to see that the documents, photostats, and other exhibits were all there . . .

"As I walked down the long marble corridors to the Senate Caucus room, I wondered if I would be able to accomplish what I had set out to do.

"The Senate had authorized the Tydings Committee to investigate Communist infiltration of government. The Senate had given the committee power, investigators, and money to run down every lead on Communists in government which I gave them. Today, March 8, 1950, my task was to give the committee the leads which would be a basis for their investigation.

"In the back of my mind there was faintly echoing the chairman's statement, 'Let me have McCarthy for three days in public hearings and he will never show his face in the Senate again.'

"Over two weeks had elapsed since my Senate speech which had forced the creation of the Tydings Committee. Already it had become apparent that this was to be no ordinary investigation. *It was to be a contest between a lone Senator and all the vast power of the federal bureaucracy pin-pointed in and backing up the Tydings Committee.*" (Italics added.)

Through his mind, he wrote, there flashed a memory of his "tail-gunner" days in the South Pacific, and in particular he recalled one extremely hazardous flight in which his task had been to take close-up pictures of Japanese installations. "McCarthy why are you here?" he said he had asked himself. And himself had answered: "Hell, somebody has to do the job. It might as well be me."

Then his mind flashed to those days just before the Tydings hearings when he had spent "ten saddle-sore days" on a "desolate but friendly cattle ranch" in the Colorado hills, relaxing and gathering strength for his great ordeal. "So it was that I walked into the huge, red-carpeted Caucus room on that Wednesday morning more than two years ago," he continued. There, waiting for him, was the committee of his peers, three Democrats and two Republicans, seated behind a long mahogany table. "The Republican members of the committee had not been given counsel," he wrote insinuatingly, ignoring at this point the fact that they shortly were given a counsel of their own choosing, Robert Morris, one of the foremost Congressional committee witch hunters. As McCarthy took his seat, he noticed an inimical, if not positively subversive, press.

". . . Elmer Davis, easy to identify by his heavy black-rimmed glasses, was seated at one end of the table," he wrote. "I remembered that Davis had headed the Office of War Information. Many of the cases I was about to present had once been employees in the OWI under Davis and then had moved into the State Department.

"As I glanced at Davis I recalled that Stanislav Mikolajczyk, one of the anti-Communist leaders of Poland, had warned the State Department, while Davis was head of the OWI, that OWI broadcasts were 'following the Communist line consistently,' and that the broadcasts 'might well have emanated from Moscow itself.'

"There could be no doubt about how Davis would cover the story."

This kind of character assassination of some of the nation's ablest journalists went on and on. At another press table, McCarthy noticed "one of Drew Pearson's men," and he charged that Pearson at one time had had a couple of Communists on his "limited staff," one of whom had written pieces about the House Un-American Activities Committee. "No doubt about how Pearson would cover the story," he concluded. And then there was the nationally syndicated and highly respected columnist, Marquis Childs. "I saw Marquis Childs stop Senator McMahon on his way into the Committee room to chat with him. As I saw Childs with his hand on McMahon's shoulder, I remembered that Childs had defended both Remington and Hiss and had bitterly attacked General MacArthur's headquarters for exposing Communist Agent Agnes Smedley who later was to will her estate to Chu Teh, one of the Chinese Communist leaders." Even the *Christian Science Monitor* did not escape. McCarthy wrote that he saw "Richard L. Strout of the *Christian Science Monitor* shaking the hand of Rob Hall of the Communist *Daily Worker*," and he added: "I was doubly disturbed with the thought that if a columnist for a paper like the *Christian Science Monitor* could so closely follow the Communist line, *no publication and no institution in the entire country could be secure from Communist infiltration.*" (Italics added.)

It was a picture of a journalistic cabal marshaled in awesome phalanx to discredit upstanding Joe McCarthy in his one-man battle against the forces of evil. It was a technique McCarthy was to employ again and again. He always studiously ignored the fact that large and powerful segments of the press supported him and whooped him on. He pictured the dissenting minority as representative of the majority, and he tried to pin the communist label on every critic who questioned his claims. In time even such eminently conservative publications as *Time* magazine and the *Saturday Evening Post* would be accused by McCarthy of following the communist line after they had printed unflattering appraisals of him. No demagogue ever devised a neater ploy. If an isolated critic or publication hit a sensitive nerve, its disclosures were instantly discounted; for, according to McCarthy's rationale, this was exactly what was bound to happen when the press was infiltrated and dominated by dangerous "leftist" elements. In these circumstances, the failure of proof became in itself proof of the existence of conspiracy.

IT WAS MARCH 8, 1950, when McCarthy went before the Tydings committee and read in the faces and attitudes of the journalists there evidence of overwhelming hostility. Senator Tydings presided, backed up on the Democratic side by Senators McMahon and Theodore F. Green, of Rhode Island. The Republican minority consisted of Senators Lodge and Bourke B. Hickenlooper, the conservative Iowan.

It is customary in most Congressional committee investigations to accord the lead-off witness the privilege of making an opening statement, to organize and present his case in his own words to the best of his ability. When he is finished, he is questioned by the committee's counsel and individual members of the committee on the details. But in this case Senator Tydings could not wait. Before McCarthy had a chance to open his mouth, Tydings went on the attack.

The Democrats by this time were well aware of McCarthy's faux pas on February 20 when he had become so ludicrously entangled in his Cases 14 and 41, making the same man a villain in the first and a hero in the second. And so Tydings obviously had decided to harass and embarrass McCarthy at the very beginning. He demanded that McCarthy state whether he proposed to make a charge against "the high State Department official" whom he had accused of using pressure to force witnesses to change their affidavits in Case 14. Could McCarthy name that official? Tydings wondered.

This instant attack brought an instant counterattack from the Republican minority on the committee. Senators Lodge and Hickenlooper shouted protests. Lodge declared that Tydings was following "an amazing procedure," that he was breaking the continuity of McCarthy's testimony and was denying the witness "the ordinary courtesy of being allowed to tell his own story in his own way." Hickenlooper, reminding Tydings that he had said the hearings would be "neither a witch-hunt nor a whitewash," cried out: "A label may have to be attached to this thing if the proceedings go on like they are now!"

Tydings responded with heat that he had "a label" in mind for the Republicans, too, but his retort seemed feeble in contrast to his blunder. Here at the very outset, before a word of testimony had been taken, he had handed the Republicans an ideal propaganda issue—the contention that the Democrats had loaded the dice against McCarthy and that any conclusions to which the Tydings committee might come in the future would constitute "a whitewash."

As for the issue that Tydings had raised, it got all but lost to public view in the acrimonious exchanges between committee members. McCarthy, as he was so often to do, blunted the issue for the moment by temporizing: Wait until tomorrow, he said, and he would handle fully the issue of "the high State Department official." After the hearing, he acknowledged to reporters that he didn't even know the name of the official, but again, using another of his favorite ploys, he shifted the onus from himself to the committee. The name was in the files, he said, and could be easily ascertained by the committee—if the committee had any real desire to get it.

The next day, March 9, featured more bitter wrangling and some of the fanciest footwork by a witness ever seen on Capitol Hill. Tydings continued to hammer hard. If such an official had twisted arms to get witnesses to repudiate their affidavits against a man who was a security risk, it was a vile deed and "a matter of the highest importance," Tydings contended, and it should be pursued at once. Would McCarthy say for the record whether his files contained the name of "the high State Department official?"

McCarthy naturally would not. He dodged and twisted and made so many counteraccusations that he transferred all guilt to the Democrats. He accused Senators Tydings, McMahon and Green of acting as "tools" for the State Department. They weren't interested, he said, in getting "the names of disloyal persons"; all they wanted was the identity of the "loyal Americans" in the department who had given him his information. If he yielded to their demands, he said, "heads would roll" among his informants.

The Democrats protested as the Democrats were always to protest in this era. They had no such intention, they said; what they wanted was to determine whether McCarthy was operating on a basis of facts or guesswork. Wouldn't he, without making the name public, simply state whether the name of such "a high State Department official" existed in his files?

McCarthy said he had "a strong suspicion" of the identity of the official; it was possible that the name was in his files, but "the best way" for the Democrats to get the name was to subpoena the State Department files and find out.

The frustration of the Democratic members of the committee is apparent from the record. McCarthy was more slippery than any eel, and every time they tried to get a simple answer out of him, he squirmed away and imputed to them some lack of Americanism or investigative zeal. Senator McMahon, the only one to attack McCarthy on an issue of basic principle on February 20, grew angrier by the minute; and, at the end of a fruitless cross-examination in which McCarthy had dodged any direct answer as to whether he had the name or not, McMahon snapped:

"I am left with the unfortunate opinion that Senator Mc-Carthy has material in his possession which he refuses to turn over to this committee."

"You are not fooling me," McCarthy shouted. "You want the information so that heads will fall in the State Department.

"I am surprised that this committee would become the tool of the State Department—not seeking to get the names of bad security risks, but seeking rather to find out the names of my informants so they can be kicked out of the State Department tomorrow."

His face and his knuckles white with anger, McMahon replied:

"I am profoundly shocked by the irresponsible speech just made by the Senator from Wisconsin. His imputation of any such motive is something I repudiate and denounce. It is unworthy of any Senator of the United States."

Then, directly facing McCarthy, McMahon admonished:

"When you start making charges of that sort about me, you had better reflect on it—and more than once."

"I have reflected," McCarthy replied imperturbably.

If McMahon had right and logic on his side, McCarthy had gained the propaganda advantage, and his party seized it immediately. Nothing could have pleased the Republicans more at this juncture than the browbeating of McCarthy by the Democrats, and on March 12 Senator Owen Brewster, the ultraconservative Maine Republican, roared to the attack with charges of an impending Tydings committee "whitewash."

Brewster calculated with great precision the minutes—and even seconds—that McCarthy had been allowed to testify freely, and he contrasted this figure with the minutes and seconds during which McCarthy had been "heckled" by Democrats on the committee. Brewster contended that, during his first 250 minutes on the stand, McCarthy had been allowed to testify without interruption for only seventeen minutes and 30 seconds, a mere 7 percent of the time. During the first two days of hearings, he said, McCarthy had been interrupted by the Democrats eighty-five times.

"On at least thirteen occasions," Brewster charged, "Senator McCarthy was forced to plead that he be allowed to answer the question of one Democratic member before being required to answer the question of another Democratic member who had interrupted or heckled him." The result, he said, was that Mc-Carthy "has been forced to spend the overwhelming portion of his time on the witness stand in defending himself against personal insinuations and abuse instead of presenting evidence which the subcommittee is instructed by the Senate of the United States to obtain.

"It is deplorable that a member of the United States Senate, regardless of party affiliation, should be subjected to filibuster tactics by a committee at any time."

The martyrdom—and canonization—of Joseph R. McCarthy had begun.

By all the rules of logic, it would seem that McCarthy most certainly should have begun his prepared presentation by bombarding the Tydings committee at the outset with his strongest case. It is significant then that the very first menace to the security of the republic whose name he dragged from his bulging brief case turned out to be a former municipal court justice in New York City who had had only the most tenuous relationship with the State Department.

This prime McCarthy target was former Judge Dorothy Kenyon. A stocky, strong-jawed woman with wide-set, sparkling eyes, Miss Kenyon was perfect for McCarthy's purposes in one respect, if in no other: she was an activist. In the free-wheeling and healthier atmosphere of the Roosevelt era, she had embraced numerous causes—and in some of them she had brushed shoulders with Communists professing similar concerns. Mc-Carthy and his investigators had catalogued all of these actions that had now become hideous indiscretions; and in his appearance before the Tydings committee on March 8, McCarthy reported in shocked tones that Miss Kenyon had been "affiliated with at least twenty-eight Communist-front organizations."

He did not let the simple charge rest there. "The Communist activities of Miss Kenyon," he told the committee, were "not only deep-rooted but extend back through the years." And he added: "It is inconceivable that this woman could collaborate with a score of organizations dedicated to the overthrow of our form of government by force and violence, participate in their activities, lend her name to their nefarious purposes, and be ignorant of the whole sordid and un-American aspect of their work."

This, then, was the charge. McCarthy was later to add, as a further justification for making it, that Miss Kenyon's case was in his opinion "extremely important in that it will shed considerable light on the workings of our loyalty program." The implication was that Miss Kenyon, despite all of these allegedly subversive associations, had been cleared by the State Department's loyalty procedures for government service—and that this in itself showed how defective those procedures were.

All of this led, of course, to a basic question: Just how did Miss Kenyon influence policy in the State Department? The answer was simple. Miss Kenyon had not been an employee of the State Department at all. Hers had been an honorific appointment; she had been named in 1947 to serve as an American delegate to the United Nations Commission on the Status of Women. Her term had expired at the end of 1949; this had been her only connection with the State Department; it had not involved any high-level formulation of policy; she had not been privy to any foreign policy secrets. And so, as both she and the State Department freely acknowledged, she had never been run through the mill of the department's loyalty screening processes. There was no reason she should have been.

A peppery and outspoken individual, Miss Kenyon replied to McCarthy instantaneously and unequivocally; she called him "an unmitigated liar." And she noted: "Senator McCarthy comes from Wisconsin, sometimes called the state of the great winds. He is a wonderful example."

On another level, perhaps mindful of McCarthy's February 20 pledge that he would make no charge on the Senate floor that he wouldn't make off it, both Miss Kenyon and the American Civil Liberties Union, of which she had been a director since 1931, challenged him to repeat his charges in a forum in which he could be sued. "Senator McCarthy is a coward to take shelter in the cloak of Congressional immunity," Miss Kenyon declared. And Dr. John Haynes Holmes, ACLU chairman, and Patrick

Murphy Malin, ACLU director, dared McCarthy to repeat his charges and called his statements "unworthy of a member of the U.S. Senate." Joe gave no indication that he had heard.

Miss Kenyon demanded and was promptly granted the right to appear before the Tydings committee. She took the stand on the afternoon of March 14, 1950. She had indicated to the press that she hoped McCarthy would be present for a face-to-face confrontation, but this was a meeting that he ducked. He had been present at the morning hearing, reading more charges into the record, but then he vanished. It was simply impossible for him to attend afternoon sessions, he said.

By his absence, McCarthy indicated that he possessed at least some small degree of discretion, for it quickly became apparent that, in the lady judge from New York City, he had drawn a tartar. Miss Kenyon's reply could not have been more forthright. She testified:

"I am not and never have been a Communist. I am not and never have been a fellow-traveler. I am not and never have been a supporter of, or member of, or a sympathizer with any organization known to me to be, or suspected by me of being, controlled or dominated by Communists.

"As emphatically and unreservedly as possible, I deny any connection of any kind or character with communism or its adherents. If this leaves anything unsaid to indicate my total and complete detestation of that political philosophy, it is impossible for me to express my sentiments. I mean my denial to be all-inclusive."

Miss Kenyon described herself as "an independent, liberal, Rooseveltian Democrat" interested in a variety of causes to promote human welfare, and this concern, she conceded, might have led her at times to join organizations "that later proved to be subversive but which at the time seemed to be engaged in activities or dedicated to objectives that I could and did approve." But she had never, she said, continued active in an organization once she got a whiff of communist conniving in its management.

As for the twenty-eight communist front organizations (actually the number was only twenty-four, for McCarthy's arithmetic was again awry), Miss Kenyon acknowledged that she had been affiliated in the past, in one way or another, with twelve. Other alleged associations she could not recall, and in some instances, it appeared, her name had been used on letterheads without her consent.

Some of the organizations with which Miss Kenyon admitted an affiliation dated back to the late 1930s and derived from her opposition, like that of millions of other Americans, to the policy of the Roosevelt Administration and of the British and French governments toward the Spanish Civil War. It seemed to many liberal activists at that time (and the event was to prove them correct) that this policy played into the hands of Hitler and Mussolini, allowing them to overthrow the legitimate Loyalist government of Spain, to set up another Fascist dictatorship, and to take another long stride down the road that led inevitably to World War II.

In this context, Miss Kenyon had been active in such organizations as the Coordinating Committee to Lift the [Spanish] Embargo in 1939 and the Lawyers Committee on American Relations With Spain in 1938 and 1939. Her name had appeared, though she denied any knowledge of it, in an advertisement for the Veterans of the Abraham Lincoln Brigade in the *Daily Worker* in 1940, and as one of the signers of an open letter circulated by the Washington Committee to Lift the Spanish Embargo in 1939. Only one of these organizations, the Veterans of the Abraham Lincoln Brigade, had made the Attorney General's list of "front" organizations—and this not until 1947. The taint of the others depended on findings by either the California Committee on Un-American Activities or the House Un-American Activities Committees in 1944 and 1948.

McCarthy's accusatory list included other organizations with which Miss Kenyon admitted connections, such as the American Committee for Democracy and Intellectual Freedom, the American-Russian Institute, the Conference on Pan-American Democracy, the Consumers' National Federation, the League of Women Shoppers, and the National Council of American-Soviet Friendship. Miss Kenyon's sponsorship of the last-named organization capsuled much of the idiocy of the idea of retroactive heresy. She had joined the council in 1943 during World War II when Russia was our ally and when hopes were high for continued amicable postwar relationships with the Soviet. She had had eminent associates on the board of sponsors. They included: Joseph E. Davies, former ambassador to Moscow and the father-in-law of

Senator Tydings; former Republican Senator Arthur Capper of Kansas; and Democratic Senators James E. Murray of Montana, Claude Pepper of Florida, and Elbert D. Thomas of Utah. When the political climate changed in the postwar era, Miss Kenyon testified, she had severed her connection with the National Council of American-Soviet Friendship about 1946, and in 1949 she had written the organization a strong protest after she found that it was continuing to use her name.

This pattern of joining organizations whose ostensible and laudable aims coincided with hers at times when they were not in any way suspect—and of later severing ties with them when she discovered that communists were worming their way into positions of control—was a thread that ran throughout Miss Kenyon's testimony. One especially striking example dealt with her activities in the American Labor Party in New York. This was a dissident, third-party movement that initially corraled a lot of liberal support but eventually came under communist domination and was destroyed. Miss Kenyon was one of the liberals in the ALP who fought strenuously in 1940 against the increasing communist control of the party; and when that fight failed, she quit.

She offered documentary evidence to prove her contention that in 1939 she had committed the sin of sins for communists by denouncing the Hitler-Stalin Pact. And she had been one of the original members of William Allen White's Committee to Defend America by Aiding the Allies. This again was a stand in diametric opposition to communist policies, for the American Communist Party, adhering to the line laid down in Moscow, vigorously opposed all such aid to the allies in the war against Hitler and demanded American isolation and noninvolvement.

Even more significant had been Miss Kenyon's recent conduct in her United Nations assignment. Her appointment as the American delegate to the Commission on the Status of Women had stemmed from her long and active championship of women's causes, and at meetings of the U.N. commission she had battled vigorously with the Soviet delegate, Mme. Elizavieta A. Popova. Miss Kenyon's attitude was expressed in one speech in 1948 when she told a women's club audience: "Women in Russia undoubtedly have more equality in a greater number of jobs than do American women, but it is the equality of slavery." The Russians had been incensed at this pronouncement, and the Soviet short-wave radio had accused Miss Kenyon of "slandering the Russian people" with "irresponsible drivel."

Such was the woman whom McCarthy had accused of "deep-rooted" communist activities. In her eloquent final summation of her activities and beliefs, Miss Kenyon declared:

"With all the mistakes and errors of judgment which the best of us can and do commit only too frequently, I submit that the record proves without a question that I am a lover of democracy, of individual freedom, and of human rights for everybody, a battler, perhaps a little too much of a battler sometimes, for the rights of the little fellow who gets forgotten or frightened or shunned because of unpopular views . . . The converse of these things: dictatorship, cruelty, oppression and slavery are to me intolerable. I cannot live in their air, I must fight back. This is not perhaps a very wise or prudent way to live, but it is my way."

That it was indeed "her way" was attested in a statement signed by thirteen eminent New York lawyers who had long known Miss Kenyon. They declared that of their "own knowledge," Miss Kenyon "never had the slightest sympathy with communism in any of its forms." The signers included Robert P. Patterson, former Secretary of War, and John W. Davis, the conservative Democrat, Liberty League backer, counsel for Morgan Wall Street interests, and one-time Presidential candidate.

Such was the first McCarthy "case" intended to show dangerous subversion in the State Department. With McCarthy unfortunately unable to attend any afternoon sessions and with Senator Lodge absent, the luckless Senator Hickenlooper was left alone to do battle for his party. He led Miss Kenyon through a long cross-examination about her connections with the various organizations on McCarthy's list, and he taxed her with having committed the unpardonable sin of questioning the justice of the conviction of Alger Hiss. She acknowledged that, in a speech in Troy, N.Y., she had said the Hiss prosecution was "a product of hysteria created by the House Committee on Un-American Activities." She had said further that "in the present temper of the country" it was doubtful that Hiss could obtain a fair trial, and she had charged that there was "not a shred" of direct evidence against him except for the testimony of Whittaker Chambers, an admitted perjurer, and the documents that Chambers had produced. These, she told Senator Hickenlooper, were still her opinions.

In the end, Hickenlooper virtually threw up his hands. There was, he declared, not "the least evidence" or "the least belief" on his part that Miss Kenyon had ever been "in any way subversive or disloyal." But then, trying to salvage something from the disaster, Hickenlooper argued that McCarthy had meant only "to suggest that your membership in organizations later termed subversive was a matter for concern so far as security risks go in the State Department."

Miss Kenyon, who had said in her direct statement that McCarthy's charges had "seriously jeopardized if not destroyed" the reputation of a lifetime, told Hickenlooper that she was trying to keep her temper, but that she had been charged "with a great deal more than that." As, indeed, she had.

This scuttling of the first specific charge made by McCarthy before the Tydings committee should have exposed him, one would have thought. But the Republican Party could not admit of failure; its investment in him was already too great. And McCarthy in his own inimitable way blunted the impact of the Kenyon exposure by smothering it in a blanket of new charges. As Senator Taft had advised, "If one case doesn't work, try another."

THERE IS AN INNATE TENDENCY to sensationalism in the techniques of the American press. It is tied to the drawing-power of eight-column headlines. A charge that is challenging, startling or seemingly earth-shaking becomes "news" and the later exposure of that charge as utterly false and preposterous becomes a let-down of anticipations—and of eight-column headlines. Probably no politician in America ever understood this weakness of the American press better, or took greater advantage of it, than did McCarthy. Every time one of his charges collapsed, he would dig into his bottomless bag of innuendo and come up with new and even more explosive headline material before the truth could catch up with his past charges.

On the same day that McCarthy fired his initial barrage at Miss Kenyon, for instance, he injected in his testimony before the Tydings committee, almost as an aside, a name so prestigious that it was certain to make headlines even after Miss Kenyon's case had been laid quietly to rest. Promising darkly that he would deal with the gentleman more fully later, he mentioned Professor Philip C. Jessup, U.S. Ambassador at Large.

In a one-sentence reference, McCarthy denounced Ambassador Jessup as having "an unusual affinity . . . for Communist causes." Jessup, he declared, was "now formulating top-flight policy in the Far East affecting half the civilized world." And, finally, he tarred Jessup as having been a sponsor of the American-Russian Institute, an organization later adjudged subversive by the Attorney General. This was McCarthy's first reference to a diplomat whom he was to hound for years, comparing him on more than one occasion to the man whom Republicans labeled the "arch-traitor," Alger Hiss.

In attacking Jessup, however obliquely, McCarthy was aiming his darts with unerring instinct, in terms of the building public hysteria. Like Hiss, Jessup was an intellectual who epitomized the suave university types who had been brought to Washington by the New Deal. In addition, Jessup was a prominent figure who had filled several key roles in the State Department and so fitted the prerequisites of a propaganda that pictured just such men as the ones who had caused all our troubles—who had betrayed us in the Far East.

Superficially, Philip Caryl Jessup seemed tailored as a perfect target. When one probed deeper, there were complexities and contradictions; like most men Jessup did not fit neatly under one all-inclusive ideological label. But this was not so instantly apparent; and to millions of Americans in the perfervid atmosphere of the Nightmare Decade, it never did become apparent.

Jessup was a professor of international law at Columbia University. During leaves of absence from his university post, he had served in a variety of high-level capacities in the State Department. He had been a prominent figure on the board of directors of the prestigious Institute of Pacific Relations, a research organization highly regarded for its expertise in Far Eastern affairs—and one that had now become highly suspect as a vehicle of communist propaganda. Capping all this, as if events were conspiring with McCarthy, Jessup was abroad on a fact-finding tour for the State Department at the very moment that McCarthy injected his name into the Tydings hearings. He had left on December 30, 1949, on a trip that had taken him to Japan, Korea, Formosa, Hong-Kong, the Philippines, Vietnam, Thailand, India, Pakistan, Afghanistan, Indonesia and Singapore.

Apprised of McCarthy's attack, Ambassador Jessup flew back from Europe, arriving at New York International Airport at 7:30 A.M. on March 15. He declared that there was "no substance at all" to McCarthy's charges of communist influence in the State Department, then departed by train for Washington. Five days later, he took the stand before the Tydings committee; there, he denounced McCarthy and repudiated his charges.

Two principal themes ran through Jessup's defense. He called McCarthy's charges "false and irresponsible" and declared that they showed "a shocking disregard" of the national interest; and he argued that he should be judged, not on the basis of any associations, but on the basis of what he had actually *done* throughout his entire career. In stressing the first point, Jessup argued:

"If Senator McCarthy's innuendoes were true, the representatives of foreign governments with whom I spoke would be entitled to believe that my statements to them were deceitful and fraudulent. They would be entitled to believe that no confidence should be placed in the declarations which I made on behalf of our government. If it were true that the President and the Secretary of State had sent on such a mission a person who was a traitor to his own Government they might well feel that they could place no confidence in the statements made by any of the representatives of the United States abroad.

"It may be relatively unimportant whether the character of a single American citizen is blackened and his name is brought into disrepute, but in the present serious situation of international relations throughout the world today it is a question of the utmost gravity when an official holding the rank of Ambassador at Large of the United States of America is held up before the eyes of the rest of the world as a liar and a traitor. I am aware, Mr. Chairman, that Senator McCarthy has not used those words. But if his insinuations were true, those words would certainly be appropriate."

In such fashion Jessup laid down the gage of battle; so he drew the larger issue—that of patriotism. It was an appeal that was to be scorned.

Taking up his own defense, Jessup detailed his family history. His ancestors had come here from England in the seventeenth century. One of his great-grandfathers had been a delegate to the 1860 Republican National Convention that had nominated Abraham Lincoln and had been chairman of the committee that drafted the platform on which Lincoln ran and was elected. Jessup's father had been a lawyer in New York City and a lay leader in the Presbyterian Church. Jessup himself had served as a private in the 107th Infantry in France in World War I. After the war, he had worked for a time as assistant to the president of the First National Bank of Utica, N. Y.; he had been superintendent of the Sunday School of the First Presbyterian Church; and he had commanded the local post of the American Legion. He was still a member of the Legion.

His experience as a soldier in World War I had had a profound effect upon him, and the revulsion at the horrors of war that was to lead America into the isolationism of the 1920s developed in Jessup "an overwhelming desire to devote my life to promoting the cause of international peace." Resigning from his bank job, he entered Columbia University Law School, later studied at Yale, served in the State Department and began to lecture at Columbia.

His mentor throughout the early stages of his career had been Elihu Root, the eminent Republican statesman whom he had originally met while a student at Hamilton College. He had accompanied Root as his assistant to one Geneva conference on the World Court, and he had later, with full access to Root's papers and memoranda, written Root's official biography. During Herbert Hoover's Administration, he had served for nine months as the legal adviser to the American Ambassador to Cuba; and in the succeeding years, in different administrations, he had filled a variety of roles. Throughout this part of his career, Jessup had been the technician, the man with expert knowledge, one of the many faceless consultants who operate in the background, beyond the public ken. But in 1948 all this changed.

Russia's Andrei Vishinsky was then the terror of the United Nations General Assembly. A loud-roaring orator, he out-shouted and out-bluffed Western diplomats until neutral delegates described him as "a matador fighting with cows." Then Jessup took his seat as the American delegate, a lanky, rumpled, professorial figure; and almost at once, he tangled with Vishinsky in a debate so bitter that it quickly became apparent the Russian had met his match. The Soviet press responded with its usual diatribes, listing Jessup among the "capitalistic warmongers."

On the Far Eastern tour on which he had been when McCarthy attacked him, he had denounced Russian foreign policy with such vigor that on March 3, 1950 (just five days before McCarthy's denunciation), *Izvestia* had erupted in frothing rage:

"At a press conference arranged on Feb. 23 in Delhi, Jessup set out to obtain a change of view in Indian public opinion. Jessup brought into action all kinds of means: flattery and the publicizing of American 'assistance to backward regions' and most of all, of course, slanderous fabrications against the U.S.S.R. . . . in general, Jessup tried with all his might, but he had little success. The imperialistic aggressive character of the policy of the United States throughout the world, and in Asia in particular, is so evident that no hypocritical speeches and anti-Communist philippics could hide it."

This put Jessup in the unique position of having been denounced almost simultaneously by Joe McCarthy for his "unusual affinity" for communist causes and by *Izvestia* for his slanderous anticommunist statements.

That such a man could have been the tool of Soviet policy made still less sense when Jessup read into the record encomiums from two of America's most distinguished leaders, men who had known him long and well and who had had opportunity to observe him in action at close hand—General George C. Marshall, former Secretary of State, and General Dwight D. Eisenhower, then president of Columbia University.

Writing that he was "shocked and distressed" at the attack made on Jessup, General Marshall added: "Throughout your entire service with me while I was Secretary of State you were clearly outstanding as a representative of the Government both as to your masterful presentations and the firmness of your opposition to all Soviet or Communist attacks or pressures."

General Eisenhower added this tribute: "Your long and distinguished record as a scholar and a public servant has won for you the respect of your colleagues and of the American people as well. No one who has known you can for a moment question the depth of sincerity of your devotion to the principles of Americanism."

This was the record—the record of a diplomat who had championed American causes in face-to-face showdowns with some of the toughest delegates the Soviet Union had sent to the United Nations. He had faced them down over the Berlin blockade, which he had denounced as a naked use of force that threatened the peace of the world; he had condemned Soviet intrigues in China for their "continuation of the Tsarist-Russian imperialism in the Far East." What, then, was left? The malicious interpretation of a few associations in the long life of a busy public figure.

McCarthy, in his original denunciation of Jessup, had harped on just one association, describing the ambassador as a "sponsor" of the American-Russian Institute. This turned out to be a wild exaggeration, if it was not, indeed, a deliberate misrepresentation. Jessup had never "sponsored" the institute. He had on two occasions, in 1944 and 1946, permitted his name to be used, along with those of hundreds of other eminent Americans, as a sponsor of two *dinners* the institute had given. The purpose of the second dinner had been to pay posthumous tribute to President Franklin D. Roosevelt. Furthermore, as Jessup pointed out in his testimony, the Attorney General had expressly excluded the American-Russian Institute of New York from the original lists of subversive organizations and did not include it until April 21, 1949.

McCarthy later broadened his attack against Jessup, directing his fire at the Institute of Pacific Relations, with which Jessup's relationship had been much closer. IPR had been organized in Honolulu for the express purpose of promoting understanding of Far Eastern problems. It had been supported financially by some of the largest American corporations and foundations, and it had been international in character, deriving additional assistance from other nations and business firms of other nationalities in the Pacific area. Its finance committee had been headed at various times by such ideological irreproachables as Henry Luce, publisher of *Life*, *Time* and *Fortune*; Juan Trippe, the presiding genius of Pan American Airways; and William Herrod, who later became president of International General Electric Company. If there were any validity to the theory of guilt by association, these corporate emperors should have been considered suspect, too.

It is often argued that extremely busy executives like these simply do not have the time needed for close supervision of the inner mechanisms of the organizations they create to do their good works. This task inevitably devolves upon a working staff, which becomes a semiautonomous bureaucracy of its own, and McCarthy's case against Jessup was that, over the months and the years, Jessup had functioned on just such a crucial, intimate, directorial level. Not only had he been on the IPR board of trustees from 1933 to 1946, but in 1939 and 1940 he had been chairman of the institute's American Council; from 1939 to 1942, he had been chairman of its Pacific Council; and in 1944, he had been chairman of the IPR's Research Advisory Committee.

In these various roles, Jessup had been thrown into close association with Frederick Vanderbilt Field, who was secretary of the American Council at the same time that Jessup was its chairman. Field was certainly a Communist, and he left the American Council in 1940 over Jessup's strenuous protests to set up a Communist Party front, the American Peace Mobilization. There can be no question from the evidence that Jessup had a high opinion of Field, and it is clear that when the IPR ran into deficits, despite hefty contributions from the Carnegie and Rockefeller Foundations and similar organizations, Field became its financial angel of last resort. What this established was that Philip Jessup certainly had worked in close harness with a man who later turned out to have been a Communist. The vital question, of course, remained: Did Jessup know this? There was never a shadow of proof that he did. Even Professor Louis Budenz, a former Communist turned informer and a most obliging witness before Congressional committees in identifying their chosen targets as one-time Reds, shied away from making any such accusation against Jessup. "I never heard him mentioned as a member of the party," Budenz testified on one occasion. And he added: "Now, you must understand, I do not know whether Dr. Jessup knew fully what Mr. Field intended to do . . ."

A great effort was subsequently made to show that articles published in IPR's magazines, *Pacific Affairs* and *Far East-*

ern Survey, were heavily weighted on the side of communist propaganda. One technique involved the tabulation of the number of writers later identified by informers before Congressional committees as having been secret communists and the drawing up of a score card, like at a baseball game, to show the number of articles these suspects had contributed and the percentage of the magazines' contents this represented. Another method involved an analysis of articles on the basis of their attitude toward the China of Chiang Kai-shek. Any questioning of Chiang's perfection became per se a proof of ideological waywardness. Ideas, of course, do not lend themselves to a percentage game like a baseball batting average. Ideas are fluid, involving countless intricacies of fact and logic and judgment. And so it is not unusual in the real world—as distinguished from the fantasy world of the propagandist—to encounter situations in which the ultrarightist and the radical leftist are taking identical stands on a given issue. Perhaps no career illustrated this point better than that of Philip Jessup.

Ironically, one of the least appreciated and least publicized facts of the Jessup case was that Jessup had been an America Firster. Not only had he belonged to this ultraconservative, isolationist organization in its early prewar days, but he had remained a member of the America First Committee for a long time. There had been, of course, a period when the aims of America First and the Communist Party coincided. During the time of the Hitler-Stalin Pact, America First stood for isolationism —and so did the Communists. After Hitler attacked Russia, the Communist Party line whirled like a weather vane in a high wind, and a shrill clamor arose for American intervention. But, significantly enough, Jessup didn't change. He remained with America First, advocating American noninvolvement.

It should be obvious that the only sane way to judge any man is on the basis of his entire career, not on isolated friendships or associations. Dwight Eisenhower and George Marshall, who had known the total Jessup, not McCarthy's piecemeal Jessup, had rendered this kind of judgment.

But the Republicans and McCarthy would not let up. They gnawed at the Jessup case like a dog on his favorite bone. At the Tydings hearings, Senator Lodge, as usual, was absent, but Senator Hickenlooper was there, yapping like a terrier at the witness. When Jessup denounced the theory of guilt by association, Hickenlooper hedged by demanding whether there was not "something to the doctrine of risk by association." Jessup retorted: "By this theory, the wartime photographs of American G.I.'s shaking hands with Russian troops in Germany would mean that the G.I.'s were guilty of communism by association."

Not getting very far with this line, Hickenlooper turned to the Hiss case. He appeared shocked that Jessup should have appeared as a character witness for Alger Hiss.

"My understanding," said Jessup, "is that there is a very simple part of our American system under which a person accused is entitled to have testimony regarding his reputation."

"Are you of the same opinion now about Hiss?" Hickenlooper demanded.

"The testimony I gave," Jessup replied, "was to his reputation. I see no reason to alter the statement I made at that time . . ."

The Tydings committee exonerated Jessup, but this meant nothing to McCarthy. For the next year and a half, he went up and down the country, attacking Jessup in speech after speech. "Why does Jessup always join Communist fronts? Why not anti-Communist organizations?" he shouted. The truth, of course, was that Jessup belonged to many organizations as American as apple pie—the American Bar Association, the Foreign Policy Association, the American Philosophical League and the American Legion, to name just a few. The American Legion Post in Utica, N.Y., which Jessup had commanded but which even McCarthy did not contend had been subverted by that experience, was so outraged that it passed a resolution defending Jessup and declaring that McCarthy's "reckless and despicable conduct in this instance cannot be condoned by any right-thinking American."

This almost unprecedented outburst by a Legion post was followed by an equally remarkable scene on the floor of the U.S. Senate. In a speech on August 9, 1951, McCarthy had charged that Jessup had helped to defend Alger Hiss and had "negotiated with the Russians much as Hiss negotiated with them at Yalta." Senator Lehman responded with an acid indictment, saying that "the time was long past when we should have rebuked" McCarthy, and adding: "Jessup has served his country well [and] . . . does not deserve the shabby and dastardly treatment accorded him on the Senate floor under the cloak of Senatorial immunity."

Republican sensibilities were instantly outraged by the application of the word "dastardly" to one of their members, and Minority Leader Kenneth Wherry shouted that Lehman should be silenced for violating the rules of the Senate club by "impugning the motives" of a fellow Senator.

"I move to amend my remarks by striking out 'dastardly' and substituting 'cowardly,'" Lehman shot back.

Such oratorical fireworks served as little more than a prelude to the final showdown in the Jessup drama. In October, 1951, President Truman nominated Jessup to serve on the American delegation at the United Nations under Warren R. Austin, a Republican stalwart and former Senator from Vermont. Jessup had been approved for diplomatic posts five times without objection, but now McCarthy made his appointment a personal issue, denouncing Jessup again.

A subcommittee of the Senate Foreign Relations committee sat for days, going over McCarthy's so-called evidence. McCarthy held the floor for more than ten hours, rehashing his charges. The committee was by turns shocked and incredulous. Its bewilderment became apparent after McCarthy had recited again his "evidence" about Jessup's sponsorship of two dinners of the American-Russian Institute. McCarthy said he wasn't prepared to determine the extent of Jessup's affiliation with the institute beyond these two instances.

"I have given you the evidence," he told Senator J. William Fulbright, the Arkansas Democrat who was later to become a rallying point for opposition to the Vietnam war. "You can evaluate it."

"What evidence?" Fulbright wondered. "You can put together a number of zeroes and still not arrive at the figure one."

"If you consider belonging to an organization cited as a Communist front is a zero, then I'm wasting my time," McCarthy raged.

After more hours of this, Fulbright turned to his colleagues and said:

"This is perfectly ridiculous. Are all of his cases just as flimsy?"

McCarthy, sweating from his exertions, red-faced at being treated so cavalierly, turned almost savagely on his fellow Senators.

"Men of little minds," he snarled, "are trying to make this a political issue."

"You wouldn't try to do anything like that, would you?" Fulbright wondered in his characteristic mild, professorial tone tinged with sarcasm.

The audience tittered, and McCarthy, further enraged, lashed out wildly: "I can't keep all the details in my head," he said furiously. "I'm dealing with too many of these slimy creatures to do that."

The "slimy creatures" remark obviously applied to Philip Jessup, and there was a moment of stunned silence in which even McCarthy apparently appreciated that he had gone too far. He flushed, sputtered and qualified with the lame excuse: "I am referring to Communist-front organizations, not individuals."

As he left the stand, Senator Fulbright declared icily: "I want to say for the record that in all my experience in the Senate, never have I seen a more arrogant or rude witness before any committee."

It seemed obvious that McCarthy had all but scuttled his own cause against Jessup, and so he sent out an appeal for help. In answer to his drowning cry, up popped Harold Stassen. The one-time Governor of Minnesota, ex-glamour boy of young Republicanism, perennial candidate for President—and any other office that might be up for grabs—owed McCarthy a political debt for help in the Republican primary in Wisconsin in 1948. And so now he attempted to verify McCarthy's charges about Jessup's having followed the "Communist line."

As proof, Stassen recalled that the late Senator Arthur Vandenberg, the Michigan Republican who had been one of the godfathers of the bipartisan foreign policy, had told him that Jessup had recommended stopping aid to Nationalist China at a White House conference on February 5, 1949. Leaving aside the issue of whether such a recommendation would have demonstrated communist leanings or just plain common sense, the embarrassment to Stassen and to McCarthy lay in the quickly demonstrated fact that U.N. records showed beyond cavil that Jessup had been in New York attending to U.N. business at the exact time he was supposed to have been offering subversive advice to the White House. Stassen's second item of proof turned out to be no better than the first. He recalled attending a State Department panel conference at which, he said, Jessup sounded to him like a procommunist; but when the State Department promptly released a verbatim transcript of the conference, newsmen examining it failed to find any indication of Jessup's alleged waywardness.*

Against this tissue of innuendoes was the solid endorsement of Jessup, not only by Marshall and Eisenhower, but by Warren Austin and General Lucius D. Clay. Austin told the committee that Jessup was a "powerful protagonist" of American interests, "with no traces of Communist sympathies." And General Clay, who was occupation commander in Germany, said that Jessup had taken a "firm" and "realistic approach toward the Russian problem," especially at the time of the Berlin blockade.

When the subcommittee hearings concluded, Senator H. Alexander Smith, a New Jersey Republican, complimented Jessup and told him: "I have known you too long to have any doubts about your loyalty or integrity. I know darn well that you are not a Communist."

By late 1951, however, Joe McCarthy had become a power in the nation; he aroused the wildest passions against anyone whom he attacked; his irate followers deluged the Senate with protest mail. Fellow Senators opposed him at their own peril. When the Senate subcommittee voted on Jessup's confirmation, three of the five Senators voted against him. And the swing vote was cast by none other than H. Alexander Smith, the man who had had no doubt about Jessup's loyalty.

---

* A striking example of the reliance on falsehood in this case was seen in the final flareup over Jessup. Seth Richardson, by this time, had been succeeded as chairman of the Federal Loyalty Review Board by another impeccable Republican, former Senator Hiram Bingham, of Connecticut. On October 2, 1951, McCarthy told reporters Bingham had assured him that, if the Loyalty Review Board had possessed the authority to "turn him [Dr. Jessup] down as a bad security risk, it would have done so." Joe's source instantly disowned him. "I never told McCarthy any such thing," Bingham said. He added that since his review board had considered Jessup's case, he had had "no communication with Senator McCarthy" of any kind. He had never, he said, expressed an opinion of his own to anyone about Dr. Jessup as a security risk. (See *The New York Times*, Oct. 3, 1951.)

PART THREE

The Opening Salvos

11

The Case of Owen Lattimore

IN MID-MARCH, 1950, after the folly of the Dorothy Kenyon case, after the fumbling first attack on Philip Jessup, McCarthy desperately needed the big one—the case that would justify his sensational charges that Communists were formulating policy in the State Department. In this exigency, he began to toy with the name of Professor Owen J. Lattimore; and as the need intensified for a new headline to cover up the fact that yesterday's had not quite panned out, Lattimore grew in menace until he became, in McCarthy's version, the subversive Svengali of American diplomacy.

The frenzy of those days was captured by Jack Anderson and Ronald W. May:

"Senator Joe McCarthy put on his act under the white-domed Capitol, a Big-Top in marble and pillars.

"The crowd, subdued by the stately environment, would surge into the hearing room; Joe, arriving at the last minute, would walk into an electrical storm of exploding flashbulbs; reporters would scramble for seats at the long picnic tables spread with yellow scratch paper; the newsreel and television crews would focus their photographic field artillery on the target area; klieg lights would produce sudden sunrises and sunsets in the room, plunging the proceedings into alternate glare and gloom. And Joe, in the role of the accuser, would be ready to deliver another dramatic, finger-pointing harangue on the subject of Communist spies and international intrigue."

In this atmosphere, on March 13, McCarthy first attacked Lattimore, then director of the Walter Hines Page School of International Relations at Johns Hopkins University. A frequent consultant of the State Department, Lattimore was at that moment with a United Nations mission in Afghanistan, discussing a program for Point Four economic aid. McCarthy's initial charge was that Lattimore had a "pro-Communist record going back many years."

His principal specific charge, like that against Jessup, centered on Lattimore's role as a trustee for the Institute of Pacific Relations, his editorship of its magazine, *Pacific Affairs,* and his association there with such "pro-Communists as Frederick Vanderbilt Field and Philip Jaffe." In addition, Lattimore had delivered a speech on February 11, 1941, before the Washington Committee for Aid to China, an organization later termed subversive by the House Un-American Activities Committee. Another speaker at this meeting, McCarthy added, had been Field.

"Here again," he intoned, "we have the old familiar pattern of a member of the important policy-making group of the State Department collaborating with known Communists under the sponsorship of organizations officially declared subversive."

At first glance these charges did not seem much different from those McCarthy had been making against others. But now in mid-March things were getting rough for McCarthy, and something more spectacular was required. Despite his February 20 pledge to get out of the Senate if he ever failed to repeat off the floor charges he had made on it, he refused to name names on an

NBC television program, where he did not have Congressional immunity to protect him from libel. Also, he was embroiled with the Tydings committee, which kept insisting that he put up or shut up—that he give it the entire list of names that he had claimed to have back in February. McCarthy kept dodging such precise details; and, perhaps to camouflage his evasiveness, began to feed the press hints of a super bombshell to come.

He was about ready to name "the top Russian espionage agent in the United States." This was the man, he suggested darkly, who had been the "boss" of Alger Hiss "in the espionage ring in the State Department." The press began to feature this impending sensation; reporters panted for the name—for heaven's sake, Joe, *the name*. He toyed with them until he had reaped all the mileage possible from his mystery. Richard Rovere, who was on the scene trying to evaluate these tantalizing intimations, was later to write: "I have always been convinced that when he first talked about his 'top espionage agent,' he hadn't the slightest notion which unfortunate name on his list would be singled out for this distinction." Finally, in an off-the-record press conference —a forum in which nothing he said could be attributed to him and it would be difficult to nail him for libel—McCarthy confided to a group of journalists the precious secret. With Jack Anderson, the colleague of columnist Drew Pearson, he went even further. He not only told Anderson that his "top Russian spy" was Professor Owen J. Lattimore, but he embellished this revelation with a hair-raising story about four Russian spies who had landed on the Atlantic coast by submarine and then had gone straight to Lattimore for their orders.

McCarthy appeared so confident of his case that he finally —and on the record—plunged beyond the border of sane retreat, declaring: "I am willing to stand or fall on this one. If I am shown to be wrong on this, I think the sub-committee would be justified in not taking my other cases too seriously." It was a bit of bravura like his earlier pledge to get out of the Senate.

THE ATTACK ON LATTIMORE, even more so than that on Jessup, was double-barreled: there was the smearing of the individual, and the smearing of the policy-making machinery of the State Department. As Jessup had told the Tydings committee, the harm done to individuals by McCarthy's shotgun charges was serious enough, but that done to the nation was infinitely worse. Probably no case illustrated this better than that of Owen Lattimore.

In striking at Lattimore, McCarthy was playing to one of the most paranoid streaks in the American psyche—the delusional trauma over the "loss" of China. Owen Lattimore became the symbol of this frustration and failure; and he came to represent to the public all the diplomats in the Far Eastern branch of the State Department.

The cost to the nation has been incalculable. Only belatedly —and perhaps a bit shamefacedly—have some Americans begun to acknowledge that in the State Department in the 1940s we possessed a Far Eastern elite corps that was the envy of many foreign chancelleries. It was composed of career men who knew Asia probably better than any other single group in the West. Many of these experts were the sons of American missionaries who had spent their lives in China; several had been reared and educated in China and knew the language, the people, and the problems of that huge, war-wracked land.

Owen Lattimore was one of these valuable men. His entire life had been bound up with the problems of the Orient. He spent his first twelve years in China, then went to school in Switzerland and England. In 1919 he returned to Shanghai and went into the import-export business. But he was an intellectual, not a businessman, and soon turned to travels and journalism. In 1926 and 1927 he explored the little-known interior of Central Asia, an experience that led to his first books—*Desert Road to Turkestan* and *High Tartary*. He lectured to the Royal Central Asian Society in London and the Royal Geographical Society, which gave him an award for his explorations.

After graduate work in anthropology at Harvard, he returned to Asia, traveling in Manchuria and Inner Mongolia. He was in Jehol in 1933 and saw the Japanese overrun 100,000 square miles of territory in ten days. He was in Peking when the Japanese cut through Northern China. These experiences made him passionately anti-Japanese. In reaction to Japanese ruthlessness, he began to look to Chiang Kai-shek as the best hope for China, the one national figure about whom the prostrate nation might rally.

In 1938 he became the director of the Walter Hines Page School of International Relations at Johns Hopkins University. Because of his expertise, he was used more and more frequently as an adviser. In 1941, before the American involvement in World War II, he was named personal American aide to Chiang Kai-shek, with the approval of President Roosevelt. (At this point, he was in the personal employment of Chiang—not of the State Department.) After Pearl Harbor he resigned and was made Deputy Director of the Office of War Information, in charge of Pacific affairs. In this capacity he traveled to Chungking in the late summer of 1942, renewed relations with Chiang, and es-. corted Madame Chiang to America when he returned to San Francisco in November. In the latter days of the war, he accompanied Vice President Henry Wallace to Siberia and China. After the war he was consulted from time to time, but he was never attached in any official capacity to the State Department. His role had been that of an independent scholar.

The knowledge of men like Lattimore should have been considered invaluable. It was all to become suspect; it was all to be sacrificed. The men who possessed it were to be exiled to private life, and in the vacuum of knowledge so created, America was to fumble like a blindfolded giant, applying the rigid policies of a militaristic anticommunism to alien cultures where the problems were political, economic and nationalistic in nature; we were to act from ignorance, self-delusion, and fanaticism; and in this repression of reality we were to progress inevitably into the costly folly of Vietnam.*

* James C. Thompson, Jr., a Far East expert and assistant professor of history at Harvard, served in the White House and the State Department from 1961–66, throughout the period of the formulation of our Vietnam policy. In the April, 1968, *Atlantic Monthly*, he wrote a devastating critique, "How Could Vietnam Happen?" It emphasized that "a first and central ingredient" of our fatally mistaken policy "was the legacy of the 1950s—by which I mean the so-called 'loss of China,' the Korean War, and the Far East policy of Secretary of State [John Foster] Dulles." He explained that the State Department's Bureau of Far Eastern Affairs "had been purged of its best China expertise, and of far-sighted, dispassionate men, as a result of McCarthyism." The bureau that remained had become "the most rigid and doctrinaire" of State's regional divisions. Its resident officials held fixedly to the idea of the containment and isolation of China. "Another aspect of the legacy [of the 1950s] was the special vulnerability and sensitivity of the Democrats on Far East policy issues. The memory of the McCarthy era was still very sharp, and Kennedy's margin of victory [in the 1960 election] was too thin . . ." The result was Kennedy's adoption of a more aggressive policy in Vietnam, and "the experts, the doubters and dissenters" who might have

The tragedy that must be the lot of any nation that embraces such unreality is perhaps best illustrated by a look at the expressed views of Owen Lattimore.

In 1949 Little, Brown & Co. published *The Situation in Asia* by Professor Lattimore. Its opening paragraphs, twenty years later and in light of the disaster of Vietnam, read almost like prophecy:

"Asia is out of control. From Suez to the Western Pacific we face one problem after another, in one country after another, which we cannot settle either by an American decision or by joint action with countries that we consider our allies.

"From the Arab countries to China, the old forms of ascendancy, protectorate, or rule cannot be reasserted by military action. We have already had experience enough to prove that the more modern and highly equipped is the military force that is used, the more expensive is the failure eventually inflicted on it by cheap methods of guerrilla warfare that require no industrial support . . .

"Nor can Asia be starved or coerced economically. Everywhere in Asia the local resources are ample enough to enable the people to survive without being more miserable even if they resist military coercion; and that degree of misery is one which they are prepared to endure . . ."

The collapse of the colonial system in World War II had led to a great wave of nationalism in which millions were caught up, regardless of party. As a result of the war, many of these former colonial subjects had obtained armaments; the old power brokers had lost face; and new men had arisen who voiced the national aspirations of their people and wanted a share of power for themselves.

"Both in reacting emotionally to moral issues and in making what we think are hardheaded decisions in power politics, Americans are the most unrealistic political thinkers in the world,"

---

restrained him were gone. Their departure had cast an inhibiting pall over their successors. "Career officers in the State Department, and especially those in the field, had not forgotten the fate of their World War II colleagues who wrote with frankness from China and were later pilloried by Senate committees for critical comments on the Chinese Nationalists. Candid reporting on the strengths of the Viet Cong and the weakness of the Diem government was inhibited by memory . . ."

Lattimore wrote. "Until we get some of the illusions shaken out of us, we are certain to go on stumbling into the same kind of mess that we stumbled into in China in 1948 . . ."

In an Asia "out of control," he saw two major forces at work —"nationalism and revolution. Of these two, nationalism is the more elemental force. To a large extent, nationalism is 'revolutionary' simply because the change is from subjection to independence and from arbitrary government by imposed authority to forms of government that are made possible only by 'the consent of the governed' and at least the crude beginnings of representative government."

The Russians, as "professional revolutionaries," were ideally situated to take advantage of such nationalistic drives and upheavals; we were not. We had found no way to make our form of democracy a revolutionary ideal. "Unless we can learn to match the Russians in professional skill in the art of influencing revolutions which we cannot control, the advantage will be with them." But, again most perceptively, Lattimore foresaw that Russia would "not be able to stroll in and nonchalantly take over" China.

Further, Lattimore wrote that "in the social transformation that accompanies the achievement of national independence, the bitterest struggle has not been between the capitalists and the proletariat but between feudal landholders and the peasantry . . ." In Asia, only possession of the land counted, and the land was held in fief by great feudal baronies, capable of grinding down the peasants and tenant farmers. Land reform, the desire to throw off such long servitude, became the crucial issue in a revolutionary time.

But the trouble was that America had placed its power on the side of the ruling class of the repressive feudal system. This, as Lattimore saw it, was the situation in Korea, and some two years in advance of the event he predicted with uncanny accuracy the outbreak and the course of the Korean War.

In South Korea he saw that we had affiliated ourselves with those forces that had collaborated with the Japanese during the Japanese occupation. Only token land reform had been undertaken, with most of the arable land finding its way again into the hands of feudal landlords and collaborators who manipulated the power structure. "If there is to be a civil war," Lattimore wrote, "South Korea would not be able to subdue North Korea without a great deal more American help than is now available. North Korea would be able to overrun South Korea without Russian help, unless stopped by American combat troops . . ."

Regarding the situation in Indo-China, Lattimore was equally perceptive. Ho Chi Minh, he wrote, derived his strength from the fact that he was the hero of his country's struggle for national independence, not from the fact that he was a Communist. "All French efforts to split up the nationalist movement by isolating the Communists have failed; there are not enough Communists to isolate," he wrote, adding:

"The hardest of hard facts in Indo-China is that the country will become independent . . . Reconquest of Indo-China cannot be made a national cause in France, and for America the diversion of military forces needed to reconquer the country for France would be a military absurdity and a political impossibility."

F R O M O U R P R E S E N T P E R S P E C T I V E , we can appreciate Owen Lattimore's foresight. But in 1949 the truths he perceived were rejected. The failure of the American policy to "hold" China against communism was a terrible psychological blow to Americans. Here was abject defeat where only complete success would have been acceptable. There was virtually no popular understanding of the complexities of China, of the internal factional morass in which we had involved ourselves. American information media could not have cared less until suddenly the collapse and fall of Chiang made our "loss" of China a headline item. Then the public platform was immediately preempted by the screamers and shouters, not the men of reason. They gave a quick and easy explanation: great, all-powerful America, the nation that could do literally *anything*, must have been betrayed. And it followed from this formula that anyone like Lattimore who had foreseen the defeat—and had argued against the commitments that made it so damaging—became automatically suspected of treason.

The entire thrust of the Lattimore episode can only be understood, then, by a look at the vital Chinese realities on which these Far East experts had argued American policy must be based. For an entire century, China had been a nation in name only. From 1840 until the end of World War II, Britain, France and Russia tore into this ancient and defenseless empire, immobilized in its Confucian isolationism; and later, Japan, Germany and the United States joined in the orgy of economic exploitation.

This century of Western piracy victimized one of the world's proudest peoples. The Chinese had only contempt for the Western "barbarians" who, because they possessed new sources of industrial and military strength, had raped their land. Their hatred of the white, imperialistic foreigners led to the bloody Boxer rebellion of 1900; and when this was finally quelled by Western military might, the days of the Manchu dynasty were numbered. In 1912 the Manchus, who had ruled China for 268 years, were toppled, and the Republic of China was proclaimed. But the republic, like the nation, existed in name more than in fact. Independent war lords ruled vast areas; the Communists began to contend for power; and foreign invaders continued their ruthless conquests. The Japanese were the last and most hated of these foreign conquerors. They tore into China in 1937, seized the vast area of Manchuria north of the Great Wall, and drove ever deeper into the vitals of China, their clear intent eventual subjugation of all China. During the entire thirty-seven years from the fall of the Manchus in 1912 to the Communist conquest of 1949, there was unending civil and foreign war.

During these decades of upheaval two leaders emerged who were to polarize the contending forces in China—Chiang Kai-shek, the disciple of Sun Yat-sen, and Mao Tse-tung, the disciple of Marx and Lenin. Sun Yat-sen was the middle-class, intellectual revolutionary who had inspired the overthrow of the Manchus. But in seeking to consolidate power in China, he had turned to the only source of help available to him—the Soviet Russia of Joseph Stalin. A pact was concluded whereby Communists, as individuals, were permitted to join Sun Yat-sen's Kuomintang (National People's Party), and Russia, in return, pledged herself to aid Sun in his effort to unite his nation. As one result of this agreement, Sun's young military aide Chiang Kai-shek was sent to Russia to study and negotiate military aid. On his return, he founded the Whampoa Military Academy to train officers for the Kuomintang's armies.

When Sun Yat-sen died, Chiang succeeded to power in the

Kuomintang and began the drive that was to subject the war lords of China to his authority. As his power increased, he decided that the time had come to end the uneasy truce with the Communists, and in 1927 he ordered his armies to search out and destroy all the followers of Marx and Lenin. In the bloody purge that followed, thousands of Chinese Communists were liquidated, imprisoned or tortured. But Chiang failed to get them all. Mao Tse-tung gathered about him refugees from the slaughter; took to the mountain fastnesses of the interior; and finally led some 100,000 on the gruelling, 6,000-mile Long March that took them across China and into the wilds of Shensi Province in the extreme northwest. Fewer than one third of those who had begun the Long March survived it; but with this nucleus Mao set up his capital in Yenan and began all over again to organize Communist strength in China.

Mao's forte lay in his understanding of the peasants, just as Chiang's fatal weakness lay in his incomprehension. Of peasant ancestry himself, Mao was to turn Marxist theories upside down. Marxism was based upon the belief that revolution in an industrialized society must come from the uprising of the working classes in the great cities. Mao's formula virtually ignored the cities and concentrated on the countryside. As a young Communist in 1926, he had witnessed a spontaneous peasant revolt in his native Hunan Province. In a report at that time, he wrote:

"The main targets of the peasants are the local bullies, the evil gentry and the lawless landlords . . . In force and momentum, the attack is just like a tempest or a hurricane; those who submit to it survive, those who resist perish. As a result, the privileges the feudal landlords have enjoyed for thousands of years are shattered to pieces . . . A rural revolution is an uprising, an act of violence whereby one class overthrows the authority of another. A rural revolution is a revolution in which the peasantry overthrows the authority of the feudal landlord class. If the peasants do not use the maximum of their strength, they can never overthrow the deeply rooted, age-old authority of the landlords."

Thus, early in his career, Mao outlined his prescription for the eventual takeover of China.

The Japanese invasion brought a brief and uneasy truce between the Communists and Chiang. Even the Communists recognized that Chiang was the only figure of national stature about whom the country might rally against the foreign invader. But, as in the days of Sun Yat-sen, the truce was for the political convenience of the moment only; each side waited for the opportunity to slit the other's throat.

During all the years of World War II, this internal enmity vitiated Chinese resistance to the powerful Japanese armies. General Joseph W. (Vinegar Joe) Stilwell, a field commander who came to fight, was frustrated in his attempts to get Chiang (whom he called "The Peanut") to fight the Japanese instead of husbanding his strength for the eventual showdown with the Communists. The acerbic exchanges between the American general and the Chinese Generalissimo reached a stage where, it seemed to Washington, there was only one choice: Stilwell was relieved of his command and called home, and a more diplomatic general, Albert C. Wedemeyer, succeeded him. But even Wedemeyer could not get Chiang's armed forces to put up an effective resistance, and Japanese armies in the final stages of the war tore ever deeper into China, forcing American air bases ever further into the interior—and away from important Japanese targets.

When the war ended, China was in utter chaos. Thousands of Japanese troops wandered around the countryside, fully armed, with no one accepting their surrender. John F. Melby, in a day-by-day diary he kept at the time, reflected in bewilderment upon this anomaly. On December 27, 1945, he noted: "I still don't understand about the Japanese. Officially they are being disarmed, but the fact is they never seem to be. In Shanghai fifteen thousand still walk the streets with full equipment. In Nanking the high Japanese generals are bosom buddies of the Chinese. In the north tens of thousands of Japanese soldiers are used to guard railroads and warehouses and to fight the Communists. If you ask what this is all about the answer is either a denial or in more candid moments a 'Shhh, we don't talk about that.'" In another entry on January 30, 1947, a good sixteen months after V-J Day, Melby noted that, though it was being kept "very quiet," there were "eighty thousand holdout Japanese troops in eastern and northwestern Manchuria who are fully equipped, fighting the Communists."

Melby, who had been acting director of the U.S. Office of

War Information in Moscow in 1944, had been sent to China shortly after V-J Day because the State Department reasoned that a man with knowledge of the Russians might be able to find out what the Russians were up to in China. He was on the scene throughout the period of General Marshall's abortive mission to China (later to become the focal point for one of McCarthy's most vicious diatribes), and he was to stay for four years, down to the collapse of Chiang's regime in 1949. His experiences have now been recounted in his book, *The Mandate of Heaven,* a combination diary-exposition that is one of the most vivid accounts of the period.

From Melby's first days in China in the fall of 1945, two problems assumed paramount importance in his eyes—the problem of Manchuria, that vast and rich northern province that the Japanese had transformed into an industrial heartland; and the problem of the corruption, brutality and ineptness of Chiang Kai-shek's regime. At the end of the war, the Russians had swept over Manchuria like a swarm of locusts, stripping it of everything movable. They left behind a quagmire in which a whole regime could drown, and Chiang Kai-shek, possessed of the delusion that every inch of China belonged to him, was perversely determined to drown in it.

From the outset Chiang saw everything in terms of military conquest; he was blind to the crying need of his people for land reform. Here was the basic reason that Chiang, even with powerful American support, could never in the end "hold" China. In the contest of brutality, Chiang and the Communists canceled each other out; but the Communists had the advantage that they offered hope, while Chiang offered only the perpetuation of his own corrupt palace circle. Given such alternatives, the Chinese people had little choice.

The failure of Chiang was not a failure of power, but a failure of morale and competence. At the outset, Chiang's armies outnumbered the Communists by a margin of 5 to 1; by December, 1945, Melby writes that "the United States had completed the equipping of the previously promised thirty-nine divisions with heavy materiel and transport." This automatic and unthinking support of Chiang's regime had placed America in a position in which we could only lose. Some of the first entries in Melby's diary convey this. On November 9, he wrote:

"As far as we are concerned, we have by now jockeyed ourselves into a position where there is no longer any good answer. No matter what we do, we are wrong . . . nothing in this country has the remotest chance of popular appeal which does not call for agrarian reform. In Canton there is even an organization known as the South Seas Basketball Association for Agrarian Reform!"

Yet Chiang continued obdurately on his way. He ignored the warning of General Wedemeyer that if he plunged beyond the Great Wall into Manchuria he would dangerously overextend himself, as Napoleon had in the march to Moscow; and he reaped in the end precisely the disaster that Wedemeyer had foreseen. He ignored the repeated warnings of General Marshall that his military victories were hollow triumphs that in the end could only bleed and exhaust his regime.

On December 8, 1945, Melby, referring to a student strike in Kunming, noted: "The murder and brutality going on there are shocking. A lot of Kuomintang people are genuinely horrified by it, but it still goes on.

"One of the great mysteries to me is why one group of people retains faith, whereas another from much the same origins and experience loses it. Over the years the Communists have absorbed an incredible amount of punishment, have been guilty of their own share of atrocities, and yet still have retained a kind of integrity, faith in their destiny and will to prevail. By contrast, the Kuomintang has also gone through astonishing tribulations, has committed its excesses, has survived a major war with unbelievable prestige, and is now throwing everything away at a frightening rate because the revolutionary faith is gone and has been replaced by the smell of corruption and decay . . ."

On January 15, 1946, Melby made this entry in his diary: "Shortly after I arrived here we found that the police who guard the Embassy were stealing our gasoline. Someone notified the Foreign Office. That night every one of them was shot. Some time ago one of our Chinese press monitors was arrested on unspecified charges. Despite all our efforts, he was not returned to us until two days ago. He was dead, and what had happened to him first was appalling . . ."

Such was the government to which we had committed ourselves and our prestige—one that was steadily alienating itself from its own people, some of whom were beginning to mutter that "conditions were better under the Japanese." The dissident liberals in China were without a leader of national stature; they were a splintered, ineffective group, men of ideals who lacked the ruthlessness that leads to power. But even they were being driven into the Communist camp. Melby quotes one of them as saying: "As between a Fascist Kuomintang supported by the United States and a Chinese Communist party supported by the Soviet Union, the [Democratic] League will support the Communists because they are fighting the greatest menace of all, Fascism. Furthermore, even though Communism in China will allow no more scope for the activities of the liberals than does the Kuomintang, still Communism means greater good for the mass of the people and should be supported . . ."*

The inevitable point was reached: Chiang's soldiers refused to fight their own people. These soldiers had been conscripted against their will into the army in the first place, and they simply had no desire to fight. Whole divisions went over to the Communists without striking a blow. Arms, ammunition and supplies sent by the United States to Chiang were either filched and sold to the Communists by Chiang's corrupt commanders or were meekly turned over to the Communists by troops who surrendered. The Chinese Communist armies became so well-equipped with the war materiel we had sent to Chiang that they fought most of the first half of the Korean War with these American guns and supplies.

The fragmentation of Chiang's regime and the erosion of

---

* The deep-seated hatred of America which persists in China today stems from our unblinking support of Chiang. Felix Greene, a British Broadcasting Company reporter, in two long trips into China in the latter 1950s, described this feeling in his book: *China, The Country Americans Are Not Allowed to Know*, Ballantine Books, New York, 1962. He expresses the prevalent Chinese feeling: "Do Americans not realize with what hatred we recall those last dreadful years of Chiang's regime? Do they not know of the countless thousands killed or tortured by Chiang's secret police? Or of the fortunes made by his politicians while our people everywhere were starving? Can they not realize that this persistent support of a man who was inflicting the most gross injuries on his own people convinced us that American policy was designed in no way for our benefit, but to prevent us from controlling our own country? In spite of countless official reports, articles by reputable American reporters, eyewitness accounts, documented proof of his cruelty and corruption, Washington has persisted to this day in giving Chiang money, arms, and all the moral support that she can muster." The quote is from pp. 269–270. Pearl Buck has called Greene's volume "the most realistic book that has yet been written about the China of today."

morale proceeded at such a pace that in November, 1948, Major General David Barr, then the senior American officer advising Chiang, summed it up this way:

"I am convinced that the military situation has deteriorated to the point where only the active participation of United States troops could effect a remedy . . . No battle has been lost since my arrival due to lack of ammunition or equipment. [The Kuomintang's] military debacles in my opinion can all be attributed to the world's worst leadership and many other morale-destroying factors that can lead to a complete loss of will to fight. The complete ineptness of high military leaders and the widespread corruption and dishonesty throughout the armed forces could, in some measure, have been controlled and directed had the [necessary] authority and facilities been available. . . ."

This was the judgment of a high-ranking American military officer, and like the judgment of the civilian experts who were to be McCarthy's targets, it implied that we could have prevailed in China only if we were to indulge in all-out war, sacrificing millions of American fighting men to do the job that Chiang's regime could not do for itself. One shudders at the price America would have had to pay to save Chiang for our "free world." Fortunately, the Truman Administration, in one of its more sober moments, refused to pay such a price—and so brought down upon itself the wrath of the yahoos.

O N E O F T H E E A R L I E S T V I C T I M S of this irrational outcry was a career diplomat who had been one of the foremost of "the old China hands" in the Far Eastern branch of the State Department. He was John Carter Vincent, and he had been "Case Number 2" and one of "the big three" in McCarthy's speech to the U.S. Senate on February 20. At the time McCarthy attacked him, Vincent was the American minister to Switzerland, a post from which, according to McCarthy's horror tale, he had slipped secret government documents to the Russians.

Vincent, then forty-nine, had been a foreign service officer since 1924. He had spent many years in China, acquiring an intimate knowledge of the country. His expertise had led to his being made assistant chief of the division of Far Eastern Affairs of the State Department in 1943. He had become chief of the division of Chinese Affairs in January, 1944, and had been director of Far Eastern Affairs during 1945, prior to his appointment as minister to Switzerland.

McCarthy pinpointed Vincent as one of his prime targets when he turned over his list of names to the Tydings committee in private session. In this forum and in speeches he tied Vincent to Professor Lattimore—the man whom he had called the Number 1 Soviet spy in America. Vincent, he contended, had belonged to the Lattimore clique in the State Department that had "betrayed" China into the hands of Russia.

At his post in Switzerland, Vincent ignored the uproar, and when questioned, contented himself with saying that the State Department would make whatever answer it felt was necessary. The department did. Deputy Under Secretary of State John E. Peurifoy, in charge of department security, told the press that there was no evidence in Vincent's entire personnel file which would "even remotely substantiate Senator McCarthy's charge" that he had been a spy for Russia. This statement made little impression on a nation caught up in the fever of the witch hunt; it was brushed off as just the kind of denial one might expect from an accused, harassed (and doubtless guilty) administration. The attack went on, and Vincent became something of a minor cause célèbre.

Bernard F. Fensterwald, Jr., who was then a young lawyer in the State Department and who was later to have a long career as an assistant to various Senators, including Senator Kefauver, recalls the tempest well, for he was assigned by the department to prepare Vincent's defense.

"Vincent was an old Georgia boy who was probably to the right of Torquemada," Fensterwald says. "He was so appalled by the whole thing that he would do virtually nothing to prepare his own defense. He took the attitude that, if things had reached this point, if even *he* could be considered a Communist, the hell with it; the world was going to the dogs, and there was just nothing to be done about it. So all he wanted to do was to go off and play golf.

"It was left up to us to put together the best defense for him that we could. This was based largely upon an analysis of literally thousands of cablegrams that had gone back and forth between him and the department while he was in China. What these showed was that it was true that Vincent had urged cutting off all further aid to the Chinese Nationalists after he discovered that more than 50 per cent of the arms and supplies we sent them were being filched and sold to the Communists.

"If that kind of judgment makes him a Communist, then he was a Communist—but that's the only way you could ever make him one."

If this was truth—and all credible evidence says it was—this was also an age in which truth could always be overcome by the big lie. Tarred by McCarthy's charges, Vincent saw his professional career ruined. He was called home and allowed to retire from the State Department, fading quickly into obscurity, one of the less conspicuous of McCarthy's victims.

Professor Owen Lattimore—to whom McCarthy had tried to link Vincent to the latter's lasting damage—was made of sterner stuff. Not an employee of the State Department, he was less hampered by inbred official caution, more his own man, and not the kind to say the hell with it. The event might demonstrate that Vincent's was the wiser and more realistic course. Those who stood up to the witch hunt did so at their peril. Lattimore was one who stood—and suffered.

A ROUND-FACED, prissy-looking man, with thinning hair and a mousy little mustache, Owen Lattimore was in Kabul, Afghanistan, on March 25, 1950, when he received a cablegram from the Associated Press in Washington. It informed him that Senator McCarthy "says off record you top Russian espionage agent in United States and that his whole case rests on you." Lattimore, who didn't look at all like a tiger but who had a lot of tiger in him, fired off this answer:

MC CARTHY'S OFF RECORD RANTINGS PURE MOONSHINE STOP DELIGHTED HIS WHOLE CASE RESTS ON ME AS THIS MEANS HE WILL FALL FLAT ON HIS FACE STOP EXACTLY WHAT HE HAS SAID ON RECORD UNKNOWN HERE SO CANNOT REPLY IN DETAIL BUT WILL BE HOME IN A FEW DAYS AND WILL CONTACT YOU THEN STOP.

So the battle line was drawn. What Lattimore could hardly have been expected to realize at the time was the incredible danger he courted by this defiance. McCarthy had proclaimed

that he would "stand or fall on this one"—and the ultraconservative forces that were marshaling behind him could not permit
him to fall. The same thing had happened to William Remington
when Elizabeth Bentley had accused him of having been a spy;
he could have retired humbly and been forgotten. But he chose
to fight. By so doing he challenged Bentley's credibility. If she
were wrong on this, her most prominent headline case, what
value could be attributed to her other tales of espionage? Bentley
had to be rehabilitated and sanctified, and in this cause Remington *had* to be convicted. The result was the tortured fabrication
of a case in which Bentley's original testimony was altered
beyond recognition; when this case was thrown out of court, a
second indictment was brought, based on Remington's alleged
perjuries in defending himself the first time; and, so hounded,
Remington was eventually convicted, imprisoned—and murdered
in prison. A similar, though not so final and tragic, fate was in
store for Owen Lattimore almost the instant he threw down the
gage to McCarthy.

In Afghanistan, Lattimore could hardly imagine what was
happening at home, and imagination could hardly do justice to
the reality. In Baltimore, his wife, Eleanor, caught the brunt of
the storm. After McCarthy's initial testimony before the Tydings
committee, Baltimore papers broke out in a black rash of headlines. The *Evening Sun* screamed: MCCARTHY CALLS LATTI-
MORE 3 OTHERS PRO-RED AT PROBE! The Hearst *News-Post*
competed with: LATTIMORE BAD RISK TYDINGS PROBERS TOLD.
Both papers printed Mrs. Lattimore's denial that her husband
was or ever had been a Communist—but the impact lay, as
always, with the accusation.

During the next ten days the pot simmered as McCarthy
hinted mysteriously to newsmen that he was about to name the
top Russian spy in America. Finally McCarthy whispered to newsmen (off-the-record and in strictest confidence, of course) that
the Johns Hopkins professor was the man he had in mind.

Mrs. Lattimore first learned of these "secret" murmurings on
March 23 when a journalist from the San Francisco *Chronicle*
telephoned her. "I suppose you have heard about the charges,"
said he. Mrs. Lattimore assumed that he meant the charges she
had been hearing for ten days, but her caller quickly disabused

her. "No," he said, "I mean the new ones, that he [Lattimore] is the top Russian spy in this country."

Mrs. Lattimore sought help. One of Lattimore's closest friends, Joseph Barnes, who had been Lattimore's assistant in OWI during World War II, agreed to sound out Washington newsmen whom he knew. They told him that, two days before, at an off-the-record press conference, McCarthy had dropped Lattimore's name, but that no one had dared to use it yet for fear of libel.

That evening, pursuing his researches, Barnes went to a party where he met McCarthy himself. Mrs. Lattimore later wrote: "Joe [Barnes] tried to convince him that he couldn't be more wrong about Jessup and Lattimore. Others at the party were telling the Senator that he was crazy. But he had seemed completely unshakable. From others Joe heard incredible stories about the methods by which McCarthy planned to substantiate his charges. It was very frightening."

Mrs. Lattimore realized that the case was so serious defense action would have to be initiated before Lattimore could get back from Afghanistan, so she appealed for help to a lawyer whom she remembered having met at a party—Abe Fortas. Fortas was then regarded as one of those rare human beings—a truly courageous lawyer who was willing to risk his reputation and devote his time and talents to the defense of an underdog in an unpopular cause. His partners in one of the top-flight law firms in Washington, Thurman Arnold and Paul Porter, agreed without hesitation that Fortas should take up Lattimore's case. Their only question to Mrs. Lattimore was: "Will he fight?" She assured them that her husband would, indeed, fight.

Now, as was inevitable, the name dropped "off the record" began to get on the record. McCarthy, that past master at manipulating the American press, knew full well that when you tell a roomful of journalists a headline story "off the record," some of them are going to find a way to make it public. Hearst's New York *Journal-American* got around the difficulty by headlining a page-one story that pointed out that "the description" of McCarthy's mysterious "Mr. X" fitted what was known about Lattimore. Eric Sevareid adopted the same cautious, circuitous approach in a newscast that also served to connect Lattimore's name with "top spy" in the public mind. Drew Pearson now decided that it was time to act.

Pearson's colleague Jack Anderson, who had been spoon-fed the story about submarine-landed spies reporting to Lattimore, knew that McCarthy had put on record in private testimony before the Tydings committee at least the essentials of his "off the record" charges. Drew Pearson had also learned that Lattimore had acted as the sponsor and protector of a small group of Mongols who were refugees from Communist terror. They were at Johns Hopkins, working with Lattimore on his Mongolian studies. Of them, Mrs. Lattimore later wrote:

". . . The oldest of this group was a 'Living Buddha,' a very high dignitary of the Lama Buddhist Church, who had been a close friend of ours ever since 1931 when he had had to flee from the Communist government in Outer Mongolia. The younger men, who were here with their families, had been very active in the anti-Communist Mongol nationalist movement, and both had held trusted positions in the anti-Communist National Government of China. They had all had to get out of China before the Communists took over, and since Owen had been their chief sponsor in this country and had spent much time and money getting them established here, Mr. Pearson thought they were a living argument that Owen could not be a Communist."

And so, on Sunday night, March 26, 1950, Drew Pearson went on the air and stated flatly as fact what others had reported as rumor and speculation. He opened his broadcast this way: "I am now going to reveal the name of the man whom Senator McCarthy has designated the top Communist agent in the United States. Senator McCarthy has said that he would rest his entire charge of State Department communism on this case. The man is Owen Lattimore of Johns Hopkins University."

Pearson then described how Lattimore had aided the Mongols. He made it clear that, in his scale of values, this action carried greater weight than the accusatory words of McCarthy, and closed his broadcast with a personal tribute: "Now, I happen to know Owen Lattimore personally, and I only wish this country had more patriots like him."

The next day the press descended upon the refugee Mongols at Johns Hopkins. The Living Buddha, clad in a dark red robe, and scarlet and gold brocaded vest, sat behind Lattimore's own desk and told the press how Lattimore had befriended him ever since he had had to flee from the Communists in 1931. His two acolytes, flanking him, identified themselves; one as the former bodyguard, the other as the secretary of "Prince Teh, who is still holding out, with an army of five to ten thousand, against Communist domination in western Mongolia."

All during this period of uproar, McCarthy had been having his tribulations with the Tydings committee. The frustrated Democrats on the committee kept demanding that he support his charges with some kind of evidence. McCarthy's response was to counterattack with the cry that the Democrats wanted to identify his informants in order to persecute them. While insisting that he was exposing a matter of the utmost gravity, he maintained that he wasn't making "charges" against anyone, but was merely pointing out the situation. He put the onus of substantiating his own sweeping charges upon the Democrats. If they were really sincere, he said, they could discover all the evidence they needed by having President Truman release "the files," and he implied they were conspiring to cover up a treasonous mess if they did not.

The effect of his hedging was often ludicrous. At one of the early sessions, he appeared rumpled and breathless, brief case bulging. He informed the committee it would be just impossible for him to go on because there was a crisis in the Senate that demanded his immediate attention—a debate on a housing bill. He took off for the door under a full head of steam, only to be brought up short when one member of the committee informed him that the crucial housing debate had been postponed. That was wonderful news, McCarthy said, just wonderful, because some Wisconsin constituents had just come to town, were waiting to see him—he just had to dash off right away to meet them. The committee refused to let him go, sat him down, and made him go on testifying.

Now, confronted with the living evidence of the refugee anti-Communist Buddhists, McCarthy went into a new gambit. On the afternoon of March 27, he got Senator Hickenlooper to read the Tydings committee a letter in which McCarthy expressed his regret that he was "inescapably" absent from the hearing, but promised a new sensation. He was going to tell all in a Senate speech the next day; the utterance was going to be of such importance that he hoped FBI Director J. Edgar Hoover would "have one of his agents available so that I may turn over to him documents in the Lattimore case which I consider of some importance."

It was a tactic right out of the quack doctor's bag of tricks. What, my last nostrum didn't cure you? Well, my friend, just try my new super elixir.

I T W A S M A R C H 3 0 before McCarthy rose in the Senate to make his much-trumpeted speech denouncing Owen Lattimore. The galleries were packed. Cheered on by the crowd, McCarthy held the floor for four hours in a speech that ranged from denunciation of Lattimore to denunciation of our entire foreign policy.

The speech opened with a shocker: McCarthy had a witness who would testify that Lattimore had been a Communist Party member for years—"high up" in party circles. (This mystery man turned out to be Louis Budenz, and his testimony turned out to be more suspect than convincing; but, of course, that could not have been known then.) Having established a foundation through the supposedly unimpeachable imminent testimony of this mystery witness, McCarthy stormed ahead. He accused Secretary of State Acheson of being a puppet—"the voice and mind of Lattimore."

He asserted that American policy in the Far East had followed a line advocated by Lattimore—and welcomed by the Soviet Union.

Two branches of the State Department—the Far Eastern Division and the Voice of America—were "almost completely controlled and dominated by individuals who are more loyal to the ideas and designs of communism than to those of the free, God-fearing half of the world."

There were other witnesses, McCarthy assured the Senate, who would support his mystery witness in documenting the charge that Lattimore had been a Communist. He had an affidavit "closely tying" Lattimore with John Stewart Service, another Far Eastern expert who had been arrested in 1945, but later cleared, in connection with the theft of secret government documents that had been used as the basis of articles in the Far Eastern magazine *Amerasia*. One deposition, McCarthy said, came from a witness who was a guest on the night before this arrest and who saw Lattimore going over "documents." Lattimore supposedly explained that he had been "declassifying secret documents in favor of some friends"—a preposterous allegation on the face of it because Lattimore wasn't even in government service at the time and could not possibly have "declassified" any documents.

As the horror tale unfolded, the galleries broke out in applause, shattering the decorum of the Senate. McCarthy was challenged by only a tiny handful of courageous souls on the floor; it was notable, as *The New York Times* reported, that "the senior Democratic members of the Senate had nothing to say to him."

In the Republican ranks, only the veteran Senator Tobey protested this demagoguery to which the leaders of his party were either overtly or secretly committed. He interrupted, protesting against McCarthy's tactic of reading from documents "only such portions as he selects." The full texts should be put into the record so that Senators might weigh and judge for themselves, Tobey argued.

McCarthy arrogantly slapped him down: "Regardless of whether any Senator disagrees, this is the procedure I am going to follow."

Senator Lehman followed up Tobey's thrust: "Have you made available to the [Tydings] subcommittee the information of which you are now speaking?"

Haughty and contemptuous, McCarthy told him: "The answer is 'No.'"

"Why is the answer 'No?'" cried Lehman in rising anger. "That is the place to which charges should be referred rather than to submit here only parts of your charges after eliminations have been made that suit your purposes. You are making a spectacle to the galleries here and to the public where a man accused has no right to answer."

McCarthy bellowed: "The traitors will cause many men not to have a chance . . . Crocodile tears are being shed for traitorous individuals, but forgotten are 400,000,000 people [the Chinese] who have been sold into slavery by these people. I have told the committee exactly where it can get the material."

In one of his earlier passages, McCarthy had cited a 1943 letter from Lattimore, then director of Pacific operations for the Office of War Information, to his friend and deputy, Joseph Barnes. This letter showed, McCarthy charged, that Lattimore had been "seeking to get rid of all the Chinese in OWI who were loyal to the National Government." Referring to this, Lehman now shouted angrily that McCarthy was "attempting to damn and blacken individuals" by reading excerpts, and he demanded specifically that McCarthy make public the full text of the 1943 Lattimore letter. McCarthy then invited Lehman to step across the aisle to the Republican side of the Senate "so that I can show him why a fuller disclosure would be completely unfair."

Lehman called his bluff. Striding across the aisle, he held out his hand and said determinedly, "I want to see the letter."

Instantly McCarthy took back his words. "I don't yield any further," he bleated, refusing to show the letter.

And at this point the galleries actually applauded him.

The reason for his failure to make good on his proffer to Lehman became obvious later, when the full text of the Lattimore-Barnes letter was read into the Tydings record. Its entire content was the *very opposite* of what McCarthy had represented it to be. The letter was a careful analysis of Chinese pressure groups, and its intent was to make certain that Chinese personnel hired by OWI were not secret agents for Chinese cliques. Far from recommending the dismissal of Chinese favorable to the Nationalist Government, it contained a specific warning against the hiring of Communist-affiliated Chinese. Lattimore had written:

"In the circumstances we have to be extremely careful about our Chinese personnel. While we need to *avoid recruiting any Chinese Communists* we must be careful not to be frightened out of hiring people who have *loosely been accused* of being Communists . . .

"For our purposes, it is wise to recruit as many unaffiliated Chinese as we can, to pick people whose loyalty will be reasonably assured on the one hand by the salaries which we pay them and on the other hand by the fact that *they do not receive salaries or subsidies from someone else*." (Italics added.)

No wonder Joe McCarthy clutched that letter tight! On March

30, of course, neither the Senators nor the galleries could know why he did such a sudden about-face.

Senator Brien McMahon, another of the courageous few, picked up McCarthy's wild ranting about "traitors"; he asked if McCarthy would apply that term to Dorothy Kenyon, Ambassador Jessup and others he had named before the Tydings committee. McCarthy hedged, saying that he had not accused Miss Kenyon of being a traitor and that he regarded Jessup as being only "the dupe of Lattimore." The "traitors" remained, as usual, faceless.

Under pressure, McCarthy now began to hedge his bets on Owen Lattimore—the case on which he was to "stand or fall." He told the Senate:

"I fear that in the case of Lattimore I may have perhaps placed too much stress on the question of whether he is a paid espionage agent.

"In view of his position of tremendous power in the State Department as the 'architect' of our Far Eastern policy, the more important aspects of his case deal with his aims and what he advocates: whether his aims are American aims or whether they coincide with the aims of Soviet Russia.

"The administration's disastrous Far Eastern policy reflects point by point Mr. Lattimore's recommendations and advice."

It did nothing of the sort, of course; if it had, we would never have become embroiled in the Korean War, then about to break, and we would never have quarantined China for the next twenty years as a pariah not to be admitted to human discourse. But these facts, self-evident now and fairly evident to the more perceptive even then, bore little relation to the web of fantasy McCarthy was weaving.

Now McCarthy soared higher in a fanciful argument that convulsed the press gallery, finally declaiming, "I believe you can ask almost any school child who the architect of our Far Eastern policy is, and he will say, 'Owen Lattimore.' "

Ridiculous? Of course. But the curtain rang down, as it had on February 20, on another tremendous public triumph for Senator McCarthy.

THE NEXT ACT belonged to Owen Lattimore. Unlike other McCarthy victims, who had confined themselves largely to their own defense, Lattimore returned to the United States on April 1, and in a press conference launched an all-out attack, arraigning McCarthy as "a base and miserable creature," a "hit-and-run politician," and a man whose charges had been made "falsely, irresponsibly and libelously." McCarthy's attacks, Lattimore claimed, were "seriously damaging" the American position in the world. The Soviet Union, he declared, should decorate McCarthy for "telling the kind of lies about the United States that Russian propagandists could not invent."

In his own defense, Lattimore was positive and unequivocal: "I am not and never have been a member of the Communist Party or a Communist sympathizer, or affiliated or associated with the Communist Party. I have never advocated or supported the cause of communism either in the United States, in China, in the Far East or anywhere else in the world." He added that anyone who called him a communist was a perjurer and should be prosecuted.

McCarthy counterattacked. He challenged the State Department to make public the text of a "secret" memorandum that Lattimore had prepared for it, implying that the document was subversive. The department replied that Lattimore had been just one of some thirty foreign policy experts whose views had been solicited, and it did not feel free to single out and release the text of his memorandum. So Lattimore himself released it.

Like the Lattimore-Barnes letter, the memorandum contained nothing even faintly resembling what McCarthy had implied. It expressed much the same views that Lattimore had expounded publicly in *The Situation in Asia*. He opposed the policy of continued aid to the regime of Chiang Kai-shek, but on the other hand he argued forcefully for continued efforts to draw China *closer* to the United States and *away* from the Soviet Union.

China, he reasoned, could not be economically coerced; nothing could be more dangerous than for us to delude ourselves that the Communists could not achieve at least enough economic stability to make their regime politically secure. He thought that Russia would not try to take direct control of China because the task was beyond her capabilities, but that it would be a mistake for the United States to wait for the Chinese Communists to come to us "hat in hand," begging for our aid. He also argued that South Korea was more of a liability than an asset as far as

American interests were concerned, and he doubted that the South Korean regime could be "kept alive" long without our armed intervention.

On all these counts, history seems to have justified Lattimore's analysis. Equally significant, in the context of his struggle with McCarthy, were recommendations in the memorandum that would hardly have been made by a dedicated follower of the Communist Party line: for example, that the major aim of U.S. foreign policy should be to convince Far Eastern countries that they "can get along with the United States" and Western Europe —and that they could do without Russia to a great extent. In another judgment, that seems to have found its vindication in Vietnam, Lattimore had also written: "The kind of policy that failed in support of so great a figure as Chiang Kai-shek cannot possibly succeed if it is applied to a scattering of 'little Chiang Kai-sheks' in China or elsewhere in Asia."

Lattimore's release of this memorandum on April 3 set the stage for his appearance before the Tydings committee on April 6. In the meantime, his life and career had undergone close scrutiny in the press. One significant fact became apparent in the context of McCarthy's charges: Lattimore had *never* been an employee of the State Department. Lattimore himself contended that no one had less influence than he on American foreign policy because his views were never heeded. It was a statement that belittled Lattimore's role. The professor had been a figure of considerable prestige and private influence; his views on the problems of China and the Far East had been widely quoted and had influenced the thinking of many Far Eastern experts. It was true, however, that this private stature and the consideration given his views had not been reflected in the final formulation of policy. Under the pressures of the Cold War and the demands of domestic politics, the Truman Administration had adopted courses of action that were virtually the opposite of what he had recommended.

The April 6 showdown attracted an audience that packed the caucus room of the Senate Office Building. Admission was obtained only by means of passes signed by Senators, and those unable to find seats stood around the perimeter of the room. Owen Lattimore was sworn and took his seat; not fifteen feet away sat Joseph McCarthy. The professor glared at McCarthy, but the Senator would not meet his eye and appeared, as *The New York Times* reported, "pale and impassive" under the glare of the klieg lights.

Lattimore's denial of all of McCarthy's charges was as unequivocal as it had been in his earlier press conference; and it was now made, as he himself said, in the full realization that he was testifying under oath and therefore could be subject to a perjury charge. He expounded his views on China and the Far East as he had in his books and his State Department memorandum, but it was his contemptuous denunciation of McCarthy that stirred his audience to applause:

"He has violated it [the responsibility of his high office] by impairing the effectiveness of the United States Government in its relations with its friends and allies, and by making the Government of the United States an object of suspicion in the eyes of the anti-Communist world, and undoubtedly the laughing stock of Communist governments.

"He has violated it by instituting a reign of terror among officials and employees of the United States Government, no one of whom can be sure of safety from attack by the machinegun of irresponsible publicity in Joseph McCarthy's hands.

"He has without authorization used secret documents obtained from government files. He has vilified citizens of the United States and accused them of high crime, without giving them an opportunity to defend themselves.

"He has refused to submit alleged documentary evidence to a duly constituted committee of the Senate.

"He has invited disrespect to himself and his high office by refusing to live up to his word. Twice on the floor of the Senate he stated that any charges he made under the cloak of immunity, he would repeat in another place so that their falseness could be tested in a court of the United States. He said that if he should fail to do this he would resign. He has been called to repeat his charges so that they could be tested in a court of action. He has failed to do so. And he has not resigned."

It is doubtful whether any Senator of the United States has ever sat and listened to a more harsh indictment of himself. It was high drama. And *The New York Times* noted that the crowd reaction was far different from what it had been a few days earlier when McCarthy was playing to packed galleries in the Senate.

At the close of Lattimore's statement, Senator Tydings told Lattimore: ". . . I owe it to you and to the country to tell you that four members of this subcommittee [the three Democrats and Senator Lodge] recently had a complete summary of your loyalty file read to us in the presence of Mr. J. Edgar Hoover, head of the Federal Bureau of Investigation.

"At the conclusion of the reading, it was the unanimous opinion of all members of the subcommittee and of all others in the room [these included Attorney General J. Howard McGrath] that there is nothing in the files to show that you have ever been a Communist or have ever been connected with espionage.

"So that the FBI file puts you completely, up to this moment at least, in the clear."

McCarthy, who had been claiming that the files would prove his charges, was asked about this failure of the Lattimore file to show anything. Unshaken, he answered: "Either Tydings hasn't seen the files or he is lying. There is no other alternative."

Tydings, who had made his statement about what the Lattimore file did not show in the presence of his full committee, retorted, "I'll let my reputation for accuracy stand. It is significant that no member of the subcommittee contradicted the statement when I made it."

When the afternoon session opened, McCarthy was not there; he was again "inescapably" absent. The victory clearly belonged to Owen Lattimore. This, one might have thought, should have made some public impact. But it did not. Perhaps one reason was that most of the press accounts featured Lattimore's denials, but conveyed little of the drama of his scathing, personal denunciation of McCarthy. This was, somehow, not such exciting news. And McCarthy always buried whatever damage might have been done to him by rushing off to harvest new headlines. Here is the way *The Nation* described McCarthy's confrontation with Lattimore and its immediate aftermath:

"He [McCarthy] sat tight-lipped and pale, directly behind the subcommittee and facing Lattimore through the early hours of the hearing. Then he went up to Passaic, New Jersey, to accept an 'Americanism' award from a Marine Corps group. Here he shrilled defiance at Lattimore, daring him to sue on the basis of this attack made outside the privileged forum of the Senate. Reporters hastily pointed out, however, that McCarthy had not repeated his Senate charges—had said neither that Lattimore was a Communist nor that he was an espionage agent."

In this first test of courage and veracity, Owen Lattimore clearly triumphed, but in the Nightmare Decade the winning of such a victory could cost a man far more than a quick, quiet and ignominious defeat—as Lattimore, in a hounded future, would ultimately discover.

12

The Tydings Windup

THE TYDINGS HEARINGS had hardly begun before Mc-
Carthy began to play with great gusto a new role—that of super-
sleuth masterminding his own private version of the FBI. Before
many weeks had passed, the operation had sprawled out into
hideaways separate from McCarthy's official Senate quarters.
One of these counterspy cubicles was tucked away in Room 5-A
in the basement of the Senate Office Building and another in
Room 316 in the Congressional Hotel on Capitol Hill. Former
FBI men and assorted private sleuths ducked in and out of these
gopher holes, amassing their harvest of gossip and rumor.

This frenzied activity was under the overall supervision of
McCarthy's counterintelligence chief, Don Surine, a former FBI

239

agent who had been fired from the bureau in early 1950 on the charge that he had been found consorting with a Baltimore beauty whom he had been supposed to be investigating on a white slavery charge. Surine insisted it was all a great misunderstanding—a question, as he said, "of the development of an informant which involved my taking a practical means to a desired end." A few weeks after the bureau had disagreed with him about the "means" he had taken to the "desired end," Surine went to work for McCarthy and soon became a kingpin in the counterintelligence service of the great crusade.

Seldom has Washington witnessed such a blatant extralegal operation. Normally, investigators are employed by Senators or Representatives who head legally constituted committees charged with a specific investigative task, like the Kefauver probe into organized crime. Such investigations are officially sanctioned and serve a legitimate purpose. But McCarthy's operation had no such sanction. It was privately financed, a form of vigilantism, invested with impressive semiofficial trappings, but responsible actually only to the caprices of McCarthy.

In these circumstances, the antics of McCarthy's private legion rapidly became the talk of Washington. Joseph and Stewart Alsop in *The Saturday Evening Post* wrote what was to become the often-quoted, classic description of this endeavor. They described it in these words:

"A visit to the McCarthy lair on Capitol Hill is rather like being transported to the set of one of Hollywood's minor thrillers. The anteroom is generally full of furtive-looking characters who look as though they might be suborned State Department men. McCarthy, himself, despite a creeping baldness and a continual tremor which makes his head shake in disconcerting fashion, is reasonably well cast as the Hollywood version of a strong-jawed private eye. A visitor is likely to find him with his heavy shoulders hunched forward, a telephone in his huge hands, shouting cryptic instructions to some mysterious ally.

" 'Yeah, yeah, I can listen, but I can't talk. Get me? You really got the goods on the guy?' The Senator glances up to note the effect of this drama on his visitor. 'Yeah? Well, I tell you. Just mention this sort of casual to Number One, and get his reaction. Okay? Okay. I'll contact you later.'

"The drama is heightened by a significant bit of stage business. For as Senator McCarthy talks he sometimes strikes the mouthpiece of his telephone with a pencil. As Washington folklore has it, this is supposed to jar the needle of any concealed listening device."

In such fashion did Senator McCarthy seek to "get the goods" on Owen Lattimore and his other targets.

THE MONEY that supported this far-flung counterespionage operation came, as was later disclosed, from an infinite variety of sources—in dollars-and-dimes contributions from exercised Americans on the grass-roots level, and in four- and five-figure donations from some of the wealthiest men in America. At the beginning, however, a major source of financial and ideological help was doubtless the China lobby.

The China lobby was a propaganda operation financed by the National Government of Chiang Kai-shek. It was devoted to the task of convincing American lawmakers and the American public that the fate of the free world was bound up with keeping Chiang's halo untarnished. It is doubtful whether any other foreign-financed lobby ever exercised such a pervasive influence on American foreign policy, or ever so successfully tortured that policy to serve the ends of a foreign potentate rather than the best interests of the American people.

The hidden hands in this operation were five shrewd Chinese diplomats—Chen Chih-mai, Peter T. K. Pee, W. K. Lee, K. H. Yu and P. T. Mow. They worked from quarters inside the Chinese Embassy and reported directly to Chiang, using the code signature "Kung," meaning "group." A series of these secret cables fell into American hands through the good offices of a Chinese code clerk. They were funneled to the outspoken Senator Wayne D. Morse (D., Ore.), and Morse had them translated by the Library of Congress.

These cables showed a desire for another world war, in which United States involvement would have the effect, as in World War II, of serving Nationalist Chinese interests. One cable, dated December 5, 1949, reported regretfully that there were few signs Soviet-American relations would deteriorate further. Then came this sentence: "Our hope of a world war so as to rehabilitate our country is unpalatable to the [American] people."

In another cable dated July 14, 1950, just three weeks after the Korean invasion, hopes appeared to be on the rise. The "Kung" gave this analysis: "Whether the Chinese Communists send troops to Korea or not is of secondary importance, but the war in South Korea will be extended in any case. We must be patient at this time. Whether or not the war will extend to other places in Europe and Asia, we should make little comment and wait for the development of the situation."

Another cable, especially significant in the light of McCarthy's imminent attack upon General Marshall, indicated that the Chiang faction was deeply disenchanted with this distinguished American who had refused to put their interests above the interests of his own nation. "In the past years we have been very patient with General Marshall," the cable read, "but he has never changed his attitude towards us. But in order to avoid a direct break with the American administration, it is better for us not to attack him personally." This diplomatic reticence did not, of course, foreclose a vicious attack upon Marshall by an irresponsible mouthpiece in the Senate of the United States.

The shadowy "Kung" had its more visible counterparts—the overt shakers and movers who furthered the designs of the China lobby. The two most prominent front men were William J. Goodwin, a one-time follower of Father Charles Coughlin's Christian Front, and Alfred Kohlberg, a New York importer of Chinese lace. Goodwin was paid $25,000 a year by the Chinese News Service, the propaganda arm of the Nationalist Government, and his activities were described by Anderson and May in these terms:

". . . For the benefit of thirsty Congressmen, he threw fancy parties at the Mayflower Hotel and the Metropolitan Club in Washington and at the Wee Tappee Tavern in New York. In an interview with Edward R. Harris of the St. Louis *Post-Dispatch*, Goodwin estimated that he had entertained more than one hundred Congressmen a year and had converted half of them to support more aid for Nationalist China. And Goodwin added boastfully that he had 'helped materially' to lay the groundwork for Senator McCarthy's attacks on the State Department."

Equally vigorous in cultivation of McCarthy for the purposes of the China lobby was anticommunist Alfred Kohlberg. Kohlberg, indeed, was probably the first of the pro-Chiang coterie to sense the possibilities in McCarthy. About three weeks after Wheeling, Kohlberg took McCarthy to dinner and discoursed at length upon his favorite theme, the "sell-out" of China by subversive elements in the State Department. Kohlberg's success in indoctrinating McCarthy with his viewpoint became obvious when the Senator followed the Kohlberg line on Ambassador Jessup and Owen Lattimore, sometimes almost word for word. For instance, in the August, 1949, issue of *China Monthly*, Kohlberg had charged:

"Professor Jessup must therefore be honored by our State Department as the initiator of the smear campaign against Nationalist China and Chiang Kai-shek, and the originator of the myth of the democratic Chinese Communists."

Less than a year later, in his March 30, 1950, speech in the U.S. Senate, McCarthy had said:

"Professor Jessup must therefore be credited by the American people with having pioneered the smear campaign against Nationalist China and Chiang Kai-shek, and with being the originator of the myth of the democratic Chinese Communists."

Equally significant was the history of the Lattimore-Barnes letter that McCarthy had refused to show Senator Lehman. As Lattimore later wrote, "the letter had been used as long ago as 1948 by Kohlberg, in a magazine article in *China Monthly*— and used with exactly the same distortion McCarthy used, creating the strong presumption that the letter came into McCarthy's hands from Kohlberg." Though McCarthy was later to return with great fanfare a $500 check mailed to him by Kohlberg and though he shunned public association with anyone Chinese, his tie to the China lobby seems well-established by his own words.

DON SURINE, four other former FBI men and a number of private eyes devoted a great deal of time and energy to the attempt to substantiate McCarthy's charges against Owen Lattimore. Though even McCarthy himself had been forced to acknowledge that the "Number 1 Soviet spy" gambit was too preposterous for belief, he had put his entire credibility on the line when he had bragged that he would "stand or fall on this one"; and, consequently, it became imperative to save him from falling flat on his face. Hence began the desperate effort to pillory Lattimore at all costs.

The pivotal figure in this effort was Louis Budenz, the former editor of the *Daily Worker* and a Communist high in the party who, like many of his fellow creatures, had "seen the light" and made the swing from extreme left to extreme right. From 1946 through 1949, Budenz had sung his informer's song to the FBI, indulging the bureau with more than 3,000 hours of personal recollections about the great communist conspiracy and those who took part in it. In these 3,000 hours it must be presumed that he had had every opportunity for total recall of the names of every communist, every fellow traveler, every menace to the security of the republic. Now, however, with McCarthy's witch hunt *in extremis* because of the wild-flying charges against Lattimore, Budenz discovered that he had suffered a mental lapse during those hours of recollections, culled over a period of three years with the probing help of the diligent FBI. Somehow he had overlooked Owen Lattimore.

The rumors that Budenz was McCarthy's trump card, the mystery witness of his March 30 speech, had been flying around Washington for weeks. In the brief moment of euphoria after Lattimore's appearance on the stand, and his seeming victory in his face-to-face confrontation with McCarthy, there had been speculation that Budenz might not be produced. Abe Fortas, however, suffered from no such illusion. Lattimore later recalled a visit to Fortas' office at which the lawyer broke the news to him.

"He shut the door behind us, looked at me squarely, and said nothing for what seemed like a long, long time," Lattimore wrote. "Then he said, 'McCarthy is a long way out on a limb. The political pressures that are building up are terrific. The report that Budenz will testify against you has shaken everyone in Washington. It is my duty as your lawyer to warn you that the danger you face cannot possibly be exaggerated. It does not exclude the possibility of a straight frame-up, with perjured witnesses and perhaps even forged documents. You have a choice of two ways of facing this danger. You can either take it head on, and expose yourself to this danger; or you can make a qualified and carefully guarded statement which will reduce the chance of entrapment by fake evidence. As your lawyer I cannot make that choice for you. You have to make it yourself.'

"'Abe,' I said, 'I don't see how we can do any pussyfooting on this. I want to meet this thing head on and slug it out. I owe it to myself and the issues that are at stake.' Then I turned to Eleanor. I said, 'Do you agree?' And she said, 'Of course.' "

So a new battle line was drawn.

At this point, Lattimore got a break. He was tipped off that Dr. Bella V. Dodd, a New York lawyer who had once been a member of the top committee of the Communist Party but had later broken with the Communists and been viciously attacked by them, might testify that she had never heard Lattimore's name mentioned in any way in connection with party activities. Since she had been in a position to know, her testimony could be of great value. Abe Fortas went to New York to see her. Having suffered so greatly from the malice of her former Communist comrades, Dr. Dodd was extremely reluctant to call down upon her head new waves of vituperation by embroiling herself in the defense of a man whom she did not even know.

But Fortas, the able and persuasive advocate, told her: "You are going to find it hard to live with yourself if Lattimore is successfully framed. You will never be able to forget that you might have helped by exposing the lies told against him. Or put it the other way round. If he wins out, you will always regret that you did not join in a good fight well fought."

Dr. Dodd yielded and signed an affidavit for Lattimore's defense. The next day, April 20, 1950, Louis Budenz took the witness stand before the Tydings committee.

The hearing room again was crowded—but this time, as Lattimore noted, with an entirely different audience. Budenz, when he recanted his communist faith, had embraced Catholicism; and now, among those waiting to hear his testimony, was "a strong representation of Catholic priests, whose black garb made them stand out conspicuously." The Daughters of the American Revolution happened to be holding its convention in Washington at this time; and a number of the DAR dowagers helped to swell the crowd, hanging on every word of the informer.

It was testimony that rambled all through the labyrinth of communist plots and intrigues. It was, for the most part, an excellent example of what Elmer Davis had called the "double-think," an exposition of deluded communist faith on the one hand and a completely unrealistic assessment of the degree of the menace on the other. But when it came to specifics, Budenz was anything but specific. The best he could produce against Owen

Lattimore was arrant hearsay. He recalled that Earl Browder, one-time head of the Communist Party, and Frederick Vanderbilt Field had told him that Lattimore was subject to Communist discipline and that his mission was to organize American writers to put over the deceptive idea that the Chinese Communists were simple agrarian reformers.

This was the remotest kind of testimony, and it left Senator Lodge decidedly uneasy. He asked Budenz for "a specific instance when an order or an instruction" was issued to Lattimore by the Communist Party and carried out by him.

Budenz said the order to represent the Chinese Communists "as agrarian reformers was certainly carried out," but "specifically I do not know because I did not hear the detailed report on the matter."

"Is that the most concrete and specific illustration there is?" Lodge asked.

"That is the most concrete, yes, sir," Budenz replied.

This, as it turned out, was not quite accurate. Given still another year to perfect his recall, Budenz's recollection became more fertile. In 1951, before the McCarran Committee, he finally came up with the kind of specifics he had not been able to produce for Lodge. He charged that John Carter Vincent and Lattimore, acting as "members of the Communist Party," had been "relied on" to guide Vice President Wallace "along the paths" desired by communism during his mission to China in 1944. The columnist Joseph Alsop, whose sympathies are far more right than left, promptly denounced Budenz and suggested that he should be prosecuted for perjury because this testimony, the first that offered a check-point with fact, was the very reverse of the truth.

Alsop had a very simple way of knowing this. As it happened, *he* had played a major role in guiding Wallace on his Far Eastern tour; Vincent, he said, had been helpful in furnishing information. As a result of this information and this guidance, Wallace had recommended the dismissal of General Stilwell, who had wanted closer relationships with the Chinese Communists because they fought well, and the appointment as his successor of General Wedemeyer, a stout anticommunist who is to this day one of the heroes of the American ultraright.

"This was the strongest blow that could then be struck at the

Communist cause in China," Alsop wrote. ". . . Hence the facts glaringly contradicted Budenz's sworn testimony. When asked to explain, Budenz only entangled himself in a further web of contradictions. This reporter . . . therefore felt bound to recommend that the case of Louis Budenz be submitted to the Justice Department for investigation for perjury . . ."

This recommendation was ignored. In a society bewitched by the informer syndrome, the informer must be protected at all costs because only he can give the low-down on the menace. The man who opposes him will be prosecuted for perjury if he can somehow be trapped into making an incautious or injudicious answer, but the informer remains untouchable, the indispensable handmaiden of the government.

The Lattimore case eventually was to illustrate all this to perfection, but at the moment, on April 20, 1950, all that was apparent was that the utterly damning exposure of Lattimore that McCarthy had promised in his March 30 speech was fizzling like a damp fuse. The Republicans, anxious to salvage some headlines from the wreckage, clamored for adjournment the instant Budenz left the stand. If they could strangle facts at this point, the morning papers would be left with little choice but to headline Budenz's accusation that Lattimore had been a Communist. The insubstantial nature of this charge might become apparent to readers who waded through the story; but the impact-producing headlines would be based on the denunciation.

Abe Fortas fought this tactic. He demanded and won the right to present a strong rebuttal witness. This gave the defense the opportunity to spring its own surprise by calling to the stand retired Brigadier General Elliot R. Thorpe, who had been chief of counterintelligence during the Pacific war for that redoubtable hero of the American right, General of the Army Douglas MacArthur. Thorpe had known Lattimore well, both during the war and during 1945–46 in the postwar occupation of Japan. With the full cooperation of the FBI, he had investigated Lattimore's loyalty record on three separate occasions, and each time he had found that there was no question about Lattimore's loyalty; each time he had cleared Lattimore, giving him access to "top secret" information. He testified that "during the early days of our occupation of Japan I asked and received his [Lattimore's] assistance in dealing with matters pertaining to the USSR of a confidential nature. His assistance was of material value."

General Thorpe concluded his statement with these words:

"For me to say that I know the innermost thoughts or all the secret acts of Owen Lattimore would be absurd. I can only say that were I called on to commit my personal safety and that of my command on information by Dr. Lattimore, I would do so with the confidence that he would always act as a loyal American citizen."

Having been dealt this all but mortal wound by a high-ranking military man of unimpeachable integrity, the Republicans fought for and obtained an adjournment. Abe Fortas, still on the counterattack, immediately released Bella Dodd's affidavit to the press. The pertinent paragraph read:

"I have never met Owen Lattimore. I never heard of him until the present controversy. In all my association with the Communist Party I never heard his name mentioned by Party leaders or friends of the Party as a Party member or a friend of the Party."

Dr. Dodd could hardly have remained in ignorance had Lattimore been given, as Budenz charged, the crucial task of brainwashing all American writers on the Orient. Subsequently, the rest of Budenz's hearsay evidence was impugned. Earl Browder, the former head of the Communist Party, one Budenz source, testified that he did not know Lattimore and that, furthermore, he had never heard Lattimore's name mentioned in Communist circles. Frederick Vanderbilt Field, the other source for Budenz's hearsay, denied emphatically that he had ever told Budenz what Budenz testified Field had told him; to the best of his knowledge and belief, Field said, Lattimore was *not* a Communist.

The case on which Joe McCarthy had chosen to "stand or fall" appeared to be a shambles.

T H E E F F E C T on the denizens of Room 5-A in the basement of the Senate Office Building was little short of devastating. The unpersuasive testimony of Budenz made it imperative for the McCarthy legions to shore up his story with some credible, corroborative testimony. Additional witnesses, about whom McCarthy had bragged so freely in his March 30 speech, simply must be found. The hunt began, and one of the first to feel the heat was Emmanuel Sigurd Larsen, a former specialist in the China Division of the State Department's Bureau of Far Eastern Affairs.

Larsen, to his own everlasting damage, had been involved in the 1945 *Amerasia* case. *Amerasia* was a magazine edited in New York by Philip J. Jaffe, a Marxist theoretician. Agents of the Office of Strategic Services, the original American spy outfit and predecessor of the Central Intelligence Agency, had discovered that *Amerasia* was publishing articles, parts of which, at least, were almost verbatim reproductions of secret American reports on Far Eastern developments. Long weeks of sleuthing by the FBI had established that Jaffe was in contact with Larsen and others in Washington; that he also visited Earl Browder and the Russian consulate in New York; and that official government documents were being funneled to him by his Washington collaborators. When Jaffe's New York headquarters was raided, some 1,700 government documents that had no business being there were found.

The Hearst and Scripps-Howard press in New York, among other newspapers, built up the *Amerasia* case into a great spy sensation. The *Amerasia* affair undeniably had a nasty odor about it, but as a spy case it had one immediately obvious flaw: no spy in his right mind would ever advertise his spying by publishing in a publicly distributed magazine the information he had stolen. The outcome was, therefore, a letdown of the anticipated sensation. Charges against only two of the defendants survived in court. Jaffe was fined $2,500 on a conspiracy count; Larsen, $500.

In an epilogue that was as weird as the case itself, Larsen rushed into print in September, 1946, just as a crucial Congressional election was coming up, with the thundering accusation that the *Amerasia* case had been characterized by "a mysterious whitewash of the chief actors." Since Larsen himself, on the record, had been one of the "chief actors," the accusation was mystifying, to say the least. Significant, however, was the vehicle in which it was made. Larsen's article appeared in the first issue of a new magazine called *Plain Talk*, edited by Isaac Don Levine, a rightist journalist who had been the original confidant of Whittaker Chambers—and so a figure in the background of the Alger Hiss case. Perhaps it was this indication of a cooperative attitude toward the political right or perhaps it was just Larsen's well-known intense dislike of Acheson that led McCarthy to hope he might be helpful in the collapsing case against Owen Lattimore.

In any event, as Larsen was later to testify, he received a telephone call from McCarthy in April, 1950. Larsen at the time was about to testify in a Loyalty Board review of the case of John Stewart Service, another Foreign Service officer implicated in the *Amerasia* case. In response to McCarthy's call, Larsen visited the Senator's office. McCarthy, he said, warned that he might attack Larsen himself for his role in the *Amerasia* case unless— The thought was not quite completed, but McCarthy said that "everything would go much easier" for Larsen himself if he testified "correctly" about Service.

At this point, Don Surine entered McCarthy's office. The Senator introduced Larsen to Surine, and Larsen accompanied McCarthy's chief of staff down to the basement counterespionage nest. He later described his experience in these terms:

"So we went downstairs to Room 5-A. That is their chamber of horrors, bristling with dictaphones and recording machines. There must be eight or ten of them there. We sat down at a desk, he on one side and I opposite."

They sparred verbally; then, according to Larsen, Surine said:

"If you give the evidence we want . . . if you string along with us, then it will go easier for you."

Surine further suggested, Larsen said, that Larsen's role in the *Amerasia* espionage case left him little choice but to co-operate with McCarthy. Larsen objected heatedly to the term "espionage"; *Amerasia*, he conceded, had involved the theft of documents—but for publication, not for espionage.

Surine reared up behind his desk, and roared, "Are you defending *Amerasia*?"

"No, Mr. Surine, I am defending myself," Larsen said he replied.

Larsen's description of the scene continued:

"He kept standing up. The phone rang, obviously the master upstairs, McCarthy. He gave some instructions because he [Surine] said, 'Uh, uh, uh, all right, all right,' put it [the phone] down, and so almost simultaneously I said: 'I think I'll have to go home.'

"I thought, 'I am not subpoenaed. I don't have to take this kind of stuff, I can walk out of here any time I please—at least I hope so.'

"Surine said: 'I'm leaving you now. I will have to talk to you later. Thank you very much for coming, Mr. Larsen.' And I went out and I thought, 'The heck with that Gestapo stuff.' "

Having failed to make any progress with Larsen, McCarthy and Surine flew to New York a few days later for an evening conference with J. B. Matthews, one of the earliest and most indefatigable of the witch-hunting pack. Matthews had begun his career under Martin Dies as an investigator for the original Dies Un-American Activities Committee. He now served William Randolph Hearst, the Lord of San Simeon, as the Hearst chain's superspecialist on the menace.

His official title was "special assistant to the publisher of the New York *Journal-American*." Shortly after Wheeling, when it became obvious that McCarthy was whipping up passion in the boondocks, Hearst had deputized Matthews to investigate and determine whether McCarthy was "sufficiently clean" to merit support. It was like sending one fanatic to find out whether another fanatic was fanatic; the finding was almost automatic. With Matthews' clearance, McCarthy began to get a good press, with Hearst columnists beating the drums for the great crusade. Foremost among the drum-beaters were George Sokolsky and Westbrook Pegler, a one-time great journalist who had become almost unhinged by his hatred of the entire Roosevelt clan and the New Deal.

McCarthy's attention was said to have been directed to Dorothy Kenyon by some information in Matthews' files on which he had seized in a moment of desperation. Now, in a similar moment, he and Surine repaired to Matthews' London Terrace penthouse in New York, where they met with a man named John J. Huber. Huber was apparently the Mystery Witness Number 2 whom McCarthy had built up in his March 30 speech as the authority who would corroborate his Mystery Witness Number 1 —Louis Budenz.

Huber had been a handy informer for the FBI for years. In

the 1930s, he had served as a minor WPA official, and, in his spare time, had been an occasional bartender at Communist Party rallies. As soon as the FBI became aware of him, Huber began to lead a double life, serving up liquor on the one hand and information on the other.

Between the years 1938 and 1947, Huber had kept a meticulous, day-by-day diary that ran to a thousand pages. On three occasions during the fall of 1949 he had testified before the McCarran Subcommittee of the Senate Judiciary Committee on "Communist activities among aliens and national groups." His testimony covered more than one hundred printed pages, and he named hundreds of names. Like Louis Budenz, Huber would seem to have had, especially with the aid of his diary, abundant opportunity to perfect total recall—but he seemed never to have mentioned the name of Owen Lattimore. This was an oversight that McCarthy and Surine now hoped to rectify.

No details of the Matthews' penthouse conference ever found their way into the official record, but the subsequent sequence of events seemed to indicate that enough transpired to raise the hopes of McCarthy and Surine. When they returned to Washington, they were accompanied by Huber and Lawrence E. Kerley, a Hearst journalist whose duties seem to have been twofold—to "get the story" and to wet-nurse Huber. Arriving in Washington, Kerley and Huber registered at the Carlton Hotel and awaited their cue.

The summons came that very evening. Kerley took the stand before the Tydings committee in public session, ostensibly to identify Huber as a trusted FBI informant. Having made this point, Kerley began to explain the details of Huber's expected testimony regarding Lattimore. The story was that Huber had spotted Lattimore attending a party in 1946 at the home of Frederick Vanderbilt Field. The object of the gathering was to boost the Committee for a Democratic Far Eastern Policy, a group that had been later labeled subversive by the Attorney General.

When Kerley began to relate what Huber was supposed to testify to, Tydings called a halt. This was all hearsay, he said, Kerley's version of what Huber had told him; and, if there was to be evidence on this point, it should be given by Huber himself. And so the call went out: "John J. Huber." There was silence. No Huber.

Kerley offered an explanation tailor-made for an eight-column headline in the Hearst press. Huber, he said, had been stabbed in the hand by two sinister-looking men who had attacked him on a Bronx street the previous Saturday night. One of these villains had told Huber: "You SOB, we're going to kill you!" This assault, in Kerley's rationale, must have so unnerved Huber that he had taken a powder.

The Bronx police promptly doused the stabbing story; no such incident had occurred, they said. A few days later, Huber himself turned up, back in New York, bearing no visible sign of a wound. No, he said, no one had stabbed him; no one had threatened him. His explanation was simple: "I blacked out."

The Tydings committee threatened to drag him back to Washington and compel him to testify, but it was forced to abandon this plan when it received a letter from a doctor attesting that Huber was "on the verge of mental collapse."

McCarthy, with the egg figuratively dripping from his face, offered an explanation: Huber had agreed to testify—but only at a private session. Crowds made the poor man nervous, and when he found he was going to have to appear in public, he simply panicked and fled.

Many suggested uncharitably that the real difficulty probably lay in Huber's concern that what he was supposed to say on the witness stand did not jibe with the contents of his thousand-page diary or his previous McCarran testimony. It was suggested that the haunting specter of a possible perjury rap may have been the real cause of his "blackout."

Perhaps Huber should not have been so concerned: the perjurious government informer is a well-protected creature. But, as the Lattimore case was ultimately to show, such consideration is not given the accused.

WHAT HAD BECOME of McCarthy's constant bleat that "the files" would prove his charges? From the very beginning, from his February 20 speech in the Senate almost to the end of the Tydings inquiry months later, McCarthy had declaimed time and again that the evidence was all in "the files"—if the Democrats would only produce them. The insinuation was that the Truman Administration's refusal to open "the files" was tantamount to proof of its guilt.

It seemed like the safest of all ploys. President Truman was a stubborn man. He had closed all executive department loyalty files to Congressional committees in 1948—and he was not likely to change his mind. Thus McCarthy could be relatively certain that Truman would never call his bluff.

Republicans in the Senate picked up the trumpet and blew loud and long. As early as February 23, Senator Wherry was demanding that Secretary of State Acheson be served with a subpoena "to produce the files" and be cited "for contempt if he refuses." When the Tydings inquiry began, Truman refused to let the committee see "the files," and Republican members of the committee badgered Tydings to subpoena them. Tydings argued that there was no way to compel the President to make the files available even if he did issue a subpoena, and he reasoned that he might accomplish more by a conciliatory approach—an effort to persuade Truman to change his mind.

On March 27, in an attempt to quiet the uproar, Tydings called as witnesses Attorney General McGrath and FBI Director J. Edgar Hoover. Both declared that it would be unthinkable to release "the files" to the Tydings committee for two reasons: if there were leaks (and there had been in the past) the identity of witnesses whom investigative agencies wished to protect might be revealed, and irreparable damage done to the national security machinery; and, in the second place, the release of raw, unevaluated data would spatter many innocent individuals.

Hoover's testimony in particular should have been most devastating, especially in superpatriotic circles where he was most admired. He testified that "98 or 99 per cent of the time" the mere fact that the FBI had not forwarded a case to the Justice Department for prosecution meant that it didn't feel there was a conclusive case. The rare exceptions occurred, he said, when the bureau considered it best to let a suspect run loose under surveillance in the anticipation that he might lead agents to others in the ring. Since there had been no wave of prosecutions and no demand from the FBI for such action, this testimony should have done much to discredit McCarthy's charges that a legion of subversives were running riot in the State Department.

On the second major issue involved, Hoover's testimony was equally cogent. He emphasized that the loyalty files contained "complaints and allegations" as well as some facts, and that their release might damage individuals who, after subsequent and more thorough investigations, had been established to be innocent.

"The files do not consist of proved information alone," he said, validating the contention of Senator McMahon on February 20. "The files must be viewed as a whole. One report may allege crimes of a most despicable sort, and the truth or falsity of these charges may not emerge until several reports are studied, further investigations made and the wheat separated from the chaff . . .

"I would not want to be a party to any action which would 'smear' innocent individuals for the rest of their lives. We cannot disregard the fundamental principles of common decency and the application of basic American rights of fair play in the administration of the FBI."

When President Truman followed up Hoover's convincing testimony by repeating his refusal to release "the files," Senator Wherry, the Republican floor leader and a stout McCarthy partisan, erupted in a froth of denunciation. The President's decision, he said, "must be shocking to the American people." Truman's announcement "climaxes a build-up to smear the efforts of Senator McCarthy and those of us who are disturbed by the infiltration of left-wing radical socialist plotters in the Government." The Senate inquiry, he declaimed, was being "thwarted and hamstrung by the President's shameful refusal to cooperate in this patriotic effort upon which the security of our country may depend." The only possible inference was that President Truman was a traitor.

The Republican Senate Policy Committee, under the guidance of Senator Taft, met to consider the possibility of serving a subpoena directly upon the President, but Truman let it be known that he would refuse to honor such a subpoena, and no action was taken. Though Taft kept insisting that the party was not bound irrevocably to McCarthy and his charges, the reality swore at his pretensions. When Representative Franklin D. Roosevelt, Jr., rose in the House to praise Dr. Jessup as "one of our eminent statesmen and one of our loyal Americans," he was almost drowned out by the hoots and jeers coming from the Republican side of the aisle.

This unceasing and unseemly furor was all grist for the public relations mill of Joe McCarthy. Appearing at a radio round-table discussion of Tydings inquiry issues, he declared: "The President is afraid to make those [loyalty] files available. It seems inconceivable that the President would not trust the members of the committee with the files."

The uproar had its inevitable effect upon the national mood. What was in those files anyway? It seemed to many logical that they must contain some horrendous and damning secrets, just as McCarthy had charged. Otherwise, why couldn't they be made public? Lost and buried in the public consciousness was the fact that J. Edgar Hoover had already given scrupulous answers to such questions. What registered was that the Administration must be hiding something.

With the Democrats buffeted from all sides over the issue of "the files," Truman suddenly did a complete about-face. He announced on May 4 that he would let the Tydings committee examine the files of the 81 persons whom McCarthy had finally named. The reason he was doing this, the President explained, was that these files had already been released to Congressional committees anyway. The cases were those examined by four Republican committees of the Eightieth Congress in 1948 without a single adverse finding.

Truman had done at last what he should have done first. The Democrats, some of them, must have known almost the instant McCarthy opened his mouth on February 20 that he was culling his cases from these old Congressional lists. Instant exposure should have been the first Democratic priority; but Truman, by withholding the material for months, had handed the opposition a gold-plated issue. The belated decision to open "the files" could not undo the damage.

The sequel touched ludicrous heights. Almost the instant that Truman disclosed he would let the Tydings committee see "the files," McCarthy began to bleat a new tune. Now, incredibly, he cried that "the files" would prove nothing. How could this be? McCarthy's answer was simple. "The files" would now prove

nothing because they had been "raped," they had been "skeletonized or tampered with." Truman was only releasing them because all the damaging material had been squirreled out. If the
files had not been so "thoroughly raped," McCarthy thundered,
the U.S. Minister in his Case Number 2 (John Carter Vincent)
would have been "fired immediately."

The Tydings committee, including its Republican members,
spent hours and days poring over the files; and, while they found
in them, as Brien McMahon and J. Edgar Hoover had foretold,
gossip, rumor and innuendo, they found no hard facts on which
to base a judgment. When Tydings finally called a halt to the
study of the files, not even Senator Hickenlooper, McCarthy's
stoutest advocate on the committee, had the heart to protest.

McCarthy, however, kept in full cry after his newly created
issue of the "raped" files. At one point, he triumphantly displayed
a letter from J. Edgar Hoover saying that the FBI had not examined the files shown to the Tydings committee by the State Department. Tydings countered by asking the FBI to reexamine
"the files" to ascertain whether they were indeed complete. From
July 15–17, FBI agents performed this task, and on July 17
Attorney General McGrath informed Tydings that the FBI investigation "reveals the files contain all FBI reports and memoranda furnished to the department in these cases prior to the
time they were turned over to your committee . . ."

No exposure, one would have thought, could have been more
devastating. None ever made less public impact.

TRUTH OFTEN COMES in tiny capsules. It came in that
form to the Tydings committee on April 5, 1950. In plain, unadorned testimony, two stalwart Republicans attempted to set
the record straight. Brigadier General Conrad E. Snow, "a Republican all my life," who headed the State Department's own Loyalty
Security Board, testified that he and his associates "always gave
the Government the benefit of the doubt" in loyalty cases that
came before them.

"If there are *any* Communists in the State Department, the
Loyalty Security Board is uninformed of their existence," General Snow told the Tydings committee.

He said that his board had never been reversed on appeal to the higher body, the Loyalty Review Board headed by Seth W. Richardson, the second man to testify.

Richardson, who had served as an Assistant Attorney General in the Administration of Herbert Hoover and, like Snow, had been a lifelong Republican, explained that his board was composed of twenty-six members, about evenly divided between Republicans and Democrats. It functioned as a kind of Supreme Court, adjudicating appeals brought before it from loyalty-board decisions in the various executive departments. Richardson, therefore, had an overall view of the loyalty issue, not just in the State Department, but in all of the executive departments. The orientation of the appeals machinery over which he presided was decidedly conservative; there could be no question, as General Snow had testified, about giving the Government "the benefit of the doubt" in any case of suspected disloyalty. Yet the number of such findings had been miniscule.

Richardson testified that his Loyalty Review Board had been responsible for 182 dismissals in all federal departments; in other cases, it had reinstated 124 workers whom departmental boards originally had found suspected of disloyalty or indiscretion. His board, he agreed, had never overruled the Loyalty Board of the State Department on any dismissal.

The loyalty machinery, in other words, had been about as airtight as it was humanly possible to make it.

These facts emerged from Richardson's testimony:

—In 10,000 full field investigations in three years of screening, the FBI had found *not one single case* of espionage in any of the federal departments.

—Neither in these screenings nor in the examination of some 3,000,000 files had the FBI found *any evidence even "directing toward espionage."*

—The loyalty program unfitness tests (standards that included not just questions of loyalty, but of homosexuality, excessive drinking and other risky personal habits), after long investigations by the FBI, had produced adverse findings about *"less than one twentieth of 1 per cent"* of federal employees.

Those were the facts.

.　　.　　.

THE DEMOCRATS IN THE SENATE now decided to do what they should have done before they gave McCarthy the national sounding board of the Tydings committee; they switched to all-out attack. Typically, the change of tactics was too little and too late. Instant exposure of McCarthy after his February 20 speech might have put truth into focus; but by May 3, two and a half months later, the barrage of sensational charges had done its work: the public was more likely to believe that the Democrats had become enraged because they had been badly hurt.

Yet the scene in the Senate on May 3 was remarkable in and of itself. In its savagery, it was unprecedented in the memory of Washington correspondents. The Democrats administered to McCarthy the most relentless verbal beating any Senator had taken in years; and it was notable that, except for the ever-faithful Kenneth Wherry, the Republican leadership abstained from the fray and let McCarthy take his lumps.

Majority Leader Scott Lucas led the attack. He began by reading a statement from John E. Peurifoy, Deputy Under Secretary of State in charge of security. Peurifoy charged with perfect accuracy that McCarthy, far from presenting the Senate with new and sensational information on February 20 as he had claimed, had simply revived shopworn charges that had been discredited even by the Republican-controlled Eightieth Congress. When Peurifoy wrote that there was "not a shred of evidence" to support McCarthy, Wherry demanded that Lucas be called to account because he was now impugning the character of a fellow member. Vice President Alben W. Barkley told Lucas to sit down, but the setback was only momentary. Lucas was soon on his feet again, picking up the reading of the Peurifoy letter at the precise point where he had left off.

When he finished, he turned to face McCarthy directly, and he harked back to the issue at which he had hammered on February 20. Had McCarthy or had he not charged at Wheeling that there were 205 Communists still actively at work making policy in the State Department? There was by now, it would seem, abundant material for a much more far-ranging and specific attack upon McCarthy, distorted case by distorted case, twisted fact upon twisted fact; but still the Democrats did not mount the kind of assault the situation warranted. They contented themselves with trying to show that McCarthy had lied at Wheeling. And McCarthy twisted and dodged, refusing to say either yes or no.

Senator Matthew Neely (D., W. Va.) shouted that, if the accusations against the State Department proved false, "those responsible should be scourged from the company of decent men." Lucas stormed: "The time has now come to call a spade a spade. I am willing to take what the press of the country said [about McCarthy's 205 charge] and not what Senator McCarthy says he said on that occasion [in Wheeling]."

On and on went the hammering.

"Will the Senator say yes or no?" demanded Neely. "Will he say he did or he didn't?"

"I did not say I had the names of 205," McCarthy responded. "I said Byrnes had said that he had the names of 205. I'm not going to discuss any rough draft [of a speech]."

"Did you give the radio station such a speech?" Neely demanded.

McCarthy's response: "I call for the regular order, Mr. President."

"Did you say yes or did you say no?" Neely pressed.

"It is perfectly evident . . ." broke in Senator Lehman.

"I call for the regular order, Mr. President!" McCarthy cried, almost in desperation.

". . . he has not denied," Lehman concluded.

"A point of order, Mr. President!" McCarthy pleaded, striking a refrain that was to become familiar during the Army-McCarthy hearings.

Senator Neely capped the attack by demanding that the Tydings committee find out "where the truth lies" regarding the Wheeling speech, and with obvious reference to McCarthy, he shouted:

"Someone whose identity is not yet officially determined is lying at the rate Ananias never lied."

Throughout the verbal hurricane, McCarthy "sat bent over his desk, and he scarcely lifted his head when in a suddenly thinned voice" he made his calls for "point of order." The Republicans "understood exactly what the Democrats were doing" in raising the question of McCarthy's honesty toward his colleagues, *The Nation* wrote, but "they either left the floor or listened quietly as McCarthy was subjected to his 'Ananias' lashing."

The Republicans were not ready yet to defend McCarthy's use of the multiple big-lie technique, but that time would come— and soon.

THERE REMAINED one brief moment that belonged to honor and to conscience. Its heroine was the lady from Maine, Republican Senator Margaret Chase Smith. On June 1, 1950, Mrs. Smith took the Senate floor to present a "Declaration of Conscience" that had been signed by her and six other Republican Senators.

"I speak as a Republican. I speak as a woman. I speak as a United States Senator. I speak as an Americn," she told the Senate.

"The United States Senate has long enjoyed worldwide respect as the greatest deliberative body in the world. But recently that deliberative character has too often been debased to the level of a forum of hate and character assassination sheltered by the shield of congressional immunity.

"It is ironical that we Senators can in debate in the Senate directly or indirectly, by any form of words, impute to any American, who is not a Senator, any conduct or motive unworthy or unbecoming an American—and without that non-Senator American having any legal redress against us—yet if we say the same thing in the Senate about our colleagues we can be stopped on the grounds of being out of order."

Though Mrs. Smith did not mention any Senator by name, there was only one to whom her words applied—and everyone knew it. McCarthy, white and silent, sat barely three feet behind Mrs. Smith, listening to her denunciation.

Speaking as a Republican, Mrs. Smith harshly criticized the lack of leadership in the Democratic Administration, but she saw the larger issue clear and whole. She saw the damage that McCarthyism—the phrase that Owen Lattimore had introduced into the language in his testimony—was doing to the nation. She saw the growth of "a national feeling of fear and frustration that could result in national suicide and the end of everything we Americans hold dear." She saw the nation "being psychologically divided by the confusions and suspicions that are bred in the United States Senate to spread like cancerous tentacles of 'know nothing, suspect everything' attitudes . . ."

"As a United States Senator," she said, "I am not proud of the way in which the Senate has been made a publicity platform for irresponsible sensationalism. I am not proud of the reckless abandon in which unproved charges have been hurled from this side of the aisle . . ."

She said that she did not wish to see her party win by riding "to political victory on the Four Horsemen of Calumny—Fear, Ignorance, Bigotry and Smear. . . . While it might be a fleeting victory for the Republican Party, it would be a more lasting defeat for the American people . . ."

At the end of her speech, she read the short "Declaration of Conscience" in which her six fellow Republicans had joined. It began with the statement: "We are Republicans. But we are Americans first." It continued: "Certain elements of the Republican Party have materially added to this confusion in the hopes of riding the Republican Party to victory through the selfish political exploitation of fear, bigotry, ignorance and intolerance. There are enough mistakes of the Democrats for Republicans to criticize constructively without resorting to political smears."

The Senators who joined with Mrs. Smith in this statement were: Charles W. Tobey of New Hampshire; George D. Aiken of Vermont; Wayne L. Morse of Oregon (then a Republican); Irving M. Ives of New York; Edward J. Thye of Minnesota; and Robert C. Hendrickson of New Jersey.

The Washington columnist Doris Fleeson assessed the impact this way:

"It [Mrs. Smith's speech] sobered and silenced her colleagues —both Democrats and Republicans—including Senator McCarthy, who shielded his face with his hand. When she finished her 'Declaration of Conscience,' Senator Lehman of New York declared in a matching burst of candor: 'This should have been said a long time ago.'

"That it was not said sooner is a reflection of the intellectual and moral confusion existing here since Alger Hiss was convicted.

"The Hiss case has seemed to paralyze the Democrats' faith

in themselves, in their own officials and in the fairness of the American people. Weeks lengthened into months and they did not defend their own Secretary of State from the floor.

"The long-frustrated Republicans have ignored every implication of McCarthyism in their hope that the gambler from Wisconsin would bring in his long shot, another Hiss case. Influential Senators, including Taft, privately encouraged him while keeping a pious distance from his methods."

Had conscience been a strong force in the Senate or in politics, the stand of the signers of the "Declaration of Conscience" would have had a sobering effect. That its impact was fleeting, for the day and the moment only, spoke volumes.

McCarthy, who had been pale and shaken by Mrs. Smith's attack and had literally fled the Senate chamber as fellow Senators of both parties gathered around her to congratulate her, made a rapid recovery. The following day, June 2, he took the Senate floor for a speech in which he made it clear that no declaration of conscience was going to stop him.

"Let me make it clear to the Administration, to the Senate and to the country that this fight against communism, this attempt to expose and neutralize the efforts of those who are attempting to betray this country, shall not stop, regardless of what any group in this Senate or in the Administration may do," he thundered.

"I hold myself accountable not to them, but first to the people of my state, and secondly to the people of the nation, and thirdly to civilization as a whole."

THE TYDINGS REPORT made public on July 17, 1950, ripped apart the fabric of Senate amenities in an indictment so harsh that it was virtually without precedent. The "Ananias lashing" to which McCarthy had been subjected on May 3 paled beside this blunt official condemnation.

America was now involved in the Korean War, and against this background of international conflict with communism—by an Administration that was being denounced as "soft on communism"—the Democratic majority on the Tydings committee wrote:

"At a time when American blood is again being shed to preserve our dream of freedom, we are constrained fearlessly and frankly to call the charges, and the methods employed to give them ostensible validity, what they truly are: a fraud and a hoax perpetrated on the Senate of the United States and the American people.

"They represent perhaps the most nefarious campaign of half-truths and untruths in the history of this republic. For the first time in our history, we have seen the totalitarian technique of the 'big lie' employed on a sustained basis.

"The result has been to confuse and divide the American people, at a time when they should be strong in their unity, to a degree far beyond the hopes of the Communists themselves, whose stock in trade is confusion and division."

The report declared that the charges "of Communist infiltration and influence upon the State Department are false." It castigated McCarthy for his "hit-and-run tactics" and declared: "He has stooped to a new low in his cavalier disregard of the facts."

The Democratic majority on the committee wrote that they had been subjected to an "organized campaign of vilification" and had been accused of "whitewashing" the investigation before it even began. Actually, the committee wrote, it would have been justified in investigating McCarthy himself because he had "perpetrated a fraud on the Senate" in making his initial charges in February when "he had no information whatever to support them."

The question of ethics posed by McCarthyism was captured:

"We have seen the character of private citizens and of Government employees virtually destroyed by public condemnation on the basis of gossip, distortion, hearsay and deliberate untruths. By the mere fact of their associations with a few persons of alleged questionable proclivities, an effort has been made to place the stigma of disloyalty upon individuals, some of whom are little people whose only asset is their character and devotion to duty and country.

"This has been done without the slightest vestige of respect for even the most elementary rules of evidence or fair play, or, indeed, common decency. Indeed, we have seen an effort not merely to establish guilt by association, but guilt by accusation alone."

Case by case, name by name, the report took up McCarthy's charges, showed the lack of evidence to support them—and dismissed them. Its conclusion was that there had been nothing, absolutely nothing (as, indeed, General Snow and Seth Richardson had testified) to justify the sweeping accusations of betrayal.

McCarthy did not have the grace to be even momentarily flustered. With his infallible instinct for turning an attack upon himself into a boomerang, he seized instantaneously upon the Tydings Report as the living proof of all his charges. The report, he trumpeted in an immediate press release, was "a signal to the traitors, Communists and fellow travelers in our Government they need have no fear of exposure from this Administration."

In vituperative frenzy, he went on:

"The most loyal stooges of the Kremlin could not have done a better job of giving a clean bill of health to Stalin's Fifth Column in this country. At a time when American blood is staining the Korean valleys, the Tydings-McMahon report gives unlimited aid and comfort to the very enemies responsible for tying the hands and shooting the faces off some of our soldiers."

Could any sane person believe that Senators Tydings or McMahon or Theodore Green of Rhode Island, the Democratic majority on the committee, were "stooges of the Kremlin" as McCarthy implied? It seemed that the Tydings report and McCarthy's condemnation of it posed the ultimate test of conscience. A choice had to be made. And where did this choice leave the Republican Party? In the arms of Joe McCarthy.

Senators Lodge and Hickenlooper had refused to sign the Tydings report and had brought in separate findings of their own. Lodge, at least, had exhibited signs of a disturbed conscience on several occasions. At one point he had remarked that he would "like to take this show off the road," referring to the public hearings of the Tydings committee; and, even in his dissent from the report, he wrote that there were "many fine people in the State Department and there are the essential elements of a good security system if it is invigorated and developed." This last suggestion that perhaps the department had been laggard conflicted with another observation by Lodge that those administering its loyalty program were doing so "in a conscientious manner."

Lodge and Hickenlooper condemned the Tydings inquiry as hasty and inadequate: "The fact that many charges have been made which have not been proved," Lodge wrote, "does not in the slightest degree relieve the subcommittee of the responsibility for undertaking a relentlessly thorough investigation of its own."

As with Lodge and Hickenlooper, so with the other Republicans in the Senate. What registered with them was not McCarthy's blatant lack of ethics. What registered was that one of their own had been condemned in language so harsh that it broke all rules of Senatorial courtesy.

Shock and fury swept their side of the aisle. The Republican Senate Policy Committee met to try to devise ways to soften or block acceptance of the report. Speaking for the committee afterward, Senator Taft denounced the report as "political" and as "derogatory and insulting to Senator McCarthy." He added that "the language used by the Democrats about Senator McCarthy was inexcusable." He did not, of course, concern himself with the issue of truth.

The polarization of the Senate along strict party lines, without regard to principle, became evident in the floor debate on the Tydings report on July 20. Tydings led the attack in a speech that lasted two hours and five minutes. He excoriated McCarthy to his face in terms that "men with long Senate experience said exceeded anything they had ever heard." He accused McCarthy of resorting to "mud, slime and filth" in making "foul and vile charges" against the State Department. He asked unanimous consent to play a recording of one of McCarthy's speeches that, he said, would show McCarthy was a liar. Indicating the record mounted on a small, heavy, portable machine on his desk, Tydings said Senators could hear for themselves if they would.

"There is a record that stands to challenge Senator McCarthy," he declared. "We have got his voice here. That's why we said the charges were a hoax and a fraud. And by the eternal God that's the truth!

"What is there here other than a fraud and a hoax? It ought to make every American's blood boil that they have been told these foul charges. Here is the record to prove what I say. And if it is broken I have duplicates. Here is a voice. And it is not the voice of truth."

Kenneth Wherry objected to the playing of the record, and Tydings yielded the point. Any Senators who were interested could come to his office and hear "the voice" at any time, he said. Then he turned upon another foe in the Senate, William Jenner, Republican from Indiana. Weeks earlier, Jenner, echoing McCarthy, had accused Tydings of conducting a "whitewash." Recalling this, Tydings walked across the Senate chamber, pointed a lean and stabbing finger at Jenner, and shouted:

"I do not start fights, but I do not run away from them. I dislike to seem immodest, but in my youth I was in some fairly hot places. [This referred to the fact that Tydings was an infantry officer in World War I and won the Distinguished Service Cross.]

"I have been in places where men, real men, were being killed in battle. When it is suggested that I would protect Communist spies in the country that I love—I find—no, I cannot say here what I would wish to say.

"I have taken punishment in the last three months from colleagues who have used every effort to blackguard me. I do not want to sink to that level. But anything I will say on the floor I will say off the floor."

Throughout it all, the Republicans fought a desperate rearguard action. It was significant that not one of them dared to make a personal defense of McCarthy. Their tactic was to try to smother the Tydings report by calling for three separate votes on different issues. On all they lost, since Democrats outnumbered Republicans in the Senate. The final vote accepting the Tydings report was on party lines: 45 Democrats voting for the report: 37 Republicans, against. Not even the signers of the Declaration of Conscience found it in their consciences to break with their party on so politically explosive an issue.

And Senator Tydings, the conservative who had had the courage to denounce the "ism" was soon to become its victim.*

---

* The furor over the Tydings report kept the Senate in turmoil for days. Senator Jenner on July 22 made one of the most violent speeches that sedate chamber had heard in years. In this, incredibly, he accused the conservative Tydings of trying to save his own "miserable political hide" by covering up the "bloody tracks of traitors in government." Of far greater significance was an exchange the preceding day between Senator Lodge and the Democrats. Asked if he believed the State Department was "harboring Reds," Lodge replied forthrightly, "I do not." He added that he believed

. . .

W H A T   E F F E C T was all of this having on the nation? The New York *Herald-Tribune* in its editorial on the Tydings report debate commented about "the general bafflement of the public about the fundamentals involved." Yet it never seemed to occur to the press during this period that it had a responsibility to replace bafflement with enlightenment.

Press coverage of McCarthy from the first had fallen into two general categories, neither helpful to public enlightenment. The more responsible newspapers devoted themselves to "straight" reporting of his charges, quoting whatever McCarthy said because his Senatorial rank gave him a quasi-official privilege. The witch-hunting press chains went all out with a barrage of eight-column headlines, treating every accusation as a new disclosure of fact. There was no sustained attempt by any large segment of the press to put the facts into focus so that the average reader could understand them and appreciate what was involved. Such attempts would be made much later, after McCarthyism had swept the nation and the damage had been done. Not until September, 1951, would the liberal New York *Post* do its full-scale takeout on McCarthy; not until late October, 1951, would *Time* magazine attempt a similar assessment; not until April, 1954, would the *Progressive* put together its documented account of McCarthyism; not until July, 1954, would Frederick Woltman, of the New York *World-Telegram and Sun*, a Pulitzer Prize winner for his communist exposés, deliver his devastating judgment. All of this came much too late.

At the time of the Tydings report, public hysteria continued to be whipped up by the redbaiting press, while the voice of more responsible journals was so muted as to be virtually unheard. The New York *Herald-Tribune*, commenting editorially on the Tydings findings, found cause for congratulation that Senator

---

there had been no communists in the department since 1945 or 1946. He also conceded under questioning by Senator Morse that McCarthy had failed to substantiate any of his charges, but he insisted he thought there should be a "more thorough investigation by an independent commission." Though Lodge and Hickenlooper criticized the Democratic majority on the Tydings committee for not having pressed on with a more thorough probe, the Democrats pointed out that neither Republican Senator had demanded such action during the life of the committee and that both had seemed willing enough to call a halt.

Lodge and the Democratic committee majority both agreed committee hearings were not the forum in which to test loyalty charges. *The New York Times* noted that McCarthy had failed to prove any of his charges; but, like the *Herald-Tribune*, it comforted itself with the thought that both Senator Lodge and the Democrats agreed there were "more responsible" ways of handling the loyalty issue. By contrast, the New York *Journal-American* seized instantly upon the red meat of propaganda. In a screaming editorial entitled "A Shameful Performance," it proclaimed:

"The Tydings committee's majority report on the McCarthy charges of Communist influence in the State Department is probably the most disgracefully partisan document ever to emanate from the Congress of the United States.

"As a public paper prepared in parlous times, it verges upon DISLOYALTY."

The *Journal-American* followed up this hysterical pronouncement by securing comments from a number of Republican Senators who hailed the editorialist's wisdom and judgment. It quoted Senator Mundt as saying: "The editorial hit the nail on the head." Kenneth Wherry contributed the thought that the editorial "tells the story in black and white as to how the Tydings committee failed miserably to do its job." Hickenlooper joined the chorus. And Senator Bricker, a close political and personal friend of Senator Taft, added that the Tydings report was "truly a shameful perfomance."

In an atmosphere in which *disloyalty* salvos were being fired by the right-wing press, in a climate in which there was no countervailing journalistic influence to seek out the truth, the nation became ever more paranoid. To be accused meant in effect to be condemned.

Typical was the experience of Haldore Hanson. Hanson was the director of the State Department's technical staff for President Truman's Point Four program for aid to underdeveloped nations. In 1938 he had been an Associated Press war correspondent in China; he had been assigned to the Communist armies; he had been impressed by their resistance to the Japanese invasion; and he later wrote a book praising the stand of the Chinese Communists—who, incidentally, were then under the supreme command of Chiang Kai-shek. Seizing upon this decade-old volume produced in a different era and a different context, McCarthy accused Hanson of procommunist proclivities. Typically, even when quoting Hanson out of context, McCarthy found it impossible to quote him accurately. He charged that Hanson had called the Communists a "group of hard-headed, *straight*-shooting realists," whereas Hanson had written that they were "hard-headed, *hard*-shooting realists." Hanson took the stand before the Tydings committee; challenged McCarthy to repeat his charges "off the floor" so that he could be sued, a challenge that McCarthy, of course, ignored; and was ultimately cleared of all taint. No action of any kind was ever brought against him. But the damage had been done by the accusation.

"For example," Hanson said in one interview at the time, "a man who feeds cattle on my farm in Virginia has been asked why he continues to work for 'that Communist.' One neighboring farmer began to refer to me last week as 'that Russian spy.'

"A petition calling my family undesirable and urging that we get out of the community was circulated in a village near my farm. Most people approached refused to sign it. Several of them were good enough to report the story to me. I understand a lawyer has now advised the drafter of that petition not to continue his activities."

As early as March 30, 1950, less than two months after Wheeling, the vituperation that is a by-product of panic had been showing up in the flood of mail received by Democratic Senators. Writing from Washington in *The New York Times*, William S. White quoted one Democratic Senator as saying: "The answers so far have plainly not caught up with the charges. We had thought earlier that they were catching up. We still hope, and think, that ultimately the public will come over to the Administration's side. But not yet, not yet."

With a grimace, the Senator tossed across his desk a typed postcard, its message heavily underlined in red ink. It read: "Why don't you get the Red rats out of the State Department?"

White concluded with this analysis: "Informants with many years of experience in evaluating postcards and letter campaigns are convinced that this one, whether misguided or not, is genuine. They are alarmed at its tone and at what they consider to be its depth in the country."

The extent of the damage being done to the nation was well illustrated in an incident cited by Elmer Davis:

". . . In Houston, a man and his wife—she a radio writer— were sitting in a Chinese restaurant talking to the proprietor about a radio program which they hoped he would sponsor—a program dealing with recent Chinese history. A man who over-heard them rushed out and telephoned the police that they were 'talking Communist;' so they were promptly arrested. What they were said to have said—whether they did say it or not is not clear—was that Chiang Kai-shek was fighting a losing battle. That may or may not have been true—especially depending on whether it meant his hanging on in Formosa or reconquering the mainland; but true or false, it was no evidence of Com-munism. Yet this couple spent the night in jail—fourteen hours in jail—before the police finally concluded they had nothing on them and let them go."

PART FOUR

The Men Behind THE MAN

13

The Power Brokers

JOSEPH MC CARTHY pulled together more successfully than any other politician in our history all the elements of an incipient American fascism. Fortunately for America, he did not have any ideological program to offer. There are some indications (newspaper columnists privy to his designs on occasion began to beat the propaganda drums) that at a later period in his career, just before his downfall, McCarthy toyed with the glorious notion of himself in the White House. Some of his most powerful backers vocally supported the idea but for McCarthy himself it was more of a passing fancy than a goal to be grimly pursued. He, for the most part, was in the game for kicks—the thrill of seeing his name in the boldest, blackest headlines. He reveled in the uproar he created, but seemed to lack any coherent or serious national purpose.

Other demagogues have come and gone, but none ever inspired the national frenzy that McCarthy did. In this century, before his time, the most famous and most feared had been Huey Long, the Louisiana Kingfish, whose slogan was "Every Man a King." Long became the virtual dictator of Louisiana, and a rampaging, unpredictable force in the United States Senate. But he remained, for all his color and dramatics, essentially a fringe figure; his appeal was to the Depression's poor and desperate and disenchanted—and to that crackpot element that will always be beguiled by ranting oratory and a slogan. A Louisiana phenomenon, he never united the disparate political elements that would have made him a truly potent national figure for one very good reason: he threatened rather than served the purposes of the big business-press-religious complex that forms the nation's Establishment.

Joe McCarthy, on the other hand, was useful to those forces—useful because he had the ability to induce a popular frenzy against the liberal elements his backers feared.

Around the figure of McCarthy rallied both the cynics of great purpose and the worried, disillusioned and unhinged. Because he was so invaluable in using the Goebbels technique of beating all liberals over the head with a communist bludgeon, he lured to his defense many of the intellectuals of the right, such as William F. Buckley, Jr., and L. Brent Bozell, who became his apologists. Press lords helped to build his image as the champion of pure Americanism—an endeavor to which the powerful McCormick, Hearst and Scripps-Howard chains devoted their talents. With the instinct of a Billy Sunday, he played to religious passions and prejudices. In his speeches, the God-fearing Free World was always pitted against the evils of atheistic communism; and so he drew to his cause much of the hierarchy of the Catholic Church—and, at the same time, he lured many Protestant fundamentalists. Behind all of these disparate elements was the indispensable force of money—big money.

In our Establishment-oriented society, it has become the fashion to belittle McCarthy's appeal to those with the big money as a matter of little consequence, involving only a few crackpot millionaires. It is a delusional view. The record shows conclusively that McCarthy went to the Senate with the backing of big-business interests in his own state and the whole-hearted endorsement of the Chicago isolationist-McCormick-America First axis. This was just a beginning. When he began his liberal-smearing anticommunist campaign, he quickly attracted additional heavy backing from financial moguls. One of these was Joseph P. Kennedy, the multimillionaire founding father of a political dynasty that was to put one son in the White House and two others in positions of national power. Though parts of the record remain obscure, Joseph Kennedy's great wealth helped to finance McCarthy's crusade, and contributed its mite to his reelection campaign in Wisconsin in 1952.

Far better publicized than the Kennedy support was the financial aid McCarthy received from the oil millionaires and billionaires of Texas. This Texas backing has often been written off as that of ignorant *nouveaux riches,* but in any realistic appraisal of our times, the rulers of the Texas oil and gas baronies can hardly be dismissed so lightly. They have been—and remain —a highly favored class. For decades, until trimmed slightly in 1969, the 27½ per cent oil depletion allowance provided that this percentage of their incomes, taken off the top, escaped any taxation at all. There were other equally invaluable, but less obvious, tax loopholes in dry-well drilling and other special allowances. Such provisions put literally billions of dollars of untaxed income at the disposal of the Texas business elite. They came to control the largest reservoir of uninhibited wealth in America; and in their desire to keep things the way they were, to protect their seigneurial privileges, they spent with a lavish hand.

McCarthy's ties to the extreme right and to American admirers of the Nazi and fascist regimes were always extremely close. In 1947, in his first year in the Senate, he had unsuccessfully tried to get a parole for William Dudley Pelley, the jailed leader of the Silver Shirts, a prewar fascist organization. As soon as he became the strident crier of anticommunism at Wheeling and in the Senate, the hate-mongers flocked to him as to a brother of the blood. Gerald L. K. Smith, who has been called "America's most notorious anti-Jewish propagandist," issued and distributed a fifty-cent pamphlet containing reprints of McCarthy's speeches in the Senate. In his news sheet, *The Cross and the Flag,* Smith called McCarthy "this fearless young statesman" who "constitutes one of the most hopeful signs that has appeared on the horizon . . ." Down in West Virginia, where it all started, the West Virginia Anti-Communist League offered the Smith-McCarthy pamphlet as part of a package deal with an effusion of the anti-Semitic Joseph P. Kamp, "Exposing Walter Winchell," and Arnold Leese's virulent tract, "The Jewish War of Survival."

In Union, N.J., Conde McGinley, editor and publisher of another frankly anti-Semitic hate sheet called *Common Sense*, leaped on the McCarthy bandwagon with a whoop and a holler. "Those Americans who wish to live as free men and enjoy Christian worship as they see best, should thank our good Lord for such a man as Joe McCarthy," he proclaimed. McCarthy, he said, was being "attacked by Marxists and their dupes and hatchetmen." McGinley saw communism as a Jewish conspiracy. The handful of admitted communists, he argued, "are only the shock troops for the Marxist-Zionists who are the brains and directors of Communism while posing as lovable, respectable men and philanthropists."

Joseph P. Kamp, the discredited Nazi propagandist, tied up all the threads in one inflammatory diatribe: "May God sustain Senator Joe McCarthy!" he wrote. ". . . Nobody in years has given the Fair Deal-New Deal pressure group in Washington such a battle as has Joe McCarthy, with his forthright assault upon Communists in the State Department . . ." The title of this Kamp effusion was *It Isn't Safe to be an American*.

No politician, of course, is responsible for the beliefs of the legions that are attracted to his banner. A Roosevelt should not be blamed because a communist happened to vote for him, nor a McCarthy because he appealed so strongly to racist fanatics, *if* in each case the recipient of the favor had made it clear that he did not agree with the views of such supporters. There is a vast difference, however, between being the helpless victim of this kind of political support and actively courting it. And McCarthy courted it.

McCarthy's willingness to dwell in these chthonian levels of politics showed most clearly in his relationship with Upton Close, the Axis apologist whose anti-Semitism had banned him from the major networks. On April 30, 1950, as his campaign was gathering steam, McCarthy went on Close's radio program and said: "I've got some very good friends over in some Federal investigative agencies, and when I started going into this [his denunciation of the State Department], one of them said to me, 'Now why don't you get in touch with Upton Close? He's got a better overall picture than perhaps any other man in Washington.' "

Close murmured appropriate appreciation, and what followed was clearly the communion of compatible souls. Close got underdog Joe to tell how he was digging down into his own pocket for from $23 to $35 a day to get information on traitors in government—a patriotic performance that was all but impoverishing him. Such a lonely and dedicated champion obviously deserved support; and, before the program ended, Close appealed for contributions from one million Americans to help McCarthy in "this crusade." Shortly thereafter, whether in response to this appeal or as a result of the passions McCarthy had aroused at the grass roots, contributions began to pour into McCarthy's Senate office. The total was never definitively established, but evidence showed that literally thousands of dollars were donated.

The McCarthy-Close axis operated for a considerable time to the benefit of both. According to William V. Shannon and Oliver Pilat, Close turned over to McCarthy "tons of material," with special emphasis on the favorite theme of Far Eastern "betrayal." Close also, Shannon and Pilat discovered, ghosted some of McCarthy's early speeches, for instance one delivered before a women's convention in Atlantic City, N.J., in May, 1950.

McCarthy reciprocated by seeing that Close got favorable mention in the *Congressional Record*. Close was producing a news sheet entitled "Closer-Ups," and McCarthy dutifully entered these documents into the *Record* as important contributions to the intellectual atmosphere of the times. Some of these "Closer-Ups" contained nakedly anti-Semitic references. One in early April, 1950, denounced "tolerance racketeers," a code word on the hate-mongering fringe that translated into the Anti-Defamation League of B'nai B'rith. Though it might be argued that McCarthy did not recognize such sophisticated synonyms, he could hardly have been blind to some of the more obvious anti-Semitic statements in the material he was introducing into the *Congressional Record*. Close, for example, argued that a negotiated peace with Germany would be bitterly opposed by Jewish organizations which hold "a strategic position in U.S. politics." He also hurled some racial barbs at Supreme Court Justice Felix Frankfurter whom he called "Felix Frankfurter from Vienna." (The very name of Frankfurter was another of those code anti-Semitisms. Whenever Conde McGinley endeavored to show the dangers to the nation of the alleged Marxist-Zionist cabal, he always dragged out pictures of Frankfurter and Secretary of the Treasury Henry Morgenthau, Jr., as examples of the kind of *éminences grises* who were betraying the nation.) Close argued that Frankfurter "taught guile" to novitiates in the State Department and that his subversion of these young and inexperienced men had encouraged belief in a planned economy and admiration of "Socialist Harold Laski of England, a friend of Frankfurter."

When some wealthy and prominent Wisconsin Jews began to read this drivel, they wrote their Senator indigant protests, spelling out Close's profascist and anti-Semitic background and demanding to know what his words were doing in the *Congressional Record*. McCarthy replied in appropriately contrite terms. He protested that he had been ignorant of Close's anti-Semitic leanings and added: "I decided it would be well to remove the Close letter from the *Record* . . . You understand there is no way of removing the news letter from the temporary *Record*, but it will not appear in the bound volume."

This acknowledgment of error soothed the Wisconsin constituents, but it created a new problem. When Close learned of the repudiation, *he* became furious—and wrote McCarthy demanding to know what the devil went on here. Caught in this precarious situation, McCarthy did a balancing act that would have been the envy of any tightrope walker. On June 26, 1950, he wrote Close a "Dear Upton" letter. In it he said regretfully that he had had to do what he had done because, unfortunately, there were a lot of evil-minded people in the world who were anxious to smear the purity of his crusade by branding it "a Catholic effort" or making "it appear there is something anti-Semitic about me or my anti-Communist drive." If such canards should gain credence, he pointed out, they could "unnecessarily impair the possibility of really getting a government house-cleaning." The tenor of the letter was that Close should understand McCarthy regarded him as highly as ever.

Close, his wounded self-esteem soothed, flaunted this letter in his very next "Closer-Up," and his alliance with McCarthy flourished as warmly as ever. More than two years later, on September 1, 1952, he was telling the Associated Press: "Anyone who opposes McCarthy is giving aid and comfort to the enemies of the Republic."

THE PORNOGRAPHERS OF HATE performed an important function for McCarthy because their humble followers helped to swell the flow of donations into his Senate office, and gave him a claque to applaud his every utterance wherever he went. Perhaps even more important was another element—the intellectuals of the right, who bestowed on him the inestimable gift of respectability.

Right-wing intellectuals saw in McCarthy a formidable champion against the real enemy—the liberals, whom they regarded as virtually indistinguishable from communists. Therefore, because the cause was just, McCarthy must be forgiven his excesses; despite occasional slips, he was really RIGHT.

The most graphic example of this sophistry that poses as intellectualism is to be found in *McCarthy and His Enemies,* the ostentatiously researched work written by William F. Buckley, Jr., the oracle of the right, and his associate on the staff of the *National Review,* L. Brent Bozell. Buckley and Bozell acknowledge repeatedly in gentle tones of sorrow that McCarthy exceeded the strict bounds of truth and responsibility on occasion. But they excuse such faux pas on the grounds that he became overzealous because he was so caught up in a noble cause.

The treatment of assumption as proven fact is essential to this sort of defense. Typical is the Buckley-Bozell apologia for McCarthy's original charges of treason in the State Department. They acknowledge that McCarthy telegraphed President Truman: "I have in my possession the names of 57 Communists who are in the State Department at present." They acknowledge that he said this, not once but twice, in the same telegram. And then they write:

"McCarthy, of course, could never hope to prove that specific charge, and hence should not have phrased it the way he did. This does not mean that there were not at that time, or that there are not today, 57 Communists in the Department of State . . ."

The truth was that McCarthy, though he strove his mightiest, never could establish the presence of even *a single communist* in the State Department of Dean Acheson; but such failure of proof becomes meaningless when the basis of argument is perverted from what *is* to what *may be*. Of course, there *might* have been 57 Communists in the State Department in 1950—or 157, for that matter—but a rational society can certainly see the distinction between what *may be* and what *is*. Yet the perpetuation of the McCarthy crusade depended on making what *might be* seem factual.

The Buckley-Bozell rationale can be seen in this passage: "Probatory evidence of Party membership is *ipso facto* hard to come by. If we have learned anything about the scope and the techniques of the Communist conspiracy it is that only a small percentage of the Communist faithful take out membership cards; and that, what is more, *many Communists are not identifiable on the basis of their overt political activities.* Whittaker Chambers has a great deal to say on the subject, as do dozens of equally authentic witnesses to the conspiracy . . ." (Italics added.)

Leaving aside the question of the authenticity of informers, a point that is infinitely debatable, the thrust of this passage is that the absence of proof means nothing because proof must not be expected. How, then, can one identify the unidentifiable? One cannot; one can only imagine the worst.

The purpose of all this tortured logic is apparent in *McCarthy and His Enemies.* The real enemies are the liberals. They are the ones who let down Chiang Kai-shek; they are the ones who have "misread" history and caused all our troubles. The Buckley-Bozell outrage at the liberals froths to a crest in this passage:

". . . Some day, the patience of America may at last be exhausted, and we will strike out against the Liberals. Not because they are treacherous like the Communists, but because, like James Burnham, we will conclude 'that they are mistaken in their predictions, false in their analyses, wrong in their advice, and through the results of their actions injurious to the interests of the nation. That is reason enough to strive to free the country's affairs from the influence of them and their works.' "

In a footnote Buckley and Bozell explain that Burnham obviously was advocating "social sanctions," whatever they may be, against the liberals—not the kind of more punitive action they themselves might seem to favor in their "strike out against the Liberals" phrase. Buckley and Bozell, in obeisance to their status as intellectuals, appropriately genuflected to the ideal of "going to the rescue" of "well-meaning liberals" who were not really procommunists, but this appears from their account to have been an exceedingly rare, if indeed not a nonexistent, species.

After having administered to McCarthy the unavoidable gentle reproofs for getting carried away in some instances (as, for example, in calling Owen Lattimore the Number 1 Soviet spy in America), Buckley and Bozell concluded that McCarthy was a reputable statesman who deserved the support of all concerned Americans. This laying-on-of-hands came in the concluding sentence of their book: "But as long as McCarthyism fixes its goal with its present precision, it is a movement around which men of good will and stern morality can close ranks."

The extremists of the right and the intellectuals of the right had both blessed Joe McCarthy. All that remained was that he should be equally blessed by the servants of God and the masters of money.

SPIRITUAL AND TEMPORAL POWERS combined behind McCarthy quite early in his witch hunt. The united effort was symbolized by the activities of Joseph P. Kennedy and Francis Cardinal Spellman. Both were enthusiastic McCarthy supporters, and both helped enormously to build the McCarthy image—Kennedy with money; Spellman with his Cardinal's prestige and the imprimatur of the Church.

Drew Pearson has written that Joseph Kennedy poured $50,-000 into McCarthy's "crusade"—and this was a kitty apart from Kennedy's contributions to McCarthy's reelection campaign in Wisconsin in 1952. Pearson insisted that he had "positive information" about a meeting in the Kennedy compound at Hyannis Port, Mass., that brought Kennedy, Cardinal Spellman and McCarthy together in the early days of McCarthy's campaign. It was at this meeting, Pearson said, that Cardinal Spellman and Kennedy "helped . . . to plot McCarthy's course."

As for Joseph Kennedy's $50,000 investment, Pearson added: "We have used that figure in our columns many times, and neither Bobby nor Jack nor anyone else has ever disputed it." The Kennedy money, he explained, was funneled to McCarthy over a period of time for the specific purpose of helping to get McCarthy's anticommunist, antiliberal drive rolling, and it had nothing to do with the subsequent and far smaller donation to the 1952 reelection campaign. About this later contribution there is no question, for Joseph Kennedy himself subsequently admitted it on several occasions.

Robert E. Thompson and Hortense Myers, who wrote a biography of Robert F. Kennedy, had interviews with Papa Joe and subsequently reported: "Joseph P. Kennedy knew McCarthy, liked him, supported his campaign against international communism and had been his host at Hyannis Port." They also wrote that Joseph Kennedy had told them he had contributed "a couple of thousand dollars" to McCarthy's 1952 reelection campaign, not to keep McCarthy from coming into Massachusetts (where young Jack was running the campaign that would unseat Senator Lodge), but "because a mutual friend of ours, Westbrook Pegler, asked me to give it to him and because I liked the fight he was putting up against Communists in our government."

Pegler had a slightly different version. The contribution, he said, was $3,000 and he hadn't "asked" Kennedy for it; he had merely pointed out that McCarthy was strapped for money in his Wisconsin campaign. The Kennedy donation, according to Pegler, was forwarded to McCarthy through a go-between with the tacit understanding that McCarthy was to stay out of Massachusetts, which he did.

Whether this last fluttering of Kennedy greenbacks into the McCarthy coffers had strings attached to it seems somewhat immaterial, for the record indicates that the ties between Papa Joe and McCarthy were close enough to prevent the GOP's favorite hatchetman of 1952 from charging into Massachusetts. Joseph Kennedy certainly never made any secret of his long and lasting attachment for McCarthy. In 1961 he told one interviewer: "In case there is any question in your mind, I liked Joe McCarthy. I always liked him. I would see him when I went down to Washington, and when he was visiting in Palm Beach he'd come around to my house for a drink. I invited him to Cape Cod."

During one of these visits to Hyannis Port, McCarthy assayed to play shortstop for the Kennedy team in a softball game on the lawn, but he made four errors in rapid succession and was "benched" by being banished to the porch. Another time, Joseph Kennedy recalled, "he went out on my boat . . . and he almost drowned swimming behind it but he never complained. . . . He was always pleasant; he was never a crab."

On another occasion Kennedy told of his initial reaction when the Wisconsin Senator began to denounce the communist menace. "I thought he'd be a sensation," he said "He was smart. But he went off the deep end." Kennedy paused and then, as he recalled "the final, bleak days" of McCarthy, his "eyes . . . clouded and his voice wavered."

The attitude of the patriarch of the Kennedy family found a reflection for a long time in the conduct of his two oldest surviving sons. John F. Kennedy, when he became a candidate for the Democratic Presidential nomination in 1960, was highly suspect in liberal segments of the party because he had not taken a forthright stand on McCarthyism when it mattered, as had Senators like McMahon, Lehman and Tydings. All kinds of excuses were made—that Jack had been desperately ill at the time, that he had had a critical McCarthy speech prepared but that he hadn't been able to appear in the Senate to deliver it, that through some inter-office snafu he had failed to make his sentiments known even by remote control. A more reasonable explanation seems to be, as the future President himself once indicated in another context, that he had grown up in his father's house and had imbibed many of his father's ideas until practical political experience with the harsh realities of modern America had broadened him and set him on a different course.

In 1950 John Kennedy, then a Congressman, felt so strongly about the anticommunist issue that he was privately cheering for Richard M. Nixon in California. That was the year in which Nixon ran his typical McCarthyite "pink sheet" campaign against Helen Gahagan Douglas, a smear technique that catapulted him into the Senate and set him on the road to higher office. Despite the nature of the campaign and the obvious principle involved, Jack Kennedy could write to his old friend, Paul B. Fay, Jr., on November 14, 1950: "I was glad to . . . see Nixon win by a big vote."

During the 1952 campaign, John Mallan, then a teaching

fellow at Harvard University, described for the *New Republic* a 1950 seminar that had been addressed by John F. Kennedy. According to Mallan, Kennedy had said that he did not think enough had been done about removing communists from government. He made it clear that he rather respected McCarthy, that "he thought he knew Joe pretty well, and he may have something." Mallan's report caused a tremendous flap in liberal circles, and the author was berated for having violated the sanctity of the lecture hall by his public disclosure. But the truth of his account was never challenged.

Another incident in the 1952 Kennedy-Lodge campaign stressed the tightness of the bonds between Joseph Kennedy and Joseph McCarthy. John Kennedy was a question mark to liberals, and he needed their support. So he rallied to his side a veteran Bostonian whose championship of liberal causes was beyond question—Gardner (Pat) Jackson, one of the defenders of Sacco and Vanzetti. Jackson succeeded in a hard-sell; he got the initially suspicious trade unions and Americans for Democratic Action to support Jack Kennedy. With so much accomplished, he reasoned that his candidate ought to begin looking and acting like a liberal. This meant to Jackson that Kennedy should take a stand on the crucial issue of the day—McCarthyism. The candidate was a bit reluctant, according to Jackson, but Jackson prepared a carefully worded newspaper advertisement, based on a statement by ninety-nine members of the Notre Dame faculty, an eminently "safe" source. The advertisement was to be headlined: COMMUNISM AND MC CARTHY: BOTH WRONG.

Kennedy, despite his doubts, agreed to sign the ad, provided the veteran Rep. John W. McCormack (who was to become Speaker of the House) would agree to go along. McCormack agreed, seemingly removing the last obstacle, and Jackson, in triumph, repaired to Kennedy campaign headquarters where the candidate had asked him to read the proposed advertisement to a circle of advisers. Almost as soon as Jackson arrived, John Kennedy ducked out of the room to do some instant campaigning, and when Jackson looked around, the reason for the sudden exit became obvious—John's father was there, sitting at a card table with some aides. Jackson began to read, and he later recounted what happened in these words:

". . . I hadn't gone two sentences when Joe [Kennedy] jumped to his feet with such force that he tilted the table against the others."

The patriarch of the Kennedy clan was so furious that it seemed for a moment as if he might physically attack Jackson; then, as an embarrassed silence deepened in the room, he gave Jackson a tongue-lashing in which antiliberal, antiunion and even anti-Semitic prejudices spewed out.

"You're trying to ruin Jack," he stormed. "You and your sheeny friends are trying to ruin my son's career."

Joseph Kennedy shouted that he liked McCarthy and had contributed to his campaign; he repeatedly excoriated liberals and unionists for trying to destroy Jack. "I can't estimate how long he poured it out on me," Jackson said later. "It was just a stream of stuff—always referring to 'you and your sheeny friends.'"

Finally, exhausted by his rage, Kennedy stalked out—and any thought of making McCarthyism an issue in that campaign was dead. In interviews in subsequent years, Joseph Kennedy denied blandly that the incident had ever happened.

The language that Gardner Jackson quoted touched a sensitive nerve. As Ambassador to England in pre-World War II days, Kennedy had been accused of anti-Semitic prejudices. And there could be no question about his antiliberalism, his support of the Franco conquest of Spain, and his cordial rapport with the appeasement-minded Tory government of Neville Chamberlain.

As for Robert Kennedy, his attachment to McCarthy's brand of anticommunism was far closer and more enduring than that of his brother. In 1953, despite Jack's protests (an indication perhaps that the older brother was already changing) but with his father's urging, young Robert accepted a job as counsel to McCarthy's subcommittee on investigations. He resigned on July 31, 1953, because he disagreed with the committee's slipshod investigative methods, but he parted on the most cordial terms and remained forever faithful to McCarthy's memory. Years later he summed up McCarthy for Thompson and Myers in these terms:

"He got so involved with all the publicity—and after that it was the number one thing in his life. He was on a toboggan. It was so exciting and exhilarating as it went downhill that it didn't matter to him if he hit a tree at the bottom . . . I felt sorry for him, particularly in the last year of his life, when he was such a beaten, destroyed person . . .

"I liked him and yet at times he was terribly heavy-handed. He was a very complicated character. His whole method of operation was complicated because he would get a guilty feeling and get hurt after he had blasted somebody. He wanted desperately to be liked. He was so thoughtful and yet so unthoughtful in what he did to others. He was sensitive and yet insensitive. He didn't anticipate the results of what he was doing. He was very thoughtful of his friends, and yet he could be so cruel to others."

That was probably as clear-eyed and perceptive an analysis of Joe McCarthy as could be made. It recognized all the realities —and yet it reserved its sympathy for McCarthy and exhibited few signs of a comparable compassion for his victims.

The same bias was exhibited by Cardinal Spellman, Joseph Kennedy's partner in the early backing of McCarthy. The Cardinal's paranoia about the communist menace almost the instant World War II ended has been noted. In later years the Cardinal consistently defended McCarthy—and this long after the Senator had wished for a club to teach patriotism to "little Ad-lie," long after he had smeared such men as General Marshall, Dean Acheson and President Truman as virtual traitors.

The Spellman attitude was made abundantly clear on October 24, 1953, in a speech to a Roman Catholic lecture group in Brussels, Belgium. He asserted:

". . . No American uncontaminated by communism has lost his good name because of Congressional hearings on un-American activities.

"However, there are many individuals who have seriously compromised themselves by a flat refusal to state whether they are now or have been Communists. It is impossible for me to understand why any American should refuse to declare himself free of Communist affiliations, *unless he has something to hide* . . .

". . . The anguished cries and protests against 'McCarthyism' are not going to dissuade Americans from their desire to see Communists exposed and removed from positions where they can carry out their nefarious plans . . ."

One has to wonder what world the Cardinal had been living in when McCarthy accused a Dorothy Kenyon, a Philip Jessup, a

General Marshall of betraying their nation by their adherence to communist doctrines, all without a shred of evidence to substantiate the charges.

Unfortunately, the Cardinal's attitude was that of a large and powerful segment of his Church. In 1953, a Catholic priest at a communion breakfast for 1,800 New York City firemen in Brooklyn asserted that "out in the forefront of those ferreting out communism is that great American, great Marine and great Catholic, Senator Joe McCarthy." In 1954, a monsignor of the church, speaking as the personal representative of Cardinal Spellman at a communion breakfast of Catholic War Veterans, declared that he "personally" knew a kitty of more than $5 million had been raised to "kick" McCarthy out of the Senate and that the "reason is solely because of his Catholic ideals"—a wild appeal to Catholic prejudice for which there was never the slightest shred of proof. And in November, 1955, preaching at a memorial Mass in St. Patrick's Cathedral, still another high prelate of the church could declare that "even now, while you are listening to me, there are untouchable traitors in high places aided and abetted by strategically placed cohorts in our country. The men who sold the Chinese into Communist slavery are planning hopefully and finally to betray and take over America . . ."

It was, indeed, the season of unreason. And the Catholics were not alone; they were joined by the Protestant fundamentalists.

This, certainly, was an anomaly. Protestant fundamentalists traditionally view the Catholic Church with deep suspicion, if not with positive enmity. They were the ones most certain that if Al Smith were elected in 1928 the Pope would have a secret tunnel into the basement of the White House. In the intervening decades they had not greatly changed (as was to be demonstrated in 1960 when Jack Kennedy, despite his appeal to the rest of the nation, could make virtually no headway in fundamentalist territory). Yet on the issue of McCarthyism the fundamentalists and the Catholic prelates were as one.

The explanation was to be found in the undercurrents of religious change that were surging against the pillars of old beliefs. The fundamentalists, who adhere to the literal word of the Bible, were affronted and alarmed by revisionist interpretations. One reaction was to attribute such tampering with the bedrocks of their religion to the insidious influence of communism. Consequently, Joe McCarthy's attacks on the menace became for them, just as for many Catholics, a kind of holy crusade with the welfare of the nation and religion equally at stake.

As a result, one found so prominent a Protestant churchman as the Rev. Dr. Daniel A. Poling, president of the World's Christian Endeavor Union and chairman of the All American Council to Combat Communism, describing McCarthy as virtually a modern Messiah come to lead his children out of the wilderness of subversion. Speaking in Milwaukee after McCarthy's primary victory in September, 1952, Dr. Poling lashed out at Adlai Stevenson, whom he found far too complacent about the menace, and lauded McCarthy in a sermon entitled, "The One and Only Issue." McCarthy's victory, he said, derived from the Senator's concern with this "one issue"—and "the United States of America; the honor and integrity of this nation; her freedom and security; her world leadership and destiny." Senator McCarthy, Dr. Poling declared, "is a symbol. He is a symbol of dynamic defense."

Dr. Poling was no lonely voice among the Protestants; he was only one in a chorus. Hailing McCarthy and all his works were such fundamentalists as Carl McIntire and the American Council of Christian Churches; Edgar Bundy and the Church League of America; John R. Rice, editor of *The Sword of the Lord;* Robert Shuler and the *Methodist Challenge;* the Rev. Billy James Hargis and his Christian Crusade; and a variety of ultraconservative Baptist groups.

In an analysis of this fundamentalist phenomenon in the McCarthy era, Warren L. Vinz, assistant professor of history at Boise State College, has written:

"There was a leadership common to both fundamentalism and McCarthyism. J. B. Matthews was the link between the two movements. Not only was he hired by McCarthy as a professional researcher for the Senate Permanent Subcommittee on Investigations, but his materials were distributed by the Church League of America as well. Not only did he testify before the House Un-American Activities Committee on subversive activities in the Protestant Church, but he was also quoted and praised as

God's servant by the fundamentalists. This is to say that an attack on J. B. Matthews was also an attack on the Church League of America, the American Council of Christian Churches, *The Sword of the Lord*, the *Methodist Challenge*, and others, for all had their share in him. Moreover, these fundamentalists tenaciously hung on to every word of the House Committee hearings relevant to their interests, quoting individual members of the committee . . . and all witnesses who by their testimony helped to confirm their suspicions. Conversely, government investigative committees used the allegations of the fundamentalists to footnote their attacks . . ."

The quotes flew back and forth, one fanatic citing another as his authority, each reinforcing the other in his conviction that Armageddon was here, and all of them together combining in a religious propaganda blitz to scare the wits out of the more sober citizens of the nation.

BACKED BY RACISTS and so-called respectable rightists deluded by their hatred of liberalism, anointed by the hierarchy of the Catholic Church and by leaders of Protestant fundamentalism, McCarthy needed to tap only one more source of power to become truly formidable—money. This he found flowing freely from the bulging wallets of Texas oil millionaires. In 1954 *Fortune* offered this interpretation of McCarthy's popularity with these magnates: "McCarthy, the rough-and-ready Marine, challenging Truman, smiting left-wing college professors hip and thigh, appealed to the Texans' combativeness as well as their conservatism. The American system was being attacked by subversives; nowhere had that system reached a fuller flowering than in Texas; nobody had more to lose should the attack succeed; McCarthy was determined that it should not succeed. It was that simple." Joe McCarthy was admired "not just for attacking Communism" but for linking it with liberals who exhibited signs of wanting to cut back on oil's special privileges.

McCarthy's relationship with the monied men of Texas went back a long way. He first met many of them in 1948, nearly two years before the dinner at the Colony and the speech in Wheeling. He was involved at the time in preprimary spadework aimed at getting the Republican Presidential nomination for Harold Stassen. Another leader in this endeavor was Dan Gainey, an Owatonna, Minn., jewelry manufacturer. As Gainey later told the story, he met many of the wealthy Texans and tried to get them interested in Stassen, but they were unenthusiastic. Getting nowhere with them, Gainey decided to let McCarthy try his hand. It was love at first sight.

McCarthy's first contact with the realm of Croesus could not have been more fortuitous. Gainey introduced him to Hugh Roy Cullen and Cullen's son-in-law, Douglas Marshall, both of Houston. Cullen was so wealthy that he had staggered the imaginations of ordinary men by philanthropies estimated at $160 million, the principal beneficiaries being the University of Houston and the Texas Medical Center. He had also invested, as has been noted, some $1 million in right-wing radio propagandizing across the nation, and he was always good for a few thousands to back candidates for Congress. In the 1952 campaign he and his sons-in-law made thirty-one contributions ranging from $500 to $5,000 to candidates for the Senate and House who were not contaminated by left-wing ideas, especially where oil privileges were concerned.

McCarthy certainly was not infected. His votes in the Senate made it clear that he thought "right." On March 29, 1950, he voted for the passage of the Kerr-Thomas natural gas bill which would have exempted producers from regulation by the Federal Power Commission. This measure was vetoed by President Truman. On September 28, 1951, McCarthy was paired against an amendment to a new tax act that would have slashed the oil depletion allowance from $27\frac{1}{2}$ percent to 15 percent, and on April 2, 1952, he voted for the tidelands oil resolution—the "giveaway" measure that turned over to the states (and, in effect, to the private oil companies) the invaluable treasure hidden under the sea in off-shore oil lands.

Such a record in the Senate made McCarthy the darling of the Lone Star State. All he had to do was to pick up a telephone and ask for $5,000 or $10,000—not just for one of his own campaigns, but to wreak vengeance on Senators like Millard Tydings who had crossed him—and the money would be there as fast as the mail could fly in a check. There were also more visible signs of the McCarthy-Texas romance. McCarthy flew all around the country in the executive planes owned by his oil-baron friends.

They wined and dined him, gave him an air-conditioned Cadillac, hosted him at a $100-a-plate dinner and whirled him off to island retreats in the Gulf or to a hunting hacienda high in the Mexico hills. Nothing was too good for Joe McCarthy.

Among his legion of worshipers in Texas, a "big four" stood out. They were four of the wealthiest men in the nation, if not in the world, and they were united in the conviction that a liberal was as much to be despised as a communist. Hugh Cullen was one. He detested internationalism and free-tradism, and distrusted highly placed Eastern Republicans of liberal bent, suspecting they had far too much influence on the Eisenhower Administration. Truman's civil rights program aimed at abolishing segregation was to him an example of totalitarian government—and "that means atheism." He advocated the abolishment of all income taxes and the substitution of federal and state sales taxes, and he predicted that such a tax system, favoring the rich at the expense of the poor, would result in "the greatest kind of prosperity." He wanted to bomb China and let Chiang Kai-shek loose on the mainland, convinced that an overwhelming popular uprising would put an end to communism in China forever.

Competing with Cullen for status as a McCarthy worshiper was Clint W. Murchison (pronounced Murkison), of Dallas, who was estimated at the time to be worth at least $300 million. His fortune, founded on gas and oil and the depletion allowance, had expanded in all directions, and in the early 1950s he had heavy investments in some one hundred firms with vast influence in many areas of American life. His corporate pawns included an insurance company in Richmond, Va.; a steamship company on the West Coast; a good part of the Transcontinental Bus system, second only to Greyhound; the Martha Washington candy company; a Dallas taxicab company; a fishing tackle firm in Michigan; the Royal Gorge Bridge and Amusement Company in Colorado; drive-in theaters, tourist courts, *Field and Stream* magazine, and Henry Holt & Co., a large New York publishing house whose policies, Murchison thought, had been influenced by some off-beat thinking before he got control. Not being able to identify precisely just who the off-beat thinkers were, "We cleared them all out," he said, "and we put some good men in."

For fun and games, Murchison had a 75,000-acre hunting and cattle ranch high in the Sierra Madre Mountains of Mexico, a spread valued in itself at some $1 million. And to get there with a minimum of inconvenience, he could rely on a fleet of executive-style DC-3s, planes that he often put at the disposal of Senator McCarthy to facilitate his trips back and forth from Washington to Texas.

Murchison's life-values were perhaps best described in an anecdote related by his brother, Frank, who, incidentally, thought McCarthy was "a hypocrite and an over-ambitious man." Frank Murchison described how his brother Clint had raised his two sons after their mother died; and, though the boys had been left a fortune, he wouldn't let them touch a cent of it.

"You know," Frank said Clint told him one day, "those boys of mine made $2,000,000 last year—all by themselves."

"What do those boys of yours need all that money for?" Frank asked him. "They've got millions of their own already."

"My god," Clint said, "what else is there for them to do?"

As a far-right conservative, Murchison departed from the script in only one respect; he was an internationalist in foreign affairs and believed in aid to underdeveloped nations. But, domestically, he saw advocates of change as apostles of communism. His political philosophy was reflected in the Eisenhower-Stevenson campaign of 1952, when he was responsible for the printing and distribution of 600,000 copies of a sheet called "The Native Texan." The tone of the headlines told the story. "With Adlai You Can't Even Pick Your Own Doctor." "Adlai's Ideas Aid Kremlin." "Washington Morals Sink to New Low." "McCarthy Charges Treason." "Truman Stays Faithful to Stalin in Oregon."

Naturally, Clint Murchison liked McCarthy. He flew the Senator to the hunting preserve in Mexico, played poker and gin rummy with him, donated some $40,000 to his various political enterprises. "I tell you," he told one interviewer, "I think he's done the greatest possible service to the country. He fears nobody and he's certainly got those Communists feared to death of him. I'm for him all the way."

For him all the way, too, was the man who was to become the richest Texan of them all—H. L. Hunt, of Dallas, who has been described in recent years as a billionaire and who in the early 1950s was probably at least a half-billionaire. Hunt, like Cullen, contributed money in multi-thousand dollar gobs to extreme right-wing causes. His *Facts Forum* and several satellite radio shows, carried by hundreds of stations across the nation, were estimated by *Fortune* at one time to be costing Hunt and members of his family "between $750,000 and $1 million annually for their support."

Hunt's fortune derived from oil and natural gas, and he too had expanded into other fields. He owned such huge cattle ranches that there was speculation he must be the largest individual land-owner in the nation, and he became active in food-processing and other fields far removed from oil. He lived in a mansion that was a lavish replica of Mount Vernon, and his political ideas were even more antiquated than this manorial period piece. One Dallas oilman who knew him well once described him in these terms: "It isn't just that Hunt is to the right of McKinley. He thinks that Communism began in this country when the government took over the distribution of the mail."

Edward T. Folliard, of the Washington *Post*, who had a long interview with Hunt, described the great billionaire's conception of foreign relations this way:

"Hunt is convinced that the world situation today, with Russia having sway over 600 million people, was plotted in Washington, D.C., in the days of Roosevelt and Truman.

"He told me, with some feeling, that Russia's expansion—the gobbling up of Poland and other satellites and the movement of China into the Communist orbit—must have been 'conceived and managed' in Washington.

"And he told me also that those American boys who were tortured and slaughtered in Korea were betrayed by some 'disloyal' people who 'surrendered' to Russia five years before."

Next to "communist" the word Hunt hated most was "liberal." This second term, he said, sounded mild but was really only a coverup for the former. Hunt's definition of a "liberal" was most imprecise. Even such men as the highly conservative Senator Tydings became suspect in his mind when they dared to oppose McCarthy; and so when McCarthy needed a few thousand dollars (as he soon would) to help him avenge himself on Tydings, Hunt was only too glad to contribute.

The fourth of the Texas moguls who looked with favor on McCarthy was the least talkative and most enigmatic of them all. He was Sid W. Richardson, of Forth Worth, a close associate of Murchison, and reputed to be just as wealthy as H. L. Hunt himself. Like the others, Richardson had gained his fortune from oil; and, like the others, he had expanded his interests to include vast cattle ranches, a drug store chain, a radio-television chain, and a half-ownership in the Texas Hotel in Fort Worth. He had also acquired a dream island twenty-eight miles long and six miles wide in the Gulf of Mexico—a retreat where he had entertained such dignitaries as President Roosevelt and General Eisenhower.

Richardson's relationship with McCarthy was far more tenuous than those of his fellow Texas monarchs. In the early days, when McCarthy was starting out, Richardson was reported in Texas circles to be one of Joe's backers, and Richardson himself said enough to lend credence to the reports. He told reporters he thought McCarthy had done "some good work" and had his value, but he was tight-lipped about his own support of the Senator. He did not fete McCarthy as the others did; he kept a cool distance, and he explained the political reasons for this. "I don't see how I could be friendly with Sam Rayburn and Lyndon Johnson and be friendly with Joe McCarthy, too," he said. Later, after McCarthy began to cause trouble for the Eisenhower Administration, Richardson, who almost worshiped Eisenhower and had been influential in getting Ike into the Presidential race, would have nothing to do with McCarthy.

These were only the biggest of the big names in Texas who backed McCarthy with money and propaganda. In a state where you did not really count unless you had at least $100 million, there were a lot of lesser figures whose bankrolls were still attractive and who were infinitely helpful. One of the most enthusiastic of these second-echelon admirers was Austin F. Hancock, a retired San Antonio insurance executive. Hancock in 1950 founded the strident American Heritage Protective Committee and in three years financed some 522 million mailings of its right-wing propaganda material. McCarthy, he thought, was the only man who could "save" the nation, and he was willing to "do anything in the world" to get McCarthy nominated for President.

Hancock's views may be gleaned from the contents of the mailings he sponsored. These contained semiliterate swipes at the Fair Employment Practices Commission as "un-American, left-wing, socialistic and/or subversive and/or communistic." As for the Federal Council of Churches, Hancock's American Heritage literature asked: "Are these new 'interpreters' of our Bible communistic or Zionist inspired?" As for civil rights: "The white man in the south is the southern Negro's best friend. Ninety per cent of all Negroes would prefer to associate, co-habitate exclusively with their own race—God created them that way—just as He did the Birds of the Air, Beasts of the Forests, Fish of the Sea, regardless of any Fair Deal, New Deal man-made mandate against the laws of nature."

Such were the forces of money, religion and racial prejudice that marshaled behind Joe McCarthy. They combined to form a formidable phalanx of power.

A G A I N S T   S U C H   P O W E R , where were the voices of reason? They were there, but they were for the most part lonely voices.

One of the first and most distinguished voices to speak out against McCarthyism was that of Republican elder statesman Henry L. Stimson, who had been a Republican Secretary of State and who had served as Secretary of War in the government of national unity that President Roosevelt had formed in World War II. Stimson early perceived the drift and dangers of Mc-Carthyism; and in a letter to *The New York Times* on March 27, 1950, he took a clear and unequivocal stand.

He made the point, first, that McCarthy's ranting charges in the Senate did not constitute "the proper way in which to insure the loyalty of government employees." If that were the accuser's "real purpose," Stimson said, "he would have used the fully developed and tested procedure of the executive branch of the Government, under which charges are investigated and weighed by men of both parties and unimpeachable integrity."

"Second," Stimson continued, "no matter what else may occur, the present charges have already spattered mud upon individuals of the highest integrity, and in the present state of the world the denial cannot always overtake the accusation. It should by now be wholly clear that indiscriminate accusations of this sort are doubly offensive; they damage the innocent, and they help protect the guilty. For if the accuser is so stupid as to connect a man like Ambassador Jessup with communism, are not all such accusations made suspect?"

More important than all this, Stimson saw, was the fact that the McCarthy campaign, "directly and dangerously impedes the conduct of the foreign affairs of our government. It creates abroad a feeling that we are frightened and suspicious of each other; it diverts our attention, at home, from the genuine and pressing problems of our foreign affairs . . ." It seemed to Stimson quite clear that "the real motive of the accuser in this case is to cast discredit upon the Secretary of State of the United States. This man is not trying to get rid of known Communists in the State Department; he is hoping against hope that he will find some." And in an acid, one-sentence analysis, Stimson wrote: "The man who seeks to gain political advantage from personal attack on a Secretary of State is a man who seeks political advantage from damage to his country."

The Stimson letter was widely quoted, and President Truman expressed the hopeful thought that it had done much good. But it was a lonely reed of reason in a hurricane of unreason.

There were other isolated, perceptive and courageous voices. Walter Lippmann in his columns tried to clarify some of the fundamental issues. The significance of McCarthyism, as he saw it, was that it indicated control of the Republican Party had been recaptured by the old isolationist forces that had done so much damage to the nation and the world after World War I. This was a new kind of isolationism. It did not adhere to the old and discredited creed of complete noninvolvement with the affairs of the world; but it was isolationist in the sense that it spurned international cooperation and insisted that, in any action abroad, we must "act alone and unilaterally, or not at all."

"The Republican campaign about China," Lippmann wrote, "though it cannot possibly restore Chiang Kai-shek, has made it impossible for this government to take any of the necessary measures of an Asiatic policy. As long as we are entangled with Chiang and indirectly at war with Red China, we are not only in conflict with Russia, but we are divided from Britain and India, and we are denied the possibility of dealing with the situation in Southeast Asia through the United Nations."

When Senator H. Styles Bridges (R., N.H.) protested to Lippmann about these views, Lippmann retorted in a stinging column. "The fearful quarrel now raging in Washington," he said accurately, reflected American concern over the "loss" of China, but the Republicans were not interested in "an impartial historical inquest." They already knew the answers.

"In the view of Senator Bridges," Lippmann wrote, "the accounting must show that we have been betrayed, that there must have been a 'master spy' who has controlled the American government for the past seven or eight years, and has contrived to destroy Chiang Kai-shek and arrange the triumph of Mao Tse-tung.

"Senator Bridges does not know who that master spy was. Nor has he one shred of proof that there is or ever was such a master spy . . ."

Though it was always "difficult to prove the negative," Lippmann added, this was one case in which that nearly impossible feat could be accomplished. The proof lay in the recommendations made by General Wedemeyer, after his mission to China in 1947. No report could have been more forthright than Wedemeyer's at that time. He found that "the reactionary leadership, repression and corruption" of the Kuomintang "have caused a loss of popular faith in the government." The situation could be saved in one way and one way only—through the virtual takeover of China by a massive American military and financial commitment. Wedemeyer recommended such action.

"It is preposterous to claim that this—the crucial decision— was the work of a master spy," Lippmann wrote. The decision was made, as Marshall told the House Foreign Affairs Committee on February 20, 1948, because such total American intervention "represents a burden on the United States economy and a military responsibility which I cannot recommend as a course of action for this government."

Such were the words of reason. They were read and understood by some, but to counteract the constant clamor of McCarthy and his supporters much more was needed—a counterbarrage of equal weight and persistence. And this was something only the Democrats could accomplish. Where, then, were the Democrats?

They were in almost complete disarray. They snapped and sniped at McCarthy. President Truman in one press conference, expressing his contempt, suggested that it would not be "possible" to libel McCarthy. Secretary Acheson in a speech before the American Society of Newspaper Editors denounced the "smear" attacks on his department as a "filthy business" calculated to destroy the confidence of the nation in the government's conduct of foreign affairs "in one of the most critical hours in this nation's history." There were other isolated attacks on McCarthy, but there was no shadow of the coordinated, relentless effort that the crisis demanded. Weeks stretched into months, and still no Democrat in the Senate had risen to say a single word in defense of Dean Acheson. William S. White saw this demoralization of the Democrats as stemming from the Hiss case, and Acheson, he thought, had been "bereft of any strong personal support . . . because of his statement of continued friendship" for Alger Hiss.

The fumbling ineptitude of the Democrats is perhaps best illustrated by an anecdote I picked up in Washington in the winter of 1969. The speaker was a former high departmental official in the Truman Administration. He recalled that, in the early stages of the McCarthy madness, a round-table conference was convened in the headquarters of the Democratic National Committe to thrash out the problem of what the party should do about McCarthy.

"Those participating were not officials of Cabinet rank," he said, "but the second-echelon men, the Under-Secretaries and Assistant Secretaries—the men who handle most of the detail work of the government departments. There were about fifteen or twenty of us there, and the discussion began and went around clock-wise, with each man, as it came his turn, giving his opinion of what should be done.

"I sat there stunned as speaker after speaker advised caution. The best tactic, they felt, was: 'Ignore him and maybe he will go away.'

"I was appalled. I felt that McCarthy was a menace who had to be fought and exposed at every turn, and when it came time for me to speak, I pounded the table and raged and said I couldn't believe what I had heard. We had to fight, fight, fight, I told them—oh, I was really worked up. But out of all those there, there were only a couple of others who felt as I did.

"Most of those present were scared, of course, but also, in some cases, it was just an honest difference of opinion over tactics. Some honestly felt it would be bad to take on McCarthy directly. And so, in the end, it was a Mexican standoff. No decision was reached. Nothing was done."

14

Vengeance at All Costs

IT WAS ONE of the most notable psychological traits of the one-time Wisconsin farm boy that he had to be *right* in whatever he did. The scathing report to the Senate in which Millard Tydings had called McCarthy's charges "a fraud and a hoax" sent McCarthy into a fuming rage. The tongue-lashing by the distinguished Maryland aristocrat was a humiliation not to be borne; it cried aloud for vengeance.

Some of those close to McCarthy at this time confided that he was so worked up he could hardly sleep. "He was so preoccupied with Tydings," one said, "that he'd sit by the hour figuring out ways to get revenge."

He was in this simmering mood when, sometime in July,

1950, two visitors walked into his Senate office. One was a brisk, red-haired Baltimore lawyer with the sonorous name of John Marshall Butler. Butler had never previously sought political office, but he was now cocking his eye at the Republican nomination for the U.S. Senate—a prize that, if he could capture it, would pit him against Millard Tydings in the fall campaign. With Butler was his campaign manager, Cornelius P. Mundy, another Baltimore lawyer.

The pair informed the Senator of Butler's ambitions and said they had come to seek his advice. McCarthy hadn't met either previously, but he was certainly interested in any candidate who might administer the *coup de grâce* to Millard Tydings. Eagerly, then, he invited Butler and Mundy to lunch; and before the meal was over, the three were joined by McCarthy's beautiful girl Friday, Jean Kerr, who was to become his wife, and Robert Morris, a conservative Republican lawyer who was to become a favorite counsel for the witch-hunting Senate Internal Security Committee. The conference concerning Butler's political prospects continued throughout the long lunch and was later resumed in Morris' apartment.

Precise details about what was said at this first meeting of minds remain obscure, but the effect on McCarthy was obvious. Shortly afterward, he dashed off to consult with one of his most enthusiastic admirers and supporters in Washington—Mrs. Ruth McCormick (Bazy) Miller, the niece of the Chicago *Tribune*'s Colonel Robert McCormick, and the principal executive voice at this time in the management of the Washington *Times-Herald.*

In the spring of 1950, after McCarthy's first big splash at Wheeling, Bazy Miller's Al Marah Arabian horse farm in the Maryland countryside on the outskirts of Washington had become the rallying point for what might be called the American counterpart of England's famous prewar Cliveden set. It was here, on these maple-dappled acres, that McCarthy met and mingled with a host of the conservative political and social elite. Among those in the circle of what Bazy's own *Times-Herald* unblushingly called "These Charming People" were Mrs. Alice Roosevelt Longworth, the venerable, acid-tongued daughter of the famous Teddy; Gwen Cafritz, the party-giving competitor of Perle Mesta; General Wedemeyer; Richard Nixon; an assortment of Nationalist Chinese, Central American and Spanish diplomats;

Mrs. Marcella Du Pont; Mrs. Preston Davie; actress Constance Bennett; Mrs. Ivy Baker Priest, who was to be Treasurer of the United States in the Eisenhower Administration; and the beautiful Mrs. William Randolph Hearst, Jr. From time to time, the gatherings of "These Charming People" were supplemented by the attendance of other important political and journalistic right-wingers. The first group included such Senators as William E. Jenner of Indiana, George W. Malone of Nevada, Homer E. Capehart of Indiana, Spessard Holland of Florida, Herman Welker of Idaho, and Representatives Charles A. Halleck of Indiana and Clarence J. Brown of Ohio. In journalistic attendance on occasion were Fulton Lewis, Jr., the right-wing columnist and vitriolic radio broadcaster; George Sokolsky, of the Hearst press; Danton Walker, the Broadway columnist; Constantine Brown, the columnist of the Washington *Star*; and Walter Trohan, chief of the Washington bureau of the Chicago *Tribune*.

The cordial relations established with a variety of such influential persons were to be infinitely helpful to Joe McCarthy over the years; and even in 1950, when he was new to this elegant scene, it seemed entirely natural that, when McCarthy decided to take up the cause of John Marshall Butler, he should run first to Bazy seeking help. Bazy fell in wholeheartedly with the scheme to rid the political landscape of the presence of Millard Tydings. She suggested that a high-priced Chicago press agent, Jon M. Jonkel, should be hired to run Butler's campaign.

Some of Butler's friends were aghast at this suggestion, pointing out that a specific provision of the Maryland election laws forbade the hiring of a campaign manager from outside the state. Butler, however, following the advice of his new and powerful backers, discounted such timorous counsel. He kept Mundy as a "front man" campaign manager to maintain the appearance of legality, but the actual direction of the campaign was turned over to Jonkel.

ON THE FACE OF IT, it seemed absurd to try to defeat Millard Tydings with a political unknown. The Tydings name in Maryland was almost as much a household word as "Kennedy" was later to become in Massachusetts. A decorated hero of World War I, four times elected to the United States Senate by comfortable margins, the decisive victor over even Franklin Roosevelt when the President tried to purge him in 1938, Millard Tydings seemed unassailable. If he was to be beaten, it could only be by a colossal campaign effort to arouse the passions of the Maryland electorate—and such an effort would require heavy financing. Joseph McCarthy could meet this need of the hour.

Down in Texas, Clint Murchison had not yet met his favorite politician, but he had been hearing and reading a lot about how McCarthy was making "those Communists feared" of him in Washington. Therefore, he was predisposed to act when the telephone call came.

The caller was a man whom he knew, one of the backers of John Marshall Butler, and he told Murchison that Senator McCarthy would like to talk to him. As Murchison himself later recalled it: "The Senator asked me for some help against Tydings. I was glad to do it. Tydings was part and parcel of an administration that was entirely too friendly to communism. So I sent up $10,000—not so very much . . ."

This penny-ante contribution from Murchison was only one among several driblets that helped to fuel the anti-Tydings drive. H. L. Hunt contributed $5,000 to the cause. So did Bazy McCormick Miller of the Washington *Times-Herald*. Jean Kerr, McCarthy's secretary, invited Jonkel over to her apartment to meet Alvin Bentley, a Detroit businessman, who contributed another $5,000. Senator Owen Brewster put up $1,000, and Alfred Kohlberg of the China lobby another $1,000. Wherever McCarthy spoke, he asked for contributions to fuel the anti-Tydings *putsch* in Maryland. Probably the full amount of money raised will never be known, as is indeed the case in most political campaigns, but in any event it was so much that, after the stench of the election became overwhelming, Jonkel hastily filed a "supplementary" accounting showing that at least $27,100 in out-of-state contributions had been poured into Maryland in the "get-Tydings" drive.

What was to be the theme of the campaign? Communism. How could this work against a well-established and conservative Senator? Very simply. The Tydings report had been a "whitewash." And it followed as simply as an algebraic equation that the whitewasher, Senator Tydings, had been coddling communists.

As McCarthy himself promoted this line from the campaign stump in his arm-waving, earnest, country-boy style, listeners by the thousands were impressed by what seemed his overpowering sincerity. But John Marshall Butler and his aides didn't have the earnestness-sincerity technique so well perfected. If the communist canard about Tydings was to be believed, some kind of tangible proof was going to be necessary. This was no problem.

McCarthy conceived the idea of printing a four-page tabloid campaign sheet, *From the Record*—a title well chosen to imply authenticity. He broached this idea to Bazy McCormick Miller, and asked about the possibility of printing and distributing one million copies. Mrs. Miller thought this was a splendid idea; agreed that the *Times-Herald* would handle the printing; and eventually did order her presses to run off 500,000 copies at a total charge of only $1,414—"only about half the real cost," as Tydings later charged.

McCarthy gave Jean Kerr a leave of absence from his office to assist Jonkel in writing campaign literature and raising money. Mrs. Miller kept Jonkel happy by supplementing his $1,200-a-month salary with personal loans, and she detached her chief editorial writer, Frank M. Smith, who became Butler's assistant after the election, to work with McCarthy's hatchet brigade on *From the Record.*

The tabloid, according to its masthead, was sponsored by an organization called Young Democrats for Butler. Senate investigators later found that this was really a front organization; the "club" had only six members, held only one meeting, and knew nothing about the tabloid it was "sponsoring" until the sheet had been printed and distributed.

The paper was illustrated. One photograph showed Senator Tydings listening attentively while ex-Communist boss Earl Browder gave him some whispered words of wisdom. This incident, portrayed so graphically for the gullible voters of Maryland, had never occurred. The pictorial "evidence" that a reader saw was an outright fraud, accomplished by the simple photographic magic of taking out of the newspaper morgue separate pictures of Browder and Tydings, cropping them to eliminate extraneous detail, and then rephotographing them to make it appear that the two men were together, in intimate chit-chat.

The picture caption read: "Communist leader Earl Browder,

shown at left in this composite picture, was a star witness at the Tydings committee hearings, and was cajoled into saying Owen Lattimore and others accused of disloyalty were not Communists. Tydings (left) answered, 'Oh, thank you, sir.' Browder testified in the best interest of those accused, naturally."

Only the attentive reader caught the giveaway in that word "composite." The impact was visual: here was Senator Tydings in intimate conversation with Earl Browder, the two of them concocting a way to protect traitors in the State Department.

In the Senatorial post-mortem, those who had had a professional hand in the production of *From the Record* professed to see nothing wrong with the composite picture. Frank Smith, the *Times-Herald* editorial writer and supervisor of production for the tabloid, protested that it was "not a fake . . . not a fraud." Garvin E. Tankersley, assistant managing editor of the *Times-Herald* who was to graduate to the status of Bazy McCormick's new husband, insisted he couldn't see anything wrong with printing and distributing the picture. Jean Kerr declared that the composite picture was "the type of literature that should go out in a campaign. The voters should be told what is going on and this certainly did it."

Her only criticism was that the tabloid hadn't gone far enough. This led Senator Thomas C. Hennings, Missouri Democrat, to wonder who had toned it down. "Who," he asked sarcastically, "was the sissy in the crowd?"

On the other hand, those who were more remote from responsibility for the tabloid were quite candid in their appraisals of it. Cornelius Mundy, who had been supplanted by Jonkel as campaign manager, but had remained as treasurer, said frankly that the composite picture was "stupid, puerile and in bad taste," and he insisted he had had nothing to do with it. William Christopher, a volunteer worker in Butler's headquarters, declared that the tabloid had been "an insult to people's intelligence." He felt so strongly about it, he said, that he had performed a deed of personal sabotage: he had burned or sold for scrap paper some 150,000 copies.

The Browder-Tydings picture was not the only transparently phony item in *From the Record*. It headlined stories that, as Tydings later charged, were "a tissue of lies from beginning to end." Some of the headlines that cried aloud to ignorance and fear read: TYDINGS GROUP HELD UP ARMS . . . TYDINGS BLAMED FOR HIGH KOREAN CASUALTIES . . . TYDINGS WHITEWASH COMMITTEE ORDERED [WILLIAM REMINGTON] KEPT ON COMMERCE DEPARTMENT PAYROLL.

The Remington case had been developed by Republican witch-hunting committees in the campaign of 1948; Tydings and his committee had never had anything to do with it or with keeping Remington on any payroll. Similarly, as every member of the Senate knew, neither Tydings nor the Senate Armed Services Committee had ever held up military aid to Korea—nor could they have, even if they had wished, because such shipments were in the hands of the Defense Department.

One of McCarthy's favorite canards was emblazoned in the headlines of *From the Record*. This was the charge that Tydings, as chairman of the Senate Armed Services Committee, had sent South Korea only $200 for bailing wire, out of millions of dollars appropriated.

The truth was that $495,700,000 worth of materiel had been shipped to South Korea before the invasion from the north. A detailed list of this military aid had been released by the Defense Department and published in the *Congressional Record* of August 16, 1950, more than two months before *From the Record* went to press. Yet the tabloid had printed the bailing-wire story, and McCarthy, for more than a year, in speech after speech, continued to charge that traitors within had left South Korea defenseless because we had spent only $200 "to load some bailing wire on a ship."

The charge was so minutely specific that it seemed no man would make it if he did not have the hard facts in his possession; so the "bailing wire" tale always got a big hand from McCarthy's audiences.

IN HIS ELECTORAL CONTESTS in Wisconsin, McCarthy had always had success with his "personalized" postcard technique. This tried-and-tested tactic was now transplanted to Maryland to aid John Marshall Butler.

A Baltimore printer named William Fedder was given two Butler campaign contracts. He was to fold, address and distribute the tabloid, and he was to hire crews of penwomen to sign Butler's

Joe McCarthy and two of his
three brothers, during their
boyhood on the family farm
near Grand Chute, Wisconsin.
Left to right: William,
Howard and Joe. *Right:* This
post card was circulated
during the 1946 Senatorial
campaign in Wisconsin.
It shows McCarthy as a tail
gunner in the marines,
a circuit court judge and
a marine intelligence officer.

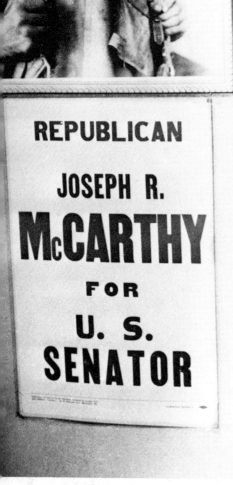

REPUBLICAN

JOSEPH R.

McCARTHY

FOR

U. S.

SENATOR

Joseph McCarthy in a victory pose just after he had defeated
Senator Robert M. La Follette, Jr., for the Republican nomination
for U.S. Senator, August 15, 1946.

Senator Millard E. Tydings, chairman
of the subcommittee of the Senate
Foreign Relations Committee that
investigated McCarthy's charges of
subversion in the State Department.
Along with the other Democrats on
the committee, Tydings ultimately
termed McCarthy's charges "a fraud and
a hoax," in the committee report made
in July 1950. In the next elections
McCarthy threw his weight behind
a political unknown, John M. Butler, to
prevent Tydings' reelection in Maryland.
Tydings is shown here after his defeat,
as he appeared before a Senate election
subcommittee in 1951 to testify that
"fraud and deceit" had been used against
him in the Senatorial campaign. *Right:*
Judge Dorothy Kenyon, the first
person falsely accused of having
leftist associations, when Senator
McCarthy made his initial appearance
before the Tydings committee.

Philip C. Jessup, United States
Ambassador at Large, whom McCarthy
unjustly accused of having "an unusual
affinity for communist causes," before
the Tydings committee in March
1950. *Below:* Professor Owen Lattimore
and his wife. In the background,
former Communist Louis Budenz arrives
to testify against Lattimore before
the Tydings committee, April 20, 1950.
McCarthy had falsely charged that
Lattimore was the "Number 1 Soviet
spy" in America.

Senator Pat McCarran, chairman of the Senate Judiciary
Committee, whose subcommittee began investigating
McCarthy's charges of communism in government in 1951.

Presidential candidate Dwight D. Eisenhower
speaks to a whistle-stop audience in
McCarthy's home town of Appleton, after
being introduced by the Senator on
October 3, 1952. Governor Walter Kohler
of Wisconsin is in the center. *Right:*
Governor Adlai E. Stevenson of Illinois
addresses the opening session of the 1952
Democratic National Convention in Chicago
at which he received the Presidential
nomination. *Below:* Senator McCarthy
delivers a slashing attack on Presidential
nominee Adlai Stevenson in a nationwide
telecast from a fund-raising dinner in Chicago
on October 27, 1952. Several times during
the speech he linked Stevenson to Alger
Hiss by saying, "Alger—I mean Adlai . . ."

Joseph McCarthy and the former Miss Jean Kerr leave St. Matthews Roman Catholic Cathedral after their marriage on September 29, 1953. *Below:* Several thousand New York City policemen at the Holy Name Society Communion breakfast in April 1954 hear McCarthy pledge to continue his fight against communism. At the right is Francis Cardinal Spellman; next to him is Msgr. Joseph McCaffrey.

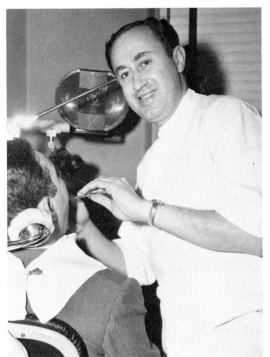

Above left: Former Army Major Dr. Irving Peress, accused by Joe McCarthy of being a "Fifth Amendment Communist." McCarthy's cry "Who promoted Peress?" led to his grilling of Brigadier General Ralph W. Zwicker, who was the commandant of Camp Kilmer, New Jersey, where Peress had been stationed. *Above right:* Brigadier General Ralph W. Zwicker. It was McCarthy's abusive treatment of Zwicker that was a key factor in precipitating the Army-McCarthy hearings. *Below:* The Army-McCarthy hearings, held in the Senate Caucus Room, April–August, 1954.

UPI

UPI

Joseph McCarthy with Roy Cohn, counsel to McCarthy's investigating committee during the Army-McCarthy hearings. *Right:* Private G. David Schine at the Army-McCarthy investigation. One of the major issues at the hearings was Roy Cohn's repeated attempts to get preferential Army treatment for Schine.

Army Secretary Stevens (left) conferring with his counsel, Joseph Welch.
Below: Francis Carr (center), staff director of McCarthy's investigating committee, who was accused by Secretary Stevens of participating in the attempts to obtain favored treatment for Private Schine. Shaking hands are Senator McCarthy and Senator Henry M. Jackson.

Army counselor John G. Adams, as he was being questioned by Roy Cohn. *Below:* Committee counsel Ray Jenkins listens to Senator Everett McKinley Dirksen.

Opposite page, above: Senator Stuart Symington clashes with Chairman Karl Mundt. Senator John L. McClellan is in the center. During the hearings Senator McCarthy referred to his colleague as "Sanctimonious Stu." *Below:* Senator Joe McCarthy, as he appeared at various points during one day of the Army-McCarthy hearings. *Above:* Army counsel Joseph Nye Welch shows the committee the original group photograph of (left to right) Army Secretary Robert Stevens, Private G. David Schine and Air Force Colonel Jack T. Bradley. On the table is various doctored picture showing Stevens and Schine alone. *Right:* Assistant Secretary of Defense H. Struve Hensel, falsely accused by McCarthy of misconduct in office.

Robert Kennedy, counsel for the Democractic minority of the Senate investigating committee during the Army-McCarthy hearings, listens to Joe McCarthy. Senator Henry M. Jackson is in the center. *Right:* Senator Ralph E. Flanders, the first Republican in the Senate to attack Joseph McCarthy in 1954.

The opening hearings of the special Senate committee formed to consider the censure of Senator McCarthy, on August 31, 1954. At the committee table are (left to right): Senator Samuel Ervin, Senator Francis Case, assistant counsel Guy de Furia, committee counsel E. Wallace Chadwick, chairman Senator Arthur V. Watkins, Senator John Stennis and Senator Frank Carlson. At the facing witness table are Senator McCarthy and his attorney, Edward B. Williams. *Right:* Senator Arthur V. Watkins, chairman of the censure committee, calls the hearings to order.

During the 1956 Presidential
campaign, Vice-President
Richard M. Nixon is greeted
on his arrival at Milwaukee
Airport on October 1, 1956,
by the two Wisconsin
Republican Senators, Joseph
McCarthy and Alexander Wile
Left: Joseph McCarthy and
his wife, Jean, with their
newly adopted daughter,
Tierney Elizabeth,
on January 13, 1957.

name to tens of thousands of postcards to be mailed to Maryland voters. Between the two tasks, Fedder found himself swamped with work; and, in addition, some of his penwomen, who were being paid $15 a thousand cards for their services, began to get writer's cramp and lose enthusiasm. The Butler camp started to worry that not all the postcards would get into the mail on time; and so, evidently to reassure Fedder and stimulate him to superhuman effort, Butler wrote the printer a personal note. It was a guarantee of payment, and it read:

"At this time I want to give you my personal assurance that I do guarantee payment for any of your services that have not been paid for at the time the campaign is completed. This assurance applies to materials that have been delivered and to materials that were not shipped in time for use in the campaign."

It was signed: "Sincerely, John Marshall Butler."

Butler evidently was not aware that, by penning this note, he had put himself in a precarious position. Fedder at the time had more than $11,000 coming to him, and Maryland's corrupt practices law specified that a candidate must limit his spending to $5,000. When McCarthy and his aides learned about this indiscreet letter, they evidently determined to try to get it back. The result was the midnight "ride" of William Fedder about which there was to be much subsequent controversy.

As Fedder later told the story, he was instructed to meet McCarthy's principal private eye, Don Surine, at midnight in the Emerson Hotel in Baltimore. Fedder went to the rendezvous, but instead of Surine, he found Ewell Moore and George Nilles, two other McCarthy handymen, waiting for him. Fedder testified:

"I asked for Don Surine, and they said he would be here soon. We left the hotel, took the finished cards from my car, and went into the post office. We took a rough count, and it was about 5,000 cards. They mailed those cards. They continued to bother me about a group of cards I had said I mailed earlier. I told them I would explain it to Don Surine when he arrived. Surine arrived about 1 a.m. . . .

"I told [Surine] that we had only three stops to make, which should be completed in an hour, and when he picked up the finished work and the leftover stamps, that he would see for himself that they would check out. Then Surine became abusive, too. His eyes looked like they were going to pop out of his head. I said that he was working himself up for nothing, that three more girls were waiting for us to pick up their work. 'Let's get this done and over with. I'm tired and I want to go home.' As I made this statement, I started walking toward the door, intending to have them follow me, so we could pick up the rest of the work. Surine reached out and jerked me back by the coat. He said: 'Listen, I want that letter back.'

"I said: 'What letter?' He said: 'The guarantee letter that you got from Butler.' I told him that he wasn't going to get the letter. He told me that if I didn't give him the letter, they would fix me up and put me through a McCarthy investigation. He bragged about being good at that sort of thing. I told him that I couldn't give him the letter even if I wanted to—that this letter was in my attorney's office.

"He then asked if I knew Kriss. I said I didn't. He said he meant Captain Kriss of the police department, who was a friend of his and could make it tough for me. I said the police don't worry me because I haven't done anything wrong. I asked him to please let me finish and go home. He said that where they came from, my kind would be lucky to get home at all.

"I sat in the back seat but was too frightened to think about anything, because I didn't know what was going to happen next. There was absolutely no conversation. We were riding around for no purpose, going no place, and I was getting sicker by the minute."

The seemingly interminable ride, according to Fedder, had one intermission at about 4 A.M. when the Surine-led group stopped at Fedder's home to let the printer pick up a $500 check which, Surine claimed, he owed them for not finishing the post-cards. In his terror, Fedder wrote out the check and brought it back to the car. He expected that would be the end of the ride, but, he testified, "Surine said: 'We're not through with you yet—get back in the car.' And with the three men crowding me, I ended up in the back seat again."

The aimless night ride was resumed. Finally, Fedder said, his custodians stopped at an all-night restaurant where, under duress, he signed two statements presented to him by Surine. The first outlined the work he had been doing for the Butler forces; the second, evidently designed to counteract the potential danger of Butler's letter, stated that the candidate owed the printer nothing. With the signing of these two statements, McCarthy's aides released Fedder, and the nightmare ride ended.

Such was the anti-Tydings campaign. When the votes were counted, the supposedly invincible Tydings was completely flattened. John Marshall Butler, the political unknown, defeated him by a margin of 45,000 votes. Joe McCarthy had his revenge —along with a significant added dividend, something even more important.

What happened to Tydings was an object lesson that sent shudders of apprehension down the spines of politicians across the nation. If this could happen to Tydings on his home turf in Maryland, who was safe? The defeat of Tydings marked the birth of a legend that was to make Joseph McCarthy the terror of the political world. Like most legends, this one had just enough truth in it to insure it widespread acceptance. Time and again, Senators who had had the fortitude to stand up to McCarthy went down to defeat. The general election in November, 1950, wrote a story that any politician could read. Candidates whom McCarthy supported won; those whom he opposed lost.

Millard Tydings was just one victim among many. Majority Leader Scott W. Lucas, the man who had presumed to heckle McCarthy so persistently about those 205 Communists mentioned at Wheeling, was opposed in Illinois by Everett McKinley Dirksen. McCarthy campaigned vigorously against Lucas—and Dirksen won. McCarthy went into Idaho and gave a helping hand to another Republican Senatorial candidate, Herman Welker— and Welker won. In Utah, McCarthy's outcries against communism and subversion took fertile root and played a major role in electing another new Republican Senator, Wallace F. Bennett.

In every election, there are, of course, many factors—a combination of issues and the contrasting personalities of the candidates. Dirksen, with his mellifluous, Shakespearean actor's voice and love of dramatics, was a colorful figure in his own right and went on to win election after election and become the Republican power in the Senate. Sophisticated analysis of the election returns could show that McCarthy's influence on the outcome in some of these election contests had been minimal, but the impact was made by the results. When two such powers in the Senate as Tydings and Majority Leader Lucas could be overthrown, it seemed to many that to oppose McCarthy was to court political annihilation.

AFTER THE MARYLAND votes had been counted, Fedder, the Baltimore printer, revealed to Tydings the story of his midnight "ride" and filled the defeated Senator in on the activities of McCarthy's operatives. Tydings asked the Senate to determine whether the nature of Butler's campaign should disqualify him from holding his seat, and an elections subcommittee of the Senate Rules Committee was empowered to investigate. The committee was headed by Senator Guy M. Gillette (D., Iowa), and its other and more active members were Senators A. S. (Mike) Monroney (D., Okla), Thomas Hennings, Robert C. Hendrickson and Mrs. Margaret Chase Smith.

The committee held lengthy hearings throughout the early part of 1951. The story of the out-of-state financing, of the printing and distribution of *From the Record,* of the Browder-Tydings composite picture, of Fedder's midnight "ride," all came out in the committee inquiry. The testimony of Surine, Moore and Nilles, of course, was different from that of Fedder. They agreed they had met Fedder on the night in question. They agreed the long midnight ride had taken place. But there had been no threats; Fedder had made up all that business about being in fear for his life. They had been merely riding about with him, all three McCarthy aides insisted, to pick up the final Butler postcards for mailing. The committee "invited" McCarthy and Butler to appear, but neither Senator took advantage of the opportunity to get his side of the story into the record. On August 3, 1951, both Republican and Democratic members joined in filing a unanimous report.

It was a scathing indictment. The committee wrote that it "unreservedly denounced, condemned and censured" the tactics used to elect Butler. It said that, under the existing rules of the Senate, there was no basis for unseating Butler, but it recommended that the rules be changed to make the use of defamatory literature in a campaign adequate grounds for such expulsion in the future.

The committee noted that Jonkel, Butler's manager, had already pleaded guilty to the charge of violating Maryland's election laws and had been fined $5,000. There was "no specific evidence that Butler had full knowledge of the manner in which Jonkel and others committed acts that have been challenged," the committee wrote, but Butler was a leading Maryland lawyer and he must have been aware of the election laws of his own state that forbade the hiring of an out-of-state campaign manager.

In one of its more acid paragraphs, the report noted that two distinctly different types of campaign had been run in Maryland.

"One was the dignified 'front street' campaign conducted by Candidate Butler in his speaking coverage of the state . . .," the report noted. "The other was a despicable 'back street' type of campaign which usually, if exposed in time, backfires. The 'back street' campaign conducted by non-Maryland outsiders was of a form and pattern designed to undermine and destroy the public faith and confidence in the basic American loyalty of a well-known figure [Tydings]."

The committee wrote that it might be an exaggeration to call this a "big lie" campaign, but it was certainly a "big doubt" campaign. It emphasized that Jonkel himself had characterized "the heart and theme of the campaign strategy as 'exploiting the doubt.'" The techniques used in this "exploiting the doubt" were condemned by the committee in harshest terms.

It used the word "infamous" in referring to the Browder-Tydings composite photograph; it said the picture was "too odious" for any but its creators to defend. The entire *From the Record* tabloid, the committee found, "contains misleading half truths, misrepresentations and false innuendoes that maliciously and without foundation attack the loyalty and patriotism not only of former Senator Tydings, who won the Distinguished Service Cross for heroism in World War I, but also the entire membership of the Senate Armed Services Committee of 1950."

Probing deeper, the committee recognized a fundamental issue of far greater consequence that the personal damage done to Tydings himself. It couched this issue in these terms:

"If one candidate's campaign chooses to inject into an American election the poison of unfounded charges and doubts as to alleged subversive language, this tends to destroy not only the character of the candidate who is its target, but also eats away like acid at the very fabric of American life.

"The right of disagreement is an inherent American right and privilege. But to recklessly imply to those with whom you disagree the taint of subversive leanings will rob democracy of its priceless heritage of the right to make up its mind as it sees fit. It is not sufficient defense to say, 'let the people themselves judge the charges.' The fact is that the people themselves are not in possession of sufficient reliable information upon which to judge irresponsible accusations of disloyalty."

As for McCarthy himself, the committee made it clear that it regarded him as the principal villain. "From the testimony it appears that Senator McCarthy was a leading and potent force in the campaign against Senator Tydings," the report declared. It noted that he had made his staff available for the preparation of *From the Record;* that campaign funds had been funneled through his office; and that his office staff had acted as couriers between Washington and Baltimore in the management of the campaign.

The committee recommended that the Justice Department examine the conflicting testimony of Fedder and Surine regarding the midnight ride incident. Someone certainly had committed perjury, the committee felt. It indicated it was not entirely happy with Fedder's testimony, and it expressed positive disenchantment with Surine. The difficulty in Fedder's case stemmed from the fact that, if his testimony about the threats was true, he had had several opportunities to use a telephone during the nightmare night—and yet not once had he used it to call for help. Surine's testimony, on the other hand, the committee wrote, "contains an apparent willful and knowing misstatement of a material fact." This referred apparently to Surine's sworn testimony that he had resigned from the FBI before going to work for McCarthy when, in fact, he had been dismissed and when, in fact, as the FBI reported to the committee, the bureau had felt so strongly about his case that it had refused to permit him to gloss over the dismissal by tendering his resignation.

In recognition of McCarthy's role in the campaign, the elections subcommittee included in its report a recommendation that conduct like McCarthy's should not go unpunished. In a paragraph that could apply to only one member of the Senate, it wrote:

"The question of unseating a Senator for acts committed in

a Senatorial election should not be limited to the candidates in such elections. *Any sitting Senator, regardless of whether he is a candidate for election himself, should be subject to expulsion by the Senate,* if it finds such Senator in practices and behavior that make him, in the opinion of the Senate, unfit to hold the position of United States Senator." (Italics added.)

This was an unprecedented suggestion to come from a select committee of the Senate. Yet this was the third time that Mc-Carthy, by his conduct, had called down upon himself the condemnation of his peers. The Senate Armed Services Committee had in effect reprimanded him for the slurs that had driven Senator Baldwin back to Connecticut in the Malmédy investigation; the Tydings committee had condemned him for the "fraud and hoax" of his campaign against the State Department; and now the Senate elections subcommittee had denounced him and even suggested the possibility of his expulsion for his masterminding of this scurrilous campaign.

What was Joe McCarthy's reaction to all this? The Butler campaign report was an attempt to "whitewash Tydings," Mc-Carthy said.

"My first reaction to this report," he stated, "is surprise at how politicians continue to underestimate the intelligence of the American people. I am not as surprised at the actions of the two 'Republicans' on the committee—after all they were on record last year [this was a reference to Mrs. Smith's Declaration of Conscience, which Hendrickson had signed]—but I am surprised that the Democrats have not learned that the American people just do not like whitewash.

"As long as puny politicians try to encourage other puny politicians to ignore or whitewash Communist influences in our government, America will remain in grave danger."

It was a response befitting the man who once told interviewers: "I don't answer charges; I make them."

15

Big Man of the Senate

WHEN THE EIGHTY-SECOND CONGRESS convened in Washington in January, 1951, only eleven months after Wheeling, the change in Senator McCarthy's status was so marked as to be ludicrous. Where previously he had been shunned like a leper, he was now courted like a potentate.

William S. White, watching developments on Capitol Hill for *The New York Times*, reported the striking change. In the last year of the Eighty-first Congress, in those uncertain months before the voters spoke in November, few members of "the gentlemen's club" had wanted to risk soiling themselves by being seen in intimate association with Senator McCarthy. Even McCarthy's fellow Republicans, White explained, had arranged their daily routines so that there would never be an occasion for them to pass near his desk. They had done this casually, unobtrusively. But the snub had been plain. "If Mr. McCarthy was a member of the historic club, he was a rather lonely one," White wrote. The dark, heavy-featured junior Senator from Wisconsin had sat in a virtual pool of isolation, and he had smiled through it all with an unfailing façade of good humor, just as though he hadn't noticed.

Then came the fall campaign—and after that everything changed. Single-handedly, Joseph McCarthy had toppled Senator Tydings, one of the most powerful men in the Senate. In many other Senatorial campaigns he had been instrumental in causing defeats of Democrats. Indisputably, the election returns had made McCarthy a power.

Recognition of that fact came swiftly in the Senate. No longer did Senators elaborately skirt McCarthy's desk. Now it was safe, even perhaps politically advantageous, to be seen in friendly conversation with him. For now he had become a symbol of resurgent Republicanism.

The effect on both parties was profound. The lessons of the elections, White wrote, "have not been lost . . . on the Republicans. Nor have the Democrats ignored McCarthy, as so long they tried to do . . . The Republicans have responded with an obvious new deference to McCarthy. For in the hard, objective books of politicians, there is beside his name the entry of success.

"The Senate Democrats, for the first time as a group, have made a response of their own. In their pre-Congress caucus of this week, they decided to put a reservation about seating Senator Butler . . . This action was the first occasion that Democrats of the right, center and left had come together without a break on the issue of Senator McCarthy's activities."

Even though the Democrats recognized that they probably could not unseat Butler—as, in the event, indeed they could not —they had banded together for the first time for the investigation that exposed McCarthy's techniques in the Maryland election. The reason for this belated unanimity was revealed in the remark of one Democratic Senator. White quoted him as saying, "For whom does the bell toll? It tolls for thee."

The issue, obvious from the moment McCarthy spoke at Wheeling, had finally registered with the Democrats. If Tydings could be unseated no man was safe. It was a lesson that the Republican Party had yet to learn.

THE REPUBLICANS could hardly wait to reward their new hero. On January 30, 1951, the Republican Committee on Committees named McCarthy to the powerful Senate Subcommittee on Appropriations, with life-and-death power over appropriations for the State Department. The Washington *Times-Herald* reported that McCarthy was "elated" at this sign of party favor—and well he might be. It was a public sanctification of his acts, and it invested in him greatly increased powers. But there were others not so elated. One of these was Senator William Benton (D., Conn.), himself a former Assistant Secretary of State, a one-time partner in the advertising firm of Benton and Bowles, and publisher of the *Encyclopaedia Britannica*. Benton was so disturbed that he took the almost unprecedented step of pleading publicly in the Senate with leaders of the opposition party to change their minds for the good of the nation.

In his Senate speech, he described a visit he had recently paid to the aging former Secretary of State Cordell Hull. He had found Hull extremely worried by the trend of the times—by what Hull called "days of chaos and unspeakable danger." Now, Benton said, the Senate by its own internal machinery "has added immeasurably to the chaos and unspeakable danger of today's world."

"I refer to the appointment of the junior Senator from Wisconsin to the Senate Appropriations Committee's subcommittee which is responsible for the budget of the Department of State," Benton said. "I think that even in normal times we could question a procedure which would give the potential power of life or death over any government department . . . to any Senator who had proved himself an implacable and, in this case, an irresponsible enemy of the Department concerned . . .

"I myself have been the victim of Senator McCarthy's attacks or libels. He came into my state three times to speak . . . He charged that Senator McMahon and I supported policies which gave aid and support to Communists everywhere . . . In his speeches in Connecticut, Senator McCarthy again and again sneered at Dean Acheson . . . as 'The Red Dean of Fashion'

. . . Here is a phrase to rival the best from the propaganda mill of the Kremlin. This kind of phrase is a perfect example of the worst and most terrifying aspect of the Russian propaganda."

Benton asked, How could one expect good and capable men to serve in the State Department in such circumstances? "The junior Senator from Wisconsin is to be the judge, the jury and the prosecutor of the State Department," he said. "He becomes his own kangaroo court . . . I should like to call upon the responsible leaders of the Republican Party to re-examine this appointment in the terms of the national interest in a time of crisis . . . If this appointment cannot be reversed, all of us in the Senate, all of us who cherish the sober, judicious and honorable traditions of the Senate, must now be doubly vigilant to speak up against the first signs of the new and worse siege of irresponsibility which I predict lies ahead."

No prediction was ever more solidly based upon the events of the past or foresaw more clearly the trend of the future. But the Republicans were not to be moved. Joseph McCarthy retained his new position of power. Soon his status was enhanced by the acquisition of a new and most powerful ally. He was Senator Pat McCarran, of Nevada—the bosom pal of Nevada gambling interests, then largely in the hands of the underworld, an ardent worshiper of Spanish Dictator Francisco Franco—and a Democrat. No Administration in power was ever more viciously betrayed by one of its own than was Truman's by Patrick Anthony McCarran. McCarran was one of the most shrewd, petty, ruthless and arrogant men ever to descend upon Washington.

He had ridden the Roosevelt landslide to victory in 1932 with campaign posters proclaiming, "A New Deal with Roosevelt, Garner and McCarran." No sooner had he landed in Washington, however, than he forgot all about the coattails he had ridden, turned his back on his campaign rhetoric, and established himself as one of the most reactionary men in the capital.

Since he came from a sparsely settled state, with a total population of only 160,000, it normally took only some 30,000 votes to elect him, and McCarran was the kind of political power broker who, with federal patronage to dispense, could always rustle up that handful of votes. Thus he had kept coming back to Washington for eighteen years; thus he had become the sixth in seniority in the Senate—and virtually the first in power. Since the Senate's rigid seniority system places a premium on mere survival at the polls, regardless of brains or character or ability, McCarran had become the hard-fisted boss of one of the most potent committees in government, the Senate Judiciary Committee. He had the power of personal veto over judiciary appointments; no Senator could get a U.S. attorney or an assistant U.S. attorney appointed in his district without dealing with McCarran. Attorney General J. Howard McGrath, a fellow Catholic, was virtually a puppet of McCarran's; and when Truman replaced McGrath with James P. McGranery, McCarran stormed in public and threatened to hold up the appointment until an accommodation was made. When that happened, McCarran suddenly became all sweetness and light.

The low regard in which McCarran was held was all but universal. *Time* magazine in 1950 listed him as among the eight Senators who were "most expendable" and called him "pompous, vindictive and power-grabbing." A group of political scientists polled by Denver University listed McCarran as eighty-seventh in merit among the ninety-six Senators.

McCarran's toast-drinking camaraderie with Franco during a visit to Spain and his subsequent ardent championship of multi-million-dollar bequests to Franco's regime had led Drew Pearson to dub him "the Senator from Madrid." His detestation of labor unions, his unswerving championship of big business, his subservience to mining interests in his own state had won him the sobriquet "the Senator from Kennecott Copper." Even more expressive of the inner man were two of the most detested and repressive acts passed by Congress during the Nightmare Decade —the McCarran-Walter Immigration Act and the Internal Security Act of 1950.

The new immigration law, for which McCarran was primarily responsible, was predicated on a Nazi-like racial bias that favored the Aryan strains of northern Europe and restricted almost to the point of elimination southern Europeans like the Italians, Greeks and Czechs. Communists and subversives were barred from admission to the United States, but no such prohibition was imposed on Nazis, Fascists and Falangists. The Internal Security Act sanctified internal repression. It set up a five-man Subversive Activities Control Board with broad authority to probe into the thoughts and beliefs of American citizens; it provided for the registration of communists and others who were deemed subversive; and it established, for the first time in America, some half-dozen concentration camps. Suspected subversives could be clamped into these camps any time an emergency was proclaimed. The camps, McCarran contended, were just detention centers for aliens left over from World War II, but millions of dollars were spent refurbishing and maintaining them in anticipation of their new usefulness. Though Supreme Court decisions in the 1960s found many provisions of the 1950 act unconstitutional and left the Subversive Activities Control Board in a moribund state, the nation is still saddled with the vestiges of McCarran's legislation. The Subversive Activities Control Board still exists; so do the concentration camps; and efforts were made in Congress in 1970 to pass legislation that would circumvent some of the Supreme Court rulings and revivify the apparatus.

Such was the legacy of Patrick Anthony McCarran. It is little wonder that blunt-spoken Harold Ickes called McCarran "one of the most socially retarded members of the Senate" and added: "It is doubtful whether history, at least during this generation, could offer a rival to McCarran as the most undesirable member of the Senate. Compared with him, the late Bilbo of Mississippi was a knight in shining armor."

Such was the man who took up McCarthy's cause with a vengeance. His support was invaluable. For now McCarthy was being confirmed by a Democrat—and what could Democrats say to that?*

The closing of Democratic ranks after the defeat of Tydings, about which William S. White had written, had had no effect upon McCarran. A virtual czar presiding over his own fief in the

---

* Archibald MacLeish celebrated this McCarran-McCarthy alliance in rhyme in the New York *Herald-Tribune*. The opening stanzas of his verse read:

> Says McCarran to McCarthy,
> What's platform or party!
> We sport the same feather:
> Let's fight this together.
> I'll tear them in two
> If they criticize you.
>
> Says McCarthy to McCarran,
> Sweet Rosie of Sharon
> My truth and my honor
> Shall fly to your banner.
> If they light into you
> They're commies, that's who.

Senate, he had no fear that the bell might toll for him, too; or perhaps to insure that it did not, he created a special investigating committee of his Senate Judiciary Committee and set out on the trail of subversives.

THE COLLABORATION began with a cloak-and-dagger farce.

The correspondence and papers of the Institute of Pacific Relations, the Far East research organization that was the *bête noire* of the far right, had been stored in a barn on the farm of Edward C. Carter, former secretary-general of the IPR, in Lee, Mass., not far from Pittsfield. In the summer of 1950, after McCarthy's attacks on Jessup and Lattimore had pictured IPR as a nest of communist intrigue, Carter had thrown open the files to government agencies. At his invitation, some dozen or more FBI agents had spent several weeks examining every last scrap of paper in the Carter-IPR files. What they found evidently did not seem to them of monumental import, for no official action of any kind resulted from their activities.

Enter now the helpful amateur. Thomas Stotler, a young Maine schoolteacher, was visiting his aunt, Mrs. James Markham, who was the caretaker of Carter's "Sunset Farms." He discovered the stack of steel filing cabinets in a dusty corner of the old barn, and the patriotic juices began to flow. On December 21, 1950, Stotler stepped into the middle telephone booth in a row of five at the Pittsfield railroad station and placed a collect call to McCarthy's sleuth of sleuths, Don Surine, in Washington. He told Surine about the "secret" IPR files he had discovered, and loyally offered his services to help smuggle out the documents.

Great now was the excitement in the McCarthy camp. Unaware that this "secret" cache was no secret but had already been analyzed to the last comma by the FBI, the bee-hive went into a frenzy of activity. On January 4, 1951, Surine telephoned Stotler in Portland, Maine, and perfected arrangements for the coup of the ages. Then he scurried up to New York to confer with J. B. Matthews, the Hearst high priest on the subject of subversion. Arrangements were made with Matthews to photostat the documents Stotler and Surine would squirrel out of the Carter barn.

Now began the subterranean task of pilfering thousands of

IPR documents, smuggling them into Manhattan, and photostating them in Matthews' office in the Hearst headquarters at Eighth Avenue and 57th Street. By February 3, more than 1,800 documents had been filmed. But at this point the intrigue began to get out of hand.

Though Surine remained blissfully unaware of the fact, his crew had been shadowed by a competing crew—investigators for the House Un-American Activities Committee. The HUAC sleuths tailed Surine and his helpers to the Carter barn, kept a tabulation on how many file drawers they smuggled out, and tracked them back to the photostating cubicle in the Hearst building.

There was worse. Elated at finding this gold mine, the discoverers found it simply impossible to keep the news about the precious nuggets to themselves. It was almost like the Gold Rush days in California; everybody had to get in the act. The confidants came to include William Randolph Hearst, Jr.; Senators Homer Ferguson and Karl Mundt; and Hearst columnists George Sokolsky and Westbrook Pegler. It was just too much to expect of human nature that everybody would keep discreetly silent.

The sequence, as it was later pieced together, showed that Sokolsky, who had himself been connected with IPR, telephoned Carter and tipped him off to the surreptitious raids that were being made on his barn. Then Sokolsky, playing a double role as usual, contacted Robert Morris and warned him that the news about the smuggled documents was "all over town." Something had better be done, and swiftly, to legalize the illegal—the theft of documents and the transporting of these stolen goods across state lines.

Sokolsky's call to Morris was made just at the time that other delicate negotiations were going on between McCarthy and Pat McCarran. Jack Anderson and Roland May had their own informant inside McCarthy's spy nest, and in a confidential memorandum dated February 8, 1951, their source advised them that McCarthy was exerting all his muscle to get Morris named "for the job as counsel for the new Senate committee to be set up by McCarran to investigate subversive activities and McCarthy's charges." Morris had been the counsel for the Republican minority on the Tydings committee, and he had been recently interviewing "witnesses for McCarthy at the University Club, NYC, of which he is a member."

In another memorandum nine days before Morris' appointment was officially announced, the same informant tipped off Anderson and May that the deed had been done.

"Morris' appointment is regarded as a victory for McCarthy," he wrote. "McCarthy put up a terrific fight to get this job for Robert Morris, and as a practical matter, Morris' appointment as chief counsel, with the sole right to select his assistants, will give McCarthy a great deal to say about the Senate sub-committee on internal security."

The committee, in effect, became a McCarthy committee parading under a McCarran "Democratic" front, and the ideology of its chief counsel left little doubt about its bias. In the October 30, 1950, issue of the *Freeman,* an ultraright magazine financed in part by Alfred Kohlberg, Morris had written an article in which he denounced the "secret liaison between the Communists, [Owen] Lattimore, the [Tydings] subcommittee, and the Democratic administration."

In any event, the McCarthy-McCarran-Morris axis, just being cemented at this time, became a source of rescue after the Sokolsky telephone calls had triggered panic. That the fear in the McCarthy camp was not totally exaggerated was illustrated later when the FBI did summon Surine and Matthews for extended private questioning about the IPR documents. If the FBI had acted sooner, it would have been much more embarrassing because McCarthy's men would have been caught with the pilfered goods. So the decision was made: the Carter-IPR documents were *smuggled back* into the lonely barn from which they had come.

But the intriguers, naturally, could not bear the frustration of forgoing the benefits of their coup. The problem now was how to get the documents back a second time—and this time legitimately so that use could be made of them.

Pat McCarran provided the solution. McCarthy arranged with him for the issuance of a subpoena by his Senate Internal Security Committee. This bit of legal paper would sanctify the deed already done. Its use led to the final scene in the whole hilarious cloak-and-dagger sequence.

On the afternoon of February 7, 1951, three strangers presented themselves at the Sheraton Hotel in Pittsfield and asked for a room to accommodate all of them. The men who didn't want to be separated identified themselves as Donald Surine, of Washington, D.C.; Thomas Stotler, of Cape Elizabeth, Maine; and Frank W. Schroeder of Delaware City, Del. They had hardly ensconced themselves in their hotel room when it began to snow, and soon a blizzard worthy of the Russian steppes was howling through Pittsfield. Well after nightfall, the three strangers, chins buried in upturned coat collars, battled their way in the teeth of the storm up Fourth Street to the office of the Associated Transport Company. There they called upon the night dispatcher, a man known as "Red" Wilbur, and demanded that he furnish them with a truck, a driver and a helper.

Wilbur was at first suspicious, but Schroeder banished doubt by identifying himself as an agent of the Senate Internal Security Committee, and assuring Wilbur they were there on important government business. The truck, driver and helper were supplied, and the raiding party descended upon the Carter farm. There they served Mrs. Markham with their subpoena, loaded the IPR filing cabinets on the truck, and high-tailed it for New York, plowing through snow-clogged roads all the way. Once in the city, the Treasury Department provided an armed convoy that, with sirens screaming, led the way to Washington.

It was headline-grabbing melodrama. The next day the nation's press featured headlines like: RED PROBERS SEIZE SECRET 'LATTIMORE' PAPERS IN FARM RAID. PROBERS PROMISE FULL STUDY OF SEIZED FILES. DARING RAID NETS IPR FILES.

Puffed up with self-satisfaction, McCarthy naturally could not refrain from taking credit for it all. In a speech in Racine, Wisconsin, he described dramatically how Carter's isolated barn had been "crammed with documents." Then, even getting some fun out of the situation, he added in his Peck's-bad-boy way: "I succeeded in—I don't like to use the word 'stealing'—let's say I 'borrowed' the documents."

The public, of course, had no realization at the time that FBI agents had examined all of the "secret" documents months earlier; that the whole blizzardy midnight raid had been pointless nonsense. Nor could anyone know at the time that some memoranda of Owen Lattimore's, found among the thousands of items in the cache, would become the springboard for one of the most relentless inquisitions in American history.

·　　·　　·

WITH POWERFUL FORCES in politics and business cheering his every invective, with only a shadow of spasmodic, disorganized opposition, the year 1951 was filled with McCarthy's clamor. As the sound and fury mounted, the American people came more and more to adopt as holy verity that backwoods homily: "Where there's smoke, there's fire."

The rodomontade ranged from the silly to the incredible, from the physical slugging of columnist Drew Person to the long 60,000-word tirade picturing the austerely upright George Catlett Marshall as a deep-dyed traitor. The Pearson episode had its origins in an encounter at the end of 1950; and when Pearson slapped McCarthy and a legion of his friends with a $5.1 million libel suit, the ensuing hearings made headlines for weeks.

It all started on the evening of December 12, 1950, when Pearson and his wife went to the fashionable Sulgrave Club at 1801 Massachusetts Avenue N.W. in Washington to attend a dinner party in honor of Senator James H. Duff (R., Pa.). It was Pearson's birthday, he later remembered ruefully, but his wife suggested that, instead of a private birthday party, they go to the Duff affair to which they had been invited for "a nice, quiet time."

The "nice, quiet time" became unstuck almost the moment the Pearsons walked through the door of the Sulgrave Club. The first person to greet them, glass in hand, was Senator Joseph McCarthy. Pearson, almost speechless from shock, said afterward that he wouldn't have come at all if he had had any idea McCarthy was to be there.

"He greeted me with a sort of mock effusiveness," Pearson later testified. ". . . He pretended to be very cordial. He said, 'I'm really going to tear you apart on the Senate floor tomorrow . . . I'm really going to tear you to pieces.' "

McCarthy then insisted on getting Pearson a drink, spilling a little of it from his tremulous hand as he made the delivery. Then, throughout the evening, in a loud voice, according to Pearson, McCarthy kept repeating to him and to any others within earshot pronouncements like: "I'm going to murder you. When I finish with you, there isn't going to be anything left of you."

It was embarrassing. Pearson kept trying to shy away from his tormentor, telling McCarthy to "forget it" so as not to embarrass their hostess, but wherever the columnist went the Senator popped up right after him, obviously well-oiled, and telling everyone in range of his voice: "I'm certainly sorry Drew is here . . . This is very embarrassing to me to meet his wife at this time for I've got this speech and I'm really going to murder him."

The climax came at the end of the evening when Pearson accidentally encountered McCarthy in the cloakroom. At the sight of him, Pearson said, McCarthy lost all control, attacked him, kicked him in the groin, and, as he doubled up in pain, began to belabor him about the head with his prize-fighter's fists. Pearson was rescued finally when other guests at the party intervened and pulled McCarthy away.

It was one startling act in what was to become a famous feud, and what happened subsequently tells much about the times. Pearson, warned of the imminent McCarthy blast in the Senate (which came, in fact, just three days later), sought some assistance in defending himself before he could be irretrievably damaged. Since, not being a Senator, he couldn't speak on the Senate floor, he sought out a Senator who could. The man he went to was one with whom he had been friendly and who certainly knew that he was no communist—Lyndon B. Johnson. Johnson was not yet the all-powerful Majority Leader he was to become, but he had already made his mark as an extremely forceful and capable Senator. He was a man who could help. But when Pearson asked him, Johnson turned him down cold.

Asked in 1969 whether he would seek such aid in similar circumstances should they ever occur, Pearson said: ". . . Yes, I wouldn't hesitate to go to a Senator who knew me and knew that I was not a Communist and ask him to say that I was not. I would have no hesitancy in doing so. If you're being unjustly attacked on the Senate floor where you don't have privilege and the attacking Senator does, I would like to have a little help. Fortunately, they didn't believe what he said about me, but I couldn't be sure in advance."

Some of the things McCarthy said about Pearson were, indeed, savage and destructive. He called the columnist "an unprincipled liar," capping this with the charge that he was a "Moscow-directed character assassin."

This was not all. Pearson's popular radio program was sponsored by Adam Hat Stores, Inc. McCarthy called for a public boycott on Adam hats, implying that anyone who purchased an Adam hat was helping to finance the designs of Moscow. It seemed a sign of the lack of courage in these times that Adam Hats shortly thereafter dropped its sponsorship of Pearson's radio program. Charles V. Molesworth, president of the hat company, insisted that the action had nothing to do with McCarthy's charges; the decision had been made before McCarthy spoke, he said. But the timing of the action appeared to many to speak for itself.

Pearson concluded that he was being made the object of a vendetta aimed at destroying his reputation and livelihood—and he retaliated with his $5.1 million libel suit. He asked heavy damages from McCarthy personally for what he called the unprovoked assault in the Sulgrave Club, and he included in the suit a whole swatch of McCarthy supporters. Those named included the McCormick Washington *Times-Herald,* Westbrook Pegler, Fulton Lewis, Jr., and Don Surine. They and others, Pearson charged, had joined in a conspiracy to destroy him.

The suit led to more verbal fireworks. Lengthy pretrial depositions were taken. When McCarthy himself was examined, William A. Roberts, Pearson's attorney—who had been one of McCarthy's dinner companions and counselors at the Colony—began to probe into the mystery of McCarthy's income tax difficulties back in Wisconsin. McCarthy whirled on Roberts, his one-time friend, and snarled: "I don't like to see shysters taking part in it. These are the most shysterish tactics I have ever seen."

"Are you implying I am a shyster?" Roberts demanded.

"Yes," snapped McCarthy and he grabbed up his bulky brief case and stalked out of the hearing room.

In the end, nothing came of the suit. Roberts was never able to serve legal papers on some of the defendants who lived outside the district and kept out of the reach of his process servers. The case dragged on for months, costs mounted, a key legal associate who was handling many of the details for Pearson died—and, finally, as happens many times in such suits, out of sheer war-weariness, Pearson gave it up. It had been a teapot tempest—but one not without significance. When even a columnist as powerful as Drew Pearson could not get a Senator with whom he was friendly to speak up for him, when he could lose his radio sponsor in circumstances that suggested a caving-in under pressure, a lot had been said about the climate in a nation that was running scared—very scared.

The most famous, or rather, infamous, speech that McCarthy ever made was delivered on the floor of the Senate late in the afternoon of June 14, 1951. The speech was an all-out attack on General George Catlett Marshall, then Secretary of War.

The speech was delivered in a time of national turmoil. President Truman had cashiered General of the Army Douglas MacArthur, summoning him back from Japan, where he had ruled as a virtual viceroy, and relieving him of his command of the United Nations forces in the Korean War. The action had precipitated a political storm. MacArthur, the great hero of the Pacific island-hopping campaign in World War II, was envisioned by some segments of the American far right as the man on horseback who would be the savior of the nation from radicalism. Republicans in Congress seized upon his dismissal to launch another full-scale attack on the Truman Administration.

McCarthy leaped instantly into the fray, using the kind of extreme verbiage that came naturally to him. In a speech on April 12, 1951, he charged that "treason in the White House" had been accomplished by "bourbon and benedictine" in the hands of men who knew how "to get the President cheerful." He added: "The S.O.B. should be impeached." When he was asked about these remarks later on the floor of the Senate, he offered only one amendment of his language. "Perhaps," he said, "I should have used the word 'benzedrine.'"

When the Senate Armed Services and Foreign Relations committees began a joint investigation, behind closed doors, of the MacArthur dismissal, McCarthy horned in, though he was not a member of either committee, popping out of the hearing room at regular intervals to give reporters his version of the testimony. Though the transcript of the hearing was declassified as rapidly as censors could go through it and strike out pertinent wartime information that might be of value to the enemy, Senator McCarthy was always way ahead with his method of instant declassification, and he became, for the moment, a reporter's best friend. Thus his name was kept in the story in a peripheral "McCarthy says" sense, but the real drama was being played out on a stage where he had no part.

Naturally this was an insupportable situation. Here was an issue that was exercising the nation's electorate, and it was imperative that he get on top of it. Early in his anticommunist crusade, in the 1950 forensics resulting from his initial charges and the Tydings investigation, he had taken some passing swipes at Marshall, but these had gone relatively unnoticed in the greater hullabaloo he had raised about Philip Jessup and Owen Lattimore. Now, in the light of the MacArthur recall, George Catlett Marshall was in a more vulnerable public position: he had supported the recall.

The brashness of McCarthy's resulting action can be fully appreciated only when one assesses the character of his victim. Other men in American life had climbed to higher positions than Marshall. As wartime leaders, Eisenhower and MacArthur were greater popular heroes. But it is doubtful if any American of his generation had built throughout his career a loftier image *as a man* than George Catlett Marshall. Richard Rovere put it well in this description:

". . . He was, above all, a man of vast and palpable dignity. The dignity was in his bearing and in his entire mien, in his aloofness from controversy, in the silence with which he had borne disappointment and defeat and sorrow, with which he was well acquainted. He was the very image of the strong, noble, gentle Southern man of arms who could be no more dishonored by enemies and critics, if he had any, than the great progenitor of the tradition, Marshall's fellow Virginian, Robert E. Lee . . ."

This was the man Joseph McCarthy now proposed to brand a traitor. Hefting a bulky sheaf of manuscript, McCarthy took the Senate floor late in the day after routine business had been transacted. Few Senators were present in the chamber. Kenneth Wherry, ever helpful, ever solicitous, thought that McCarthy should have a larger audience, and suggested a quorum call, just as he had back on February 20, 1950. But this time Senator McCarthy was magnanimous. A quorum call was not necessary, he said; he had such a long speech to deliver that he did not want to impose on his fellow Senators by making them sit through all of it.

Then he took out the document, all 60,000 words of it (later circulated in book form under the title: *America's Retreat from Victory: The Story of George Catlett Marshall*), and he began to read. Rovere suggests that this may have been the first time McCarthy himself had read the words that came tumbling from his mouth; and, preposterous though the suggestion seems, the speech does bear much internal evidence of having been prepared for him by others. It was not typical McCarthy prose. Take, for example, this esoteric aside:

"I am reminded of a wise and axiomatic utterance in this connection by that great Swedish chancellor Oxenstiern[a], to his son departing on the tour of Europe: He said, 'Go forth my son and see with what folly the affairs of mankind are governed.'"

Rovere believes that the origins of the speech are obvious. "It is a product," he writes, "of a school of revisionist historians who have in common the view that American diplomacy since the early thirties and into the early fifties was a failure because it failed to focus single-mindedly on Soviet power. Roosevelt was mistaken in recognizing the Soviet Union in 1933; wrong in aiding the Russians in 1941; wrong in seeking the total destruction of German and Japanese power in 1945; wrong in inviting the Russians into the Pacific War; wrong in insisting that Chiang Kai-shek hold his fire for the Japanese—wrong in nearly all his major decisions. The leaders of the school were Charles Callan Tansill and Stefan Possony of Georgetown University. Georgetown was, and is, its headquarters, and there seems little room for doubt that McCarthy's speech was the work either of a member of the Georgetown school or of someone heavily influenced by it. . ."

The speech was evidently too long and involved for the taste of its ostensible author. After reading the first 20,000 words, McCarthy quit and simply introduced the whole thing into the *Congressional Record*.

The speech was a long and didactic analysis of historical events, as seen with a peculiar astigmatism concerning the menace of fascism in the thirties. In this perverted revisionism of history all events were reinterpreted on the premise that there had been, and there remained, only one genuine menace in the world—Russian communism. Thus it followed that any decision that had resulted in some future accretion of Russian power had been wrong and blind—or even, possibly, downright subversive.

It was a viewpoint that ignored, for instance, the question of what might have happened to the world if Hitler had not been promptly crushed. Suppose Hitler, granted the grace of a few more years' time, had been able to wed the power of the atom to the rocket delivery system his scientists *had perfected* at war's end?

This shuddery thought seemingly never occurs to right-wing revisionists. Only by ignoring the fact that fascism, not communism, was the real menace of the thirties could one decide that measures necessary in the exigencies of a life-and-death struggle were wrong because, with victory, Russia emerged as a mighty world power.

The technique is obvious in some of the specifics of McCarthy's indictment. He faulted Marshall for opposing Winston Churchill's desire to invade the Balkans before the Russians got there, ignoring the fact that this would have been a dilution of our military strength in another peripheral campaign, delaying the Western Front strike at the heart of Germany—an invasion that became a race against time as the increasing effectiveness of the V-2 rockets over London demonstrated. Marshall was faulted also for the decisions at the Teheran and Yalta conferences, especially those designed to bring Russia into the Pacific war, and making concessions to her for her help—ignoring the fact that virtually all of our military experts, in those days before the atom bomb changed the science of war, regarded Russian collaboration as vital, and evaluated it as probably saving one million American casualties in the projected invasion of the Japanese homeland. Marshall was faulted, of course, above all for "the creation of a China policy" that had resulted in "the loss" of China, and for his opposition to sending further aid to Chiang Kai-shek.

This kind of reasoning goes on and on throughout the speech, most of it calm and dispassionate in tone, wearing all the spurious trappings of pedagogical research. In only one place did the speech lose its cool; and this was a section that was pure, visceral McCarthy—the passage that was to make the speech live in infamy.

"How," McCarthy asked, "can we account for our present situation unless we believe that men high in this Government are concerting to deliver us to disaster? This must be the product of a great conspiracy, a conspiracy on a scale so immense as to dwarf any previous such venture in the history of man. A conspiracy of infamy so black that, when it is finally exposed, its principals shall forever deserve the maledictions of all honest men . . . What can be made of this unbroken series of decisions and acts contributing to the strategy of defeat? They cannot be attributed to incompetence. If Marshall were merely stupid, the laws of probability would dictate that part of his decisions would serve his country's interest."

McCarthy was to contend forever after that he had not called General Marshall a traitor. He had not, of course, in so many words. But innuendo is often as deadly as a direct charge and more difficult to answer, and McCarthy was a past master of the art. When he spoke of "a conspiracy on a scale so immense as to dwarf any such previous venture in the history of man," when he referred to an "infamy so black . . . its principals shall forever deserve the maledictions of all honest men," he had proved himself a master of circumlocution and, if the English language has any meaning, he had indeed indicted George Catlett Marshall as a traitor.

It may seem incredible, yet it was, in effect, this speech and this passage that drove General Marshall out of government service and into private life. The demoralization of the Democrats was so complete that, as in the case of Dean Acheson, McCarthy's charges echoed through a silent Senate chamber. Marshall stayed on as Secretary of Defense for a few months longer, but he had been denounced publicly—and without any compensatory rebuttal by his party—as a perfidious man, and his usefulness had been impaired. In the end, with what grace could be mustered in the situation, General Marshall at last retired (a surcease from public cares that the tired and aging veteran would have welcomed under any other circumstances), and he was succeeded for the remainder of Truman's term by the highly capable Robert Lovett.*

* Richard Rovere in his book on McCarthy wrote that "it is no exaggeration to say that it [this speech] destroyed George Catlett Marshall," explaining that by "destroyed" he meant that the speech put an end to Marshall's usefulness as a public servant. In those days, a man's ability to operate was crippled once the finger of suspicion had been directed at him; and, as Rovere wrote, McCarthy had left Marshall with "mud on his uniform, and no President . . . could ever again advance national unity" by bringing him out of retirement.

There was an epilogue in 1953. Perhaps as a reflection of world opinion about some of the benighted antics in America, General Marshall was given the Nobel Peace Prize. When Senator McCarthy was asked what he thought about it, he replied: "No comment."

IT WOULD BE FRUITLESS as well as boring to catalogue all of those McCarthy accused of subversion or fellow-traveling in this frenetic year of 1951. There was always a new speech before some veterans' group; there was always some imagined crisis that simply demanded McCarthy bring enlightenment to his confreres in a Senate address. In such performances, the "lists" of names proliferated. Some were mere repetitions of names he had attacked before, dragged out again on some flimsy pretext, belabored again with some new twist of rhetoric. Other "lists" included some new victims, obscure, unknown to the public, faceless images of treason. In all of this, there was one case that deserves mention because it tells so much about the treachery of fanatics and informers.

In late 1950 President Truman named Mrs. Anna M. Rosenberg, of New York City, to the post of Assistant Secretary of Defense. Mrs. Rosenberg had had a long and distinguished career. A public labor and personnel relations consultant, she had served previously in a variety of governmental capacities— as regional director of NRA, regional director of the Social Security Board, regional director of the War Manpower Commission in World War II. She had been the personal representative of both President Roosevelt and President Truman in the European theater, reporting on the problems of returning soldiers. She had filled many other official and semiofficial positions in a busy lifetime, and had been the recipient of several medals. Hers was a record that appeared to be above reproach. But there were some opposed to her appointment; Mrs. Rosenberg was Jewish.

Gerald L. K. Smith, dean of the art of pandering to racial prejudices, was at the center of the web that was now spun to ensnare Mrs. Rosenberg. Smith moved into a secret headquarters in Room 405 of the Congressional Hotel in Washington; established a liaison with Joe McCarthy, whose role as the nation's savior he had already well-publicized; and put McCarthy's sleuth

Don Surine in touch with informants in New York who, it was promised, could prove the subversive ties of Mrs. Rosenberg. The charge against her was that she was a former communist and had been a member of the John Reed Club in the thirties.

Surine, accompanied by Edward Nellor, a factotum of Fulton Lewis, Jr., arrived in New York City at their favorite witching hour, midnight of December 5, 1950. There they contacted one of Smith's informants, Benjamin Freedman. They handed Freedman a note from Smith that read:

> Dear Mr. Freedman:
>
> Congratulations on the terrific job you are doing in helping to keep the Zionist Jew Anna M. Rosenberg from becoming the director of the Pentagon. This is to introduce two gentlemen who are helping in this fight. One is the bearer of this note. I understand that he is Mr. Nellor, the chief aide to Mr. Fulton Lewis. Mr. Lewis and Mr. Nellor should be treated very kindly. You should give any information that will help them, because Mr. Lewis is doing a magnificent job in the Rosenberg matter.
>
> Please destroy this upon reading it.
>
> > Sincerely yours,
> > Gerald L. K.

Smith's last admonition about destroying this introductory note was fortunately ignored, and the note became part of the literature of the case when the Senate Armed Services Committee probed the cabal. Freedman, in pince-nez and pin-striped suit, took the witness stand before the committee, where he squirmed and dodged a bit but finally admitted that he had had a telephone call from Gerald L. K. Smith to alert him to the impending midnight arrival of Surine and Nellor. There was much dispute afterward about whether the two investigators had posed as agents of the Senate committee itself (they insisted indignantly that they had not); but, in any event, with Freedman steering them, Surine and Nellor were directed to a witness who seemed ideal for their purposes. He was Ralph DeSola, an ex-communist, and he told the two agents exactly what they wanted to know.

When DeSola was produced on the witness stand before the Senate committee, he "positively" identified Mrs. Rosenberg as his former associate in communism. McCarthy was ecstatic at this triumph; and Fulton Lewis went on the air, saying that DeSola's emphatic identification reminded him of another occasion "when Alger Hiss was confronted across the table by Whittaker Chambers."

Mrs. Rosenberg's anger and anguish showed in her response to DeSola.

"He is a liar," she told the Senate committee. "I would like to lay my hands on that man. It is inhuman what he has done to me in the past few days . . . Now if this man is crazy or a Communist, I want to face him, Senator. I have never been a member of the John Reed Club; I have never been a Communist; I have never sympathized with Communists; I have spent my life trying to help my country.

"I tried to think—where do I know this man? How do I know him from some place? How can a human being do this to some one? What can he have against me? I don't know him . . . I plead with you finish this. If you don't think I'm fit to take this office, say so. I don't care what you charge me with, but not disloyalty, Senator. It is an awful thing to carry around with you."

It was a cry from the heart. And, fortunately, in this instance, it was heeded.

The case against Mrs. Rosenberg was such a flimsy tissue of lies that it collapsed of its own weight. Witnesses who were supposed to corroborate DeSola disowned him instead. And the FBI finally settled the issue beyond all doubt. It discovered there were two Anna Rosenbergs. Since this was not an uncommon name, there were probably thousands; but, for the purposes of this case, the Anna Rosenberg who had been a member of the John Reed Club and a former communist lived on the West Coast and had had no connection at all with the distinguished New York public servant.

With this revelation, the New York Anna M. Rosenberg was confirmed as Assistant Secretary of Defense; and even Senator McCarthy, who had been so ready to give credence to the siren song of Gerald L. K. Smith, ended up voting for her.

This shabby affair might have been expected to open the eyes of many. But it did not. It became only a forgotten minor contretemps in the career of the great Pied Piper.

16

The Reluctant Dragon

THE DEMOCRATS now had a champion thrust upon them, and never was a badgered and beleaguered party less enthusiastic about its own defense.

The man of principle was the tall and scholarly Senator from Connecticut, William Benton. Having spoken to a deaf Senate when he had pleaded with Republicans to refuse to invest increased authority in Joe McCarthy, having read the report of the Senate elections subcommittee that had branded McCarthy with the onus for the "despicable" campaign against Tydings, Senator Benton rose in the Senate on August 6, 1951, and introduced a resolution to kick Senator McCarthy out of "the gentlemen's club."

He based his demand on "the indictment of the practices of Senator McCarthy" in the Tydings contest. "I submit that a very high percentage of the members of this body would resign forthwith if such a report were written about them, agreed to unanimously by five of their colleagues," Senator Benton said. Knowing McCarthy, however, he did not expect him to be swayed by any such considerations of honor, and so he asked the Senate Rules Committee to authorize an investigation looking to McCarthy's ouster.

This unprecedented demand by one Senator for the expulsion of another rocked the staid chamber. Republicans were so surprised that Kenneth Wherry was reduced to the whimper that Benton had "only political motives in mind" and that it was "unfortunate" he had introduced his resolution before the full Rules Committee had accepted the Tydings election report, a quibble if there ever was one.

McCarthy was not present when Benton introduced his resolution, but when he heard of it, he erupted with typical volcanic verbiage: "I am sure that Owen Lattimore and all the Alger Hisses and William Remingtons still in government will agree with Benton's resolution," he said. "Tonight Benton has established himself as the hero of every Communist and crook in and out of government.

"Benton today has performed the important service of helping to properly label the administration branch of the Democrat party as the party which stands for government of, by and for Communists, crooks and cronies."

The vituperation wound up with a phrase that McCarthy savored so much he was to repeat it often afterward. "Lucky for this country," he said, "that Connecticut's mental midget does not run the Senate."

Never was there a more reluctant dragon than the Democratic Party. The defeats of Tydings and Scott Lucas, however achieved, were political facts of life, and made Senators who would soon have to face the electorate (except the incautious Benton, who was up for reelection in 1952) exceedingly chary about risking their hides. The antediluvian Southern wing of the Democratic Party was as rabid on the issue of communism as McCarthy himself, and hated the liberal tinge of the Truman Administration. In addition, many powerful Democratic Senators were in thrall to the same Texas and Southern oil interests that were financing McCarthyism. The result was that Benton's daring challenge did not rouse a host to storm the enemy barricades. Instead, it sent a shudder of apprehension through Democratic ranks. Even at this late date, all many Democrats wanted was to lie low.

The prevailing mood found expression in *The New York Times'* headline just three days after Benton had flung his challenge. DEAD END AWAITS DRIVE ON M'CARTHY, the headline read. The story beneath it said that Benton's demand "appeared today to be headed for a sub-committee pigeonhole." It quoted Senator Guy M. Gillette (D., Iowa), chairman of the subcommittee to which the Benton resolution had been referred, as saying he had "no plans for hearings or any other action." And it added that other subcommittee members "said privately that they did not favor the investigation demanded by Senator Benton. . ."

But the Democrats who would have liked to lie low hadn't reckoned on Senator Joseph McCarthy. He was always his own worst enemy. He wouldn't let them.

WHENEVER MC CARTHY WAS ATTACKED, he had one reflex response—the cry of "smear." Even before there were any signs an investigation would be authorized, he began to bellow. The trouble was that, in his wild and premature flailing about, he violated all the rules of "the gentlemen's club" by impugning the characters and motives of fellow Senators, some of them among the most respected in the chamber.

He lashed out at two Senators of his own party, Margaret Chase Smith and Robert Hendrickson, both of whom had signed the Declaration of Conscience and both of whom had signed the subcommittee report on the Tydings campaign. They should disqualify themselves from sitting on the Benton ouster committee, McCarthy implied, because it was obvious they were so prejudiced against him that he could not get a fair deal. Then he swung around and hurled a typical innuendo at Senator Thomas Hennings.

McCarthy charged that one of Hennings' law partners, John Raeburn Green, had served as counsel for John Gates, communist editor of the *Daily Worker,* on Gates' appeal to the U.S. Supreme

Court from a conspiracy conviction found against him and ten other communist leaders. Hennings' law firm had also represented the St. Louis *Post-Dispatch* (generally regarded by journalists as one of the best newspapers in the nation). The *Post-Dispatch* had shown its colors by consistently criticizing McCarthy and agreeing editorially with the two Supreme Court Justices who had dissented from the court's decision upholding the conviction of the communist leaders. The plain implication was that Tom Hennings himself was tainted by these associations.

Hennings, who was one of the more mild-mannered men in the Senate and who was highly regarded by the conservative Southern contingent, exploded in a rare rage. He fired off this warning telegram to McCarthy:

"I propose to discuss you in the Senate on Friday. I hope that you will have time to be there even if it requires your temporary absence from inventing smears and lies about others."

McCarthy didn't show up for the face-to-face confrontation, just as he hadn't shown up to face the ire of Dorothy Kenyon. In his absence, then, on Friday, August 21, 1951, Hennings took the floor and delivered the most blistering attack that had been made in months by a Senator not affiliated with the Northern, liberal wing of the Democratic Party. He charged McCarthy with using a "technique of distortion and misrepresentation." He called McCarthy's attack "a thinly veiled attempt to discredit the work of the [Tydings election] subcommittee and invalidate its findings by devious means and irrelevant attacks upon members." And he castigated McCarthy for striking "at the honor of the Senate" and the reputation of a lawyer, John Green, who, incidentally, had just been saluted editorially by the *Journal of the American Bar Association* as exemplifying "what is pure and noble in our profession."

As a lawyer and a former judge, McCarthy was certainly well acquainted with the canon of his profession providing that a defendant, however much his lawyer may disagree with his beliefs or his deeds, is entitled to the best possible defense. Yet in the Green case, as in others, McCarthy tried to traduce a lawyer by implying that this representation indicated the advocate's sympathy with his client's philosophy. Large segments of the public were all too ready to adopt this simplistic line of reasoning, and one effect was that a climate was created in which, at times, it became virtually impossible for ideologically tainted defendants to get capable counsel. (The Rosenberg atom spy case was an example.) Only a few exceptionally courageous lawyers like Green and Joseph Rauh were willing to risk their reputations on behalf of such defendants. In Green's case, McCarthy's one-sided citation of the attorney's record was especially despicable.

The facts were clear. Green was a corporation lawyer whose anticommunism was beyond question. He had represented Gates on appeal because he felt that fundamental American rights were being threatened; many others were similarly concerned about the Truman Administration's stretching of the "conspiracy" statute to a point where no specific deed or specific conspiracy had to be proved. The danger, as many saw it, was that conspiracy charges could be tortured to cover not only a multitude of sinners but a multitude of innocents.

Ironically enough, in defense of a similar principle, Green had represented extremists at the opposite pole of the political spectrum. He had handled the causes of right-wingers Gerald L. K. Smith and the Rev. J. Frank Norris, a fundamentalist Baptist preacher. In these two cases, Green had argued that both Smith and Norris had a right to speak from the platform of the St. Louis Municipal Auditorium.

In a letter to Hennings, which Hennings read into the Senate record, Green explained his advocacy of both Gates and Smith, writing: "In my view, the views of the Communist Party and the views of [Smith's] Christian Nationalist Party are almost equally fraught with death to our free institutions. But freedom of speech includes the freedom of the thought we hate."

McCarthy's smear attack upon Green—and, by extension, upon Hennings because he was Green's law partner—boomeranged. A Democratic-controlled Senate, which had been all but determined to keep its head buried in the sand, was virtually compelled by McCarthy himself to eschew the ostrich role. William S. White noted the change in sentiment.

" . . . A distinguished Southern Senator," he wrote in *The New York Times,* "on the morning before Hennings spoke, had explained the situation to this correspondent in approximately these words:

" 'McCarthy will never be got by the Bentons. He will never be got, here, by the State Department. But a while back, in June, he made a big mistake by attacking Marshall. He made a mistake down in Georgia the other day by asserting that some Senators have Communists on their payrolls.

" 'But he has made the biggest mistake of all now in taking on Tom Hennings. Tom is one of us. He didn't come to Washington fighting anybody and he hasn't done anything to McCarthy.

" 'McCarthy is like a man running in a broken field. He had been getting by nicely so far but now he is getting into our safety zone with this sort of thing. He had better look out.' "

The attack on Hennings, coming on top of the massacre of Tydings, was teaching even conservative Democrats an obvious lesson. They were being forced to recognize that McCarthy threatened not only the liberals, who in the code of the South were fair game, but even stalwart Southern conservatives who had the misfortune to get in his way or to cross his path. The shadow of this modern Robespierre hung over all. There would have to be a Senate investigation of Joseph McCarthy.

STILL THE RELUCTANT DRAGON dragged its feet. As gingerly as a man testing the hot water of his bath, Senator Gillette agreed to hear what Benton had to say. McCarthy, when asked if he would present his side of the story to the Gillette committee, responded with characteristic arrogance:

"No. I have said before I am not going to waste my time on that mental midget [Senator Benton]."

And so, on September 28, 1951, Benton appeared alone before the Gillette committee and presented a 25,000-word indictment of the acts of Joe McCarthy. He called McCarthy "an amoral man who uses the lie as an instrument of policy." He called him a man of "corruptibility and mendacity," a man of "gross irresponsibility" who had followed "a pattern of distortion and deceit."

To back up these thundering charges, Senator Benton cited ten specific acts of McCarthy. They were: the use of the 205 figure at Wheeling and McCarthy's denial he had used it; the $10,000 payment from the Lustron Corporation for the housing booklet prepared by his staff; the attack on General Marshall (a speech of "towering lies miles from . . . honesty or honestly intended interpretation and analysis"); misrepresentations in his March 30, 1950, speech to the Senate; the "despicable" campaign

against Tydings; the failure ever to make good on his solemn
pledge to the Senate that he would say nothing on the floor he
would not say off it; deliberate deception of the Senate on February 20, 1950, by dressing up years-old cases as new and startling
information; his role as defender of the Nazi murderers of
Malmédy; and the roles of Don Surine and a foreign spy of Mc-
Carthy's, Charles E. Davis, who had been arrested in Switzerland
and had been charged by the Swiss with forging a document that
reflected upon the patriotism of John Carter Vincent.*

"All Senators," Senator Benton said, "naturally shrink at the
thought of facing up to the fact that the Senate has an amoral
man who uses the lie as an instrument of policy. Only when one
case piles upon another case, when incident piles upon incident,
and story upon story do we learn to face up to the terrible reality,
a reality which is a source of shame to us all."

He pleaded with the five members of the subcommittee to
throw off the shackles of inhibition imposed by the traditions of
"the gentlemen's club"; he tried to make them see that more was
involved than the honor of the Senate. The honor of the nation
was at stake.

"A United States Senator," he said, "carries a heavy burden
of his country's prestige and honor. The issue here this morning
is thus not merely the issue of the moral conduct of a single Senator. It is the mighty symbolism of the Senate itself.

"If your committee, with its high responsibility, tolerates corruptibility and mendacity in a United States Senator, shame is

---

* Though the Senate committee largely ignored it, the Davis case represented
another small object-lesson of the danger implicit in placing unquestioning
trust in informers. Davis, a left-wing radical who had gone to Europe as a
journalist, had hobnobbed in international communist circles, but when Mc-
Carthy began his campaign, he became "enthralled," as he later said, and
switched sides. He contacted McCarthy's European agent and was deputized
to conduct a counterespionage operation in Switzerland. The object evidently was "to get the goods" on the much-abused minister to Switzerland
and one of McCarthy's early targets, John Carter Vincent. Swiss police arrested Davis and accused him of having sent a "faked" telegram to Vincent,
one ostensibly coming from a well-known communist that could be used
as "proof" of Vincent's communist associations. At Davis' trial, the
Swiss prosecutor declared positively that "a copy of this odious document,
this faked telegram, was sent to McCarthy's emissary in Paris for the manifest purpose of discrediting Vincent and establishing a link between him
and extreme left Swiss circles." Davis was convicted of political espionage
and sentenced to eight months in jail. Since he had already been held eleven
months awaiting trial, he was then deported. McCarthy, as soon as his agent
got in trouble, promptly disowned him, saying that his information had
been of little consequence.

brought to a whole people. Such toleration undermines on a world scale the capacity for leadership of that people in a world desperately requiring that leadership."

And, in closing, he went to the heart of the whole issue of McCarthyism in these words:

"I submit that there is one act of hypocrisy which most offends the deepest convictions of the Christian conscience and also the American spirit of justice and fair play. That act is to put the brand of guilt upon an innocent man.

"I submit that there is no one who has erred more recklessly and maliciously in this respect than Senator Joseph McCarthy. Let us now remember the words of Isaiah:

" 'Woe unto them that call evil good and good evil.' "

It was a ringing call to arms, but the committee's reaction seemed to suggest that Senator Benton was a lonely general marching into battle under the delusion that an army was following him. Chairman Gillette hastily pointed out that his committee had not yet decided even to grant the investigation for which Benton had asked. This was just a preliminary hearing, he pointed out; the committee would still have to decide what to do. The chairman's response did not augur well for the future.

COULD THE DEMOCRATS have rallied the nation at this time by resting their case on the principles of free thought, free speech, and protection of the innocent? There is some evidence that they could.

A Gallup public opinion poll taken in August, 1951, in the same month that Benton asked for McCarthy's ouster, showed that the bell-ringer from Wisconsin had won the approval of only 15 percent of the American people. Twenty-two percent disapproved of him. And 63 percent, nearly two-thirds, professed to have *no opinion*.

Taken at face value, these figures would indicate that more people were opposed to McCarthy than favored him, and that the overwhelming majority of the electorate were still on the fence, their allegiance to be won if the issues could be presented in terms of a clear choice they could understand. Some other evidence, however, suggests that at least some among that 63 percent may not have been undecided—but just plain running scared.

By the end of December, 1950, an English observer was reporting in the *New Statesman and Nation*:

"Freedom of opinion always depends on a pretty large minority of ordinary sensible men who have some convictions and some information, but who also have families and something to lose. In present-day America they keep quiet . . .

"The rift between what you can say in your own living room and what you can say in public is already clear and wide. We from Europe know what thick wedges can be driven into that rift."

Graham Greene, the well-known British novelist, interviewed in Washington, discussed the fear of communism. "America *was* the land of freedom," he said. "People came here not to win television sets or refrigerators, but to gain freedom from house spies, informers and a military regime. But there are a lot of informers working here now." Greene compared the hysteria in America to that in seventeenth-century England resulting from fabricated stories that the Jesuits were planning to assassinate Charles II. Catholics were persecuted, condemned to death in the courts, lynched by mobs. "In that frenzy," Greene said, "they [the Catholics] lost their heads. In the present one in America, the victims lose their jobs."

The vitality of a once free-wheeling and courageous people was being sapped by the fear of being tarred by an accusation. This was illustrated in a survey made in upper New York state by the Rochester *Times-Union*. Sensing the new cowed mood, the newspaper sent out reporters to see what kind of answers they could get to the most innocuous question. The question was simply this: "Do you think you are getting your money's worth out of increased taxes?"

Nothing, it would seem, could have been more deliberately calculated to get a roar out of the public, but in an editorial, the *Times-Union* described what happened:

" . . . alarming was the report of Ann Conroy, correspondent in Geneva, that she had to ask this question of dozens of people to get one reply for publication.

"An employee said, 'Don't quote me, unless you ask my boss.' (The boss said no.) A grocer said he couldn't talk without losing customers. A merchant didn't want to be quoted by name to the effect that the people 'better wake up to the fact that Socialism is sweeping over us faster than we think.' "

The *Times-Union* pointed out: "Such replies are not like America." And it asked: "What happened? Have we become so craven that we can't speak our minds right out in public? Has the climate of America so subtly shifted to intolerance of others' opinions that people are actually fearful of having their say?"

Despite this erosion of the American spirit, the probability exists that American opinion at this time was largely in a state of flux. Given the proper stimulus, a certain percentage of the 63 percent "undecided" group could probably have been persuaded to oppose McCarthyism.

The tragedy was that the Truman Administration lacked the vision to recognize the kind of battle it was in and the kind of battle it should wage; and its party in Congress was hampered by an incredible cargo of dead wood that did not want to wage any battle at all, even now. Harry Truman had to drag this lethargic crew behind him to the fray; and, to give him his due, he tried in his own way—a way that, unfortunately, was the wrong way, one that did not make the basic issues clear.

Truman's strategy was twofold: he lashed out repeatedly at McCarthy, calling him all kinds of names without ever mentioning his name; and at the same time he kept hammering away at the theme of how hard he and his Administration had fought the communist menace. This latter tactic had the effect of confirming McCarthy's principal contention—that there *was* a menace. Truman's admission opened the gates to all kinds of confusion and double-talk about how well the menace had been fought.

Truman's twin themes showed in one of his earliest references to McCarthy. In a speech before the Federal Bar Association in Washington on April 24, 1950, Truman emphasized that he had established a loyalty program for federal employees, described how well it had worked, and added archly:

"I've been surprised to see how much ignorance and misunderstanding there is about this loyalty program—even on the part of persons who should know better. It has occurred to me that, perhaps, they do know better—or perhaps there is some element of politics in their accusations. Of course that couldn't be the case."

In contrast to McCarthy's vivid accusations, this was pretty pale stuff. "Give 'em hell" Harry could do much better than that —and ultimately he did.

In the speech that contained this passing slap at McCarthy, Truman devoted far more space to his own stalwart anticommunism. He emphasized that his Administration had convicted the eleven top communist leaders; that it had "successfully prosecuted many other persons for crimes *related* to communism"; that at that moment it had under investigation the cases of over 1,000 citizens "to determine whether steps should be taken to revoke their citizenship on grounds involving subversive activities." In citing these procedures, Truman was oblivious to the fact, as Carey McWilliams later wrote, that once a witch hunt has begun "some demagogue—and if not McCarthy, then some other —would shout that the testing procedure had been inadequate or that it had been conducted by the 'wrong' agency or that the standard of loyalty was defective."

After McCarthy's slur of General Marshall, Truman stepped up the attack. Still, coyly, he refused to mention McCarthy's name, though obviously his references could apply to only one man. On August 15, 1951, speaking at the dedication of the new million-dollar headquarters of the American Legion in Washington, Truman lashed out at character assassins "who are trying to divide and confuse us and tear up the Bill of Rights." All Americans were in peril, he said, "when even one American—who had done nothing wrong—is forced by fear to shut his mind and close his mouth." He pointed out that even loyal Legion members "have no way of telling when some unfounded accusation may be hurled at you, perhaps straight from the halls of Congress," and he declared that "the scurrilous work of the scandalmongers gravely threatens the whole idea of protection of the innocent in our country today."

Secretary of Labor Maurice J. Tobin followed this up with a speech in which he attacked "irresponsible slander from the privileged sanctuary of the Senate of the United States." He added: "It is my view that the men who founded this nation did not intend the Senate of the United States to be a citadel for slanderers to hide from libel suits." Again no one was named, though it was obvious that the description fitted only Joe McCarthy.

What was said in such speeches was good enough as far as it

went, but it was still shadow-boxing. Truman's tactics were essentially defensive, his championship of American freedoms general rather than specific, his counterattack more personal than principled. The facts were there to expose the fraud, the facts put into the Tydings hearings record by Republican Seth Richardson—the fact that 10,000 full FBI investigations had failed to uncover a single instance of espionage; the fact that full screening by the FBI of 3 million personnel files had uncovered no evidence even hinting at espionage; the fact that "less than one twentieth of 1 per cent" of federal employees had suffered adverse findings for any reason. These were the facts, but Truman threw them all away for his own preferred pose of toughness. And so played into Joe McCarthy's hands.

The McCarthy riposte was entirely predictable. Replying to Truman's American Legion attack, he said: "It ill befits the President of this great nation to try to protect the dupes and stooges of the Kremlin by using his high office to attack—not the facts—but whoever attempts to bring the facts to the attention of the American people." The American people, he added, speaking, naturally, for all of them, were "getting extremely sick and tired of the Administration's clever method of defense by smearing whoever exposes Communists and corruption in government."

It was a tactic that let McCarthy play one of his favorite roles, that of the martyr persecuted by an all-powerful Administration. Some of the highest leaders of his party were soon to join him in stressing the same theme. The tawdriness of this device could have been exposed only if the Democrats had devoted themselves to a full-scale probe of McCarthy and his methods. The Benton resolution afforded them the opportunity, and Senator Gillette announced on October 9, 1951, that he had ordered his staff to begin an investigation and report by November 1. But he still said his committee would have to meet again "to decide where we are going."

THE CONGRESS of the United States has never seen a more lame-and-halt investigation than the Gillette committee's probe of Senator McCarthy. From the outset, McCarthy was openly contemptuous of the committee—and the committee ran scared of him.

One might have thought that an innocent man, arraigned before his peers in the Senate in an indictment as scathing as Benton's, would have come roaring to battle, outraged and anxious to confront his accuser and clear his name. But McCarthy could not be induced, persuaded, cajoled to take such a course. From a safe distance he bellowed that the whole thing was a frame-up; he would have nothing to do with it.

On nine separate occasions during a period of nearly one and a half years, the committee pleaded with McCarthy in its most dulcet tones to please come forward and give his side of the story. It abased itself before him in a fashion inconceivable in any other case in which a Congressional committee might want the testimony of an American citizen. Any day that would be convenient for the Senator to testify would be convenient for the committee. Wouldn't he *please* honor the committee with his presence?

His letters in response to these pleas became ever more arrogant and ever more sarcastic. On October 4, 1951, he wrote Gillette:

"Frankly, Guy, I have not and do not intend to even read, much less answer, Benton's smear attack. I am sure you realize that the Benton type of material can be found in the *Daily Worker* almost any day of the week and will continue to flow from the mouths and pens of the camp-followers as long as I continue my fight against Communists in government."

In McCarthy's absence, balked by his refusal to make a fight of it except in the newspapers, the baffled committee assigned its investigators to do some quiet background research into those incidents that Benton had attacked. There were no explosive public hearings, just some sub rosa inquiries; but these apparently touched a sensitive nerve, for McCarthy began to erupt in righteous indignation. He challenged the committee's authority to investigate his past, and accused it of all kinds of chicanery. In a letter to Gillette, dated December 6, 1951, he charged that "a horde of investigators hired by your committee at the cost of tens of thousands of dollars of taxpayers' money" had been employed for months "for the sole purpose of digging up campaign material against McCarthy . . .

"While the actions of Benton and some of the committee members do not surprise me, I cannot understand your being willing to label Guy Gillette as a man who will head a committee which is stealing from the pockets of the American taxpayers tens of thousands of dollars and then using this money to protect the Democratic Party from the political effect of the exposure of Communists in government."

Gillette always read these denunciations of himself in the press before the fuming communiqués could be delivered to him officially. He protested plaintively against this "impropriety" and discourtesy, but naturally this had no effect. McCarthy continued to treat his official correspondence with the committee like press releases.

On December 15, 1951, he outdid himself in a vituperative letter to Gillette, writing: "As I have previously stated, you and every member of your subcommittee who is responsible for spending vast amounts of money to hire investigators, pay their traveling expenses, etc., on matters not concerned with elections, is just as dishonest as though he or she picked the pockets of the taxpayers and turned the loot over to the Democratic National Committee."

The committee members at that time were Gillette, Hennings, Monroney, Mrs. Smith and Hendrickson, and they did not take kindly to being called pickpockets. They were incensed, too, at McCarthy's wild exaggeration about the "horde of investigators." Actually, as they later told the Senate, they had employed only three investigators for a brief period; their total salaries had come to $3,200; and they had been engaged not solely on the investigation of McCarthy, but also in checking on the 1950 Senatorial election in Ohio.

Though the committee members burned over McCarthy's effrontery and aspersions, they burned for a long while quietly. In fact their immediate reaction to his attacks was to lean over backward still farther until they virtually leaned themselves out of the ball park. In late November, Gillette announced that all action was being put off until 1952, and after the first of the year, there arose more excuses for delay. The membership of the committee was changed despite Benton's protests that this was like changing a jury in the middle of a trial. And a new consideration of extreme delicacy to politicians raised its head: McCarthy was running for reelection in Wisconsin in 1952; would it be "fair" to expose him to a public investigation in a campaign year?

There had never been any great zeal to give Benton what he

wanted and what was needed—an all-out investigation of Joseph McCarthy; but the Republican leadership moved quickly as the 1952 session opened to check any enthusiasm that might develop. McCarthy had protested loud and long against permitting Mrs. Smith and Hendrickson to sit on the committee in judgment of him; and in early January, 1952, the Republican leadership gave Mrs. Smith another committee assignment and replaced her with Herman Welker, an ardent champion of McCarthy. William S. White wrote that this made "the prospect of any action . . . even more remote," and he added: "The upshot of all this has been to leave Senator McCarthy in a place of indisputably increased power and prestige in the Senate."

For months the Republican leadership had done its covert best to increase McCarthy's power and prestige, no matter what his offenses against his fellow Senators, including respected members of his own party. The Republican hierarchy coddled him with good committee assignments, and adopted as its very own his slogan of "communism and corruption."

Even so, there was the rare instance when someone remembered conscience. One such moment came on April 10, 1952, when even Guy Gillette's patience became exhausted at the vituperation to which McCarthy had subjected him and his cohorts. And so he appealed to Carl Hayden (D., Ariz.), chairman of the parent Rules Committee, and Hayden appealed to the Senate. If the Senate had no faith in the honesty and integrity of the Gillette committee, Hayden said, let the Senate say so; let it discharge the committee in disgrace and either drop the whole business or find others to handle it.

Invited to a showdown in which it must stigmatize five of its own if it wished to uphold McCarthy, the Senate quailed. No Senator could find it in his heart to call the committee members thieves; but McCarthy's partisans wriggled on the hook, and some of the exchanges became acrimonious.

"I say to the members of the Senate," declared the doughty Mrs. Smith, who was no longer a member of the committee but who was determined to have her say, "that Senator McCarthy has made false accusations which he cannot and has not had the courage to even try to back up."

This was calling McCarthy both a liar and a coward, and Senator Hickenlooper, who had been McCarthy's stoutest defender on the Tydings committee, was obviously pained. He professed to be "mystified" about what had occasioned all the fireworks.

"Will the Senator from Iowa tell me whether he was ever accused of being a thief?" Mrs. Smith demanded.

"There has not been a thing in the book that I have not been called at one time or another, until I finally developed an immunity of some kind," Hickenlooper replied.

"Would the Senator ever become calloused enough to not mind being called a thief by a fellow member of the Senate?" Mrs. Smith wondered.

That silenced Hickenlooper.

Mike Monroney and Blair Moody (D., Mich.) became so enraged during the debate that their faces turned alternately red and white. Everett McKinley Dirksen, the Republican basso profundo from Illinois, commented in his most orotund tones that he saw "just a little bit of thin-skinned attitude in this proceeding." Moody retorted that he was "sorry" to see Dirksen adopt the attitude "that what has been happening amounts to nothing, that it is inconsequential, that the American people do not deserve better from the Senate than the junior Senator from Illinois would give them."

Dirksen, shaking his white mane, shot back that Moody did not have to be sorry for him; he could take care of himself in Illinois, he said, and he intimated he could take care of Moody in Michigan, too, if it came to that—an implied threat to invade another Senator's state hunting for his scalp. Dirksen rumbled on that he hoped McCarthy would be reelected in November; but there he stopped—short of defending McCarthy's conduct, which was the whole point.

And so in the end, kicking and screaming, even the Republicans were forced to give the Gillette committee a vote of confidence. The final vote was unanimous, 60 to 0. It was a complete exoneration of the committee, a complete repudiation of McCarthy's tactics—and it meant absolutely nothing; it changed nothing. No 60-to-0 vote on a point of honor was going to stop McCarthy; he roared straight ahead, unchecked—and the Gillette committee shattered before him.

.   .   .

ON APRIL 10, 1952—the very day that the Senate had repudiated his tactics—McCarthy filed a resolution demanding that the Gillette committee investigate Senator Benton. He charged Benton with a procommunist bias and with failing to report a campaign contribution from Walter Cosgriff, a bank president.

The committee agreed to take up McCarthy's charges as it had taken up Benton's, and on July 3, 1952, McCarthy appeared before it—not, of course, to answer any questions about himself, but to fire broadsides at Benton. He called his accuser "the chameleon from Connecticut," charged that Benton had surrounded himself with "a motley, Red-tainted crowd," and named seven persons "dangerous to America," who, he said, had served under Benton when he was in the State Department. As always, the emotion-laden phrases defied any precise definition; but for five hours the resounding accusations went on. McCarthy wound up by saying he hadn't determined whether Benson was "a deliberate tool of the Communist Party." But, he assured the committee, "he is doing as much damage as though he were."

As soon as McCarthy had subsided, Benton met his charges head-on—a decided contrast to the evasive maneuvers of his antagonist. Benton accused McCarthy of using the "tactics of blackmail," and told the committee:

"You have here today an example of proof of my charge of perjury. You have had example after example of a pattern of fraud and deceit and deception. You have had the star witness."

It was a ringing denunciation, but it could not offset the guerrilla warfare that was being waged against the committee. This had begun in late December, 1951, when Daniel R. Buckley, an investigator for the committee whose services had been terminated because they were no longer needed, had issued a press release charging that the committee was conducting a one-sided investigation to get McCarthy. According to the committee's subsequent report, telephone company records showed repeated calls between Buckley and Jean Kerr in McCarthy's office and between Buckley and Fulton Lewis, Jr., on the day the publicity blast was issued.

Then, on September 8, 1952, the day before the Wisconsin primary in which McCarthy was running, Jack Poorbaugh, another Senate investigator, resigned with a similar denunciation of the committee—a communiqué that was released to the press before the committee itself received it, and was nicely timed to hit front pages in Wisconsin just before the voters went to the polls. In its subsequent report, the committee wrote: "Information from a reliable source reported that Poorbaugh had conferred with associates of Senator McCarthy, including Fulton Lewis, Jr., just prior to his resignation in order to assist Senator McCarthy in the primary election."

Contributing to the impression that this most wishy-washy of all committees was out to sink a hatchet in McCarthy's skull was the resignation of Senator Herman Welker on September 9. Following Poorbaugh in what seemed like a planned one-two punch, Welker denounced the committee as dishonest and declared he would have nothing more to do with it. This unnerved Senator Guy Gillette, that least militant of committee chairmen, who decided he had had enough and sent in *his* resignation on September 10. Senator Monroney was about to take off on a long trip to Europe, and because he was going to be absent for so long, *he* quit.

This left the committee's ranks so decimated that there was really no committee left. Only Hennings and Hendrickson remained of the original group. Carl Hayden, chairman of the parent Rules Committee, joined them in order to swell their skeletonized ranks to halfway respectable proportions; and so, finally—at a time when the march of events, dramatized by McCarthy's reelection in Wisconsin, had robbed the inquiry of any real effect, without having held a single public hearing to put before the nation the evidence relating to Benton's charges—the committee on January 2, 1953, brought in a report that, in effect, condemned McCarthy's conduct and raised serious questions about his ethics and his acts.

THE REPORT is pocked with inadequacies. It bears witness to the half-hearted efforts of the committee to probe for the full truth about McCarthy. Typical was its gingerly handling of a crucial deed of demagoguery whose significance must have been clear to anyone—the attack on the patriotism of General Marshall. The committee acknowledged that this raised a question: Was McCarthy the mouthpiece of the China lobby? However, because McCarthy had charged that Benton's resolution "was communist inspired and any criticism or investigation of him was an aid to communism—the Subcommittee has been reluctant to conduct any extensive inquiry of this matter or to discuss it in this report." Could any Congressional committee more supinely adopt the strategy and contention of the accused? Having tied its own hands in this manner, the committee contented itself with reporting that "there was contact between Senator McCarthy's office in Washington and Alfred Kohlberg in New York City on at least nine separate occasions during the period from April to September, 1952."

The handling of most of the other charges was similarly baffling and inconclusive. However, even though reticence had been carried to an extreme in this investigation, the report did contain many details of McCarthy's past conduct. It documented his ties to Pepsi-Cola, to the real estate lobby; it recited his acceptance of $10,000 from Lustron, tracked his adventures in the securities market and noted his income tax troubles. It also inquired pointedly into the manner in which McCarthy had handled the thousands of dollars that had poured into his office to aid him in his fight against communism.

"The Subcommittee received unconfirmed reports that Senator McCarthy's office received a substantial number of contributions, some of which at least he was using for his own benefit and unrelated activities," the committee reported.

The report detailed a complicated series of financial transactions. On May 5, 1950, shortly after his anticommunist campaign began to arouse the boondocks, McCarthy opened a special checking account (as distinguished from his general checking account) in the Riggs National Bank at Pennsylvania Avenue and 15th Street N.W. in Washington. On September 7, 1950, he opened a savings account at the National Savings and Trust Company in Washington, and soon afterward he began a weird shuffling of cash out of this account and into soybean futures on the commodity market through his favorite brokers, Wayne Hummer & Company.

This second McCarthy "savings" account was opened with a deposit of $10,500. Of this amount, $500 in cash apparently came from the Riggs special account, withdrawn the same day the National Savings account was opened, and $10,000 from two checks drawn by Rep. Alvin M. Bentley (R., Mich.) and his former wife, Arvilla P. Bentley. The Bentley transactions could only be described as peculiar.

Bentley told committee investigators he had given McCarthy a $3,000 check to fight communism. How, then, did the check wind up in the private "savings" account? Bentley didn't know, but he said that, though he had sent the $3,000 as an outright donation to the cause, McCarthy had later suggested that he accept a non-interest-bearing note and so he had taken "McCarthy's five-year note as evidence of indebtedness." Just why would McCarthy insist that $3,000 given him outright to fight communism should become a personal note-bearing obligation? Bentley indicated that he didn't much care how the $3,000 was used, but volunteered he would be disappointed if he learned McCarthy "had used the money for gambling or to advance his personal financial condition."

Mrs. Bentley's contribution was greater than her ex-husband's, and the circumstances surrounding it were even more mysterious. Mrs. Bentley had sent McCarthy a check for $3,657 on March 22, 1951, then had given him another for $7,000, which he had deposited when he opened his new account at National Savings. After this account had been in existence for only three weeks, McCarthy sent Jean Kerr to National Savings with this note: "This is to authorize Miss Jean F. Kerr of my staff to withdraw $10,000 from my savings account for me." The committee's investigation showed that the $10,000 was used to purchase a draft in the name of Harry J. Van Straten, a long-time friend of McCarthy's; that the draft was endorsed by Straten; and that it financed the soybean gambit with Wayne, Hummer.

Whether Congressman Bentley was "disappointed" by all this, as he had indicated he might be, the record discloses not, and it is even more vague about the purposes and reactions of his ex-wife. When committee investigators tried to question her on November 26, 1952, she told them two things: she wanted to talk to her attorney, and she was too ill to see them. Two days later, on November 28, her attorney passed along the word that she had taken her physician's advice and left for Florida. And then she simply vanished from the committee's ken. Drew Pearson asserted in a column that she had left for Nassau in the Bahamas the same day she arrived in Miami. He added the details that she had used the name Mary Peterson and had taken a Pan American World Airways flight, accompanied by Harvey Matusow, an ex-communist who had become one of McCarthy's stable of informers. In such fashion, Mrs. Bentley remained out of reach until the committee had expired.

It is revealing to take a closer look at the first "special" account McCarthy opened at the Riggs National in May, 1950. The initial deposit had consisted of $35 in cash and forty-five checks totaling $1,292. The account grew until it totaled $20,732.97 by November 11, 1952. The committee traced a couple of the checks deposited in this account, and it seemed clear that at least these represented intended contributions to the anticommunist cause.

One check for $1,000 had been sent by Craig R. Sheaffer, president of the Sheaffer Pen Company, Fort Madison, Iowa. Investigators found that Sheaffer had written the Senator that he would like to make a contribution to the anticommunist crusade if this would not cause embarrassment. McCarthy had replied that he would not be embarrassed. He had a lot of expenses in connection with his war on communism, he said, and he would appreciate help. So Sheaffer sent him $1,000.

In another instance, Bernard Peyton, president of the New York Air Brake Company, heard McCarthy speak at a businessmen's luncheon, was greatly impressed by him, and later asked the Senator how he could help. McCarthy replied that he could use contributions to help him run down "the rascals and Communists in government," and so Peyton sent him a check for $500— a donation that wound up in the "special" account in the Riggs bank.

The investigation, as far as it went, seemed to indicate that this account (and the committee pointed out it never did ascertain whether there were similar accounts in other banks) represented contributions that had been made to fight communism. The crucial point then became: How were these funds used?

The committee found that a lot of records concerning McCarthy withdrawals from the account were strangely missing or illegible. However, a few items of interest were identifiable. One was a check for $73.80 to the Collector of Internal Revenue at a time when McCarthy's regular account was overdrawn; another was a check for $1,300 to his administrative assistant, Ray Kiermas; and then, of course, there was the $500 cash withdrawal that had coincided with the opening of the second account in National Savings. The implication to be derived from the committee's examination of both accounts was that considerable sums of money donated by concerned citizens to combat the communist menace had wound up furthering the personal welfare of Joe McCarthy.

With its usual leaning-over-backward delicacy, the committee did not put the issue quite so bluntly. It contented itself with pointing out that McCarthy had refused to give any explanation, adding: "However, at least without explanation, no connection could be established between many of the disbursements from this [Riggs] account and any possible anti-Communist campaign . . ."*

W H A T , T H E N , were the conslusions of the investigation?

The committee disposed of McCarthy's charges against Benton by administering the Connecticut Senator a slap on the wrist. It found that Benton had accepted $600 from Cosgriff, and had not reported it as a campaign contribution. Benton explained (and the record backed him up) that Cosgriff had not given him the money to help his political campaign in the ordinary sense, but to help defray the cost of reprinting and distributing a speech Benton had made backing the recommendations of the Hoover commission for government reorganization. Cosgriff was greatly interested in these proposals, and his contribution helped to make possible the distribution of 102,000 copies of Benton's speech, almost entirely to Benton's Connecticut electorate. Later, when Cosgriff was named for a federal post, Benton supported him, and this, the committee thought, raised the specter of a conflict of interest.

As for McCarthy, even this restrained committee expressed

---

* Anderson and May in their book on McCarthy indicated that the contributions sent to the Senator far transcended the sums mentioned in the official committee report. They wrote that the committee in its closed-door investigation "had struck a gold mine of canceled checks, made out to McCarthy but never reported on his income tax returns." Carl Hayden, they wrote, kept the evidence "under lock and key," but "one Senator, who had examined the list of canceled checks, told the authors the total was roughly $148,000."

its bitterness. "For reasons known only to Senator McCarthy," it wrote, "he chose . . . to charge that the allegations were a smear and that the Subcommittee was dishonest and was doing the work of Communists." McCarthy's actions, it wrote, "might appear to reflect a disdain and contempt for the rules and wishes of the entire Senate body . . ." The committee cited its repeated efforts to get McCarthy to tell his own side of the story, and added: "The record leaves the inescapable conclusion that Senator McCarthy deliberately set out to thwart any investigation of him by obscuring the real issue and the responsibility of the Subcommittee by charges of lack of jurisdiction, smear and Communist-inspired persecution . . ."

The committee concluded by saying it was not making any recommendations. "The record should speak for itself," it wrote. "The issue raised is one for the entire Senate." And it added that this was "a matter that transcends partisan politics and goes to the very core of the Senate Body's authority, integrity and the respect by which it is held by the people of this country."

If the Senate still retained a core of integrity, it was not observable in the aftermath. The report, another indictment of Senator McCarthy by his peers, was buried and forgotten with the most unseemly haste.

The same was true in the nation at large. The reaction of the press was notable, not only for its lack of indignation, but even for its lack of elementary curiosity. The New York *Post* editorially summed up the situation several days after the report was issued:

"The heavily-documented Senate report exposing the devious financial operations of Sen. McCarthy was released last Friday. Following is a summary of editorial comment on the report in other New York newspapers:

"*The Times*—no comment.

"The *Herald-Tribune*—no comment.

"The *Daily News*—no comment.

"The *Mirror*—no comment.

"The *Journal-American*—no comment.

"The *World-Telegram & Sun*—no comment."

Ten days after the filing of the report, the *Post* commented again:

"McCarthy's fellow Senators have been speechless. With some honorable exceptions, the nation's press—usually enthralled by news of Washington sin—gave inadequate space to the report; there has been an even more amazing silence in the editorial pages. (In this city only *The Times* and *The Post* have taken editorial notice of the findings.)

"Is McCarthy untouchable? . . ."

PART FIVE

The Menace and the Downfall

17

The Halo and the Hatchetman

FOR REPUBLICANS 1952 was the year of the halo and the hatchetman. Out front running for President was that national wartime hero, General of the Army Dwight David Eisenhower, and on the subterranean level, developing the visceral theme of "communism and corruption," was Joseph R. McCarthy.

It was obvious in the waning months of 1951 that "McCarthyism" would be a major issue in the Presidential contest—and that the Republicans expected to make the most of it. The Washington columnist Marquis Childs, writing in October, 1951, found that most Republicans held to the belief that McCarthy hadn't been damaged by his excesses, not even by his attack on General

Marshall. Childs found three major reasons for McCarthy's resilience and continued power:

". . . One is the fact that a great many people have come to believe that communism in government is a threat and that Mc-Carthy has been working effectively to remove it. Another is his sheer demagoguery; his ability to come into a meeting that may be indifferent or skeptical and get them on their feet cheering.

"A third reason is the conviction of many businessmen who are Republicans that anything goes in driving the Democrats out. They are sometimes frankly cynical about it."

This last motive was fundamental. The twenty-year succession of defeats at the hands of Democratic Presidential candidates had so frustrated the Republican Party that it was reduced to the most abject depths of irresponsibility. The climactic blow had been the stunning upset defeat of Thomas E. Dewey by Harry Truman in 1948. Such a disaster must never happen again.

In their frenzy to restore the old business order to domination, the Republicans were perfectly willing to pay the price of inflicting Joe McCarthy's tactics on the nation. McCarthy must be rehabilitated and protected for the great services he could perform in the campaign of 1952. And so there was not just a shuffling of forces to guard him from possible prying by the Gillette committee, but a concerted drive to pervert the realities of political discourse by pinning the label "smearer" on those who had been smeared.

THE TACTIC that was now adopted was a marvel. Its object was to transform the indisputable master of the smear into the lamblike victim of the smear. This campaign had begun almost the moment President Truman and Secretary Tobin assailed those unnamed hate-mongers and character assassins. On September 30, 1951, twenty-five Republican Senators rallied to the defense of the unnamed assassin, issuing a manifesto in which they denounced "some persons and groups" in the Truman Administration for using "smear tactics and propaganda techniques" to silence all opposition.

"There is evidence," the signers of the manifesto said, "that no man can criticize our government today and escape intemperate reprisals."

Senators Homer Ferguson and Styles Bridges were among the leaders in drafting and promulgating the manifesto. Senator Bricker, Taft's Ohio cohort, another of the signers, muttered darkly about the dangers of incipient dictatorship. McCarthy himself, of course, was happy to sign this denunciation. And he was joined by his own camp-followers—Welker, Hickenlooper, Mundt, Jenner, Butler, Capehart—and, among others, by William Knowland, of California and Ralph Flanders, of Vermont.

The Republican leaders who had risen to such conscientious defense of poor, besmirched Joe were soon joined in the endeavor by a cross-section of eminent men from the world of entertainment, business, the universities and the literary arts. In May, 1952, a ten-page pamphlet entitled "Senator McCarthy" was widely distributed by a group called Freedom Clubs, Inc. The pamphlet was mailed out in envelopes bearing the return address of Alfred Kohlberg, of the China lobby, and it was given the imprimatur of many headline personalities who were listed as members of the advisory committee of Freedom Clubs.

Written by Dr. Kenneth Colegrove, professor of political science at Northwestern University, the pamphlet was a ringing endorsement of McCarthy, describing him as the victim of "one of the most vicious smear campaigns in American history." The pamphlet acknowledged that McCarthy's first attacks on the State Department had been "rude and crude," but it excused his excesses as justifiable under the circumstances. His "brutal charges" were a natural reaction to the "pugnacious refusal of the Truman Administration to assist Congressional investigation of the loyalty of Federal employees." Besides, the pamphlet contended, Senator McCarran's McCarthy-supporting probe had "already substantiated a large part of the charges of Senator McCarthy, and well may lead to proof of all of these charges."

Among the Freedom Clubs' advisers whose names became connected with this endeavor were such well-knowns as these: Bing Crosby; Fulton Lewis, Jr.; General Wedemeyer; Dr. Roscoe Pound, dean emeritus of the Harvard Law School; Dr. Robert A. Millikan, prominent physicist of the California Institute of Technology; Dr. James W. Fifield, Jr., pastor of the First Congregational Church of Los Angeles, largest of its denomination in the nation; Erle Cocke, Jr., past commander of the American Legion; Cecil B. de Mille, the movie magnate; Rupert Hughes and Felix Morley, authors; Dean Clarence Manion, of the University of Notre Dame Law School, still one of the foremost promulgators of ultraright doctrines; Dr. Norman Vincent Peale, noted New York clergyman and one-time head of the Committee for Constitutional Government; Eddie Rickenbacker, President of Eastern Air Lines; George Sokolsky; and James B. Selvage, head of one of New York's largest public relations concerns.

Such were the respectables from many walks of life, such the politically powerful, who were lining up behind Joseph R. McCarthy.

THE ATTITUDE of the hierarchy of the Republican Party, as distinguished from its ultraconservative Midwestern wing, was never really in doubt. The high command intended from the start to make the fullest use of McCarthy's rabble-rousing talents.

Senator Taft, the most eminent of the party's eminents, had suffered one bad moment, a temporary case of qualms, after McCarthy's denunciation of General Marshall. Speaking in Des Moines on October 22, 1951, Taft tried gingerly to put a little clear water between himself and McCarthy, whose witch hunt he had secretly encouraged from the outset.

"I don't think one who overstates his case helps his own case," Taft commented in this moment of reasonableness. "There are certain points on which I wouldn't agree with the Senator.

"His extreme attack against General Marshall is one of the things on which I cannot agree with McCarthy. I think some criticism of General Marshall was justified, but he should not have been accused of any form of affiliation with communism."

Even so, Taft could not bring himself to disown McCarthy completely. After staking out this small area of principle, he gave McCarthy a pat on the back in these words:

"However, Senator McCarthy brought to attention the wide extent of communism in Government. There are some Communists left in Government, and some Communist tendencies, but they are not so much of a threat now."

When McCarthy was asked for comment about this mild

reproof and this minimizing of the menace, he told reporters: "I will not believe it until I get his word that he said it. I just don't think Bob Taft will join the camp-following elements in campaigning against me and I will have a definite comment if I get confirmation from him that he said it."

This amounted to saying that if he did not want to be labeled a "camp follower," Taft had better not criticize McCarthy. Whether Taft heeded the threat, or whether it was that he was so badly bitten by the Presidential bug that he felt he just couldn't afford to lose McCarthy, the fact remains that it didn't take "Mr. Republican" long to climb right back on the bandwagon.

The turnabout came in a speech in Beloit, Wisconsin, on January 21, 1952, when Taft told the Rock County Women's Republican Club: "Certainly McCarthy's investigation has been fully justified by repeated dismissals of employees of doubtful loyalty, by the revelations regarding the insincerity of the State Department's Loyalty Board, by the dismissal of [John S.] Service and by other evidence showing that the investigation must be pressed to a conclusion."

Only a new Administration (obviously one he hoped to head) could clean up the State Department, Taft said, and he sounded more and more like McCarthy himself as he continued: "This Administration has been dominated by a strange Communist sympathy, by a complete absence of consistency and principle and by the worst of judgment."

By late March, "Mr. Republican" was even more enthusiastically in McCarthy's corner. In another Wisconsin speech, he lauded McCarthy for having "dramatized" the issue of communist penetration and influence in the State Department, and praised him for having "done a great service to the American people."

Taft was by no means alone in these accolades. Appearing on a Washington television program, "Youth Wants to Know," Guy George Gabrielson, the Republican National chairman— who had been personally testing out the communist-subversion theme in West Virginia at the same time as the Wheeling speech —rebuked a youthful questioner for referring to McCarthy as "Jumping Joe." He did not "like that way of speaking," Gabrielson said severely, and he informed the young skeptic that the American people "should be proud of what the Senator has done."

Instead of investigating McCarthy's charges, he continued, the Truman Administration had "started persecuting McCarthy."

"It took a man of Senator McCarthy's nature, determination and stick-to-itiveness or else he would have been swallowed up," Gabrielson declared.

By February, 1952, two years had passed since the Wheeling speech, and a full year since the McCarran committee had made its raid on the document-filled Massachusetts barn. Those years had been filled with McCarthy's unceasing clamor about the communist menace; new names, new charges and elaborations on old ones had flitted in and out of the pages of the press, with nothing proved—but nothing disproved either. Two things seemed certain: a sizeable portion of the American electorate had become convinced that the Truman Administration had been riddled with communists and their sympathizers, and hence the battle cry in the fall campaign would inevitably be those alliterative twins, "communism and corruption." Sensing the hysteria in the nation, politicians—a breed that always gives self-preservation a high priority—began to fall all over each other to get into the superpatriotic witch-hunting act. And none was more eager than the heavy-featured, silver-maned Senator from Nevada—Pat McCarran.

It did not matter to McCarran that the principal victim of his endeavors would be the national leadership of his own party. The alliance McCarran and McCarthy had formed in early 1951 held firm. McCarran's investigators had spent an entire year doing spadework for McCarthy. They had examined the thousands of documents seized in the Carter barn raid. They had gathered evidence for a series of public hearings on communist influence in official policy-making and the media. And now, in the perfervid political atmosphere of 1952, they were ready to put their show on the road and reach for the headlines.

Their first target was Owen Lattimore. Here was the man who had stood up to McCarthy and done him the most damage, pinning upon him and his party the label of "McCarthyism." Lattimore's was the case on which McCarthy had promised to "stand or fall," and he had certainly fallen badly in the showdown before the Tydings committee nearly two years earlier. But the Tydings report had been smothered in cries of "whitewash," and Tydings himself had been defeated. Now was the time—with

McCarthy himself running for reelection—to complete the vindication of Joe McCarthy. And so, in February, 1952, McCarran subpoenaed Lattimore to appear before him for a new inquisition.

The atmosphere was reminiscent of the beginning of the Tydings inquiry. If Tydings had cast himself in the role of "hanging judge," his performance paled before that of McCarran. But the impact of the two performances on the public mind was vastly different for two reasons: Tydings had harried a Senator bulwarked by official position and power—McCarran was taking out after an ordinary and relatively defenseless citizen; McCarthy had had the support of a powerful political party eager to scream "whitewash" and to make the label stick—Lattimore, in the craven Democratic mood of the time, had no supporters at all.

It was obvious to everyone that Owen Lattimore came to his "trial" already condemned in the mind of his accuser, who was also his judge. Recognizing that fact, he came nevertheless to do battle, armed with his slingshot—a twelve-thousand-word opening statement in which he denounced McCarran to his face, charging him with smearing innocent persons and with conducting "a reign of terror" among U.S. diplomats abroad.

The Associated Press, describing this confrontation, reported: "Committee members interrupted so frequently, however, that the one-time government consultant on Far Eastern affairs got through only eight sentences of his fifty-page statement in three hours of testimony. At that rate it would take him 75 hours to read it all."

When Lattimore said that he had "no hope your committee will fairly appraise the facts," McCarran retorted that such language had been heard before from known communists—and it had landed some of them in jail. Abe Fortas protested against the constant interruption and harassment of Lattimore as he attempted to read his statement (just as the Republicans had when McCarthy appeared before the Tydings committee), but this time there was no committee opposition to McCarran to force him to mend his ways. At the close of the hearing Lattimore remarked that "the kind of examination to which I have been subjected has been rather markedly lacking in the examination of others who have made charges against me."

The pillorying of Lattimore by McCarran went on for twelve

days, the longest and most brutal interrogation of one man in all Congressional history up to that time.

The Washington *Post* commented on this relentless cross-examination.

"The subcommittee seems determined to beat Owen Lattimore into sheer physical exhaustion, to make fatigue and despair extort admissions which he would not make of his own free will. When Mr. Lattimore pleaded fatigue and asked for a respite the other day, Senator McCarran said the members of the subcommittee were tired too. The subcommittee with half a dozen members and two staff lawyers, all acting as prosecutors, has been able to question this lone witness in relays. For nine days it has subjected him to an incessant drumfire of interrogation—in a process uncomfortably like that which the Russians so commonly employ to break down innocent men. He has stood up to it well enough . . . But it is a frightening spectacle, as one foreign journalist put it, to see a committee of the United States bully and torment a witness in this fashion—as though he were in an arena, at bay, providing sport for the public. Perhaps the subcommittee chairman, Senator McCarran, needs to be reminded that bull-fighting, so popular in Spain, has never had much appeal in the United States."

Events a decade old were raked up and examined—and on the premise that Lattimore must be capable of instant, complete and infallible recall. Admittedly, Lattimore, being human, failed this test. He was in error about the precise timing of some of these years-old events. And some of the correspondence seized in the Carter barn was used against him with devastating effect. The most important of these barn-raid items was a letter from Lattimore, then editor of the Institute of Pacific Relations' *Pacific Affairs*, to E. C. Carter on July 10, 1938. It became the McCarran committee's Exhibit 4, and it read:

"I think that you are pretty cagey in turning over so much of the China section of the inquiry to Asiaticus, Han-seng and Chi. They will bring out the absolutely essential radical aspects, but can be depended upon to do it with the right touch.

"For the general purposes of this inquiry it seems to me that the good scoring position, for the IPR, differs with different countries. For China, my hunch is that it will pay to keep behind the official Chinese Communist position—far enough not to be covered by the same label—but enough ahead of the active Chinese liberals to be noticeable. For Japan, on the other hand, hang back so as not to be inconveniently ahead of the Japanese liberals, who cannot keep up, whereas the Chinese liberals can. *So the chief thing is to oppose the military wing of Japanese aggression in China, counting on a check there to take care of both the military and civilian components of aggression in Japan.* For the British—scare the hell out of them, always in a polite way, but usually in a way that looks as if it might turn impolite. The British liberal groups are badly flustered; but being British, the way to encourage them to pull themselves together is to fluster the Tories. For the U.S.S.R.—back their international policy in general, but without using their slogans and above all without giving them or anybody else the impression of subservience. . . ." (Italics added.)

This letter, referred to sarcastically by the McCarran probers as the "cagey" letter, was flaunted as proof positive that Lattimore had been promoting Soviet policy. Indeed, the letter itself left little doubt, but it was being considered in 1952 in a context entirely different from that of the time in which it was written. It is clear from his other writings that in 1938 Lattimore's overriding concern was with Japanese aggression in China. To him, any sane national policy certainly involved the encouragement of Chinese resistance, and the Communist guerrillas had proven themselves the most effective fighting force in the effort to thwart Japanese militarism abroad and discredit it at home. The fact that Russia was supporting the Chinese Communists did not alter this picture; Russia and China, to Lattimore, were two separate nations, and he had little fear that Moscow would ever swallow Peking. Similarly, support for the international policy of Soviet Russia at this time also made sense to him; for Russia, had she not been treated as a pariah by the right-wing governments of France and Britain, was the one great power in Europe that had been prepared to unite with them in defense of Czechoslovakia prior to the sellout at Munich. These stands could be defended on the grounds that they were realistic and pragmatic in the context of the issues of 1938; and they were indeed positions that were to be ratified in official policy when World War II forced the very kind of collaboration Lattimore had envisaged. But by 1952 the strains and perils of the late 1930s had largely faded in public memory; by 1952 it was sufficient to show that a man had advocated policies the Soviet had also advocated: ergo, he must have been a communist.

A more valid and damaging point, at least to Lattimore's academic prestige, arose inescapably from this so-called "cagey" letter. As editor of *Pacific Affairs*, Lattimore had been assumed to be an impartial expert, but obviously he had not been. He had been immersed in promoting a definite policy line, and articles in the magazine he edited had been slanted to accord with that line. Many in academic circles felt that they had been deceived by his pose of impartiality, an offense for which they could not forgive him.

The McCarran evidence also disclosed that many articles in *Pacific Affairs* had been heavily weighted toward policies favored by the communists. Even some of Lattimore's supporters had been affronted by the ideological content of articles that pictured the Chinese Communists not as bloody revolutionaries but as simple agrarian reformers, comparable to our Midwestern Populists of the 1890s. Lattimore's attitude had involved him in repeated clashes. In one of these, with William Henry Chamberlin in 1938, Lattimore had even defended Stalin's ruthless purges, an exercise in brutality that had shaken the faith of many American communists.

All of this could easily have been read as an ideological blind spot, such as many had in the different crises of that time, when the great menace to the peace of the world was posed by the Fascist powers. But to interlocutors like Pat McCarran and Robert Morris, to whom the lightest tinge of pink was seen as deep-dyed red, there was not the slightest doubt: such a record said to them that they were dealing with an agent of communism.

They harped upon Lattimore's admittedly close relationship with Frederick Vanderbilt Field. Lattimore at first testified that he hadn't realized Field was a communist until 1940–41, after he had ended his editorship of *Pacific Affairs*. But some of the correspondence found in the Carter barn indicated that awareness must have come much earlier than that. One IPR memo from Field to Lattimore warned that, in a certain article, "the analysis is a straight Marxist one and . . . should not be altered." Lattimore, confronted with such evidence, finally acknowledged that he had erred by "about two years" in his original testimony about the date he first became aware of Field's communist ties.

Despite the clarity of many of Lattimore's perceptions, despite his action in harboring anti-Communist Buddhists, despite his effort as revealed in the Barnes letter to make certain OWI did not employ Chinese Communists in wartime, McCarran's investigation had produced revelations that, in the fevered atmosphere of 1952, were dynamite. The findings of the inquisitors became a foregone conclusion. McCarran presented them to the Senate on July 2, 1952, in a speech that began:

"Mr. President, twenty-five years ago a small group of men interested in the Far East made a deal with Russia . . . Today we know that from that deal in Moscow there developed an operation, directed by the Soviet, that was a major factor in the loss of a valuable ally to the United States . . .

"I am convinced from the evidence developed in this inquiry that, but for the machinations of the small group that controlled and activated that organization [the IPR], China today would be free and a bulwark against the further advance of the red hordes into the Far East."

The committee's 225-page report denounced Lattimore in these terms:

"Owen Lattimore was, from some time beginning in the 1930s, a conscious articulate instrument of the Soviet conspiracy."

In denying this and insisting upon his innocence, Lattimore had committed perjury, the committee found. It charged he had lied on five points: he testified that Outer Mongolia was independent until after World War II when he knew it was Soviet-controlled; he denied knowing that Chi Ch'ao-ting was a communist; he denied knowing that Frederick Vanderbilt Field was a communist at the time he was associated with Field in IPR; he testified that he did not know that the author of some articles in *Pacific Affairs* was a communist; and he gave an inaccurate account of his relationship with a former student who, the committee contended, had written about its hearings "on assignment" from Mrs. Lattimore.

The great difficulty with the McCarran charges lay in the fact that so much depended on an interpretation of what had been in a man's mind some fifteen years earlier, on what he had known about persons with whom he associated at that time.

There was documentary evidence that Lattimore must have known about Field's communist ties before the date he originally testified he did, but so many of the other charges depended on the "he-must-have-known" school of reasoning. The stands Lattimore had taken were clear, but the answer to the vital question —Why?—depended on reading his mind for his motives. This feat was not difficult for Pat McCarran. He leaped easily to the conviction that Lattimore had been a communist agent; and, from this, he pole-vaulted to the crowning absurdity that the "loss" of China had been brought about by a small group of American conspirators, with Lattimore acting as their evil presiding genius.

To the Washington *Post*, all this was "extravagant nonsense." And Nathaniel Peffer, professor of international relations at Columbia University, an authority on the Far East and himself an original member of IPR, wrote a devastating critique for the *New Republic*.

"What, then, was it that produced the upheaval in China that culminated in Communist control?" he asked. "It was not the slow, progressive decline of the republic since 1911; not the decade of pillage by warlords; not the eight years of Japanese invasion and the devastation, economic paralysis and demoralization brought with it; not the carpetbaggerism that followed the war and the degeneration of the Nationalist government under Chiang Kai-shek. Not even the Chinese people had anything to do with it. It was all the making of the IPR, an organization 6,000 miles from China, composed of a few hundred Americans—a small number of rich businessmen, a larger number of middle-class businessmen and professional men and still more professors. The most extraordinary political feat since Hammurabi!"

Peffer pointed out that the McCarran report gave the most sinister interpretation to the famous three-day State Department conference in October, 1949, when a group of about twenty-five consultants met to discuss American Far Eastern policy. Peffer wrote:

"It is said that at that meeting a majority, who were active in the Institute of Pacific Relations, strongly advocated recognition of the Communist government in China. (I happened to be one of those present and though not active in the Institute of Pacific Relations I, too, advocated recognition and still think there was more to gain than lose by doing so.) But what is passed over lightly in the McCarran report is that among the majority were men who are also the heads of great corporations with headquarters in and around Wall Street. It must be added, too, that a large proportion, if not a majority, of Americans in the Far East, whether officials, missionaries or businessmen, also advocated recognition then."

As for one of the specific charges against Lattimore—that he had lied in denying he knew Chi Ch'ao-ting was a Communist —Peffer wrote that "many, myself included, were never certain and some still are not." In conclusion, Peffer thought it "inconceivable that this will ever get to a grand jury, even in a time of hallucination and hysteria."

In this he underestimated McCarran. The Nevada Senator hounded the Justice Department relentlessly for months, demanding that it indict Lattimore for perjury. And so, eventually, it did. Though the indictment ultimately fell flat on its face and was thrown out of court, in the atmosphere of the times *the mere finding of an indictment* could be as damning as a jury verdict of guilty. So, to many, Lattimore was condemned by the very accusation. And it escaped general notice that the McCarran committee in hounding to earth its chosen quarry had thrown its mantle of protection over its own nest of informers. As the Washington *Post* commented, "the subcommittee never put to the test the interesting issue of Louis Budenz's credibility . . . Lattimore suggested that the subcommittee ask the Department of Justice to review the record and prosecute for perjury whichever of the two appeared to have been guilty of it. But despite the fact that many witnesses of high repute [including Joseph Alsop] contradicted Budenz's sworn assertions, the subcommittee carefully shielded him from any judicial test requiring him to submit to cross-examination."

It was an illustration of a new double standard in American justice, whereby the informer—that most distrusted rogue of ages past—becomes highly valued. His victim can be required to meet every test, even fantastic tests of logic and memory— but not the informer, for without him there would be no victim. And this was and remains, to a large degree at least, a society that must have its victims, lest it be compelled to look into the face of truth.

The indictment against Owen Lattimore was returned December 16, 1952, by a federal grand jury in Washington, and it was distinguished as much by what it did *not* say as by what it *did*. Here was reflected no trace of McCarthy's "Number 1 Soviet spy" charge. Lattimore was not accused of having been a spy; he was not even accused of having been a communist. He was charged with perjury for errors of recollection concerning events that had taken place from ten to fifteen years previously. Right-wingers quivered with anticipatory delight. David Lawrence chortled in print in a column to which the New York *Herald-Tribune* attached the headline: LATTIMORE'S TRIAL EXPECTED TO OVERSHADOW THE HISS CASE.

The exultation turned out to be premature, for it was obvious from the outset that this peculiar indictment posed some tricky and delicate questions.

The first count against Lattimore was the key. It accused him of committing perjury when he told the McCarran committee: "I am not and have never been a Communist, a Soviet agent, a sympathizer or any other kind of promoter of communism or Communist interests, and all these are nonsense." The indictment picked apart this statement most carefully. It did not challenge the items that might be susceptible to proof—that Lattimore had never been a communist nor had he ever been a spy; but it indicted him for denying he had been a "sympathizer" or a "promoter" of "Communist interests."

Just how was one to define a "sympathizer"? One man's "sympathy" is another's common sense; it was an item outside the realm of specifics, not susceptible of proof. Similarly, what were "Communist interests"? No specific "interest" or action was alleged, and so how, Lattimore's lawyers asked, could he be expected to disprove a charge that was not even defined?

". . . From the longest interrogation of a single witness in congressional history," they wrote, "the prosecution fishermen, unable to produce a whale, have come up with minnows . . .

"Here are to be found only the puny charges that he [Lattimore] knowingly and wilfully perjured himself when he denied (1) that during the war years he was told that a certain obscure Chinese was a Communist; (2) that in the late 1930s he 'knew' that a certain obscure writer under the name of Asiaticus was a Communist; (3) that in *Pacific Affairs* . . . he published articles by persons *other than Russians* whom he knew to be Communists; (4) that in 1941 before the United States was involved in World War II . . . he had luncheon in Washington with the Russian Ambassador before, not after, the Hitler invasion of Russia . . .; (5) that in 1942 he was requested to and did take care of the correspondence of Lauchlin Currie while Currie was away on a trip; and (6) that as long ago as 1937 he made 'pre-arrangements' with 'the Communist authorities' to visit Yenan, just after the Chinese Communists had submitted to the political and military authority of Chiang Kai-shek. This is a matter of record."

In an acid comment on the conduct of the McCarran hearings the lawyers—Abe Fortas, Thurman Arnold and Paul A. Porter—went on to say that Lattimore "was never confronted by the witnesses against him and in the course of the cross-examination to which he was subjected he was repeatedly denied the right to refresh his memory, he was ordered to answer without attempting to refresh his recollection, *indeed he was once ordered to answer but not to think,* and several times his counsel was enjoined by the Chairman of the Committee not to speak unless spoken to." (Italics added.)

Now began a long court battle, stretching over the months and years, during which the Department of Justice exerted every effort to hang Owen Lattimore any way it could. The first blow against the government's case was struck on May 2, 1953, when Federal District Judge Luther W. Youngdahl, a Republican and former Governor of Minnesota, threw out four of the perjury charges against Lattimore, including the key first count of "sympathizing." The judge wrote that "this charge is so nebulous and indefinite that a jury would have to indulge in speculation in order to arrive at a verdict. Sympathies and beliefs and what they mean to different individuals are highly nebulous and speculative at best . . . It is fundamental that a jury should not be asked to determine an issue which can be decided only on conjecture." All of this, the judge wrote, was in clear violation of the First Amendment guaranteeing freedom of thought and speech.

Though he let three charges stand, the judge commented that he had a "serious doubt" about their validity also. Rocked back by this decision, the Justice Department appealed Judge

Youngdahl's ruling to the Court of Appeals. There, on July 8, 1954, the court by an 8-to-1 vote sustained the dismissal of the key first count of the indictment, but reinstated two of the other counts Judge Youngdahl had dismissed. It was another serious setback. U.S. Attorney Lee A. Rover acknowledged that he considered the first "sympathy" count the core of the indictment.

Trying to reestablish this core, Rover took the Lattimore case before a new federal grand jury and secured a new indictment on October 7, 1954. This contained two counts and was intended to bolster and validate the "sympathy" charge which constituted the heart of the government's case. It detailed twenty-five topics on which, it said, Lattimore's views paralleled what it defined as "the Communist line." Lattimore, peppery as ever, snapped back that, under the government's definition, anyone who had ever expressed any opinion that happened also to be held by a Communist would be culpable. In such case, he held, even Presidents Roosevelt, Truman and Eisenhower might have been considered liable to prosecution.

With the new indictment, an attack began upon Judge Youngdahl. In a virtually unprecedented step, Rover asked the judge to disqualify himself from presiding at the trial, charging that the judge had "a fixed opinion" that Lattimore was not guilty and that the government could not get "a fair and impartial trial" at his hands. Arnold, Fortas and Porter called the charges "scandalous" and asked for an appointment with Attorney General Brownell to discuss them. They charged: "The affidavit is an attempt to manipulate the administration of justice and an effort to subordinate the judiciary to the prosecuting arm of the government."

Judge Youngdahl spurned the Justice Department's demand that he quit. He denounced Rover's affidavit as a "hit-and-run attack" that might touch upon "any judge of the United States" unlucky enough to have to hear the Lattimore charges. He called the affidavit an attempt to discredit and intimidate the courts.

The next-to-the-last act in the drama came on January 18, 1955, when Judge Youngdahl threw out the new two-count indictment. He ruled that it was no more effective than the first "sympathizing" count in the old indictment which both he and the Court of Appeals had held defective. "To require defendant to go on trial for perjury under charges so formless and obscure as those before the court would be unprecedented and would make a sham of the Sixth Amendment and the Federal rule requiring the specificity of charges," Judge Youngdahl declared.

The Sixth Amendment provides that, in criminal trials, the defendant shall be "informed of the nature and cause of the accusation" against him.

This ruling sounded the death knell of the Lattimore case. The Department of Justice could have fought Judge Youngdahl's decision in the Court of Appeals, but after weighing its alternatives for six long months, it announced on June 28, 1955, that it was dropping the prosecution. The case on which Joe McCarthy had boasted he would "stand or fall" had finally and irretrievably fallen.

T H R O U G H O U T the summer and fall of 1952, Pat McCarran's supplement to the McCarthy witch hunt had been roaring on across the nation, filling up columns in the press. On August 26, 1952, McCarran's Internal Security Subcommittee came out with a denunciation implying wholesale subversion of the radio industry. The report charged that a small band of "pro-Communists" had seized control of the Radio Writers Guild, a subsidiary of the Authors League of America. It stressed that members of the guild produced 90 percent of the scripts broadcast by the radio networks—the implication being that the vast majority of scripts included some subtle form of indoctrination.

Though McCarran himself said that "less than 100 pro-Communists" (note the "pro") had taken over the 1,200 to 1,500-member guild, he obviously considered this indicated that radio script-writing had been contaminated across the board. And he expanded this assumption into a warning to the television industry that it had better be on the alert and clean its own house because the same kind of subversive termites were planning to infiltrate it, too.

This clamor was based largely upon the fact that *two* radio script writers had claimed the privileges of the First and Fifth Amendments when haled before McCarran's committee—and on the additional horror tales supplied by "cooperative" witnesses. One of these willing collaborators was Vincent W. Hartnett, a former naval intelligence officer who, in 1950, published a 213-page book, *Red Channels*, listing 151 radio and TV stars, writers, producers and directors as red-tainted. The mention of one's name in the *Daily Worker* or in testimony before the California Un-American Affairs Committee or the House Un-American Activities Committee (however suspect the source might be and however inconclusive the testimony) was certain to win one a listing in *Red Channels*. The book had become the bible of Madison Avenue; advertising agencies, sponsors, radio and TV executives consulted it to determine whether they were running any risk in employing a writer, actor or announcer. Hartnett had kept up his drumfire of charges by founding a news sheet called *Aware*. This produced a steady stream of new names, new suspects, and Hartnett became virtually a one-man clearing house for the radio and TV industry. For the payment of appropriate fees, he traced the backgrounds of employees and prospective employees; and so it came about, in the nature of his business, that the more suspects he uncovered, the more hysteria he created, the greater would be the demand for his services. The McCarran report, naturally, gave no intimation that Hartnett had a business interest in perpetuating the witch hunt.*

The release of the report brought an instant and more public embarrassment. Among the "cooperative" witnesses cited in the report was Welbourn E. Kelley, one of the founders of the Radio Writers Guild in 1939 and the guild's Eastern regional vice president in 1947. Kelley was credited in the report with having identified a whole string of his guild colleagues as dangerous "pro-Communists."

When Kelley read the transcript of his testimony, he dashed

---

* For a full account of one dramatic courtroom case resulting from Hartnett's activities see John Henry Faulk's *Fear on Trial*, Simon and Schuster, New York, 1964. Faulk had been riding the crest of prosperity with his own hour-long radio show on CBS' flagship station in New York when *AWARE* attacked him as a pro-Communist, largely through citing mentions of his name in the news columns of the *Daily Worker*. One such listing consisted of the mere statement that Faulk "was to appear at Club 65, 13 Astor Pl., N.Y.C.—a favorite site of pro-Communist affairs." Faulk lost his radio show, became virtually unemployable and was ruined professionally. He sued. With Louis Nizer as his attorney, after a long and harrowing courtroom ordeal, he won a $3.5 million verdict against Hartnett, *AWARE* and the estate of Laurence Johnson, a Syracuse supermarket operator who had furnished muscle for Hartnett's operations by banning from the stores in his chain the products of any company that persisted in hiring persons blacklisted by Hartnett.

off an angry letter to McCarran. In this, he charged, in effect, that the whole meaning of his testimony had been distorted. Kelley had not been, as the report indicated, a willing witness; he had appeared before the committee only with great reluctance and after he had been served with a subpoena that gave him no choice. And, even then, he had testified in executive session.

"At the outset of my testimony," Kelley wrote, "I stated that I could not say of my own knowledge that any member of the Radio Writers Guild was a Communist; that I bore no malice or ill will toward any member of the guild; and that I did not wish to say anything which might harm, either personally or professionally, any member of the guild. At this point the Subcommittee counsel, Mr. Richard Ahrens, called the discussion off the record, as will be noted on page 78 of the printed document, and none of my statements mentioned above are included in the printed record. During the discussion that ensued while off the record, Mr. Ahrens gave me to understand that anything I said was confidential . . . During this off-the-record discussion, Mr. Ahrens also requested that I not refer to a certain faction within the guild as 'Left Wing,' a term I had been using, but that for the purpose of clarification I refer to the two Guild factions as 'Pro-Communist' and 'Anti-Communist.' I demurred at this, stating that there were people in the 'Left Wing' faction for whom I had the greatest respect, and who in my opinion were neither Communists nor pro-Communists; however, I agreed to use the terms requested on the assumption that what I had to say was in confidence and would remain so."

It was significant that a spokesman for the committee, while not admitting quite so much, acknowledged enough to lead any reasonable man to conclude that Kelley's contention was true. The spokesman admitted there had been an "off-the-record discussion in which Kelley was instructed that the Subcommittee was not interested in receiving opinions of witnesses that any individual was a left-winger, or left-of-center, or radical, because we were seeking information about Communists, not about radicals. Communists and communism are terms that have definite meaning . . ."

And "pro-Communist," was a term that had no definite meaning, depending wholly on individual interpretation. Yet it was a far more potent term than "left-winger" and thus served the purpose of inflating Kelley's uncertain and unwilling testimony.

The incident told much about the ethics of the investigators; and it was only one among many. Out across the nation, the alarum was sounded unceasingly in the press. One of the loudest and most irresponsible criers was Harvey Matusow, that ubiquitous agent of the witch hunt who had been passed from hand to hand, from McCarthy to McCarran. The Great Falls, Montana, *Tribune* gave this account of a Matusow speech in the Great Falls High School:

"His appearance was sponsored by the American Legion— one of the few organizations that he did not accuse of being Communist-infested—the Junior Chamber of Commerce and the Speaker's Bureau.

"He cited cases to show how religion in the United States is being used by the Communists. He said the government is plagued by Reds and the press, radio, television, movies employ many Communists.

" 'The Sunday section of the *New York Times* alone has 126 dues-paying Communists,' he declared. 'On the editorial and research staffs of *Time* and *Life* magazines are 76 hard-core Reds. The New York bureau of the Associated Press has 25.'

"He said in order to get a job as a radio writer or director in New York City, 'you must be a member of the Communist Party.'

"In New York City, he declared, 500 high-school teachers are dues-paying Communists. The situation is similar in Los Angeles, San Francisco, Milwaukee—'and maybe in Great Falls,' he asserted.

"He claimed 'every major college in the country' has at least one Communist member.

"Some organizations he said were Red-infiltrated: Columbia Broadcasting System, State Department, Boy Scouts, YWCA, USO, United Nations, Voice of America and Farmers Union.

"He declared most churches are Communist-infiltrated and when a woman in the audience asked if there were any that aren't, he said, 'I don't believe the Catholics or Mormons are.' "

This was the kind of arrant nonsense that was being peddled across the nation. The specifics seemed so specific—and many, unsophisticated about the technique of the big lie, were taken in. Yet the time would come when an aggrieved government would confess that Harvey Matusow's word was unreliable, and would jail him for perjury after he had had the temerity to recant some of the tales he had told under oath as an informer.

WHEN DWIGHT EISENHOWER won the Republican nomination for President in 1952, the immediate question was: What would Ike do about Joe McCarthy?

General Eisenhower owed his career to General Marshall, whom McCarthy had most foully traduced. Marshall had been almost like a father to the rising young Eisenhower; he had jumped him over the heads of senior officers and given him the commands that had made him the nation's greatest war hero. It was inevitable, then, that the Democrats should try to put Ike instantly on the spot by demanding to know what he intended to do about the Wisconsin Senator who had besmirched his great benefactor—and who, many believed, remained his party's extra-special weapon in its drive to recapture the White House.

Senator Mundt, who was chairman of the Republican Speakers Campaign Bureau, announced almost at once that Eisenhower would "endorse and campaign actively" for McCarthy. James C. Hagerty, Ike's campaign secretary, commented cryptically: "The general speaks for himself." It remained to be seen just what the general would say.

In Denver on August 23, 1952, asked about McCarthy, the new candidate spoke in these terms: "I am not going to support anything that smacks to me of un-Americanism—that is un-American in character, and that includes any kind of thing that looks to me like unjust damaging of reputation, where the man has not the usual recourse to law. Therefore, it is impossible for me to give what you might call blanket support to anyone who holds views of this kind: who holds views that would violate my conception of what is decent, right, just and fair."

But the general was now a politician. He acknowledged that he felt he would have to be a loyal party man and back the candidates of his party down the line. Eisenhower had originally scheduled his visit to Wisconsin for September 5, a date just four days before the Republican primary. The advantage of the timing was that, with a primary contest on, he would not be expected to endorse anybody; he could show himself in Wisconsin, and get out without having to endure the political embrace of Joe McCarthy. But the Wisconsin Republican machine balked. Ike was told bluntly to stay out of the state until after the primary, when the anticipated renomination of McCarthy would put him on the spot—and the man of principle yielded.

The primary on September 9 was the anticipated triumph for McCarthy. He polled 181,238 votes, outscoring all other candidates in both the Republican and Democratic primaries by a margin of nearly 70,000 votes. Headlines billed the result as a "smashing" and "overwhelming" victory, which indeed it was, and from this moment on, there was virtually no hope of downgrading his role in the national campaign. By September 17, Senator Frank Carlson, of Kansas, a top Eisenhower adviser, was telling newsmen that Ike's managers were going to extend McCarthy an invitation to campaign widely outside his own state on the communist-in-government issue. IKE HQ TO PUT MCCARTHY RIGHT UP FRONT, read one headline.

The dilemma became obvious when Eisenhower paid his postponed visit to Wisconsin on October 3. He toyed with the idea of doing what he wanted to do—repudiate McCarthy in his home state. According to Emmet John Hughes, Eisenhower had bristled with indignation after having suffered the embrace of Senator Jenner in Indiana ("I felt dirty from the touch of the man"), and he had become excited at the daring idea of paying "a personal tribute to Marshall—right in McCarthy's back yard." Therefore, in the speech that Hughes wrote for Eisenhower to deliver in Milwaukee, there was included a clear exposition of the meaning of freedom, leading up to this declaration:

". . . The right to question a man's judgment carries with it no automatic right to question his honor.

"Let me be quite specific. I know that charges of disloyalty, in the past, have been leveled against General George C. Marshall. I have been privileged for thirty-five years to know General Marshall personally. I know him, as a man and as a soldier, to be dedicated with singular selflessness and the profoundest patriotism to the service of America. And this episode is a sobering lesson in the way freedom must not defend itself."

This passage was never uttered. Eisenhower reportedly let McCarthy know in advance the gist of what he planned to say, and the Senator paid the Presidential candidate a clandestine visit, after which everything changed. McCarthy denied blandly that he had had anything to do with Ike's changing his mind, but *The New York Times* and the New York *Post* both reported he had let Ike know that he felt any defense of General Marshall had better be made before some other audience. Whatever language was used, it was obvious that the heat was on. Eisenhower's own campaign strategists wanted to make the fullest use of the passion-arousing talents of the Wisconsin Senator and it was hardly possible to use the man and attack him. The result was that Eisenhower's incursion into Wisconsin brought the disheartening spectacle of McCarthy's shouting he wished he had a club so he could teach patriotism to "little Ad-lie"—and of Ike's being forced to swallow this affront to decency, and being forced to appear with Joe and to say he was for good Republicans everywhere.

Now the forces of the extreme right marshaled behind McCarthy, intent upon casting him in a pivotal role in the campaign. Financing was required, and it came from the two disparate wings of extremism—the oil millionaires of Texas and the old, Midwest "America First" crowd centered in Chicago. The reasons were twofold: McCarthy himself was running for reelection, against weak Democratic opposition, in Wisconsin; Senator Benton, his arch-foe, was up for reelection in Connecticut. Funds were needed to support McCarthy; to derail Benton. This was on the immediate, practical, political level. Looking to the future, there was a further aim—to put McCarthy in the spotlight before a nationwide radio-television audience in the role of the destroyer of Adlai Stevenson; to make him the hero of the campaign, the man who elected Eisenhower.

In the service of such good causes, the pouches of Texas oil tycoons automatically fell open. Clint Murchison, who had contributed $10,000 to defeat Tydings, thought it was worth $15,000 to get rid of Benton. H. R. Cullen, who was trying to buy elections wholesale with his thirty-one contributions (including one of $5,000 to help McCarthy in Wisconsin), couldn't devote so much to a single vendetta, but he nevertheless found a spare $1,000 to ship to William Purtell, Benton's Republican rival in Connecticut.

Financing the nationwide radio-television extravaganza called for more cash. The Texas money bags had already been squeezed, but still they gave some more. Murchison donated another $1,000; W. L. Goldstan, of Houston, put up $500; E. B. Germany, of Dallas, another oil man and head of Lone Star Steel, kicked in $250. The donations built up and were supplemented with funds contributed by Midwest right-wing industrialists to buy air time for McCarthy. General Robert E. Wood, the old America Firster, promoted a fifty-dollar-a-plate dinner in the grand ballroom of Chicago's swank Palmer House, and he rallied an audience of 1,150 cash customers eager to hear McCarthy serve up shredded Stevenson on the night of October 27, 1952.

The speech that they heard was McCarthy at his invidious worst. It was replete with the usual citations of the unimpeachable, tangible source ("I hold here in my hand an article . . ."). Repeatedly, he invited "my friends" in the press to come up and inspect his "documents" when he was finished. He was the most compassionate of men. There was the regret that anyone of sensitivity must feel just before he sinks the knife in under the fifth rib—"Now I perform this unpleasant task because the American people are entitled to have the coldly documented history" of Adlai Stevenson.

He began with a repetition of the charge he had made against Marshall, though this time, outside the sanctuary of the Senate floor, the villains remained nameless—"those who are in charge of our deliberate planned retreat from victory." America had become the victim of a great conspiracy, and Adlai Stevenson was deeply implicated as "part and parcel of the Acheson-Hiss-Lattimore group." Twice during the course of his speech, he used one of those coy innuendoes for which he was infamous, saying as if by mistake, "Alger—I mean Ad-lie."

The "proof" of all of this, or most of it, rested upon the old guilt-by-association criteria—upon the "shadiness" of the characters surrounding Adlai Stevenson. He named Wilson Wyatt, former head of Americans for Democratic Action; Arthur Schlesinger, Jr., the liberal historian and Stevenson speech writer; James Wechsler, editor of the New York *Post*, a member of the Young Communist League in his youth, but for years an anticommunist liberal, who was another Stevenson speech writer; Bernard DeVoto, the writer and historian who had presumed to criticize the excessive power of the FBI; and Archibald MacLeish, the poet and former Librarian of Congress, who had presumed to satirize the camaraderie of McCarran and McCarthy. All were tainted in one way or another in McCarthy's telling—and their taint rubbed off on Adlai Stevenson.

McCarthy's inability to deal with facts without distortion showed up most transparently in his attack on Schlesinger. He quoted from an article Schlesinger had written for *The New York Times* of December 11, 1949. McCarthy said:

"I quote, he said, 'I happen to believe—I happen to believe that the Communist Party should be granted freedom of political action and that Communists should be allowed to teach in universities.'"

The McCarthy advance text released to the press had included the remainder of the Schlesinger quote—an important qualifying clause dropped completely from the oral version given his radio and television audiences. This clause read: "*. . . so long as they do not disqualify themselves by intellectual distortions in the classroom.*" (italics added.)

Emerging from the sinuosities of the McCarthy text were certain cardinal charges. At one point, McCarthy cited General Walter Bedell Smith, Eisenhower's one-time chief of staff and later head of the Central Intelligence Agency, as his authority for the charge that Stevenson had "connived" to advance communist power in Italy after the fall of Mussolini. Bedell Smith "in his testimony and in his book," McCarthy said, "has told what that foreign policy established by Stevenson was—listen to this if you will—he says that foreign policy, here's his testimony, Page 35 and 37, he says that foreign policy was to 'connive,' to 'connive' to bring Communists into the Italian Government and to bring the Italian Communist leader, Togliatti, back from Moscow."

Reporters, checking the alleged source—Smith's book *My Three Years in Moscow*—found nothing of the sort. Smith never used the word "connived" and never accused Stevenson of "conniving." Smith had written that "we in the West" had done our best to set up a democratic government in Italy. He had written that "we in the West" had needed the help of communists in Italy in 1943 because they were "the rallying point for Italian opposition to the Germans," especially in industrialized Northern Italy. He had written that the communists formed "the hard core of the partisan movement" and that, to advance wartime collaboration against the Nazi enemy, we had indeed brought Togliatti back from Moscow. But there was no intimation that Stevenson, who had headed a Foreign Economic Planning mission to Italy and who was hardly in a position in any event to make foreign policy, had had anything to do with such decisions: they had been, obviously, measures considered necessary, or at least helpful, in winning the war.

In another instance, McCarthy challenged Stevenson to a test of truth. Stevenson had called false a previous McCarthy assertion about communist infiltration of the State Department and the alleged wholesale use of false passports, claiming that McCarthy was referring to an incident more than twenty years old. McCarthy insisted Stevenson had lied. He launched into his proof:

"I hold in my hand, and you people in the television audience can see it, Docket No. 51-101, a case of James P. McGranery, Attorney General vs. the Communist Party, dated July 28, 1952, that is after the Truman party nominated their candidate . . .

"I will read to you the passage to which the Democrat candidate took exception: 'Illegal passports have been used to expedite travel to foreign countries by members of the Communist Party. Plans have been discussed by leading members of the party and agents of the Soviet secret police, to obtain blank American passports from the U.S. State Department, from Communists employed in the State Department.' "

This demonstrated, McCarthy thundered, that he was dealing with a current and dangerously subversive situation.

It took boundless effrontery to stage this demonstration in order to prove a charge that had been already disproved by its source. As far back as September 4, Attorney General McGranery himself had denounced McCarthy's previous attempt to exploit the issue, and had explained that this paragraph referred to an incident that took place in 1928 in the Administration of Calvin Coolidge!

McGranery had pointed out that the quotation McCarthy used cited as its principal source the testimony of Paul Crouch, a government informer. McGranery had read Crouch's testimony, which was that he had been approached by the head of the Russian Secret Police in 1928 about the *possibility* of obtaining blank passports. He had been asked, Crouch said, if there were communists in the State Department, "and I replied there were no such members and he directed me if it were possible to try to get such members employed by the State Department . . ." McGranery had concluded: "Nowhere in the entire hearing is there any testimony that the plan was put into effect." Yet it was this aborted attempt that had taken place nearly a quarter of a century earlier that McCarthy now dragged out and refurbished.

Such was the nature of the widely ballyhooed speech that had been expected to "destroy" Adlai Stevenson. Reactions were extremely varied. There was deep silence in Eisenhower's headquarters. The Democrats were enraged. The extremists were delighted. Down in Texas, Austin F. Hancock, San Antonio insurance executive and McCarthy worshiper, claimed long afterward that McCarthy "helped elect Eisenhower more than any man alive. That speech he gave at Bob Wood's dinner in Chicago got more votes than anything else in the campaign." Among the Republican stalwarts only Everett McKinley Dirksen was open and vocal in his praise. "The left-wingers cannot answer the facts Senator McCarthy exposed," he said, "so they have only their usual recourse—to smear the man who made them public . . ."

Much of the leading press comment was unkind. *The New York Times,* which was supporting Eisenhower, denounced the speech. The Washington *Post* saw it as a shining example of an old, discredited political device known as the "roorback," used against James K. Polk a century earlier. The *Post* commented that it would take "at least a week" to check up on all of McCarthy's citations, adding that "in one instance . . . we have been unable to find the reference at all."

In Europe, the universal press reaction—left, right and center—was one of scorn and condemnation. In Paris, one paper characterized the speech as "madness"; in Rome, a progovernment journal said McCarthy's repetition of "stale, fantastic stories" had stripped the speech of any effectiveness. In London, every daily newspaper without exception either denounced the speech outright or discredited it by publishing sly barbs about McCarthy and his methods.

But perhaps the most perceptive comment was written by the veteran columnist Walter Lippmann, who was a supporter of Eisenhower.

"This has been an ugly campaign," he wrote, "not quite so foul it seems to me as the campaign of 1928, but in the perspective of the times we live in, much too ugly." He deplored equally a slurring attack made by Truman upon Eisenhower and the suggestion "that that most authentic, that original and classic American, who is Governor of Illinois, needs to be clubbed by Joe McCarthy in order to make a good American out of him.

"What, in heaven's name, has happened to us? What have we done that our public life should be so defiled, so debased? One of these two men will be the President of the United States. Is it not intolerable that on his way to that high office and to its agonizing burden he should have to suffer the indignity of having to defend, not his political beliefs, but the very honor of his soul?"

THE OUTCOME IN 1952 was never much in doubt. The Republicans had the best of two disparate worlds. They traveled the high road under the halo of Eisenhower and the low road under the aegis of hatchetman Joe McCarthy. No reputation, no intellectual brilliance could withstand the two-way attack from above and below. Adlai Stevenson went down to defeat, and the American people began their long love affair with the hero-general who had become a soothing father figure. But in the father's shadow lurked Joe McCarthy, made more powerful than ever by new triumphs—his own reelection in Wisconsin; the defeat of his archenemy, William Benton, in Connecticut.

The simplistic interpretation of these events—McCarthy wins, Benton loses (just as Tydings had lost)—magnified the menace and the stature of McCarthy; made him a colossus of politics. Yet a closer look at the election figures—the kind of analysis that is not apparent to those who hastily read the headlines—demonstrates clearly that McCarthy had been no tower of strength to his party. In fact, it is evident that he would probably have been defeated for reelection in Wisconsin if he had not ridden Eisenhower's coattails.

Eisenhower carried the state by 357,569 votes over Stevenson; McCarthy defeated Thomas Fairchild by only 139,042 votes, running nearly 220,000 votes behind Eisenhower. He also came out of the election as the weakest candidate on the statewide

Republican ticket. Governor Walter Kohler won by 407,327 votes; Wisconsin secretary of state Fred R. Zimmerman, an outspoken foe of McCarthy, piled up a huge 505,300-vote margin, Only Joseph McCarthy, the supposed bellwether of his party, lagged in the final tabulations.

The same lack of McCarthy drawing power at the polls was demonstrated in Connecticut, which he had invaded three times in pursuit of his personal vendetta with Benton. With his usual felicity of phrase, he had charged up and down the state, declaiming that "Joe Stalin could not have had a top agent in the United States who could have done a better job than Benton has done." Despite this, despite all the money that had been poured into the state in the purge-Benton effort, there was no indication that Benton had been damaged to any appreciable extent by being the lone target of McCarthy. An in-depth study of the election returns later showed that Benton's vote percentage paralleled that of his party in the state. Furthermore, the vote analysis showed that he had improved on his 1950 norm, when he had not been opposed by McCarthy, in 71 towns in the state; had stayed even in 51, and had fallen behind in only 47. His defeat, quite clearly, had been brought about by the fact that, with Eisenhower heading the ticket, 1952 was a heavily Republican election year.

In the immediate post-mortems, these more subtle facts, buried in the overall election figures, were generally ignored. Overlooked also was the failure of McCarthy, though he tried mightily, to save the scalps of some of his closest Republican supporters in the Senate. He made an especially strenuous effort to save Senator Harry Cain in Washington; but, though Eisenhower carried the state by 100,000 votes, Cain lost to Henry Jackson by 134,00. In Missouri and in Montana the results were similar; even in this year of Eisenhower triumph, McCarthy's active campaigning proved insufficient to rescue Senators James P. Kem and Zales N. Ecton. The results, if soberly interpreted, demonstrated that McCarthy, despite his rabble-rousing talents, posessed no magic formula for victory.

They also demonstrated something else—that the American people, *if informed,* still possessed the balance and judgment to turn thumbs down on the demagogue. *The Progressive,* the liberal news magazine founded by the elder Bob La Follette, later pointed out: ". . . The evidence is overwhelming that McCarthyism cannot long survive where the people are given the truth about the character of his 'crusade.'

"The most convincing proof was the 1952 election in Wisconsin. McCarthy carried every county in the state where all or a majority of the newspapers supported him, or refused to expose his contemptible conduct, or stood silent. *But he lost every county in the state in which either a daily paper or a labor weekly fought him with the facts.*

"Milwaukee County, by far the largest in the state, is a good example. Although it had tipped the election to McCarthy in 1946, Milwaukee turned against him by nearly 100,000 votes in 1952—mainly because the Milwaukee *Journal* had conducted a crusading campaign against the man and his methods. Dane County (Madison) rejected McCarthy 48,000 to 29,000, largely because of the superb exposure of McCarthyism by the Madison *Capital Times.*"

The importance of having an unfettered and probing press—something that, by and large, this nation did not have then and does not have now—was perhaps never more clearly demonstrated. When the press is dominated, except for rare and honorable exceptions, by publishers of a single political faith, when these publishers headline every charge, however irresponsible, that reinforces them in their beliefs and prejudices, the public's opportunity to learn the facts is diminished, and it is left to follow blindly the Pied Piper featured as a hero in the headlines. McCarthy was favored throughout the early years of his career by just such a partisan press on the one hand and, on the other, by more responsible papers hamstrung by their own fetish of Olympian objectivity, who headlined whatever McCarthy said simply because he said it. There was for a long time virtually no disposition to take a critical look at the man or to probe into his charges. The combination of deliberate build-up and mirror-like reflection made McCarthy a Gargantuan figure in the American imagination—and even the Eisenhower Administration itself would pay the forfeit.

18

The Witch Hunt Continues

THOSE WHO HAD BELIEVED, like Walter Lippmann, that an Eisenhower victory would put a restraining rein on McCarthy were quickly disillusioned. To deprive a demagogue of the issue that has made him famous is like trying to take raw meat from the jaws of a hungry tiger.

It made no difference that Eisenhower was in the White House. It made no difference that the Republicans, riding the Eisenhower coattails, now had control of both houses of Congress. Joe McCarthy had vaulted from back-bench obscurity into heady national prominence. Without the menace to feed on, he was a nonentity; and he would hound it to the end, even if it meant turning on his own Republican Administration. The portents of the future, the indications that McCarthy and the Eisenhower Administration were on a collision course, were there to be read almost as soon as the votes had been counted.

"Any conclusion that I shall not continue to interest myself deeply in the Communist menace is completely unwarranted," McCarthy declared in Phoenix, Arizona, on November 8, 1952. The Scripps-Howard press had speculated that he might turn from communism to the issues of graft and corruption, and McCarthy hastened to set the record straight.

Before the month was out, he was laying plans for a greatly expanded witch hunt. One result of the November victory that had given Republicans control of the Senate was that McCarthy had been catapulted into the chairmanship of one of the true power complexes of the Senate—the Committee on Government Operations. This committee has the broadest kind of investigative powers. It is authorized to probe almost at will, not only the entire federal structure, but any business, industry, school or charitable organization having contracts with the government or receiving tax relief or subsidies from it. The committee maintained its own investigating subcommittee, with a permanent staff of investigators, and McCarthy made no secret of his intention to chair both the parent committee and the investigating subcommittee. This was power—the kind of concentrated, far-reaching, official power that McCarthy had never previously wielded.

Stewart Alsop sized up the potentialities and shuddered in print in a column in the New York *Herald-Tribune* in late November. Alsop pointed out that McCarthy, almost from the moment he had dropped his bombshell in Wheeling, had raved and ranted about "the files." Alsop explained that anyone who took a government job, especially in a sensitive agency, was checked out by the security agents of the employing agency and the FBI. The agents reported everything they were told, true or false, just as they were given it, and the result was that the raw files were a potpourri of "personal enmity, or sheer malice or simple stupidity. In the raw files of one able government employee, for example, a source is quoted as describing him as a dangerous radical. Subsequent investigation revealed that this charge was based on the fact that the employee, a Vermonter, had actively supported Vermont's liberal Republican Senator, George Aiken."

This was the kind of material for which McCarthy hungered, but in the past he had been frustrated in his efforts to get it. Now, as chairman of a powerful Senate committee, he would be in a position to demand, and Alsop was horrified at the prospect. He wrote: "One can almost hear McCarthy—'I have in my hand an official report from the Federal Bureau of Investigation,' and so on. He would use the raw files to 'prove' what he has conspicuously failed to prove heretofore—that the American government is crawling with spies."

Alsop's crystal ball was working well. Even before the new Congress met, even before the new Administration took office, McCarthy was off baying down the trail in tones that indicated the menace was more menacing than ever. Honored at a dinner arranged by Alfred Kohlberg in New York on December 10, 1952, McCarthy proclaimed that there would be no slackening in his drive against communism—a fight that "can't abate until we've won this war or our civilization has been destroyed."

"Communist thinkers," he said, labeling the new enemy, would "redouble" their efforts to infiltrate the incoming Eisenhower Administration. "We have only scratched the surface of this battle," McCarthy announced. "We've won the first skirmish in this tremendously important battle against communism, and we'll need your support badly in the next three to five years."

How was a 100-percent American to identify the enemy? "You can't tell a Communist by looking at him," McCarthy told his audience. This was most disturbing; why, *anyone* . . . the thought was best left unfinished. McCarthy furnished only one clue. The battle, he said, was not so much against "the man who looks like a Communist, with long hair, but the Communist thinkers, the suave, intellectual individual found at Washington cocktail parties." It was frustrating to have the easy "long hair" identification taken from one, but it was at least a little comforting to learn about the suave intellectual cocktail-drinkers. Perhaps if one shunned cocktail parties—especially Washington cocktail parties—one could avoid contamination.

Two days later, taking the sun in Puerto Rico in the company of Robert Thompson, of Dallas, McCarthy further discussed the imminent Eisenhower years.

"In any government, especially one that has been in power a long time," he said, "you are bound to get a number of traitors, saboteurs and crooks. And of course the Communists will keep trying to infiltrate. We will have to start investigating the Republican Administration in six months or a year . . ."

WHEN CONGRESS CONVENED on January 2, 1953, the shape of things to come became almost instantly apparent. McCarthy's powerful Government Operations Committee was stacked with kindred spirits. Second in command was the ever-faithful Karl Mundt, and joined with McCarthy and Mundt were these other Republican camp followers: Senators Henry Dworshak (Idaho), Dirksen, Butler and Charles E. Potter, of Michigan. Only Mrs. Smith represented a potentially dissident voice. The Democrats had three minority members on the committee, and their new Senate leader, Lyndon B. Johnson, had appointed to serve with the veteran, John L. McClellan, of Arkansas, two newly elected Senators who would not have to face the electorate for another six years and so could possibly afford to be obstreperous: Stuart Symington, of Missouri; and Henry M. Jackson, of Washington.

It was evident from the beginning that there was going to be intense competition for headlines. McCarthy's success had inspired a whole crew of Republican imitators, anxious to gain similar notoriety. The Senate Internal Security Committee was still in business, chaired now by Senator Jenner, the man whose touch had made Eisenhower shudder, and Pat McCarran was still on the premises as the ranking "Democrat." The House Un-American Activities Committee took on a new lease on life under the chairmanship of Rep. Harold H. Velde, a former FBI agent. Normally these two committees, with their awesome investigative powers, would have been considered more than adequate to deal with security matters, and McCarthy's Government Operations Committee might have been expected to devote itself to the problems of graft and corruption in government. But McCarthy had no intention of being shoved out of the headlines by competitors poaching upon his chosen preserve.

Joining him and his ideologically heavily weighted committee was a whiz-kid attorney whose attitudes coincided perfectly with those of the maestro. He was Roy M. Cohn, a precocious prosecutor who, despite his youth, was selected by McCarthy to become the committee's chief counsel.

Cohn was the son of Justice Albert Cohn, of the Appellate Division of the New York Supreme Court. He had received his law degree from Columbia University Law School at the age of nineteen, and he had had to wait two years before he became old enough to take his bar examination. Once admitted to the bar, he leap-frogged almost instantly into a position of public prominence as the confidential assistant to Myles J. Lane, then U.S. Attorney for the Southern District of New York.

Possessed of a furious, driving energy and the unbounded conviction that any case claiming his talents must represent a milestone in the law, the mercurial Roy Cohn became a familiar figure to reporters around the Federal Court House in Foley Square. His person almost dripped with gadgets—it would hardly have caused surprise to find he had a hidden recording device tucked under his big toe. His first assignments plunged him into investigations of narcotics traffickers and stamp and currency counterfeiters—blackguards whom Cohn pursued with zeal, dramatizing each case as the most important ever.

He became so fascinated by the wiliness of the underworld characters to whom his investigations had introduced him that, on one occasion, he entertained visitors by showing them how difficult it was to tell the difference between forged and legitimate postage stamps. The demonstration had a convincing sequel, one that caused consternation around the Federal Court House. The young prosecutor himself became so confused that he dispatched a batch of his personal mail adorned with the counterfeiters' forgeries.

Under Irving H. Saypol, Lane's successor as U.S. Attorney, Cohn's career took off in a new direction. He switched to the prosecution of spies and subversives. He was Saypol's faithful shadow throughout the controversial prosecution of Julius and Ethel Rosenberg, who were ultimately executed as the atom bomb spies. He became an all-around troubleshooter for Saypol. In this capacity he worked on the William Remington perjury case, and assisted in obtaining a perjury indictment against Owen Lattimore.

Not yet quite twenty-six when McCarthy named him chief

counsel, Roy Cohn was like a whirling dervish, avid to strike out in all directions at enemies of the republic, real or fancied. It soon became obvious that, brilliant as he was, he lacked those very qualities that his unstable boss most needed in an assistant —balance, a sense of restraint and scrupulousness in the preparation of his cases. The union of McCarthy and Cohn was the partnership of kindred souls, each fueling the excesses in the other.

THE NATURE OF THE FIRST BLOW foretold the havoc to come. It was leveled at the Voice of America, the radio propaganda arm of the State Department's International Information Administration. The Voice broadcast the American message in some forty languages to a potential audience of 300 million persons in eighty-seven countries. It put more program hours on the air than NBC and CBS combined. It was an invaluable instrument in the Cold War battle for men's minds. And it was at this instrument that McCarthy and Cohn chose to strike.

Their investigation was preceded by the typical fanfare, a succession of leaked, sensational stories that prepared the public to accept the verdict before any evidence had been placed on the record. The Washington *Times-Herald* broke out on February 13, 1953, with this headline PROBERS TOLD OF ANTI-U.S. PLOT IN VOICE—INFILTRATION CALLED APPALLING. The story began:

"A Senate investigation of Communist influence in the Voice of America headquarters here has uncovered amazing evidence of a conspiracy to subvert American policy in this nation's radio propaganda broadcasts abroad.

"Scores of witnesses questioned by day and by night in the past week have involved high officials in a detailed account supported by documentary proof which indicated deliberate sabotage of American objectives in foreign propaganda."

The New York Times on the same day headlined the promised sensation this way: MC CARTHY SIFTING VOICE OF AMERICA—HEARINGS ON MISMANAGEMENT AND SUBVERSION CHARGES TO BE HELD NEXT WEEK.

In Cleveland, on February 14, the *Plain Dealer* story explained: ". . . McCarthy said most of today's evidence dealt with 'a vast amount of waste running into tens of millions' but he declined to elaborate. The rest of the evidence dealt with subversion."

When McCarthy opened his hearings on February 16, 1953, it at once became apparent that, at the heart of his widely ballyhooed charges of subversion, lay the story of Baker East and Baker West—the two most powerful short-wave radio transmitters in the world. The equipment had been built for the Voice of America in the hope of breaking through Russian jamming zones and carrying the American message behind the Iron Curtain. McCarthy sought to show that the sites chosen for the location of the stations were not the best, but the worst; that they had been deliberately selected by disloyal officials in the Voice to sabotage the whole program.

The cardinal factor, obviously, was the location of the two powerful transmitters. Some sites are much more subject to magnetic storms than others, and highly technical calculations were involved in selecting the most propitious areas for breaking through the heavy Russian jamming. The State Department, recognizing this, had sought the aid and advice of a whole complex of major research organizations—the Massachusetts Institute of Technology's Research Laboratory of Electronics, the Radio Corporation of America's Radio Propagation Laboratory, the Bureau of Standards and the U.S. Army Signal Corps. After all the technical information had been assembled and evaluated, MIT recommended two sites: one in the Cape Hatteras area of North Carolina for Baker East and one near Seattle for Baker West.

Personalities now created dissension. Lewis McKesson, who had been an engineer for the Voice, had favored different sites. He had wanted Baker East located in Florida; Baker West, in Southern California. McKesson contended that the Hatteras-Seattle sites were more susceptible to interference by the auroral absorption belt (magnetic storms far above the earth extending for about a thousand-mile belt around the north geomagnetic pole), and he had pressed his view with such persistence that the Voice had asked the MIT research laboratory to reevaluate its findings. This had been done. On December 26, 1951, MIT emphatically confirmed the previous selection of the Hatteras and Seattle sites. Dr. Jerome B. Wiesner, director of the

MIT laboratory, wrote the State Department that McKesson's "method of analysis is so oversimplified as to lead to erroneous conclusions."

How could even Joe McCarthy build a sinister plot out of this? By ignoring the mass of countervailing evidence and relying on McKesson as the witness who had the infallible word. Using this one-sided technique, McCarthy succeeded in raising a headline storm about colossal waste and sabotage in the Voice program.

The method exposed itself in the series of leading questions that McCarthy posed to his star lead-off witness, Lewis McKesson. McCarthy loaded his interrogation with all the desired implications in this fashion:

"As well as the question of waste, what other significance do you find in this location of Baker East and Baker West? . . . Assume I do not want that [voice] to reach Communist territory. Would not the best way to sabotage that voice be to place your transmitters within that magnetic storm area? . . . Now has it ever been suggested by those who have worked with you in the Voice that this mislocation of stations, the waste in the construction program, has not been entirely as the result of incompetence, but that some of it may have been purposely planned that way?"

With a cooperative witness indicating that McCarthy was right all the way, the headlines inevitably reflected a bias in favor of the sabotage theory.

McCarthy was interested only in testimony that would support his lurid assertions; he excluded all else. Expert engineers who would have testified were never called. One, Andrew Ring, a private radio engineering consultant, attended the hearing of February 16, 1953, expecting to testify. Dr. Wilson Compton, administrator of the Voice, referring to Ring, told McCarthy: "He is right here." McCarthy repeated, "He is right here"; and then, just as he had done in his housing hearings when he sidetracked witnesses he did not want to hear, he went right on asking a string of questions, prolonging the session and never calling Ring. Later Roy Cohn contended that Ring was not available when he was wanted, and McCarthy berated the State Department for giving him the names of potential witnesses who were "out in the Pacific and not available." According to the department, Ring was in the country all the time, even though he did not attend every hearing, and it would not have been too difficult to get him for a witness if McCarthy would just have had him.

Even more remarkable was the complete distortion of the role of Dr. Wiesner. As the controversy raged on through those early weeks of 1953, the Voice asked Dr. Wiesner for yet another reappraisal. Was it possible that the original decision had been wrong? Was there any new scientific data that might alter the equation? In a reply on February 21, 1953, Dr. Wiesner confirmed the original choice for the sites of Baker East and Baker West. He conceded that there might be times when transmissions from Seattle would be poorer than those from Southern California, but on the whole "under favorable conditions transmissions from Seattle would provide stronger signals than more southerly points." As for Baker East, several points on the East coast were almost equally advantageous, but MIT, relying on RCA data "which we still believe to be reasonable," thought the Cape Hatteras site was "slightly better than most other locations."

If Dr. Wiesner had been called to testify, the McCarthy case might have been exposed as a fraud. There was even a momentary danger that this might happen. Senator Mundt, usually the most faithful of followers, became disturbed about the one-sided nature of the testimony, and he and some other Senators pressed Roy Cohn to find out the views of reputable scientists. The result was that Cohn telephoned Dr. Wiesner at MIT. On March 3, 1953, he gave the committee the results of this conversation in these words:

"The staff contacted Dr. Wiesner at MIT. We talked to him, three of us on the line for over an hour. Dr. Wiesner stated that it was his conclusion that Baker West, from the standpoint of efficiency and reliability, should be moved south and away from Seattle and that he would just as soon not come down and testify as that would be his opinion."

Months later, Dr. Wiesner was still enraged at what he called this complete misrepresentation of his views. Frederick Woltman, the New York *World-Telegram and Sun* journalist who had won a Pulitzer Prize for his communist exposés, had become convinced that McCarthy was doing more harm than good, and he questioned Dr. Wiesner about the Cohn statement.

"I told Cohn my technical judgment was still to put Baker

West in Seattle. We had a long, heated discussion in which he tried hard to get me to agree that the Seattle site was inferior. I refused. He misrepresented my position.

"Also, at the end of our final discussion, Cohn said: 'I don't intend to subpoena you but you are free to come down and make any statement you want to.' He did not ask me to come. Since I had no idea he was going to misrepresent me, I thought I had no need of coming.

"I told Cohn I saw no evidence of sabotage. I felt at the time and still do that the sabotage charge was completely unfounded and ridiculous."

With Dr. Wiesner unheard in the wings and misrepresented by proxy, the probe into sabotage wound up, paradoxically, by sabotaging a vital American propaganda program. McCarthy's committee produced a face-saving report that was a masterpiece of unverified assertion and innuendo. The original, specific charge that there had been "deliberate sabotage" of the Baker East-Baker West program vanished; but virtually the same effect, a miasma of suspicion and subversion, was retained by the claim that the probe had "uncovered waste and mismanagement of such a magnitude to *suggest* deliberate sabotage as *a possible alternative* to hopeless incompetence." (Italics added.)

Not content with this, McCarthy obscured the facts with a blizzard of other charges. MIT had been paid $600,000 for its study, he shouted at one point; actually, it had received only $6,000. McCarthy's probe had "saved" the government more than $18 million, he declared; actually, the two Baker transmitters had cost $8,434,000—and, as a result of McCarthy's strident obstructionism, a panicked State Department scrapped the whole project. The result was that the world's two most powerful radio transmitters were declared surplus property and left to gather dust and rust in government warehouses.

Journalist Frederick Woltman, certainly no friend of communism, judged the probe as ". . . one of the most disgraceful, scatter-brained, inept, misleading and unfair investigations in Congressional annals." He said it had given "a totally distorted picture" of an agency that had become "a potent force in the psychological war against communism," and the result had been the disruption and demoralization of the Voice and damage to America's prestige abroad. "It was a mighty victory for the Kremlin."

.   .   .

IT WAS ALSO A PERFORMANCE that had a tragic sequel.

One of the contentions of supporters of McCarthy was that he really did no harm to innocent persons. It was a theme upon which McCarthy himself often expounded with self-righteousness. In an interview for the New York *World-Telegram and Sun* in early June, 1953, he protested vigorously: "I have hurt no innocent person, but I have consistently fought to drive Communists and pro-Communists out of public life." And he asked challengingly: "What innocent person have I injured? I've asked that question lots of times—on forums and in speeches—and nobody ever tells me. I've never yet had anyone give me the name of a single innocent person who has been hurt by my methods . . ." Needless to say, the innocents whom he had injured ranged from the high and distinguished, like Ambassador Jessup and General Marshall, to literally thousands of inconspicuous, average American citizens.

One of those, who could no longer answer McCarthy's challenge, was Raymond Kaplan, the Voice engineer who had done much of the technical spadework on the Baker projects. At the height of the public furor created by McCarthy, with dark charges of "sabotage" flying wildly in the headlines, Raymond Kaplan threw himself under a truck in Boston. McCarthy promptly disclaimed any responsibility for the suicide, announcing that he had no evidence of "any wrongdoing of any kind" against Kaplan.

But in suicide notes to his wife and son, Kaplan fixed the responsibility for the pressures that had driven him to take his life. He wrote that he had been made "the patsy." And added: "You see, once the dogs are set upon you, everything you have done from the beginning of time is suspect."

IT HAD BEEN GENERALLY ASSUMED that a Republican Administration, headed by a much-revered military hero, would be immune to intimidation by the bullyboy from Wisconsin, but it quickly became apparent that it was not. It lay before McCarthy's trampling feet as supine as the Democrats. One reason may be that the Republicans had swallowed their own poison; they came to office fearful that they might be surrounded on every side by spies—that the betrayals they believed had taken place in the Truman Administration might also happen in theirs.

Emmet John Hughes in his *Ordeal of Power* has described how completely the Republicans had become the prisoners of their own myths. They just *knew* they would find in some subterranean vault of the State Department secret treaties telling of our dealings with the Russian infidel; and so they spent endless weeks hunting for these traitorous agreements, finally becoming convinced they did not exist and never had. Then, unwilling to confess so much, they spent additional agonizing hours drafting language by which they could get Congress to repudiate deeds that had never been done and pacts that had never been drafted.

A craven Democratic Party, doubting its own soul, connived with the Administration in this slitting of its own throat. Hughes reflects in wonderment on the willingness of the Democrats under the aegis of Lyndon Johnson to go along with the Eisenhower Administration by pledging to repudiate secret treaties, if found. The fact that no such treaties existed was thus obscured in the public mind. The Democrats themselves were admitting the possibility.

With even the Democrats conceding so much, the incoming Republican Administration was hagridden by the specter that thousands of employees in the government departments might be subversive. John Foster Dulles, the new Secretary of State, was especially prey to such doubts and pressures. As soon as he took office, he wrote a letter to all State Department and Foreign Service officers demanding what he called "positive loyalty." To many, this communication was an insult.

Dulles followed up this initial blunder by a whole series of abject obeisances to the witch hunt. For instance, six days after he took office, he implied in a television speech that State Department officers had given away to the Russians many of our secrets, including the secret of the atom bomb. And he capped all previous performances by issuing an ill-considered and ludicrously worded directive on February 19, 1953, that read:

"No material by any Communists, fellow travelers, et cetera, will be used under any circumstances by any IIA [International Information Administration] media."

The imprecision of the anti-communist vocabulary had now

been carried to its logical conclusion. One must beware of those "et ceteras."

The effect of this asinine rule, promulgated only after serious and detailed consideration on the highest levels of the department, was to forbid American information officers even from quoting Stalin to show that Stalin had lied. Alfred H. Morton, a radio executive who had become chief of the Voice of America, fired back an angry protest in which he said that he would continue to quote communist sources when by doing so he could show their duplicity. The department's policy desk promptly rapped his knuckles with an admonitory ruler: the new order stood; the Voice must not sully itself by the use of *"any* words for *any* purpose by a Communist or an 'et cetera.' "

Evidence that the department was indeed honeycombed with spies—right-wing spies, not left-wing spies—came with the receipt of Morton's protest. McCarthy's agents revealed that they were fully aware of its contents as soon as the department was, proof positive that his underground was keeping him informed of the minutest developments within the department. The reaction to this disclosure was panic. Under Secretary Walter Bedell Smith *publicly suspended* Morton from his post. The following day, when saner second thoughts prevailed, Morton was reinstated, but he had already been discredited.

Another stunning example of the incredible political naiveté of the Eisenhower Administration was the appointment of R. W. Scott McLeod as the new security chief of the State Department.

McLeod was well known as a loudly aggressive superpatriot. A former FBI agent, he had attached himself to New Hampshire's Senator Styles Bridges, and Bridges had brought him to Washington as his administrative assistant. Bridges, of course, was one of McCarthy's most ardent supporters and closest collaborators in the all-out assault on the State Department. It followed that McLeod's appointment was almost universally interpreted as conclusive proof of McCarthy's power: He had installed his own man in the most sensitive post in the State Department and Dulles had yielded to him.

But as Emmet John Hughes tells the story the appointment came about in a most haphazard way. Hughes writes:

". . . The Under Secretary of State for Administration, Donald B. Lowrie, had come to Washington, from the presidency of

Quaker Oats, with somewhat less preparation for the political scene than Charles E. Wilson. A serious and conscientious citizen, Lowrie had known virtually not a single citizen in Washington prior to his appointment. Idly conversing with a neighbor in Chicago, who happened to be an ex-FBI agent, he had picked up the name of Scott McLeod. The name came to mind again, as he settled into his Washington office. He called McLeod. They lunched. He liked him. He gave him a new job. And he conscientiously spent a large part of the next months mourning his own folly."

This chance selection of McLeod set the stage for the world-shaking controversy over President Eisenhower's appointment of Charles E. (Chip) Bohlen as Ambassador to Russia. Bohlen was widely respected, both within and without the department, as one of the most capable Foreign Service officers. He and George F. Kennan, whom he was to succeed as Ambassador, were unquestionably the two diplomats most knowledgeable about the Soviet Union. Yet, almost the instant Bohlen was named, McCarthy and his allies in the Senate kicked up a terrific furor. McCarthy implied that McLeod had refused to clear Bohlen after examining his FBI dossier; Secretary Dulles said there were no differences between McLeod and himself on the matter; and McCarthy came back with the charge that the Secretary simply was not telling the truth.

Senator Taft and Senator John J. Sparkman (D., Ala.) constituted themselves a jury of two to examine Bohlen's file. They found in it nothing discreditable or treasonous, and Taft put his prestige on the line in a rousing Senate speech, completely vindicating Bohlen. This seemed, for the moment, like a severe setback for McCarthy.

But now Charles Bohlen, because of his sense of honor, unintentionally gave McCarthy a leg up. Bohlen had served as Roosevelt's interpreter at Yalta, the summit meeting that Republicans had charged represented the acme of sellout. In testimony before the Senate Foreign Relations Committee, Bohlen stoutly defended the Yalta agreements as in the best interests of the United States at the time they were made, though unforeseeable subsequent events had cast a different light on them. In effect, Bohlen told the Senate committee that he did not want to go to Russia as Ambassador if the price he had to pay for his confirmation was the repudiation of Roosevelt.

Here was ammunition for the know-nothing brigades. McCarthy and his far-right legions raised an emotional outcry about Yalta and betrayal. They failed. Most Senate Republicans could not bring themselves to repudiate their own President; most Democrats refused to vote so openly to condemn themselves. The result was that Bohlen was confirmed by a 74–13 vote. On the surface, it was a victory for the Eisenhower Administration over Joe McCarthy; but on another level, even in losing, McCarthy came out a winner in the public eye.

William S. White, in *The New York Times,* wrote in summing up that "there were many who thought that Senator McCarthy had emerged, in a way, as the hero of the piece, if only because the public seemed to have gotten the idea that he alone was making the fight against Bohlen and Yalta. A Democratic Senator who in this controversy was relatively detached told this correspondent that of forty wires and other urgent communications he had received on the eve of the Bohlen vote every one mentioned McCarthy and none mentioned any other participant in the drama. And most of the forty were against Bohlen and Yalta."

There were other episodes that strengthened the growing popular impression of McCarthy as a man who towered over the State Department and the White House. Three times in one week in February, 1953, McCarthy forced the State Department to reverse itself on stated policies involving internal operating procedures. In one instance, it was because Dulles tried to take a stand in the case of the much-maligned John Carter Vincent. Hounded by the McCarran Committee after McCarthy's initial bellowings, Vincent had again been called before the Loyalty Board, which had decided that perhaps there was "a reasonable doubt" about Vincent's loyalty. Dulles reviewed the record—and couldn't find the "reasonable doubt." He reinstated Vincent. McCarthy scowled and growled that he didn't like it one little bit— and the Secretary of State decreed hastily that Vincent had better retire because he did not meet the "standards" of the department.

So it went. The effect on the Foreign Service was devastating.

C. L. Sulzberger, chief of *The New York Times'* foreign bureaus, writing from Paris, quoted one West German official as observing: "The technique of character assassination reminds me of the way the Nazis took over our own foreign office twenty years ago." George Kennan, the architect of the policy of containment, had not even been consulted by Secretary Dulles after the death of Stalin, and was being retired from the department. And, Sulzberger added, "Charles Thayer, one of Washington's few experts on Soviet affairs, has resigned—in this case because of the Wisconsin Senator."

The demoralization of the Foreign Service was illustrated in Sulzberger's observation that "many cautious individuals are now restricting their operational efficiency to avoid doing the slightest thing that might be viewed unfavorably in later years." He cited the specific example of the meetings of the Economic Commission for Europe in Geneva. Here our diplomats had rubbed shoulders with those from communist-bloc countries; they had been able to exchange ideas, pick up bits of useful information vital to any understanding of the realities of life within the Soviet orbit. But now this avenue of information had been closed off. "At the last ECE meeting," Sulzberger wrote, "no American dared to be seen reaching for a sandwich by the side of a known Communist."

THE VOICE OF AMERICA INVESTIGATION had been raging on many fronts for months. It was highlighted by the performance of the Abbott and Costello of McCarthy's crusade: Roy M. Cohn and G. David Schine. Cohn, short, dark, with slightly protruding agate eyes and an aggressive, cocksure demeanor; Schine, tall, wavy-haired, with regular good-looking features and a languid manner, the perfect playboy. They were of the same age, a bumptious twenty-six, and Schine had come into the McCarthy camp as chief consultant on the menace by a circuitous route that led through the ubiquitous George Sokolsky.

Schine was the son of Morris Schine, of Gloversville, N.Y., who owned a chain of movie houses, radio stations and hotels. The hotel chain, which boasted it was the "Finest Under the Sun," included the Roney Plaza and Boca Raton at Miami Beach and the Ambassador in Los Angeles. Young Schine, who had a supervisory role in his father's hostelries, owned a Cadillac equipped with telephone service; had been a press agent for Vaughn Monroe's orchestra; and had dated Hollywood starlets, the best known being Piper Laurie. On the intellectual plane, he had authored a six-page pamphlet, "Definition of Communism," which he had thoughtfully placed at the bedsides of all the customers in the "Finest Under the Sun" hotels.

Richard Rovere later described this master work in these terms: "It puts the Russian Revolution, the founding of the Communist Party, and the start of the First Five Year Plan in years when these things did not happen. It gives Lenin the wrong first name. It confuses Stalin with Trotsky. It confuses Marx with Lenin. It confuses Alexander Kerensky with Prince Lvov . . ."

This "anthology of wrong dates and mistaken identities," so the story goes, came to the attention of Rabbi Benjamin Schultz, who headed an organization called the American Jewish League Against Communism. The rabbi, while staying at a Schine hotel in Florida, read "Definition of Communism" and "was so dazzled by its depth of understanding" that he introduced the young author to Hearst columnist George Sokolsky. Sokolsky passed Schine along to Roy Cohn, and Cohn performed the introduction to McCarthy. There were some uncharitable souls who later speculated that one of David Schine's major recommendations for employment as a witch hunter was not his knowledge of the menace but the fact that he was young, wealthy, and powerful in the management of fancy hotels located in warm, attractive places.

Richard Rovere found the partnership of Cohn and Schine preposterous. The mind, he wrote, does not boggle at the idea of Torquemada, a fanatic monk, presiding over "the roasting of two thousand of his fellow men," but it finds it difficult to accept "the thought that a Grand Inquisitor might either be or pretend to be Punchinello, say, or a common tumbler. Ridiculous!—the clown's disguise would never occur to a heresy hunter, for a heresy hunter must be a man full of earthly vanity or of spiritual pride. A Torquemada in motley—impossible! A fool turned inquisitor—absurd! Heresy hunting would never occur to a clown."

But there on the stage of the Nightmare Decade was the vaudeville team of Cohn and Schine. They were indeed ridiculous

—and yet they had the power to humiliate honest men, to destroy careers.

The inquisition into the Voice produced some of the most callous displays of the McCarthy era. One shameful performance illustrates the role of Roy Cohn. It was March 3, 1953, and McCarthy was questioning Reed Harris, with Cohn sitting at his elbow and egging him on.

Harris was a State Department official who had headed the International Information Administration in the brief interregnum during the changeover of Administrations. He had spent nineteen years in government service, and was regarded as a faithful and highly able public servant. He was to be vilified by a hectoring McCarthy cross-examination and a month later he resigned.

Twenty years earlier, fresh out of college, Harris had written a book called *King Football,* which had decried the overemphasis on athletics and had advanced some harsh criticisms of higher education in general. McCarthy fastened upon a few passages of this long-forgotten book in a merciless grilling of Harris. He also drew the darkest inferences from the fact that in 1932 the American Civil Liberties Union had offered to defend Harris when he was suspended from classes at Columbia because the administration felt some of his editorials in the *Spectator,* the campus daily, were in poor taste. The question-and-answer sequence went like this:

Harris: I had many offers of attorneys and one of those was from the American Civil Liberties Union, yes.

McCarthy: The question is: Did the Civil Liberties Union supply you with an attorney?

Harris: They did supply me with an attorney.

McCarthy: The answer is "Yes?"

Harris: The answer is "Yes."

McCarthy: You know that the American Civil Liberties Union has been listed as a front of the Communist Party.

Harris: Mr. Chairman, this was 1932.

McCarthy: I know this was 1932. Do you know that they since have been listed as a front doing the work of the Communist Party?

Harris: I do not know that they have been listed so. I have heard that mentioned, or read that mentioned.

What was incredible about this performance was that the

American Civil Liberties Union had *never* been listed as a Communist front by the FBI, the Attorney General's office, or any committee of Congress. But even worse was involved. Richard Rovere explained:

"Those of us who watched this particular exchange observed that McCarthy, just before asking Harris if he knew about the political coloration of the Civil Liberties Union, paused and looked hesitantly, inquiringly at his chief counsel, clearly asking Cohn's approval of what he was about to do. Cohn responded with a lack of response, a silence that was McCarthy's cue to press forward, to lay on, and with that silence new ground in political morality was broken. For the fact of the matter was that less than three weeks earlier—on Abraham Lincoln's birthday, to be precise—Roy Cohn, chief counsel, had attended and addressed and by his remarkable little presence endorsed an American Civil Liberties Union conference at the Henry Hudson Hotel in New York City."

Cohn and Schine, having played the jackanapes at home, now took their road show on a whirlwind tour of Europe. It was a jaunt that fascinated an incredulous world.

The pair popped up in Paris on Easter Sunday, April 4. The trip seems to have been set up on the spur of the moment; it cost the American taxpayers some $8,500; and its stated purpose varied from press conference to press conference. First, in Paris, Cohn and Schine said they were examining overseas offices for inefficiency, but in Bonn they said they were looking for subversives. Asked in Munich to explain this discrepancy, Cohn proved equal to the task by having it both ways. Efficiency, he said, "included complete political reliability," and so when they spoke of inefficiency, this included subversives. When McCarthy, back home, said that the purpose of their trip was to discover how much money was being spent "in putting across the Truman Administration" in Europe, Cohn acknowledged that he'd never heard about this purpose, but it was all right with him. "Anything the chairman of our committee says, if he said it, goes with us," he declared loyally.

As Cohn and Schine flitted about Europe, visiting twelve cities in six countries in just seventeen days, reporters and photographers thronged about them, watching their every movement, recording their every uttered word. Even their exchanges with hotel clerks were noted for posterity. McCarthy, in his attacks on the State Department, had stooped to implying it was riddled with homosexuals, and when registering at hotels, Cohn and Schine seemed to derive huge delight from asking for adjoining—but separate—rooms. With an archness that they evidently considered the height of wit, they would explain the "separate room" request by telling uncomprehending hotel clerks, "You see, we don't work for the State Department."

Probably the most publicized incident of the tour came when Cohn and Schine had an altercation, as a result of which, according to reputable journalists, Schine chased Cohn around a hotel lobby, flailing him over the head with a rolled-up magazine. Both participants insisted vigorously that the incident had never happened, but it became firmly fixed in legend, perhaps because it seemed so perfectly to epitomize the whole excursion.

As investigators, Cohn and Schine were often ludicrous. They sought the opinions of hotel clerks and taxicab drivers. They huddled furtively with an occasional foreign informer. They had a rendezvous with Hede Massing, a devotee of the witch hunt and the former wife of Communist leader Gerhart Eisler.

In Vienna Cohn and Schine paid a hasty visit to the Soviet Information Center, where they were observed going through the file cards to determine what works of American authors were deemed acceptable to the Soviet. Armed with this evidence, they then walked the three blocks to the U.S. Information Center—a unit of the much-attacked International Information Administration—and there they conducted some eager researches into *our* card files to see if *we* were distributing books that the Russians found acceptable. By this astute cross-checking, they made a momentous discovery. The works of Mark Twain were on display in *both* the American and Russian information centers.

This was shocking, indeed, and the two young researchers were encouraged to examine the periodicals our information center was displaying. To their horror, they noted that the center did not have copies of those two distinguished American periodicals, *The Freeman* and the *American Legion Magazine.* The functionary in charge of the periodical room confessed regretfully that he had never heard of *The Freeman,* an obscure right-wing propaganda sheet, and he hadn't thought there were enough American legionnaires in Vienna to make it worthwhile stocking the American Legion's contribution to modern literature. Cohn and Schine cluck-clucked at this exhibition of incompetence, left Vienna, and eventually headed home.

If they had done nothing else, they had revived an old-time vaudeville line so that correspondents (and many others) took to chanting in derision: "Positively, Mr. Cohn! Absolutely, Mr. Schine!"

Even the humor, however, had a sickness about it as a response to a performance so humiliating for the entire nation. Emmet Hughes perhaps capsuled the effect best in this anecdote:

"One small personal incident, expressive of the shame of it all, still stings in my memory. It came with a visit to my White House office, one spring afternoon, by a crippled German friend whom I had known years earlier in Berlin. The young man had almost blown himself to pieces with a grenade during World War II—in the course of making one of the anti-Nazi underground's several vain attempts upon Hitler's life. And both anger and anguish trembled in this man's voice, as he spoke of the only matter he could discuss. 'You have just sent us, you Americans, two visitors—two new-style American ambassadors, I suppose you call them,' he said. 'Whatever fantastic harm they have done elsewhere, can you imagine their impact in Germany— and on Germans still looking a little skeptically at free government? *You* are supposed to be the models for all us authoritarian-minded Germans. Tell me, my friend—*what* do I say to my German friends, when they gape at Messrs. Cohn and Schine, and then ask me: 'Is *this* what you call democracy?' "

THE COHN AND SCHINE INVASION of Europe marked only one phase of McCarthy's assault upon the International Information Administration. Dr. Robert L. Johnson, president of Temple University, had been persuaded by President Eisenhower to occupy the hot seat of IIA administrator as a patriotic duty because, the President said, the agency was so vital in the effort to win friends for America around the world. Johnson brought Martin Merson with him to Washington as his chief assistant; what follows is from Merson's account.

Dr. Johnson and his aide quickly discovered that they were

like targets for knife throwers. McCarthy and his cohorts in Congress were out to destroy IIA, and they didn't care how they did it. At the very outset, Representative Cliff Clevenger (R., Ohio), chairman of the subcommittee that was to hold hearings on IIA appropriations, told Johnson: "Dr. Johnson, you seem like a nice man. We've heard nothing but good things about you, but your agency is full of Communists, left-wingers, New Dealers, and radicals, and the best thing you can do is to take the funds you have on hand, liquidate it, and go back to Temple."

Despite resounding official pronouncements from the White House about the tremendous importance of the agency, Johnson and Merson found themselves surrounded by Congressional McCarthyites slashing away at their budget—and unable to get any help, unable even to get an audience at the White House. In desperation, they appealed to the great white father of Republicanism, the party's last President, Herbert Hoover, isolated in his apartment in the Waldorf Towers in New York. But they discovered to their dismay that Hoover's mind was in tune with McCarthy's. When they asked for his help, he replied flatly, "No." He declared, in Merson's words, that "the IIA was so permeated with leftists that the only solution was to liquidate it completely, firing all of its present personnel."

The bogeymen were everywhere. Just how one identified them no one could say; and so the only solution—like the one Clint Murchison had adopted at Henry Holt & Co.—was to get rid of them all. Never was the absurdity of this "solution" exposed more completely than in Dr. Johnson's IIA.

Johnson told Scott McLeod: "I'll back you to the limit: You send me the information on anybody you think is a risk, and I'll fire him."

Merson shuddered at this sweeping pledge because no one had yet defined with any precision just what constituted a "security risk" and because Johnson's promise, in effect, put all 9,000 IIA employees at the mercy of Scott McLeod, McCarthy's favorite scalper. Yet the results were ludicrous. Even Scott McLeod couldn't identify those ubiquitous subversives. On information he supplied, only six persons out of 9,000 were dismissed as "security risks"—and, as Merson wrote, "not one IIA official in all my five months was brought up on any charge involving loyalty . . ."

Despite the evidence, Johnson and Merson quickly learned the lesson that most of Washington was learning in those days —that they were literally at the mercy of Cohn and Schine. The pair kept hounding IIA, and Merson "spent endless hours with them—on the phone, at luncheon, dinner, and in meetings in our offices. . . . They kept on referring casually to chats with the Vice President and other senior members of the Executive and Legislative branches . . . They produced lists of officials who on some personal charge or other should be fired if we weren't to get into trouble with 'Joe'—and names of others whom we ought to hire in their place."

When the steep budget cuts dictated by the McCarthyites forced the firing of 1,500 IIA employees, an unexpected howl went up from Cohn and Schine. "In the process of weeding out officials of low seniority," Merson wrote, he and Johnson had unknowingly lopped off the heads of "persons who had made private contact with the McCarthy Committee. Quite unintentionally, we were breaking up McCarthy's underground network at the Voice and shutting off the informers from their promised reward." Schine announced he was "going to see the Vice President about this, and he was sure the President would 'go along.'" Cohn complained that employees who had "cooperated" with McCarthy were being fired and many who had not cooperated were being retained; he was furious and named specific persons and specific jobs he wanted straightened out.

The beleaguered administrators sought a face-to-face meeting with McCarthy—but he was more elusive than a ghost. Vice President Nixon himself finally promised Johnson that he would get Johnson and Merson together with McCarthy; a meeting was arranged—but McCarthy didn't show. The reason for the standup was that he wasn't yet satisfied Johnson and Merson were "cooperating" enough. Settling for *les enfants terribles*, Merson and Johnson set conferences with Cohn and Schine for April 24 and again for April 27. The pair broke both dates. On April 28, however, the two young men brazenly stalked into IIA offices, and, Merson wrote, "we listened to another speech about whom we should hire and fire."

Above the storm sat the nation's hero-general-President, refusing to hear their case or to intercede with McCarthy. Johnson and Merson tried to get C. D. Jackson, an executive of *Time* and one of the President's closest advisers, to arrange a White House audience for them, but Jackson told them he wouldn't dream of it; it was Eisenhower's "passion," he said, "not to offend anybody in Congress."

In desperation Johnson and Merson turned to the mediator of last resort—George Sokolsky, a close friend of Herbert Hoover's, and a man who had never been able to refuse bounties from powerful pressure groups while posing as an impartial journalist. He had been exposed by the Nye committee in pre-World War II days as a secret dealer in munitions while working for *The New York Times;* he had been exposed by the La Follette Committee as a lecturer and propagandist for the National Association of Manufacturers and the Iron and Steel Institute (*Time* put his stipend at $40,000) while he was pontificating in the columns of the *Herald-Tribune*. He had finally wound up in the arms of Hearst and had devoted his talents to redbaiting. No more bitter commentary on the morally enervating American scene of 1953 could be made than the mere fact that Johnson and Merson had felt compelled to carry their case to such a man in the hope that he could do for them what the President of the United States could not or would not do.

Appealing to this arbiter without portfolio, Johnson invited Sokolsky to dinner one evening in May. "In the course of the evening," Merson wrote, "the famous columnist produced a little black book from which he read out accusations against IIA officials who, he said, should be fired. It was the list of McCarthy and his boys all over again. I lost my temper and challenged him for proof. He had none that made sense to me."

There were more dinners with the journalistic intermediary, more conferences, more efforts to get the mighty McCarthy to condescend to a meeting. Finally, on May 23, 1953, the objective was attained. McCarthy consented to dignify with his presence a dinner hosted by Dr. Johnson in the Presidential suite of the Statler Hotel. McCarthy, having satisfied his ego by the sight of suppliants on their knees, was almost benign. He chided Johnson about certain "subversives" still in IIA, received Johnson's assurance of cooperation, and promised to forward more specific information about his "cases." It had taken all of this maneuvering and self-abasement to accomplish virtually nothing, and the fact that McCarthy could put high officials through such a wringer in so futile an exercise was just one more illustration of his power.

The harmony of this summit affair was marred by only one untoward incident, and this, curiously enough, was provoked by George Sokolsky himself. He "got into an argument," Merson wrote, "with Cohn and Schine on the subject of purging American composers of reputedly leftist associations, Sokolsky arguing over his long cigar that he didn't want to see Aaron Copland put on the blacklist, whatever his politics and associations, since he personally considered him one of America's greatest composers."

Needless to say, no one was horrified by the mere suggestion that there should be such a blacklist. Music had been added to sound effects as a potential vehicle for ideological contamination. One illustrative incident took place in Vienna. The IIA office there had decided it would be a good idea to stage a cultural exhibit, and it wanted to use a collection of photographs of America's leading composers. It queried the State Department for "clearance" on the ideology of these musicians; and State questioned the ideological purity of twenty-three of the composers, including the late Walter Damrosch. The result: the entire cultural exhibit had to be canceled.

IF BABY-GURGLERS AND COMPOSERS could fall under such a blight, what about those dangerous individuals who deal in words and thoughts? McCarthy, with the fly-by-night Cohn and Schine researches in overseas libraries as his basic documentation, now launched a campaign to smite writers. Author after author was called and grilled about writings that seemed to the inquisitors to contain traces of dangerous thoughts. When even Reed Harris' youthful criticism of the commercialization of college football could be used as a springboard for attack, virtually no thought and no author was safe.

Writers are especially vulnerable because by the very nature of their work they deal with ideas and make their beliefs obvious. Many writers are penurious, dependent on a regular job for bread and butter while they create in their spare time. Their employers, fearful that business would suffer if it were intimated they were harboring a suspect person, threatened such writers with instant dismissal unless they "cleared" themselves with Mc-Carthy.

There was only one way of winning such clearance. McCarthy's hearings were now a regular television feature, beamed across the nation, and an author hailed before his committee, if dependent upon an employer for his livelihood, had to abase himself in public, to disown his past beliefs, and to promise never again to wander into such ideological error. The humiliation that was visited on many is almost too painful to relate. One writer who needed his job to support his family was summoned to appear before the new supreme literary critic in Washington. The procedure in such cases was clearly charted. The victim was grilled first in private session; if his responses established that he would be sufficiently cooperative, he was then placed on public display before the television cameras. This particular writer had been told by his employer in explicit terms just what he might expect. He must go before McCarthy and apologize humbly for every offending word he had ever written. If he did that, he could keep his job; if he didn't, he would be fired on the morrow. "We will be watching your performance on TV," his employer told him. And so he did what he had to do: he went and performed and testified by rote.

There were some who were more fortunately situated or perhaps just constitutionally more defiant. One of these was James A. Wechsler, the fighting liberal editor of the New York *Post*. Wechsler had never made any secret of the fact that he had belonged to the Young Communist League in his youth; but he had broken with the ideology early and had been known for years as one of the strongest and most forceful opponents of communism, earning for himself the encomium of angry denunciations in the *Daily Worker*.

In May, 1953, on eighteen hours notice, Wechsler was called to Washington for his first, private session with McCarthy. In his case, there was to be no second, live television performance; for Wechsler, in seventy minutes of give-and-take, made it clear what kind of show he would put on.

The pretense for calling him was that he had written a book that had been found in IIA's overseas libraries. "The hearing never even revealed which book it was, or where it was found," Wechsler later wrote. McCarthy himself dropped the pretext almost as soon as it was advanced and began to grill Wechsler on the real issue—the *Post*'s attacks upon the sacred figure of Senator Joseph R. McCarthy, which obviously could only have been inspired by communism.

Wechsler assumed that the printed attacks upon him in the *Daily Worker* would be of some relevancy in demonstrating that he was not beloved by communists. But as soon as he offered copies of these articles, "the faint, familiar smile" vanished from McCarthy's face.

"Did you write that statement?" McCarthy asked suddenly.

Wechsler was stunned. "At first I wondered whether I had heard him correctly," he later wrote. "When he made it clear that I had, I asked whether the question was facetious. He repeated it, broadening it this time to ask whether I or one of my deputies had inspired the Communist attack upon me.

"In what I will always recall as one of the most preposterous moments of my life, I thereupon solemnly denied under oath that I was the author of the Communist statement denouncing myself!

"McCarthy's realm is often described as the place where men are held to be guilty until they prove their innocence. But now I can personally report that it is also a place where *the existence of proof of innocence becomes damning evidence of guilt.*"

THE OVERSEAS LIBRARIES of the International Information Administration were a hunting preserve, stocked with helpless prey. The United States at the time was maintaining 192 libraries in the major cities of sixty-five nations. More than two million volumes were on the shelves. They covered all categories of literature. In Europe, five borrowers out of every eight wanted new American novels; but in South America, the Middle East and the Far East, three out of four wanted factual books. In these regions, "know-how" books on technical subjects, and works on American history were especially popular. Those millions of volumes were the ideal target for Joe McCarthy's favorite numbers game.

He came up with a headline-worthy figure: IIA's overseas libraries harbored 30,000 volumes subversive of American interests. And American taxpayers' money had been used to purchase these books. "Where in the name of Heaven, we asked ourselves, did he get such a figure?" Martin Merson later wrote. The mathematical mechanics gradually became clear. Over a period of weeks, McCarthy's hounds had demanded information about 418 authors, playwrights and artists whose works were on display in the overseas libraries. They had not been tagged absolutely as communists; it was merely implied that their loyalty was suspect. If one simply multiplied the 418 authors by the number of their volumes on the shelves, one would get about 30,000—a figure that was pure breathtaking magic.

"The McCarthy list itself was a shocker," Merson later wrote. "A few obvious names such as William Z. Foster and Howard Fast had been lumped with some of the most respected names in our literature. I recall the name of Foster Rhea Dulles, cousin of the Secretary of State, and the names of such anti-Communist liberals as Elmer Davis and Arthur Schlesinger, Jr. Some of the most prominent educators and historians were listed: John Dewey, Robert M. Hutchins, Henry Steele Commager, Zechariah Chafee, and Bernard DeVoto. And when it came to novelists, poets, playwrights and critics, the roll call read like a Who's Who of contemporary American writing: Franklin P. Adams, Sherwood Anderson, Brooks Atkinson, W. H. Auden, Stephen Vincent Benét, Louis Bromfield, Van Wyck Brooks, Theodore Dreiser, Edna Ferber, Archibald MacLeish, Quentin Reynolds, both Carl and Mark Van Doren, Edmund Wilson and many others."

On June 15, when Merson went to see Secretary Dulles on "the book question," he found this highest arbiter of American foreign policy baffled.

"Why have they got my cousin on that list?" the Secretary wondered plaintively.

NOW THE WORKS of communists, fellow-travelers, leftists and those "et ceteras" vanished from our overseas libraries as a panicked State Department genuflected before the Thunderer on the Hill. Nowhere was the precipitate retreat more destructive of American foreign policy than in West Germany.

We had forty IIA branch libraries in Berlin and West Germany, and they had been visited in 1952 by an estimated 15,000,-000 persons. Now books by a score of American writers vanished from the shelves. The works of those who had been critical of Chiang Kai-shek automatically were consigned to the darkest corners of the storage rooms. Writers who fell under this ban included Edgar Snow, former staff member of *The Saturday Evening Post*; Theodore White, formerly of *Time* magazine; Anna Lee Jacoby, who had become Mrs. Clifton Fadiman; Lawrence K. Rosinger, formerly associated with the Foreign Policy Association—and, of course, Owen Lattimore.

Even books that had no ideological bias were banished, not because of their contents but because of the political coloration of their authors. A book of fiction, *Return to the Vineyard*, by Walter Duranty and Mary Loos was adjudged to have acquired from its authors a taint that made it unacceptable for display. Similarly barred were the mystery books of Dashiell Hammett—unfit because their author had taken the Fifth Amendment in his appearance before a Congressional committee.

As High Commissioner John J. McCloy had noted in July, 1952, one of the basic purposes of our libraries in Germany was to combat the intellectual stagnation of the Nazi era, "counteracting the effect of twelve years of isolation and one-sided information." Now we were emulating the very kind of thought control that had marked Hitler's regime, and in the process we were exposing ourselves as the most timorous of the Western Allies administering occupation zones in Germany. As *The New York Times* reported: "The British and French information services continue to present the Germans a broad cross section of opinion from their own countries. The British display the left-wing journal, *New Statesman and Nation*, and the French provide several opposition publications."

We not only wouldn't allow dissent—we began to burn books.

The number, contrasted with the two million volumes on IIA shelves, was infinitesimal (only eleven, according to Secretary Dulles), but it was the symbolism of the act that counted. The Nazis, too, had burned books. Overseas libraries in Sydney, Australia, and Singapore had actually consigned offending volumes to the bonfire. Secretary Dulles, shocked by this overzealousness on the part of aides, ordered the book burnings stopped; but the psychological damage had been done.

Under the pressure of these events, President Eisenhower came momentarily out of his shell. On June 14, 1953, the President addressed the graduating class of Dartmouth College at Hanover, New Hampshire.

"Don't join the book-burners," he told the graduates. "Don't think you are going to conceal thoughts by concealing the evivence that they ever existed. Don't be afraid to go to the library and read every book so long as that document does not offend your own ideas of decency—that should be the only censorship."

To deny a man the right to have ideas, to record them in a book, and to place that book in a library where all may read it "is not America," the President said.

It was a forthright statement and seemed to be aimed directly at the junior Senator from Wisconsin. But Eisenhower's lofty stand on principle lasted for just three days before there began the characteristic wavering, the retreat from showdown. In a press conference on June 17, he was bombarded with questions about his Dartmouth speech. In response, he defended free access to knowledge; he even urged the reading of the basic doctrines of Karl Marx and Joseph Stalin as essential to an awareness of communist designs; he favored the retention of "merely controversial" books on the shelves of libraries both here and abroad. But he approved the destruction of books advocating the overthrow of the U.S. Government; and when he was asked specifically about Joe McCarthy, he insisted that he never dealt in personalities, that he had not intended the Dartmouth speech as an attack or reflection on anyone.

This suggestion that in some instances even book burning was not reprehensible, was gleefully seized upon by McCarthy and his Congressional coterie. "I think he [the President] has given a commendable clarification of the Dartmouth speech, which apparently has been misunderstood by many newsmen," McCarthy declared. Senator Mundt hailed Ike's remarks as "a 100 per cent endorsement" of McCarthy's investigations and said they bore out "our feeling that his remarks [at Dartmouth] were not aimed at McCarthy." The inevitable conflict had been averted for the moment by Eisenhower's temporizing.

Even so, the Dartmouth statement had had some effect: it had helped to put some semblance of backbone into the flab of the State Department. In late July, State announced a new policy. In the future books would be banned, not automatically because of the names and philosophies of their authors, but only if their contents were judged deleterious to American interests. It became safe once more to read the detective stories of Dashiell Hammett; these, along with a lot of other proscribed books, would now go back on the shelves of overseas libraries. In its new directive, the State Department also acknowledged its regret that, on February 25, it had ordered the destruction of the July, 1946, *Annals* of the American Academy of Political and Social Science, one of our more prestigious scholarly organizations. That issue of the *Annals* had dealt with "one world government and one-world citizenship," a topic whose very mention had been considered heresy, and so the publication had been consigned to the flames. No responsible publication would suffer such a fate in the future, the department promised.

With this ruling, some small measure of sanity returned to our posture.

UNCHECKED BY THIS FAINT REBUKE, McCarthy raged on across the American scene. On July 24, 1953, the Senate Appropriations Committee held hearings on the budget for the new U.S. Information Agency, which was to succeed the battle-scarred IIA. Senator Styles Bridges was the committee chairman, but he had been incapacitated in an automobile accident, so Senator Homer Ferguson was in the chair. Usually appropriations hearings were held in a small room of the Capitol, but this one had been mysteriously transferred to the large and ornate Senate Caucus Room, with television crews in abundant attendance. Senator A. Willis Robertson, a conservative Virginia Democrat, wondered querulously who had ordered this change. It was the Senator from Wisconsin who stepped forward and explained that he had persuaded Senator Bridges to use the caucus room so that press and public could be accommodated—and so, as soon became obvious, thespian Joe McCarthy could get national exposure.

When the hearing began, McCarthy virtually took command. He hectored General Walter Bedell Smith, the Under Secretary of State, telling Smith he did not know what he was talking about when he insisted that the State Department no longer purchased works of communist authors. He clashed with Senator J. William Fulbright over the student exchange program that

Fulbright was sponsoring. He sneered that it was a "half-bright" program, and at one point, he grabbed the gavel out of the nerveless hand of Senator Ferguson, banged it loudly two or three times, and snarled that he wanted Fulbright to answer a question —one that Fulbright had already answered.

"Mr. Chairman, who is running this committee? Is Senator McCarthy its chairman?" Senator Allen J. Ellender, Sr. (D., La.), interjected.

Ferguson retrieved the gavel and attempted to act like the chairman. He ruled that Fulbright had already answered the question and that he could go on with his testimony. McCarthy kept interrupting. Finally, he dramatically announced that he had to depart for the Senate floor to look after a matter of vital interest. "I don't want the witness [Fulbright] to disappear while I'm gone," he barked.

Even Ferguson rebuked him for this, saying "there is no justification" for implying Fulbright would take refuge in flight; McCarthy stormed out, leaving behind him the kind of chaos that he delighted in creating.

The camera crews were appreciative; the ranting, badgering and insinuating of the star performer had made good television.

19

The Hidden Flaw

I T S E E M S N O W that the month of July, 1953, marked the
turning point. It was then that the seeds of defeat were being
sown. But McCarthy was still striding across the national stage,
apparently as invincible as ever. No one could have known that
the curtain would soon come crashing down.

It can be seen as a downfall predestined by the flawed characters of those who joined the demented crusade. Of course no
character was more flawed than that of McCarthy himself, but
his own weaknesses were compounded by the deficiencies of
those attracted to his grubby banner. The combination was bound
to lead to disaster. How could one suppose that the bizarre team
of Cohn and Schine, which had gained some mysterious domi-

nance over its master, could fail to bring the master to ruin?

But at the time it seemed that it would all go on forever. The press was filled with McCarthy's clamor. As chairman of the permanent investigating subcommittee of his own Government Operations Committee, he continued to stage daily spectaculars. He called before him processions of quavering witnesses, browbeat them, denounced them and banished them to the dark limbo of un-Americanism. So overwhelming was the performance that no one could foresee that two events—one public, the other taking place backstage—were conspiring in a great pincer movement to crush the maestro.

T H E   C A T A L Y S T in McCarthy's first public contretemps was that veteran of decades of professional redbaiting for the Hearst chain, J. B. Matthews. Matthews had played a key undercover role in McCarthy's career, first in persuading Hearst to back him, and then in helping with the photostating of the documents sneaked out of the Carter barn. Now, with McCarthy heading his own investigating committee, the time had come for Matthews' reward.

The prelude to Matthews' official elevation was a dinner and rally of reactionaries in the Waldorf-Astoria Hotel in New York on February 13, 1953. Some three hundred guests rendered homage to Matthews at the $12.50-a-plate dinner. They included some of the most notorious anti-Semites and ultrarightists in the nation. The toastmaster, inevitably, was George Sokolsky; the principal speaker, inevitably, was Joseph McCarthy. Congratulatory messages were read from Vice President Nixon, from editors and officials of the Hearst chain, and from the original official witch hunter, Martin Dies himself. Russell Maguire, the former Christian Fronter who had acquired control of the *American Mercury* and turned that esteemed magazine, of which H. L. Mencken had been editor, into a redbaiting sheet, table-hopped all over the dining room, urging everyone to read Matthews' latest opus. It told all, it was entitled "The Reds in the White House," and it was contained in the latest issue of the *Mercury* in abundant supply at all tables.*

* It is perhaps appropriate to note here that the Hearst chain, which did so much to promote McCarthy, looked back on his performance twenty

Turning out for this bash were such as Harry Jung, former publisher of *The American Gentile,* Merwin K. Hart and Joseph P. Kamp. The latter pair, perhaps for fear anti-Semitism would show too clearly in public acknowledgment of their presence, were not included in the guest list, but Kamp sat at Table 6 and Hart at Table 33, from which vantage points they applauded Alfred Kohlberg, of China lobby fame and currently president of the American Jewish League Against Communism, as Kohlberg made a speech lauding Matthews.

Plaques and testimonials were presented to the guest of honor by the American Legion, the Catholic War Veterans, the American Coalition of Patriotic Societies, the American Jewish League Against Communism, the Joint Committee Against Communism, and Harding College—a fount of intellectual right-wing paranoia in Searcy, Ark., whose president, Dr. George Benson, paid appropriate tribute to Matthews. (Both Dr. Benson and Harding College, little known to the public at the time, would be in the forefront of the superpatriotic movement of the early 1960s—an effort to reincarnate McCarthyism and to fan prejudices against the liberal Administration of John F. Kennedy.)

Others included in this 1953 gathering of kindred spirits were: Victor Lasky, the journalist who was to denigrate President Kennedy in *JFK, the Man and the Myth;* Mr. and Mrs. William F. Buckley, Jr.; John T. Flynn, the one-time America Firster who had done his bit for the cause in *The Road Ahead:* Miss Elizabeth Bentley, the Mata Hari of informers; Earl Harding, the former head of America's Future, that spawn of the Committee for Constitutional Government; Mr. and Mrs. Westbrook Pegler;

---

years later with regret and distaste. William Theis, chief of the Washington bureau of the Hearst newspapers, with the aid of a panel of Hearst reporters, wrote a long article tracing the rise and fall of McCarthyism for publication on the anniversary of the Wheeling speech. He noted that McCarthy had "generated panic and hysteria" throughout the nation for five years "with his claims that communists lurked under practically every rock." He wrote that McCarthy had developed a "style of witch hunt" that became known as McCarthyism and that in his "demagogic execution" of his role "he demeaned and denounced two Presidents, terrorized the Senate and struck blows at the State Department from which Secretary of State William P. Rogers says it is 'just now fully recovering.'" Theis' article, naturally, did not mention the Hearst role in promoting McCarthyism; and, ironically, it viewed with alarm the continued existence of conditions that had allowed McCarthyism to flourish in the 1950s. The article was read into the *Congressional Record* by Senator Henry M. Jackson (D., Wash.) on February 19, 1970.

Philip Scanlan, of the Brooklyn *Tablet;* Julius Cahn, counsel of the Senate Foreign Relations Committee; Eugene Lyons; Igor Cassini, Hearst journalist and columnist; journalists from the Chicago *Tribune;* and Harvey Matusow, not yet fallen from grace because of the injudicious announcement that he had used his imagination under oath.

Murray Kempton, of the New York *Post,* who described it all, commented: "There is a society of professional anti-Communists; J. B. Matthews is at once its Ulysses and its Circe. It has the sadness of all emigre societies, and its members backbite each other like so many jungle monkeys. But they carry over from their old days . . . a species of false good fellowship, so all of them call J. B. Matthews 'Doc,' the name given him by Martin Dies out of a semi-literate's respect for the scholar."

"Doc" Matthews had come out of Hopkinsville, Ky., born into a family of shouting Methodists. He had become a fundamentalist Methodist preacher. Seeking larger fields for his talents, he had come to New York, had been caught up for a time in communist-front peace movements, and then, in the mid-thirties, he had made the almost conventional switch from extreme left to extreme right and gone to work for Martin Dies, ferreting out the infidels. After Dies, he had gravitated inevitably to Hearst as keeper of the files on the menace; early, he had recognized the Heaven-sent potential of Joseph McCarthy, and had counseled and guided him. No one could say that old "Doc" Matthews had not given his all.

In this feastly atmosphere of a celebrating clan, everyone paid proper tribute to everybody. Old "Doc" Matthews told one and all that, when he listened to George Sokolsky on the radio, "I think of the Prophet Amos almost invariably." McCarthy brought down the house with his references to "the great Red Dean, Acheson." And then he went out on the longest limb of all. Ignoring Matthews' role in helping to whip up the hate chorus against Anna Rosenberg, McCarthy lauded the guest of honor by declaring that "never did an unjust or unprovable word pass his lips."

If this was not just superficial rhetoric tailored to the occasion, if McCarthy really believed it, he was suffering from a delusion for which he would soon pay, and dearly.

. . .

T H E O U T C O M E O F T H I S E X E R C I S E in mutual admiration was all but inevitable. Joe McCarthy, feeling that he
needed at his right hand the ultimate voice on the treacheries
surrounding us, summoned "Doc" Matthews to Washington on
June 22, 1953, and made him the $11,600-a-year executive di-
rector of his subcommittee's investigative staff.

The action, unfortunately for McCarthy, virtually coincided
with the arrival on the American literary scene of Matthews' latest
endeavor. Having polished off "The Reds in the White House,"
he had embarked upon his masterwork: an exposé of Reds in
the pulpits of the nation's Protestant churches. This diatribe appeared in the July, 1953, issue of the *American Mercury*, which
was on the newsstands just at the moment its author was settling himself comfortably into his new chair in Washington.

This literary effort minced no words. The opening sentence
read: "The largest single group supporting the Communist apparatus in the United States today is composed of Protestant
clergymen." Later in the article, Matthews expanded on this
assertion by writing that in the past seventeen years the Communist Party had "enlisted the support of at least 7,000 Protestant
clergymen" as party members, fellow-travelers, espionage agents,
party-line adherents and dupes.

This was the man McCarthy had praised for never having
uttered an "unjust or unprovable" word.

The effect was profound. McCarthy, by the deed of his mentor and agent, was implicated. The Democrats, so long recum-
bent under McCarthy's trampling feet, bestirred themselves.
Even they recognized the madness of the notion that Protestant
pastors were secret agents of the Kremlin. Senators Jackson,
Symington and Monroney had already begun to look for a way
to throw a roadblock across the path of McCarthy's runaway
investigations, and this attack on the Protestant clergy won them
a powerful cohort—Senator John L. McClellan, the conservative
Arkansas Democrat (who now heads the same committee Mc-
Carthy then ruled). McClellan was enraged by the tone and
opening paragraphs of Matthews' "Reds and Our Churches," and
he promptly assumed the leadership of the Democratic dissi-

dents and demanded a face-to-face showdown with McCarthy.

A planning session was held early in the day of Thursday, July 2, and that same afternoon the rebellious Democrats confronted McCarthy with the Matthews article. His first reaction was to disclaim responsibility and to belittle the entire incident. The article had been written before he appointed Matthews, he said; he had known nothing about it, and anyway, however regrettable, it was simply a "well-intentioned" error. McClellan refused to accept such exculpations. He demanded that McCarthy take "appropriate action" by firing Matthews; and, in the end, McCarthy threw up his hands and said: "Gentlemen, you appear to have me over a barrel."

The words were prophetic, but the surrender they implied was a chimera. McCarthy would never learn how to step back and counterpunch; he had only one technique—that of the windmill aggressor. And so, before the hour was out, he issued a press statement aligning himself solidly with Matthews. The Democrats responded by calling for Matthews' ouster. The battle was joined.

McCarthy's defense of his intemperate mentor had put him in an untenable public position. It led him to utter incredible statements in defense of the indefensible. "As a free lance writer he [Matthews] wrote many articles," he said. "I have not read them and don't intend to. I do not set myself up as a censor." And again: "I feel I have no right to censorship over anyone"— this coming from the man who had set himself up as the supreme literary censor of America!

The two-facedness was obvious, but this was nothing new. What really mattered now was that McCarthy, for the first time, had aligned himself against a powerful conservative segment of the American Establishment. Protestants were outraged. A flood of mail began to flow into Senatorial offices and the White House. Even Republican Senators who were usually solidly in McCarthy's corner began to waver. Senator Charles E. Potter, a wheelchair survivor of World War II, whose strength lay in Michigan's Protestant Bible belt, demanded that Matthews be fired and announced that he would vote with the Democratic opposition on the committee to achieve it. Even Senator Mundt announced plaintively that he had opposed the hiring of Matthews from the beginning.

Still, McCarthy would not yield. With typical arrogance, he tried to ride out the storm. He announced that Matthews had submitted his resignation—but that he had refused to accept it. He met with the members of his rebellious committee on Thursday, July 7. Dirksen didn't show. Mundt left early. For the first time, deserted by his allies, McCarthy was left alone to face four determined opponents. If a vote could have been taken, four members of the seven-man committee—McClellan, Symington, Jackson and Potter—would have voted to oust Matthews. McCarthy knew this, and so prevented a vote. In a bitter two-hour wrangle, he faced down his opposition, contending arrogantly that the hiring and firing of "non-professional" staff members was the sole prerogative of the committee chairman. Of Matthews' resignation, he said: "I did not accept it and have no present intention of accepting it."

Now other wheels were set in motion. Watching the uproar from the sanctity of the White House, Emmet Hughes and Deputy Attorney General William Rogers (made Secretary of State in 1969) decided that the attack on the Protestant clergy offered a perfect opportunity to administer a rebuke to McCarthy. Rogers, who was one of the closest confidants of Nixon, reported to Hughes that the Vice President agreed. All that was needed was some device to give the President an excuse for acting, and to achieve this the White House contingent contacted friends in the National Conference of Christians and Jews in New York.

The religous leaders cooperated and sent the President a telegram that said: "The sweeping attack on the loyalty of Protestant clergymen and the charge that they are the largest single group supporting the Communist apparatus is unjustifiable and deplorable." The telegram was signed by Msgr. John A. O'Brien of the University of Notre Dame; Rabbi Maurice N. Eisendrath, president of the Union of American Hebrew Congregations; and the Rev. Dr. John Sutherland Bonnell, pastor of the Fifth Avenue Presbyterian Church in New York.

Sherman Adams, Eisenhower's "deputy president" in the White House, had been apprised of the contemplated squeeze-play on McCarthy and welcomed it. He agreed to take Hughes' draft of a stinging Presidential denunciation to Eisenhower for approval. With all in readiness, there now occurred an eleventh-hour snafu.

Rumors were flying all over Capitol Hill that McCarthy was closeted with Mundt, who was persuading him to see the light, and that he was about to dump Matthews. The White House staffers wanted the President's statement to get out first to take the headline play away from McCarthy; but, just at this critical juncture, the President was in conference with important visitors and could not be reached, not even by Sherman Adams. On the Hill, Rogers was almost frantic. "For God's sake," he telephoned Hughes, "we have to get the message out fast or McCarthy will beat us to the draw." Finally, as the anxious minutes ticked away, Adams got in to see the President. Eisenhower read Hughes' draft, approved of it in principle—but he wanted a few changes made in the wording. New stencils had to be cut. More delay.

Almost in desperation, Rogers telephoned Hughes again from the Vice President's office: "Mundt and McCarthy have been meeting and are on their way here right now with, I'm sure, Matthews' resignation."

Hughes told him to stall McCarthy, to keep him away from the press for ten minutes; by then, the White House would have its statement out.

Rogers and Nixon staged a wily delaying action. When McCarthy arrived, they were so solicitous about his plans that he could hardly believe it. As Rogers later described the scene to Hughes: "Dick and I kept asking him all kinds of thoughtful questions . . . He even looked a little puzzled at our sudden interest. As he was rambling on, of course, your message got to the press, which he had no way of knowing. So as he headed for the door finally, he said with a big grin, 'Gotta rush now—I want to be sure I get the news of dumping Matthews to Fulton Lewis in time for him to break it on his broadcast.'"

It was too late. For once, McCarthy had been upstaged. The President's stern and unmistakable rebuke was already on the press wires, and it preempted the next morning's headlines. In his response to the protest of the religious leaders, Eisenhower said: ". . . I want you to know at once that I fully share the convictions you state. The issues here are clear. Generalized and irresponsible attacks that sweepingly condemn the whole of any group of citizens are alien to America. Such attacks betray contempt for the principles of freedom and decency. And when these attacks—whatever their professed purpose be—condemn such a vast portion of the churches or clergy as to create doubt in the loyalty of all, the damage to our nation is multiplied."

Joe McCarthy had suffered his first sharp setback—and the Eisenhower Administration had taken one long stride toward the inevitable confrontation.

Nonetheless, as he had so often done before, McCarthy now tried to camouflage the fact of the Matthews debacle by rushing into the headlines with a sensational new charge On July 10, 1953—the same day the newspapers featured Eisenhower's rebuke and Matthews' ouster—*The New York Times* ran this headline: "M'CARTHY STRIKES AT ALLEN DULLES. Says Intelligence Agency Head Balks Inquiry Into Aide, Who, He Charges, Helped Hiss."

The lead of the story said that McCarthy "struck close to the White House itself today" by announcing in a Senate speech that he intended to subpoena Allen W. Dulles, brother of the Secretary of State and head of the Central Intelligence Agency. The CIA aide whom McCarthy attacked was William P. Bundy, whom he accused of contributing $400 to the Alger Hiss defense fund. McCarthy had demanded the right to question Bundy about this, and he had also badgered the State Department not to grant Bundy a passport for a vacation abroad, the sinister implication being that Bundy was too dangerous to be permitted to leave the country. Allen Dulles had defied McCarthy, ordering his CIA aides not to testify before Congressional committees; and now McCarthy was dragging out the story in a moment of desperate need.

This time, for the first time, it did not work; nothing worked. McCarthy had blundered so badly in the Matthews affair that he had lost what he had always prized most—the initiative. The Democrats now had it. They had lifted Matthews' scalp, and they wanted Roy Cohn's to go with it. Beleaguered now, McCarthy tried to fight them off.

At a committee meeting on July 10, McCarthy insisted it was his sole right as committee chairman to hire and fire the staff. The Democrats demanded a say in the selection of vital personnel. The issue was put to a vote, and this time the four Republicans in the majority closed ranks and voted as a bloc. (Some interpreted this as yet another Administration effort to appease McCarthy and soothe his ruffled feathers.) The result of the strict party-line division was that McCarthy won; but immediately the unexpected happened. The three Democrats—McClellan, Symington and Jackson—walked out. They would have nothing further to do with the committee, they said, since they would have to accept, if they stayed, a measure of responsibility for McCarthy's actions "without any voice, right or authority" in regard to them.

The Democratic leadership in the Senate upheld the walkout. Not a single Democratic Senator would accept appointment to any of the three vacant seats. This left McCarthy alone, bereft of the façade of bipartisanship—and it left the Republicans, no longer quite so enchanted with him, with full responsibility for him and his actions.

Now another blow fell. On July 13, in a blunt and hard-hitting speech, Mike Monroney denounced McCarthy for his plan to investigate the CIA. Such an investigation, he said, "would disclose to our enemies information and data that even the Kremlin's best spy apparatus could not get for them."

He continued, scornfully: "I question the oft-stated claim that only the Senator from Wisconsin stands between us and complete internal subversion," Monroney said. "I doubt that he has a monopoly within this government of despising, exposing and prosecuting Communists and their fellow-travelers.

"I doubt that Messrs. Cohn and Schine, J. B. Matthews, or even the distinguished junior Senator from Wisconsin measure up in ability to the Federal Bureau of Investigation."

When Monroney finished speaking, Senator John Sherman Cooper (R., Ky.) strode across the aisle in full view of the press to shake Monroney's hand. And Senator Alexander Wiley, the veteran Republican whom McCarthy had tried to unseat in his first Wisconsin Senatorial campaign, congratulated Monroney: "Mike, that was a terrific speech!" The next day, after a conference with Allen Dulles, McCarthy announced that he was dropping his loudly touted investigation of the CIA.

It was the first time he had fallen so hard on his face without a better sensation to pick him up. He had been hurt badly, and he knew it. But he could not change. He snarled that perhaps the boycotting Democrats did not dare to look into the misfeasances of the Truman Administration; then he turned upon them the other side of his nature and almost humbly pleaded with them to be good boys and return to the committee. He was "quite distressed" by their attitude, he said; and, if they would only return and take their seats, he would welcome them with open arms—all would be forgiven.

Not caring a fig for his forgiveness, the Democrats spurned all overtures; and so for the rest of 1953, he had to go it alone, consoled only by the presence of Cohn and Schine.

IT WAS DURING these steaming summer months of 1953 that the second event—the one that would lead to the ultimate downfall—was taking shape backstage.

The United States Army was making threatening gestures to induct G. David Schine into the service of his country. Roy Cohn could not abide the thought of his buddy's fate; nor could Joe McCarthy bear to see Roy distressed.

According to a synopsis of the action released by the Army in March of the following year, it was some time in mid-July, 1953, that Major General Miles Reber, then chief of the Army's Legislative Liaison branch, received a telephone call that Senator McCarthy desired to see him. Reber went to McCarthy's office on the Hill, and there the Senator told him that he was most anxious to secure a direct commission for G. David Schine, who, otherwise, would soon be inducted into service as a buck private. During the discussion, Roy Cohn entered McCarthy's office and emphasized to Reber that it was essential to get the deed done swiftly.

On July 15, according to the Army, Schine telephoned Reber's office and asked if he could come to the Pentagon that very afternoon and "hold up his hand." He was advised that it wouldn't be so simple. First, he would have to come in and fill out a formal application. He did.

The gravity of the matter was, of course, obvious from the start. Senator Joseph McCarthy was no one to trifle with, a fact of life recognized by the Army as well as by everyone else in Washington. And so, during the last two weeks of July, some of the Army's highest brass weighed the delicate matter of granting a commission to G. David Schine. The Commanding General of the First Army in New York (it would be nice to keep G. David close to home, available for consultations with the McCarthy committee), the Chief of Transportation (it had been suggested that Schine's hotel experience might qualify him for a commission in the Army Transport Service), and the Provost Marshal General all batted around the question of the hour: to commission or not to commission? Their collective judgment was not to commission. General Reber ratified this decision, and Schine was informed of the verdict by letter, dated July 30.

The reaction came almost the instant the mail was delivered. On August 1, Cohn telephoned Legislative Liaison and asked about the possibility of getting Schine a commission in either the Air Force or the Navy. These services weighed the matter, but they, too, refused to commission Schine. Cohn was given the tragic news sometime during the month of August, but he was not deterred by this universal coolness of the services to the merits of his protégé. On September 30, he telephoned Secretary of the Army Robert T. Stevens and said he had two important matters he wanted to discuss with the secretary. An appointment was made for a meeting on October 2.

Cohn appeared, accompanied by Francis Carr, the successor to the departed Matthews as executive director of the McCarthy investigative staff. The conference with Secretary Stevens lasted for about thirty-five minutes. The two important matters on Cohn's mind turned out to be: McCarthy's plans for an investigation of the Army's Signal Corps laboratories at Fort Monmouth, N.J.—and favored treatment for G. David Schine. Cohn insisted it was most important to the national interest that Schine be kept available to the committee for staff consultations on the pending Fort Monmouth inquiry, and he argued that the Army must have several posts in the New York area at which it could accommodate one extra body for so vital a purpose. Secretary Stevens seemed to think that it would be best for Schine to be treated just like any other young man being inducted into service.

This did not satisfy Roy Cohn. He returned to the attack during the period October 14–17, asking Stevens to assign Schine to temporary duty in the New York area after his induction. It was essential, Cohn argued, that Schine be allowed to complete his work for the McCarthy committee. Secretary Stevens thought it might be possible to give Schine fifteen days' grace between induction and the beginning of basic training.

A fifteen-day reprieve did not mollify Cohn. According to the Army's account, made public months later, Cohn was on the phone almost every day prior to Schine's November 3 induction, arguing for a permanent New York assignment for his favorite.

While all of this was going on behind the scenes, McCarthy himself was preoccupied with romance. The object of his affections was Jean Kerr, the twenty-nine-year-old former college beauty queen who had been so active in his office in preparing the Lustron booklet and helping with the campaign against Tydings. Theirs had been a stormy romance, and according to Roy Cohn, Jean Kerr had despaired at times of ever becoming Mrs. McCarthy. But on September 17, 1953, their engagement was announced, and on September 29 they were married in St. Matthew's Roman Catholic Cathedral in Washington.

The press noted with some interest those who graced the nuptials with their presence and those who did not. Vice President and Mrs. Nixon were there; President and Mrs. Eisenhower sent their regrets. But the White House was represented by important Eisenhower aides, headed by Sherman Adams. There were in the audience numerous Senators and Representatives—and Jack Dempsey, the former heavyweight boxing champion.

The brief honeymoon was hardly over before McCarthy became entangled in the affair of Cohn and Schine. He had started closed hearings on the security situation at the Army's chief Signal Corps laboratory at Fort Monmouth, N.J., and in mid-October he and his bride had a conversation with John G. Adams, the Army counsel, at the Federal Courthouse in New York's Foley Square. "Senator McCarthy at this time told Mr. Adams that Mr. Schine was of no help to the committee, but was interested in photographers and getting his pictures in the paper, and that things had reached the point where Mr. Schine was a pest," the Army later charged. McCarthy added that he hoped the Army would treat Schine just like any other young man; and when Adams asked his permission to repeat this remarkable statement to Secretary Stevens, McCarthy assured him that he hoped he would—and quickly.

A few days later, Secretary Stevens, Adams and McCarthy

were together, and Adams raised the Schine issue. "Senator Mc-
Carthy," the Army account said, "told Secretary Stevens and Mr.
Adams that Mr. Schine was a nuisance, but that Senator Mc-
Carthy did not want Mr. Cohn to know of these views of Mr.
Schine." This, certainly, was a bewildering statement. It seemed
to indicate that Cohn exercised some kind of Svengali-like hold
over McCarthy—and that McCarthy, of all persons, was not
quite his own man where Roy Cohn and G. David Schine were
concerned.

From October 18 to November 3, there was an increasingly
intensified pressure campaign on the part of Cohn to get the
Army to "do something" for Schine. Cohn kept badgering Adams,
according to the Army's account; and Adams, annoyed by it all,
aware of McCarthy's unrevealed attitude, told Cohn that the
Army had an obligation to 300,000 other young men it was in-
ducting into service every year, that to single out Schine for
special treatment would not be in the national interest.

"Mr. Cohn replied," the Army declared, "that if the national
interest was what the Army wanted he'd give it a little and then
proceeded to outline how he would expose the Army in its worst
light and show the country how shabbily it is being run."

On November 3, Private Schine was inducted, but the behind-
the-scenes struggle to get him the most preferential treatment
possible abated not at all.

In this acerbic conflict, the basis had been laid for the
eruption that would finally destroy Joe McCarthy. But the public,
as yet, had no knowledge of it. The headlines were being preempted at the time by a new McCarthy horror tale—the charge
that traitors and spies had riddled the security screen of one of
the Army's most sensitive installations, the Signal Corps laboratories of the Fort Monmouth complex, where some of the most
advanced radar and electronic research was being conducted.

FORT MONMOUTH is located in Eatontown, N.J., a few
miles inland from the Monmouth County seashore resorts of Long
Branch and Asbury Park. During World War II, it had grown
from a pigmy into a giant, spawning satellite installations around
the Monmouth County countryside—laboratories that bore the
names of Evans, Coles, Squier and Watson. This sprawling com-

plex became the nerve center for research and development in radar, all kinds of countermeasures, nucleonics, thermionics, and applied physics. The most advanced forms of radar, so invaluable in the latter stages of World War II, had been developed and perfected here.

Long before McCarthy became interested, Fort Monmouth had been shaken by spy sensations. The first, the most serious and indeed the only case to be authenticated, involved the activities of Julius Rosenberg, who was later convicted and executed with his wife, Ethel, on charges that they stole and gave the Russians the secret of the atom bomb. Rosenberg had been employed at Fort Monmouth; he had known some of the civilian scientists there; and the "Rosenberg ring" had had additional contacts with employees of firms producing devices developed at Monmouth. The FBI investigation of the Rosenbergs had broken up this network, and this first rumble of espionage, dating back to World War II days, had died down, but had left in its wake a lingering aura of suspicion.

This miasma of doubt had led to a second temblor that had shaken the installation. In December, 1951, Lt. Col. Ollie J. Allen, then executive officer of the Signal Corps intelligence agency, had dictated a two-and-a-half-hour tape recording alleging that a serious security situation existed at Monmouth. Allen had backed up his own taped description of the threat with a petition signed by himself, two other officers and seven civilian employees of his investigative agency, requesting that Congress undertake a full-scale probe of the security-espionage situation at Fort Monmouth.

The Allen charges were headline stuff at the time. Though the full contents of the tape never were revealed, it was disclosed that Allen and his investigative colleagues had made these basic charges: fifty-seven top-secret documents were missing from Signal Corps files; seven civilian employees were involved in suspicious activities that might equate with espionage; and one employee of the Central Intelligence Agency with ties to Monmouth was accused of communistic associations.

The House Un-American Activities Committee, a legislative band ever thirsting to relive the glory days of the Hiss case, took up the chase—but then, oddly enough, the whole sensation expired without even a death rattle. In its report of December 28,

1952, HUAC dismissed the Allen charges in a scant two pages. The mystery of the missing fifty-seven documents had turned out to be no mystery at all; in every instance, the documents had been found, or official certificates authorizing their destruction had been located. One former employee of the Signal Corps investigative agency had admitted communist sympathies to HUAC investigators; but, except for this, the committee's staff had "added no substantial information to that gathered by the Army investigators concerning the accused employees."

As for the CIA agent branded by Allen, he had been investigated by both the CIA and the FBI until, in the words of General Walter Bedell Smith, "I think he is black and blue." This rigorous double-inquiry had resulted in the agent's complete exoneration; absolved on all counts, he was retained in his job by the CIA. The evidence certainly indicated that, if even HUAC could not smell out subversion at Fort Monmouth, it was highly improbable any existed there. But, naturally, this lack of substance did not deter McCarthy.

The McCarthy attack on Fort Monmouth that erupted now in the fall of 1953 was given a semblance of validity by the confusion caused by Eisenhower's new loyalty security program. Victims of their own propaganda that had pictured all Washington as riddled with spies and traitors, the Republicans had decided not to trust anything the Truman Administration had done in the security sphere—not even the Loyalty Board screenings supervised by such stalwart Republicans as Conrad Snow and Seth Richardson. The new Administration must have a far more strict program, one that would make it impossible for a single tainted employee to remain in federal service. And so, with this end in view, President Eisenhower promulgated his famous April 27 Executive Order 10450. As his press secretary, James C. Hagerty, explained it, this order provided:

—All new applicants for federal jobs, whether in sensitive or nonsensitive posts, would be investigated. Those in nonsensitive posts would be screened only by their own departments, with an additional "name check" in FBI files.

—In sensitive agencies, everyone must undergo a "full field investigation"—that is, an FBI check of their backgrounds, family relationships, associates, employers and civic and fraternal activities.

—All past investigations that had not been completed would be finished.

—All persons who had received a full field investigation during the Truman Administration would be investigated again—and this applied to those in nonsensitive as well as sensitive jobs.

—All employees who had had adverse information of *any kind* filed against them were to undergo a full field investigation. Any derogatory information indicating an employee might be a security risk would result in immediate suspension.

In addition, unlike the Truman program, which had been administered by boards composed of distinguished citizens, both Republicans and Democrats, the new Eisenhower security measures were placed exclusively in the hands of government employees. The American Civil Liberties Union felt that this provision jeopardized an employee's right to a full and impartial review. "Under the new order," it said, "Government employees who must sit in judgment on other Government employees may be prejudiced against them, because to pass favorably on these cases, especially sensitive border-line cases, could result in themselves being called security risks."

In effect, the dice had been loaded against any federal employee who had the misfortune to be accused. And to the average American, it seemed suspicious and scary—almost tantamount to a finding of guilt—that employees who had been suspended and run through the security mill once were now to be suspended and investigated again. That must mean that something was *really wrong* . . .

Such was the atmosphere created by the new program. At Fort Monmouth, already slightly tarred in the Rosenberg case, the situation was especially sensitive. When scientists who had been suspended and then reinstated in their jobs were accused and suspended again, it all seemed highly suspect to the public.

J O S E P H   M C   C A R T H Y opened his hearings into espionage at Fort Monmouth in the Federal Courthouse in New York's Foley Square on October 8, 1953. These were executive hearings, all the testimony taken behind closed doors with press and public excluded. The accounts that filtered out to the press depended solely on the veracity of Senator McCarthy. The press put its trust in a Senator's honor that what he said had happened behind those closed doors was what had happened, and a succession of headlines battered the public mind. Here is a sample of a hysteria-making headline sequence:

SPYING IS CHARGED AT FORT MONMOUTH (October 13); ARMY RADAR DATA REPORTED MISSING (October 14); ROSEN-BERG CALLED RADAR SPY LEADER: MC CARTHY SAYS RING HE SET UP "MAY STILL BE IN OPERATION" AT MONMOUTH LABORA-TORY (October 16); RADAR WITNESS BREAKS DOWN; WILL TELL ALL ABOUT SPY RING (October 17); ESPIONAGE IN SIGNAL CORPS FOR TEN YEARS IS CHARGED (October 18); "MORE THAN 12" OUT IN RADAR SPY CASE (October 21); MC CARTHY CHARGES SOVIET GOT SECRETS (October 23); MONMOUTH FIGURE LINKED TO HISS RING: FOREMAN IN SIGNAL LABORATORY QUESTIONED—27 SUSPENDED NOW IN MC CARTHY INQUIRY (October 27).

The suspensions had nothing to do with McCarthy's probe, but he got the credit. They resulted largely from the Army's reopening of old cases as a result of Eisenhower's Executive Order 10450, and several suspensions had taken place before McCarthy held his first hearing. But with the headlines reflecting the most sinister disclosures in the secret testimony as interpreted and relayed by McCarthy, both press and public were largely deluded into accepting the thesis that the new cleanup at Fort Monmouth was the result of the diligence and perseverance of one knight in shining armor.

Just what *was* taking place behind the closed doors of Joe McCarthy's hearing room?

The veil was lifted on this inner sanctum by an irate attorney, Harry Green, of Little Silver, New Jersey. Green was a lifelong Republican, with some close ties to the conservative New Jersey Republican organization. He and Ira J. Katchen, of Long Branch, a Democrat, eventually came to represent most of the forty-five Fort Monmouth employees who came under the cloud of 10450 and McCarthy. In taking these cases, Green and Katchen had both announced publicly that they would refuse to represent anyone unwilling to testify under oath—and so lay himself open to a possible perjury prosecution—that he had never been a communist. Theirs was a decidedly conservative legal representation of the accused; and, in the circumstances, Harry Green's denunciation of McCarthy and his methods carried with it the ring of authenticity, of honest outrage. In the *New Jersey Law Journal*, Green wrote this description of a typical session with the Mc-Carthy inquisitors:

". . . You walk in with your client, in a room bustling with movement and excitement, and with guests of the committee chairman and counsel; you are placed before a long table with four or five inquisitors thereat . . .

"Counsel for the witness is immediately told off, as follows: 'You will be permitted to sit with your client, you may consult with each other, but you are not to participate in any other manner in the hearing. You are not to ask questions, you are not to cross-examine, you are not to make objections, you are not to argue. You may remain under these conditions.'

"Your client is then subjected to a hydra-headed interrogation from all around the table, and to say that he is confused is to put it mildly.

"You sit there like a 'wooden Indian,' and you hear questions that seem incredible. Here is an inquisitorial example:

" 'I am troubled by what a witness testified to yesterday. I asked him if you [your client] were a Communist and he refused to answer upon the ground that it might incriminate him. Why should he refuse to answer? It seems to me from this that you are a Communist.'

"At this point, I could take it no longer and I stated that it was not fair—why not ask my client if he was a Communist, etc.? Silence. I then turned to my client and asked him to state on the record whether he was a Communist, or a Communist sympathizer, or whether he could be one and client stated emphatically that he was not and could not be.

"Please bear in mind that my client is one of the top radar men in the country with the Signal Corps Laboratories for thirteen years and, like everyone at the Fort doing top-clearance work, has been investigated and re-investigated by the FBI and by military intelligence, and that my man enjoys the full confidence and support of his superiors at the Laboratories, and no question whatever has been raised about his loyalty or any improper conduct on his part."

McCarthy demanded that men who had been previously suspended and investigated turn over to him all their records, including transcripts of testimony before the appeals boards that had reinstated them. He threatened to charge the accused men with contempt and have them indicted by a grand jury if they defied his order. In a letter to McCarthy, Green protested the high-handedness of this procedure. Some of the material McCarthy requested, he pointed out, had been marked "confidential" by the government itself; and so, if the defendants yielded to McCarthy's demands, they would be subjecting themselves to the possibility of indictment on another count—the disclosure of "confidential" information. Furthermore, if they parted with all their records, they would be handicapped in defending themselves the second time around against charges that were largely a repetition of those on which they had once been cleared.

Challenging McCarthy directly in a letter, Green painted a vivid picture of the atmosphere that had been created at Fort Monmouth. He wrote:

"You know of the ordeals that these men and their families went through, on charges which turned out to be trumped-up and false. These men were suspended for about a year and a half. Neither their accusers were named, nor were they confronted by their accusers in violation of every concept of justice or fair play. They had to defend themselves against 'phantoms.' They had to make extensive investigations to try to determine who their accusers were, so as to demonstrate their complete innocence. They and their families were dependent upon relatives and friends for support in the interval. The wife of one of the men has suffered a grave nervous ailment. Their cases came before several Boards, they were found not guilty of any disloyalty or of being a security risk, they were restored to duty with back pay . . .

"You must realize, Senator McCarthy, what a terrible effect this has had upon the states of mind and morale of these men and their families, and their being summoned before your committee. They had been investigated, re-investigated, checked and re-checked by every investigative agency of the Federal Government and of the military service, and it is fair to say that nothing turned up against them, otherwise they never would have been reinstated . . .

"There has been a reign of terror in these wholesale suspensions at Fort Monmouth during the past few years on the flimsiest of charges, wholly uncorroborated and unsubstantiated, gossip and rumor of the wildest character, 'poison pen' letters, reports and statements of disgruntled, jealous, intolerant and bigoted persons; and these suspensions have injured loyal men and women to an extent that shocks all standards of decency and fairness."

McCarthy didn't deign even to acknowledge this letter. Instead, Green got a telephone call from Dan Buckley, one of the investigators on McCarthy's staff. "In a sharp and peremptory tone of voice," Green wrote McCarthy in a second letter, Buckley ordered both Katchen and himself to appear before the committee on Wednesday of the following week with their clients and all the records McCarthy had requested. He warned that the attorneys themselves should be prepared to take the witness stand.

"I asked him," Green wrote, "to be good enough to send a letter to me to this effect, he said that no letter nor anything else was going to be sent to me, and that this was an order from you. I told him he cannot order me about in this fashion and he hung up."

Such conduct, Green protested, was naked "intimidation of a member of the bar who is trying to represent clients in accordance with the best traditions of English-speaking lawyers." Not expecting any reply from McCarthy, Green fired off an indignant protest to Senator Hendrickson in which he denounced McCarthy's subcommittee, not for its ostensible purposes, "but the manner in which it acts, the *in terrorem* atmosphere it creates and the fear that it instills in persons summoned before it. It smacks of Star Chamber and the Inquisitions of old, and what you hear about Behind-the-Iron-Curtain countries . . ."

THE MONMOUTH COUNTY AREA in which Fort Monmouth is located was a hotbed of Ku Klux Klan rallies in the 1920s, the scene of German-American Bund activity in the 1930s. In 1953 it was a fertile territory for McCarthy-inspired hysteria. Though it has become less rural and more cosmopolitan in the postwar growth of suburbia, it retains today a strong John Birchite flavor. In the wartime expansion, employment in Monmouth's laboratories ballooned from 150 to 14,000; and, among the new employees, there was a heavy sprinkling of Jews and Negroes.

Harry Green in his *Law Journal* article had hinted broadly at the underlying bigotry and viciousness that had played a role in spattering the reputations of many of the defendants. The Anti-Defamation League of B'nai B'rith, after an extensive investigation of its own, challenged the Army to examine the files of six hundred employees at Forth Monmouth to determine whether charges against Jews were handled in one fashion and similar charges against gentiles in another. The Army replied, a bit huffily, that it had found no evidence of anti-Semitism in the loyalty program at the fort; but, significantly, it never made the test the Anti-Defamation League had requested.

The league's own investigation showed that about 25 percent of the civilian employees in the Signal Corps complexes were Jewish. One witness told league investigators it was "common knowledge" that "only inferior Christian engineers were working at Fort Monmouth, since the better ones were able to get employment in private industry." Conversely, "since Jewish scientists and engineers of superior ability cannot readily get outside employment, they had to take jobs such as those at Monmouth."

In its forty-four-page brief filed with the Army, the league accused one particular security agent of being a "prime factor" in the suspensions and the losses of security clearances. There was, it said, "sufficient evidence and persuasive hearsay" that this individual "personally is an anti-Semite." The Army, in its reply, said only that its investigation of this agent showed the issue was "by no means clear." This was something less than a rousing affirmation of open-mindedness.

There had been other background indications of racial prejudice and bigotry. When veterans returned from the war, efforts were made to evict some of the Monmouth employees from housing projects on the grounds their incomes exceeded the project limits. These efforts failed. Additional friction was caused when some Monmouth workers fought racial discrimination in schools and businesses; and, when these activities led them to join organizations that some older residents deemed dangerously liberal, there was a further outcry.

This background of prejudice must be understood, for it helped to create the fevered atmosphere in which the charges flung at many of the Fort Monmouth victims were taken seriously. One technician was suspended as a security risk because, among other things, his mother had taken him to meetings of the Young Pioneers of America in 1933 and 1934 when he was twelve and thirteen years old. An electronics engineer was suspended because he "favored the 'leftist' policies of Max Lerner," the New York *Post* columnist, who, far from being radical, seems more often than not to leave an impression of ambivalence about where he stands on critical issues. A physicist was suspended because he had "attempted to transmit" a reprint of a scientific paper to a Czechoslovak professor who had requested it. Shades of the Rosenbergs! But in reality the comparison was ridiculous. In the first place, the scientific paper the Czech wanted was one that had been published and was public property; in the second, the physicist did not try to transmit it secretly but went to his superior and asked what he should do; in the third, the superior had thought it would be a good idea to send the reprint, along with a letter extolling the virtues of American democracy—a bit of propagandizing that had been scotched by a higher authority in calling off the whole transaction.

Now McCarthy and Roy Cohn raised a tremendous hue and cry in the press about "Fifth Amendment Communists." Witnesses who claimed the privilege of the Fifth against possible self-incrimination were convicted out-of-hand in their judgment. This ignored the possibility that taking the Fifth might well indicate not guilt but simple common sense—a protection against an all-too-easy frameup by informers whose dedication to veracity was uncertain. This was the very reason that the Founding Fathers, fearful of the overweening power of autocratic governments using *agents provocateurs,* had considered the Fifth Amendment so essential as a guarantee of the liberties of the individual.

The outcry about "Fifth Amendment Communists" created in the public mind the impression that the Fort Monmouth complex was literally crawling with subversives. Yet nothing could have been further from the truth. The witnesses who did take the Fifth Amendment before McCarthy inquisitors were either those who had been employed at Fort Monmouth in the period from World War II to 1947 when the Rosenbergs were active, or those who had been employed, not by the Signal Corps, but by firms in private industry. The significant fact was that all of the employees who had been suspended in 1953 took the witness stand, swore under oath that they were not communists—and so accepted the threat of perjury prosecutions if they were not telling the truth. In the entire McCarthy inquiry, nothing was adduced to cast even a sustainable suspicion on any employee of the fort after about 1947–48.

The ethics of the inquisitors was best illustrated, perhaps, by a horror story that McCarthy built up whole-cloth from an episode that took place during those private hearings whose significance he was interpreting for the press. On October 17, 1953, *The New York Times* broke out this page-one headline: RADAR WITNESS BREAKS DOWN: WILL TELL ALL ABOUT SPY RING.

The story that followed began:

"An 'important' employee of the Army's Fort Monmouth, N.J., radar laboratories, a close friend of Julius Rosenberg, executed atom spy, broke down yesterday and agreed to tell all he knew about espionage rings."

McCarthy called this a "most important development," immediately placed the witness in "protective custody," and proclaimed that he did so because the witness "is afraid for his own personal safety." Adding the appropriate touch of cloak-and-dagger to the event, McCarthy pleaded with newsmen: "I want to ask a favor. If by chance you learn the identity of the witness, please don't use his name!"

The Senator, on his word of honor, said that the witness had given testimony regarding members of a suspected spy ring. Originally, he said, the radar expert had denied knowing the Rosenbergs, had denied any knowledge of espionage, but "under some rather vigorous cross-examination by Roy Cohn the witness broke down and began to cry." Then he had promised to tell all.

Reporters got a glimpse of this crucial witness as he slumped in a chair in an anteroom, "his face ashen." A doctor and nurse hurried in with stimulants, and under their ministrations, the witness, "shaking with fright," finally revived. McCarthy was in his glory. "The witness," he said, "has indicated a great fear of the spy ring which *is operating within Government agencies, including the Signal Corps.*"

Nothing could be more specific. But a month later there was a quite different story—this time one that did not rate page one. The Asbury Park *Evening Press*, in Asbury Park, N.J., broke this story, and the Associated Press carried it on its national wires. *The New York Times* dealt with this shocker on an inside page in a subdued headline that read: MYSTERY WITNESS DISPUTES M'CARTHY.

The story identified the mystery man as Carl Greenblum, thirty-seven, an electrical engineer, of Wanamassa, N.J., a suburb of Asbury Park. Greenblum denied that he had ever lied, denied he had any knowledge of espionage, insisted he had always been a loyal American, and announced that, though he had been suspended from his job at the Evans Radar Laboratory, he had now been cleared and restored to his former position. What had happened when he was questioned by the McCarthy inquisitors, he said, was this: his mother had died two days previously, then he had been summoned by McCarthy, had been battered by a barrage of questions cross-fired at him by those hard-eyed inquisitors grouped around the table—and it had all become too much for him; he had broken down and cried. He had never been an intimate of Julius Rosenberg, he said. Rosenberg had been in his class at the City College of New York; he had had a nodding acquaintance with Rosenberg and with Morton Sobell, a fringe figure convicted with the Rosenbergs. But that was as far as it had gone. He knew nothing about any espionage ring; he had never promised to "tell all" because he had had nothing to tell.

He was speaking out now, Greenblum said, because he was being harassed in his home town. His German-born wife, Marianne, described these incidents:

"One day we came home and the phone rang. I answered and a woman's voice told me to look on my front door. I did and found a note saying: 'Get out of town, you Nazis.'

"Another day a painting of a hammer and sickle was placed against the back of our house. One other time it involved our 3-year-old son, David.

"He came home and said another boy called him a 'pie.' David can't pronounce 'spy.' The child also told David he couldn't play with him because David had a bad daddy."

After Greenblum defended himself, he was almost instantly suspended from his job for the second time. Major General Kirke B. Lawton, the commandant of Fort Monmouth, a martinet who had made no secret of the fact that he personally went about the post prying into desks after hours to see if anyone was squirreling away secret material, called a "restricted" meeting of several hundred post personnel—and warned them bluntly that anyone caught talking to a reporter would be suspended on the spot. In speeches over the next several months, the general sounded almost like McCarthy himself. According to the Asbury Park *Evening Press,* he linked the spread of the Red menace to certain eminent American universities, naming specifically City College of New York, the Massachusetts Institute of Technology, Columbia and Harvard Universities, and the Universities of Chicago and Minnesota. General Lawton also continued to give a blanket endorsement to Joe McCarthy and his methods. He had been impressed, he said, by McCarthy's "fairness and courtesy" in handling witnesses.

As for that "fair and courteous" man himself, what did he have to say? Confronted with Greenblum's statement, challenged on a point of simple veracity, McCarthy told the press: "I would not want to comment on that."

And that was virtually the last anyone heard of the great, currently functioning espionage ring at Fort Monmouth.

DURING THIS PERIOD of investigations at the Federal Courthouse in New York, there was one episode that had a significance all its own because its sequel proved out in legal terms a supreme irony: everything that McCarthy had done as the chairman of his subcommittee investigating subversion had been flagrantly illegal.

The duties of the Committee on Government Operations had been clearly defined in the Senate resolution creating it. It was empowered to investigate budget and accounting measures, and reorganizations in the executive branch; it could study government operations at all levels in the interest of economy and efficiency; it could examine intergovernmental relationships between the federal, state and municipal governments. But one thing it specifically could *not* do was to probe into subversive activities.

The limitation was explicit in these words: ". . . It is also intended that certain aspects of improper influence in Government shall be investigated, but any inquiries undertaken will in no way *interfere or transgress* those investigations which other Senate and House of Representatives committees may be engaged in making in comparable areas of Government operation, *such as subversive activities.*" (Italics added.)

The issue emerged in an historic court case involving Dr. Corliss Lamont, a Columbia University professor of philosophy and, by avocation, an author. No one would ever question that Corliss Lamont's political beliefs placed him far to the left of William McKinley and Herbert Hoover. During the 1930s Lamont unquestionably had been oversold on the nobility of Stalin's regime in the Soviet Union. And he continued to promote Soviet-American friendship long after the Cold War had made it a myth. His activities had left him wide open to charges of being a "fellow traveler," a "party liner," even "a Communist."

Lamont appeared to be a perfect sitting duck for McCarthy, but like that other professor, Owen Lattimore, he was courageous and obstinate—something of a tartar. McCarthy subpoenaed Lamont to appear before him on September 23, 1953. McCarthy's only excuse for dragging Lamont into the investigation of the Army was that some of Lamont's writings dealing with the Russian scene had been quoted in books purchased for distribution by the federal government. This, McCarthy trumpeted, was "Communist infiltration" for which Lamont was obviously responsible.

The Columbia professor came to the confrontation girded for battle. He was convinced that his beliefs were his own affairs; he was not in government, he held no position of public trust, he had no access to classified information. What he thought and said and wrote, he was entitled to say and think and write under the First Amendment to the Constitution. He meant to take his stand on that vital principle.

He made just one concession to McCarthy. He testified: "To dispose of a question causing current apprehension, I am a loyal American and I am not now and never have been a member of the Communist Party." Beyond this, Lamont would not go, telling the grand inquisitor bluntly that he had no business prying into the political beliefs or private lives of American citizens.

This confrontation took place in executive session, where the testimony was supposed to be secret; but the instant it ended McCarthy called in reporters, expelled Lamont and his counsel,

Philip Wittenberg, and gave the press his own one-sided version of what had taken place.

Now came an incident that cast a telling light on McCarthy's complete lack of scruples. At the close of the executive session, Lamont had agreed to identify some of his writings and the quotations culled from them by others. McCarthy had ordered Lamont and Wittenberg to appear before him again in Washington the following Monday at 1 P.M. "Incidentally, 1 o'clock means 1 o'clock, not 1:30, because I'm going to be tied up all afternoon," McCarthy had snapped in his usual intimidating fashion.

On Friday Wittenberg received a telephone call from a member of McCarthy's staff, informing him that Lamont's appearance had been postponed and that he would be notified later when to appear. With a lawyer's caution, Wittenberg refused to accept this telephonic notification as valid and said Lamont certainly would appear on Monday unless notified in writing to the contrary. Shortly thereafter, Wittenberg received this telegram from McCarthy: "Lamont's appearance before the subcommittee in Washington on Monday September 28, 1953 postponed. Mr. Lamont is continued under subpoena however and you will be notified when his presence is required." Lamont received a similar telegram, bearing the name of Senator McCarthy as its author.

As a result, Lamont and Wittenberg were not present when McCarthy called his hearing to order in Washington on Monday, September 28. "Mr. Lamont has not been subpoenaed," McCarthy said in his most unctuous manner. "He was notified that he could come here today and purge himself of the contempt of failure to answer last week. Is Mr. Lamont here?"

Naturally, Mr. Lamont wasn't there—and McCarthy then proceeded to move fast. He made public the minutes of the executive session the week before and recommended the Senate cite Lamont for contempt.

In the ensuing Senate debate, what was most notable, as always, was the paucity of men with courage. Only Herbert Lehman, William Langer of North Dakota, and Dennis Chavez of New Mexico argued that the Senate should postpone action at least until it had taken a close look at the Constitutional issues involved. Ironically, Wayne Morse, the great libertarian, led the fight to shut off all debate, to cite Lamont immediately for contempt and to let the courts handle it. By an overwhelming 71–3 vote, the Senate did just that. And Lamont automatically was indicted.

Philip Wittenberg now challenged the legality of the indictment in New York Federal Court. But he based his challenge, not just on Corliss Lamont's cherished First Amendment grounds, but on the proposition that McCarthy had had no authority to conduct his one-man subversion probes, and hence that virtually everything he had done had been illegal. Judge Edward Weinfeld later upheld this contention, ruling on July 27, 1955, that the indictments against Lamont and two other similar defendants should be dismissed for this cause alone. "This disposition makes it unnecessary to determine," he wrote, "the constitutional and other issues so vigorously pressed for disposition by the defendants."

The Justice Department fought the case to the Court of Appeals—and again lost. On August 14, 1956, the three-man appeals tribunal upheld Judge Weinfeld. It chided the government for "attempting to hang onto and retain for trial indictments for offenses which cannot be supported in law," and it held McCarthy's committee had been acting in a field in which it had absolutely no authorization. The vital First Amendment issue, which Lamont had hoped would be resoundingly affirmed, was left in limbo; but at least, after three long and harrowing years of legal battles, the courts had administered a decisive verdict on the inquisitorial excesses of McCarthy.*

.   .   .

* This fatal legal flaw in the McCarthy caper was first dragged out into the light of day during the Army-McCarthy hearings in 1954. During his cross-examination of McCarthy, Joseph Welch asked by what authority McCarthy had held his far-flung one-man hearings into communism and subversion. Had he been empowered to do so by the Senate? No. Had his own full Government Operations Committee passed a resolution granting him the right? No. Perhaps the first person to realize the significance of McCarthy's admissions was Jesse Gordon, public relations man for *The Nation,* who was also doing some work for Lamont. Reading the transcript of McCarthy's testimony in *The New York Times* one day during the Army-McCarthy hearings, he came across the admission by McCarthy that he had never bothered to obtain proper authorization for the activities of his investigative subcommittee. "I said to myself, 'That's it!' Gordon recalls, and he sat down and wrote a letter to Lamont. It was a discovery that changed the whole course of the legal battle, much to Lamont's own disgust, for the professor had wanted to fight the issue on First Amendment grounds, had hoped to get a ringing reaffirmation of First Amendment guarantees from the courts—and had been prepared to go to prison if he did not.

ONE OF THE MOST AMAZING ASPECTS of the entire Fort Monmouth episode was that McCarthy's charges were flatly disputed by high officials of the federal establishment.

The challenge was posed directly by Secretary of the Army Stevens himself. In a press conference on November 13, 1953, Stevens announced that the most rigorous investigation by the Army's G-2 intelligence unit had failed to produce any evidence of current espionage at Fort Monmouth. "I think there was espionage there in the days of Rosenberg," Secretary Stevens said, but he declared flatly that the Army had been "unable to find anything relating to espionage" since that time.

McCarthy and Roy Cohn, however, continued to rant about the horrors they were going to prove. Senator Allen J. Ellender (D., La.) challenged McCarthy on the floor of the Senate on February 2, 1954. Ellender wanted to know whether McCarthy was rehashing old cases, whether he had anything new, and McCarthy replied:

"I may say to the able Senator from Louisiana that I am not only of the opinion that there was espionage at Fort Monmouth but I know there was espionage at Fort Monmouth. We have sworn testimony to that effect from witness after witness."

Asked whether he was talking about espionage that had taken place ten years or twenty years previously, McCarthy insisted that he was talking about *current espionage.**

Roy Cohn was equally explicit. Shortly after Secretary Stevens had made his no-espionage pronouncement, Cohn and liberal lawyer Joseph Rauh tangled in a radio debate on the National Broadcasting Company's *American Forum of the Air.* Rauh declared bluntly that the whole Fort Monmouth investigation was "a hoax on the public." Cohn countered with the

---

* Despite McCarthy's emphatic assertions that there was current espionage at Fort Monmouth, he had begun as early as December 15, 1953 to shift his ground to a stance where proof would not be expected of him. He said at a hearing in New York at that time that his purpose was to expose "potential espionage"—a broad term that might or might not include the deed; that his role was to alert security officers to the danger, not to "take over the job of the Justice Department and prove espionage cases beyond a reasonable doubt." As in the Tydings inquiry, McCarthy shifted the burden of proving his sensational charges onto the shoulders of someone else. His committee investigation, he said, was building up a list of persons who might be cited and jailed for contempt, but that was the most anyone should expect from him—and that, indeed, was all that his committee ever did achieve.

declaration that public hearings "will bear out everything Senator McCarthy has said." And he added ominously: "Wait until Tuesday."

Rauh sneered at Cohn's threat: "Senator McCarthy held hearings at Fort Monmouth for weeks. He charged espionage at press conferences twice a day . . . I predict that they will have nothing on Tuesday to support their hoax."

Rauh chuckles today when he recalls this exchange and its aftermath. The reaction he encountered was a vivid example of the panic of the times.

"When I came back to Washington," he says, "I found that my friends were appalled. They called me up and told me that was the stupidest thing I had ever done, to stick my neck out like that. 'How can you be sure that they won't find a Communist by Tuesday?' they asked. . . .

"Well, my position was: How could you answer the kind of tactics McCarthy and Cohn were using unless you called their bluff and took a chance? How could anyone know what they might produce by Tuesday? Fighting McCarthy was always a gamble, but that was the only way you could fight him. He was a gambler—and you had to be willing to gamble, too. The trouble was most people weren't gamblers; they weren't willing to risk their own hides.

"I'll never forget it. I waited for Tuesday to see what they would produce. I waited until after midnight, and then I walked down and got the first edition of Wednesday's Washington *Post* and went through it—and found nothing, of course."

Events were to show that Rauh had gambled correctly in ridiculing Cohn's "Wait until Tuesday" threat, for the world is still waiting. On June 8, 1969, the current commandant of Fort Monmouth, Major General William B. Latta, in a long interview with the Asbury Park *Sunday Press*, was asked specifically what had become of the charges made during the McCarthy era. He replied:

"It's unfortunate that many people construe 'publicity about' something to mean it must be true. It's a fact that seven employees of Fort Monmouth were dismissed as security risks [a far broader label than espionage] in 1954. But the record shows that the matter was appealed through higher echelon channels and *all were reinstated eventually.* Thus those investigations established *no security risks.*" (Italics added.)

Not even with the help of a security system in which the government did not have to prove guilt but had to establish only a doubt, a suspicion, had the McCarthy inquisition been able to establish *anything.* Fort Monmouth, far from producing a flourishing spy ring or a nest of communists, in the end could not even produce a security risk!

20

The Inevitable Showdown

M C C A R T H Y   S A I L E D   I N T O   1 9 5 4 with no premonition that disaster lay a scant four months ahead. He had survived, apparently unscathed, a whole series of exposures, any one of which might have been expected to destroy a politician less adept at the manipulation of the press and public opinion. There had been the collapse of the Wheeling charges, the unconscionable Voice of America probe, the ridiculous European escapades of Cohn and Schine, the shame of the book purges, the fiasco of J. B. Matthews, the Fort Monmouth charges that had produced absolutely nothing. Yet none of this seemed to have slowed McCarthy down by so much as half a stride. His visceral appeal to a great portion of the public remained unimpaired; he was still considered a potent factor at the polls; and the Republican Administration in Washington—those knights of the great crusade who had taken office to bring shining purity back to national government—seemed most concerned about how to employ the talents of the scalper from Wisconsin, and least concerned about the damage he was doing.

In this vacuum of ethics and courage, McCarthy became carried away with the image of his own omnipotence: he delivered what was virtually an ultimatum to his own party. In a radio and television speech on November 24, 1953, he treated the Eisenhower Administration almost as rudely as he had previously treated Truman's. He castigated the State Department of John Foster Dulles for not having dismissed John Paton Davies, Jr., an old China hand, and for sending "perfumed notes" to foreign chancelleries in "the style of the Truman-Acheson regime." He also laid down the battle line for the coming 1954, midterm Congressional elections. These battles must be fought out, as he saw it, on one basic issue—the necessity of retaining Republican control of Congress so that he, Joe McCarthy, could keep his seat of power in control of his investigating committee, unhampered in his mission of ferreting out communists.

The speech was taken by many as a clear warning that the Republican Party must be remade, not in the decent image of Eisenhower, but in the demagogic mold of McCarthy. Arthur Krock, of *The New York Times*, reported that the speech "angered" the President and all his aides, "alarmed most of them and forced them nearer to their inevitable battle with him [McCarthy] for the mind and spirit of the Republican Party." It was a most perceptive analysis, but there were not yet any signs, either in the White House or in Congress, of a willingness to do battle.

The White House forces were split into two opposing camps: those who felt that McCarthy was a disgrace and that Ike would have to take him on, and those who still wanted to appease him so that they could use him. The feelings of the first group were reflected in a letter that C. D. Jackson, the former *Time* executive, wrote to Sherman Adams, Eisenhower's deputy in the White House. Boiling with indignation over McCarthy's November 24 speech, Jackson wrote:

"I hope this flagrant performance will open the eyes of some of the President's advisers who seem to think that the Senator is really a good fellow at heart. They remind me of the people who kept saying for so many months that Mao Tse-tung was just an agrarian reformer . . ."

This, as Adams later wrote, was "a barbed criticism of the attitude of a few members of the President's official household who maintained friendly relations with McCarthy in an earnest effort to avoid a complete blow-up between the Senator and the White House. The principal protagonist in this behind-the-scenes drama was Richard Nixon."

Nixon had risen to fame and power through his own exploitation of the communist menace, and he was in many respects a kindred spirit—"McCarthy with a white collar," as Adlai Stevenson once called him. From the earliest post-Wheeling days, there had been contact between McCarthy and Nixon, and Nixon had loaned McCarthy some of his files in the effort to help him substantiate some of his charges before the Tydings committee. At the same time, Nixon had warned McCarthy about the danger of irresponsible attacks. Don't be specific about the number of card-carrying Communists in the State Department, he had advised, because this can't be proved, but concentrate on persons with "Communist-front affiliations and associations" because "this you can prove."

McCarthy, of course, had not accepted this counsel of restraint; he had gone his own irresponsible way. Nevertheless, he and Nixon remained friendly, and Nixon throughout the early Eisenhower years was the mediator, the man who strove hardest to prevent a complete rupture with the White House. His motives were purely political, and there is no sign that he ever considered the evil that McCarthy represented or the harm that he was doing to the mind and soul of the nation. Nixon's attitude has been described by his official biographer, Earl Mazo, in this passage:

"As the one most responsible for the first effective anti-Communist investigation, Nixon was not particularly awed, from a personal standpoint, by McCarthy's power. But he was anxious that the party benefit however it could from the Senator's influence with bloc-voting Democrats and extreme Republicans. Nixon also felt that an affront to McCarthy would split the Republican Party. From the start Nixon was sympathetic to McCarthy's zeal in fighting Communists. He saw such vigor and enthusiasm as a decided long-term asset, if sensibly channeled. The Vice President told me he never shared the belief of some of the Eisenhower Administration that 'Communism to McCarthy was a racket.' Nixon felt that the Senator 'believed what he was doing very deeply.'"

So motivated, Nixon made one final effort to keep the McCarthy hatchet from cleaving Republican craniums. He and Deputy Attorney General Rogers were spending the Christmas season of 1953 in Key Biscayne, Florida. McCarthy arrived on December 30, 1953, for a conference. Mazo quoted Nixon as telling McCarthy:

"Don't pull your punches at all on Communists in government. It doesn't make any difference if they are in this administration or in previous ones, if they are there, they should be out. On the other hand, remember that this is your administration. That the people in this administration, including Bob Stevens, are just as dedicated as you are to cleaning out people who are subversive. Give them a chance to do the job."

Coupled with this "give them a chance" plea was the suggestion that McCarthy should shift his focus and place major emphasis on the pursuit of corruption, mismanagement, inefficiency and favoritism in government. If he would do this, the Administration promised to dig out all the old files of the Truman era and turn over to him whatever rich material could be found on which he could feast. McCarthy seemed amenable. In fact, while he was still in Florida, he told newsmen his committee was going to "broaden" its investigative field by inquiring into tax cases that had been settled by the previous Administration "at ridiculously low figures."

Evidently assuming that a pact was a pact, Nixon subsequently leaked the details of the McCarthy truce to the press. The implication was that McCarthy was now going to become more of a statesman, less of a redbaiter, and that the principal "commie-hunting" would be done by the Senate Internal Security Committee headed by Senator Jenner. When he read this, McCarthy blew his cool. Pact or no pact, he simply could not bear the thought of abandoning the rich field that had put his name in headlines.

"It's a lie," he shouted, according to Mazo, undeterred by the fact that the man he was accusing of lying was the Vice President of the United States.

N O W   M C   C A R T H Y   Z I G Z A G G E D to his last great triumph. Despite the fact that he had repudiated the "pact" of Key Biscayne, despite the fact that he had in effect called Nixon a liar, he now did a swift about-face. The raucous, intemperate demagogue was suddenly replaced with the soft-talking, reasonable junior Senator from Wisconsin. The motivation for this sudden switch was obvious: McCarthy needed funds to finance the work of his committee—and only the Senate could grant him those funds. He was, therefore, in a bind. He could not afford to offend both the Democrats and the representatives of his own Administration; it was a time to walk softly and hide the big stick.

In this exigency, his first move was to placate the Democrats who had walked off his committee in 1953 and stayed off. He obliged them with a mock surrender. He agreed to abandon his contention that he alone could hire and fire the staff; personnel would be picked in the future by a majority vote of his committee. Since his Republican cohorts controlled the committee, this concession was relatively meaningless, but it mollified the Democrats who seemed to think they had gained something. Senators McClellan, Symington and Jackson announced they were rejoining the committee.

Having protected this flank, having emphasized to his own party how vital his services would be in the upcoming 1954 campaign, he next sought funds. He began by calling loudly for a hefty increase in his appropriation; and, having panicked everyone with the exorbitant nature of his demands, he suddenly switched to his sunny and reasonable self and agreed that he could perhaps get along on the same $214,000 allowance his committee had been granted the previous year. Here was the crucial issue—the vote that could end it all. Did the Senate have the courage and the conscience to act?

The matter came to a vote on February 2, 1954. For three hours, Senators Ellender and McCarthy bandied back and forth the issue of what McCarthy had shown, what evidence he had. It was in this debate that McCarthy insisted he had evidence of "very, very current espionage" at Fort Monmouth, and he went on to claim that these hearings would "prove the most productive we ever held from the standpoint of decimating the ranks of the Communist Party."

"The party is going to bleed very heavily," he predicted. "We will send its leaders to jail, not for technical convictions for espionage, but for contempt of this committee."

Did Senator Ellender, he wondered suavely, oppose ferreting out communists? The suggestion naturally shocked the Senator from Louisiana; and, by his response, he painted himself into a corner—Joe McCarthy's corner.

He murmured weakly that he was just as opposed to communists as McCarthy, but he thought the Federal Bureau of Investigation was the agency to investigate and contain them. McCarthy, of course, always proclaimed his fealty to J. Edgar Hoover and the FBI, but his contention was that his committee could do things the FBI could not do. In the end, Ellender was beaten into full retreat. He even said he would "acknowledge" there had been laxity under "the past administration" (the Democratic Administration of his own party) and that he would concede McCarthy had "done a lot of good in dramatizing the Communist issue before the country."

After that, there was no hole left in which a Democrat could hide. When the vote was taken, McCarthy got his funds by a lopsided margin of 85 to 1. The lone dissenter was the Senator from Arkansas—J. William Fulbright.

Having won a virtually unanimous vote of confidence, McCarthy's ego propelled him to heights of vilification which even he had never attained before. He began to trumpet in speeches up and down the country that the Roosevelt and Truman Administrations represented "twenty years of treason"; and in the same week in which he had won the backing of every Senator except Fulbright, he returned to the scene of his first great triumph—West Virginia. There, in a speech in Charleston, he labeled every Democrat a traitor to his country.

"The hard fact," he cried, "is that those who wear the label —Democrat—wear with it the stain of an historic betrayal."

The very term "Democrat," he said, was "a political label stitched with the idiocy of a Truman, rotted by the deceit of an Acheson, corrupted by the red slime of a [Harry Dexter] White." Other political leaders in the nation, he assured his audience, felt just as strongly about this as he did, but they thought it was not "gentlemanly" to talk this way; they just didn't have the raw guts.

The performance in Charleston was only the first in a series of eight cross-country Lincoln Day speeches arranged for Senator McCarthy by a Republican National Committee intent on wringing the last drop of political advantage out of his intemperate accusations. And intemperate they were. Everywhere McCarthy went he spoke on the theme of "twenty years of treason," and everywhere his language was characterized by the same kind of indiscriminate vilification he had used at Charleston. This was the culmination, the frank and open expression, of the ideological propaganda campaign that dated back nearly twenty years to the Committee for Constitutional Government.

ALL DURING THIS PERIOD of committee hearings, Senatorial debates and Lincoln Day speeches, Private G. David Schine —away from the public eye—had been on his tour of basic training at Fort Dix, New Jersey. But this was no ordinary private.

The first faint hint of the brewing upheaval crept into the press on January 30, 1954, just three days before McCarthy won his vote of confidence in the Senate. On that day, *The New York Times* reported that the Army had begun to investigate complaints that Schine had received incredibly favorable treatment during his indoctrination into service at Fort Dix. Fellow recruits in Company K of the Forty-Seventh Infantry Regiment had complained that Schine had gotten weekends and holidays off when they couldn't; that he had suffered only one brief period of KP; that he had skipped guard duty and target practice; and he had chatted familiarly with officers, as no other recruit would dare to do, trading on his connection with the McCarthy committee and pretending that he was on an official mission to check up on morale at the base. Inspector General James J. Fogarty had started questioning Private Schine's fellow recruits in Company K on these charges, the Army said.

Interestingly, it was just at this time that McCarthy embarked on an unremitting campaign against the Army. He wanted its loyalty-security files; he was demanding the right to grill members of its loyalty board; he was summoning servicemen, one after another, for questioning. It would be fruitless to recall the many officers he badgered and harassed, for in the end only one case really mattered. At Camp Kilmer, N.J., just outside New Brunswick, McCarthy finally and triumphantly discovered an officer who apparently was a communist. He was Irving Peress—a dentist.

Peress, who lived in New York City, had been inducted into service on October 15, 1952, under the doctors' draft law, and he had been commissioned a captain, as the regulations provided. In filling out his personal-history and loyalty forms, Peress invoked the Fifth Amendment to questions about possible subversive activities and affiliations. This, in the lexicon of the day, automatically stigmatized him as a "Fifth Amendment Communist." In the paper flood inundating the Pentagon, this tell-tale stain went undetected for months. It was not until sometime in February, 1953, that the Army began an investigation. This was finished in early July, and the report to First Army Headquarters in New York recommended that Peress be separated from the service.

What happened next gave McCarthy the opportunity to raise a sensational storm about the Peress case. On October 23, 1953, while the Army was still debating what to do, Peress was promoted to major along with 7,000 other doctors and dentists whose promotions had been made mandatory by an amendment to the doctors' draft law calling for a general readjustment of grades based on civilian medical experience.

Sometime in December, 1953, the Army's personnel board decided that it should by all means get rid of Irving Peress. But how was this deed to be accomplished? The Army could court-martial Peress. But for what? He had not committed perjury; from the first, he had openly claimed his Constitutional privilege. He had not violated orders; he had given the Army no opening on which to attack him. The court-martial procedure (especially since the Army had tried and lost a similar case) therefore seemed inapplicable. Alternatively, the Army might give Peress a dishonorable discharge; but, if he fought such an action, as he well might, he could tie the Army up in legal actions for at least a year—and he might win in the end. The only other alternative, especially if Irving Peress were to be gotten rid of quickly, was to give him an honorable discharge. This was the course the Army elected to follow.

It did not, however, move swiftly enough. McCarthy had been tipped off (the speculation was that he learned of the Peress case from a leak of testimony the Army itself had given another Congressional committee in secret) to the possibilities of the Peress case, and he summoned Peress to appear before him in New York on January 30, 1954. Peress invoked the Fifth Amendment, declining to answer thirty-two questions about communist affiliations. The following day, Peress applied to Camp Kilmer for immediate discharge, and McCarthy fired off a letter to the Pentagon, demanding that it hold and court-martial Peress. There was now a race against time. McCarthy's letter evidently lagged behind the urgent suggestion from Kilmer that the Army rid itself as quickly as possible of Major Peress. The Pentagon acted on the suggestion. On February 2, it gave Major Peress an honorable discharge—and Senator McCarthy the headline sensation he had been so avidly seeking.

"Who promoted Peress?" McCarthy screamed.

He repeated the question over and over—and set out to get the answer.

IT WAS THURSDAY, February 18, 1954. The scene: a closed hearing in New York. The inquisitors: Joe McCarthy and Roy Cohn. The witness: Brigadier General Ralph W. Zwicker, the commandant of Camp Kilmer, New Jersey.

General Zwicker, a graduate of West Point, was a much-decorated hero of World War II. Unlike McCarthy, he had not spent his time shooting up coconut trees, but he had led a special reconnaissance unit ashore during the early hours of the D-day landings in Normandy; and afterward had commanded the 38th Regiment of the Second Infantry Division in the Battle of the Bulge. His decorations included the Silver Star, the Legion of Merit with Oak Leaf Cluster and the French Legion of Honor and Croix de Guerre with Palm.

The general was a man in the middle. He, personally, had had nothing to do with the Peress case except to follow the directions of his superiors. The investigation had been handled by Army specialists even before he had been assigned to the command of Camp Kilmer; the issues posed by Major Peress had been weighed in the higher echelons of the Pentagon beyond his ken; the orders to give the controversial dentist his honorable discharge had come down to him through First Army Headquarters in New York. General Zwicker had merely done what he had been ordered to do; and, under Army regulations, he was not even permitted to discuss security matters—he could be cashiered from the service if he did.

All of this meant nothing to McCarthy. He was only interested in getting the answers to two questions: Who had promoted Peress? Who had given him an honorable discharge? He had before him a sitting duck in uniform. The question-and-answer sequence released later by McCarthy himself—as if it were something of which to be proud—revealed that General Zwicker was subjected to a hectoring, humiliating inquisition.

McCarthy tried to hang the general from his inquisitorial yardarm by propounding a ridiculous analogy. Would the general have given an honorable discharge to a soldier if he had been informed at the last minute that the soldier had stolen fifty dollars? Would he give such a man an honorable discharge as he had Major Peress who "was a part of the Communist conspiracy"?

The whole basis of the proposition was, of course, false. The issue of a fifty-dollar theft was something that could be left to the discretion and authority of a post commandant; investigations of communist ties were handled by Army specialists on a higher level. Zwicker tried to explain this, tried to point out that he had only been following orders handed down to him. McCarthy cut him short roughly: "Don't you give me that double-talk."

Zwicker insisted: "I had no authority to retain him [Peress] in the service." And again: "I was never officially informed by anyone that he was a part of the Communist conspiracy, Mr. Senator."

Brushing all such explanations aside, McCarthy harped upon his hypothetical theft.

Question: Would you tell us, general, why fifty dollars is so much more important to you than being part of the conspiracy to destroy a nation which you are sworn to defend?

Answer: Mr. Chairman, it is not, and you know that as well as I do.

McCarthy agreed he did indeed know this. "That is why I cannot understand you sitting there, general, a general in the

Army, and telling me that you could not, would not, hold up his discharge . . ."

Boring in, grilling his victim ruthlessly, McCarthy demanded that Zwicker tell him whether he thought that a hypothetical general—one who had acted just as Zwicker acted in the Peress case—"should be removed from the military." Zwicker answered: "He should by all means be kept if he were acting under competent orders to separate that man."

McCarthy persisted in misunderstanding. He persisted in holding Zwicker himself responsible—as if he were the authority itself, the man who "originated the order directing the separation." Should such a general be kept in service? Zwicker protested that this was a hypothetical question in the first place and that, in the second, it would not be for him to decide but for the Army higher command to decide. McCarthy demanded Zwicker's personal opionion.

"You are ordered to answer, general . . . You will answer that question unless you take the Fifth Amendment. I do not care how long we stay here. You are going to answer it."

Answer: Do you mean how I feel about communists?

Question: I mean exactly what I asked you, general, nothing else. And anyone with the brains of a five-year-old child can understand that question . . .

The image of this hypothetical child untangling the tortured syntax of McCarthy's hypothetical question added the final touch of absurdity. The badgering continued. Finally Zwicker said that he thought that the general in McCarthy's hypothetical question —a mythical figure whose actions were not at all comparable to Zwicker's and whose assumed conduct indeed had no relation to the reality of security investigations—should not be "removed from the military."

"Then, general," McCarthy thundered, soaring to the denunciatory heights he so relished, "you should be removed from any command. Any man who has been given the honor of being promoted to general and who says, 'I will protect another general who protected Communists,' [something, of course, that Zwicker had not said at all] is not fit to wear that uniform, general. I think it is a tremendous disgrace to the Army to have this sort of thing given to the public. I intend to give it to them. I have a duty to do that . . . You will be back here, general."

This branding of an honorable and heroic general as "unfit to wear the uniform" was so outrageous it was not to be borne. Combined with the still-obscured saga of Private Schine, it was now to detonate an explosion on the political scene.

ROBERT STEVENS, Eisenhower's honorable and fair-minded Secretary of the Army, was enraged. His early training in his family's textile business had not prepared him for the intrigues and jungle warfare that are trademarks of Washington official life. But Bob Stevens knew one thing: that the man at the top must accept responsibility, that he must stand up for his subordinates when they have been unjustly attacked.

What especially incensed Stevens was that he had done this at the very outset. He had been in Europe when the Peress storm broke, but as soon as he returned to Washington, he had looked thoroughly into the case. He had acknowledged in a letter to McCarthy that the case had uncovered defects in the Army's procedures; he had promised vigorous action if further investigation disclosed anything irregular about the promotion and discharge; he had pledged to revamp the handling of such cases to see that the same thing did not happen again. But he had said there had been no grounds, so far as he could see, for the court-martial of Peress. McCarthy had stormed that the letter was "double-talk" and had plunged ahead to harass General Zwicker.

Immediately after the Zwicker hearing, Stevens obtained an affidavit from the general about the treatment to which he had been subjected, and on February 21, the Secretary threw down the gage of battle to McCarthy. He said in a press statement that he had "ordered" General Zwicker not to appear for a scheduled second session with McCarthy in New York the following Tuesday. "I cannot permit loyal officers of our armed forces to be subjected to such unwarranted treatment," Stevens said. "The prestige and morale of our armed forces are too important to the security of the Nation to have them weakened by unfair attacks upon our officer corps." If McCarthy insisted upon pursuing the matter, the Secretary said, he would take the witness stand and testify himself, and he demanded that the hearing be in public.

Roy Cohn answered for McCarthy. "The favorable action in the case of this Fifth Amendment Communist," he said, referring to Peress, "was stupidity at best and treason at worst. Those who committed it are now being shielded by order of the Secretary of the Army." This official protector of stupidity or treason would certainly be summoned to testify at a public hearing in Washington, Cohn promised.

Washington's Birthday now intervened. In memory of the Father of His Country, McCarthy, speaking in Philadelphia at a Sons of the American Revolution luncheon, read selected portions of the Zwicker transcript as a part of his speech and marveled at his own generosity and forbearance. "As I look it over today," he said, "I was too temperate. If I were doing it today I would be much stronger in my language."

Secretary Stevens and Senator Karl Mundt were flying to Valley Forge where both were to receive awards from the right-wing Freedom Foundation. Stevens gave Mundt a ride in his Army plane, and all the time they were airborne Mundt kept trying to convince Stevens that he was making a bad mistake in brawling with Joe McCarthy. Mundt asked Stevens whether he had read the Zwicker transcript; Stevens said he hadn't because he hadn't yet been able to get a copy from McCarthy. Mundt said he better read it; he might be surprised. After this effort at shaking the Secretary's confidence, Mundt raised what he considered an even more fundamental question—the Senate's prerogatives. He pointed out to Stevens that he was, in essence, putting the Army on a special plane, immune from the legislative branch of the government, if he persisted in his ruling that his officers were not to testify before Senate committees. "Bob, it's a most unfortunate issue," Mundt warned solemnly. "Joe's worst enemies would support him on this one. I think that would lick you hopelessly."

The softening-up process that was eventually to rob Stevens of all dignity had begun, but the Secretary was still bull-dog determined. In his Valley Forge speech, he said bluntly: "I intend to accept responsibility . . . pleasant or unpleasant. I intend to support the loyal men and women of our Army."

The speech earned Stevens the sobriquet of "Fighting Bob," but already knives were being sharpened for his back.

What mattered most to the great crusaders who had come to Washington was that an all-out confrontation must be avoided. They were hagridden by the fear that an internecine quarrel would have two disastrous effects: it would tear the party apart, causing it to lose the 1954 Congressional elections; and, if the Eisenhower wing were to survive, the party almost certainly would lose the services of its most valuable demagogue. Weighed against these all-important considerations, the traducing of an honorable Army officer was inconsequential.

Nobody was more wedded to that creed than Vice President Nixon. Horrified at the thought of the damage that might be done to the party, he called a conference in his Capitol hideaway. He summoned Senate Republican Leader William Knowland, a Californian of rightist persuasion; Senator Dirksen; Army lawyer John G. Adams, whom McCarthy had evicted from the Zwicker hearing when Adams tried to protect the general; Stevens himself; Deputy Attorney General Rogers; and two White House aides. Adams and Stevens were isolated in the party pressure-cooker, and the hand of the White House itself must have seemed evident to them in Nixon's handling of the affair. Though Stevens stoutly maintained his position, others at the conference banded together to impress these points upon him: the Army had a bad record in the Peress case; McCarthy could blunt the effect of his browbeating of General Zwicker by shifting his emphasis to Peress; a public free-for-all could only harm everybody; and an effort should be made to get together with McCarthy, have him call off his public showdown with Stevens, and then have his committee draft a new set of rules governing the conduct of his one-man show. Overborne, Stevens agreed to try the recommended remedy.

Dirksen and Mundt next went to work on McCarthy in Mundt's office. McCarthy was obdurate at first, but the mellifluous and persuasive Dirksen pointed out to him that he had nothing to lose by agreeing to talk with Stevens. On the other hand, just possibly, there might be much to gain. McCarthy agreed to a luncheon date with Stevens on February 24.

The Army Secretary, shortly after noon on that day, broke off a briefing session with his aides; and, without telling them what he was about to do, went with Senator Mundt to the

Capitol's Room P-54. Sherman Adams was later to write that Adams had been assured this would be "a secret affair," but when he arrived, he found "a crowd of a hundred reporters milling around the corridor in front of Dirksen's office waiting for him." This was the living proof that Stevens had been double-crossed from the start; and, when he walked on into the luncheon conference, he was described by one Washington wag as looking "like a goldfish in a tank of barracudas."

The menu, appropriately, featured fried chicken. Nixon himself was not at the repast, but he had been its instigator, and from his nearby office, he kept in close touch with developments. Present in addition to Dirksen and McCarthy were the other Republican members of McCarthy's committee, Mundt and Potter. The famous "fried chicken" luncheon lasted for more than two hours. At the outset, it found Stevens and McCarthy in bitter confrontation. "I'm not going to have my officers browbeaten," Stevens told McCarthy. And McCarthy snapped back: "I'm not going to sit there and see a supercilious bastard sit there and smirk."

Mundt elected himself the mediator. "Joe," he said, "you're not dealing with Dean Acheson any longer. Let's look to the future."

The "future" meant, of course, the political future, not the nation's future. This reminder that all good Republicans must stick together lest the Democrats squirm their way back into Washington gradually turned the tide. The Senatorial cabal ganged up on Stevens; and Stevens, feeling perhaps mistakenly that this party pressure had the blessing of the White House behind it, finally yielded. Mundt drew up a typewriter and happily pecked out a document he called a "Memorandum of Understanding." It had four points: "Communists must be rooted out"; Stevens would make "everyone involved" in the Peress case available for McCarthy's questioning; Zwicker's reappearance before McCarthy would be postponed; and Stevens' appearance before McCarthy was "canceled."

There had been, Stevens afterward insisted, a further and explicit understanding that Army officers called before McCarthy's committee would never again be subjected to the "Zwicker treatment"; that they would be questioned fairly. However, there was no mention of this understanding in the "Memorandum of Understanding" that was read to the press by Mundt with Stevens standing, poker-faced, beside him and McCarthy on the other side grinning contentedly, with his left fist clenched in a half-raised arm in a hooray-for-me gesture.

The Army Secretary, threading his way out of the crush of newsmen and photographers, returned to his office and told his aides he had won the round; he had obtained all he wanted—a guarantee of free treatment for his officers. There were congratulations all around. The euphoria lasted only as long as it took for newspapers to begin hitting the street. New York was typical. STEVENS BOWS TO MC CARTHY, *The Daily News* proclaimed. "Stevens' Surrender Rocks GOP; Adlai Hits 'Betrayal' of Zwicker," said the New York *Post*. "Stevens Case Stuns Capital; Pentagon Bitter and Gloomy," *The New York Times* reported. The headline verbs were SURRENDERS, CAPITULATES, RETREATS. At first, the Secretary was furious at what he considered distortions of the press, but then he read that McCarthy had told a newsman Stevens could not have caved in "more abjectly if he had got down on his knees."

With that, even the Secretary realized that his situation had become virtually untenable. Army brass stopped calling him "Fighting Bob" and substituted "Retreating Robert." Embittered wisecracks made the rounds of Washington. A typical one: "Private Schine is the only man in the Army today with any morale." Sensing the changed atmosphere, a humiliated Stevens began to telephone Senators, insisting there had been an important additional agreement; that his "surrender" was not as abject as McCarthy had portrayed it. Some of those whom he called told newsmen he was sobbing on the phone and saying he would have to resign because he had "lost standing" at the Pentagon.

Now the slumbering White House of Dwight Eisenhower roused itself and tried to repair the damage. Joseph and Stewart Alsop wrote that, on the morning after the fried chicken luncheon, "the atmosphere suggests Berlin after the Reichstag fire, with Stevens in the role of Van der Lubbe, the dullwitted Dutchman who committed the arson; with Eisenhower as the aging Hindenburg and with Hitler played by you-know-who." Eisenhower, the Alsops wrote, had been prepared to back Stevens all the way, but he had been undercut by the appeasers on his own staff; and Stevens, sworn to secrecy about the luncheon in advance, had gone to meet "three of the toughest characters on Capitol Hill" unaware of the President's real attitude.

Horror-stricken at the havoc that had been caused and at the prospect of McCarthy's destroying the morale of the Army as he had that of the Foreign Service, the White House mapped a counterattack. At Nixon's suggestion, it was said, Senator Dirksen was called in to see if he could be persuaded to use his talents to undo what he had just helped to do. The White House gave Dirksen a rough draft of the kind of statement it would like the Senatorial cabal to issue. This contained three points: an admission by McCarthy that he had abused Zwicker; a statement that assurances had been given Stevens of McCarthy's future good conduct; a hint that calling Army officers in the Peress case might not be necessary. "I'd like to see if you can do this," the President told Dirksen. Dirksen promised to try.

An all-day huddle on the Hill proved fruitless. McCarthy, having won all his points in the "Memorandum of Understanding," laughed at the idea he should concede anything. He was willing to grant, he said, that Bob Stevens was a nice fellow— and that was all.

About 4 P.M. Nixon brought the Senators' meaningless statement to the White House. A conference was held in the East Room while Eisenhower was out practicing chip shots on the South Lawn. At 5:30 the meeting broke up. Then a smaller group of advisers huddled for about half an hour with the President in his second-floor study. It was decided that Stevens should issue his own statement. And Eisenhower, who for so long had shunned a direct clash with McCarthy, would back him 100 percent.

At 6:15 P.M. reporters were called into the office of Presidential Press Secretary James C. Hagerty. There Stevens read his statement.

"I did not at that meeting [recede] . . . from any of the principles upon which I stand," he said. "I shall never accede to [Army personnel] . . . being browbeaten or humiliated . . . From assurances which I have received from members of the committee, I am confident that they will not permit such conditions to develop in the future."

As soon as Stevens had finished, Hagerty added:

"On behalf of the President, he has seen the statement. He approves and endorses it 100 per cent."

Finally, at long last, Joe McCarthy had been called by the man who held all the aces.

McCarthy reacted with his customary name-calling. Informed of Stevens' statement, he denounced the Secretary of the Army as a liar, saying he had made "a completely false statement" about any assurances having been given him along with the fried chicken. But the next day, confronted with the Presidential presence, some of his luncheon companions began to beat a retreat. Senator Mundt, the author of the "Memorandum of Understanding," conceded that Stevens was right; he had received promises of fairer treatment for Army officers. Senator Potter agreed.

In the post-mortems, James Reston, of *The New York Times*, wrote that at the luncheon Stevens had "made the worst deal since Yalta, but, in an administration that came to office spouting copy-book maxims, he was the one man who tried, however ineffectually, to fight for the right and moral thing. He became the goat because he placed too much faith in the moral pronouncements of the President. He started out to fight for principles he had heard the President pronounce, but when he turned around, the crusaders were talking tactics."

F R O M   T H E   M O M E N T that Eisenhower committed his long-husbanded Presidential prestige, Fate, for so long blind, seemed to conspire against Joe McCarthy. He was like a juggler who has kept ten balls whirling in the air to the amazement of his audience; then he drops one, and the rest begin to bounce off his head.

The bullyragging of General Zwicker had been too much. In New York, the late Edward R. Murrow, then the emcee of one of the most courageous shows on television, CBS' *See It Now*, asked his staff to put together all of the available film clips on McCarthy. On March 2, after finishing his regular telecast, Murrow signed off with a teaser. He remarked on "the retreat into unreasoning fear that seems to be part of the climate in which we live. We shall try to deal with one aspect of that fear next week." It was a veiled disclosure of a decision he had already made—to do a full-length half-hour program on McCarthy on his next telecast, March 9.

In the meantime, other voices began to be raised in the chorus that would soon expose McCarthy to a national television audience. One of the principal catalysts in the unfolding drama was Adlai Stevenson. On March 6, in a radio-TV speech from Florida, he jabbed a spear into the hide of the elephant.

"And why . . . have the demagogues triumphed so often?" Stevenson asked. "The answer is inescapable; because a group of political plungers has persuaded the President that McCarthy-ism is the best Republican formula for political success . . . It seems to me that this Stevens incident illustrates that . . . a political party divided against itself, half McCarthy and half Eisenhower, cannot produce national unity."

McCarthy clamored at once for air time to answer Stevenson, but the Administration moved swiftly to checkmate him, inform-ing the NBC and CBS networks that it wanted time in the name of the Republican National Committee. Vice President Nixon spoke for the party. By indirection he both praised and criticized McCarthy. He lauded "men who in the past have done effective work exposing communism," but deplored "reckless talk and questionable methods" that had made such men themselves the issue. And he dropped into the speech a line that was to be much quoted as showing that Nixon himself was not above the use of the "questionable methods" he had just criticized. He said: "Incidentally, in mentioning Secretary Dulles, isn't it wonderful, finally, to have a Secretary of State who isn't taken in by the Communists, who stands up to them?"

McCarthy was enraged both by the networks' decision and the Nixon speech. He stormed that he was "delegating no one to answer the attack made upon me," and he threatened the net-works, declaiming that they "will grant me time or learn what the law is." But the networks paid no attention to his threat.

With rockets streaking into the political skies and exploding in star bursts in all directions, the mild-mannered and much-respected Republican from Vermont, the late Senator Ralph E. Flanders, took the Senate floor late on Tuesday afternoon, March 9, and delivered the most scathing attack any Republican had made on McCarthy since Eisenhower had come to power. Flan-ders accused McCarthy of trying to "shatter" the Republican Party, of trying to set up "a one-man party—McCarthyism." Then he launched into this description of McCarthy in action:

"He dons his warpaint. He goes into his war dance. He emits his warhoops. He goes forth to battle and proudly returns with the scalp of a pink Army dentist. We may assume that this represents the depth and seriousness of Communist penetration at this time."

That same evening, like the second part of a one-two punch, came the Ed Murrow *See It Now* telecast. Murrow's staff had spent a frantic week piecing together their documentary on Mc-Carthy. There were inevitable gaps in the recital. They had been unable to find any tape of the Wheeling speech, and there was no footage available on the questioning of General Zwicker, since that had taken place in closed session. But Murrow's camera crews had gone to Philadelphia and had caught McCarthy in action during the Washington Birthday speech in which he had read with such relish the Zwicker transcript. There was also a long film record of McCarthy's questioning of Reed Harris, a sequence that showed the grand inquisitor at his browbeating worst.

It is perhaps significant that, before putting the show on the air, Murrow and his producer, Fred W. Friendly, felt the same kind of compulsion for self-examination that I was later to feel in writing about the Alger Hiss case. Friendly has described how they called together their entire unit and went from man to man asking whether there was "anything in their own back-grounds that would give the senator a club to beat us." Friendly later wrote: "One man told us that his first wife had been a Communist Party member but that their marriage had been dis-solved years before." Since this was the only taint among the staff, and this a taint long ago removed, Friendly and Murrow felt safe in airing their McCarthy documentary.

Television has probably never been used with more devastat-ing effect. The camera eye caught all the hectoring, bullying man-nerisms of McCarthy. Murrow let McCarthy expose McCarthy; and, whenever necessary, he set the record straight. He showed McCarthy telling Reed Harris that the American Civil Liberties Union had been exposed as a communist front, and then, in dry and controlled tones, Murrow set down the facts: that the ACLU had never been so designated and that it held "in its files letters of commendation from President Eisenhower, President Truman and General MacArthur."

At the end of the program, Murrow summed up in a scathing editorial close. He said: "It is necessary to investigate before legislating, but the line between investigating and persecuting is a very fine one, and the junior senator from Wisconsin has stepped over it repeatedly. His primary achievement has been in confusing the public mind as between [the] internal and . . . external threat of communism. We must not confuse dissent with disloyalty. We must remember always that accusation is not proof, and that conviction depends upon evidence and due process of law. We will not walk in fear, one of another. We will not be driven by fear into an age of unreason if we dig deep in our history and our doctrine, and remember that we are not descended from fearful men . . ."

Murrow had done what so many of the great news media had so long refrained from doing; he had laid bare the soul and techniques of a demagogue. The reaction was swift and overwhelming. CBS stations across the nation were deluged with telephone calls, letters and telegrams. So great was the outpouring that, as Friendly later wrote, no complete tabulation could be kept, but the response was overwhelmingly favorable to Murrow. In New York the messages were anti-McCarthy by 15 to 1. Chicago narrowed the margin to 2 to 1, but in San Francisco it was again 15 to 1. The response seemed to indicate that the American people could be depended upon when they were given the kind of leadership and information to make an intelligent choice possible.

Undeterred, McCarthy and Cohn kept pounding down the Army witch-hunt trail. During the height of the Peress hysteria, McCarthy had interjected into his harassment of the Army the spicy detail that Annie Lee Moss, an Army "code clerk" handling "topmost" secrets, was a member of the Communist Party. The evidence depended upon the testimony of Mrs. Mary Markward, an undercover informer for the FBI who had wormed her way into high position in communist ranks in Washington. Mrs. Markward had testified that she had learned during her undercover work that an Annie Lee Moss worked in the Pentagon, but admitted she could not identify the woman by sight.

The Army had replied that Mrs. Moss, a Negro, was not a "code clerk," but merely the operator of a machine transmitting coded messages, a job that involved no knowledge of the secrets of the codes. Now, on Thursday of this tumultuous March week, Mrs. Moss herself took the witness stand before McCarthy's committee. McCarthy began the questioning in a low key, then turned the witness over to Roy Cohn. Almost at once, the ballyhooed spy case began to fall apart. Mrs. Moss explained that she had no access to the code room, knew nothing of the secrets of the codes, and had never heard of the designations "confidential," "secret" and "top secret." McCarthy interrupted, citing Mrs. Markward's testimony that "while she never met you personally at a Communist meeting . . . your name was on the list of Communists who were paying dues."

Mrs. Moss protested that she knew nothing about any dues. She had never paid any. She did not know Mrs. Markward. There were, she explained, three other women named Annie Lee Moss in the District of Columbia. A dim light began to break through: Mrs. Markward had seen the name Annie Lee Moss on a Communist dues roll; there was an Annie Lee Moss in the Pentagon. The instant leap to accusation reminded some of the Anna Rosenberg case.

Senator Symington broke into the questioning. "Did you ever hear of Karl Marx?" he asked. Annie Lee Moss, looking bewildered, asked: "Who's that?" And the hearing room erupted in laughter.

With the witness beginning to make her inquisitors look ridiculous, McCarthy suddenly recalled that he had "an important appointment" to keep (it turned out he was to appear on Fulton Lewis' radio show), and he rose and left the hearing room. Murrow's cameramen, who were there, panned to the empty chair as the grand inquisitor fled.

McCarthy's departure left Senator McClellan in command of the hearing, and he and his Democratic colleagues took over the questioning of Mrs. Moss. Her ignorance of the simplest details of communism seemed so obvious that Senator Symington said, "I may be sticking my neck out, but I believe you're telling the truth." The audience cheered.

McClellan and the Democrats then went after Cohn. They denounced him for having introduced into the record the hearsay testimony of Mrs. Markward, and they upbraided him for claiming he had corroboratory evidence but could not produce it. The hearing became a shambles for the McCarthy-Cohn axis. Annie Lee Moss emerged as the victimized heroine of the occasion and was soon restored to her Pentagon job.*

THE ANNIE LEE MOSS CASE served as a prelude to the next big explosion. The public still did not know of the Cohn-Schine time bomb ticking away quietly behind the Washington scene, but insiders in the Pentagon and the Administration had, of course, been aware of it for months and had begun to assess the possibility of making use of it. On January 21, after it had become obvious that the McCarthy-Cohn attack upon the Army was assuming the characteristics of a vendetta, Henry Cabot Lodge had suggested that it was time the Administration considered some course of action. As a consequence, a meeting was called in the office of Attorney General Herbert Brownell, with Lodge, Brownell, Sherman Adams and John Adams present. It was at this conference that John Adams described for the others the still-secret story of the efforts to get favored treatment for G. David Schine. Sherman Adams later wrote that it had seemed to him like "a strange and incredible" story, and when he learned that the Army had kept a full record of all the Cohn-Schine maneuvers, he advised John Adams to "draw up a detailed chronological account of the whole affair and confront the subcommittee with it."

This had been done, the report had been given to Senators on McCarthy's subcommittee, and the press, "not entirely by accident," as Sherman Adams later wrote, had been tipped off to the hidden sensation. Thursday, March 11, there was a frantic

---

* Cohn in his book, *McCarthy*, still insists he was right in the Annie Lee Moss case. He belittles the identity issue by saying Mrs. Moss claimed "there must be" another Annie Lee Moss, something considerably less specific than she did claim. He also asserts that the Subversive Activities Control Board in 1958 obtained FBI documents showing that the Communist Party's own records contained the notation that Annie Lee Moss, 72 R Street, S.W., Washington, D.C., "was a party member in the mid-1940s." Cohn leaves the implication that the R Street Annie Lee Moss was the Pentagon's Annie Lee Moss, but this remains by no means so certain. In the Senatorial debate on the censure of McCarthy, Senator Welker, who obviously had access to all the relevant information in the case at the time, identified the Pentagon's Annie Lee Moss as having lived at 525½ Second Street N.E. in 1943 and for a short time in the 600 block of Second Street N.E., an entirely different section of Washington.

scrambling among the Washington press corps, and by late evening, reporters had obtained copies of the document. The full text was carried by several papers the next day.

It shocked the nation as had nothing else in the whole long record of McCarthy investigations. Yet, even so, there was evidence that the Army had watered down its account. Brigadier General Thomas R. Phillips, the military analyst of the St. Louis *Post-Dispatch*, wrote that Assistant Secretary of Defense Fred Seaton had reduced the original seventy-five-page report, which had been embellished with many direct quotes, to a stark thirty-five-page chronology. "The Army record contained stenographic transcriptions of conversations filled with obscenities and vituperation of a nature which would not be published in the *Congressional Record* or in any newspaper," Phillips reported flatly.

Joseph and Stewart Alsop obtained a similar account from their sources inside the Pentagon. They wrote that "the whole [original] document was studded with disgusting obscenities in which Cohn indulged whenever he was bullyragging Army Department officials to give Schine special favors."

Defanged though it was, the Army account revealed, not only the desperate preliminary efforts that had been made to get a commission for David Schine, but the persistent attempts carried on over a period of months to ameliorate his lot after he was inducted. As the Army pointed out, it was a standard rule at Fort Dix that, during the first four weeks of basic training, recruits were not permitted to leave the post evenings nor were they allowed weekend passes.

Schine arrived at Fort Dix November 10, 1953. The very next day, Francis Carr and Roy Cohn showed up and asked General Ryan, the post commandant, to see Private Schine. The request was granted. The following day, November 12, Private Schine was granted a weekend pass. More passes followed; evenings off from the post became an almost established routine. Finally, on December 6, 1953, General Ryan telephoned Army Counsel John Adams, complaining that "the matter of handling Private Schine was becoming increasingly difficult since the soldier was leaving the post almost every night." He was also returning "very late at night," General Ryan said, and unless the Army objected he was going to put an end to the granting of week-night passes for Private Schine. Adams told him to go ahead, but to make Schine available on weekends if the Mc-Carthy committee wanted him.

This treatment of Schine brought an almost immediate protest from Cohn, according to the Army. At a committee hearing on December 9, Cohn discussed Schine's situation with Adams, then "broke off this conversation in the middle, turning his back on Adams in the Senate caucus room." After the hearing, Adams followed McCarthy to his office and there discussed the Cohn-Schine importunities. McCarthy agreed to write Secretary Stevens a letter saying "that the committee had no further interest in Private Schine and that he hoped Private Schine would be treated the same as other soldiers." McCarthy delayed carrying through on this promise, but he finally did write such a letter on December 22, the Army said. Cohn, in the meantime, learned that Adams had appealed to McCarthy and telephoned Adams, screeching that "he would teach Adams what it meant to go over his head."

Cohn's pressure was unremitting, according to the Army. In a telephone call to Adams on December 11, the Army said, he upbraided Adams for what he called the "double-cross" of Schine on the matter of a commission. The strange ambivalence of McCarthy, who time and again revealed himself as virtually the hand-bound captive of Roy Cohn, was one of the most intriguing aspects of the report. In New York on December 17 prior to a committee hearing, the report said, McCarthy told Adams "that he had learned of the extent of his staff's interference with the Army with reference to Schine and that he wished to advise Adams thereafter to see that nothing was done on the committee's behalf with reference to Schine."

After the hearing, McCarthy, Cohn, Francis Carr and Adams were together. Adams, hoping to get McCarthy to express himself in front of Carr and Cohn, deliberately brought up the subject of Private Schine. "Cohn was vituperative in his language," the Army report declared. "During this discussion, Senator McCarthy remained silent."

The report continued: "The party rode uptown in Cohn's car and Cohn continued his statement. Twice during the ride uptown and as Adams was getting out of the car, Senator McCarthy asked Adams to ask Secretary Stevens if the Secretary could find a way to assign Private Schine to New York." McCarthy even suggested that Schine might investigate "the textbooks at West Point" to see whether they "contained anything of a subversive nature."

Schine continued to be given regular weekend passes—and the crisis continued to build. The Army, after testing Schine at Fort Dix for his capabilities, decided that he was best qualified to become an army investigator—and so should be sent to the Provost Marshal General School at Camp Gordon, Georgia, a long way from New York City. This insensitive decision almost drove Roy Cohn up the wall, according to the Army's version. Cohn wanted to know if Schine would have to live on the post, if he could have his own car, who could be contacted at Camp Gordon to relieve Schine of duty "when necessary."

On one occasion, in early January, while Adams was speaking at Amherst College in Amherst, Mass., he reported that he got a telephone call from Carr. Carr told him Cohn had been trying to reach him; the indignity of indignities had just been inflicted upon Private Schine, still stationed at Fort Dix—he had been "scheduled for KP duty on the following day, a Sunday." Adams told Carr he could do nothing for Schine from Amherst, and when Cohn placed a follow-up call, Adams refused to accept it.

Conferences over the fate of Private Schine once he had survived the rigors of Camp Gordon continued over the next few weeks and took up much of the time of some of the Army's highest brass. When Cohn learned that the chances were "nine out of ten" that Schine might be assigned to overseas duty after Gordon, he threatened to "wreck the Army" and cause Stevens to be "through as Secretary of the Army," the report charged. It was throughout this January–February period, while the tug-of-war over Schine was going on, that Cohn and McCarthy kept hounding the Army with the Fort Monmouth and Camp Kilmer investigations. The Army report left little room for doubt that, in its opinion, its refusal to coddle Private Schine had resulted in a vengeful determination on the part of Cohn and McCarthy to besmirch Stevens and "wreck the Army."

Near the conclusion of the report, the Army described a three-hour visit by John Adams to McCarthy's apartment in Washington on January 22. McCarthy had requested the meeting. There were two items on the agenda for discussion: McCarthy's desire to question members of the Army Loyalty-Security

Appeals Board; and the possibility of getting Private Schine a New York assignment. Though McCarthy himself had repeatedly expressed his lack of interest in Schine, he had never been willing to make such statements in the presence of Cohn, and it was now quite obvious that he was pressing Cohn's case in making this final appeal to the Army to do what he had agreed it should never do.

"Senator McCarthy pointed out that the Army was walking into a long-range fight with Cohn and that if Cohn resigned or was fired from the committee staff, he would carry on his campaign against the Army thereafter from outside Washington," the report said.

"Senator McCarthy suggested that Cohn through the medium of connections with various newspaper elements would begin getting published articles alleging favoritism on the part of the Army in numerous other cases."

At the same time, McCarthy sympathized with Adams over what he had had to endure, the report stated. Referring to the way Cohn had berated the Army counsel during the automobile ride to uptown New York on December 17, "Senator McCarthy stated that he would not have blamed Adams that day, in view of the abuse from Cohn, if Adams had walked out and refused ever to speak to Cohn again."

The Army report concluded with the account of a February 16 telephone talk between Carr and Adams. The McCarthy committee, Carr said, wanted to call a number of witnesses from Camp Kilmer in the affair of "the pink dentist," and Adams expressed the fear that this was going to be Fort Monmouth all over again.

"Carr stated that if the Army would be reasonable, probably the committee would be reasonable," the Army report declared. "Adams inquired how Carr thought that the Army should be 'reasonable' and Carr answered rather facetiously that, if the Army would only do all that had been requested of it, the Army's problems would be at an end."

MC CARTHY'S REACTION to the publication of this material was entirely predictable.

He stormed before the television cameras and a gaggle of reporters, accusing the Army of "blackmail." He charged that the

Army had held Schine as a "hostage," refusing him fair treatment unless McCarthy abandoned his Army investigations. He accused Secretary Stevens of trying to persuade McCarthy's committee to switch its probe to the Navy and Air Force and promising to supply it with "plenty of dirt" if it did.

McCarthy released eleven memoranda from his subcommittee files to support his sensational counteraccusations. The key document was labeled simply "Memorandum for the Files." It bore nothing to indicate to whom it was addressed or who had prepared it. It purported to be an account of a meeting with Secretary Stevens on November 6, 1953, concerning the Fort Monmouth Signal Corps hearings. It pictured Stevens as saying "if we brought out everything, he would have to resign." It added:

"Stevens asked that we hold up our public hearings on the Army. He suggested we go after the Navy, Air Force and the Defense Department instead. We said first of all we had no evidence warranting an investigation of these other departments.

"Adams said not to worry about that, because there was plenty of dirt there, and they could furnish us leads. Stevens thought this was the answer to his problem."

Another memorandum from Roy Cohn to McCarthy, dated January 14, 1954, accused Adams of trying to pressure him for a lucrative law partnership in New York. "Adams said this was the last chance for me to arrange that law partnership in New York which he wanted," Cohn wrote. "One would think he was kidding but his persistence on this subject makes it clear he is serious. He said he had turned down a job in industry at $17,500 and needed a guarantee of $25,000 from a law firm."

Stevens responded by calling the charge that he had offered to furnish dirt about the Navy and Air Force "utterly untrue." Adams said the "blackmail" charge was "fantastic and false." He added: "If there ever had been any basis for such a charge, it is inconceivable that no complaints were ever made to the Secretary of the Army. And none was."

The issue was out in the open. On the highest levels of government, someone was lying, and a public hearing to determine who it was now became inevitable.

21

The Army-McCarthy Hearings

J O E   M C   C A R T H Y tore around Washington like a human
hurricane. He fired off statements, dashed from crisis to crisis
in such a whirlwind of activity that his own staff sometimes lost
track of him. A vivid picture of McCarthy in perpetual motion
was painted by a *Time* reporter who followed him about on the
evening of Thursday, February 25—the day that Secretary Stevens, speaking from the White House, had given his version of
the luncheon conference; the day that McCarthy, for the first
but not the last time, had called the Secretary a liar.

McCarthy was "charging in and out of his Senate office,
snatching up telephones, rushing to the Senate floor to answer
quorum calls, dictating statements to reporters," the *Time* man

wrote. "As he dashed about, his office staff lost track, believed a rumor that he had emplaned for New York. Then Joe stomped in from the corridor, stuffed a briefcase, said, 'Come on,' to a waiting reporter and hurried out. Behind them came a job seeker from Wisconsin, carrying the briefcase.

"The three got into the Senator's air-conditioned Cadillac (a wedding gift from Texas admirers) and started for Joe's new home (bought by his mother-in-law) a few blocks away. The Senator had not yet figured out the best way to drive to his house, and he had to circle a block before he found the alley to the back door. He stumbled up the four brick steps, found a key, entered, groped for a light switch. In the dark, the Wisconsin job seeker banged into the door."

Jean McCarthy was in a hospital in New York at the time, but she had ordered a pile of groceries by telephone. These were stacked up in the kitchen. Joe and his trailing reporter "walked through a dining room stacked high with boxes, perhaps 200 of them—wedding presents that the busy McCarthys (married in September) have not got around to opening."

Joe sank exhaustedly into a big red chair in the still half-furnished green living room. He waved a hand at the television set. The reporter tuned it in and flipped from channel to channel until he found a newscast, and the Senator watched himself at his snarling best as he declared that Secretary Stevens had made an "absolutely false" statement. Satisfied, he waved the TV off.

"Meanwhile," the *Time* man wrote, "the job seeker from Wisconsin knew what to do. Digging into the groceries, he started to get dinner. He found some frozen pork chops, which he broiled (he is not looking for a cook's job), a fine Maryland ham, a Wisconsin cheese, some bourbon, some seltzer.

"The phone began to ring. Between 7 p.m. and 11 it rang 100 times. The Senator took perhaps one call in ten, sometimes listening for a moment and then saying, 'The Senator is not here.' The doorbell began to ring. During the evening, some 20 or 30 people trooped in and out. They did not have appointments; most seemed to have no specific business. They came, as it were, out of the wood-work, as they always come to hover around a man of power. Some got the Senator in a corner and talked earnestly to him. Some wandered into the kitchen and sampled the bourbon. Some just stood around. Between conversations and phone calls, the Senator ate dinner in the kitchen. The broiler of pork chops, having eaten his fill, made a serious pitch for a job, but the Senator promised nothing.

"Several times during the evening, the Senator sank exhausted into his chair, muttering, 'I'm getting old.' He is 44. His digestion is bad, and he has sinus trouble. But he is not slowing down, and he is decidedly not mellowing."

Such was Joe McCarthy at the zenith of his power.

THERE WAS A LAST, FUTILE EFFORT to avoid the great confrontation by belittling the whole affair. It was, McCarthy said, "a tempest in a teapot," a quarrel over one unimportant Army private—and, really, it couldn't concern him less.

In the executive sessions of the Government Operations Committee, Senator Dirksen tried his best to bury the whole controversy "by simply letting the grass grow over it." What good would a public airing do? Dirkson wondered. "Let us forget about it and start with a clean page," he pleaded.

Senator McClellan would have none of it. During McCarthy's earlier and repeated affronts to honor, McClellan had habitually stood quietly in McCarthy's corner. When Democratic leaders counted noses on a McCarthy issue, there had always been three of their own on whom they could not count: Pat McCarran; John McClellan, the conservative Arkansan; and James Eastland, the Mississippi primitive. It was the J. B. Matthews affair and the slur on the Protestant clergy (Protestantism is strong in Arkansas) that had first brought McClellan out of his conservative shell. He was now facing a stiff reelection fight in Arkansas; and, on the whole, the time was right for him to assert the claims of conscience in leading the Democratic battle against McCarthy.

Opposing Dirksen's suggestion, McClellan argued in a voice deep-toned with righteousness that this simply could not be done. "This is already out in the open," he said, "and it is a national issue today . . . It is before the public, and this committee cannot afford to do anything that would look like we are trying to hush it up or whitewash it."

McClellan argued further that McCarthy had been haling ordinary citizens before television cameras; he had browbeaten and berated them; he had gotten the Senate to vote charges of contempt against them. "Now you have it at the top level thrown open to the public," he said, "and I do not believe this committee can maintain its prestige and command public respect if it does less than bring these principals . . . before the committee and let them testify, just like you do to the commonest or anyone against whom accusations are made."

Except for Dirksen, the Republicans kept an unhappy silence. None of them felt they could adopt the "let the grass grow over it" approach. Even formerly zealous Karl Mundt sniffed the political winds and decided that this was not the time to be a McCarthy militant. Mundt wanted some other committee to handle the dispute, but none would. Since McCarthy himself was a principal and would be a witness, he could not act as chairman—and the next man in line for the honor was Mundt himself. He attempted to disclaim this post in the limelight, but he couldn't get off the spot. He was it. McCarthy, taking himself temporarily off the committee, selected another stalwart fellow-traveler of his, Senator Henry C. Dworshak, of Idaho, as his replacement on the committee. Dworshak voted against accepting this honor, but he, too, was overruled by other members of the committee. No one could get off the hook—and nobody was happy.

The next decision involved the selection of legal counsel. The committee was to have its own counsel to handle the questioning of witnesses; Stevens and the Army were to have separate counsel, with the right to cross-examine. After one false start when it selected a lawyer who turned out to be an avowed McCarthyite, the committee picked for its legal representative Ray H. Jenkins, of Knoxville, Tenn., an expert criminal trial lawyer noted for his courtroom dramatics. Stevens and the Army, to the surprise of many, selected a relatively unknown Boston attorney, Joseph Nye Welch.

The opposing lawyers were a study in contrasts. Jenkins was a rugged, square-jawed six-footer who had been born in the eastern Tennessee hills fifty-seven years before. He had come down out of the mountains to establish a law practice in Knoxville, and he had quickly earned a reputation as an advocate who could save clients from the electric chair and even, unless the case was airtight, win their vindication. In action in the courtroom, he habitually loosened his collar, unbuttoned his coat, untied his tie and went to work, throwing himself into his defense with such energy that jurors were impressed. In one of his first cases, he had to defend a professional bondsman who had fired a shot at a newspaper photographer. The cameraman had taken a picture of the bondsman in the very act of firing. It seemed that nothing could save the bondsman from a long prison stretch. Jenkins stalled the case, winning several delays; and when it finally came to trial, he had his client brought into the courtroom on a stretcher attended by a nurse. He contended that the bondsman was both mentally and physically ill; he argued that the poor man had been hounded and harassed by the photographer until he was goaded into shooting. His client got off with a light fine and sixty days in the workhouse.

Welch was a different type. Born in Primghar, Iowa, the son of William and Martha Welch, he was now sixty-three years old. He had graduated from Grinnell College in 1914 and Harvard Law School in 1917. He entered the Army in World War I, was an officer candidate and was commissioned after war's end. Having fallen in love with Boston during his years at Harvard, he had remained there the rest of his life, becoming a member of the staid Boston law firm of Hale & Dorr. He was known as a man who loved trial work, as one who often represented Harvard students without fee when they got into trouble; and he now agreed to represent Secretary Stevens and the Army without payment of any kind, even for his expenses.

Welch's manner and appearance were deceptive. A chunky man, with wide lips, a long face, a large broad nose, high-arched quizzical eyebrows and a balding head, he dressed like a proper Bostonian—conservative suit, little bow tie, an inevitable vest. He appeared at times almost sleepy and indifferent, and he spoke in tones deceptively dulcet. It was all a camouflage; it gave to what he said the effect of a delayed time fuse. It took a confronted witness several startled seconds to realize that this gentle-seeming man had actually impaled him on the harshest of harsh questions or had demolished him with barbed, sardonic humor.

The iron hand in the velvet glove became apparent on April 15. The bill of particulars that Welch filed with the Mundt committee repeated the earlier Army charges, but hardened the line, putting the onus squarely on McCarthy for the Schine affair. It also added this final, deadly charge: "On or about February 16,

1954, and on several other occasions, Carr and *a person purporting to act as a representative of Senator McCarthy* indicated that
the investigations of the Army then contemplated by this subcommittee would either be terminated or be conducted along
reasonable lines if the Army would accede to Senator McCarthy's
and Cohn's request for a special assignment for Private Schine."
It was McCarthy's loudly trumpeted "blackmail" charge turned
back upon its author. The "person purporting to act as a representative" of McCarthy was not identified at the time, but Secretary Stevens was later to name him as George Sokolsky, the
Hearst columnist, McCarthy collaborator and go-between in the
McCarthy-Cohn-IIA rumpus.

McCarthy and Cohn fired back with their own bill of particulars, which typically attempted to smother the issue in question with a new charge. It accused H. Struve Hensel, Assistant
Secretary of Defense, of having profited from government contracts during World War II while he occupied a "top procure-
ment" post in the Navy. Hensel, McCarthy alleged, had helped
organize a ships' supply company; and, in the years 1943 through
1945, he had drawn a total of $56,526.64 from the firm, "which
was operating with Government sanction and priorities." When
McCarthy started to investigate this conflict-of-interest situation,
he said, Hensel had tried to block his probe, and this explained,
in part, the motivation for the "attacks" by the Army on Mc-
Carthy, Cohn and Carr.

Hensel denounced McCarthy's accusations as "barefaced lies."
If McCarthy would just repeat his charges outside the privileged
forum of the Senate, Hensel promised to slap the Senator with a
libel suit that would curl the few remaining hairs on his head.

McCarthy was down in the friendly land of Texas when he
was informed of this challenge. Naturally, he declined to repeat
his charges, implying that strategic necessities of the moment
compelled his reticence, but he cloaked discretion with an implied
threat. "If at some future time," he said, "Hensel still wants this
material repeated—and I don't think he will—away from the
committee, I see no harm in that."

THE ARMY-MC CARTHY HEARINGS that were to hold
the American people spellbound in front of their television sets

opened in the ornate Senate Caucus Room on April 22, 1954. In an atmosphere of high tension, under the hard white glare of the television lights, to the accompaniment of popping flashbulbs, with a limply draped American flag in the background, the members of the McCarthy committee that had now been transformed into the Mundt committee ranged themselves along one side of a long hearing table, confronting the witnesses in this climactic showdown scene. There had been some doubt about what role McCarthy himself would play. He had said several times in the weeks preceding the hearings that he intended to ignore the whole thing because it didn't concern him, and in a speech just the night before in Houston, Texas, he had referred to the hearings as "this television show of Adams versus Cohn." But the instant the television cameras were focused, McCarthy was there, striding into the spotlight, turning the hearings into a direct contest between himself and the Army.

Senator Mundt had hardly opened with a prefatory statement before McCarthy broke in. "A point of order, Mr. Chairman, may I raise a point of order?"

It was a haranguing refrain that was to be repeated endlessly during the next interminable weeks. In this instance, at the outset, he objected to the bill of particulars filed by Welch because it contained the notation "Filed by the Department of the Army." Welch, he contended, did not represent the Army; he represented Stevens, Adams and Hensel. "What I object to is an attempt to make this a contest between me and the Army," McCarthy declaimed, ignoring the fact that he himself had made it such a contest. The wrangle served at least to show the American public the rampaging image of Joe McCarthy. Mundt himself finally cut McCarthy off and instructed Ray Jenkins to call his first witness and get on with the hearing.

The Army opened its case with Major General Miles Reber, who described in direct testimony McCarthy's first request to him for a commission for Schine and the subsequent, persistent efforts of Roy Cohn. In questioning Reber, Ray Jenkins played an unprecedented dual role: first he led the witness in direct examination as a lawyer would in presenting his own case—and then he turned around and cross-examined as if the witness were testifying for the opposition. In this cross-examination of General Reber, Jenkins attempted to show that concern about G. David

Schine on the part of McCarthy and Cohn was only natural because the possibility existed that the very fate of the republic was bound up in the communist-hunting expertise of Schine. Though there were abundant indications by this time that McCarthy's Fort Monmouth espionage headlines of the previous fall had been a fraud upon press and public, no faintest glimmer of this possibility showed in the questioning by Jenkins, as was shown by this sequence with General Reber:

Question: You knew of the tremendously important work in which Senator McCarthy was then engaged, did you not?

Answer: I certainly did, sir.

Question: And that was the investigation of communists and of the infiltration of communists in industry, in every branch of government, as well as the Army?

Answer: That was my understanding.

Question: General, you would regard that as a work than which there could possibly be no more important work insofar as the security of this nation is concerned, would you not?

Answer: I certainly think it is vital, sir.

This witness was obviously not inclined to question the great crusade, but when McCarthy got his chance to cross-examine immediately after the general had finished his direct testimony, he leaped at once for the jugular.

Question: Is Sam Reber your brother?

Answer: Yes, sir.

The significance McCarthy attached to the witness's brother became quickly apparent. Sam Reber had been acting deputy high commissioner in Germany during the overseas library inquisition of Cohn and Schine, and McCarthy thundered that Sam Reber "repeatedly made attacks upon them" and "appointed a man to shadow them throughout Europe and keep the press informed as to where they were going and where they were stopping." Ray Jenkins, Mundt, McClellan and virtually everyone else seemed to think that McCarthy was incorporating testimony into his questions—testimony about what might or might not be facts. Jenkins also wondered what General Reber's brother had to do with the issues at stake, and McCarthy insisted he was trying to show bias on the general's part, trying to establish that General Reber had been so prejudiced he had given Private

Schine a raw deal and had exaggerated the pressure applied to him by Cohn.

General Reber insisted that, while he knew Cohn and Schine had had some trouble with the State Department in Europe, he had never been aware of any direct conflict between them and his brother. "Are you aware of the fact that your brother was allowed to resign when charges that he was a bad security risk were made against him as a result of the investigation of this committee?" McCarthy thundered.

This, certainly, was slandering an uninvolved bystander on nationwide television without, as Senator McClellan pointed out, any "testimony that the statements that the Senator makes as facts are true." General Reber protested: "Until the Senator brought up this question a few moments ago, I had never heard a single word about my brother being investigated in any way by this committee."

Joseph Welch proposed that General Reber testify about "his knowledge of the reasons lying back of his brother's retirement from his position." This suggestion made McCarthy almost apoplectic. "Mr. Chairman, a point of order," he screeched. Although he himself had raised the issue, he now protested that it would be "completely unfair" for General Reber to answer Welch's question and say what he knew about his brother's case. "I would not ask him that question," he said righteously. "It has to do with the type of security, whether it is Communistic activities."

General Reber, his back up, demanded that he be allowed to tell what he knew about his brother's retirement. He protested that "a very serious charge has been made against my brother in this room"; he would like to answer it to the best of his ability. He finally won his point. He then said, ". . . as I understand my brother's case, he retired as he is entitled to do by law upon reaching the age of 50 . . . I know nothing about any security case involving him."

The general left the stand, his testimony about Cohn's efforts on behalf of Schine unshaken, and Senator Mundt congratulated him on "the frank and cooperative manner in which you have handled your part of this discussion." Senator McCarthy's first resort to dirty pool had backfired.

.   .   .

SECRETARY STEVENS followed General Reber to the stand. In a long prepared statement, he backed up under oath the charges originally made by the Army in the Cohn-Schine affair. In addition, he disclosed that after Cohn had failed to get Schine a commission through regular Army channels he had tried an end run by appealing to Gen. Walter Bedell Smith, then Under Secretary of State. Stevens' testimony was interrupted so that General Smith could testify about this novel approach. The general read into the record a letter he had written to Secretary Stevens in which he said: "I asked Cohn why he came to me, as I was no longer in active military service. He replied that Army authorities had not been cooperative, that General Reber had promised to arrange a commission for Schine and had not done so, that I knew all the senior officers in the Pentagon and would know who to talk to."

General Smith said that he had tried to see whether anything could be done for Schine, but that the responsible officers in the Pentagon had told him just what they had told Reber—that few direct commissions were being granted except for special experts like doctors or dentists and that Schine simply didn't have the necessary qualifications.

Resuming his testimony, Secretary Stevens spelled out in detail the efforts that had been made, first to get Schine a commission, then to get him favored treatment. From mid-July, 1953, to March 1, 1954, he said, "Senator McCarthy or members of his staff" made "more than sixty-five telephone calls" on behalf of Schine. There were in addition nineteen meetings between Army personnel and members of the McCarthy staff on the problem of doing something for G. David. Between November 10, 1953, and January 16, 1954, Private Schine at Fort Dix "obtained fifteen passes from the post," while the majority of his fellow inductees were granted no more than three.

Summing up, Stevens testified: "I may say that during my tenure as Secretary of the Army, there is no record that matches this persistent, tireless effort to obtain special consideration and privileges for this man."

He then described a visit that he, some of his officers, McCarthy and members of the McCarthy staff had made to Fort

Monmouth on October 30, 1953. They had flown down from New York in an Army plane, and they were joined at the base by Senator H. Alexander Smith and Representative James C. Auchincloss, the Republican who represented the Third New Jersey District. During the tour of the base, the party came to a laboratory engaged in secret work, where special security clearance was needed. Stevens was aware that not everyone in his party had such clearance. "I made an on-the-spot decision that I would take the responsibility for inviting those who had been elected to public office to enter with me," Stevens testified.

This left Roy Cohn and some others standing around outside.

"Upon leaving the laboratory," Stevens continued, "I could see that Mr. Cohn was extremely angry at not having been allowed to enter. Colonel BeLieu informed me that Mr. Cohn, upon having been denied entrance, had in substance said:

" 'This means war . . . Don't they think I'm cleared for classified information? I have access to FBI files when I want them . . . They did this on purpose just to embarrass me. We will really investigate the Army now.' "

The Secretary added that he had attempted to mollify Cohn by explaining that he had intended nothing personal.

Turning next to McCarthy's charges against the Army, Stevens denied that he had ever tried to "blackmail" McCarthy; denied he had ever suggested that McCarthy "go after" the Navy and the Air Force; denied he had ever promised to furnish McCarthy "plenty of dirt" on the other services. He then quoted a series of press statements McCarthy had made voluntarily to newspaper reporters *after* the time that, he said, Stevens had tried to blackmail him. In these, McCarthy had called Stevens "a very fine fellow," "honest," and a man who "is doing a good job."

"Is that the description of a blackmailer?" Stevens asked.

"The fact remains that this most serious charge is still on the record. I therefore state that it is absolutely false."

Now, with Stevens undergoing cross-examination on April 26, Ray Jenkins sprang a surprise. He asked Stevens if he had ever asked to have his picture taken with David Schine. It seems obvious from the transcript that the Secretary was puzzled by the question. He said there were always photographers around when he went to Army bases, and perhaps he and Schine had been photographed together sometime; he just couldn't recall.

This didn't satisfy Jenkins. He wanted to know if the Secretary had ever said " 'I want my picture taken with David' and have it done."

"I am sure I never made a statement just like you made there," Stevens told him.

Jenkins now whipped out a picture and gave it to Stevens. It showed the Secretary and a soldier posed together, apparently at the Maguire Air Force Base near Fort Dix during a trip Stevens made there with McCarthy. Stevens had some trouble recognizing the soldier, but finally acknowledged he looked like David Schine. Jenkins suggested that the picture showed just Schine and Stevens posed "alone," and he seemed to consider it documentary evidence that Stevens was being "especially nice and considerate of this boy Schine . . . in order to dissuade the Senator [McCarthy] from continuing his investigation . . ." Wasn't that true? Jenkins asked. "Positively and completely not," Stevens replied.

The mystery of the buddy-buddy picture of the private and the Army Secretary was left there for the day, but next morning came the explosion. Joseph Welch strode front and center and made his first impact upon the television audience of millions. Welch charged that Jenkins ". . . yesterday was imposed upon, and so was the Secretary of the Army, by having a doctored or altered photograph produced in this courtroom as if it were honest."

To many with long memories, the charges triggered an instant recall—shades of the Browder-Tydings "composite" picture.

Welch now drove home his point. He produced a copy of the original photograph. It showed Stevens and Schine standing with a third man (Air Force Colonel Jack T. Bradley), and the sleeve of a fourth appeared at the outer edge of the picture. The full picture showed, Welch argued, that Stevens had not posed "alone" with Schine; they had been photographed "in a group" and the picture with which Jenkins had confronted the Secretary the previous day had been deliberately cropped to convey a false impression. Jenkins protested at once that he had had no idea such cropping had taken place, and Welch assured him he had not the faintest doubt about Jenkins' own integrity.

McCarthy, though he disclaimed any responsibility for the

phony picture, leaped instantly into the fray. "Mr. Chairman, a point of order," he cried. Welch, he said, ". . . makes the completely false statement that this [the second picture] is a group picture, and it is not."

Senator Symington broke in: "I would like to say if this is not a point of order, it is out of order."

"Oh, be quiet," snapped McCarthy.

"I haven't the slightest intention of being quiet . . . ," retorted Symington.

". . . I am getting awful sick and tired of sitting down here at the end of the table and having whoever wants to interrupt in the middle of a sentence," Joe raged. ". . . Call it a point of order or call it what you may, when counsel . . . makes a statement and he is allowed to do it without interruption, and if that statement is false, do I have a right to correct it, or do we find halfway through my statement that Welch should not have made his statement and therefore I cannot point out that he was lying? I think that is an important question."

In succeeding testimony, the committee tried to find out just who had been responsible for pawning off the cropped picture on Jenkins, and what developed was pure farce. Witness after witness testified that *he* had barely touched the picture, that *he* hadn't even *seen* it, that *he* had no idea how the group picture had become one portraying a tête-à-tête. It all began where so much began—with Roy Cohn.

Cohn admitted he had told Jenkins there was a picture of Schine and Stevens; he knew this because he had seen the picture on Schine's office wall in New York. Were there other persons in this picture? Cohn's memory failed him at this point. The only figures that had registered with him, he said, were those of Schine and Stevens, the only two men who mattered anyway.

Cohn's recall was much more perfect about events that had taken place at the Maguire Air Force Base months earlier. His memory was clear that, almost the moment their plane touched down, Secretary Stevens had walked over to Schine and said: "This is a picture I would like to have. It is one I wanted, so let's have it taken now."

"I heard that, Senator McCarthy heard that and Mr. Carr heard that," Cohn testified.

About other details Cohn was much more vague. When

Jenkins expressed interest in the picture, Cohn testified, he sent Private Schine up to New York to get it. "He procured that picture. He brought it down. I did not see it." His staff had handled the rest. The picture had been "taken downstairs to have copies made" and the two-man blowup that resulted had been delivered to Jenkins—but Cohn had not seen it.

Asked about his thoughts during the sequence of questioning in which Jenkins had hammered at Stevens and flourished the picture as proof that the Secretary was telling less than the whole truth, Roy Cohn confessed that he had missed the whole point. "I did not catch the word 'alone' put in there by Mr. Jenkins," he said. "I did not hear that word, and I did not catch that, Senator McClellan."

"Now, don't you think in the interest of keeping the record straight, so that there couldn't be any dispute, that you should have called attention to the fact that this picture might not be complete?" McClellan asked.

And Roy Cohn, who indisputably possessed one of the wiliest legal intellects extant, could only protest: "Sir . . . in response to your question, I did not catch the word 'alone,' and I did not attach any significance to it then, and I don't recall even hearing it."

Just who had tailored the photo? Ray Jenkins, who wanted to find out as quickly as possible, suggested as the afternoon hearing of April 29 began that Secretary Stevens should be excused from the stand so that he could question Private Schine. The Secretary, Jenkins said, must be "exhausted" from six days on the witness stand, and the committee should clear up the photograph issue before proceeding further. There was a dispute with McCarthy even about this. McCarthy said he would agree to the change in the order of witnesses if Secretary Stevens himself would plead fatigue. The Secretary wouldn't. McCarthy then protested against excusing the Secretary and calling Schine, but the committee overruled him. And Private Schine, tall and handsome in his Army uniform, took the witness stand.

He testified that he had gone to New York, that he had brought the uncropped picture back to Washington and had delivered it to George Anastos, a lawyer on the subcommittee's staff. And that was all *he* knew about it.

Question: Do you know now, Private Schine, how Colonel Bradley, one-third of the characters in the play, disappeared from the cast?

Answer: I have absolutely no idea, sir.

Anastos testified that when Schine passed the picture package on to him it was delivered "onto the desk of Frank Carr" and that Mrs. Frances Mims, secretary of the subcommittee, was the only other person present. Had Anastos seen the photograph? "No, Sir; no, Sir," he replied. Had he ever at any time seen the original photograph? "No, Sir." Did he know anything about how the picture came to be cropped? "No, Sir." He conceded to Welch that this was, indeed, "a hot picture." What had he done with "the hot picture?" He had sent it along, sight unseen, to James N. Juliana, of the subcommittee's investigative staff.

Mrs. Mims testified that she, too, hadn't seen a thing, not a thing. After Private Schine came in, "I saw the package lying later on the desk, and I didn't see what was in it, and I didn't know what was in it, and I don't know what became of it."

The trail was narrowing down to the man who simply had to know something—James Juliana, a former FBI agent who had been employed by the McCarthy committee for about two years. Juliana said that when he received "the hot picture," he had sent it along to Don Surine to have enlargements made. He had instructed Surine to make two sets of blowups—one set of the whole picture; one set showing just Stevens and Schine. When the enlargements came back from Surine, he had tucked those of the full picture away in a filing cabinet and had sent Jenkins just the picture showing two figures. Why had he done this? Juliana insisted again and again, in testimony that neatly avoided fixing responsibility on anyone, that he had been under the impression "Jenkins and/or Cohn" wanted just "a picture of Secretary Stevens and Private Schine."

This was a situation perfectly tailored for the trial talents of Joseph Welch. In cross-examination, he pinned down the hapless Juliana the way a taxidermist might a butterfly. He got Juliana to describe how he had whispered into Cohn's ear the news that "the picture" had arrived. Was Juliana under the impression Cohn wanted a picture of Schine and Stevens "alone?" Juliana protested that he did not "know," that this was an "unfair" question. Welch, in his mildest but most persistent manner, demurred: Juliana could certainly say what was his "understanding" of the matter.

Welch: When you leaned over to tell this glad, good news to Mr. Cohn, were you under the impression that he was hoping to hear you had a picture of the Secretary and Private Schine alone?

Juliana: I was under the impression that this was glad news to Mr. Cohn . . .

Welch: I find myself so puzzled to know why you just did not take a photostat of the picture that was delivered to you that afternoon and hand it over to Mr. Jenkins. Would you tell us how come you did not do that?

Juliana: I just mentioned or just stated that I was under instructions to furnish a picture of only the two individuals.

Who had given him such instructions? "Jenkins and/or Cohn."

Welch wondered why any enlargement at all had been necessary. Why hadn't Juliana simply delivered to Jenkins the picture that came off Schine's wall? "I wasn't asked for that, and I didn't deliver that," said Juliana. He next protested that, though he had had the original picture in his hands, he didn't even know what was in it. This led to an exchange in which McCarthy called down upon himself the kind of ridicule he had so often administered to others. The sequence began in this fashion:

Welch: . . . You were asked for something different than the thing that hung on Schine's wall?

Juliana: I never knew what hung on Schine's wall . . .

Welch: Did you think this came from a pixie? Where did you think that this picture I hold in my hand came from?

Juliana: I had no idea.

At this point McCarthy thought he saw an opening and was lured into a challenge of wits with Joseph Welch.

"Will counsel for my benefit define—I think he might be an expert on that—what a pixie is?" McCarthy asked.

Rapier sharp came the instant riposte.

"Yes, I should say, Mr. Senator, that a pixie is a close relative of a fairy. Shall I proceed, sir? Have I enlightened you?"

Laughter shook the hearing room. Roy Cohn's lips tightened into white angry lines, and McCarthy glowered in his fury.

.   .   .

THE BATTERING of Secretary Stevens on the witness stand
went on for fourteen interminable days. It was a brutal, repeti-
tive, ugly ordeal. Every question that could possibly have been
asked had been asked and answered, not once but several times,
yet every time it came his turn to question the Secretary, Mc-
Carthy went at him again in his most hectoring manner. He demanded that the committee put on the witness stand members
of the Army's Loyalty Board, Attorney General Herbert Brownell,
Sherman Adams, indeed practically the entire hierarchy of the
Eisenhower Administration. Even Senator Mundt had to gavel
down these demands in an effort to keep the hearing within
bounds.

Throughout it all, Secretary Stevens emerged as the somewhat pitiful victim of the Eisenhower Administration's policy of
appeasement. The Secretary's ordeal on the witness stand left
him gray-faced under the harsh television lights, and as a result
of the incessant hammering, his right eye sometimes blinked
uncontrollably and his right cheek twitched. These signs of strain
were the by-products, not just of the relentless grilling, but of
the untenable aspects of the Secretary's position.

He had done his utmost to "cooperate" with committees of
Congress, he said—a policy mandated from the White House
itself—but this "cooperation" had been carried to such extremes
that his position as an independent executive had been frequently compromised. Undeniably, Stevens had gone to humiliating lengths in his efforts to placate McCarthy and take some heat
off the Army. At the very outset of the secret Fort Monmouth
hearings, he had taken McCarthy and staff to lunch three times
at the swank Merchants Club, in handy walking distance of the
Federal Courthouse, and he admitted that he had told them to
dine there as often as they wished—and put it all on his tab. He
had made his private plane available to ferry McCarthy's staff to
Boston; he had attended McCarthy's wedding; and when he
learned that McCarthy was unhappy about Stevens' pronouncement there was no espionage at Fort Monmouth, he had hastily
lunched with McCarthy and had rushed out a conciliatory statement saying that this was just what the Army's own investigation
had showed; he didn't mean another inquiry might not find
espionage there. On the flight down to Eatontown on the day

on which Roy Cohn allegedly had issued his "declaration of war," Stevens had been trying to get McCarthy to "suspend" his probe; he had had a statement all prepared in which the Senator would graciously say that he was giving the Army a chance to clean its own house. Stevens explained this maneuver by emphasizing he was just as much opposed to communists and espionage as anybody else—but that he had wanted a "different" type of investigation. Wheeling and dealing to obtain this objective would have made sense to the public only if someone had exposed the type of hearings McCarthy had been conducting for what they were. And neither Stevens nor anyone else in the Eisenhower Administration had had the grit to do that.

In his questioning of Stevens, Ray Jenkins sometimes brought outbursts of laughter from the audience as he showed that Schine had received fifteen leaves in eight days; had hired another draftee to clean his rifle; had ridden in a truck cab on rainy days instead of in the open with his fellow privates; and had told his astonished company commander that he was in service only because he had a mission to modernize the Army.

This spate of questions and answers drove McCarthy into a frenzy in which he whirled from one objection to another even more far-fetched. The questions about Schine were unfair, he cried, because they posed facts that had not been proved. This argument caused titters in the audience, probably from those who recognized that this very tactic was a principal weapon in McCarthy's own arsenal. Further, McCarthy argued, it was "unfair to the Army and the mothers of America" to picture soldiers being packed into trucks in the rain "like cattle or sheep"—a contention that brought guffaws from every ex-GI in the audience. Finally he was driven to argue that no charge should be brought against a man unless he was present in the room to defend himself: "This committee has a rule stating that, and we have always followed it."

"Then why wasn't it followed last Thursday when accusations were made against General Reber's brother when he was not here to defend himself?" snapped Senator Jackson.

Jackson's question became even more pertinent on May 4 when McCarthy tried to pull another fast one on the committee. In cross-examining Stevens, he flourished under the Secretary's nose what purported to be a January 26, 1951, report from J.

Edgar Hoover warning of the dangers of espionage at Fort Monmouth. The report had been labeled "confidential" by the FBI, a designation that in bureau lexicon was the equivalent of "top secret." Questions instantly arose. How did such a document come into McCarthy's possession? And could it be used in a public hearing?

In the investigation that followed, it came out that McCarthy's document purported to be a verbatim copy of an FBI report—but that the FBI had made no such report. It bore the signature of J. Edgar Hoover, but Hoover had never signed such a document. What had happened was this: the FBI had forwarded to Military Intelligence a fifteen-page report covering information it had gathered about employees at Fort Monmouth. Some paragraphs of this report and the McCarthy document were identical. It became apparent that some hand, identity unknown, had condensed the FBI's fifteen pages into a two-and-a-quarter page summary—and, in the process, had placed an individual interpretation upon the contents. Both documents contained the names of thirty-four persons, but the FBI had not attempted to make any evaluation, to render any judgment. In line with its long-established practice, the FBI had simply forwarded all the information it had gathered, however reliable or unreliable. But the secret hand that had slipped McCarthy the condensation had rendered judgment, appending after each name the notation "derogatory" or "no derogatory."

The wrangle over the purloined report lasted for three days. Robert A. Collier, a former FBI agent serving as a committee investigator, testified that FBI Director J. Edgar Hoover had told him he had never signed such a document as McCarthy had presented; that no such document existed in the FBI files. Hoover said, however, that some phrases had been lifted verbatim from the FBI's fifteen-page report. Welch cross-examined Collier.

Question: Now, Mr. Collier, as I understand your testimony, this document that I hold in my hand is a carbon copy of precisely nothing. Is that right?

Answer: I will say that Mr. Hoover informed me it is not a carbon copy of a memorandum prepared or sent by the FBI.

Question: Let's have it straight from the shoulder. So far as you know it's a carbon copy of precisely nothing.

Answer: So far as I know it is. Yes. But that again is—

Question: And so far as you know, this document in this courtroom, sprung yesterday by Senator McCarthy, is a perfect phony. Is that right?

Answer: No, sir. I—That is your conclusion, I will not draw any such conclusion.

When McCarthy took the witness stand later that same day, May 5, he twisted this testimony around to suit his own purposes, congratulating himself by saying "it has been testified that it's a complete word-for-word verbatim transcript of the FBI report. I was very happy to learn that this morning." A little later in his testimony, even he conceded that what he had was "an evaluation" of the FBI original, and he admitted that, though thirty-four persons were named, "I don't have the report on each individual."

He testified on direct examination by Jenkins that his summary bearing the name of J. Edgar Hoover had been given to him by a young Army Intelligence officer who was disturbed because no action was taken. (Everyone at the hearing ignored the fact, by now so obvious, that many of the persons named in the FBI's unevaluated collection of gossip and rumor had been run through the security mill, some for the second time, and had been cleared of all suspicion. Indeed, some of these new clearances were being announced at Fort Monmouth even as the hearings were taking place.) When Welch tried to learn from McCarthy the identity of the author who had passed him the summary, McCarthy told him: "You will not get that information from me." He insisted that he would protect his informants at all costs.

The following day, May 6—and on several occasions thereafter—McCarthy made it clear that he considered himself the supreme arbiter of what information he should receive and what he should do with it. Attorney General Herbert Brownell, in a letter to the committee, declared that neither the fifteen-page FBI original nor McCarthy's bobtailed version should be declassified. The McCarthy document, Brownell wrote, "constitutes an unauthorized use of information which is classified as confidential and . . . it is my opinion it should not be made public."

McCarthy, in a lengthy statement, said in effect that no one was going to muzzle him. ". . . when I received FBI material which is disseminated and is in the hands of loyalty boards with

Communist records," he said, recklessly impugning the patriotism of Loyalty Board members, "I can no longer respect any classification of them . . ." He stormed on in involved syntax, declaring that "there is no human directive . . . [that] will keep me from making available to the public the type of information which we have here showing neglect."

On May 28 and again on June 15, McCarthy explicitly appealed to federal employees to disregard all rules and regulations to send him information. On the first occasion, he said he would like to notify the millions of federal employees "that I feel it is their duty to give us any information which they have about graft, corruption, Communism, treason, and that there is no loyalty to a superior officer which can tower above and beyond their loyalty to their country." On the second occasion, he declared that "I have instructed a vast number of these employees that they are duty-bound to give me information even though some little bureaucrat has stamped it 'Secret' to protect himself."

These open and repeated declarations that McCarthy would observe no rules regarding classified information was, as Walter Lippmann wrote, a pernicious doctrine which placed the whim of one man above all the constituted agencies of government.

FOR FOURTEEN DAYS McCarthy hounded Stevens in a bullying persecution that could not help but build up sympathy for his victim.

Joseph and Stewart Alsop wrote that McCarthy was conducting a filibuster designed to stalemate the hearings and force a halt short of complete disaster. Joseph Welch, on the eleventh day of the hearings, had expressed the same thought in these words: "For days I have passed when I have been given an opportunity to ask questions. For days the committee members have passed when given their opportunity. I suggest that it's time the country heard this simple thought—that the Senator is now engaged in a filibuster by the device of cross-examination."

The filibuster, the Alsops wrote, "was designed to keep the monitored [telephone] conversations out of the record" and avoid exposure of "the full nastiness of the whole business." This would "quickly happen," they added, the instant unadorned transcripts of the words that fell from the principals' mouths went into the record. Though the filibuster obviously "did McCarthy and Cohn great harm in the country"—as, indeed, was shown by Gallup polls reflecting overwhelming support for Secretary Stevens— it was a tactic of desperation that served a second, secret McCarthy purpose. It made everyone so disgusted and weary of the whole business that there was a chance the hearings might be cut short, leaving McCarthy with the victory of a drawn battle.

Such a result, indeed, was precisely what Senator Dirksen tried to achieve. On May 10, the thirteenth day of the hearings, he offered a resolution providing that, after Stevens left the stand, McCarthy should be called to testify—and that, then, all other witnesses should be heard in executive session, with testimony released to the press at the end of the day. This would have served the purpose of taking the show off television, dampening the whole dispute. For two days, the committee fussed and fiddled with this proposal.

Assistant Secretary of Defense Hensel, against whom not a word of proof had been offered in support of McCarthy's charges, took the position that he would not oppose curtailment of the hearings if the committee dismissed the charges as unproved. Chairman Mundt indicated plainly that he would like to vote for the Dirksen proposal, but he wanted the agreement of Secretary Stevens. At this point, however, the much-abused Secretary refused to compromise. The position of the Army, he said, was that "every witness who has a place in this hearing should be brought here and should testify and should get all the facts on the table."

On the second day of debate over the curtailment issue, Dirksen offered some slight amendments to his original resolution, and Mundt pressed Welch to find out how Stevens felt. Welch consulted the Secretary and reported that Stevens did not "think it fair and equitable that I should be stuck on the stand for fourteen days and that one or two of the parties on the other side and perhaps one on my side, Mr. Adams, should never be there at all." Mundt protested that this still didn't answer his real question which was, in effect, would the Secretary "go along?" Welch consulted his client again and reported:

"A.—He does not wish to accept from the Chairman a proxy to cast your vote. He thinks, Mr. Chairman, that is outside his province.

"Secondly, as to fairness, he says, 'I continue in my view that the proposed resolution would not result in fairness.'"

This was probably Stevens' finest hour. He had spurned compromise, and so, as Thomas L. Stokes wrote, he had "completely foiled some of the slickest political operators in the business, and the nation's Capital is chuckling about it." Senator Mundt, having failed to cajole the Secretary into making the decision for him, reluctantly joined with the Democrats in defeating Dirksen's coverup proposal by a vote of 4 to 3.

The televised hearings would go on; refuge from the public eye was denied McCarthy.

ONE OF THE SURPRISE twists of the hearings came when the Army's much-bruited, monitored telephone talks were introduced into the record. They didn't begin to show what their advance billing had heralded. The "full nastiness" of the whole business, which the Alsops had predicted would become instantly revealed, was still obscured. One reason, perhaps, was that John Adams, the Army counsel, had not begun monitoring his telephone calls until nearly the end of February—and by that time he and Roy Cohn were not on speaking terms. The result was that there was no record to substantiate Adams' charges that Cohn subjected him to wild vituperation and obscenities.

The calls that had been monitored were largely those between Secretary Stevens and McCarthy, between the Secretary and some Democratic members of the McCarthy committee, and between Adams and Francis Carr, the successor to J. B. Matthews as the committee's staff director. What these calls showed was the excessive concern exhibited by the Secretary of the Army for one lowly private, G. David Schine.

One especially revealing call, placed by the Secretary on October 21, 1953, showed Stevens in most humble, humiliating posture. Talking like a father to his favorite son, the Secretary had assured Schine he had done everything possible for him; he had taken his case all the way up to the top—up to Secretary of Defense Charles M. Wilson himself. Unfortunately, service regulations were such that both Wilson and himself had been compelled to decide they could do nothing for Schine at the moment; but the Secretary assured his favorite private-to-be that, if he would just go to Fort Dix and take his basic training, "there is an excellent chance that we can pick you up and use you in a way that would be useful to the country and yourself . . ."

In similar vein, the monitored talks between Adams and Carr showed that the Army counsel was constantly trying to assure the committee director of the Army's eagerness to cooperate, to do almost anything possible to soothe the ruffled feelings of the McCarthy clique. In the whole mish-mash, there was just one monitored call that was really helpful to an Army contention —the contention that McCarthy was not really a free man in the Schine affair, but was being prevailed upon by Cohn. In one talk with Stevens, McCarthy said: "If he [Schine] could get off weekends—Roy—it is one of the few things I've seen him completely unreasonable about. He thinks Dave should be a general and work from a penthouse in the Waldorf."

The monitoring revealed that Secretary Stevens, in his desperation to put an end to the hounding of the Army, needing help wherever he could get it, had appealed to the Democrats. With McCarthy and Mundt the Republican powers on the committee, the Secretary had turned to McClellan and Symington for support. He had called McClellan after the General Zwicker affair, informing him that he was not going to let Zwicker testify again and that McCarthy was threatening to subpoena him. McClellan suggested that Stevens should move in fast before McCarthy could serve him with a subpoena. "Beat him to the punch . . . Just announce that you definitely have requested the opportunity to appear."

Symington, who had been Secretary of the Air Force before he became a Senator and so had a special interest in the armed services, had also been consulted at length by Stevens. One monitored call quoted Symington as telling Stevens he had better forget "the Marquis of Queensberry Rules" if he were going to "play" with McCarthy because McCarthy played "rough." Seizing upon these disclosures, McCarthy began to thunder that it was all a Democratic plot against him, and he demanded that Symington should leave his committee post and be compelled to testify under oath about his relations with Stevens. "As the chair knows," he thundered, "the Marquis of Queensberry Rules are the rules for fair fighting, the rules that provide you must not hit below the belt, you must not cheat, you must not lie, you must not gouge." Obviously he spoke as a man who would never stoop to such tactics himself.

Symington, imperturbable, responded that he had indeed warned Stevens that he had "better look out because if he got in a scrap he might find that the junior Senator from Wisconsin would not use rules which were decent or right or fair—and I based that on things I have seen as a member of this committee and also on the campaign of 1952 in Missouri."

For the next two days, McCarthy grabbed the spotlight before the television cameras as the hearings opened, repeating over and over again his aggressive demands that "Sanctimonious Stu" should be compelled to testify. Each time he did, Symington sank in the harpoon, needling McCarthy about his refusal to testify before the Senate committee that had investigated Benton's charges. "Nobody in the Senate knows more about how to avoid testifying than the junior Senator from Wisconsin. And everybody in the United States knows that that fact is true," Symington remarked on one occasion. He also suggested to McCarthy: "You better go to a psychiatrist."

The repetitious battle, always precipitated by McCarthy, got so bad that even Senator Mundt moaned about "this mid-morning madness" and protested about the prodigious waste of the committee's time.

FROM BEHIND THE SMOKE SCREEN of all this sound and fury, there gradually emerged a clear picture of the youthful Svengali of this imbroglio, Roy Cohn. The image that was formed from bits and pieces of testimony, all melding together, was that of a young man stuffed with conceit and a ruthless sense of power. It was a montage built from the testimony, not only of what others said about Roy Cohn, but of what Roy Cohn said about himself.

Cohn took the witness stand with the self-important announcement: "Roy Cohn is here speaking for Roy Cohn, to give the facts."

He boasted that he had no attorney; he was his own counsel. Kindly Joseph Welch looked at this specimen sitting in the witness chair before him, and he began, ever so gently, to sink in the barbs.

"Mr. Cohn, I assumed you would like it understood that although I sit at the same table, I am not your counsel."

"There is no statement that has been made at this hearing with which I am in more complete agreement," Cohn answered. ". . . I have no counsel here . . ."

"In all modesty, sir," came the soft Bostonian voice, "I am content that it should appear from my end that I am not your counsel."

Welch produced the original, full photograph from which the famous Schine-Stevens picture had been cropped and asked Cohn to look at it. Cohn suggested that the picture be brought closer. "I confess," he said, "to a slight case of near-sightedness."

"I think you have," said Welch, oozing sympathy, "betrayed some near-sightedness."

Murray Kempton, recounting this by-play, wrote: "Roy Cohn gulped and gasped like a mud-sucker aspiring to be a trout and flexed his fingers and said he could not hope to match Mr. Welch's quips. Joseph Welch laved poor, suffering Roy with his healing glance and said, 'Oh, Mr. Cohn,' and it sounded like, 'Bless Your Soul.' "

Directing Cohn's attention to the uncropped picture, Welch suggested that Secretary Stevens had a "grim" look on his face. Didn't Cohn think so? Cohn couldn't really tell. Well, could Cohn be sure that the Secretary was really looking at Schine—and not at Colonel Bradley, who was standing just the other side of Schine? "It would take someone with clairvoyance to know at whom Secretary Stevens is looking, would it not?" Welch asked.

"No sir," said Cohn. "I don't think so. It would take somebody with common sense who can look at a picture and see what's in it."

Welch was unshaken. "I think I observe on Colonel Bradley's face a faint look of pleasure. Do you, sir?"

Roy Cohn, to his undoing, ventured to match wits with Joseph Welch.

"I would say," he replied, "I know that Colonel Bradley had a good steak dinner shortly afterward. Perhaps he was anticipating it."

With a lightning rejoinder that convulsed the audience, Welch shot back: "If Bradley is feeling good about a steak dinner, Schine must be considering a whole haunch of beef!"

It had perhaps nothing much to do with the issues at stake, but it was a marvelous show and its effect was undeniable. Here was the young terror of the McCarthy committee, the purger of books, the ruthless inquisitor, being given lessons in a technique more suave and deadly than his own, and made to look puerile and ridiculous.

The portrait of an arrogant young man running amuck was sketched in great detail by John Adams, the Army counsel who had dealt so often with Cohn. One of Adams' most vivid recollections derived from the ride to uptown New York after a luncheon near the Foley Square Courthouse on December 17, 1953. Adams wanted to catch a train back to Washington from Pennsylvania Station and was going to take the subway, but Cohn said, "No, I can get you there quicker," and they began to ride up Fourth Avenue in Cohn's car. Cohn was seething over the Schine affair, and during the whole ride he was extremely vituperative and abusive, Adams said.

". . . Cohn's anger erupted again, and as it erupted, it was directed on this occasion more toward Senator McCarthy than it was to me," Adams testified. "And as we were riding uptown Senator McCarthy turned around to me and on two or three occasions . . . he asked me if I couldn't, when I got back to Washington, talk to Mr. Stevens and arrange an assignment in New York for Schine . . ."

At Thirty-Fourth Street, Cohn wanted to make a left-hand turn to go across town to Penn Station, but no turn was permitted at the intersection. Cohn waved some kind of special-privilege card under the nose of the traffic cop and said he had to get Adams to the station, but the cop roared, in effect, "Who the hell is Adams?" and told Cohn to get moving up the avenue. They zipped through the tunnel under Grand Central Station, and the first thing Adams knew they were at Forty-Fifth Street going rapidly in the wrong direction. He protested to Cohn "and in a final fit of violence he stopped the car in the middle of four lanes of traffic and said 'get there however you can.' So I climbed out of the car in the middle of four lanes of traffic between Forty-Sixth and Forty-Seventh Streets on Park Avenue . . ."

A few days later, Adams testified, Carr told him "that he didn't think I should feel badly about the way I was put out of the car, because he said I should have been there to see the way

Senator McCarthy left the car a few blocks later . . . He said
. . . I should have seen the way Senator McCarthy was put out
of the car in front of the Waldorf-Astoria."

Though Cohn denied he ever used obscenities—he did not,
he said, use any more "cusswords" than the average man and
there were no novel expressions in his repertoire—repeated incidents of this kind reinforced the picture of a man-child throwing uncontrollable tantrums when he was unable to get his way.

There was the "declaration of war" incident at Fort Monmouth. Though Cohn denied he had ever said any such thing—
the whole idea was preposterous, he said, how could *he* "declare
war" on the Army?—there was much testimony on the Army side
that he had indeed used just such a threat, and even Cohn himself admitted that he had been exceedingly angry at the affront
of being barred from the secret laboratory at Monmouth.

Adams testified that Frank Carr told him on one occasion
"he felt the Army should be aware of the fact that as long as
Mr. Schine's assignment did not suit Cohn, that the Army was in
for trouble with this committee."

Virtually the same word had been conveyed to him, Adams
said, by that shadowy figure in the background of the McCarthy
entourage, George Sokolsky. Sokolsky was introduced into the
drama by Frank Carr, Adams said. Carr kept telling him that
Sokolsky had powerful influence with McCarthy and kept urging
him to get in touch with Sokolsky. Adams did. He testified that, in
a forty-nine-minute telephone talk on February 5, 1954, Sokolsky
suggested that Schine, who had just been sent to Camp Gordon,
be placed immediately in a special program called Course 95.
Regulations provided that trainees had to finish eight weeks of
basic training before they could be assigned to this course, but
Sokolsky urged that this rule be waived for Schine and promised
that if it was he would "move in" and settle things. There were
other conversations with Sokolsky, Adams testified. The final
one came on February 16. Adams described it this way:

". . . Sokolsky asked me what was going to happen to Private
Schine with reference to Course 95 and I told him Schine was
not going to enter Course 95.

"He stated to me that the Army was being very foolish, that
we were just asking for a two-year fight and that we were just
going to be in trouble that long."

Senator McClellan wondered why the Army hadn't yielded, and Adams said:

"Well, I guess as good a reason as any was that we had— well, we had 25,000 men killed in Korea who didn't have the money or the influence to get themselves a New York assignment."

McClellan asked whether it was unusual for the counsel for the Army or the Secretary to get a call to keep a private off KP (the purpose of the Carr-Cohn calls to Adams at Amherst), and Adams replied: "It's so unusual, sir, that it's nothing short of fantastic."

In summation, Adams testified:

"And the abuse I took with reference to Schine during this period, if you would pile together all of the abuse that I had from all the other members of Congress and all of the other Congressional employees over a period of five years, it would not compare to the abuse I took over this situation."

Question: The abuse from whom?

Answer: Mr. Cohn.

All of this was capped by one vivid, off-the-record vignette. It occurred after the close of the June 11 hearing. Senator Jackson had been putting Senator McCarthy through a vigorous cross-examination and, shortly after the cameras were turned off, Cohn clashed with Robert F. Kennedy. Young Bobby, then just beginning his career, and placed with the committee through his father's influence, was serving as counsel to the Democratic minority. It was a minor role, and it was no secret that he and Cohn cordially detested each other. But until this day, they had preserved an appearance of amenity. Now, in seconds, their tempers flashed. Reporters overheard a part of the exchange. According to Kennedy and Jackson, Cohn threatened to "get" Jackson—ironically, one of the strongest boosters of the military and an unyielding hard-liner in foreign affairs—by bringing out "stuff about his being favorably inclined toward Communists."

The exchange between Cohn and Kennedy began low-voiced, but the anger of the two struck sparks and as tempers rose so did their voices. Reporters overheard Cohn accuse Kennedy:

"You have a personal hatred . . ."

"If I have, it's justified," snapped Kennedy.

Cohn, raging: "Do you want to fight now?"

Kennedy, equally furious: ". . . You can't get away with it, Cohn. You tried it with McCarthy and you tried it with the Army. You can't do it."

"Do you think you're qualified to sit here?" shouted Cohn.

Kennedy turned his back in cold contempt and walked away.

Afterward, Cohn denied he had made any threat to "get" Jackson, but Kennedy said:

"I told him he had a —— nerve threatening me. I told him he had been threatening all the Democrats and threatening the Army and not to try it on me."

THE HEARINGS DRAGGED ON interminably. They continued to twitch like a dying snake in the sunset long after Joseph Welch had delivered the *coup de grâce* in a scene of unforgettable drama that blotted out most of what had gone before and all that came afterward. The climax came on June 9, 1954, while Roy Cohn was on the stand. Welch was taking Roy over the high hurdles in regard to the Fort Monmouth inquiry. His point was that Cohn and McCarthy had had the purloined FBI letter in their files for months; they had uncovered what they said was shocking information about Fort Monmouth —and yet weeks had gone by and they hadn't informed the Secretary of the Army in their own Republican Administration about the situation so that he could take swift and appropriate action. Why?

Welch, needling, sarcastic, impaled Roy Cohn in this sequence:

Question: And on September 7 when you met him [Secretary Stevens] you had in your bosom this alarming situation about Monmouth, is that right?

Answer: Yes, I knew about Monmouth then, yes, sir.

Question: And you didn't tug at his lapel and say, "Mr. Secretary, I know something about Monmouth that won't let me sleep nights?"

Answer: I don't know.

Question: You didn't do it, did you?

Answer: I don't, as I have testified, Mr. Welch, I don't know whether I talked to Mr. Stevens about it then or not . . .

Question: Don't you know that if you had really told him what your fears were and substantiated them to any extent he could have jumped in the next day with suspensions?

Answer: No, sir.

Question: Have you, did you have, any reason to doubt his fidelity?

Answer: No, sir.

Question: Or his honor?

Answer: No, sir.

Question: Or his patriotism?

Answer: No, sir.

Question: And yet, Mr. Cohn, you didn't tell him what you knew?

Cohn could only repeat that he did not know. Welch suggested that, if one possessed the kind of information Cohn claimed to have had, it would be advisable to move "before sundown," and he sank another barb with this puckish advice: "May I add my small voice, sir, and say whenever you know about a subversive or a Communist or a spy, please hurry. Will you remember those words?"

Listening to all this, Joe McCarthy was almost beside himself with vexation and impatience; he was driven to the imprudent leap. Thrusting himself into the middle of the confrontation without even a cry of "point of order," he charged before the television cameras, a grin on his face as he obviously envisioned the annihilation of the gadfly lawyer.

". . . In view of Mr. Welch's request that the information be given—what we know of anyone who might be performing any work for the Communist Party, I think we should tell him that he has in his law firm a young man named [Frederick G.] Fisher whom he recommended, incidentally, to do the work on this committee, who has been for a number of years a member of an organization which was named—oh, years and years ago—as the legal bulwark of the Communist Party . . ."

Roy Cohn, a more wily and perceptive man than his master, whatever his faults, sat slumped in the witness chair, his legs dangling, shaking his head in silent protest, his lips at one point even seeming to frame the silent caution, "Stop, stop!"

But nothing could stop McCarthy now. He plunged recklessly

on, charging that Welch had tried to have Fisher named "as the assistant counsel for this committee," despite the fact that Fisher had belonged for a number of years to the National Lawyers Guild, an organization that had been labeled subversive by the House Un-American Activities Committee. McCarthy blustered:

"Now I have hesitated bringing that up but I have been rather bored with your phony request to Mr. Cohn here that he personally get every Communist out of government before sundown. Therefore we will give you the information about the young man in your own organization.

"Now I'm not asking you at this time why you tried to force him on this committee. That you did, the committee knows. Whether you knew he was a member of that Communist organization or not I don't know. I assume you did not, Mr. Welch, because I get the impression that while you are quite an actor, you play for a laugh, I don't think you have any conception of the danger of the Communist Party. I don't think you yourself would ever knowingly aid the Communist cause. I think you're unknowingly aiding it when you try to burlesque this hearing in which we are attempting to bring out the facts or . . ."

Senator Mundt broke into the tirade to set the record straight.

"The Chair wishes to say," he intoned almost sepulchrally, "that he has no recognition or no memory of Mr. Welch recommending Mr. Fisher or anybody else as counsel for this committee."

His veracity challenged even by his long-time supporter, McCarthy whirled around, muttering he would get a news story to substantiate his charge. Welch just stared at him. He no longer resembled a puckish actor. His face had gone white with anger.

"Senator McCarthy," he began in a voice that shook, "I did not know, Senator—Senator, sometimes you say, 'May I have your attention.' May I have yours, Senator?"

McCarthy, contemptuous, paid no heed, but walked over to James Juliana and called in a loud voice for the production of the newspaper clipping he wanted.

"I'm listening to someone in one ear and you in the other," he told Welch.

"Now this time, sir, I want you to listen with both," Welch snapped.

"Yes, sir."

McCarthy, displaying his indifference, went right on giving instructions to Juliana about the material he wanted to place into the record.

"Senator, you won't need anything in the record when I finish telling you this," Welch told him in a voice shaking with anger, tears glistening in his eyes. "Until this moment, Senator, I think I never really gauged your cruelty or your recklessness.

"Fred Fisher is a young man who went to Harvard Law School and came into my firm and is starting what looks to be a brilliant career with us. When I decided to work for this committee I asked Jim St. Clair, who sits on my right, to be my first assistant. I said to him: 'Jim, pick somebody in the firm to work under you that you would like.'

"He chose Fred Fisher and they came down on an afternoon plane. That night when we had taken a little stab at trying to see what the case was about, Fred Fisher and Jim St. Clair and I went to dinner together.

"I then said to these young men: 'Boys, I don't know anything about you except I've always liked you, but if there's anything funny in the life of either one of you that would hurt anybody in this case, you had better speak up quick.'

"And Fred Fisher said: 'Mr. Welch, when I was in law school and for a period of months after I belonged to the Lawyers Guild,' as you have suggested, Senator.

"He went on to say, 'I am the secretary of the Young Republicans' League with the son of the Massachusetts Governor and I have the respect and admiration of my community and I'm sure I have the respect and admiration of the twenty-five lawyers or so in Hale & Dorr [Welch's law firm].'

"And I said, 'Fred, I just don't think I'm going to ask you to work on the case. If I do, one of these days that will come out and go over national television and it will hurt like the dickens.'

"So, Senator, I asked him to go back to Boston. Little did I dream you could be so reckless and so cruel as to do an injury to that lad. It is true he is still with Hale & Dorr. It is true that he will continue to be with Hale & Dorr.

"It is, I regret to say, equally true that I fear he shall always bear a scar, needlessly inflicted by you. If it were in my power to forgive you for your reckless cruelty, I would do so. I like to think I'm a gentle man, but your forgiveness will have to come from someone other than me."

The Senate Caucus Room was hushed, its audience held spellbound by the sudden and potent drama. Few there—and doubtless fewer still in the television audience—realized that this had all been disclosed before; that Welch himself had related the circumstances the very day he had sent Fisher back to Boston, and that *The New York Times* had carried the story, together with Fisher's picture. Joseph Welch, sensing the character of the enemy, had tried to be above-board about it, hoping to forestall the very kind of television sensation McCarthy was now attempting to create. Only the sensation wasn't developing quite the way McCarthy had anticipated. Even he could feel the force of Welch's anger and contempt; even he could sense the gathering emotions in the hearing room. He fumbled with some papers before him, and then he tried to bluster his way through the storm he had created, rumbling in self-justification that Welch "has been baiting Mr. Cohn here for hours" and "I just want to give this man's record . . ."

Welch, who had been caught up in the emotion of his statement, now had full control of himself again. His eyes were cold and hard, and his tone frigid: "Senator, may we not drop this? We know he belonged to the Lawyers Guild."

"Let me finish this," cried McCarthy.

"And Mr. Cohn nods his head at me. I did you, I think, no personal injury, Mr. Cohn."

"No, sir."

"I meant to do you no personal injury, and if I did, I beg your pardon. Let us not assassinate this lad further, Senator. You've done enough. Have you no sense of decency, sir? At long last, have you left no sense of decency?"

"I know this hurts you, Mr. Welch," snarled McCarthy.

"I'll say it hurts."

"May I say, Mr. Chairman, as a point of personal privilege, that I'd like to finish this."

"Senator, I think it hurts you, too, sir," said Welch.

McCarthy rumbled on, trying to show that Welch had attempted to get the committee to hire Fisher as an assistant counsel, an allegation whose truth Mundt again denied. McCarthy attempted to ask Welch a question, and Welch froze him with his final rejoinder:

"Mr. McCarthy, I will not discuss this further with you. You have sat within six feet of me and could ask, could have asked me about Fred Fisher. You have seen fit to bring it out, and if there is a God in Heaven it will do neither you nor your cause any good.

"I will not discuss it further. I will not ask Mr. Cohn any more questions. You, Mr. Chairman, may, if you will, call the next witness."

It was over. It took a few seconds for the realization to sink in; then the caucus room rocked with the thunder of applause. Even the press photographers, for the first time in the memory of Washington observers, were so moved that they dropped their cameras and clapped for Welch. Senator Mundt, who had tried to prevent such demonstrations in the past, bowed his head to the gale as this one swept the hearing room—then quickly called a five-minute recess.

Joe McCarthy sat slouched in his chair, breathing hard. Spectators and reporters shunned him. Feeling the universal hostility, he looked around, spread out his hands in puzzlement, and asked as if to himself: "What did I do wrong?"

22

Censure

THERE WAS NO CHANCE of stopping the toboggan; it was all downhill now for Joe McCarthy.

His Nemesis was to all appearances one of the least likely men in the Senate for that role. He was Ralph E. Flanders, the Republican from Vermont, certainly no shouting radical. Flanders had criticized Senator Tydings to his face for the manner in which he had conducted the original investigation into McCarthy's communists-in-government charges; he had applauded many of McCarthy's early efforts to root out communism; he had been one of the twenty-five Republican Senators who had signed the manifesto of 1952, attacking the Truman Administration for its "smear" attack on McCarthy. Clearly, Ralph Flanders was no "fellow-traveler" out to crucify Joe McCarthy for his attacks on communism.

He was, on the contrary, a man who had literally lived the legend of Horatio Alger. His father, in his youth, had been "bound out" to any neighboring farmers who would give him his keep for his work. The family had known the hard, scrabbling life of farming on Vermont's rocky acres. Upon leaving school, Flanders had become a machinist's apprentice, gradually fighting his way up from job to job—and ultimately marrying the boss's daughter. He had become a leading industrialist and president of the Federal Reserve Bank of Boston.

Now seventy-three, completely bald, slightly stooped, somewhat paunchy, Ralph Flanders was a mild-mannered, folksy man with a little graying mustache. He viewed the world from behind rimless spectacles through eyes that held a perpetual twinkle—eyes that had lost some of their kindly humor after the General Zwicker episode that had led Flanders to make his first anti-McCarthy, "war dance" speech. The Army-McCarthy hearings had followed in short order; and, viewing that carnage, looking back upon the long trail of McCarthy's misdeeds, Ralph Flanders felt that the time had come for the Senate, for its own honor's sake, to put an end to the caperings of the junior Senator from Wisconsin. It was an entirely independent decision on his part.

On June 1, eight days before Joseph Welch publicly skinned McCarthy and hung him up to dry, Flanders took the Senate floor and flung down the gage of battle. He called McCarthy an adult "Dennis the Menace" who was dividing the country, dividing even his own Catholic Church and causing fear and foreboding among minorities. The Jews especially were apprehensive, Flanders said—and with reason. For McCarthy's "anticommunism so completely parallels that of Adolf Hitler as to strike fear into the heart of any defenseless minority." McCarthy's usefulness as an investigator "is continually asserted, but never documented," Flanders said. "Let him also be investigated . . . Were the junior Senator from Wisconsin in the pay of the communists, he could not have done a better job for them."

By any standard of judgment, this should have been headline news, but a press that had persistently and uncritically headlined McCarthy's charges was not greatly interested. Flanders himself later wrote: "My experience in getting my case before the public has been baffling. The radio to some degree and the newspapers to a lesser extent made note of my speeches. Should I give voice to a criticism on the Senate floor, my opponent could make instant rejoinder, since the television was always at his disposal in the committee room. On the morning of June 11 the thought came to me that it would be useful if I shared in the Senator's advantages. Since he had complained that I had given him no notice of my last previous speech (though I asked one of my secretaries to notify his office) it seemed proper to give him notice of the one prepared for that day.

"So I entered the big hearing room and began to look about for a clear way to the witness table where the Senator was testifying. Immediately the reporters sensed that something unusual was in the air and voices saying 'This way—this way' came to my ear. The hot blast from the lights and the eyes of the television cameras were pointed my way. I reached the table and handed this letter to the Senator, which he read aloud:

" 'This is to inform you that I plan to make another speech concerning your activities in the Senate this afternoon as soon after the morning hour as I can get the floor.

" 'If you desire, I would be glad to have you present.' "

Millions of Americans were watching their television sets that morning, and there was now no way for the media to ignore Ralph Flanders. He had achieved the breakthrough he desired.

True to his word, he rose on the Senate floor that afternoon and introduced Senate Resolution 261. It read: "Resolved, That the conduct of the Senator from Wisconsin [McCarthy] is unbecoming a member of the United States Senate, is contrary to senatorial traditions, and tends to bring the Senate into disrepute, and such conduct is hereby condemned."

Two days later, Flanders appeared before another huge television audience on NBC's *Meet the Press*. He served public notice that he intended to keep up his attack in an effort to persuade the Senate to take action against McCarthy. McCarthy, he said, "seeks to be the sole private eye, prosecutor, judge, jury and sentencer" with no one above him—not even the President, not even the people whose interests he pretended to serve.

"This is so clearly in the direction of fighting communism with Fascism that I am seriously disturbed," Senator Flanders said.

This maverick attack by the usually mild and courtly Senator from Vermont enchanted the politicians of neither party. The Democrats, still timorous, pondered the wisdom of an all-out attack on McCarthy. President Eisenhower had sent Flanders a brief note of thanks after the Senator's March "war dance" speech, but his further attacks upon McCarthy met with no response from the White House. Flanders was left in doubt about the real attitude of the Administration. As he later wrote:

". . . I began to surmise, and do still wonder, whether he [the President] did not find me an embarrassment as so many other rock-ribbed Republicans did. Some White House sentiment was surely adverse, for in those last weeks of July I had a visit from a leading Cabinet member (and I mean *leading*) saying that a number of his associates had been discussing the matter, and he had come to tell me that they thought I should lay off. He talked very reasonably, but I had to tell him that the strength of my position lay in being unreasonable."

This refusal of Flanders to yield to pressure, his insistence that his resolution must be considered, forced a three-day Senate debate, July 30 and 31 and August 2. Senator William F. Knowland, of California, the Republican Majority Leader, headed off an immediate vote. Senator Dirksen raged that the Senate would be playing into the hands of the communists if it moved against McCarthy. "The Senator from Vermont and the *Daily Worker* are on the same side of this issue," he intoned. Senator Capehart saw Flanders' move as "an attack on the Congress of the United States. It is an attack on the right of Congress to investigate." Senator Welker warned ominously that, if McCarthy were allowed to fall, Jenner and Velde, who headed the Senate Internal Security Committee and the House Un-American Activities Committee, would be the next to feel the ax.

On the other side, Senator Fulbright was Flanders' principal supporter. He told the Senate: "It is necessary for one to see him [McCarthy] in action as chairman of his committee fully to appreciate his talents; they cannot be described adequately by words. Fortunately, many millions of Americans including, I assume, all members of this Senate have observed the technique and methods of the junior Senator from Wisconsin . . ."

McCarthy, as he always did, trumpeted that he wanted Senators who desired to investigate *him* to come forward and be put under oath and compelled to testify. He sneered at Fulbright as "Halfbright." And he referred to Flanders as "senile. I think they should get a man with a net and take him to a good quiet place."

In the end, it was all just too much. McCarthy had defied too many canons of honor and common decency, and even the Senate, which had demonstrated an almost infinite capacity for stomaching him, could restrain itself no longer. To prevent an outright vote of censure, Knowland introduced a resolution for the appointment of a select committee of six Senators to hear the case against McCarthy. It carried 75 to 12 and was opposed mainly by those like Flanders and Fulbright who felt that the record was abundantly clear and condemnation should be voted out of hand. Judgment had been postponed, but Joe McCarthy, at long last, had been called to account by a jury of his peers.

O N A U G U S T 3 1 , 1 9 5 4 , after thirty-six days of hearings during which some two million words of testimony were taken, the Army-McCarthy committee headed by Senator Mundt issued its report. It was a split decision, the Republicans arrayed on one side, the Democrats on the other. But both sides, varying only in degree, were devastating to McCarthy.

Midway in the hearings, the Republican majority by a strict party-line 4 to 3 vote had washed out the charges against Frank Carr and H. Struve Hensel. McCarthy had not attempted to introduce into the record a single word of proof in substantiation of the conflict-of-interest charges that had catapulted Hensel's name into such glaring prehearing headlines, and the Democrats raged at the decision of the Republicans to let the charge fall by default without pinning McCarthy with responsibility for the fraud.

What was left, then, for the committee to decide was the two basic issues that had been there from the beginning: Had McCarthy hounded the Army in the effort to get favorable treatment of Schine? Had the Army used Schine as a "hostage" in an attempt to "blackmail" McCarthy into dropping his investigation of it?

The Republicans held that the evidence did not establish Mc-

Carthy's "personal involvement" in the efforts made on Schine's behalf, but it rapped his knuckles for not having "exercised more vigorous discipline in stopping any member of the staff from engaging in unduly persistent or aggressive efforts in behalf of G. David Schine." The Republicans found that Roy Cohn had, indeed, been "unduly aggressive and persistent" and that under the circumstances, with the committee investigating the Army as it was, such actions "take on an aspect of impropriety which otherwise might not be present." However, the Republicans held, the Fort Monmouth investigation "was not designed or conducted as a leverage to secure preferential treatment" for Schine.

McCarthy's countercharge of "blackmail" was dismissed. The Republicans decided that Stevens' motives were "beyond reproach," but they reprimanded him for "placation, appeasement and vacillation" and said he should have settled the whole Schine issue the instant it was raised by voicing a decisive and resounding "No." Stevens and Adams, the Republicans concluded, "failed to exercise their responsibilities appropriately." As for the direct and irreconcilable conflicts in the testimony, the Republican majority announced that a full transcript was being sent to the Justice Department to determine whether perjury prosecutions were warranted.

The Democratic minority report was longer, gave a much fuller summary of the evidence, and denounced McCarthy in uncompromising language. The Democrats computed that Private Schine, in sixty-seven days of training at Fort Dix, had received "passes for all or part of 34 days." They ridiculed the argument that this extraordinary consideration had been justified by the pressure of committee work. They demonstrated that, according to the testimony, Schine had been given no new assignments after it became obvious in July that he was soon to be drafted; they emphasized this left him with four months to clean up his desk and tidy up unfinished business—"yet not one memorandum written or dictated by Mr. Schine during those days was produced." The Democrats remarked sarcastically: "It is hardly credible that such an allegedly prodigious worker could leave such minute traces of his labor."

The evidence established, the Democrats contended, that whatever work Schine had performed before entering the Army was "insignificant and unimpressive" and certainly did not justify his receiving any special consideration. In the light of these facts, the Democrats ruled that Roy Cohn "knowingly misrepresented" the need for Schine's services and so "misused and abused the powers of his office and brought disrepute to the Subcommittee." The evidence clearly demonstrated to the Democrats that McCarthy knew all this, that he "acquiesced" and "condoned" Cohn's conduct, and in the hearings "undertook to defend" it. "For these inexcusable actions Senator McCarthy and Mr. Cohn merit severe criticism," the Democrats wrote.

Like the Republicans, the Democrats found McCarthy's "hostage" and "blackmail" charges against the Army "wholly unsubstantiated." And like the Republicans, they criticized Stevens for his efforts to appease McCarthy and Cohn, and for granting incredible special privileges to Schine. "We have grave doubts that any other draftee in basic training ever received such high-level attention and consideration or was ever permitted so to interfere with the proper function of our Defense Establishment," the Democrats said.

Zeroing in on McCarthy, they declared that he merited "severe criticism" for these additional actions: for "attacking the character and impugning the loyalty of individuals who were in no way associated with or involved in the proceedings"; for attempting to use the spurious "top secret" FBI document, and for appealing to government employees to violate the law by pilfering and giving him other classified documents.

The combined effect of the two reports was a condemnation of McCarthy. The best his Republican cohorts had been able to achieve for him was a lame technical clearance that loaded all onus on the shoulders of Roy Cohn, of whose activities McCarthy had been well aware and for whom, as the chairman of his own investigating committee, he had been responsible.

P R O B A B L Y there were never six United States Senators more unhappy than those drafted by the leadership of both parties to hear censure charges against Senator McCarthy. There were no volunteers for this task. Every member of the Senate had vivid memories of what had happened to associates who had crossed McCarthy's path—to Raymond Baldwin, to Millard Tydings, to

Guy Gillette; and none was anxious to expose himself to similar treatment. The result was that the leadership of both parties had to tap the condemned men on the shoulder.

A scrupulous effort was made to select Senators who had kept quiet about McCarthy, who had no known bias. The committee was truly bipartisan, composed of three Republicans, three Democrats. Its chairman was Senator Arthur V. Watkins, a Utah Republican. His Republican associates were Frank Carlson, of Kansas, an admirer and close friend of President Eisenhower, and Francis Case, of South Dakota, who was known as one of the Senate's most artful compromisers, a Republican who had been able to remain on good terms with even Wayne Morse.

The Democratic contingent was composed of Senator Samuel J. Ervin, Jr., of North Carolina, a former judge; Edwin C. Johnson, of Colorado, a member of the Senate's exclusive and dominant conservative-oriented inner club and the mentor of another Johnson, Lyndon B. Johnson, of Texas; and John C. Stennis, of Mississippi, a reserved, quiet, tolerant conservative who had been a lawyer and judge before he came to the Senate.

This was the committee that held nine hearings from the last day of August through mid-September. In the final Senate debate, Senator Flanders had flung a blizzard of charges against McCarthy, arraigning him on thirty-three separate counts. These the committee and its counsel—E. Wallace Chadwick, a former Pennsylvania Congressman—reduced to five major categories.

The charges were all based upon incidents of McCarthy's career about which there could be little dispute. They involved: his contemptuous conduct toward the Gillette committee that had investigated Senator Benton's charges; his appeal to federal employees to violate the law and secrecy classifications to furnish him information; his use of classified data—the spurious FBI report he had flashed at the Army-McCarthy hearings; his berating of Senators Hendrickson and Flanders by calling one "a living miracle" and the other "senile"; and his conduct with respect to General Zwicker.

The hearings were held in the same Senate Caucus Room that had been cluttered with cameras and crawling with cables during the Army-McCarthy hearings. But this time there was a distinct difference in the atmosphere. Senator Watkins was determined to run his hearings with an authoritative hand and a maximum of decorum. The hearings were open to press and public, but television and newsreel cameras were banned. From the standpoint of public interest, it was perhaps just as well, for the censure hearings featured long readings of reports and transcripts of evidence already taken. Chadwick read for hours, for example, the texts of the correspondence that had taken place between Gillette and McCarthy in the Benton investigation, and there were similar long readings from the transcripts of the Army-McCarthy hearings and the examination of Zwicker by McCarthy.

McCarthy had chosen for his attorney one of the best in Washington, Edward Bennett Williams. Williams had made McCarthy promise to be a good boy and let Williams run the show. It was a most difficult promise for McCarthy to keep; and, at the very outset of the hearings, he tried to raise a terrific storm about an article that had appeared in the Denver *Post*, quoting Senator Edwin Johnson as saying he personally loathed McCarthy. Johnson denied that he had ever expressed such a sentiment. This wasn't enough for McCarthy. As Senator Fulbright had warned his colleagues in advance, McCarthy attempted to create chaos and divert the attention of the committee from himself to Senator Johnson. He demanded to know whether Johnson had checked with the Denver *Post*'s editor about the quote. What had he learned?

Watkins was determined that his committee should hew to the main issues and not be distracted by diversionary tactics. He ruled that McCarthy's charge was "extraneous" and that the committee should not waste time with it. If McCarthy wanted to know more, he could talk to Johnson privately. "The Senator is out of order," he ruled, banging his gavel at McCarthy.

McCarthy: Can't I get the Senator to tell me—

Watkins: The Senator is out of order.

McCarthy: —whether it is true or false?

Watkins: The Senator is out of order . . . We are not going to be diverted by these diversions and sidelines.

By holding such a tight rein on the proceedings, Watkins avoided the kind of diversionary madness that had disrupted the work of the Baldwin and Gillette committees. By keeping the focus on the charges against McCarthy, he gave McCarthy little room to maneuver, for the proof of many of these charges was already in the public record. Williams attempted to argue on McCarthy's behalf that the report of the Gillette committee was without validity because the committee had never been specifically authorized by a Senate vote to investigate McCarthy. It was a legal quibble that Watkins rejected, pointing out that Benton's resolution had been referred to an appropriate committee of the Senate as was customary in such cases and that the committee had full authority to pursue it. As for McCarthy himself, his testimony was largely a rehash of positions he had previously taken. He reviewed the Peress-Zwicker affair, contending that the general had not given him straightforward answers about the honorable discharge of the pink dentist; he argued that he was within his rights to ask federal employees to give him information when they knew about wrongdoing; he refused to soften in any way the personal aspersions he had cast on Senators Hendrickson and Flanders; he said that he had told Senator Gillette he would testify about Benton's charges if he was "ordered" or subpoenaed to do so, but that he wouldn't appear voluntarily unless he was given the right to cross-examine witnesses.

None of this was very dramatic nor did it alter the essentials of the case against McCarthy. And so on September 27, 1954, Senator Watkins' committee filed its report. It recommended the censure of McCarthy on two counts.

The first involved his contemptuous refusal to have anything to do with the Gillette committee that had been appointed to hear Senator Benton's charges. He had denounced Senator Hendrickson as "a living miracle without brains or guts" because Hendrickson had remained on the committee and signed the final report with Senators Hennings and Hayden. He had insulted all the members of the committee, including those whom his tactics had driven off it, by insinuating they were no better than thieves or pickpockets, and he had refused to explain any of the serious charges against himself—charges that went directly to the issue of his personal honor. Of all this, the Watkins committee wrote:

"It is our opinion that the failure of Senator McCarthy to explain to the Senate these matters: (1) Whether funds collected to fight communism were diverted to other purposes inuring to his personal advantage; (2) whether certain of his official activities were motivated by self-interest; and (3) whether certain of his activities in senatorial campaigns involved violations of the law; was conduct contumacious toward the Senate and injurious to its effectiveness, dignity, responsibilities, processes and prestige."

The committee called McCarthy's conduct in the General Zwicker affair "reprehensible" and advocated that he be censured on this count also. It wrote that "the conduct of Senator Mc-Carthy toward General Zwicker was not proper. We do not think that this conduct would have been proper in the case of any witness, whether a general or a private citizen, testifying in a similar situation . . . the conduct of Senator McCarthy toward General Zwicker in reprimanding and ridiculing him, in holding him up to public scorn and contumely, and in disclosing the proceedings of the executive session in violation of the rules of his own committee, was inexcusable. Senator McCarthy acted as a critic and a judge, upon preconceived and prejudicial notions . . ."

The committee decided not to censure McCarthy on the additional counts of encouraging federal employees to give him confidential information; for receiving classified documents (the spurious FBI report) from executive files; and for abusing other members of the Senate. In this last category, the committee decided that McCarthy's description of Senator Flanders as "senile" and his suggestion that the little men come with a net to put him in a quiet place, while "highly improper," had been in part provoked by Flanders' own previous breach of Senatorial etiquette by comparing McCarthy's methods to those of Adolf Hitler.

The issue now went to the Senate—and McCarthy burst the bounds of the control Edward Bennett Williams had imposed. In a letter to Watkins, he accused three members of the committee of "deliberate deception" and "fraud" for failing to disqualify themselves; in a statement to the press on November 4, he described the pending Senate debate on the report as a "lynch party"; in a nationwide radio-TV show on November 7, he called it a "lynch bee"; in a press statement on November 13, he charged Watkins himself was guilty of "the most unusual, the most cowardly thing I've ever heard of," and he added that Watkins was "stupid" and that his committee had served as the "unwitting handmaiden," the "involuntary agent" and "attorneys in fact" of the Communist Party.

The Senate debate began on November 10, 1954, and continued through seven sessions. While it was in progress, right-wing forces marshaled to put pressure on the Senate. The aim was to gather ten million signatures on petitions opposing censure.* Many of the leaders in this petition drive were extremists who were to become even more prominent in spearheading the superpatriotic rallies of the early 1960s that attempted to revive McCarthyism.

Heading the group that called itself Ten Million Americans Mobilizing for Justice was Lieutenant General George E. Stratemeyer, retired Air Force commander in the Korean War. Rear Admiral John G. Crommelin was the chief of staff in headquarters set up in New York's Roosevelt Hotel. Seven vice chairmen were: Admiral William H. Standley, retired Chief of Naval Operations; Charles Edison, former Secretary of the Navy and a notorious backer of far-right causes; General James A. Van Fleet, retired Eighth Army commander in Korea; Mrs. Grace L. H. Brosseau, president of the American Coalition of Patriotic Societies and president-general of the Daughters of the American Revolution; John Francis Neylan, a California lawyer; Lieutenant General Pedro A. del Valle, retired commander of the First Marine Division at Okinawa; and John B. Trevor, president emeritus of the American Coalition.

On November 11, McCarthy zealots, rallied by this organization, poured into Washington by train and bus from New York, Boston and other cities. One train from New York alone brought 873 wild-eyed McCarthyites, one man carrying a net to snare Senator Flanders as McCarthy had suggested, others waving placards expressing their sentiments. Some of the signs read: "Senator McCarthy Deserves a Citation Instead of Censure"; "You Can't Hide the Truth with Censure"; "Senator McCarthy Is the Man Who Fulfilled the Ike Campaign Promises"; "Why Did Alger Hiss Want Trial in Vermont? Do You Know, Senator Flanders?"

That evening in a rally in Washington's Constitution Hall, Senator Welker called the attack on McCarthy "foul play" and "dirty work" and denounced it as a communist conspiracy that

* On the day of the final censure vote, a Brink's armored truck drew up before the Capitol and delivered a protest petition said to contain 1,000,816 signatures. No one challenged the validity of the claim.

had lured some Republican support. "If the fight against Joe Mc-Carthy succeeds," Senator Welker said, "then I am willing to predict here tonight that the next big fight will be over the admission of Communist China to the United Nations." And that, obviously, was a specter to chill the stoutest American heart.

The debate in the Senate followed similar lines. Barry Goldwater, who had been a Senator from Arizona for only one year, joined Herman Welker in describing the attack on McCarthy as a communist plot. He told the Senate that "the labeled Communists have wisely moved aside and have allowed these naive recruits to handle all the heavy artillery . . ." McCarthy, he said, had been accused of "relatively trivial offenses"; and he predicted in a voice of doom: "I suggest to the Senate at this time that if this censure movement against the Senator is successful the next attack will undoubtedly be made upon J. Edgar Hoover."

It went on that way until Senator Watkins faced down the Senate and drew the line. On November 16, he challenged his Senate colleagues in these words:

"Continuous guerrilla warfare has been waged against us by the junior Senator from Wisconsin and his journalistic friends and radio commentators and satellites throughout the United States in an effort to put us in bad with the people of the country. It was abuse heaped upon abuse."

Watkins told the committee that the current debate had given it a priceless opportunity to see and evaluate McCarthy in action; it had seen a vivid example of his "hit-and-run" tactics in the personal assault he had made on Watkins' own courage and intelligence. With this preface, he put the entire Senate on the hook as he said:

"I am asking all of my colleagues in the Senate—and it must be remembered that we members of the Select Committee were practically drafted for the job, and so far as I am concerned it was the most unpleasant task that I have ever had to perform in my public life—I am asking all my colleagues, 'What are you going to do about it?'

"Some people are inclined to say that what Senator McCarthy did with respect to the Gillette-Hennings subcommittee took place in another session and that all of that is outlawed, and therefore nothing can be done about it by the Senate. I ask my colleagues: 'What about the attack right here in your presence?'

"That is what I want to know. That is what all members of the Select Committee want to know from all Senators . . ."

The issue had been drawn in uncompromising terms. The Senate had to act against Joe McCarthy—or discredit itself. Forced into this corner, the Senate reluctantly composed the softest rebuke that its genius could devise. It retained in the final resolution the Watkins committee's first count, the one based upon McCarthy's cavalier contempt for the Gillette committee and the slur cast upon Senator Hendrickson's physical and mental capacities; it threw out the recommended censure for his berating of General Zwicker—and so, by implication, exonerated him for his browbeating of all witnesses; and it substituted a new second count, based upon his wild-swinging charges against the Watkins committee. For all this, it did not "censure," it simply "condemned" him.

In the final vote, this "condemnation" of McCarthy was approved by the Senate, 67 to 22. The Republicans split evenly, 22 casting their votes for McCarthy, 22 opposing him. The hard-core supporters who remained solidly in McCarthy's corner with hardly an exception through a series of telltale roll calls, included: Barry Goldwater, Karl Mundt, Roman L. Hruska, Styles Bridges, Everett McKinley Dirksen, William F. Knowland, Herman Welker, Homer Capehart.

Though, contrary to many reports, Vice President Nixon himself had had no hand in changing the word "censure" to "condemn," he did take occasion in commenting on the final decision to emphasize that the Senate had not really "censured" McCarthy, it had merely "condemned" him. In this, the McCarthyites took great solace, buoyed by the wishful thought that nothing had really changed.

THE SINGLE most incredible aspect of Joseph McCarthy's career was the lightning speed of its disintegration. The dirigible *Hindenburg* went up in flames and smoke in half a minute, and McCarthy collapsed almost as swiftly once the Senate had "condemned" him.

He had not been "lynched." He had not been ousted from the Senate. He had not lost his committee assignments. He was no longer chairman of the Government Operations Committee simply because Democrats had recaptured control of the Senate in the 1954 elections, but this had been a midterm contest in which the tide traditionally runs against the party in power, and no one placed the onus for defeat on McCarthy. All that had really happened was that he had been spanked in public, lightly at that, and perhaps the essential character of McCarthy and his "crusade" was revealed in the fact that so light a punishment could bring such swift and utter demoralization. Once the Senate had discovered within itself the courage to spank him, he could no longer terrorize it with character assassinations as he had in the past; once he lost the power to bully, he lost everything.

The irony was that he still retained an immense base of potential power, but he had lost the ability to use it. In the nation at large, he had been damaged, but he had not lost the hard core of his frenzied following—and this was a legion that numbered in the millions. Gallup polls reflected not only the overall damage he had suffered, but the size of his fanatical army as well; mass meetings and public demonstrations expressed the fervor of the undying faithful.

In January, 1954, a time when only Senator Fulbright had mustered the courage to vote against McCarthy, a Gallup poll showed that 50 percent of the people approved of McCarthy; only 29 percent opposed him, with 21 percent undecided. By August, 1954, after the Army-McCarthy hearings, after the nationwide exposure on television, sentiment had shifted dramatically. A new Gallup poll on August 22 showed that 51 percent of the public opposed him, 36 percent were still for him, and 13 percent were still undecided.

Thirty-six percent of the American public, still not disillusioned, still not shaken in its faith, represented a truly enormous personal following, and its feverish dedication to the man who was its hero was demonstrated by a number of events.

On July 20, after the debacle of the Army-McCarthy exposure, McCarthy announced with deepest regret that he was accepting the resignation of Roy Cohn as chief counsel for his committee. He also transferred Don Surine from the investigative staff to his personal office payroll. Cohn, in his letter of resignation, attributed his action to what he politely called "a lack of unanimity" among committee members about "continuing my services as chief counsel." McCarthy wept his regret in his bitter acceptance, writing: "The resignation of Roy Cohn must bring great satisfaction to the Communists and fellow travelers. The smear and pressures to which he has been subjected make it clear that an effective anti-Communist cannot long survive on the Washington scene."

On July 28 more than 2,500 persons turned out for a "memorial" service for Roy Cohn in New York's Hotel Astor. McCarthy was there to pay tribute, and Rabbi Benjamin Schultz, who officiated, had to plead with the congregation "in the interests of discipline" not to rush forward to the dais to seek the healing touch of the master.

It was, by and large, the same old crowd—Westbrook Pegler, William Buckley, Fulton Lewis, Jr., George Sokolsky, the disciples of the Sons of the American Revolution, the Ancient Order of Hibernians, the Veterans and Citizens Against Communism, the Minute Women of Maryland, the Pro-American group from Dallas, the Daughters of I Will Return. Roy Cohn was called "the American Dreyfus." His downfall was compared to "the loss of a dozen battleships." *The New York Times* and the New York *Herald-Tribune* were excoriated as little better than cousins of the *Daily Worker,* and Fulton Lewis assured the faithful, "We must fight the devil with unpleasant weapons." He added the estimate that whatever section of the press "believes in integrity and fair reporting is 10,000 percent behind Roy Cohn." It was all great catharsis for ravaged spirits convinced of the impending doom of America.

These obsequies for Roy Cohn were eclipsed by the great outpouring of affection that laved Joe McCarthy after the Senate in its brutishness had betrayed the soul of America by condemning him. The Committee of Ten Million Americans Mobilizing for Justice was still going strong, despite the failure of its petition drive to stir the Senate's conscience, and it turned out a massive crowd of 13,000 screaming McCarthyites in a New York rally on November 29. McCarthy himself could not be there. He was just out of Bethesda Naval Hospital, his arm in a sling after one of his mysterious and increasingly frequent bouts with physical misfortune; but Jean McCarthy and Roy Cohn appeared as his stand-ins. "Who promoted Peress?" screamed the faithful, as if one pink Army dentist must have contaminated all the molars that he had drilled. And the crowd jumped and roared when told that the Peresses of this world would go marching on in triumph as long as "we soothe the injured feelings of a crybaby general." Praise was lavished on McCarthy by Admiral Standley, Charles Edison, Utah Governor Bracken Lee, Mrs. Brosseau, and Alvin M. Owsley, of the American Legion. Roy Cohn, speaking for the incapacitated guest of honor, beamed on all as he associated himself and his master with the real Americans. "Joe McCarthy and I would rather have American people of this type than all the politicians in the world," he said.

The intensity of the passions that had been aroused among a large segment of the 36 percent who refused to be disillusioned with McCarthy was apparent in wildly vituperative reactions to anyone who wrote critically of him, no matter how solid the writer's own anticommunist credentials.

In July, 1954, the New York *World-Telegram and Sun* ran a series of articles by Frederick Woltman called "The McCarthy Balance Sheet." Probably no journalist in the nation had more impeccable anticommunist credentials than Frederick Woltman. He had been awarded a Pulitzer Prize for his early journalistic exposés of the communist menace; he was so hated by the party that the *Daily Worker*, with its unfailing delicacy of phrase, had denounced him as "Freddie the Fink." Yet, when Woltman wound up and let fire with the conclusion that McCarthy "has become a major liability to the cause of anti-communism," he called down upon his head the wrath of the furies.

The Brooklyn *Tablet*, official publication of the Brooklyn Catholic Diocese, called him "a hatchet man." (The *Pittsburgh Catholic*, organ of the Pittsburgh Diocese, balanced this somewhat by praising Woltman's effort as "a study which the country needs and for which it has been long waiting.") Subscriptions were canceled, and irate readers announced they would boycott the paper on the newsstands. Sackfuls of mail, containing many letters of praise but others that were virtually unprintable in their vituperation, deluged the *World-Telegram and Sun* office. Among the more temperate and printable comments were these judgments: "indefensible," "rotten," "a grave injustice to the average man's intelligence," "a new low in journalism." One reader summed his feelings up in one word: "Stinks." "Thoroughly disgusted," wrote another. "I have read it with a little nausea," confided a third. "I paid a perfectly good nickel to get a picture of

Sen. Joe McCarthy out of your phony rag," another announced. And finally an enraged reader, expressing a theme that occurred again and again, screamed: "Did Russia award a prize to Mr. Woltman? . . . Get over to Russia where this column belongs."

Richard Rovere had a similar experience, an ominous one that demonstrated that even the passage of time had not dimmed the passions McCarthy had aroused. In 1958, after McCarthy had died, Rovere wrote an article for *Esquire,* giving his estimate of McCarthy's deeds and character.

"Then the furies descended," he afterward wrote. "I have half a file drawer full of suggestions that I walk into the Atlantic Ocean until my hat floats, that I ask God's forgiveness for my acts of desecration, that I buck for the next Stalin prize and so forth . . . what impressed me most was the volume of the letters from terribly anguished men and women who would not stand idly by while McCarthy's name was dishonored. The letters were ugly, threatening, in many cases vile. Yet they bespoke a love for the man which, though it was doubtless a form of self-love, was not entirely without the power to be affecting. Three hundred subscriptions, or a lot, to *Esquire* were cancelled, and this was a tribute . . ."

It was a tribute, not just to the man but to the brainwashing that for decades had aroused such animal passions in so many Americans.

J O S E P H   M C C A R T H Y lived on for two and a half years after the censure vote, but he lived as only the pale ghost of his former self. The stuffing had been knocked out of him by the condemnation in the Senate, and no one paid attention to him any more. The Administration, which had quailed before him, now refused even to consider his choice for postmaster of Appleton, Wis. When he rose to speak in the Senate, the chamber emptied, and reporters in the press gallery, who had once hung on his every word, decided it was a good time for a coffee break. The so-called journalistic "goon-squad" that had been detailed to shadow him and record his every utterance was disbanded. He was no longer "news." Handouts from his office, struggling to grab new headlines, were consigned to the wastebaskets of the newsrooms. And the White House, in a gratuitous slap, announced that, of all the members of Congress, Senator and Mrs. McCarthy would not be welcome on its guest lists for 1955.

He fumbled around for a new issue, even as he had been fumbling before the dinner at the Colony; he got L. Brent Bozell to write some high-toned, intellectual speeches on foreign and military policies. One of these, as Rovere later wrote, "described with remarkable prescience our lag in missile development"; it was a truly important speech; but the ears of the press and America were tuned out, no one was listening, no one paid the slightest attention.

Where he had been the ultimate weapon of his party in the Presidential campaign of 1952, he was the forgotten and discarded warrior of 1956. He did not even go to the Republican National Convention that renominated Eisenhower. He had let it be known that he personally favored either J. Edgar Hoover or Herman Welker as the Republican candidate, and when the party persisted in ignoring his advice, he ignored the campaign. When some other Senator was holding a headline-making hearing as he himself had done in the old days, he would sometimes try to horn in on the act, prowling the hearing room, peering at witnesses, wearing his familiar dark, ominous scowl. Photographers, out of kindness, would sometimes snap his picture, knowing even as they took it that, now, it would never be used.

He was a hollow shell of the man he had been, and his physical and spiritual disintegration became daily more visible. One of the psychiatrists who had made one of those tentative appraisals of him had written:

"When intellectual devices—rationalizations—fail, McCarthy is able to fall back on physical illness. This may be real or exaggerated in his mind. Illness gives him a chance to withdraw, if the going is rough . . . Fatigue is his enemy.

". . . McCarthy is now on a downgrade course. With the resilience of his mental makeup, he is unlikely to become overtly insane. It is more likely that he will become a prey to physical ailments. Alcohol may be used increasingly to allay anxiety . . . This form of alcoholism, if it should occur, is the desperate type, to reduce acute feelings of disturbance."

McCarthy began to prove the perceptiveness of that analysis. He had always been a heavy drinker, but he drank ever more heavily now and his physical system, ravaged by all the strains he had placed upon it, could no longer tolerate the intake. Where he had been able formerly to carry a heavy load without visible effect, now two or three drinks were his undoing. He was frequently in and out of the hospital with ailments that were obscure or that were deliberately made so in the official announcements. "There was endless talk of back trouble, leg trouble, liver trouble, prostate trouble, lung trouble, heart trouble, herniated-diaphragm trouble, and—always—bottle trouble," Rovere later wrote.

McCarthy had been warned by his doctors to leave liquor alone, but he could not do it. He would try to behave for a while; for weeks he would drink nothing more potent than beer. He would try to diet. On one occasion, he and his doctors said, he lost forty-one pounds in a short period of time—and he looked worse than ever; he looked ghastly. Too late, he tried to change, to redeem his life's errors. He spoke at times of retiring with his wife and adopted daughter, both of whom he obviously loved deeply, to "a small cattle-spread in Arizona." The desire impelled him to mend his spendthrift ways. He no longer squandered money as fast as he made it. He no longer gambled so heavily on the ponies or at poker; instead, he began to build a fortune in the stock market. Guided by friends with "inside" knowledge, he plunged into oil and uranium ventures; he built up a fancy paper profit, hung on—and then lost heavily, disastrously, when his "friends" dumped their stock and took their profits without bothering about him while he was out of touch in the wilds of Wisconsin.

It was the last betrayal. "He fell off the wagon in a heap and never got back on again," Rovere wrote. On April 28, 1957, he was taken once more to the Bethesda Naval Hospital. Mrs. McCarthy told the press that he had gone there for "a knee injury," but Washington speculated that he was being dried out again. Navy doctors eventually announced that he was suffering from "peripheral neuritis," an inflammation of the nerve ends farthest from the central nervous system, an affliction often associated with acute alcoholism. But it all remained something of a mystery.

What actually happened, according to one inside version in Washington, was this:

On the sixteenth floor of the Bethesda Naval Hospital was a series of private rooms, not elaborate but conveniently isolated.

The area is known in Washington parlance as Tower 16, and it is reserved for the exclusive use of eminent leaders of our governmental establishment when they have become overloaded with more booze than their systems can tolerate. They are taken to Tower 16 to dry out, and there are times when the tower does a rushing business.

McCarthy had been a frequent visitor to Tower 16. Toward the end, when he really went on a bender, he had a tendency to become "a mean drunk." The attendants at Tower 16 had had considerable trouble with him on previous occasions, but when he came in this last time, he was literally uncontrollable. He grabbed a chair and broke it over the head of one of the enlisted personnel who were trying to take care of him, and the force on the floor, unable to control him, shoved him into "the tank," a padded cell where he could do no harm to himself or anyone else. There he passed out.

Poisons built up in his system, and by the time he was taken to his bed in his private room in Tower 16, the damage was irreversible.

"Bethesda was embarrassed by it," says one Washington insider. "There was some feeling that, if they had put him in a straight-jacket and gotten him to bed and treated him earlier, he might have lived. But there was no reason why anyone should have felt guilty, really. If it hadn't been this time, it would have been the next because he couldn't give up the liquor; he couldn't stop."

The end came on May 2, 1957, at 6:02 P.M., just one hour after he had been administered the last rites of the Catholic Church. The first bulletin gave no cause of death. Later ones spoke of "acute hepatitic infection" and "hepatitic failure," but the cause almost certainly, as *Time* magazine reported, was cirrhosis of the liver, an ailment most often induced by alcohol which turns this essential organ into a spongy mass unable to filter out in bile all the accumulating poisons in the system

In any event, however ingloriously—and, indeed, tragically —the end had come. McCarthy was dead. But his legacy went marching on.

PART SIX

The Legacy

23

The Victims

T H E   D A M A G E that Joe McCarthy did is incalculable. There are no scales on which to weigh his impact on the soul of the nation, but it is safe to say that he left America less free than he found it. He made dissent suspect. He made rational debate of major political issues impossible. He imposed a straitjacket on foreign policy. No President from his day to this has been able to act solely on the basis of intelligence, conscience and conviction in foreign affairs; all have had to look over their shoulder and worry lest by any act of theirs they should lay themselves open to the charge of being "soft on communism."

This pressure from the right has exercised an inhibiting influence on foreign policy ever since McCarthy's day. The ultraconservative forces that had made McCarthy their hero did not vanish with his death, and no President has felt free to ignore those 36 percent of all Americans who remained committed even after the exposures of the Army-McCarthy hearings. From the moment that McCarthy and his Republican allies raised their outcry about "the loss" of China by betrayal, American policy in Asia has been tortured by an irrationality that has made us the wonder and despair of our staunchest allies.

Turning our backs on reality, we have tried to pretend that Communist China is either not there or is an aberration that will collapse—and that, therefore, it should not be admitted to the United Nations. Clayton Fritchey, who served as an aide to Adlai Stevenson at the UN, has made the point that no Administration for the last twenty years has really believed in the policy of freezing out China—but that, at the same time, no Administration in the last twenty years has had the guts to break with the fetish. Fritchey quotes John Foster Dulles, that most committed of anticommunist warriors, as saying: "We ought to be willing that all nations should be members [of the UN] without attempting to appraise closely those which are 'good' and those which are 'bad.' Already that distinction has been obliterated by the present membership of the UN." This was a policy of reason that no Administration has felt free to adopt. Instead, we have followed a rigid policy of trying to quarantine, trying to contain China militarily—a policy fraught with incalculable risks, when a hostile China, turned inward upon itself and feeding on its own frenzies, becomes fully possessed of nuclear weapons and intercontinental delivery systems.

The idiocy of this policy has been clear for a long time. "John F. Kennedy," Fritchey writes, "frankly told his top associates that he thought U.S. China policy was 'irrational.' Most of them agreed with him; and many senior officers of the Johnson Administration felt the same way . . . Still, when the chips were down, these Administrations backed away from any change."

This inability to change, this inability to act realistically underlies our tragic involvement in the quagmire of Vietnam—an episode in futility that has cost us more than 40,000 American lives and more than 300,000 total casualties, a shocking 12 percent of the wounded totally disabled, maimed for life. Our involvement is founded on all the old delusions—that we must contain China; that communism is a monolithic menace; that, if South Vietnam fell, there would be a fateful "domino" effect that would cause virtually all else to fall. Such beliefs are still adhered to fanatically by the American right, by all the old devotees of McCarthyism, and no President in our time has dared to defy their imperatives.

President Eisenhower, tepidly and reluctantly, committed us to Vietnam, sending economic aid and a small corps of American military "advisers." President Kennedy stepped up the aid and greatly increased the number of advisers as part of the militant, anticommunist policy that every President—and especially all liberal Presidents—has felt compelled to adopt ever since the days of Joe McCarthy. But Kennedy came to have his doubts—and felt it would be politically suicidal to act upon them.

Kenneth O'Donnell, President Kennedy's White House chief of staff, and an intimate of the Kennedys, has disclosed that Kennedy, shortly before his assassination, had determined to change American Vietnam policy after his reelection in 1964. The first shock to Kennedy, O'Donnell writes, came as early as 1961, when both General Charles de Gaulle and General Douglas MacArthur warned him against any military involvement on the Asian mainland.

The MacArthur warning especially impressed the President, for MacArthur, after his dismissal by President Truman during the Korean War, had become a hero of the American right, and efforts had been made to start a Presidential boom for him. MacArthur was also recognized as probably the greatest of modern American military strategists. Therefore, Kennedy was stunned by the old soldier's blunt advice at their first meeting shortly after the Bay of Pigs debacle. MacArthur warned him that Asian manpower was virtually unlimited and that "even if we poured a million American infantry soldiers into that continent, we would still find ourselves outnumbered."

Later the President and the general talked at the White House. Kennedy was so fascinated that he kept MacArthur for three hours and ruined the whole day's appointment schedule. Again, MacArthur was extremely critical of the advice the President had been getting from the Pentagon; again, in O'Donnell's words, he "implored the President to avoid a U.S. military buildup in Vietnam, or any other part of the Asian mainland, because he felt that the domino theory was ridiculous in a nuclear age . . . Kennedy came out of the meeting somewhat stunned. That a man like MacArthur should give him such unmilitary advice impressed him enormously."*

In 1962 Senator Mike Mansfield, the Democratic majority leader, made a trip to Southeast Asia; and, after his return, he pressed upon Kennedy the same advice MacArthur had given. Kennedy was at first angered, especially so when, in 1963, Mansfield repeated his views in front of the Congressional leadership at a White House breakfast. Afterward, however, O'Donnell writes, the President grabbed his arm and told him, "Get Mike and have him come to my office." O'Donnell sat in on much of the conversation that followed, and he reports that the President told Mansfield he now agreed on the need for our complete military withdrawal from Vietnam.

"But I can't do it until 1965—after I'm reelected," Kennedy said.

O'Donnell sums up:

"President Kennedy felt, and Mansfield agreed with him, that if he announced a total withdrawal from Vietnam before the 1964 election, there would be a wild, conservative outcry against returning him to the Presidency for a second term.

"After Mansfield left the office, the President told me that he had made up his mind that after his reelection he would take the risk of unpopularity and make a complete withdrawal of American forces from Vietnam. 'In 1965, I'll be damned everywhere as a communist appeaser. But I don't care. If I tried to pull out completely now, we would have another Joe McCarthy red scare

---

* Though Kennedy was surprised by MacArthur's views, the general had previously warned against any American military involvement on the Asian mainland; and, as far back as 1957, as a corporation executive speaking to his stockholders in Sperry Rand, he had denounced "the continuous stampede of patriotic fervor" that had pressured us into committing "exorbitant funds" to the military. In another speech to the Congress of the Republic of the Philippines, he had called for disarmament and the abolition of war, arguing that this policy was no longer "the vague imagining of a visionary" but an absolute necessity in the nuclear age. Science, he said, had made "mass destruction a reality" and "we must go on or we will go under." These speeches had received almost no notice in the American press, though I had used quotes from them in The Warfare State in 1962. Kennedy, however, according to O'Donnell, had gone to his first meeting with MacArthur expecting to encounter a rigid, militaristic mind and had come away dumbfounded by the brilliance of MacArthur's conversation and his intellectual range and insights.

on our hands, but I can do so after I'm reelected. So we had better make damned sure that I *am* reelected."

It was not to be. And Kennedy's successor, Lyndon B. Johnson, plunged us into full-scale war in Vietnam, adopting the military advice against which MacArthur had warned, and trumpeting that he was not going to be the first President to preside over an American military defeat—a battle cry that has been echoed almost word for word by President Nixon. Such was the most tragic legacy of McCarthyism.

WAS THERE ANY REAL BASIS for the movement that has had such profound and lasting effects upon the American public and the formulation of American policy? Was there any substance to it at all?

It has often been said of McCarthy that, despite his sensational headline charges that communists were everywhere, he never discovered and produced a single communist. It is true. He never did. His most publicized cases, once subjected to tests in Loyalty Board hearings or in the courts, collapsed. The case against Owen Lattimore, the case on which he would "stand or fall," fell. The great Fort Monmouth spy sensation could not in the final analysis produce even one "security risk." These results were typical.

In December, 1953, after the Eisenhower Administration had been in office for eleven months, after McCarthy had been crying out about the communist menace for nearly three years, the Associated Press tried to determine just how much substance there was in the charges that were making wild-flying headlines. Associated Press reporters consulted the staffs of the Senate Internal Security Committee and the House Un-American Activities Committee, groups that had been dedicated to the witch hunt for five years. What had they established in that time, at least to their own satisfaction? That out of a total of 2.5 million federal employees, only some seventy-five could even be accused of communist activities. Of this miniscule number, two, Harold Ware and Harry Dexter White, had died. Of the remainder, just two, Alger Hiss and William Remington, had been tried and convicted on perjury charges. Both of these cases had been developed in 1948 before McCarthy exhibited any awareness of the communist menace, and both have remained infinitely suspect prosecutions, tainted with dependence upon perjured informers and the over-zealousness of federal prosecutors.

It is true that in the 1950s the FBI developed the Ethel and Julius Rosenberg atom spy case, the Judith Coplon case (which eventually collapsed on legal grounds) and a number of other minor spy sensations. But a clear distinction must be made here. No nation is ever going to be immune from the occasional spy who, out of ideological motives, greed, frustrated ego, or personal weaknesses that subject him to blackmail, can be induced to betray his country. But the isolated case of espionage was not the gravamen of McCarthy's charge. His was a much more insidious, sweeping and damaging indictment than that.

From the moment he spoke in Wheeling on February 9, 1950, down to the instant of his condemnation by the Senate in late 1954, his unvarying thesis was that the American system on the highest levels was riddled with subversives; that communist infiltrators had been placed and protected in high policy-making positions; that they had betrayed the nation. For all of this, he never offered one word of credible proof. Yet he made this pre-posterous charge so stridently that many came to believe it.

Vast portions of the American public never realized that the whole performance was a "hoax and a fraud," as the Tydings committee had proclaimed. It did not register that neither Mc-Carthy nor the Eisenhower Administration nor any agency of the federal government—not even the Congressional witch hunters —could substantiate any part of McCarthy's extravagant claims.

The Eisenhower Administration, committed by the campaign rhetoric of 1952, tried for a time to put some foundation under the communists-in-government charge, but it found proof beyond its capacity. All it produced was a shifting numbers game, reminiscent of McCarthy's own, that made its own credibility on the issue infinitely suspect. On February 18, 1954, the Adminis-tration announced that there had been 2,200 "security risk" fir-ings—but only twenty-nine had involved charges of disloyalty. By February 21 the Administration raised the disloyalty-firing figure to forty-one. In March the figures were revised upward on three different occasions until the Administration finally pro-claimed that, out of a total of 2,429 dismissals, 422 involved "subversives." This figure was certainly far more impressive than the original twenty-nine; but, even if one is not made suspicious by the constantly changing statistics, even if one concedes this final figure was true, it still represented less than two-hundredths of one percent of all 2.5 million federal employees. Not even a Republican Administration fully determined to uncover the worst had been able to show any high-level betrayals in the Truman Administration. All it had managed to establish was that some ninety-nine and ninety-nine-hundredths percent of all federal employees were loyal Americans.

IN THE CONFUSIONS of the time, facts did not register; only the perfervid rhetoric did. Millions of Americans became convinced that communists, burrowing from within, had caused all the troubles of the decade. The nation's policies were formed in this atmosphere of paranoia; and in the unceasing effort to find some evidence to support the delusion, victims were hounded on every level of American society, from the highest to the lowest.

The first, the heaviest, the most relentless blows fell on the State Department. Here was the handy scapegoat for "the loss" of China. The idea that Secretary of State Dulles, a Republican, would be able to stand up to McCarthy, another Republican, became one of the first casualties of the Eisenhower era. Dulles pursued a policy of appeasement toward McCarthy and his followers. One after another "the old China hands" were purged from the department in disgrace. McCarthy trumpeted each dismissal as the proof of how right he was; and, in this atmosphere, each firing only paved the way for the next. The effect was to leave the State Department ultimately bereft of any experts with an intimate knowledge of China.

The case of John Paton Davies, Jr., perhaps best illustrates the cravenness of Dulles before the blustering of McCarthy. Davies, a veteran Foreign Service officer, had been the political adviser of General Stilwell in China in 1943 and 1944. He had sensed the decadence and corruption of Chiang Kai-shek's regime, and though he had recommended that we should continue to support Chiang as long as was feasible, he had warned that we should prepare ourselves for an eventual Communist takeover. The objective of American policy in that eventuality, as he saw it, should be to keep a door open to China—not to drive China into the arms of Russia, but to endeavor to drive an American wedge between the two. To those who viewed communism as a monolithic menace, immune to the rivalries and jealousies that haunt all other ideologies, this attitude had been proof-positive of Davies' questionable loyalty.

Ironically Davies was a conservative-oriented figure of the intellectual Eastern Establishment. He was a hard-liner in his attitude toward the Soviet Union. In 1950, some months after the first Russian atomic explosion, he had advocated "a preventive showdown with the Soviet Union." He had also devised a super-secret, cloak-and-dagger project known as Tawny Pipit (a code name taken from an English bird akin to the lark) aimed at using disaffected Communists inside China to disrupt the Chinese Communist regime while its grip on national power was still insecure. Paradoxically, the McCarthy witch hunters seized upon this project and flaunted it as proof of Davies' dangerous ideological bent—ignoring the fact that Tawny Pipit had been conceived as an anticommunist project. In a speech in November, 1953, McCarthy conceded that the Eisenhower Administration had swept out a lot of Truman "bad security risks," but he then harried it for not firing Davies, whom he described as "part and parcel of the old Acheson-Lattimore-Vincent-White-Hiss group which did so much toward delivering our Chinese friends into Communist hands."

Eight times Davies had been called before Loyalty Boards; eight times his record had been put under the most searching microscopes—and eight times he had been cleared. But now, panicked by McCarthy, Secretary Dulles decided to give it a ninth try. He sent the Davies case to a five-man board headed by a lieutenant-general. Even this panel decided that Davies had not been "disloyal in the sense of having any Communist affinity," but he had been indiscreet in advocating the policies he favored and so had shown "a definite lack of judgment, discretion and reliability." Dulles tried to get Davies to retire quietly. Davies refused. If the Secretary wanted to get rid of him, he said, he would have to do the deed himself.

On November 4, 1954 (this, remember, was after the Army-McCarthy hearings had already inflicted their damage on McCarthy) Secretary Dulles called in Davies for a brief confrontation. "The board has found against you," he told Davies. "Do you agree?" Davies challenged. "Yes," said Dulles. "I am sorry," Davies told him, turning his back and walking out of the office and out of the Foreign Service for good. A few days later, he received word from Dulles that he could use the Secretary's name as a recommendation for any new job he might seek.

The damage inflicted upon the Foreign Service by this case, capping as it did a whole succession of earlier dramas, can hardly be overestimated. "The message of the Davies decision," as John W. Finney later wrote in *The New York Times,* "was clear: henceforth any Foreign Service officer who dared to question policy, who sent back reports that did not support policy or associated with individuals deemed questionable by the security office, ran the danger of being declared unreliable."*

The assaults of McCarthy, the supine attitude of Dulles combined to achieve the complete demoralization of the Foreign Service. This was demonstrated in a multitude of ways. Where in the past many of our brightest college students had looked forward to careers in government service, now they shunned the whole idea. A committee appointed to study the problem told Secretary Dulles in May, 1954, that *no junior officers* had been appointed since August, 1952, and the Foreign Service had declined from 1,429 to 1,285. The same committee, to test morale, sent a questionnaire to forty-three chiefs of mission in foreign countries; thirty-three replied that, in their judgment, morale was either low or "very low." Indicative of the smothering blanket of conformity was a comment made in 1960 to Professor Tillet by a State Department official. He said it had been *eight years* since any chief of mission abroad had forwarded to the department a report with which the chief of mission disagreed, but one that contained information or a viewpoint of which he thought the department should be apprised. In other words, Washington was being told only what it was assumed Washing-

---

* Even after John F. Kennedy had brought the courageous New Frontier to Washington, no one dared attempt to right the wrong that had been done Davies. Davies had served under Averell Harriman when the latter was Ambassador to Russia; he had played an important role in briefing Harriman and leading him to his early skepticism about Soviet intentions. Harriman repeatedly tried to get the Kennedy Administration to clear John Paton Davies' record, but the old fear of the "soft on communism" canard blocked any action on the highest levels. It was not until mid-January, 1969, in the eleventh hour of the Johnson Administration that Davies was vindicated when, after a thorough review of all the evidence in his case, the government announced he had been given a security clearance.

ton wanted to hear. And what Washington wanted to hear was being determined on the highest policy levels not by facts, but by slogan-inspired emotionalism.

M C C A R T H Y I S M affected not just American foreign policy and the high-level officeholder, it affected the quality of American life on every level. Under the loyalty security program, the long arm of suspicion reached out and tapped the shoulder of the common man—the toolmaker, the plumber, the butcher. The charges came out of the night, affecting not just government employees, but additional millions of workers in private industries holding government contracts. The evil had begun under Truman with the institution of the loyalty program, but McCarthyism intensified the mood of suspicion in the country and drove the Eisenhower Administration to proclaim that everyone who had been investigated under Truman would have to be subjected to a new and more rigorous inquisition. The communists-are-everywhere fantasy reinstituted and reinvigorated the witch hunt; and in this climate, Eisenhower's Executive Order 9835 had far-reaching and profound effects on individual lives.

Take the case of Charles Allen Taylor, a toolmaker for the Bell Aircraft Corporation in Buffalo, N.Y. Taylor had worked for Bell from 1941 until 1956, earning in good times about $5,000 a year. On September 6, 1956, without prior notice or warning of any kind, a paper fluttered out of the Office of Industrial Security Review of the Defense Department and landed on the desks of executives of Bell Aircraft. It stated that Charles Allen Taylor was no longer cleared for access to defense information; this meant that he could no longer work for Bell. He was fired on September 11, 1956.

Now began a long legal battle, a David-and-Goliath struggle of a lone worker against the massive bureaucracy of the Defense Department and all the other federal power complexes the department could rally to its aid. The department's "Statement of Reasons," received by Taylor after he had been fired, alleged that in 1942 and 1943 he had held a membership card in the Communist Party, had paid dues to the party, and "may still have membership in the Communist Party."

On November 1, 1956, Taylor appeared for a hearing before

the Defense Department's security board in New York. The board
made it instantly clear, as Joseph L. Rauh, Jr., Taylor's attorney,
later wrote, that "it would produce no evidence in support of the
charge of Communist affiliations nor even inform the petitioner
of the names of his accusers." The chairman of the board admitted that he did not have the alleged Communist Party membership card, or the equally alleged Communist Party "transfer"
card, in his possession; but he made it clear that the board intended to proceed on the assumption "that these documents
exist." It was up to Taylor to defend himself before a tribunal
that obviously had already judged him on the basis of evidence
it had not seen, but whose validity it assumed, based on reports
by governmental investigative agencies.

This represented a complete reversal of a principle held
sacred in America. The fathers of the Constitution had built a
safeguard for the common man in the Sixth Amendment, which
provides that the accused must be "informed of the nature and
cause of the accusation"—and that he must "be confronted with
the witnesses against him . . ." Under this provision a man could
not be condemned on the word of some secret informer or the
report of the secret police, as had happened so frequently under
tyrannical regimes in Europe; on the contrary, the State must
present its evidence, its witnesses, and prove its case. But now
this precious American principle was junked. Now the accused
had to prove his innocence. He had to prove it without having in
his possession any of the essentials of proof. He had to prove it
without even knowing the identity of his accuser, without having
the opportunity to confront him, to test his veracity in cross-
examination. It was like shadow-boxing in a fog.

Nevertheless, Taylor and his attorneys undertook the all-but-
impossible task. And what emerged from the hearing was what
was to emerge from many others of a similar nature—a vivid
portrayal of a man whose every *public action* belied the veracity
of the charges and the evidence that the government kept hidden
behind its precious smoke screen of "security."

Taylor belonged to the United Automobile Workers Union.
During the war years, there had been one clear-cut test of communist policies in the union's ranks. The Communist Party in its
all-out support of its ideological mother, Russia, had advocated
adoption of a no-strike pledge and, in an even more sinister move,

had fought for the adoption of a piece-work, speed-up, incentive program to turn out more materiel for Russia. It was, as has been said, a platform on which the Communist Party and the National Association of Manufacturers were in perfect ideological accord, and only Walter Reuther and a small coterie of labor leaders affiliated with him had the courage to stand up against the pressures exerted by a following bewitched by dollar signs.

Charles Taylor testified that he had actively and strenuously opposed the communists within the Union on this issue. His testimony was backed up by that of eleven other witnesses. These witnesses charged that the Communist Party leader in Taylor's UAW local in 1942–43 was a man named Allie Brodose. John Maturski defeated Brodose for the leadership in 1943, running on an all-out anticommunist platform, and he testified that Taylor had supported him, publicly opposing Brodose and the communist-sponsored ticket. Another witness, Joseph Rosmyslowski, testified that Taylor had denounced Brodose to his face on one occasion and had repeatedly attacked Brodose as "a red." Still a third witness, Leon Meyers, testified that Taylor had warned him against associating with Brodose because "you know he's a Commie." A fourth, Gilbert McGovern—a man who described himself as the most notorious redbaiter in Taylor's local —declared he had never considered Taylor either a communist or a communist sympathizer, that he had been "shocked" when he heard of the government's charges, and had volunteered his testimony to help defend Taylor.

After three days of hearings, there was, as Rauh later wrote, "not a word in the record" to support the government's charges, and there was a large-sized volume of testimony that seemed completely to refute them. Nevertheless, the hearing board, relying on the sanctity of its secret and untested information, declared on June 14, 1957, that it found the government's charges "true as stated." It refused Taylor a security clearance; he was still banned from his job.

An appeal was taken to the Secretary of Defense. In this, it was suggested that the government's informants might have been confused and named the wrong man. There had been an Alvin Taylor in Charles *Allen* Taylor's UAW local, and Alvin Taylor had had the reputation of being a close ally of Brodose. Could it be possible that this was a case of mistaken identity?

Five months passed without any word from the office of the Secretary of Defense, and so Rauh filed suit in Federal District Court in Washington. This legal action triggered a fast reaction. The Defense Department announced that Taylor's case was being returned to the hearing board for "further proceedings," but at the same time it defended the original verdict against Taylor as "neither arbitrary nor capricious" but "reasonably supported" by the undisclosed "evidence."

Two years had now passed—years in which Taylor, working at whatever odd jobs he could get, had scratched out the most miserable kind of income. After his discharge from Bell in early September, 1956, he had earned only $181.70 for the balance of that year; in 1957, his total income had been $1,718.07; and in 1958, up to September 9 when he filed his affidavit, his earnings had totaled only $497. Such was the specter of impoverishment that haunted workers should they call down upon themselves the curse of the government's secret informers.

Taylor's second hearing before the New York security board served just one purpose: to demonstrate the obstinate persistency with which bureaucracy, caught out in error, defends untruth as truth. There was in this second hearing a delicate change in the tenor of the government's charges—an amendment suggesting that the uncertain recollections of informers become much more precise when *someone else* has furnished them with a skeleton of established fact on which to build their fantasies. The charge that Taylor "may still be" a communist was dropped, and the charge that he "had been" a communist was amended sufficiently to try to make it conform to the overwhelming weight of evidence produced for Taylor in the first hearing. The charge now was that he had been "expelled" from the Communist Party in 1943 because he had "opposed the 'no strike pledge' and 'incentive pay' policies supported by the Communist Party." A new charge was also introduced: Taylor was accused of perjury because he had denied communist affiliations in defending himself the first time.

Rauh and his legal associates demanded again that Taylor be given the right to confront his accusers and that he be permitted to examine the alleged Communist Party membership card, which the government had identified specifically as No. 3060. There was a heated wrangle, but the hearing board remained adamant. Taylor could confront no one; he could see none of the alleged "evidence" against him. It became obvious, as Rauh later wrote in his appeal brief, "that *the Board itself was forced to rely on second-, third-, and fourth-degree hearsay assertions against petitioner by persons the Board itself never examined and that petitioner's accusers are not federal agents secreted in the Communist Party but merely casual informants engaged in private slander.*"

The appeal to the Secretary of Defense and the phony second hearing, whose verdict has been obviously predetermined, had produced nothing "but a fruitless nine-month delay of legal redress," as Rauh said, and so on September 1, 1958, he filed suit in Federal Court, asking for a summary judgment in Taylor's favor. With argument set for October 14, the Defense Department at the eleventh hour on October 13 rushed out its "verdict" on the second hearing. It announced that it had again refused Charles Taylor clearance; it insisted the original charges were "true as stated"; and it accused Taylor of "deliberately and knowingly" making "false or misleading" statements when he denied any communist affiliations.

The Federal District Court, though confessing it was worried about the implications of the case, performed its patriotic duty and upheld the government; and Rauh promptly appealed to the U.S. Supreme Court. The Supreme Court granted review; and, almost the instant that it did, driven up against the ultimate wall, the Defense Department performed an amazing backward somersault. Though it had held just two months previously after two exhaustive reviews that Charles Taylor was a menace to the republic, it now proclaimed on December 31, 1958, that the "clearance of Charles Taylor is in the national interest."

This capitulation, however, was not quite all that it seemed. Rauh noted that the wording differed from the standard form which read that clearance was "clearly consistent with the interests of the national security." The Defense Department had also failed to make any stipulation of its findings on the specific counts it had lodged against Taylor, though such point-by-point decisions were required by federal regulations. Furthermore, the instant Taylor reported for work at Bell Aircraft, the whole security procedure was started up again, just as if he were some new and unknown quantity. The obvious intent was one of continued harassment.

Rauh, therefore, persisted in fighting the case to its ultimate conclusion before the United States Supreme Court. Solicitor General J. Lee Rankin, who did his valiant best to uphold the Defense Department, conceded in arguments before the court on March 31, 1959, that five of the six informants against Taylor were of the "casual" type, but he argued strenuously that to disclose the names of any of them might "destroy our intelligence system." He contended that ordinary citizens would not feel free to inform on their neighbors unless guaranteed anonymity, blind evidently to the obvious—that such a protection provided the perfect cloak for the deluded and the malicious. Rankin argued —the perfect authoritarian argument, one that would have shocked our Founding Fathers—that the interests of the government and the security of the Defense Department must outweigh any incidental harm to the individual.

Chief Justice Earl Warren was plainly shocked and questioned Rankin sharply. "As to those [casual informers], wouldn't he have the right to be confronted?" the Chief Justice asked. "If neighbors accuse me . . . I have the right to confront them."

With the attitude of the court becoming obvious, the government's case now collapsed like a jerry-built house in a hurricane. Having exhausted all the resources of subterfuge, the government finally conceded that the charges against Charles Allen Taylor were false. It agreed to expunge the record against him; it promised it would never again raise such charges; it pledged its sacred honor that it would never, never again refer to that precious secret information on which for so long it had so obstinately relied.

The case had come to an end after two and a half grueling years. Vindication had come for Charles Taylor. But at what cost to him, to the government's credibility and honor, and to a public increasingly intimidated by such authoritarian procedures?*

* Such government procedures are not dead; some have endured right down to the end of 1969. *The New York Times* disclosed on October 9, 1969, that some of the nation's leading scientists had been blacklisted by the Department of Health, Education and Welfare for the past fifteen years. HEW is not a sensitive agency; it does not deal with military or foreign policy—but with such matters as mental and physical health. Yet its blacklists for more than a decade have banned hundreds of the nation's foremost scientists from its advisory panels. Those banned included presidents of learned societies, graduate school deans and researchers with international reputations. Yet HEW's National Institute of Health has persisted in maintaining blacklists of several hundred names, depriving America of the full benefits of some of

· · ·

THE LOYALTY PROGRAM affected some 10 million American workers during the Eisenhower Administration. In addition to the approximately 2.5 million federal employees, there were 3.5 million in the armed forces, 3 million in private industry, half a million merchant seamen and port workers, and 100,000 subject to clearance by the Atomic Energy Commission.

In the mid-1950s the Ford Foundation's Fund for the Republic made an exhaustive study to determine just what effect the loyalty procedures were having on the American psyche. Many of the nation's leading law firms—firms that had often handled at great sacrifice to themselves the cases of the unjustly accused and beleaguered—threw open their files to the foundation's examiners. The names of their clients were not revealed in an effort to shield them from further harm by wanton and malicious gossip, but the details in case after case, taken from the official hearing records, painted the picture of a society increasingly oriented toward the assumptions and techniques of the police state.

There was a Negro meat inspector for a federal agency in a Western state. He had been employed in this type of work, inspecting carcasses and meat products, for thirty-eight years. He earned a mere $4,955 a year; and, since the carcasses of hogs and cows contain no mysterious formulas for atomic weapons, it is rather difficult to envision him, whatever his beliefs, as a threat to the security of the republic. Nevertheless, it was deemed a matter of national importance that he should prove his loyalty —not once, but twice.

His first trial took place in 1948. Federal officials who had flown out from Washington to prosecute the case showed the defendant's lawyers what purported to be the photostatic copy of the cover of a Communist Party membership book bearing

---

its best scientific brains because these brains belonged to men who had run afoul of witch-hunting Congressional committees or had opposed the Vietnam war. "I simply can't see the point of intensive security when reviewing work to be done on, for example, arthritis studies," said one of the blacklisted scientists. Another, a psychiatrist, reacted as if the nation was still in the blackest pit of McCarthyism—as, indeed, for him, it was. "For God's sake don't use my name," he pleaded with a reporter. "Don't say what town I'm in—don't even say what section of the country I'm in. If you do, they'll be bound to find out, and I'll never get off the list."

the defendant's name. They had also, they said, brought with them an accusing witness; but when one of the government representatives left the hearing room to get this avenging angel, it was found that the gentleman had decamped.

So sorry, the government said, in effect; we cannot understand what happened to our man. We have no power to subpoena our own witness and compel him to testify if he doesn't wish to. It's now up to you; go ahead and defend yourself, if you can.

The Negro meat inspector testified that he had never been a communist. Twelve other witnesses testified for him. Some had known him for twenty-five years. All testified that he was "an outstanding Christian, family man, and church and community leader; a man of firm religious convictions and outspoken manner." The meat inspector was baffled by the charges made against him. He had been embroiled at one time, he said, in a conflict with the pastor of his church whom he had accused of "courting left-wing support in his political campaigns"; and during World War II, he had worked a night-shift in a defense plant where, to get the job, he had had to join a union that was then communist-dominated.

The government, of course, did not indicate which of these speculations about the origin of the charges might be correct. The hearing board simply weighed the secret evidence against the public testimony for about a year, and then in October, 1949, it "cleared" the suspect. The meat inspector went back to his job. But the Eisenhower Administration came to office with the dictum that everyone who had been investigated by the suspect Trumanites must stand the ultimate test of Republican purification. Thus the meat inspector was suspended once more. He was notified in May, 1954, that the security sleuths had again called his loyalty in question; and, as in the case of Charles Taylor, he was hit with an additional charge—that he had perjured himself in his first defense when he denied communist ties.

After months of delay, a second hearing was held in September, 1954. This time there wasn't even a pretense that the accusing witness would appear. The meat inspector was simply informed that he must refute charges of communist affiliation made by "a confidential informant who had furnished in the past reliable information to the FBI."

The agency lawyer contended that the documentation of Communist Party membership had been obtained by "a person who was taking considerable risk on himself and extracted copies from the records." In addition to the photostat of the alleged party membership book, the government showed the defense lists of names, written in several hands on sheets of paper, that purported to be the names of Communist Party members in the area. The agency lawyer had no information, he acknowledged, about who had gathered the names or how; he just knew the data "was given to us and taken from their regular records."

Defense attorney: "But you don't know how their regular records were kept?"

Agency lawyer: "No, I do not."

Defense attorney: "Or how accurately kept?"

Agency lawyer: "No, I do not."

As at the first hearing, the government called not a single witness. It was up to the accused to defend himself. The testimony was largely a repetition of that offered at the first hearing; but this time, zeroing in on the union involvement in the wartime defense plant, the defense called as a witness the former secretary of the union. He testified that the union had been under communist domination; that the defendant, to get a job, had had to join the union; that the communist leaders of the union sometimes used union funds for donations to communist-front causes; and that all union members received a copy of a communist newspaper that carried a page of union news. The secretary also testified that the accused meat inspector had never attended union meetings or been active in the union's affairs.

It slowly began to become apparent that the FBI's "reliable informant" had stretched what had been a force-put membership in a communist-controlled union into an allegation of Communist Party membership. But the crushing blow to the government's case was delivered by witnesses who testified that the meat inspector, just like Charles Taylor, had been an active *anti*communist. He had belonged to the local chapter of the National Association for the Advancement of Colored People, and he fought actively, witnesses testified, to prevent communists from gaining control of the local. One of the witnesses who told the government panel about these anticommunist activities of the defendant was a member of the state board against discrimination.

This discovery that a "reliable informant" had transformed an anticommunist into a communist was a bitter pill for the government loyalty sleuths to swallow. They tried their best to reject it. In summation, the agency lawyer argued in contravention of the most basic American principles that the government "does not have to prove the man's guilt by a preponderance of the evidence or beyond a reasonable doubt, but [it must show] only that there be *a doubt* that his retention in the Government service is not consistent with the interests of national security . . ." (Italics added.)

In this case, the Loyalty Board could not persuade itself that the government's case justified even "conviction by doubt." It mulled the issue over for months, but finally in April, 1955, it reinstated the meat inspector in his job and he received back pay for the eleven months he had been suspended. He was more fortunate than many.

There was a plumber-foreman on the West Coast who had worked for the same contractor for three and a half years. He was capable and so highly valued by his employer that he had been made a job supervisor. A still higher front-office job loomed ahead. Then the employer got a contract for plumbing work at a West Coast Air Force base. The plumber-supervisor handled the classified plans and blueprints, which he passed out to his work crews.

In July, 1952, the plumber-supervisor was suddenly discharged. Naturally, he went to his employer and asked what he had done wrong. Nothing, nothing at all, the employer told him; it was just that the Air Force Loyalty Board had ruled he was a bad security risk. Therefore, he couldn't handle classified blueprints—and so no job.

The shocked plumber began to knock on doors. He went to the local District Attorney, to a nearby office of the FBI, to the nearest Corps of Engineers Security officer, to the security office at the Air Force base. Nobody knew anything. Nobody could tell him why the ax had suddenly fallen on his head or what he could do about it. He finally wrote to his Congressman in Washington; and, with the Congressman's prodding, the cumbersome Air Force bureaucracy began to move. They were examining his case; they would let him know. Ultimately, they did. In September, 1953, fourteen months after he had been fired, the plumber-foreman got this one-sentence specification of the charges against him:

"You are currently maintaining a close continuing association with your wife . . ., who is stated to be engaged in activities of an organization which is Communist."

To what organization was his wife supposed to belong? The astonished plumber asked for details and got this reply: "The organization referred to is the Communist Party."

The plumber now engaged a lawyer to fight the case. In December, 1953, he and his wife submitted affidavits; three other persons submitted affidavits; and fifteen wrote letters. The acquaintanceship with these supporters varied from one to thirty years. Some had actually lived with the employee and his wife in their home; some had had unrestricted access to the employee's mail; some had been active with the employee and his wife in one of the two major political parties. All agreed that the couple never received communist literature, that they never expressed communist ideas—but, on the contrary, had been at times quite critical of Russian policies.

Since the plumber's difficulties stemmed more from a possible taint attached to his wife rather than any waywardness in himself, her affidavit was of special significane. The two pertinent paragraphs read:

"I was interviewed by two agents of the Federal Bureau of Investigation in my home . . . in the latter part of December, 1951. I was informed by them that they were calling upon me as a routine check on some names printed on a letterhead of the Spanish Anti-Fascist Refugee Committee. My name was one of those so listed. I informed these agents, I believe, that I had not authorized my name to be listed, and was not aware that it had been listed. I stated to them, if I remember correctly, that this committee had apparently used the names of everyone who was an officer of the Newspaper Guild-CIO at that time. I also told the agents that I had attended fund-raising parties given by this committee, but that I was not an officer or a member of the committee itself.

"On the occasion of that interview, I *volunteered* the information to the FBI agents that early in 1946, in Los Angeles, at a restaurant, at an impromptu gathering there and after I had had more to drink than I usually take, some person, whose name I can't remember and could not remember at the time of the interview, asked me why I didn't join the Communist Party. I don't remember my reply, but I do remember giving this person a check, as a contribution I believe. I never did join the Communist Party, never received a membership card from them, and never attended any meetings of this party. *I don't think the FBI knew of this incident before my telling them about it.*" (Italics added.)

The wife said that she had belonged to only four organizations in her life: the Campfire Girls, the Newspaper Guild, the Business and Professional Women's Club, and a young political club of one of the two major parties in California. The drinking incident that had led to the five-dollar check, which developed into the crux of the case, had occurred during a brief reunion with old newspaper friends in Los Angeles—and before she had even met the man who was to become her husband. Her anguish at the trouble she had now unwittingly caused him showed in these words of her affidavit:

"There are many people whose statements I feel I could furnish, but since I feel so terribly ashamed that such an accusation has been made against me, I am naturally hoping not to have to appeal for such reference to any more persons than are absolutely necessary to establish my innocence of the charges against me.

"It has been a terrible shock to find myself responsible for destroying the career of a man as fine and capable as my husband, a responsibility I am determined to fulfill by doing whatever possible to right the wrong I feel has been done him."

A hearing was held. The plumber testified that he had been out of work for some time, but that he was currently employed doing manual labor as a plumber. His wife, he assured his questioners, never asked him to show her the blueprints of any jobs on which he had worked.

The whole case obviously pivoted about his wife's beliefs and that five-dollar contribution she had made to someone while feeling a bit too high for her own good. The FBI agents had reported that she had said the five dollars was for Communist Party membership. She denied this. She testified, that, as far as she knew, it had been a contribution to some cause (because of the drinks, she couldn't be certain what cause); she had never received a Communist Party membership card, had never heard anything more about it; she wasn't even certain whether the check had been cashed.

She was questioned about the literature that she and her husband read. All this line of questioning elicited was a denial that they received or subscribed to *People's World,* a Marxist news sheet. Their only subscriptions, both the wife and husband testified, were to a local daily newspaper, the *Breeder's Stock Magazine, Popular Mechanics, Ladies' Home Journal* and *Cosmopolitan,* all eminently "safe" ideological fare. This was not getting anywhere, and the legal adviser determined to find out how much the husband told his wife about his work.

Question: Does your husband discuss his work with you at home, usually?

Answer: No, sir; he does not. He volunteers no information.

Question: Do you know what type of work he is doing now?

Answer: . . . I don't know. However, I don't believe it is a secret thing, but we are both very busy and the time we have at home is devoted to just being together.

After further questioning, even the Appeal Division of the Western Industrial Security Board could not discover anything subversive about the couple. It ruled that the plumber, after all, could have access to classified information. So he had won—but he had lost in winning.

The decision came twenty months after he had been discharged. He received no compensation for time lost and for the periods he had been out of work; he had to pay the fees of two attorneys—and he was now *persona non grata* with the contractor who had valued him so highly that he had been undergoing training for front-office work. He could still get a job and make a living as a plumber, but what had been a promising career with his original employer had been ruined.

T H E C A S E S go on and on. People in every walk of life came under suspicion. Workers were fired from jobs, professors were denied clearance. In many instances, it was not a person's own thoughts or conduct that caused trouble, but a wife's, a brother's.

The case of the sea-going butcher is illustrative. He had worked steadily from 1945 to 1952 in the merchant marine. Suddenly he came under the eagle eye of the Coast Guard's tightened port security program. He was fired from his job, not because of his own thoughts or conduct, but because "he has brothers who, according to this [secret] file, are *believed* to be affiliated with, and associated with the Communist Party." (Italics added.) The butcher, whose attorney was not allowed to see the sacred contents of the secret file, was asked to assist the Coast Guard in proving its "belief" by telling what he knew about his brothers. Had they helped him get his good shipboard butcher's job? No, he had gotten it through the regular union hiring hall, he insisted. Didn't he have some suspicion that there must be something wrong with his brothers, since they had been screened and beached before the Coast Guard got to him? Well, he didn't know. All he knew was that he wasn't a communist and that "outside of union activities . . . I haven't done nothing." This clearly was not what his interrogators wanted to hear. The original denial of clearance was upheld, and the butcher, after working for a few weeks in a cannery in Alaska, went on the rolls of the unemployed.

Official interrogators, in trying to discover possible heresies in the minds of the accused, frequently revealed the intense prejudices of their own. Guilt through reading matter, guilt through remote association, guilt even in the testimony of innocence—so far did the madness go.

In one case a minister was testifying. He knew the suspect well; he knew that the man associated with members of his church. The minister, in his innocence, evidently considered that this spoke well for the embattled employee. After all, if a man could be tainted by having associated in the remote past with persons who turned out to be communists, shouldn't it speak in his favor that he was now consorting with good church-going types? The Loyalty Board counsel attacked the minister's testimony. Wasn't the minister familiar, he asked, with the communist tactic of becoming a "member in good standing of churches and other worthy organizations" so that there might be people with "Communist tendencies in churches, whether or not such persons were actual party members"?

Another defendant, according to his counsel, was actually asked this question:

"Don't you think that any person is a security risk who at one time or another associated with a Communist—even though it was not a sympathetic association and even though the association terminated many years ago?"

In hearing after hearing, witnesses were questioned about the publications that they read. Under the pretense of protecting our freedom, this basic freedom to investigate all ideas was pitched overboard.

One accused employee confessed that he had committed the indiscretion of reading *Consumer Reports.* His motive, he said, had been to find the best buys available for himself, certainly a laudable 100-percent American trait, and he just couldn't believe that *Consumer Reports* was dyed with the stain of communism. He had read in the press, he said, that all members of the board of Consumers Union, publisher of the reports, had signed non-communist affidavits. Nevertheless, officials at the hearing seemed to attach considerable significance to his price researches in *Consumer Reports,* so much so that the employee's attorney later sent the security officer a letter pointing out that Consumers Union and *Consumer Reports* were no longer considered subversive even by the House Un-American Activities Committee.

Other defendants were asked whether they belonged to the Book Find Club, and one was asked: "Were you a regular purchaser of *The New York Times?*" Fortunately for that man, he was able to assure his interrogators that his regular reading fare was the San Francisco *Chronicle,* though he confessed that, upon occasion, he had bought and read the *Times.*

One wealthy West Coast executive and civic leader got himself in trouble through his numerous philanthropies. The executive held top positions in two large business concerns and was on the board of directors of a number of other corporations. One of these firms was being considered for a Navy contract, and the Navy asked that all officials, including members of the board of directors, be checked for security clearances. The top executive flunked the loyalty test.

The specifications against him alleged that his name had been used as a sponsor, and he had supported financially the following organizations: the Anti-Fascist Refugee Committee, American-Russian Institute, California Labor School, American Friends of the Chinese People, Bay Area Council Against Discrimination, and Federation for Repeal of the Levering Act.

In his reply, the executive said it had been his understanding that the organizations in several instances had a charitable, not a political, purpose and he argued that some of the organizations, at least, had been definitely anticommunist. He pointed out that, though he made gifts running into several thousand dollars a year to his favorite charity, his donations to these six organizations had been for $20 or $50 or $100.

Since the executive was a man of standing and influence, he produced a number of witnesses, including a Navy officer still on active service, who testified that he was a man of unquestioned loyalty who should not be stigmatized for his generous impulses. Nevertheless, the executive had a difficult time explaining why he had been so charitable. The Security and Legal Advisor of the Western Industrial Personnel Security Board put heavy emphasis on this point.

Question: I think, Mr. ——, that a matter of great importance to the board at the present time is to find out what procedure you are going to follow in making charitable or organizational contributions in the future.

Answer: Well, I am going to be more careful.

Question: If you see a new name among your mail at the present time naturally you are going to be a little more cautious.

Answer: Did you refer to anything specific there?

Question: No. I say if you receive a request for money from an organization that carried a high-sounding title but you knew nothing about it, you are going to be a lot more cautious in the future about giving money to it, wouldn't you?

The executive promised again that he would be more careful.

With this assurance, he was finally cleared, and it became possible for his company to get a Navy contract. But the preparation and presentation of his defense had taken some seventy hours of an attorney's time, and he had to pay the counsel fee of $1,750 out of his own pocket.

One $10,000-a-year professional engineer in an industrial plant found himself in deep trouble because it was alleged that his second wife, before they were married, had indulged in a dangerous intellectual flirtation with the *Daily Worker*. The engineer protested that neither he nor his wife read this communist bible. Naturally, the government would not reveal the source of its incriminating information, but a security officer, in questioning the engineer, incautiously stated that he had specific information the wife had received the *Daily Worker* at the apartment house where she lived in 1946.

The engineer's counsel, who had apparently done his homework most thoroughly, then stunned the hearing board by identifying its informant. She was, he said, the landlady of the apartment house where the wife had formerly lived, and he read into the record the name, address and telephone number of the landlady. He had talked to her himself, the lawyer said, and she had told him, just as she apparently had told government sleuths, that she knew the engineer's wife had been a communist because she had held communist meetings in her apartment. How, the lawyer had asked, did she *know* they were communist meetings?

"They had the candles low—the candles burning, and they spoke very lowly," the landlady had said.

24

"The Evil That Men Do..."

I T   H A S   L O N G   B E E N   a complacent ostrich-like delusion of the nation's liberal-intellectual establishment that Joseph R. McCarthy represented a temporary aberration of the American spirit. It is the fashion to believe that this historically stable nation is too sensible and too decent to be long deceived by the wild cries of extremists. Historical precedents are frequently cited for this comfortable persuasion. It is undeniably true that hate movements and radicalism in the past have crested in brief waves of frenzy, then have receded just as quickly, leaving hardly a ripple. Such was the fate of the Know-Nothings in the nineteenth century; such the story of the Ku Klux Klan that seemed about to sweep the nation in the 1920s, then receded into its

limited stronghold in the South. And so, it is assumed, McCarthyism died once its symbol was crushed, and now it can be disregarded as an ugly, momentary derangement of the past.

What such assessments conveniently ignore is one cardinal
fact: the virulent fanaticisms of the past were truly fringe
movements; they did not have behind them the power and prestige of the respectable and influential in American society. Mc-
Carthyism was different. It had the all-out support of ultraconservative big-business interests in rebellion against the twentieth
century, in rebellion against the threat of any further tampering
with their baronial privileges. Their true target had never been
communists. That was the smoke screen borrowed from Goebbels
—the tactic of fascism. The real foe was always the American
liberal—the New Dealer, the innovator, the idealist who saw the
injustices in American society and advocated the use of the in-
strumentalities of democratic government to effect reforms. To
the emperors of the status quo, such shakers and movers were
dangerous men. They must be stopped. They must be hounded.
Propaganda campaigns mounted by these powerful industrial and
financial barons in the late 1930s have never ceased. The result
is that McCarthyism did not die with McCarthy; it simply slum-
bered—for a very brief time, at that—and then was reborn in
new and more insidious guise.

The periodic rebirth and resurgence of the radical right indicates that it represents no temporary malaise of the American
spirit. It is like the tides of the sea; it ebbs and flows, but is
forever with us. Under the benign and calming influence of
Eisenhower, there came one of these characteristic brief ebbings.
But McCarthy had been buried less than two years when the
John Birch Society was formed in December, 1958, in a meeting
in Indianapolis, Ind. It had behind it the imprimatur of three
former presidents of the National Association of Manufacturers
and a whole host of regional industrial potentates.

The Birchite appeal was the McCarthy appeal, dressed up
now in activist organizational form, with frank advocacy of
"front" organizations and use of storm-trooper tactics. From this
central cancer was spawned a whole host of satellite radical-
right organizations, with Minutemen hoarding arsenals of rifles,
bazookas and field artillery, and proclaiming on one occasion

that they had their gun sights leveled on the necks of twenty-five Congressmen.*

The election of John F. Kennedy on the mildly liberal program of the New Frontier intensified the paranoia of the right, and the resurgence of the movement in all its virulence was almost instantaneous. All of the old slogans that equated liberalism with communism, and so with subversion and treason, were dragged out. The nation was engulfed in a wave of "Project Alert" rallies staged with the cooperation of the military half of the increasingly powerful military-industrial complex. Units of the armed services lent the prestige of the uniform to these flag-waving, supercharged performances reminiscent of Nazi rallies in Hitler's day. Communism was pictured as a monolithic menace sweeping the world, at the very time the split between Russia and China was demonstrating that it was not monolithic at all. We were told we stood at Armageddon, the last defenders of the free way of man: leftish governments like those of Great Britain, the Scandinavian countries and indeed most of our "free world" allies were equated with the onrushing communist wave; the movement for racial equality was all a communist plot; and the Supreme Court was so subversive that Chief Justice Earl Warren should be impeached—or, as many Texans advocated, hanged.

The assassination of Kennedy removed from the scene the principal target of this new radical right resurgence; it shocked the nation into remorse and mourning. But fanatics of the far right continued their propaganda activities and went on to new heights with the seizure of the power structure of the Republican Party and the nomination of Barry Goldwater in 1964. In state after state, especially in the West, the leaders of the Goldwater legions were also leaders in the John Birch Society. In the Califor-

---

* Frank advocacy of assassinations has become a persistent theme of extreme right organizations. On June 30, 1970, Senator Mike Gravel (D., Alaska), read to a hushed Senate chamber the transcript of a recorded telephone message in which an official of the neo-Nazi National Socialist White Citizens Party (successor to George Lincoln Rockwell's American Nazi Party) accused critics of the Vietnam war of treason. A man who identified himself as Dr. William Pierce on the party's dial-a-message tape denounced Senators Fulbright, George McGovern (D., South Dakota), and Mark Hatfield (R., Ore.), saying "the whole rotten bunch needs a bullet right between the eyes."

nia primary campaign, the storm-trooper tactics advocated by the Birchers were put on display; Nelson Rockefeller's rallies were invaded, disrupted, some of his workers physically beaten. Many voters were turned off by the obvious extremism of many of the forces behind Goldwater and the acceptance speech of the candidate himself in which he welcomed extremism; but the Goldwater debacle, while momentarily chastening, did little to curb the activities of the extreme right-wing, now solidified in its control of the Republican Party. The Goldwater activists remained a potent force behind the political scene, and they determined to a profound degree the dialogue of the 1968 campaign. Some, especially in the South, joined the third-party movement of George Wallace, but the bulk of the Goldwater underground gave its allegiance to Richard Nixon and played an important role in his nomination and election.

Changing times had altered some of the rhetoric and given currency to new catchwords, but the techniques and the scapegoats remained essentially the same. When George Wallace spoke and, later, Vice President Agnew, they appealed to the same dark, atavistic recesses of the American spirit. The targets were those suspect Eastern intellectuals, the "left-wing" media, the dissidents who disagreed with American foreign policy and "aided the communists" by opposing the war in Vietnam. And there was a new phrase—"law 'n' order"—that the hate fringe understood to mean repression of the Negro.

To understand the similarities and the derivations, let's bring Joe McCarthy back for a moment, and then let George Wallace and Spiro Agnew speak.

In 1950, after Joseph and Stewart Alsop had painted their unflattering portrait of him in that most conservative of publications, *The Saturday Evening Post*, McCarthy fumed: "The article is almost 100 per cent in line with official instructions issued to all Communists and fellow-traveling members of the press and radio by Gus Hall, national secretary of the Communist Party." In 1952 *Time* magazine similarly offended him by being critical. McCarthy wrote *Time:* "I am sure you will agree that the policy of *Time* magazine to throw pebbles at communism generally but to then parallel the *Daily Worker*'s smear attack upon individuals who start to dig out the dangerous secret Communists, is rendering almost unlimited service to the Communist cause and undermining America." He informed *Time* he was "preparing material on *Time* magazine to furnish all your advertisers so that they may be fully aware of the type of publication which they are supporting"; and he did indeed try, without any great success, to pressure advertisers to abandon *Time*.

The theme never varied; there was always some left-wing, intellectual conspiracy against Joe McCarthy. In 1952, when seventy-eight civic leaders in Madison, Wis., denounced him in a newspaper advertisement, McCarthy proclaimed that they were all "dupes and dopes of the Communist Party." The language of their advertisement, he said, "comes almost directly from the *Daily Worker*." In 1953, after the Washington *Post* had criticized him editorially, McCarthy launched an attack on J. Russell Wiggins, its vice president and managing editor, for "deliberate abuse and prostitution of freedom of the press." And in 1954, with his showdown battle with the Army just ahead, McCarthy denounced "the left-wing press" for leading "the jackal pack of Communists, Leftists, deluded liberals and eggheads" in a campaign to "get" him.

Nearly twenty years after the first witch-hunting speech at Wheeling, George Wallace became McCarthy's echo. Times were different and yet in many ways curiously the same. The unwinnable Korean War had been replaced by the unwinnable Vietnam War. The bloody racial riots of the long hot summer of 1967 were fresh in memory. A Louis Harris poll taken before the Democratic convention debacle in Chicago showed that the American people by an overwhelming 81 to 14 percent believed that law and order had broken down. The enemies they feared were black agitators, communists, the courts, youthful demonstrators and intellectual-liberal elements of the Establishment itself.

The mood was made for demagoguery—and George Wallace. In speech after speech, he pictured himself, exactly as McCarthy had, as the champion of "the folks" battling against some overwhelming conspiracy among the intellectual, liberal leaders of the Establishment. He would say:

"Them anar-kists and these newspapers, they not so smart these newspapers, you jes remember one man write edit-orial and you jes one man and jes one woman and you jes as smart and besides, there more of *us* than there is of *them*. And we goin' fix them anar-kists. One of them lays down in front of *mah* car, it going to be the *last* car he'll ever lay down in front of. . . ."

He brought audiences roaring to their feet with lines like these:

"We are going to show them in November that the average American is sick and tired of all these over-educated, ivory-tower folks with pointed heads looking down their noses at us, and the left-wing liberal press writing editorials and guidelines. So we are going to shake them up good in November."

"If you walk out of this hotel tonight and someone knocks you on the head, *he'll* be out of jail before *you're* out of the hospital and on Monday morning they'll try the *policeman* instead of the criminal . . . That's right, we gonna have a *police* state for folks who burn cities down. They aren't gonna burn any more cities."

"Well, when *I* get to be President, I'm gonna call in a bunch of *bureaucrats* and take away their brief cases and throw 'em in the Potomac River."

As the campaign drew to its close, with polls showing his support was wavering, he pictured himself as the victim of a conspiracy between the polls and the media. Smirking, grimacing, he heckled the TV camera crews covering his campaign. "You anar-kists better have your day now, 'cause after November 5th you are through in this country," he would tell them.

The passions that Wallace aroused won him nearly 10 million votes, and few doubted millions more would have voted for him, except for the pragmatic argument that has always killed third parties in America: Why throw your vote away? Richard Nixon plugged this theme long and hard, especially in the border states and the South. He spoke much as Wallace spoke, except for the violent rhetoric. The "responsible" witch hunter of the McCarthy era was now the "responsible" candidate who aped the irresponsible Wallace line. He criticized the Supreme Court; he bore down hard on "law 'n' order"; he gave the impression that he would do everything that Wallace would do—only he could be elected and Wallace couldn't.

The ideological linkage between the Wallace campaign and Nixon in the White House probably never showed more clearly than in Nixon's televised November 3, 1969, speech on Vietnam. As far back as September 16, 1968, *Newsweek* magazine in its profile of Wallace had described his constituency this way: "They are the silent America, and no one knows their number because no national politician has ever taken their census at the polls." In the November 3 speech, Wallace's "silent America" became Nixon's "silent majority," and the President called upon the silent ones to speak out in defense of his Vietnam policy of gradual withdrawal. The response was a flood of letters, postcards and telegrams that so pleased the President that he had his picture taken with the mail piled high on his desk.

But the performance of the three major television networks triggered a far different reaction. In their commentaries on the President's speech, the networks had not been ecstatic, but neither had they been hostile. The burden of their mild dissent seemed to be that nothing much had changed. The White House was irritated, and Presidential speech writer Patrick Buchanan was assigned the task of preparing a verbal salvo for Vice President Agnew to fire at a Republican rally in Des Moines on November 13.

Agnew had already demonstrated his aptitude for the task. In a speech on October 19, he had coined phrases that seemed to qualify him for the role of hatchetman for Nixon, as Nixon had been hatchetman for Eisenhower. This was the speech in which he said: "A spirit of national masochism prevails, encouraged by an effete corps of impudent snobs who characterize themselves as intellectuals." The anti-intellectualism was purest McCarthy, and the Des Moines speech was a head-on denunciation of the media in the free-swinging McCarthy manner.

The timing of the speech seemed significant. It was delivered on a Thursday night just prior to a weekend moratorium march that brought some 250,000 protesters against the war to Washington. The tactic seemed transparent: to discredit the antiwar protest in advance, blaming distortion of the news by the media for causing the hostile reaction to Vietnam policy.

Agnew made it clear that the only media reactions that would have pleased the White House would have been either praise or silence. He held that "the people of this country have the right to make up their own minds and form their own opinions about a Presidential address without having the President's words and thoughts characterized through the prejudices of hostile critics before they can even be digested."

The American people, Agnew said, would not have tolerated in government such a concentration of power as existed in the media in the hands "of a tiny and closed fraternity of privileged men, elected by no one, and enjoying a monopoly sanctioned and licensed by Government." Though Agnew disclaimed any intention to impose censorship, the clear implication was a threat that the networks' licenses could be revoked if they did not shape up.

Who belonged to this "tiny and closed fraternity of privileged men?" Eastern intellectuals, of course. "To a man," Agnew declared, "[they] live and work in the intellectual and geographical confines of Washington, D.C., or New York City . . . Both communities bask in their own provincialism and their own parochialism. We can deduce that these men read the same newspapers. They draw their political and social views from the same sources. Worse, they talk constantly to one another, thereby providing artificial reinforcement to their shared viewpoints."

This was just the opening barrage. On November 20, in a speech in Montgomery, Ala., Agnew extended his attack to the press that he had said the TV newsmen were reading and believing. He attacked specifically *The New York Times* and the Washington *Post*, two distinguished papers that had been favorite targets of McCarthy. Agnew laid the groundwork by deploring the death of five large New York City dailies and "the growing monopoly that involves the voices of public opinion." The implication again was that the public was being brainwashed by a one-sided, liberal, Eastern press. There was no recognition of the fact that the press of the nation had supported Nixon by a margin of 5 to 1 in the 1968 campaign. Agnew sneered at editorialists of the *Times* for defending the younger generation against his charge that they were ignorant; he attacked editorial writers in the *Post*'s complex of interests for "all grinding out the same editorial line"; and he stumbled into a gross inaccuracy when he charged that the *Times* "did not carry a word" about a letter from Congressmen and Senators backing the President's Vietnam stand when, as the *Times* demonstrated, it had carried the story. As in the McCarthy era, truth could never catch up with the charge, and the new Agnew attack had his Montgomery audience and a following across the nation screaming their enthusiasm.

The effect of these speeches, coming from the highest level of national government, with the implied support of the White House, was an outpouring of hate unprecedented in virulence and volume since McCarthy's day. Pete Hamill, a columnist for the New York *Post*, wrote that "since Spiro Agnew opened his mouth, the mail has been pretty wild. I don't mean the usual stuff about how much Moscow must be paying me, or how did a nice Irish boy like me ever fall in with the pinko left-wing travelers. This latest batch is really vicious stuff: they are going to kill my children; I am a 'Jew bastard' and should 'go back where you came from'; Agnew is going to put me in a detention pen or under a rock; Hitler didn't gas enough of us. It's always interesting, of course, that these big brave heroes never sign the mail. These people have the kind of courage that is based on the art of the double-bank or that slithers into a Book Depository."

Columnist Harriet Van Horne, sampling the contents of one day's mail, wrote in the New York *Post*: "Newspapers and the networks are receiving the ugliest hate mail since the days of Joe McCarthy. In a single clutch of letters I am denounced as a snob, a slob, a rat-fink traitor, a WASP witch, a Jew-Communist and other epithets not quite so gracious . . . letters on expensive notepaper, letters dictated to secretaries, are even more vicious than the scrawls on lined paper."

A nation already divided by the most unpopular war in its history, by the long-neglected problems of race and the cities and the quality of urban life, was being further split into hostile factions by an Administration that had taken office pledging "to bring us together." Incredibly, it was an Administration that either did not know or did not care what it was doing. Republicans were ecstatic at the public response Agnew had evoked; he was the campaign orator most in demand by the party faithful; and the party capitalized on his talents in the Congressional campaigns of 1970, as in 1952 and 1954 it had utilized the talents of Nixon and McCarthy. The mood at the top was perhaps most frankly expressed by Tricia Nixon, the President's eldest daughter. In an interview with United Press International, she exulted: "The Vice President is incredible. I feel I should write him a letter. He's amazing, what he has done to the media —helping it to reform itself. I'm a close watcher of the newspapers and TV. I think they've taken a second look. You can't underestimate the power of fear. They're afraid if they don't shape up . . ."

". . . The power of fear . . . afraid if they don't shape up . . ." Tricia Nixon's phrases reflected the mood of an increasingly authoritarian America—an ugly America, molded to a large degree by three decades of hate propaganda. Though many Americans may refuse to recognize the face in the mirror, this has become a nation in which "good" citizens are ready to tolerate—indeed, to welcome—the assassinations of liberal leaders. This soul-sickness was revealed in the decade of assassinations that followed so closely on the Nightmare Decade of Joe McCarthy, and the same dark streak is threaded through the violence-prone seventies.

As one who stood cursing and pounding my fist into a wall the day President Kennedy was assassinated, I have been horrified by a reaction I have encountered again and again. Take as one example a New Jersey housewife, mother of three. Her husband is a hard-working provider. These are not deranged persons; they are not psychotic persons. They are the home-loving, industrious kind that in a former generation might have been described by the term "salt of the earth." Yet they were among the millions who voted for George Wallace and contributed their mite to the Wallace war chest. And this housewife, in a casual discussion of the assassination of President Kennedy, remarked: "Well, it was a terrible thing of course—it was a terrible thing to happen to anyone—but if that was the only way we could get rid of him, *it was a good thing.*"

Again, in 1968, after Robert F. Kennedy was assassinated in Los Angeles, a sober-appearing businessman walked into my favorite restaurant and discussed the headline story of the day with a Greek waitress. She later told me: "Do you know what he said? He said, 'Well, if that was the only way we could keep him from becoming President, *it was a good thing.*' I couldn't believe it. I was *so* shocked!"

The press reported that after the tragedy in Dallas several hundred schoolchildren cheered the news of the assassination of President Kennedy. Feeling its guilt for having so long tolerated some of the most vicious radical-right cells in the nation, Dallas tried to deny that it had ever happened; but the evidence seems abundant that it did. In any event, Dallas bears no special guilt for that; Dallas was not alone. After the assassination of Robert Kennedy, a teacher in a North Jersey high school was stunned to find many students, doubtless reflecting the views of their parents, making light-hearted wisecracks about the assassination. "They were not," the teacher says, "by any means a majority of the school. They were a minority—but a sizeable minority. It was not just an isolated case or two; it was far more than that."

And now the last of the Kennedy brothers, Senator Edward M. Kennedy (D., Mass.), lives under the shadow of hate. Hate mail and threatening letters pour into his Senatorial office in Washington; every week the Secret Service comes and dutifully hauls away this virulent outpouring in bulging mail sacks.

In a nation so poised on the knife edge of hate and violence, we are embarked on a new path that can only serve to increase divisiveness and intensify passions. And this time the demagogic campaign is the work, not just of a lone Senator from a state of little political consequence, but of the White House itself. Vice President Spiro Agnew, the mouthpiece of President Nixon, with White House speech writers coining alliterative denunciatory barrages, raged up and down the nation in the Congressional elections of 1970. He coined a new term of opprobrium— "Radic-Lib." It was the ideological heir of Joe McCarthy's "pinko" and "fellow-traveler," of Robert Welch's "comsymp." It tagged every political leader, even Republicans, who opposed the war in Vietnam or fought racist appointments to the U.S. Supreme Court as a dangerous "radical" to be shunned by all "good" Americans.

The rhetoric and tactics of the campaign, masterminded by President Nixon from the White House, were purest Joe McCarthy. In opposing Senator Charles E. Goodell, of New York, one of those Republicans who had earned a "Radic-Lib" label for denouncing the Vietnam war, Vice President Agnew stooped to the kind of vituperation McCarthy would have relished. He called Goodell "the Christine Jorgensen of the Republican Party."

In the closing weeks of the campaign, President Nixon himself took the stump in state after state in a performance that demonstrated that the old "pink sheet" demagogue of the early California days had not really changed. The charge then had been that Democrats were "soft on communism." The charge now was that they were soft on the issue of law and order—that they were the party of permissiveness and that the crime and violence in the nation were largely the result of their soft-headed policies.

This simplistic demagoguery did not work. The American voters in 1970 were not made to stampede into the arms of the ultraright. President Nixon claimed a great victory, but the Republicans lost eleven governorships, lost seats in the House of Representatives, lost control of the state legislatures in Pennsylvania and California, won three Senatorial battles—and lost as many. To most, the figures seemed to say that they had not even achieved a standoff.

If there was cause for congratulation in this, there was also cause for worry. What was appalling was that the old and discredited tactics of Joe McCarthy had been trotted out and tried again, with frenzy and desperation, by the highest officials in the land. And, in the aftermath, there were no signs of shame, only these spurious claims of victory. There was no guarantee that the same techniques would not be tried again and again until, through some fortuitous combination of circumstance and crisis, the spark caught and rekindled the flames of the Nightmare Decade. Had our leadership learned so little? Could it all happen again? "Hell, yes," said Joseph Rauh, and that possibility in itself is enough to make any American shudder.

P A R T O N E Build-up to Hysteria

1 | The Way It Was

The McCarthy "Ad-lie" quote as I have used it here is from my own recollection and notes of his television appearance at the time. The Associated Press on Oct. 12, 1952, filed a story from Chippewa Falls, Wis., quoting McCarthy as telling the Wisconsin Buttermakers and Managers convention that if he were put aboard Stevenson's campaign train with "a slippery elm stick" in his hand he "might be able to make a good American" out of the Democratic candidate. Thomas L. Stokes, in a column in the St. Louis *Post-Dispatch* on Oct. 30, 1952, made passing reference to McCarthy's claim that, if he could get on Stevenson's train with "a club," he could teach the candidate "some sense."

For a vivid account of Eisenhower's deletion of all criticism of McCarthy in Wisconsin, see Emmet John Hughes' *The Ordeal of Power*, Dell Publishing Co., New York, 1964, p. 39.

Walter Lippmann's reasoning about the 1952 campaign has been referred to many times. This version comes from one of his annual, hour-long television interviews about the problems of our times.

Dulles' attitude on taking over the State Department was described in considerable detail by Clayton Fritchey in a column in the New York *Post,* Feb. 12, 1969.

Richard H. Rovere, the Washington correspondent of the *New Yorker,* on Feb. 27, 1953, described how Dulles altered policy to suit McCarthy: "Four times in these ten days, McCarthy . . . has let his views on State Department issues be known, and four times the State Department has made McCarthy's views American policy within a matter of hours." Rovere added that the department sometimes acted in anticipation of McCarthy's displeasure, suspending and dressing down officials who might possibly give McCarthy offense, thus giving McCarthy "next week's victory this week." See Rovere's *The Eisenhower Years,* Farrar, Straus and Cudahy, New York, 1956, pp. 95–99.

The Eisenhower quote on his refusal to tangle with McCarthy is from Hughes, p. 81. The next Hughes quote is from p. 78.

The Martin Merson quote is from his article "My Education in Government," *The Reporter,* Oct. 7, 1954.

This brief summary of the Hiss case is from my own earlier research on the hearing and trial records. See *The Unfinished Story of Alger Hiss,* William Morrow & Co., New York, 1958, pp. 120–121.

The Madeline Lee episode is from "Blacklist, the Panic in TV-Radio," by Oliver Pilat, in the New York *Post,* Jan. 26, 1953.

The publishing industry incidents used here were described by Corliss Lamont in a pamphlet, *The Civil Liberties Crisis,* Basic Pamphlets, New York, 1954.

The Joseph Rauh quote is from my interview with him on Feb. 13, 1969.

The direct quotes that I have used here from the Tillett survey are all taken from typed or handwritten replies Tillett received to his questionnaires. The material has been made available to me by Professor Hugh H. Wilson, of Princeton University, who has custody of it.

The Crossman article quoted here appeared in the *New Statesman and Nation,* Oct. 16, 1954.

The Jules Feiffer quote is from his appearance on NBC's *Today* show, Feb. 4, 1969.

The quotes from the graduating class of 1958 are all from "The Class of '58 Speaks Up," *The Nation,* May 17, 1958.

The Elmer Davis quotes are from his book *But We Were Born Free,* Perma Books edition, New York, 1956, pp. 14–15 and p. 41.

Drew Pearson referred several times in his nationally syndicated columns to the street polls showing Americans shocked by the words of their own Declaration of Independence and Bill of Rights. For a succinct summary, see *Never Tire of Protesting* by George Seldes, Lyle Stuart Inc., New York, 1968, p. 261.

2 | The Roots Go Deep

The Taft quote is from *The Crisis of the Old Order,* by Arthur M. Schlesinger, Jr., Houghton Mifflin Co., Boston, 1957, p. 60.

The Barry Goldwater "extremism" quote is from his acceptance speech before the Republican National Convention in 1964.

For Elmer Davis on doublethink see *But We Were Born Free,* pp. 103–111.

J. Edgar Hoover's statistics on Communist Party membership may be found in his *Masters of Deceit,* Henry Holt & Co., New York, 1958, p. 5.

The Hamilton Fish detail is from two issues of *Democracy's Battle,* a newsletter published by the liberal group Friends of Democracy, March 31, 1946, and Nov. 30, 1947.

This account of the postwar period is based in part on my own researches for *The FBI Nobody Knows,* the Macmillan Co., New York, 1964.

The Chester, Pa., episode is reported in *The New York Times,* April 29, 1919.

The electric guillotine and similar detail are from *Red Scare, a Study in National Hysteria,* by Robert K. Murray, University of Minnesota Press, Minneapolis, 1955, pp. 34–35.

The New York Times analysis is from a study by Martin Kriesberg, "Soviet News in *The New York Times,*" *Public Opinion Quarterly,* Winter, 1946–47, as quoted in an article by Les K. Adler, "The Red Menace Revisited," *Continuum,* Autumn, 1968.

The Gardiner quote is from his book *Portraits and Portents,* Harper Brothers, New York, 1926.

The first Theodore Roosevelt quote about the "money men" is from a letter to Hamlin Garland, Nov. 23, 1907, in *Theodore Roosevelt and His Time, Shown in His Own Letters,* by Joseph Bucklin Bishop, Charles Scribner's Sons, New York, 1920, v. II, p. 50. The following Roosevelt quotes are from Schlesinger, p. 19.

The Coolidge quotes are from Schlesinger, p. 57.

The Frances Perkins quote is from her book *The Roosevelt I Knew,* Harper Colophon Books, Harper & Row, New York, 1946, pp. 107–108.

The Herbert Hoover "end of the rope" quote is from Schlesinger, p. 1; the despair of the business order is from p. 4.

3 | The Equation of the "Ism"

This account of the doings of the Liberty League is based upon articles in *The New York Times*, April 16, 1934; Aug. 25, 1935; Jan. 25, 26 and 29, and March 22, 1936. A United Press article in the New York *World-Telegram and Sun*, Jan. 9, 1935, identified the great corporations whose officers were league directors; it is quoted in *Witch Hunt* by George Seldes, Modern Age Books, New York, 1940, p. 260. Schlesinger's *The Politics of Upheaval*, Houghton Mifflin Company, Boston, 1960, pp. 518–519, gives a vivid description of the Liberty League dinner. For Roosevelt's reaction see Frances Perkins' *The Roosevelt I Knew*, p. 157.

For detail on the Farmers' Independence Council, see Schlesinger, pp. 522–523.

This account of Sentinels of the Republic comes from Schlesinger, p. 82; Seldes, p. 262.

The description of the 1936 campaign, in addition to personal recollections, is based largely on Schlesinger, pp. 606–644.

For some of the material here, I have relied on the fullest account of the early activities of the Committee for Constitutional Government, which is a four-part series of articles published in *Democracy's Battle*, the publication of Friends of Democracy, Febr., March, April and May, 1950.

For a description of CCG's attempt to woo the farmer, see *Who's Behind Our Farm Policy*, by Wesley McCune, Frederick A. Praeger, New York, 1956, pp. 229–237.

The extensive references I have made here to the 1950 House lobbying investigation all come from the record of the House hearings: *Hearings on Lobbying Activities*, House Subcommittee on Lobbying, Eighty-first Congress, U.S. Government Printing Office, 1950. The CCG material may be found in Part V, beginning with the hearing of June 27, 1950.

4 | The Tide Changes

The *Editor & Publisher* survey of press support of President Nixon in 1968 was widely reported in an article moved on the national wires by the Associated Press on Oct. 24, 1968.

Roosevelt's quote on the press in the 1936 campaign may be found in Schlesinger's *Upheaval*, p. 590.

Schlesinger recounts the performance of the Chicago *Tribune* in the 1936 campaign in *Upheaval*, p. 633.

Richard Rovere's quote is from his *The Eisenhower Years*, Farrar, Straus and Cudahy, New York, 1956, p. 123.

The Jackson speech is quoted at length in Seldes, pp. 154–156.

The anti-Russian prejudice in school textbooks is taken from

Adler's article in *Continuum,* cited in Chapter II. It is based on two studies: *Civic Attitudes in American School Textbooks,* by Bessie Louise Pierce, Chicago, 1930, and "The Teaching of the Soviet Union in American Secondary School Social Studies," by Richard Wellington Burkhardt, an unpublished Ph.D. dissertation, Harvard University, 1950.

Diggins' article appeared in *The American Historical Review,* Jan., 1966, and is quoted by Adler.

John Brooks in *Once in Golconda,* Harper & Row, New York, 1969, details the hate-Roosevelt propaganda, p. 216. For an account of the Fala incident, see Frances Perkins, p. 114.

The detail on the American Democratic National Committee and American Action comes from Parts III and IV of the Friends of Democracy's four-part series on Rumely and the Committee for Constitutional Government cited in Chapter III.

For additional details on American Action and its role in the Wisconsin campaign, see *McCarthy, the Man, the Senator, the Ism,* by Jack Anderson and Ronald W. May, Beacon Press, Boston, 1952, pp. 112–113.

Lippmann's quote on democracies is from *An Almanac of Liberty,* by Justice William O. Douglas, Dolphin Books, Doubleday & Co., New York, 1954, p. 264. Jefferson's first inaugural is quoted on p. 263.

The Truman-McGrath quote is from *The Presidency and Individual Liberties,* by Richard P. Longaker, Cornell University Press, Ithaca, N.Y., 1961, pp. 59–60.

The Carey McWilliams quote is from the introduction to his book *Witch Hunt, the Revival of Heresy,* Little Brown & Co., Boston, 1950, p. 6.

The American Civil Liberties Union report is quoted by McWilliams, p. 5.

Clifford Durr's quote on his conference with Truman is from a letter by Durr to the author, Feb. 12, 1965.

This account of the headline hunting in the 1948 campaign is based upon my own earlier researches for *The FBI Nobody Knows,* the Macmillan Co., New York, 1964.

The results of the first two years of the American loyalty program are summarized in McWilliams, pp. 16–17.

The British security program is described in Douglas, p. 273.

This quotation from the Georgetown speech is from the text of an address delivered by Clifford Durr before the Episcopal League for Social Action, San Francisco, Calif., Sept. 30, 1949.

For an excellent description of the events of 1949 and their impact on the American people, see *The Crucial Decade—And After, 1945–60,* by Professor Eric F. Goldman, Vintage Books, a division of Random House, New York, 1960, pp. 91–133.

The Butler quote is from Goldman, p. 125.

For Fitzgerald's analysis of *The Road Ahead,* see p. 28, vol. V of the 1950 Buchanan committee's lobbying hearings, cited in Chapter III. The quotes from CCG correspondence are also from this volume of the hearings.

The quotes giving Flynn's philosophy are from *The Road Ahead* by John T. Flynn, Devin-Adair Company, New York, 1949; see especially pp. 9, 59, 60, 67.

For Gerard's letter and Fitzgerald's questioning of Rumely about the "scalps in our belt" phrase, see p. 59 of the Buchanan hearings.

PART TWO **The Man**

5 | *The Kind of Man He Was*

The Bricker quote is from the second article of "Smear Inc." by Oliver Pilat and William V. Shannon in the New York *Post,* Sept. 5, 1951.

The psychiatric detail is from Rovere, *Senator Joe McCarthy,* The World Publishing Company, Cleveland and New York, 1960, pp. 66–67.

There are many accounts of McCarthy's early life, but by far the most detailed research, conducted over a period of months and on the scene in Wisconsin, was done by Jack Anderson and Ronald W. May in *McCarthy, the Man, the Senator, the Ism,* pp. 6–43. Most other accounts of McCarthy's early years rely largely on their research, as I have here. For another brief account see *McCarthy* by Roy Cohn, The New American Library, New York, 1968, pp. 12–15, and Goldman, pp. 138–139.

For details of the Quaker Dairy case, see Anderson and May, pp. 44–50; also the special McCarthy issue of *The Progressive,* April, 1954, with extensive quotes from the Supreme Court decision on page 7.

McCarthy's war record is covered fully in Anderson and May, pp. 53–66; *The Progressive,* pp. 9–11; and Pilat and Shannon in the New York *Post* series previously mentioned. The Pilat-Shannon quote on McCarthy's substitution of a Guadalcanal plane crash for the shrapnel version of his war injury is in their article of Sept. 7, 1951.

The Canaan quote is from the Pilat-Shannon series in the New York *Post,* Sept. 7, 1951.

6 | *How to Make the Most Out of War*

For Mike Eberlein on McCarthy's finances see Anderson and May, p. 34.

The Cohn quote is from *McCarthy,* p. 270.

The Senate analysis of McCarthy's financial operations is from the official report entitled "Investigations of Senators Joseph R. McCarthy and William Benton," of the subcommittee on privileges and elections, a subdivision of the Committee on Rules and Administration, U.S. Government Printing Office, Washington, 1952, p. 27.

For a fuller discussion of McCarthy's tax evasion and the Tibbetts quotes see the McCarthy issue of *The Progressive*, April, 1954, pp. 19–20.

This account of McCarthy's campaign against Alexander Wiley is based primarily upon Anderson and May, pp. 67–71.

The quickie divorce scandal is covered in both the Pilat-Shannon series and in Anderson and May. Pilat and Shannon in their Sept. 6, 1951, article in the New York *Post* reported that McCarthy was kidded by his friends about being "Reno's No. 1 rival." Most of the direct quotes here are from Anderson and May, pp. 72–77.

The La Follette campaign is covered in Anderson and May, pp. 78–106; by Pilat and Shannon in the Sept. 9, 1951, article in their New York *Post* series; and in the McCarthy issue of *The Progressive*, pp. 63–65. The "Tail Gunner" and "Joe card" quotes used here are from Anderson and May; the headlines from the Communist-controlled *CIO News* in Wisconsin are from photostatic reproductions in *The Progressive*. "The communists have a right to vote" quote may be found in both the Pilat-Shannon article and in Anderson and May.

Michael Rogin's analysis of voting trends, which demonstrated that McCarthy's strength came, not from old-line Populist radicalism, but from a midwest swing to ultraconservatism may be found in his book *The Intellectuals and McCarthy: The Radical Specter*, the Massachusetts Institute of Technology Press, Cambridge, Mass., 1967. The quotes used here are from pp. 221–232.

An account of the Felix Belair interview with McCarthy and the subsequent American Action involvement may be found in Anderson and May, pp. 111–113. Pilat and Shannon deal with the American Action role in Wisconsin in the Sept. 9, 1951, issue of the New York *Post*.

The McCarthy-McMurray exchange and the McCarthy "100 per cent American" advertisement are from Anderson and May, pp. 106–110.

7 | *The Worst Senator*

McCarthy's victory dinner, arranged by John Maragon, is described by Pilat and Shannon in their New York *Post* series, Sept. 14, 1951.

The challenge to McCarthy's seating as a Senator is covered in Anderson and May, pp. 116–121. Additional detail is contained in *The McCarthy Report*, compiled by the Wisconsin Citizens' Committee on McCarthy's Record, Madison, Wis., 1952, pp. 16–17.

A partial quote from Rogers' petition is in Anderson and May, p. 120. There are fuller quotes, together with a reproduction of the pertinent paragraph of the court's decision, in the McCarthy issue of *The Progressive*, April, 1954, p. 8.

The one-wife anecdote is from the Pilat-Shannon series in the New York *Post*, Sept. 9, 1951.

McCarthy's attack on the bar commissioners is quoted in Anderson and May, p. 121.

For accounts of McCarthy's voting record in his first years in the Senate, see the Pilat-Shannon series in the New York *Post*, Sept. 4, 1951; *Time* magazine's McCarthy profile, Oct. 22, 1951; Rovere, pp. 104–109; Anderson and May, p. 3; the McCarthy issue of *The Progressive*, p. 71.

There are several accounts of the Pepsi-Cola Kid in action. The quotes used here of McCarthy's clash with Tobey are from Anderson and May, pp. 128–137. See also *The Progressive*'s McCarthy issue, p. 14; and the Pilat-Shannon series, Sept. 14, 1951.

The details of McCarthy's complicated financial transactions are taken from the Report of the Subcommittee on Privileges and Elections, Committee on Rules and Administration, entitled "Investigations of Senators Joseph R. McCarthy and William Benton," U.S. Government Printing Office, Washington, D.C., 1952, pp. 33–39.

The manner in which McCarthy maneuvered himself into the control of the Joint Housing Committee is best described by Pilat and Shannon in the New York *Post*, Sept. 11, 1951. Anderson and May add some additional details, pp. 138–147.

The Lustron case is covered in detail in the Senate investigative report previously mentioned. To set the record straight, Roy Cohn in *McCarthy* repeats without qualification (p. 271) McCarthy's quote that he had to split the $10,000 fee "with ten people who helped me." Yet the Senate report (p. 133) contains a photostatic reproduction of the check bearing McCarthy's endorsement and showing that the entire amount was deposited to his account with Wayne Hummer & Co.

For additional details on the Lustron involvement, see Anderson and May, pp. 152–157; Pilat and Shannon in the New York *Post*, Sept. 12, 1951; and the McCarthy issue of *The Progressive*, pp. 12–13.

For the Malmédy investigation and a full description of McCarthy's ties to Harnischfeger, I have relied here especially on the Sept. 13, 1951, article in the Pilat-Shannon series; on Anderson and May, pp. 158–164; on *The Progressive*, p. 70, with its direct quote from the McCarthy letter to Matt Schuh informing him that Harnischfeger was putting up the necessary collateral; and, finally, on Richard Rovere. Rovere's detailed, firsthand account of his encounter with McCarthy as the latter stormed out of the Baldwin hearings may be found in Rovere, pp. 111–118.

8 | *"I Have Here in My Hand—"*

This account of the dinner at the Colony is taken from Anderson and May, pp. 172–173, and Goldman, pp. 139–141. For a description of Father Walsh's background see George Seldes' *Never Tire of Protesting*, pp. 183–184.

The mood of 1950 has perhaps been captured best by Goldman in his chapter "The Great Conspiracy," pp. 113–133. The Hiss, Coplon, Fuchs case details derive from my own earlier researches and may be found in part in Goldman. The Capehart quote may be found in Goldman, p. 137. The inhibiting pressure of the Catholic vote was mentioned as a major force handcuffing the Democratic Administration by virtually everyone with whom I talked in Washington in 1968–69 who had been in the Administration at that time and retained a clear memory of events. For Cardinal Spellman's quotes see Goldman, pp. 130–131.

Walter Reuther's anticommunist stand, which almost wrecked his career, began during World War II, when he opposed a piece-work program ardently advocated by both the National Association of Manufacturers and the Communist Party, the former group because it stood to make greater profits from the risky speedup of its working force, the latter because it didn't care a fig how many workers might be maimed or injured in such a program as long as more goods were produced to aid Russia. Reuther's opposition to the communist cells within the United Automobile Workers continued in the immediate postwar period and is well documented. The brief account here is based on my own earlier researches for a short biography of Reuther published by Encyclopaedia Britannica Press in 1963, under the title: *Walter Reuther, Building the House of Labor*.

Cronin's quote is from *Communism: Threat to Freedom*, published by the National Catholic Welfare Conference, Washington, D.C., 1962, p. 32.

Congressman Jonkman's quote may be found in the *Congressional Record*, Aug. 2, 1948; also see the McCarthy issue of *The Progressive*, April, 1954, pp. 24–25.

The Republican National Committee's February 6, 1950, campaign statement may be found in an article in *The New York Times*, Feb. 7; also, in an article by Cabell Phillips, Section IV of the *Times*, Feb. 18, 1950.

The background of the Wheeling speech is dealt with in *McCarthy and His Enemies* by William F. Buckley, Jr., and L. Brent Bozell, Henry Regnery Co., Chicago, 1954, pp. 41–49; Cohn, pp. 1–3; Anderson and May, pp. 173–174; Rovere, pp. 124–126.

The Desmond quotes are all taken from his page one, seven-column story in the Wheeling *Intelligencer*, Feb. 10, 1950. The black, bold, off-lead line of the paper read: MCCARTHY CHARGES REDS HOLD

U.S. JOBS. The subhead: "Truman Blasted For Reluctance To Hold Probes."

The Callahan quotes are from my interview with him, June 6, 1968.

This survey of the immediate press reaction is from my own research in the files of a number of leading papers for the days and weeks immediately after the Wheeling speech. Incredible as it may seem, the staunchly Republican New York *Herald-Tribune* had not even made a mention of McCarthy and Wheeling by mid-month, and Hearst's *Journal-American*, preoccupied with the Fuchs case and its own Rushmore series on communism, let the entire month pass without a mention of McCarthy and Wheeling. The only mention in the similarly red-baiting New York *World-Telegram and Sun* came on February 25 when the paper carried a four-paragraph, page-one item announcing that the Senate was going to investigate McCarthy's charges.

For McCarthy's vacillation after the Wheeling speech, and the Woltman quote on his lost copy of his notes, see Rovere, p. 127.

The McCarthy-Valentine quotes from the tape recording of the interview may be found in "McCarthyism: How It All Began" by former Senator Millard E. Tydings in *The Reporter*, Aug. 19, 1952. The Conners quote is from the same article.

The text of the Truman telegram may be found in *Major Speeches and Debates of Senator Joe McCarthy*, delivered in the United State Senate, 1950–51, an unabridged reprint from the *Congressional Record*, U.S. Government Printing Office, Washington, D.C.

The account of the names first cited by McCarthy is from the Chicago *Tribune*, Feb. 13, 1950, and *The New York Times*, Feb. 14, 1950.

This analysis of McCarthy's changing figures and their origins is based principally upon a study made by Alfred Friendly, of the Washington *Post*, in his article "The Noble Crusade of Senator McCarthy," *Harper's*, August, 1930.

The Gabrielson and Hallanan quotes are from the Wheeling *Intelligencer*, Feb. 11 and 14, 1950.

The McCarthy-Lodge exchange is taken from the *Major Speeches and Debates of Senator Joe McCarthy*.

9 | *The Mad Hatter's Nightmare*

This account of the February 20 scene in the Senate is taken from the *Congressional Record* report *Major Speeches and Debates of Senator Joe McCarthy*, cited in Chapter VIII. Some of the principal page citations: the "twisted-thinking intellectuals" quote, p. 6; the exchange with Lucas, and the pledge not to say anything off the floor he wouldn't say on it, p. 6; the clash with Lehman, pp. 14–15; Wherry's quorum call appeals, pp. 10 and 24.

Rovere (p. 133) is the source for the statement that this was the first time in five years the sergeant-at-arms had been asked to use his authority.

McCarthy's statement that many he accused were no longer in the State Department may be found in *Major Speeches and Debates*, p. 21; his pledge to Lucas on the names, p. 17; "iron curtain of secrecy" recital, p. 28.

A comparison of McCarthy's and Kamp's charges may be found in Seldes, pp. 185–186.

See Alfred Friendly's *Harper's* article for a minute analysis of the gaps in McCarthy's cases.

McCarthy's discovery he was repeating his own data in discussing Case 77 may be found in *Major Speeches and Debates*, p. 60; his clash with McMahon, the Republican reaction, and McMahon's clash with Mundt are in the same volume, pp. 33–38. The United Press wire story account of the Mundt-McMahon clash is from the Wheeling *Intelligencer*, Feb. 21, 1950. *The New York Times* of the same date printed McCarthy's most lurid charges "straight," with no mention of the issues McMahon had raised and no analysis of any discrepancies in McCarthy's figures or performances.

The account of McCarthy's entanglement in Cases 14 and 41 is from *Major Speeches and Debates*, pp. 23 and 51. The source of the statement that McCarthy didn't know the name of the man he accused in Case 14 is *The New York Times*, March 9, 1950. Panuch's quotes are from the New York *Post*, March 10, 1950.

McCarthy's introduction to the Lorwin case (his Case 64) is in *Major Speeches and Debates*, p. 57. This account of the outcome of the case is taken from *The New York Times* and the New York *Herald-Tribune*, May 26, 1954.

The Rovere quote is from his book, pp. 135–136.

The Elmer Davis quote is from his book, p. 41.

The Taft quote is cited in Rovere, p. 136; and Anderson and May, p. 352.

10 | *The Tydings Saga Begins*

The Acheson press conference is from *The New York Times*, Feb. 25, 1950.

For Tydings' stand on the court bill and the 1938 purge, see *Yankee From the West* by former Senator Burton K. Wheeler, Doubleday & Co., New York, 1962, pp. 322 and 344.

Ickes' account of the Tydings Virgin Islands inquiry is from *The Secret Diary of Harold L. Ickes, the First Thousand Days*, Simon and Schuster, New York, 1953, pp. 390–399.

The McCarthy quotes on the March 8 Tydings committee hearing are from his book, *McCarthyism, the Fight for America,* the Devin-Adair Company, New York, 1952, pp. 1–5.

This description of the first two days of hearings is based largely upon articles by William S. White in *The New York Times,* March 9 and 10, 1950.

For an account of Owen Brewster's defense of McCarthy and his attack on the Tydings committee, see the article by Jay Walz in *The New York Times,* March 13, 1950.

The Dorothy Kenyon story was covered in detail in *The New York Times,* March 9 and 15, 1950. Miss Kenyon's reply calling McCarthy "an unmitigated liar" is from a separate story in the *Times* of March 9. The ACLU demand that McCarthy repeat his charges outside the Senate is from the New York *Post* of March 10.

Miss Kenyon's quote summing up her philosophy is from the Tydings Committee Hearings, published under the title *State Department Loyalty Employee Investigation,* U.S. Government Printing Office, Washington, D.C., 1950, p. 187.

The Kenyon case is also covered in considerable detail in *McCarthy and His Enemies,* by William F. Buckley, Jr., and L. Brent Bozell, pp. 76–85. In Appendix A, pp. 343–346, Buckley and Bozell give a complete listing of the organizations with which Miss Kenyon was accused of having some kind of relationship. It is typical of the Buckley-Bozell approach that, after calling Miss Kenyon "a reputable New York City lawyer" and having admitted more in sorrow than in anger that McCarthy made excessive statements in his accusations, they then argue that the Tydings committee did not investigate Miss Kenyon thoroughly enough and imply that perhaps there was something there after all. The concession of Senator Hickenlooper is ignored in their account, though it is plain in the Tydings record and in the March 15 article in *The New York Times* by William S. White. Another Buckley-Bozell tactic is to decide that McCarthy was justified in raising the Kenyon case because *"The Loyalty-Security Board had never held a hearing on the Kenyon case—had never even sent her a routine 'interrogatory.' "* The reason it had not, of course, was to be found in the purely fringe nature of her connection with the State Department, a fact conveniently glossed over.

For McCarthy's first attack on Jessup, see *The New York Times* account of March 9, 1950, and for Jessup's reply on his arrival from Europe, see the New York *Herald-Tribune,* March 16, 1950.

The full text of Jessup's statement to the Tydings committee was carried in *The New York Times* of March 21, 1950, and this account of Jessup's background and the quotes in which he defined the basic issues are taken from that.

The full texts of the Marshall and Eisenhower letters were carried by the *Times* of March 21, incorporated in the page one news story by William S. White. The later exchanges with Senator Hickenlooper are taken from the same article. The *Times*, from the beginning, covered the McCarthy story in detail and published texts of key documents.

For an account of Jessup's performance in the United Nations, see Anderson and May, pp. 223–226. For additional quotes from the Soviet press attacking Jessup see the McCarthy issue of *The Progressive*, p. 53. On the same page, there is the text of a letter from the State Department's Loyalty Review Board to the Senate subcommittee giving its finding that "there is no reasonable doubt of his [Jessup's] loyalty."

For another discussion of the Jessup case, see Buckley and Bozell, pp. 99–124. It is an ambivalent performance. The attitude perhaps is captured best in this sentence on page 122: "To be sure, Jessup was an America Firster and remained one until Pearl Harbor; but he was concurrently involved with pro-Communist organizations, and his remaining with America First after July of 1941 *may* have been protective coloration." Then they conclude that, though McCarthy was justified in attacking Jessup, "it does not follow that he was a loyalty risk as of 1950. In our opinion, the evidence turned up as a result of McCarthy's leads was not sufficiently incriminating to justify such a finding." They acknowledge "Jessup's consistent anti-Communist statements after 1946," but rejoice that he had been driven out of public life and had returned to teaching at Columbia.

McCarthy's continuing attacks on Jessup may be found in the following: an account of his speech on the Senate floor and exchange with Lehman, *The New York Times*, Aug. 10, 1951; Anderson and May, p. 229; and *The Times* and San Francisco *Chronicle* of Dec. 15, 1951.

For accounts of the exchange with Fulbright and the Senate subcommittee hearings on Jessup's UN appointment, see especially the *Times* of Sept. 28, 1951, and Anderson and May, pp. 230–233.

PART THREE   The Opening Salvos

11 | The Case of Owen Lattimore

The description of the klieg-lighted Tydings committee atmosphere is from Anderson and May, p. 212.

For accounts of McCarthy's first attack on Lattimore, see William S. White's article in *The New York Times*, March 14, 1950, and Bert Andrews in the New York *Herald-Tribune* of the same date.

Rovere's comment that McCarthy picked on Lattimore by chance is from his book, p. 151.

McCarthy's sly build-up of the Lattimore case, and his assertion that Russian espionage agents, landed by submarine, reported directly to Lattimore for orders are described by Anderson and May, p. 177.

Incidentally, Buckley and Bozell complain almost plaintively (p. 153) that it was not really McCarthy who should be blamed for putting Lattimore's name in headlines as the "top Russian spy" in America. They emphasize, in italics, that he had made this charge to the Tydings committee only *"in closed session,"* and add: "The words had hardly left McCarthy's mouth when Drew Pearson leaked these charges to the nation," the implication being that it was Pearson who was the villain for publicizing what McCarthy had said.

Lattimore's background is from a lengthy biographical outline prepared for use in his defense and from notes of an interview he had with *The Nation* at that time. Included in his career summary were voluminous quotes from his magazine articles and books showing that he had been critical of communism and an advocate of democracy. For example in *China Monthly* in December, 1945, he had written: "I do not believe that the spread of Communism anywhere in Asia (or indeed in Europe or America) is either inevitable or desirable . . . More than that, I believe that the country which most people in Asia would like to imitate and emulate is America rather than Russia." And at another place in the same article, he had written: "What I believe in, and what my whole record shows I believe in, is the spread of democracy, not the spread of Communism."

The opening Lattimore quotes are from his *The Situation in Asia*, Little Brown & Co., Boston, 1949, pp. 3–4. His description of nationalistic pressures is from pp. 38–39. His description of the interrelation of nationalism and revolution is from pp. 52–53. His description of the South Korean situation follows. The Indo-China quote is from p. 195.

For an analysis of the American character, with its dangerous delusion that the world must be made in its own image, see the interview with Gunnar Myrdal, the Swedish sociologist and friendly critic of America, in *Look*, Dec. 24, 1968.

One of the most concise and clear retellings of the China story may be found in *China*, by Harry Schwartz of *The New York Times*, a New York Times Byline Book, published by Atheneum, New York, 1965. Mao's quote on the peasant revolt in Hunan is from the same work, p. 45.

John F. Melby's *The Mandate of Heaven* was published by the University of Toronto Press, Toronto, Canada, 1968. The quotes on the Japanese still roaming the countryside are from pp. 56 and 183. Melby's description of Chiang's initial edge in gun power is from p. 224. The agrarian reform quote is from p. 30. The Kuomintang corruption and decay quote is from p. 44. The murder of embassy guards is from p. 75. The flight of Chinese liberals into the arms of the Communists in revulsion against Chiang's regime is described on p. 202.

The description of Chiang's conscript army is from Schwartz, pp. 60–61. General Barr's quote is from Schwartz, pp. 62–63.

The identification of John Carter Vincent as McCarthy's "Case Number 2" was made definite by the Associated Press in a national wire story out of Washington on May 13, 1950; see the New York *Herald-Tribune*, May 14, 1950.

Fensterwald's description of the Vincent case is from my interview with him on Feb. 11, 1969.

The text of Lattimore's reply to McCarthy is from Lattimore's book *Ordeal by Slander*, Little Brown & Co., Boston, 1950, p. 4.

The account of what was happening here while Lattimore was in Afghanistan is from a chapter by Eleanor Lattimore in *Ordeal by Slander*, pp. 29–54. The full text of the Pearson broadcast may be found on pages 44–46.

Both Rovere, pp. 150–151, and Shannon and Pilat in the New York *Post*, Sept. 17, 1951, describe the farcical scene in which McCarthy tried to avoid testifying because of the scheduled Senate housing debate.

The quotes from McCarthy's letter funneled to the Tydings committee via Hickenlooper are from *The New York Times*, March 28, 1950.

A full account of McCarthy's March 30 performance may be found in William S. White's story in *The New York Times*, March 31, 1950; see also Rovere, pp. 152–153.

A full text of the Lattimore-Barnes letter may be found in *Ordeal by Slander*, pp. 98–105. A partial quote may be found in *The New York Times*' account of the Tydings hearings, April 7, 1950.

Lattimore's "base and miserable creature" and other quotes on his return from Afghanistan are from *The New York Times*, April 2, 1950, which covered his press conference in detail.

The dispute over the Lattimore memorandum is from *The New York Times* of April 4, 1950. The *Times* carried the full text of the memorandum.

Lattimore's appearance before the Tydings committee was carried in detail, together with a sidebar story on a crowd reaction, in *The New York Times*, April 7, 1950. The text of Lattimore's statement and his direct arraignment of McCarthy in the quotes I have used here are from his *Ordeal by Slander*. See pp. 60–90.

The concluding quote is from *The Nation*, April 15, 1950.

12 | *The Tydings Windup*

McCarthy's private counterespionage setup was described by Shannon and Pilat in the New York *Post*, Sept. 18, 1951; Anderson and May, pp. 196–198; and Rovere, p. 144. The Alsop quote is used by both Anderson and May and Rovere, and is paraphrased by Shannon and Pilat.

This account of the China lobby, its formation and the activities of Kohlberg is based largely on Anderson and May, pp. 192–195, and Shannon and Pilat in the New York *Post*, Sept. 18, 1951. The Goodwin quote and the two descriptions of Jessup by Kohlberg and McCarthy are from Anderson and May, p. 193.

The Lattimore quote on the peregrinations of the Lattimore-Barnes letter is from *Ordeal by Slander*, p. 97.

Lattimore's own account of the confrontation with Budenz is given in *Ordeal by Slander*, pp. 109–131. The Abe Fortas quotes are from pp. 111–112; the Bella Dodd development, pp. 113–115 and pp. 130–131; General Thorpe's role p. 116 and pp. 126–130. For an on-the-spot account, see *The New York Times* of April 21, 1950. For a brief summary, see Anderson and May, pp. 215–216.

Joseph Alsop's denunciation of Budenz and the quotes used here are from his column in the New York *Herald-Tribune*, Dec. 21, 1952.

This capsule description of the *Amerasia* case is based on my own earlier treatment in *The FBI Nobody Knows*, pp. 277–283.

For a description of the Surine-Larsen episode, see Shannon and Pilat in the New York *Post*, Sept. 18, 1951. The Huber contretemps is dealt with in this same article in the *Post;* in *Ordeal by Slander*, pp. 137–140; Anderson and May, p. 215.

For the debate on the files, see the New York *Herald-Tribune*, Feb. 24, 1950; *The New York Times*, March 28 and 29, 1950; the *Herald-Tribune* and *The New York Times*, March 30, 1950; *The New York Times*, April 10, May 5, May 8, June 22, June 24, and July 13, 1950. Truman's announcement that he would let the Tydings committee see the files was made in Washington on May 4—and McCarthy's first outcry that the files had been "raped" was made in a speech in Janesville, Wis., on May 7 and reported in the *Times* on May 8.

The testimony of General Snow and Seth Richardson was covered in detail in *The New York Times*, April 6, 1950.

For the tongue-lashing to which McCarthy was subjected in the Senate, see *The New York Times*, May 4, 1950 and *The Nation*, May 13, 1950.

The Margaret Chase Smith quotes are from the text of her speech; see also *The New York Times* and the New York *Herald-Tribune*, of June 2, 1950. The *Times* also carried the text in full.

The Doris Fleeson quotes used here are from her column in the New York *Post* of June 2, 1950.

For McCarthy's reaction and the quotes used here, see *The New York Times* of June 3, 1950.

The Tydings report was covered in detail in *The New York Times* of July 18, 1950, and to a lesser degree by the New York *Herald-Tribune* of the same date. The *Times* carried extensive excerpts covering all major facets of both the majority and minority reports and the text of Senator McCarthy's reply.

For the details of the July 20 debate on the Tydings report and the quotations used here, I have relied mainly on *The New York Times* of July 21, 1950. See also the New York *Herald-Tribune* and the New York *Post* of the same date.

For editorial reaction to the Tydings report, see the New York *Herald-Tribune* of July 18 and 22, 1950, and the *Times* of July 18. The *Tribune* quote used here is from the issue of July 22.

The *Journal-American* "Shameful Performance" editorial is from its issue of July 19, 1950; the approving quotes of the Republican Senators from a news story the following day.

The Haldore Hanson quotes are from an interview in the New York *Herald-Tribune*, March 26, 1950. See also *The New York Times* account of his testimony and challenge to McCarthy, March 29, 1950. For yet another account, see Buckley and Bozell, pp. 86–96.

The White quotes are from *The New York Times*, March 31, 1950.

The Elmer Davis anecdote is from *But We Were Born Free*, pp. 14–15.

PART FOUR   The Men Behind THE MAN

13 | *The Power Brokers*

Some of the most powerful corporations in America actively promoted the radical right florescence with its hate-Kennedy motif in the early 1960s. For details, see my earlier treatment of the subject in "The Ultras," *The Nation*, June 30, 1962.

The best account of McCarthy's relationship with Upton Close is in the Shannon-Pilat series in the New York *Post*, Sept. 21, 1951.

Anderson and May, pp. 413–416, made a compilation of the accolades bestowed upon McCarthy by leading hate-mongers. Quotes used here are from that compilation.

The Buckley-Bozell quote about the 57 Communists is from their book, p. 52. The quote about the difficulty of identifying Communists is from p. 53. The "strike out against the Liberals" quote is from p. 333. The final blessing of McCarthy from p. 335.

One Drew Pearson column dealing with Joseph Kennedy's $50,000 investment in McCarthy was carried by the New York *Post*, May 3, 1968. The additional Pearson quotes used here are from my talk with him on Jan. 23, 1969.

The Thompson-Myers quotes are from *Robert F. Kennedy, the Brother Within*, the Macmillan Company, New York, 1962, pp. 99 and 103.

The additional quotes detailing the Joseph Kennedy-McCarthy relationship, including the Gardner Jackson episode, taken from a variety of sources, are all to be found in *The Founding Father* by Richard J. Whalen, New American Library, New York, 1964, pp. 426–429 and 436–437. For Joseph Kennedy's continued defense of McCarthy and tearful reaction to the memory of his last days see especially the New York *Post*, Jan. 9, 1961.

Jack Kennedy's delight at Nixon's election in California in 1950 as revealed in the quote used here is from *The Pleasure of His Company* by Paul B. Fay, Jr., Dell Pocketbook edition, New York, 1966, p. 56.

Cardinal Spellman's Brussels speech, as reported by the Associated Press, was carried in *The New York Times*, Oct. 25, 1953. The full text may be found in *U.S. News & World Report*, Nov. 6, 1953.

The additional quotes from Catholic spokesmen used here are from *The New York Times*, June 1, 1953; Nov. 9, 1954. And from the New York *Herald-Tribune*, Nov. 25, 1955.

The Poling speech is from *The New York Times*, Sept. 25, 1952.

The Vinz quote is from his article, "Protestant Fundamentalism and McCarthy," *Continuum*, Autumn, 1968, pp. 314–325.

The *Fortune* quotes on the Texan oil millionaires are all from "Texas Business and McCarthy" by Charles J. V. Murphy in the issue of May, 1954.

The account of McCarthy's 1948 contacts with the Texans is from an article by Edwin R. Bayley in the Milwaukee *Journal* of Dec. 20, 1953. Bayley also detailed McCarthy's pro-oil votes and made the point that these were votes against the best interests of his constituents in Wisconsin.

This description of the Texas "big four" and their fondness for McCarthy is derived from the following sources: the *Fortune* article mentioned above; a series of six articles by Edward T. Folliard in the Washington *Post*, beginning Feb. 14, 1954; and a series by Alvin Davis in the New York *Post*, beginning July 6, 1953. The Frank Murchison anecdote, the "Native Texan" quotes, and the quotes from Hancock's "American Heritage" propaganda are all from Davis.

The Walter Lippmann columns quoted here are from the New York *Herald-Tribune* of March 28 and March 30, 1950.

Truman's press conference quote is from *The New York Times*, April 14, 1950.

Acheson's speech was covered in *The New York Times* of April 25, 1950.

William S. White's analysis is taken from his article in *The New York Times* of June 18, 1950.

14 | *Vengeance at All Costs*

The description of McCarthy's reaction to the Tydings report and his thirst for vengeance is based on Anderson and May, p. 296.

The account of the first McCarthy-Butler meeting is from Shannon and Pilat, the New York *Post*, Sept. 19, 1951.

Bazy McCormick Miller's "These Charming People" circle was described in detail in "The Ring Around McCarthy," by Richard Wilson, *Look*, Dec. 1, 1953.

The Murchison quote on his $10,000 gift in the Tydings campaign is from an article by Alvin Davis in the New York *Post*, July 7, 1953; see also Folliard in the Washington *Post*, Feb. 16, 1954.

For a full account of other large contributions, see Anderson and May, p. 305.

For an account of the Senate elections subcommittee investigation, which includes the Fedder "midnight ride" episode, see Anderson and May, pp. 295–308. Also see the Washington *Post*, August 4, 1951, containing a detailed account of the subcommittee's report from which most of the quotes used here were taken. Another account is in Rovere, pp. 160–161.

See also the article "Political Murder Inc." by Helen Fuller in the *New Republic*, April 2, 1951.

McCarthy's statement criticizing the elections subcommittee's denunciation of him in the Tydings campaign was used in full in the Washington *Post*, of Aug. 4, 1951.

The McCarthy quote about not answering charges but making them is from an interview with him, quoted by Shannon and Pilat in the New York *Post*, Sept. 17, 1951.

15 | *Big Man of the Senate*

The William S. White quotes are from his article in *The New York Times*, Jan. 7, 1951.

The *New Republic* of Feb. 12, 1951, devoted a full page to an extensive excerpt from Senator Benton's speech pleading for Republican responsibility.

One of the best-documented accounts of McCarran's career is in an article prepared by Graham Dolan, editor of the Mine, Mill and Smelter Workers paper, the *Union*. The union itself came under attack by McCarran's committee the instant McCarran found Dolan had been researching his career. See also Anderson and May, pp. 340–350. For *Time*'s attack on McCarran, see its issue of March 20, 1950. See also Marquis Childs' column of Sept. 7, 1952.

The repressive features of the McCarran-Walter Immigration Act were widely denounced. See *The New York Times* of Dec. 29, 1952 for attack by Senator Lehman; Associated Press article in the

New York *Herald-Tribune* of Dec. 20, 1952, describing the restrictive features of the act; an editorial in the national Catholic weekly *America* in January, 1953; an attack by the National Lutheran Council meeting in Atlantic City, the New York *Herald-Tribune*, Feb. 6, 1953; editorial in the San Francisco *Chronicle*, Jan. 23, 1953. The Mine, Mill and Smelter workers in describing their confrontation with Mc-Carran (union release, Oct. 9, 1952) taxed him with the establishment of concentration camps in seven areas of the nation; McCarran contended these were "detention camps" left over from World War II, but the union alleged more than a million dollars had been spent in the past year "to make them ready to hold hundreds of thousands of decent Americans, including especially trade unionists"; that they were "built specifically to carry out the provisions of the infamous McCarran Act of 1950, and we have documentary evidence to prove it." The union contended that when its officials tried to testify, "McCarran banged the gavel and shut us off" a total of "732 times in three days." These concentration camps, a legacy of the McCarran-McCarthy era, are still in existence, still maintained by the government—waiting.

The Carter barn raid is described by Shannon and Pilat in the New York *Post*, Sept. 18, 1951, and by Anderson and May, pp. 340–346. The Anderson and May "informer" memos quoted here are from pp. 342–343.

For the filing of the Pearson-McCarthy libel suit, see *The New York Times* and the New York *Post* of March 3, 1951.

Pearson's description of the Sulgrave Club incident is taken from his testimony at the pre-trial deposition. See the Washington *Post*, Sept. 26, 1951.

The Pearson quote on seeking LBJ's intercession is from an article by Robert G. Sherrill in *The Nation*, July 7, 1969.

For the Adam Hats sequence see *The New York Times*, Feb. 22, 1952.

McCarthy's exchange with Roberts is from the Washington *Post*, Sept. 27, 1951. See also the Associated Press account carried by a number of papers on the same date.

The text of McCarthy's speech attacking Marshall is in the *Congressional Record* for June 14, 1951, beginning on page 6752. See *The New York Times*, June 13, 1951, for McCarthy's advance notice of his coming attack on Marshall; the issue of June 15 for an account of his Senate speech; the issue of June 16 for his reiterated attack on both Acheson and Marshall in a speech before the Fifth Marine Division Association in New York.

McCarthy's April 12, 1951 "S.O.B." reference to Truman is quoted in Anderson and May, p. 360.

The Rovere quotes are from pp. 172 and 177. Rovere's full account of the Marshall episode may be found in his *Senator Joe McCarthy*, pp. 170–178.

For a more sympathetic treatment of McCarthy in the Marshall episode, see Appendix F, Buckley and Bozell, pp. 388–392.

The New York *Post*, as early as Sept. 13, 1950, reported that Freedman and Smith were "already whooping up" a campaign against Mrs. Rosenberg.

Anderson and May deal with the Anna Rosenberg case, pp. 309–313; Rovere gives it brief mention, p. 162; Buckley and Bozell ignore it entirely. See also a brief account in *Jewish Life*, July, 1953.

16 | The Reluctant Dragon

For Benton's call for McCarthy's ouster and McCarthy's vituperative reply, see *The New York Times*, and the New York *Herald-Tribune*, Aug. 7, 1951.

The do-nothing mood was described in the *Times*, Aug. 9, 1951.

During this whole period, McCarthy was furious with his fellow Republican Senators who had signed the Tydings election subcommittee report. He repeatedly attacked Mrs. Smith and Hendrickson, and even flailed out in a Republican caucus at one of his staunchest supporters, Kenneth Wherry. See stories in the New York *Post*, Aug. 4, 1951; the Robert S. Allen column in the *Post*, Aug. 14, 1951; the Washington *Post*, Aug. 21, 1951.

For Hennings' rejoinder to McCarthy, see the Washington *Post* of Aug. 22, 1951, and two columns by William S. White in *The New York Times* of Aug. 23 and Sept. 9, 1951.

The gingerly manner in which Gillette decided to give Benton a hearing was described by William S. White in *The New York Times* of Sept. 25, 1951.

For McCarthy's "mental midget" comment and Benton's denunciation of McCarthy, see *The New York Times* and the New York *Herald-Tribune* of Sept. 29, 1951. The *Times* gave a case-by-case summary and breakdown of Benton's charges.

For the mood of the country, as reflected in Gallup polls on McCarthy over the years, see *U.S. News & World Report*, March 19, 1954.

For much of the following material—including the *New Statesman and Nation* and Graham Greene quotes and the Rochester *Times-Union* survey—I am indebted to an article "Witch-Hunting, 1952: The Role of the Press," by Sozier C. Cade, in the *Journalism Quarterly* of the University of Minnesota, Minneapolis, Minn., December, 1952.

The full texts of the Truman speeches quoted here were carried by *The New York Times* of March 25, 1950, and August 15, 1951. Tobin's speech was quoted at length in the *Times* of Aug. 30, 1951.

The Carey McWilliams quote is from his *Witch Hunt, the Revival of Heresy*, p. 16.

The nine occasions on which the Gillette committee pleaded with

McCarthy to appear are enumerated in its final report, "Investigations of Senators Joseph R. McCarthy and William Benton," previously cited in Chapter VII. The enumeration covers pp. 2–8 of the report. The full texts of the Gillette-McCarthy correspondence were included in the report, and these quotes from McCarthy's letters are taken from pp. 61–65.

The limping nature of the inquiry is shown in a succession of news reports. A short Associated Press story, carried by the New York *Herald-Tribune,* Nov. 31, 1951, reported Gillette had postponed the investigation until the new year. *The New York Times* reported on Jan. 17, 1952, that the Republicans were trying to remove *both* Mrs. Smith and Hendrickson from the committee; on Jan. 20, it reported that Senator Lodge had concurred in the plan "significantly to alter" the complexion of the committee; on Jan. 24 it headlined: "MRS. SMITH QUITS M'CARTHY INQUIRY." William S. White's assessment of the significance of all this may be found in his analytical story in the *Times,* Jan. 27, 1952.

On Jan. 30, 1952, the New York *Post* headlined: "Senators Shelve McCarthy Probe, At Least Until After Election Day."

The April 10 vote-of-confidence showdown on the floor was covered in detail by *The New York Times* and *Herald-Tribune* on April 11, 1952, and in the Washington column of Vance Johnson in the San Francisco *Chronicle* of April 13, 1952.

For McCarthy's one appearance before the committee and Benton's reply, see *The New York Times,* July 4, 1952.

The sequence of withdrawals aimed at discrediting the committee from the inside is summarized in the Senate report, p. 14.

The McCarthy-China lobby connection is briefly alluded to in the Senate report, p. 40.

The question of McCarthy's use of funds donated for the anticommunist cause for his own personal benefit is dealt with in the Senate report, pp. 19–27.

The Benton half of the investigation is dealt with in the Senate report, pp. 45–52.

The quotes summarizing the committee's reaction are from the Senate report, p. 11, and the final quotes leaving the issue up to the Senate are from the report, p. 45.

The New York Times commented editorially on the report on Jan. 10, 1953, and the final New York *Post* editorial quoted here appeared on Jan. 12, 1953.

For other comment, see "Who Will Stand Up to McCarthy?" in the *New Republic,* Jan. 12, 1953, and " 'If McCarthy Were a Man' " in *The Progressive,* May, 1953.

PART FIVE **The Menace and the Downfall**

17 | The Halo and the Hatchetman

The Marquis Childs quotes are from his column in the New York *Post,* Oct. 31, 1951.

The Republican manifesto was described by the Associated Press in a story out of Washington on Sept. 30, 1951, carried by a number of papers.

For an account of the Freedom Clubs pamphlet, see the Washington *Post,* May 18, 1952.

Taft's criticism of McCarthy was described in an Associated Press story from Des Moines; see *The New York Times,* Oct. 23, 1951, which also carried McCarthy's rejoinder.

Taft's change of heart was described by *The New York Times* of Jan. 22, 1952 and March 23, 1952; see also TRB's column in the *New Republic,* April 2, 1951.

Gabrielson's quote lauding McCarthy is from a United Press story from Washington, Feb. 2, 1952; see *The New York Times* and the *Herald-Tribune,* Feb. 3.

The Washington *Post* quote is from an editorial, March 8, 1952.

For the day-by-day Lattimore-McCarran exchanges, see *The New York Times* and *Herald-Tribune* and the Washington *Post,* Feb., 1952; Anderson and May, pp. 212–222; the *New Leader,* March 31, 1952.

McCarran's performance in the Senate in submitting his committee's report was described in *The New York Times* and the *Herald-Tribune* of July 3, 1952.

Nathaniel Peffer's article is in the *New Republic,* Aug. 4, 1952.

The David Lawrence column cited here was published in the New York *Herald-Tribune,* Dec. 17, 1952.

The Lattimore defense quotes used here are from the brief filed in the U.S. District Court in Washington, Feb. 16, 1953.

For Judge Youngdahl's initial ruling, see *The New York Times* and other papers of May 3, 1953; for the Court of Appeals ruling, with a breakdown of the votes of the various judges on the various counts in the indictment, see the Washington *Post,* July 9, 1954, also *The New York Times* of the same date.

For accounts of the second Lattimore indictment, see *The New York Times* and other papers, Oct. 8, 1954; for accounts of Rover's attack on Judge Youngdahl and the Lattimore defense's reply, see the issues of Oct. 14, 1954; Judge Youngdahl's refusal to step down was reported in the press, Nov. 19, 1954.

Judge Youngdahl's ruling throwing out the second indictment was reported by *The New York Times* and other papers, Jan. 19, 1955, and the account of the final dropping of all charges appeared in the issues of June 29, 1955.

For accounts of the McCarran committee's radio-infiltration report, see *Variety*, Aug. 27, 1952; the *Daily Compass*, of the same date, and *The New York Times*, Aug. 28, 1952.

The quotes from Wellbourn Kelley's letter are from a photostatic copy of the letter in my possession; the reply of the committee to his charge is from *The New York Times*, of Aug. 28.

The Great Falls *Tribune* account of Matusow's speech was reprinted in full in the *Union*, the publication of the Mine, Mill & Smelter Workers Union, from which this account is taken.

On the immediate challenge to Eisenhower on McCarthy, see the Associated Press story quoting Senator Green in the New York *Herald-Tribune*, Aug 21, 1952; see Mundt's reply in the same paper the following day.

Eisenhower's rebuff on his original plan to visit Wisconsin on Sept. 5 was described by Joseph Alsop in his column in the New York *Herald-Tribune*, Aug. 31, 1952; see also Alsop's later column, "Know-Nothings Triumphant" in the *Herald-Tribune*, Sept. 12.

Eisenhower's Denver statement of principle was covered by *The New York Times*, Aug. 23, 1952; the full text of the questions and answers at this press conference was carried by the Washington *Post*, Aug. 24, 1952.

For accounts of the McCarthy primary triumph, see *The New York Times* and the *Herald-Tribune* of Sept. 10, 1952. In a sidebar story on Sept. 10, the *Times* reported that Senator Taft was "delighted" by McCarthy's vote and quoted this additional comment: ". . . I did and do approve of his accomplishments in rooting out Communists and subversion in Government."

Emmet Hughes' account of the prepared Wisconsin speech and its significant deletion is from *The Ordeal of Power*, pp. 38–39.

See *The New York Times* and the New York *Post* of Oct. 4, 1952 for accounts of the McCarthy-Eisenhower meeting; McCarthy's version was carried in the *Times* the following day, Oct. 5.

The eagerness of Eisenhower's headquarters to have McCarthy campaign after his Wisconsin victory was described in the St. Louis *Post-Dispatch*, Sept. 17, 1952; the New York *Journal-American* and the New York *Post*, of the same date; and *The New York Times*, of Sept. 18.

Murchison's contribution to the campaign against Benton was described by Alvin Davis in the New York *Post*, July 6, 1953; Edward Folliard in the Washington *Post*, Feb. 16 and 19, 1954, mentioned the contributions of Murchison and Cullen; other Texas contributions were detailed by Edwin R. Bayley in the Milwaukee *Journal*, Dec. 20, 1953.

The quotes from McCarthy's Stevenson speech used here are from the full text as recorded by *The New York Times*, Oct. 28, 1952. In the running news story on the same day, the *Times* called attention to the distortion of the Schlesinger quote.

McGranery's exposure of the 1928 incident was dealt with in

The New York Times of Sept. 4, 1952 and in greater detail in the New York *Herald-Tribune,* Sept. 5, 1952. For the Bedell Smith analysis, see the *Times* of Oct. 31. Hancock's quote is from Alvin Davis' fourth article in his New York *Post* series. Dirksen's comment was carried in the *Times,* Oct. 29; the foreign press reaction in the *Times,* Oct. 30.

The Washington *Post* editorial, quoted here is from the edition of Oct. 29, 1952.

Walter Lippmann's quote is from his column in the New York *Herald-Tribune* of Oct. 30, 1952.

For an analysis of the Wisconsin vote in 1952, see the McCarthy issue of *The Progressive,* April, 1954, pp. 68–69.

For McCarthy's role in Connecticut, see the New York *Herald-Tribune,* Oct. 30, 1952.

This analysis of the Benton vote figures is taken from a monograph, "Toward an Explanation of McCarthyism," by Nelson W. Polsby, Yale University and the Brookings Institution, 1959, pp. 14–16.

The Progressive's quotes on the influence of the press are from the McCarthy issue, p. 5.

18 | *The Witch Hunt Continues*

McCarthy's Nov. 8 quote is from an Associated Press story from Phoenix carried by most newspapers the following day.

See *The New York Times* of Nov. 21, 1952, for the first account of McCarthy's new role as committee chairman.

The Stewart Alsop quotes are from his column of Nov. 23, 1952 in the New York *Herald-Tribune.*

The New York dinner quotes are from *The New York Times* and the *Herald-Tribune* of Dec. 11, 1952.

The threatening quote made in Puerto Rico is from a United Press story moved from San Juan on Dec. 12, 1952 and carried by a number of newspapers.

For accounts of the multiple Red investigations and the organization of McCarthy's committee, see *The New York Times* of Jan. 8 and 18, 1953; for a short profile of Roy Cohn, see the *Times* of Jan. 3, 1953.

The Voice of America investigation is handled in detail in the McCarthy issue of *The Progressive,* April, 1954, pp. 33–36. Dr. Wiesner's role and the quotes used here are from Frederick Woltman's interview with him, used in the last article of his five-part series, "The McCarthy Balance Sheet," in the New York *World-Telegram and Sun,* July 12–16, 1954. Woltman's verdict on the Voice probe, as quoted here, is from the same article.

The McCarthy-Roger Stuart interview quoted here is from

Stuart's article in the magazine section of the New York *World-Telegram and Sun*, June 13, 1953. This account of the Raymond Kaplan suicide is from Woltman's last article mentioned above.

The atmosphere of the early days of the Eisenhower Administration is described vividly in Hughes, pp. 68–77.

James Reston in *The New York Times*, March 19, 1958, detailed a whole series of submissions to McCarthy by Dulles; along the same lines see William S. White in *The New York Times*, Feb. 22, 1953, and Rovere, *The Eisenhower Years*, pp. 95–99.

The "et cetera" order and the resulting humiliation of Morton are described in Martin Merson's Oct. 7, 1954 article in *The Reporter*.

Hughes' version of the McLeod appointment is from his book, p. 75.

Articles on the Bohlen fight filled the press during the latter part of March, 1953. See especially *The New York Times* for March 19, 22, 24 and 29. The White and Sulzberger quotes used here are from the issue of March 29.

The Rovere quotes used here are from his *The Eisenhower Years*, which is the best account of the Cohn and Schine saga (pp. 125–142). See also the McCarthy issue of *The Progressive*, pp. 81–83.

The Emmet Hughes anecdote is from *The Ordeal of Power*, pp. 78–79.

The Merson quotes used here are all from his article in *The Reporter*, Oct. 7, 1954.

For accounts of Sokolsky's checkered career, see several references in George Seldes' *Never Tire of Protesting*, and a brief profile in *Time*, May 24, 1954.

The Wechsler quotes are from his article in *The Progressive*, June, 1953.

Details on the number and contents of U.S. overseas libraries may be found in *U.S. News & World Report*, June 26, 1953.

The book censorship and book burning made innumerable headlines during the month of June, 1953. Only the more pertinent items can be cited here. *The New York Times*, June 11, described the effect on West German libraries; for Secretary Dulles' admissions on the book-burning, see the *Times* of June 16 and June 18; the full text of Eisenhower's Dartmouth speech was carried by the New York *Herald-Tribune*, June 15; Eisenhower's press conference was reported in detail by the *Times*, June 18, and *The Daily News* of the same date described the happiness of McCarthy and Mundt; the change in State Department book policy was described by Homer Bigart in the New York *Herald-Tribune*, July 19; the McCarthy-Fulbright clash may be found in the *Times*, July 25.

19 | *The Hidden Flaw*

This description of the Waldorf-Astoria dinner is based on an on-the-spot report by Friends of Democracy, and a column by Murray Kempton in the New York *Post*, Feb. 16, 1953.

An excellent, detailed description of the J. B. Matthews case, its background and significance, appeared in *Congressional Report*, Vol. 2, No. 4, July 22, 1953, the biweekly bulletin of the National Committee for an Effective Congress. See also *The New York Times* of July 8, 10 and 11. The *Times* of July 10 carried the texts of the clergymen's protest and Eisenhower's response. For the British slant on the same episodes see the *Manchester Guardian* of July 11 and 17, 1953.

Hughes' account of the White House offensive is from his *The Ordeal of Power*, pp. 83–85.

For accounts of the Democratic walkout, see *The New York Times* of July 11, 14, 17 and 20. Monroney's speech attacking McCarthy was reported by the *Times* in the issue of July 14.

This account of the slow-building Cohn-Schine feud with the Army is based upon the initial Army account, the full text of which was carried by *The New York Times*, March 12, 1954.

The first extensive, probing treatment of the Fort Monmouth episode was published by *The New York Times* in an excellent three-part series written by Peter Kihss, Jan. 11–13, 1954.

For an account of the 1951 Allen charges, see an article by Walter Kerr in the New York *Herald-Tribune*, June 14, 1954.

A full description of Eisenhower's new security order may be found in the McCarthy issue of *The Progressive*, p. 32.

The listing of typical headlines is taken from Peter Kihss' first article in the *Times*.

Harry Green's exchange with McCarthy are taken from Green's article in the *New Jersey Law Journal*, April 1, 1954.

The Anti-Defamation League's charges and the Army's reply were reported in *The New York Times*, Aug. 27 and 28, 1954.

The Kihss series recounts in considerable detail the nature of the charges filed against employees at Fort Monmouth. See also the exhaustive study made by the Scientists' Committee on Loyalty and Security, of The Federation of American Scientists, issued April 25, 1954.

The Greenblum incident is covered in detail in the scientists' report. See also *The New York Times* and the *Herald-Tribune*, Oct. 17, 1953, for accounts of the original McCarthy charges; and the same papers of Nov. 17, 1953 for Greenblum's explanation. See in addition the New York *Post*, Nov. 24, 1953, for an account of Greenblum's new suspension and General Lawton's actions; and the New York *World-Telegram and Sun*, April 29, 1954, for an account of the content of Lawton's speeches.

The Lamont case has been described in great detail in *The Lamont Case,* by Philip Wittenberg, Horizon Press, New York, 1957. The book is a compendium of all the briefs and court decisions, reproduced verbatim, tied together with the briefest of narrative connecting links. The quote that I have used here on the limitations on McCarthy's committee is from a footnote in the final Court of Appeals decision, p. 311. Lamont's denial of Communist Party membership may be found on p. 23. The telegrams from McCarthy telling Lamont and Wittenberg not to appear are reproduced in engravings on p. 11.

Secretary Stevens' announcement that no espionage existed at Fort Monmouth was carried by *The New York Times* and the *Herald-Tribune,* Nov. 14, 1953.

The McCarthy-Ellender exchange may be found in the *Congressional Record,* Feb. 2, 1954, pp. 1048–1055.

Rauh's clash with Roy Cohn, as reported by the Associated Press, was carried by *The New York Times* on Nov. 23, 1953. Interestingly enough, I can find no record that the failure of Cohn to produce on his "wait until Tuesday" threat stirred any curiosity in the press or resulted in any reporting of that rather significant fact. Rauh's quotes on the reaction among his friends are from my interview with him, Feb. 13, 1969.

The Latta quote, as indicated, is from the Asbury Park *Sunday Press,* June 8, 1969.

20 | *The Inevitable Showdown*

On McCarthy's November 24, 1953, speech, see Arthur Krock's column in *The New York Times,* Nov. 30; also *U.S. News & World Report* of Dec. 11 for a partial text.

The C. D. Jackson quote and the following reference to Nixon may be found in *First-Hand Report* by Sherman Adams, Harper & Brothers, New York, 1961, pp. 136–139.

For Nixon's professed views on McCarthy and the quote used here, see *Richard Nixon, a Personal and Political Portrait* by Earl Mazo, Harper & Brothers, New York, 1959, pp. 140–141 and p. 144. The Key Biscayne meeting is described on pp. 147–148. On the same theme of the pact with McCarthy see W. H. Lawrence in *The New York Times,* Jan. 5 and 10, 1954.

McCarthy's maneuvering to get the Democrats to rejoin his committee was described in *The New York Times,* Jan. 25 and 26, 1954.

The appropriations debate and vote were described in *The New York Times,* Feb. 3, 1954; see also two analytical articles by W. H. Lawrence in the Sunday *Times,* Jan. 31, 1954 and Feb. 7, 1954.

A chronology of the Peress case and its development may be found in *Time* magazine, March 8, 1954.

This description of the Zwicker case is taken from the transcript of his testimony published in *The New York Times,* Feb. 23, 1954.

For the step-by-step development of the explosive Stevens-McCarthy confrontation. I have depended mainly on two accounts— a long roundup in *The New York Times'* The Week in Review section, Feb. 28, 1954, and an in-depth treatment in *Time,* March 8, 1954.

That Nixon's sole concern was with political tactics becomes obvious from his own account to Earl Mazo, who quotes him directly to this effect on p. 148.

Stevens' and Hagerty's statements and a description of Eisenhower's final defiance of McCarthy are from *The New York Times* of Feb. 26, 1954.

The Alsops' quote is from their column in the New York *Herald-Tribune,* Feb. 28, 1954. The Reston quote is from his column in the *Times* of the same date.

Mundt told the New York *Herald-Tribune* that he had been surprised Stevens had not requested the assurances given him would be spelled out in the "Memorandum of Understanding," but he confirmed they had been given. See the issue of Feb. 26, 1954.

For an excellent roundup of the explosive March week marked by the Stevenson, Flanders and Murrow performances see *The New York Times'* Review of the Week section, March 14, 1954. For a short profile of Flanders, see Joseph and Stewart Alsop's column in the Washington *Post,* March 12, 1954.

Nixon's reply to Stevenson is described in Mazo, pp. 149–150.

A detailed account of Murrow's McCarthy program and the Annie Lee Moss case is contained in *Due to Circumstances Beyond Our Control* by Fred W. Friendly, Vintage Books, New York, 1968, pp. 23–50.

Sherman Adams describes the Jan. 21 conference in *First-Hand Report,* pp. 143–145.

The Alsop column on the deletions in the Army Report appeared in the New York *Herald-Tribune,* March 15, 1954.

The description of the Cohn-Schine maneuverings here is taken from the text of the Army Report, published in *The New York Times,* March 12, 1954.

McCarthy's counterblast is taken from the texts of the memoranda he released, published in *The New York Times,* March 13, 1954. The Stevens and Adams replies are from texts of their statements in the same issue.

21 | The Army-McCarthy Hearings

The description of McCarthy in action is from *Time,* March 8, 1954.

For an excellent background article on Dirksen's efforts to block public hearings, and on McClellan's role, see Edward J. Milne's article in the Providence *Sunday Journal,* May 16, 1954. See also W. H. Lawrence in *The New York Times,* April 25, 1954.

See *The New York Times,* April 3, 1954, for an account of Welch's appointment; and the April 11 issue for a sketch of Ray Jenkins.

For an account of Mundt's reluctant acceptance of chairmanship see *The New York Times,* March 17, 1954.

Welch's bill of particulars was described by *The New York Times* and the *Herald-Tribune,* April 15, 1954; the full text was carried by the Associated Press and appeared in several papers on April 16.

The New York Times, April 21, 1954, carried the full text of the McCarthy charges against Stevens; Hensel's reply was carried in papers of the same date. An additional Hensel statement was carried in full by the New York *Herald-Tribune,* April 25, 1954.

The New York Times ran on a daily basis virtually the full texts of the Army-McCarthy hearings. I have relied here on this transcript. The Reber-Stevens testimony may be found in the issue of April 23, 1954; General Smith's testimony was given the same day.

The transcript detailing the beginning of the false-photo issue may be found in *The New York Times,* April 27, 1954; Welch's charges, April 28; Cohn's testimony, the same day; Schine's testimony, April 30; the testimony of Anastos, Mrs. Mims and Juliana, May 1.

In addition to the summary of Stevens' admissions taken from the transcript, for some of the color and flavor of the hearings I have relied here on a column by Murray Kempton in the New York *Post* and an article by William V. Shannon in the *Post,* April 28, 1954; also, a description in *Time,* May 17, 1954.

For discussion of the McCarthy-FBI letter, see the transcripts in *The New York Times,* May 5, 6 and 7, 1954; Walter Lippmann's observation is from the New York *Herald-Tribune,* May 10, 1954.

The Welch quote about the filibuster is from the transcript in the *Times,* May 7; the Alsop and Stokes columns quoted here are from the Providence *Sunday Journal,* May 16, 1954. On the Dirksen motion to cut off the inquiry, see the transcripts in the *Times,* May 10 and 11.

For the monitored telephone calls, see the transcript in *The New York Times,* June 4 and 8, 1954. For the clashes between McCarthy and Symington, see the issues of June 8, 9 and 10. For Cohn's first exchange with Welch, see the issue of April 28, and for the Murray Kempton quote used here, see the New York *Post* of the same day.

For John Adams' testimony, see the transcripts in *The New York Times,* May 13, 14 and 15; for Cohn's testimony see the issues of May 29, June 2, 3 and 10.

The Cohn-Kennedy tiff was described on June 12 in the *The Daily News*, *The New York Times* and the New York *Herald-Tribune*.

For the climactic scene of the Army-McCarthy hearings, see the transcript in *The New York Times*, June 10, 1954; also, Eric Goldman's *Crucial Decade*, pp. 276–279.

22 | *Censure*

For a short sketch of Flanders' career, see the *New York Times*, July 31, 1954; also Flanders' autobiography, *Senator from Vermont*, Little Brown & Co., Boston, 1961.

The quotes from Flanders' June 1 speech are from the *Congressional Record*, pp. 6976–6977.

The Flanders quotes on the difficulty he had getting his case before the public are from his book, pp. 260–262.

The *Meet the Press* quotes are from *The New York Times*, June 14, 1954.

For a lengthy account, with direct quotes from the Senate debates, see *U.S. News & World Report*, Aug. 13, 1954.

The full texts of the Army-McCarthy committee reports were printed in *U.S. News & World Report*, Sept. 10, 1954.

For profiles of the six Senators chosen to serve on the Watkins committee, see *The New York Times*, Aug. 6, 1954.

Lengthy excerpts from the transcript of the Watkins hearings were published by *U.S. News & World Report*, Aug. 13, 1954.

For the right-wing pressure drive, see *The New York Times*, Nov. 12 and 15, 1954.

Texts of the high points in the Senate debate were carried by *The New York Times* in its issues of Nov. 11, 12, 13, 16, 17 and 18.

For another description of the Senate action, including the full text of the final resolution, see Rovere, pp. 223–231. For Nixon's role, see Mazo, pp. 150–151.

For an account of Roy Cohn's resignation and the texts of the Cohn, McCarthy statements, see *The New York Times*, July 21, 1954.

Descriptions of the Cohn dinner were carried by *The New York Times* and the *Herald-Tribune*, July 29, 1954; see also Murray Kempton's column in the New York *Post* of the same date.

Much of this account of the McCarthy rally and McCarthy's last days owes a debt to Rovere, pp. 232–254.

The New York *World-Telegram and Sun* ran pages of reader's comments on the Woltman series, July 16, 17 and 22, 1954. The *Tablet* quote is from its editorial, July 17; the *Pittsburgh Catholic* quote was reprinted in the *World-Telegram and Sun*, July 22.

Rovere's account of the reaction to his *Esquire* article may be found in his book, pp. 236–237; the psychiatrist's quote is from Rovere, p. 67; the final Rovere quote is from p. 246.

PART SIX   The Legacy

23 | *The Victims*

Clayton Fritchey's quotes are from his column in the New York *Post,* Oct. 6, 1969.

The quotes dealing with President Kennedy's conversations with MacArthur and Mansfield and his change of heart on Vietnam are taken from Kenneth O'Donnell's "LBJ and the Kennedys" in *Life* magazine, Aug. 7, 1970. The O'Donnell disclosures touched off a spate of comment. See columns by Mary McGrory and Clayton Fritchey in the New York *Post* of Aug. 3 and 7, 1970, and one by Kenneth Crawford in *Newsweek,* Aug. 17, 1970.

The Associated Press survey mentioned here was published in the Los Angeles *Times,* Dec. 1, 1953.

Philip M. Stern cites the shifting Eisenhower loyalty-firing figures in *The Oppenheimer Case,* Harper & Row, New York, 1969, p. 239. He also points out, p. 500, that the Truman Administration had screened 4,756,705 persons during its tenure and had denied clearance in only 560 cases on loyalty grounds. Again, this represented only about one-hundredth of one percent of those investigated.

For a news story containing a succinct summary of the purge of the old China hands, see *The New York Times,* Jan. 15, 1969. The John Paton Davies case was fully treated in John W. Finney's "The Long Trial of John Paton Davies" in *The New York Times Magazine,* Aug. 31, 1969.

The details on the decline of State Department morale are taken from the Tillet survey, pp. 50–57, and the eight-year conformity quote is from p. 9.

This account of the Charles Allen Taylor case is taken from the transcript of the record filed with the U.S. Supreme Court in the October term, 1958, Case No. 504. Rauh's quotes are from his brief filed with the Supreme Court in arguing the appeal. See also *The New York Times* and the Washington *Post,* April 1, 1959, and an Associated Press wire story carried by several papers on April 2.

The Ford Foundation survey from which these anonymous cases are taken was entitled *Case Studies in Personnel Security,* published by the Bureau of National Affairs Inc., Washington, D.C., in August, 1955.

24 | *"The Evil That Men Do . . ."*

Prior to the assassination of President Kennedy, I described the orgy of radical right extremism which his election had inspired, identifying many of the influential businesses and magnates supporting it in "The Ultras," *The Nation,* June 30, 1962.

The 1964 Presidential campaign was marred by the fanatical propaganda of right-wing extremists. It may seem ridiculous now, but an all-out effort was mounted to paint President Johnson as "soft on communism" and a "fellow-traveler." Democrats, monitoring right-wing broadcasts, found that 1,300 radio and television stations across the nation were carrying 6,600 right-wing programs a week. Just one of these—the Manion Forum, the creation of Dean Clarence Manion, former head of Notre Dame University's law school—cost $6,000 a week to put on the air, according to Manion himself, and he declared the money came from 582 "leading industrialists, business and professional men" across the nation. For a fuller account of this propagandizing, see my "Hate Clubs of the Air," *The Nation*, May 25, 1964.

Undoubtedly the most thorough and persistent research into the growth of the John Birch Society and other extremist groups has been done by Arnold Forster and Benjamin Epstein of B'nai B'rith's Anti-Defamation League. See their book, *Danger on the Right*, Random House, New York, 1964, and their *The Radical Right*, Vintage Books, New York, 1967. In the latter volume Forster and Epstein calculate that something like $20 million a year is being invested in right-wing propagandizing. They write: "The hallmark of the phenomenon is everywhere visible; a propaganda theme that sees the United States in the grip of a deeply entrenched, well-advanced internal Communist conspiracy that maintains a stranglehold on the Federal Government, the local town council, the school board, the press, the public library and the pulpit; that names statesmen and clergymen, editors and teachers, scientists, civil rights leaders, and even singers as traitors and agents of the Great Red Plot."

The McCarthy denunciations of the press and media used here are taken from: the New York *Post*, August 9, 1950; *The New York Times*, Jan. 29, 1952, and Aug. 16, 1953; the Madison, Wis., *Capital Times*, March 17, 1952; and the New York *Herald-Tribune*, March 21, 1954.

For an account of the Wallace campaign and the quotes used here, see "Wallace and His Folks," *Newsweek*, Sept. 16, 1968; also a column by Jimmy Breslin, the New York *Post*, Oct. 9, 1968; a Wallace profile in the New York *Daily News*, Oct. 21, 1968. Details of the Harris poll on American attitudes on the eve of the Democratic convention are contained in the *Newsweek* article.

For a description of Nixon wooing the Wallace vote, see *The Resurrection of Richard Nixon* by Jules Witcover, G. P. Putnam's Sons, New York, 1970, pp. 403–404.

The text of the Agnew Des Moines speech was carried by *The New York Times*, Nov. 14, 1969; see also *Newsweek*, Nov. 24, 1969. A summary of Agnew's most-quoted lines was carried by *The New York Times'* Review of the Week section, May 10, 1970. For an account of Agnew's further attack on the press, see the New York

Post, Nov. 21, 1969, and the *Times* of the same date; also, *Newsweek,* Dec. 1, 1969.

For reactions to Agnew's performance: the Pete Hamill quote is from his column in the New York *Post,* Dec. 18, 1969; the Harriet Van Horne quote is from her column in the *Post,* Dec. 8, 1969.

Tricia Nixon's quote on Agnew may be found in *Newsweek,* March 2, 1970.

The persistent threats against Senator Edward M. Kennedy's life have been mentioned many times—by Stewart Alsop in his weekly column in *Newsweek;* by Washington columnists, Frank Mankiewicz and Tom Braden; and by the Senator's wife, Joan Kennedy, in a long interview in the *Ladies' Home Journal,* July, 1970. In their April 4, 1970, column in the New York *Post,* Mankiewicz and Braden wrote: "Twice weekly, at least, Kennedy associates talk to police about . . . threats on his life—they come by the dozens in the morning mail— which they consider most worthy of being looked into." Alsop in one *Newsweek* column wrote that the hate mail and the threats filled mail sacks that were turned over to the Secret Service every week for inspection.

Index

About the Author

FRED J. COOK was born in Point Pleasant, New Jersey, and
graduated Phi Beta Kappa from Rutgers University. He was
a reporter for the Asbury Park *Press*, and in 1944 joined the staff
of the New York *World-Telegram*, where he worked as feature writer
until the end of 1959. He has frequently written articles on subjects
relating to Senator Joseph McCarthy, and during that era he wrote
special issues of *The Nation* on the Hiss Case, the Remington Case,
and the F.B.I. Mr. Cook's pieces have also appeared in many
other magazines, including *Saturday Review, Reader's Digest,
American Heritage* and *The New York Times Magazine.*
Among his best-known books are *The F.B.I. Nobody Knows,
The Warfare State* and *The Unfinished Story of Alger Hiss.*
Mr. Cook has received numerous awards for his work.
In three successive years, he was honored with Page One Awards
by the Newspaper Guild of New York—in 1958, for best local
reporting; in 1959, for best magazine feature article in the nation;
and in 1960, for the best magazine reporting in the nation.
At present he is writing and living in New Jersey.